D0368614

The New York Times
Film Reviews

A ONE-VOLUME SELECTION

The New York Times
Film Reviews

A ONE-VOLUME SELECTION

1913-1970

Chosen from the 7-volume Set
with an Introduction and
Six Original Essays
by
GEORGE AMBERG

An ARNO PRESS BOOK published in cooperation with
QUADRANGLE BOOKS, INC.

CONTENTS

CRITICS

Some reviews are signed only with initials. The full name of the critics can be identified from the list below.

A.S. or A.D.S.	Andre Sennwald
A.W.	A. H. Weiler
B.C.	Bosley Crowther
B.R.C.	B. R. Crisler
E.A.	Eugene Archer
E.J.B.	Edmond J. Bartnett
F.S.N.	Frank S. Nugent
H.H.T.	Howard Thompson
H.T.S.	Harry T. Smith
J.P.S.	John P. Shanley
J.R.L.	Joelyn R. Littauer
J.T.M.	John T. McManus
M.E.	Milton Esterow
M.H.	Mordaunt Hall
O.A.G.	Oscar Godbout
P.P.K.	Paul P. Kennedy
R.A.	Renata Adler
R.W.N.	Richard W. Nason
T.F.B.	Thomas F. Brady
T.M.P.	Thomas M. Pryor
T.S.	Theodore Strauss
V.C.	Vincent Canby

The date line after each review gives the month, day and year, in that order, when it was printed in The *New York Times*.

FILMS IN NEWSPRINT

Our concept of contemporary man, of his position and function in the "global village," is unattainable without awareness and appreciation of modern technology and the mass communication media. Among the new media that have radically changed the way we live, the way we perceive, and the way we comprehend, the cinema occupies a singular position because it has preserved, though largely incidentally, pictorial records of the past seventy-five years. Public as well as private archives contain countless millions of feet of motion picture film, illustrating virtually every day that has passed since the new recording device was invented. Invaluable footage has been lost, destroyed, or discarded, and even more has chemically disintegrated, yet the still massive remainder constitutes a living memory of unprecedented abundance. Although seventy-five years, the mere span of a lifetime, is but an infinitesimal fraction of the story of mankind, this brief period represents not only one of the most critically eventful but also, owing to the cinema, the most comprehensively documented phase in history. Whatever intention or purpose the motion pictures fulfill—entertainment, drama, spectacle, document— they are inevitably reflections of the time and place of their origin and, as such, firsthand evidence of past events. This applies not exclusively to documentaries, factual films, and newsreels but equally to fictional narrative, comedies, and musicals. For, regardless of its particular character and style, any film whatsoever portrays implicitly the tastes and fashions, the problems and preoccupations, the mores, morals, and concerns of a particular moment in a particular environment.

Shortly before the turn of the century, two famous early pioneers, Louis Lumière in France and Thomas A. Edison in America, had predicted that the new invention had no future. As it turned out, paradoxically, the one condition that most delayed and denied its recognition as a unique, new art form was that it had no past. Primarily a product of technology, lacking the antecedents and credentials of the traditional arts, the movies were reluctantly admitted to a back seat on the art scene under the label of popular entertainment. Thus classified, the cinema was kept at a safe distance from the dramatic stage, the fine arts, and the realm of letters for the greater part of its prodigious growth. This is not denying that the movies are indeed a popular art, and that they are entertainment as well—but not exclusively so. In the present state of change, expansion, and experimentation, the generic term *cinema* must accommodate film productions of enormous diversity in scope, content, style, and value. A documentary on the rock or drug scene is as legitimately cinematic as Napoleon's defeat at Waterloo, the agonies of a family drama, or Chaplin's triumph over adversity. The prevalence of popular music, literature, art, and film is as distinctive a facet of our culture as is the restricted realm of more refined and sophisticated creations.

It is possible, in fact likely, that we still underestimate the social and cultural impact of the movies, their pervasive and inescapable influence in forming our notion of twentieth century man and his world. Owing to the easy availability of the moving image on screen or tube, we have become accustomed to rely on information once removed from actuality and often far removed from truth. Whether historical or contemporary, document or fiction, masterpiece or failure, any film is implicitly an *interpreted* version of the human scene, revealing graphically how people see themselves or, more significantly, how they wish to be seen. What makes it so difficult to experience movies purely or essentially as art is the presence of unstylized human beings on the screen, endowed with the unmistakable authenticity which the photographic process insures. Discounting trick photography and special effects, the viewer is aware that everything appearing on the screen must have been actually in front of the lens at the time of the shooting. And, as the layman persists in asserting, "the camera doesn't lie." It is mainly for this mindless reason that a large majority still considers "realism" a criterion for excellence. However, cinematic realism, especially in fictional narrative, does not refer to reality as either actuality or verifiable fact, nor yet as imaginative transformation of actuality; its functions rather literally as *a metaphor for wishful thinking*. Realism, so-called, is essentially in the viewer's mind.

During the formative years of the cinema, many tentative notions about the nature of the motion picture became unchallenged stereotypes. In this accidental way, "realism" acquired a peculiar meaning in filmic parlance and practice. It originated in the momentous discovery that the moving image is capable of creating an illusion of actuality far more suggestive than is conceivable in the traditional arts or even still photography. Unfortunately, the discovery of this unprecedented potential was made by people unable to appreciate its artistic significance but well able to exploit its popular appeal. Thus, from the very beginning, the new medium was dominated by the ambition to produce on film the closest possible equivalent of the visual world. And since the cinema could do this supremely well, it became the art of imitation in the least Aristotelian and the most literal meaning of the term: it became the realistic medium *par excellence*. However, the particular form of realism prevailing in the average film production has no more genuine authenticity, either factual or artistic, than the spectator has been conditioned to concede; it is as surely a convention as Italian opera.

The moving pictures, comparable to certain devotional images, are essentially likenesses taken on faith. It is not so absurd as it may sound that a reputable reviewer should commend an actor for his "extraordinary likeness to Christ." Under the proper physical and psychological conditions (as they prevail in the movie theatre), visual experience seems incontrovertible. The public would probably accept a square wheel, provided it were visually corroborated. While manifesting a virtually unlimited tolerance for improbable premises (*Dracula*), the audience is rigorous in its demand for the explicit form of pictorial documentation which is supposedly objective and authentic—the presupposition evidently being that only the visual (and audible), that is, the physical world is "real." The suggestion that cinema, as an extension of reality into an imaginative dimension, may have artistic validity would be lost on the average spectator. It was in fact lost on so reputable an authority as Dr. Krakauer in his *Theory of Film*, the standard work on theory.

These considerations indicate the predicament confronting a responsible critic. He has many options, but if he writes for the broad, daily readership, he must never question the presuppositions on which their illusions are founded. This raises the question of the extent to which film criticism affects the potential audience. Opinions are widely divided among the readers as well as the critics themselves, and no conclusive answer is possible. However, there seems to prevail pretty much the view that, as often as not, the vast, movie-going population makes its own choices, guided by such factors as word-of-mouth, predilection for a star or director, promotional persuasion, established reputation on the stage or in print, and, most of all, precedent and analogy. On the other end of the spectrum are the discriminating and informed filmgoers who appreciate critical analysis, challenging discourse and debate. In their opinion, the critic's special obligation is to discover, explicate, and promote the unorthodox, "difficult" films that get no proper public exposure and might pass unexamined or unnoticed. As in any area of publishing, professional competence exists on many levels. Just as books, newspapers, and magazines are published, so films are produced and reviews written with the objective of appealing to a particular segment of the population. The readers of the *New York Times* have little in common with those of the *Daily News*; the audience for *Airport* would hardly venture out to see *Viridiana*. At this point, it is necessary to propose a distinction between the *reviewer*, who is primarily a journalist concerned with the news of the moment, and the *critic,* who is primarily an analyst concerned with lasting aesthetic qualities. Summarily speaking, the reviewer cultivates his sense of topicality, the critic his sense of history. In actual practice, of course, the dividing line is fluid. The readers' final criterion for the reviewer-critic is not so much the rightness, fairness, and impartiality of his judgment than the appeal of his personality and style.

The critic's authority is fragile, depending, as it does, on the fluctuations of taste and the unpredictability of the latest film's box office appeal. Exposed in the news media, his opinion enjoys a high degree of visibility, thereby often attaining an inflated, momentary notability. Such conspicuous exposure, in turn, provokes strong public reaction. For the average reader seeks confirmation rather than information, and he is apt to resent the critic's prerogative of passing judgment. A motion picture like *The Sound of Music*, with its sensational popular response, exists virtually outside the realm and reach of aesthetic valuation. The reviewer-critic can merely observe, but not affect, the phenomenon of the triumph of the worthless. Two arguments are most frequently invoked against the legitimacy of adverse criticism; there is hardly ever any objection to favorable recommendation. The first argument amounts to a challenge, daring the critic to perform as well or better than the creator whose work he considers wanting. This is obviously an absurd request as the critic is not competing with the artist in the area of his competence but relying on his own expertise in explicating and evaluating the creator's achievement. Moreover, contrary to a cherished stereotype, a responsible critic is not a frustrated artist who has failed but a dedicated expert who has succeeded. It cannot be too strongly emphasized that his chosen metier is as valid and exhaustive a vocation as the artist's. The second argument derives from the observation that different critics of equal professional standing may arrive at radically different conclusions. This, supposedly, weakens their credibility, whereas it actually affirms their integrity. Aesthetic judgment posits no absolutes; it recommends considered options. The function of criticism is to focus attention on the essential qualities or deficiencies of a work of art rather than to impose a definitive opinion. Dissent and controversy are inherent in a critical statement. For criticism does not pursue the same purpose as an award jury which requires consensus or a majority vote. It is indeed highly questionable whether collective agreement would serve the best interests of art and artists.

These introductory comments are intended to put the reviews reprinted in this collection into the larger context of the critical profession. When the *New York Times* decided to review motion pictures, in 1913, the new medium had existed for at least fifteen years. This initial period had witnessed the development of professionalism in production, the international expansion of an ever-growing audience, the beginning of a specialized industry, and the founding of profitable business enterprises. The movies were unmistakably here to stay and to be reckoned with. In retrospect, it is easy to understand that the *New York Times* bided its time, as did other responsible publishers, because there prevailed great doubt and uncertainty about the artistic respectability of the new medium. Attempts to gain cultural prestige had been made before. The ambitious venture of the "Films d'Art", in France, had transferred theatre plays onto film, using famous stars of the stage in their productions, and the great Sarah Bernhardt appeared in America in a full-length (silent) screen version of *Queen Elizabeth*. However, this was artificial, filmed theatre, not the true, popular cinema that kept expanding regardless of prestige. From the professional point of view, it was also a question who was qualified to review films, those peculiar hybrids that were neither theatre nor fine art nor yet photography but a bit of each. For a long period of time, then, there were no film experts but trained journalists doing a job of reporting as best they knew how. And although everybody had a dim awareness that something of importance was in progress, no prophet arose on either side of the Atlantic who had a vision of the cinema's prodigious future.

A written history of the movies is one thing and surely a useful one; a collection of original documents, telling the story almost day by day, is quite another and surely a unique one. This is the enormous task the *New York Times* and Arno Press have jointly undertaken by reprinting all the film reviews that appeared in the daily paper from 1913 to 1970. The sum total amounts to the staggering figure of about 19,000 reviews, contained in seven large volumes, including a cumulative index for easy reference.* While this notable publishing event is of only limited interest for the layman because of its very inclusiveness, it is, for precisely the same reason, an invaluable resource of firsthand information for the scholar and researcher. The reader of the present selection should at least be aware of the availability of the complete edition.

The purpose of this condensed edition, divided into six sections, each covering the period of a decade, is to make the unique material accessible in an easily manageable format, adjusted to a limited budget as well as limited shelf space.

* *The New York Times Film Reviews,* 1913–1970, 7 vols. New York: The New York Times and Arno Press, 1970–71.

In addition, there were other than merely practical considerations. It appeared as a real challenge to explore how much or how little material was needed to preserve the excitement of discovery or rediscovery derived from the study of virtually every page of the original edition. Inevitably, the reader will sometimes vainly look for one of his favorites, or, conversely, wonder why others have been included. It was obvious at the outset, that such a small fraction of the total material could not be remotely representative of the richness of the original source nor satisfy everybody's expectations. But it could, and hopefully does, trace a coherent and authentic story of the movies. The samples, then, have been chosen with a view not so much for their individual merit or the artistic significance of a particular film as for their function in the continued flow of cinematic events.

It goes without saying that even 19,000 reviews do not fully cover the whole world film production over a span of six decades. They do, in themselves, amount to a selection, partly because not all films were necessarily previewed in New York, partly because the reviewers themselves exercised reasonable discrimination and, finally, because space limitations curtailed the amount of copy apportioned to the cinema. In fact, the first and most visible symptom of the growing significance of the movies as a newsworthy, public event was the steadily increasing volume of copy devoted to them. Individually judged, not all the reviews are equally absorbing or perceptive. The literary and intellectual caliber of the reviewers naturally varies and, accordingly, the insight and interest of the reviews, although not even the best reviewer can better the material with which he is compelled to work. For the history of the cinema, just like that of painting and literature, is hardly a chain of inspiring masterpieces but, for the most part, a succession of competent mediocrities. As the composite product of art, technology, and business, the movies are more immediately dependent on social, environmental, financial, and other nonaesthetic conditions than any other creative medium. The wonder is that occasionally a superior work of art emerges that justifies much previously wasted effort. This is the hope and the reward that sustains the reviewer in his day-to-day routine. Over a period of time, the collected reviews reveal two parallel developments: the increasing control of the medium on the part of those who produce films and the increasing control of the critical profession on the part of those who write about them. Eventually, some reviewers distinguished themselves by transcending the safe limits of mere reporting and exposing themselves in the more exciting but more perilous arena of critical analysis. There is a point in all responsible judgment where aesthetics infringes upon ethics, that is, when a statement implies a definitive moral stance.

If this selection should cause some surprises, they are possibly due to the fact that it is a condensation of the larger work in which the surprises are even more frequent and more startling. A close reading of the six original volumes is an enormously instructive experience on account of both what it reveals and what it omits. It would seem reasonable to expect that a continuous, chronological succession of a very large number of reviews would balance out as a fairly accurate picture of the principal world events of the several decades covered. This is true only with considerable qualifications. While there is no doubt that the movies reflect as well as affect the world in which they originate, the frequency and the extent to which it occurs as well as the nature of this reciprocity would require extensive study. On the face of it, there is no discernible, consistent pattern prevailing throughout. The evidence shows that the reviews, and the movies to which they refer, convey peculiarly fragmentary, and often ambiguous, intelligence about the events of their time. At the production end, some form of censorship may account for it or the fear of getting involved in controversial issues or other nonartistic considerations that excise, distort, or controvert the facts. A telling example for this kind of biased selectivity is the practice of portraying the "villain" by the political enemy of the moment: thus, in our country, the Nazis, the "Japs," the "Commies," have alternately represented the principle of evil, while the respective friends and allies were candidly idealized. Another factor affecting our judgment is that there are two opposite ways in which the film makers may respond to a given situation. An extended period of political, social, or financial crisis may result in depressing, gloomy pictures, but it may equally provoke a counterreaction in cheerful, escapist ones. This leads to the suspicion that the movies are questionable witnesses.

There exists a persistent paradox: on one side, no record could be more literally exact than a motion picture, on the other, the movies are the most accomplished providers of illusion. The seeker after the truth must be well aware of this duality. However, in defense of the reviewer, it is fair to remember that it is not his task to examine the truthfulness of the evidence but to judge the cinematic quality of the presentation; he is not writing for posterity but keeping account of the film news of the day. In his capacity as a reporter, he cannot be held responsible for the disconcerting fact that the world-shaking crises of our century—the major and minor wars, the fall of empires and dynasties, the redistribution of political power, the clash of ideologies, the atomic holocaust —do not figure so prominently on the record as one would surmise. At the same time, though, the documentary film assumed increasing significance as a factual, eyewitness report on the political, social, and military scene as well as an effective means of building and sustaining morale under extreme hardship. Furthermore, as another consequence of world events, first the Russians in the twenties, then the Nazis in the thirties, and eventually other countries as well, recognized the cinema's tremendous power of persuasion for purposes of propaganda. However, as the majority of those specialized films, both documentary and fictional, were designed for home consumption rather than for international distribution, they remained mostly unknown outside their intended sphere of influence. Only with considerable delay, they have finally become available for purposes of sociological and psychological analysis. Immediately after the end of the Second World War, in the midst of the ruins and chaos of the old world, began the great stylistic innovation, initiating what may be called the "modern" film as distinct from the European tradition that had been disrupted or destroyed in the cataclysm. During the same period, American film production had the benefit of a relatively undisturbed and prosperous economy. Simultaneously with this burst of creativity and the emergence of new talent, the reviews, too, reflected a definite change, disclosing interest in such cinematic aspects of the medium as structure, dynamics, composition, editing, camera work, and sound treatment.

Perhaps the least expected and therefore the most conspicuous feature of the movies is the extent to which technological progress has been taken for granted in the cinematic news. Aside from generally dull, descriptive, or instructional documentaries, there is scant mention, let alone an expression of amazement or admiration, concerning the momentous technical and scientific discoveries of our century, such as the development of aviation, radio, and television, the harnessing of nuclear energy, the conquest of space, to mention but the most obvious neglect. Equally, in the area of cinema technology proper, the advent of sound and the introduction of color, both crucial advances in the art and technique of the medium, are rather casually treated and rarely appraised by reviewers. The reason for this apparent lack of appreciation must be sought in the definition of the reviewer's objective. He felt neither motivated nor qualified to report or comment on physical innovations, so long as technical and professional publications had writers with the requisite expertise. A more significant reason was that motion picture narrative was essentially appraised in the traditional terms of the novel and the drama, on which it had indeed been chiefly dependent for the major part of its development. Accordingly, the prevailing practice was to concentrate on content analysis on the one hand and an appraisal of the performance on the other. However valid, these criteria of valuation were borrowed rather than indigenous. The realization that the cinema is a total and unique art form in its own right dawned very gradually and very late, in the world at large as well as in the newspaper community. The result of this insight is an entirely new attitude toward the art of the film, implying the recognition that film is neither literature nor drama but a complex composite of many arts and crafts. Slowly but surely, the film reviewers of the *New York Times* have redefined their responsibility by adopting a genuine critical and analytical stance and a concern with aesthetics. As the reader progresses through six decades of journalistic effort, he will surely be struck by the difference in form and substance between the earlier reviews and the later ones, a difference that logically parallels and illustrates the history of the cinema.

George Amberg

The New York Times
Film Reviews

A ONE-VOLUME SELECTION

FROM THE BIRTH OF THE MOVIES TO
"THE BIRTH OF A NATION"

Moving pictures were projected onto a screen in front of an audience for the first time in 1894. Many different people in different countries had been working simultaneously, though independently and secretly, toward the perfection of the new moving picture machine and, virtually at the same time, workable prototypes originated in France, England, Germany, and the United States. The many conflicting claims as to who was the original inventor of the cinematograph will never be settled with certainty.

The success of the new invention was instantaneous and sensational, although the first movies were very short and, by present standards, naive and artless. But within barely one decade, longer narrative films and comedies developed, together with increasing technical skill and more sophisticated equipment. Many of those early films, extending into the twentieth century, were indeed amazingly inventive and often charming, such as the delightful fantasies of Georges Méliès, the first animated cartoons by Emile Cohl, the elegant comedies of Max Linder, all three Frenchmen; in the United States originated the innumerable shorts directed by D. W. Griffith, the first films establishing the production firm of Thomas H. Ince, the innovative pictures directed by Edwin S. Porter for the Edison Company; there were also English, Scandinavian, German, and Russian films of considerable competence and inventiveness. Although today the majority of those productions is mainly of interest to the historian and scholar, this less known phase of cinema history should not be viewed as the dark ages of the movies but as a vital and exciting testing ground for emerging new talent in a new field of creative endeavor.

The key event of the second decade was the production of *The Birth of a Nation* by David Wark Griffith, followed, the year after, by *Intolerance,* an even more gigantic, though less successful venture. However, for all their originality and creative independence, these two great films did not spring from a void. During the same period, Chaplin began to develop his screen character; Mack Sennett invented his madcap comedies, with the Keystone cops, the bathing beauties, and the wild chases; two distinguished directors, Victor Seastrom and Mauritz Stiller, created artful, stylized dramatic films that established a solid artistic reputation for the Swedish cinema; Ernst Lubitsch, D. F. Murnau, and E. A. Dupont, in Ger-

3

many and Abel Gance, Louis Feuillade, and Jacques Feyder, in France, started their promising careers; at the end of the second decade, Robert Wiene's *The Cabinet of Dr. Caligari*, an expressionistic, macabre fantasy, focused attention on radically novel ways of film design and acting style. Yet, even in this respectable company and in the midst of rapid growth and some remarkable experimentation, Griffith remains the founder and initiator of cinematic art. In one large-scale, complex, enormously ambitious enterprise, he consolidated the cumulative experience of the preceding two decades and set the example for the future. At one stroke, cinema had become respectable. With *The Birth of a Nation* began the age of the cinema.

QUO VADIS

The Astor Theatre housed a moving-picture production for the first time yesterday, when the Kleine-Cines's presentation of " Quo Vadis? " was given there. The pictures, which were made in Italy, followed the events of the successful novel of that name by Sienkiwicz. The presentation was divided into three acts, which took more than two hours to show. Special incidental music was provided on a mechanical orchestral player.

The pictures represent the most ambitious photo drama that has yet been seen here. The production has many spectacular scenes and is full of pictorial effects that are striking. One of the notable things about the production is its success in fixing the atmosphere of the days of Nero. It is plain that a wealth of effort has been spent on details, and nothing occurs to destroy the illusion. The arena scenes are almost painful, so faithfully do they paint a picture of ruthless cruelty.

The two biggest scenes are the burning of Rome and the arena scene. Both employ hundreds of people, who are handled in a masterly manner, and the results are highly realistic. In the arena scene there are gladiatorial combats, chariot races, more than a score of lions, whose destruction of the Christian martyrs is managed in a way to bring gasps of horror from the audience, and finally the combat between the giant Lygian, Ursus, and the bull which carries Lygia on its back.

In none of the pictures is there the slightest suggestion of canvas and paint, all of them being taken with a natural background. It is said that a huge arena was specially built for the production, and the film gives visible proof of the statement. The films are fine examples of motion-picture photography, all of them being perfectly lighted and free from blemish. The acting of the principals was calculated to help the illusion at all times, and the handling of the small army of supernumeraries admirable. If a feature moving-picture production can fill a Broadway theatre, " Quo Vadis? " ought to be able to do it.

Ap 22, 1913

WAR "MOVIES"

Moving pictures of real warfare were exhibited in the Seventy-first Regiment Armory last night. The pictures were, for the most part, taken during the final battles between the Greeks and Bulgars in and about Salonika during the second Balkan war. Some of them showed shrapnel shells bursting in the air and men and horses of retreating artillery batteries falling under the heavy onslaught.

The "movies" proved of great interest to soldiers of the Seventy-first Regiment, who saw them by invitation, as they demonstrated that the moving-picture camera could be both a great spur to a soldier's courage and also an element capable of adding much to the shame of defeat. A film that brought applause from the military men showed a cavalry charge, in which it could plainly be seen that soldiers who came falteringly into the range of the camera dug their spurs in their horses' flanks and rushed forward after finding the camera playing upon them.

In a view of Bulgarian prisoners the Greek captors marched boldly up toward the camera, dancing with glee, while their captives held their hands over their faces or turned their backs upon the camera man. The moving pictures were taken at the command of the King of Greece, who was himself at the front for a time and was shown as an observer of one battle. They were exhibited privately last night, no admission fee being charged.

Ja 14, 1914

CABIRIA & ESCAPE

The Knickerbocker Theatre became a moving-picture house last night, when the much heralded photo drama " Cabiria," written by Gabriele D'Annunzio, was produced for the first time in America. A large audience, which included several of the representatives of the Italian Government in this country, saw the production of the Italian writer's first motion-picture play.

For the movies D'Annunzio has taken as an inspiration a period in the early history of the Roman Empire when that nation was at its mightiest. The action of the play takes place in the third century before Christ, when the Romans were fighting the rival empires of Carthage and Greece.

The story, which is romantic and partly historical, begins when Cabiria, a pretty Sicilian child of five years, is saved by her nurse on the day when Catavia, a city in Sicily, is almost destroyed by an earthquake and an eruption of Mount Aetna. After escaping

5

from the ruined city the nurse and child are captured and are about to be cast into a burning furnace as a sacrifice to Moloch. but they are rescued by Fulvio, a young Roman, and his herculean servant, Maciste.

The escape of the child and her life afterward form the nucleus of D'Anunzio's play, in which several thousand persons take part. The film was produced by the Italia Film Company of Turin with great care and attention to details. The mechanical effects are thrilling and excellent, and the photo drama is one of the most effective ever shown here.

A large chorus and an orchestra take part in the production, greatly adding to the effect of the play. A symphony precedes the presentation of the picture play.

The Cort Theatre, which up to last Saturday night housed "Peg O' My Heart," also became a moving-picture theatre yesterday afternoon, when "The Escape," a seven-reel photo play founded upon Paul Armstrong's drama of the same name, which was seen here last Winter, began an engagement.

"The Escape" treats of eugenics and sex questions and shows in an interestingly told story what Mr. Armstrong and the producers believe to be the haphazard way in which human beings select their mates and contrasts it with the alleged care used in the same selection by the lower animals.

The film is cleverly done, and there is an interesting prologue put together by Dr. Daniel Carson Goodman which traces the development of microscopic life. The photo play was produced by the Mutual Film Corporation, under the direction of D. W. Griffith.

Je 2, 1914

'THE BIRTH OF A NATION.'

Film Version of Dixon's "The Clansman" Presented at the Liberty.

"The Birth of a Nation," an elaborate new motion picture taken on an ambitious scale, was presented for the first time last evening at the Liberty Theatre. With the addition of much preliminary historical matter, it is a film version of some of the melodramatic and inflammatory material contained in "The Clansman," by Thomas Dixon.

A great deal might be said concerning the spirit revealed in Mr. Dixon's review of the unhappy chapter of Reconstruction and concerning the sorry service rendered by its plucking at old wounds. But of the film as a film, it may be reported simply that it is an impressive new illustration of the scope of the motion picture camera.

An extraordinarily large number of people enter into this historical pageant, and some of the scenes are most effective. The civil war battle pictures, taken in panorama, represent enormous effort and achieve a striking degree of success. One interesting scene stages a reproduction of the auditorium of Ford's Theatre in Washington, and shows on the screen the murder of Lincoln. In terms of purely pictorial value the best work is done in those stretches of the film that follow the night riding of the men of the Ku-Klux Klan, who look like a company of avenging spectral crusaders sweeping along the moonlit roads.

The "Birth of a Nation," which was prepared for the screen under the direction of D. W. Griffith, takes a full evening for its unfolding and marks the advent of the two dollar movie. That is the price set for the more advantageous seats in the rear of the Liberty's auditorium.

It was at this same theatre that the stage version of "The Clansman" had a brief run a little more than nine years ago, as Mr. Dixon himself recalled in his curtain speech last evening in the interval between the two acts. Mr. Dixon also observed that he would have allowed none but the son of a Confederate soldier to direct the film version of "The Clansman."

Mr 4, 1915

BERNHARDT IN PHOTO PLAY.

Her Lameness Hidden in "Jeanne Dore," Shown Privately.

The first acting done by Sarah Bernhardt since the loss of one of her legs by amputation last Summer was shown in motion pictures exhibited privately yesterday afternoon at the offices of the Universal Film Company in the Mecca Building. The film was a screen arrangement of Tristan Bernard's drama, "Jeanne Dore," and was taken in France.

It was in this play that Mme. Bernhardt was appearing in her theatre in Paris when the trouble with her leg forced her to leave the stage. Mme. Bernhardt's rôle is that of a middle-aged woman, and while she appears a trifle older in the pictures, perhaps, than on her last visit here, otherwise she looks the same wonderful artiste of other years. Her great visual charm and her marvelous facial expression are still potent.

The film itself was so arranged before it was sent to this country that all evidences of the actress' lameness because of her artificial leg have been deleted. So the film, as it reached America, never shows the actress walking. In every scene in which she appears she is shown either seated or standing, and whenever she starts to walk the scene is immediately changed through the devices of the switchback, the cut-in, or the printed legend. Thus, if Madame rises from a chair and starts to walk across the room to a window, she is seen to rise, the picture is snuffed out for an instant, and when it again covers the screen the actress is shown at her destination.

The effect is no more confusing than in the average picture, which often baffles and irritates all but the incorrigible movie fan. The picture is so focused that the feet of the actress do not show, or if they do only for short intervals, so there is nothing in the many scenes of the protodrama, which is melodramatic in the extreme, that would apprise the uninformed of her misfortune.

According to the motion picture people Mme. Bernhardt will never be able to act again on the legitimate stage. The directors who took the film so informed the company controlling the American rights. But William F. Connor, Mme. Bernhardt's American representative, denies this, and insists that she will make her American tour this Winter as planned. "Jeanne Dore" has been announced as one of the new offerings of her répertoire when she arrives. The picture shown yesterday, after further excisions and rearrangement, will be exhibited publicly within the month.

O 21, 1915

GERALDINE FARRAR SEEN BUT NOT HEARD

Theda Bara Is Presented as a Rival Carmen in a Scenario That Follows the Opera.

Geraldine Farrar, favorite prima donna of the greatest opera house in the world, came to New York yesterday. She came not in the flesh but in the shadow, not on the operatic stage nor on the concert platform but on the screen. The place was the Strand Theatre, the occasion the first New York presentation of "Carmen," an ingeniously prepared, picturesque, amorous and exceedingly physical photoplay based on the novel by Prosper Merimée. In this picture, a handsome and creditable product of the Lasky studios now released like any other in the Paramount program, Miss Farrar plays, of course, the leading rôle, and by this means makes her first New York appearance in the movies.

It is a curious commentary on the crazy economy of the theatre that a supreme dramatic soprano should give any of her precious time to a form of entertainment—to an art, if you will—wherein the chief characteristic is a complete and abysmal silence. But, though the call of the movies is audible enough, there is small reason for fear that, after Miss Farrar's success, there will be a great rush of prima donnas to California, for precious few of them could so meet the exactions of the camera.

As for Miss Farrar, let it be said that among movie actresses she is one of the best. The Strand may be besieged all this week simply because her name has long been one to conjure with, but it seems altogether probable that when, if ever, she appears in another picture, the movie patrons will crowd to see it because they cherish her as one of their own. There is every indication that new millions will soon be calling her "Our Geraldine."

This new movie star "registers," as the film folk have it. There is no doubt at all about that. She does more than make faces at the camera; she knows that in acting for motion pictures, she must do more than go through the motions. And she does. Her familiar vigor and dash are helpful, and she can make good use of the flashing Farrar smile. But quite aside from these, she brings to the richly colorful performance a degree of vitality that animates all the picture and offers a good illustration of the difference between posing and acting for the camera.

Her playing is able. Also it is bold, bald, and in dubious taste. Many portions of the film are successive pictorial studies of physical passion, and it is small wonder that in some quarter the much belabored censors winced.

Merimée's story of the gypsy has been skillfully and imaginatively adapted in the Lasky studios, and the product is pictorially handsome. Many stretches of the film are impressionistic and reveal the strides the movie directors are taking in their business. The unfolding of the film at the Strand is accompanied by a clever arrangement of music from the opera. Most of this adds considerably to the entertainment, but it is rather too bad to have the "Habanera" sung poorly offstage as it was yesterday afternoon.

The Fox film studios boldly challenged comparison with the Farrar picture by bringing a screen "Carmen" of their own to town on the very same day and displaying it to the patrons of the Academy of Music and the Riverside Theatre. This "Carmen" has in the leading rôle Theda Bara, a movie star who is widely known as "the vampire woman" of the screen and who is immensely popular in the theatres where her pictures are shown.

This second "Carmen" is an example of excellent motion picture photography, but its scenario, which follows the opera libretto rather than the Merimée story, is loose and vague, and Miss Bara seems

very mechanically seductive when compared, as she must be, with Geraldine Farrar. The Fox " Carmen " has none of the elements which make the Lasky " Carmen " remarkable, and none, it should be added, of the elements which make the latter picture objectionable.

N 1, 1915

THEDA BARA

WELL CAST IN "THE SERPENT"

The ingenuity of the men who write scenarios for Theda Bara must be hard pressed at times, because Miss Bara, according to her press agent, is a perfect specimen of the "vampire" type, and the story must be bounded on four sides by a certain kind of atmosphere. Since Miss Bara is so well fitted by looks to act this sort of creature before the camera, it would be squandering her resources to cast her in a Mary Pickford sort of role.

Whoever wrote the scenario of " The Serpent," the new William Fox picture revealed simultaneously in the Academy of Music and the Riverside yesterday for the first time, should therefore be praised in the introduction for having furnished this actress, who is no novice in the films, with a stirring story. After that the producer should receive a kind word for the little touches that go to make " The Serpent " above the average of its kind.

One of these touches comes to mind immediately, because it is in the last reel. The scene is a Russian peasant's cottage and the father of the girl portrayed by Miss Bara attempted to draw on his boot. When it won't go on he looks within and discovers a mouse. Business of close-up of the boot showing the mouse. The cat by the hearth sniffs, and when the mouse is turned out of his home, pussy is seen chasing him to a corner, and—exit mouse. Which is only one of a number of realistic touches that add interest to the picture.

The problem of having Miss Bara play the part of a vampire and still retain the sympathy of the audience is solved by making her evil deeds the figments of a dream. Vania Lazar, the serf's daughter, whom Miss Bara impersonates, dreams that the Grand Duke has ruined her life, and that in vengeance she sets out upon a career of wickedness that covers several continents.

First she goes to London and wrecks a perfectly good home by causing one brother to break a wine bottle over another's head for love of her. Then she becomes a famous actress and the Grand Duke, not recognizing her, pays court to her. From him she learns that his son is convalescing in a Paris hospital from wounds suffered in battle, and she hastens there and becomes a nurse that she may be near him and drag him into her web. Her revenge is complete when she brings father and son together and causes the son to utter this subtitle: " My Wife."

That is her dream. What really happens is that Vania falls out of bed and goes downstairs to finally gain her father's consent to wed Andrey Sobi, her real sweetheart. Thus is art and virtue served and the sympathies of the audience preserved with no sacrifice of thrills.

The interpolation of scenes illustrating episodes not directly concerned with the plot is a favorite practice of directors. Thus Vania, sitting beside the wounded son, says: " Tell me the story of the battle of Ancourt," and presto, a succession of unusually thrilling battle scenes is unreeled. They are so realistic that until the hero himself is identified leading charges one begins to believe they are scenes from the real war, and not a mimic one staged in New Jersey.

Miss Bara's following is easily accounted for by this picture. She is a clever actress with a high sense of screen values. Hers is a marvelously mobile and expressive face that can express deeper scorn by a curl of the lip or greater sorrow through an expression of her eyes than the average screen player can denote with exaggerated heavings and writhings.

Ja 24, 1916

RIALTO THEATRE OPENS ITS DOORS

THE GOOD BAD MAN

The Rialto Theatre, which for nearly a year has been building on the spot in Times Square where Hammerstein's old Victoria used to stand, opened its doors last evening to a specially invited and very imposing audience. Today and daily hereafter the clamorous public will be admitted, and so another motion picture house has been added to the thousands which dot the map of the United States. But the difference between the queer, jiggly films that used to serve as chasers on the Keith programs fifteen years ago and the elaborate photoplays of 1916 is no greater than the difference between the evilly ventilated little nickelodeons and the luxurious theatre which was opened last night.

A handsomely appointed house dedicated entirely to the movies is thus established on one of the finest theatrical sites in the world. At every turn you found some grounds for the enthusiasm of the laureate of the occasion, who in the program burst forth as follows:

"With the peal of the grand organ, the fanfare of the orchestra, and the flash of thousands of iridescent lights, a new palace of polite pleasure for thousands is born tonight."

The interior is done in ivory and gray with hangings of red. The dome over the balcony is lovely in coloring, a playground for innumerable lights of every hue. The very ushers are elegantly upholstered, each carrying an electric flash and a swaggerstick. There was some speculation last night as to whether these were to be used for prodding a sleepy patron or for hitting the critics on the knuckles, but a part of the Rialto Review showed the ushers in action. It seems they are trained in first aid work, and the swaggersticks are used in making tourniquets. The Review also transports you to the Rialto in Venice with Nevin's lovely Venetian music as the appropriate accompaniment.

Like the Strand, which preceded it and has served to some degree as the model for all of the finer motion picture theatres in America, the Rialto is an expression of the taste and ideas of S. L. Rothapfel, its managing director. Here is a goodly auditorium, with seats downstairs and in the steep cantilever balcony to the number of 2,000. Here is a big orchestra, a program that includes some singing and then no end of movies, with two photoplays and a topical review of the sort that shows a Governor dedicating something somewhere and some children doing something somewhere else, and so on.

The Knickerbocker is a fine old theatre temporarily made over into a movie house, and even the Strand is so built that at very short notice it could be converted to the uses of opera or drama, but the Rialto is a motion picture house, pure and simple. It is stageless, the screen being placed boldly against the back wall of the theatre. It is built in the conviction that the American passion for the movies is here to stay.

Triangle films seem to be the central attraction at the Rialto and the opening bill contained an abundance of the Triangle's trump card—Douglas Fairbanks. His Wild West, sagebrush photoplay, "The Good Bad Man," might have been designed by Penrod Schofield with flashes by a sentimental chambermaid, but it is full to the brim with Fairbanks. His expressive face, radiant, toothsome smile, immense activity, and apparent disposition to romp all over the map make him a treasure to the cinema. No deserter from the spoken drama is more engaging in the new work than Douglas Fairbanks. May his shadow never grow less.

Ap 22, 1916

INCE PHOTO PAGEANT SHOWN

"Civilization" Is a Spectacle of the Physical Horrors of War.

"Civilization," Thomas H. Ince's effort to rival D. W. Griffith with a photo spectacle of the scale and scope of "The Birth of a Nation," was displayed in New York for the first time last evening at the Criterion Theatre. It is an excellently elaborate photo pageant on the physical horrors of war, a big motion picture marked by lavishness in production and beauty in photography.

"Civilization" attempts to serve the pacifists as "The Battle Cry of Peace" tried to serve the cause of preparedness. Its argument is elementary, a leaf out of the pacifists' primer, a projection on the screen of something of that state of mind that was most in evidence in this neighborhood at the time the Ford expedition set forth from these shores. Its program describes it as a direct appeal to the "mothers of men."

The hero of "Civilization" is the submarine commander who, secretly wearing the purple cross of the Mothers of Men Society, refuses to torpedo a defenseless passenger vessel. In the mutiny that follows the submarine is sunk. He is drowned, and his spirit goes to an inferno inspired by Doré. There the Christ comes to him, receives him as a redeemed soul, returns among men in the discarded body of the dead man, and there takes the warlike King on such a review of war's horrors as to make him cry for peace. The King then heeds the pleas of the Mothers of Men, and the last picture shows the soldiers returning jubilant to their peasant homes.

In the earlier part of this photoplay there are many stirring battle scenes, and the whole episode of the submarine and the sinking of another Lusitania is extraordinarily graphic—so graphic, indeed, that at this point in the unfolding of the spectacle last evening Billie Burke fainted.

"Civilization" was displayed last

evening with a full orchestra in full
blast, with off-stage singing, both solo
and choral, and with a preliminary cor-
poreal pantomime of the sort employed
in " Ramona," and always of doubtful
value in the screen world. A large audience, full of notables, saw and applauded the picture at its first showing,
and at the end called for Mr. Ince, who
was led on by Al Woods, his associate
in the New York display of the film.
Mr. Ince spoke his acknowledgments
with a modesty and brevity in striking
contrast with the fulsome Ince-adulation
which makes the program such painful
reading. He has projected a philosophy
of war on a par with " War Brides," an
entertainment on an artistic level with
" Ben Hur," a dramatic photo spectacle
that falls somewhat short of "The Birth
of a Nation."

Je 3, 1916

'INTOLERANCE' IMPRESSIVE.

D. W. Griffith's New Picture Is a Stupendous Spectacle.

Ever since the remarkable film,
"The Birth of a Nation," was unreeled
before an amazed public more than a
year ago, the question of whether it
was an accident or whether D. W. Griffith, the man who directed its taking,
was really a new master of the cinema
has interested those who study the
personalities that manipulate the puppets of stage and studio. The answer
came last night when Mr. Griffith's
second big picture, "Intolerance," was
exhibited in the Liberty Theatre before
an audience that might have gathered
to witness the premiere of some favorite dramatist's latest work, so dotted
was it with prominent folk of the
theatre.

The verdict " Intolerance " renders in
the controversy concerning its maker is
that he is a real wizard of lens and
screen. For in spite of its utter inco-
herence the questionable taste of some
of its scenes and the cheap banalities
into which it sometimes lapses " Intolerance " is an interesting and unusual
picture. The stupendousness of its pano-
ramas, the grouping and handling of
its great masses of players, make it an
impressive spectacle.

An excerpt from the highly literary
program will give some idea of Mr.
Griffith's latest offering.

" The purpose of the production," so
runs the foreword, " is to trace a universal theme through various periods of
the race's history. Ancient, sacred,
mediaeval, and modern times are considered. Events are not set forth in
their historical sequence, or according to
the accepted forms of dramatic construction, but as they might flash across a
mind seeking to parallel the life of the
different ages.

" There are four separate stories, each
with its own set of characters. Following the introduction of each period there
are subsequent interruptions as the different stories develop along similar lines,
switching from one to the other as the
mind might do while contemplating such
a theme."

What Mr. Griffith has attempted to do
in his eight or nine reels of film is to
show that intolerance has always been
a vice of man. To prove his point he
has unfolded a tale of Babylon when
Belshazzar was King, has prepared a
series of a few rich tableaux of the persecution of the Nazarene, has pictured
with a wealth of atmosphere the massacre of St. Bartholomew, and paralleling these has spun a lurid, modern
melodrama in the prevailing mode of the
screen.

Shorn of the impressive bibliography
recorded on the program and of the
somewhat hazy symbolism that flickers
between the episodes, " Intolerance " is
a regulation photo-drama, superior to
the average feature picture because of
the skill with which it is handled, and
an amazingly accurate and thrilling
picture of Assyrian civilization.

The French scenes and those of the
life of Christ constitute only a smart
part of the film. They were apparently
included to develop the idea of the presence of intolerance through the ages.
In spite of their general excellence and
the faithfulness with which they have
been reproduced, tehy do nothing but
add to the general confusion and might
well be eliminated. This is especially
true of those scenes in which the
Christ is impersonated, always a questionable proceeding if the feelings of
many are to be respected.

It is the Babylonian portion of the
film that will commend it to the great
public. These pictures of the walls of
Babylon, broad enough for chariots to
pass at ease, of the great gates thronged
with picturesque caravans, of the palace
of Belshazzar with its myriad slaves
and dancing girls, and of the seige and
fall of the city are indeed masterpieces
of the cine.

They are so splendid that it seems a
pity the story was not deleted

S 6, 1916

NEW COLOR MOVIES SHOWN.

The movies have merely scratched the
surface. The enthusiasts have proclaimed all along that as they developed
they would gain in effectiveness, and
pointed to the possibilities of color
reproduction as one of the directions in
which they would develop. How infinite these possibilities are became evident at the Strand yesterday, when
color movies made by a new process
were shown for the first time.

The subjects were many and varied.

and included land and seascapes, animal pictures, and portraits of people. The irridescence of the surface of a soap-bubble in the sunlight, the glow of a woman's cheek, the brilliance of the setting sun have all been caught and reflected with amazing veracity. One especially alluring picture of a herd of cattle rounding the crest of a hill gave the feeling of a Bonheur painting come to life. The color gives a third dimension to the pictures, so that in many instances the perspective is quite remarkable. The films were made by the Prizma process.

A commendable screen version of Oliver Goldsmith's "The Vicar of Wakefield" was exhibited yesterday at the Rialto. This film had the honor of being the first one to win the stamp of approval of the recently formed Photo-play League. The movies love misery if it can be shut off in time for a happy ending, so this classic in which the woes of the Primrose family are recited conforms to the photoplay norm.

A careful selection of backgrounds has helped give an old English flavor to the picture. More than to any other one factor, however, it owes its success to the acting of Frederick Warde in the title rôle. That veteran of many rôles and years not only looks the part, but acts it with great skill and understanding.

Rex Beach's Alaskan story, "The Barrier," has been made into a strong photoplay, which was exhibited for the first time yesterday at the Broadway. The film's makers have succeeded in conveying to us something of the virility of this author's stories. The players were chosen with a sense of types. An adaptation of Winston Churchill's novel, "The Crisis," was put on exhibition at the Park.

F 26, 1917

SARAH BERNHARDT IN REAL WAR FILM

"MOTHERS OF FRANCE"

"Mothers of France," a cinematic epic of the great war, is the photo-drama for which Sarah Bernhardt acted before she sailed from France to come to America last Fall. Jean Richepin, dramatist and Academician, wrote the scenario, and the French Government offered every facility for enacting its scenes before a truly martial background. It was exhibited here for the first time yesterday at the Rialto.

"Mothers of France" atones for most of the sins of the movies; to see it is recompense for having sat through a series of atrocious and banal war films purporting to point a moral. It is pro-paganda subtle and powerful that must move even the most calloused and neutral observer. Only the pro-Teuton could see it and not be touched by its sincerity and its art—the art that is inherent in truth.

It is a brief for the women of France who are doing their bit behind the fighting lines, told in terms of the most vivid realism. The story unfolded is of the sacrifices of a small group of neighbors in a village of France. It is a tale whose various details have been duplicated in every corner of that fair land since the war began.

A woman, whose son has been wounded, leaves the base hospital at Rheims, where she is serving as a nurse, to search for him. She finds him in the first aid station to which he has been carried, and shortly after her arrival he dies in her arms. The death of her husband, a Major, in battle, is her next bereavement, but still she is brave, hiding her feelings in public and doing her part in the great work of healing torn bodies and lives. "We have not the right to curse," she tells her stricken neighbor whose son has been blinded in battle. "Those for whom we weep are dead in order that our mother shall possess all things. France never dies."

A nation at war provided the mise en scène for this universal drama of France, and that nation's greatest actress gave her services that the world might weep with the mothers of France and rejoice at their courage and the spirit, a courage that passes all understanding. Mme. Bernhardt acted the rôle of the central figure of the story, a choice that was ideal both because of her art and because more than any other living person she typifies to America the joy, the warmth, the strength, the capacity to drink to the full of life that is France.

The power of the movies to obliterate space removes the handicap of her inability to walk freely; she is always revealed standing or sitting, and one is conscious only of the wonderful expressiveness of her countenance and gestures. In one scene in particular, in which she stands before the portrait of her dead husband, the poignancy of the grief expressed seems to lose nothing through its inarticulateness.

The skill of the players, all of whom, even to the children, possess the Gallic felicity of gesture, combines with the unmistakable veracity of the scenes to make this a film unique in its power to stir the emotions. Mme. Bernhardt, in the rôle of the mother, is pictured in the hospitals, the commissary camps, and even in the very trenches with the poilus. Once she is shown waiting in the corner of a transverse to allow a squad of soldiers to run by, each carrying an aerial torpedo.

Again she stands before the statue of Joan of Arc in front of the war-scarred Cathedral of Rheims, its shattered window[...] and bag-protected buttresses plainly visible. Real chateaux, real peasant women toiling in the fields, and real munitions smoke give a flavor that no amount of paint and plaster villages and trenches filled with tin soldiers hired at a dollar a day could ever hope to approximate.

The artistic value of the film itself has been enhanced by the manner of exhibition. The singing of the "Marseillaise" precedes the showing, and throughout its course appropriate music, with the French national anthem as the recurrent theme, is played. Then by the process of double projection glimpses of Geraldine Farrar's portrayal of Joan of Arc are thrown on the screen synchronously with the other picture.

A picturization of "A Tale of Two Cities" was the new offering at the Academy of Music. "Sapho," with Pauline Frederick in the title rôle, was shown at the Strand.

Mr 12, 1917

CHAPLIN AS SOLDIER DROPS OLD DISGUISE

IN "SHOULDER ARMS"

"The fool's funny," was the chuckling observation of one of those who saw Charlie Chaplin's new film, "Shoulder Arms," at the Strand yesterday—and, apparently, that's the way everybody felt. There have been learned discussions as to whether Chaplin's comedy is low or high, artistic or crude, but no one can deny that when he impersonates a screen fool he is funny. Most of those who go to find fault with him remain to laugh. They may still find fault, but they will keep on laughing.

In "Shoulder Arms" Chaplin is as funny as ever. He is even more enjoyable than one is likely to anticipate because he abandons some of the tricks of former comedies and introduces new properties into his horseplay. His limber little stick, for instance, which had begun to lose its comic character through overuse, does not appear. Instead Chaplin, camouflaged as a tree trunk, plays destructively with one of the tree's branches. The baggy, black trousers are also gone, giving place to a uniform and such equipment as a soldier never dreamed of. The comedian begins as a rooky, the most awkward member of the awkward squad, and ends by capturing the Kaiser, the Crown Prince and von Hindenburg. Between the beginning and the end there are many laughs.

There is a Burlingham Travel Scenic on the Strand bill which shows many interesting views of wounded British soldiers arriving in Switzerland, where the people bedecked them with flowers, and there are views of a French tuberculosis hospital in the mountains.

"Shootin' Mad," with Gilbert Anderson, also at the Strand, is a Wild West photoplay without much merit, either as comedy or melodrama.

Another Wild West production was new yesterday at the Rialto. It is "The Pretender," with William Desmond, and in it there are at least comedy bits that deserve the laughter they get. The Rialto also shows "The Triumph of Transportation," which sketches the evolution of transportation from the stage of the naked negro carrying loads swung on a pole to the triumphant time of the modern motor truck. The film shows something of the construction of trucks, and their use at the front and in rural communities.

Speaking again of the Woolly West kind of film, the best of the week is at the Rivoli. It is an Alfred Henry Lewis story, "Rose of Wolf[...]lle," turned into an amusing photoplay.

"A Woman of Impulse," with Lina Cavalieri in the leading rôle, is the Rivoli's featured offering, and although Mme. Cavalieri is undoubtedly capable of good screen acting, and the director of the production, Edward Jose, succeeded in creating a number of scenes dramatically and scenically effective, the play as a whole bores one, largely because it starts out in the mood of grand operatic tragedy and then works clumsily into that of modern fictitious trash with a "happy," but weak and wan, ending.

"Midst Peaceful Scenes," the pictorial at the Rivoli, is one of Van Scoy's, released by the [...] Film Company. This will recommend it to many.

"The Making of a Sailor," an official naval film illustrating the process of sailor-making from the time a youth gazes at a recruiting poster until he becomes a full-fledged seaman, was shown last night at the Fulton Theatre to invited spectators, consisting mostly of the families of men in the service. It was enthusiastically received.

O 21, 1918

BROKEN BLOSSOMS

A screen tragedy—not a movie melodrama with an unhappy ending—but a sincere, human tragedy—that is what D. W. Griffith has had the courage and the capacity to produce in "Broken Blossoms," which opened his repertory season at the George M. Cohan Theatre last night. Mr. Griffith chose a tragic story of impossible love, love impossible in this world of passions and prejudices and brutal forces; he absorbed it in its full meaning, recast it in his mind pictorially, translated it from the written words of the author into the scenes and action of a photoplay, added what was needed to make it live in pictures, left out what pictures could not have adequately expressed—and "Broken Blossoms" came to the screen, a masterpiece in moving pictures.

The original story is "The Chink and the Child" in Thomas Burke's "Limehouse Nights." The chink is far away from his native land, living in London, a dreamer and a poet lost in the Western Chinese quarter. The child is a girl, the daughter of a cockney pugilist, who makes her his punching bag when his temper and liquor control him, which is most of the time. The chink sees the beauty of the child, but always from a distance, until one day, when the pugilist has beaten her more unmercifully than usual, she staggers through the streets and falls in the Chinaman's door. He takes her up, bathes her wounds, and places her as a princess in his room. He robes her in silk, surrounds her with flowers, burns incense at her feet—and worships her. And for the first time in her life she smiles.

But some one tells the pugilist and he discovers family honor. His child with a dirty chink! He'llearn "them both. And he does. He smashes the temple that the poet from China has built—and all three, the pugilist, the girl, and the poet, go down in the crash. It was inevitable from the beginning.

This bare narration of the story cannot hope even to suggest the power and truth of the tragedy that Mr. Griffith has pictured. All of his mastery of picture-making, the technique that is preeminently his by invention and control, the skill and subtlety with which he can unfold a story—all of the Griffith ability has gone into the making of "Broken Blossoms." Many of the pictures surpass anything hitherto seen on the screen in beauty and dramatic force. The whole is a photoplay that cannot fail to impress anyone who looks at it in any mood short of the most resolute hostility.

But though the photoplay is distinctly Mr. Griffith's achievement, it is not his alone. A number of unnamed persons must have contributed to it, in addition to the cast—and the cast was triumphantly equal to everything Mr. Griffith could expect. Leading all is Lillian Gish. Miss Gish has repeatedly, in varying rôles, proved her superior talent as a screen actress, but she has never been as human and at the same time as accomplished as in the character of the child.

The rôle is so difficult as to be beyond the reach of almost any actress whose name comes to mind, but it was within Miss Gish's grasp. She was such a child as the poor little delicate blossom must have been. Donald Crisp was violently realistic as the pugilist. Richard Barthelmess was a sensitive, convincing yellow man, and Edward Peil, as a Chinese of another character, made an impressive contrast.

The overture and orchestral accompaniment of the picture, described as thematic, and including original compositions by Mr. Griffith and Louis F. Gottschalk, heightened the effect of the photoplay, and the production was further enhanced by the suggestive decorations of the theatre.

The spectators, among whom were many well known persons, applauded enthusiastically after the presentation and refused to leave until Mr. Griffith had answered their calls for his appearance on the stage.

My 14, 1919

BLIND HUSBANDS

Many who saw Eric Stroheim as a Prussian villain in "The Heart of Humanity" and other war films may have wondered, because he seemed so completely designed for his part and nothing else, what he would do when the public no longer demanded a Hun to hiss. If they will go to the Capitol Theatre this week and see "Blind Husbands" they will know that whenever Mr. Stroheim desires to give up acting, or is not required, in pictures, he can devote all of his time to directing—and if the promise that is borne of his first performance as a director is fulfilled, the screen will be greatly enriched.

"Blind Husbands," as it stands, is superior to most of the year's productions, and, more importantly, its outstanding pictorial quality indicates that Mr. Stroheim, unlike many directors, grasps the fact that the screen is the place for moving pictures and that whatever is to be done on it with artistic finish, must be done pictorially. So many directors use moving pictures chiefly to ornament and enliven their stories. They do not depend upon them in crises. Whenever dramatic moments come, or when plot is to be unfolded or carried forward, they turn to familiar, but ineffectual, words. But Mr. Stroheim, although he has not done all that he might in the elimination of text, has evidently relied principally upon pictures and in a number of his dominating scenes there are no words at all, only eloquent pictures, more eloquent than words could ever be.

The climax of the play comes when two men, an Austrian Lieutenant, a "love - pirate" and "lounge - lizard," and an American surgeon, a man of worth-while ability, climb one of the peaks of the Dolomites together. The Austrian has boasted to women of the mountains he has climbed and he has influenced the surgeon's neglected wife, but when he stands before the steep side of a real mountain he is adequate only as to his faultless Alpine costume. He does not choose to climb, but he must The other man has forced him to it.

14

As he goes up he weakens, while the other increases in strength, and when the two stand alone on the pinnacle one is the master and the other a contemptible thing. The story gives dramatic suspense to this scene, but the suspense is heightened, the scene is developed to its full power, by pictures, for which no words are needed and few are used. And so in smaller scenes, in their intelligibility of action and genuineness of setting, Mr. Stroheim has worked and succeeded with the camera.

He needed, of course, competent actors, and found them in himself as the Austrian Lieutenant, in Sam de Grasse as the surgeon, and in Francelia Billington as the woman. H. Gibson-Gowland, as an Alpine guide, and others in supplemental rôles met all requirements for background and atmosphere.

By its pictorial quality, therefore, "Blind Husbands," not especially original in plot, and weakened somewhat by its resort to the well-worn theatrical trick of withholding important information from the spectators, is interesting throughout and at times supremely compelling. Some of its scenes are continentally frank, but they are not offensive, nor more suggestive than is necessary to present the triangle of the self-absorbed husband, the neglected wife, and the human bird of prey.

It ought to be added that Mr. Stroheim originally named his production "The Pinnacle," and, according to report, seriously objected when the cheapening title, "Blind Husbands," was plastered on it by the proprietary company.

"Tom's Little Star," one of the Stage Women's War Relief films, in which a number of theatrical celebrities are displayed, is also at the Capitol.

D 8, 1919

The second group of reviews covers the period approximately from the end of World War I to the Wall Street crash, which coincided with a major crisis in the cinema: the end of the silent era. The war years had been immensely profitable for the expanding American film industry because the war had virtually wiped out competition abroad. With the greatest ease, the American film business absorbed subsequently a major portion of the European market, dominating it for many years to come. Now that European production was virtually at a standstill, Hollywood hired available talent, reputable directors, performers, designers, and other highly qualified artists and craftsmen, especially from Germany, France, and Sweden. Hollywood grew into a fabulous super-enterprise that was as much an idea and a myth as a physical reality and a place, a compound of wealth, glamor, extravagance, vice, and scandal. Superstars were made, like so many homunculi, unreal and remote, receiving larger salaries than bank presidents, living in an artificial paradise of inconceivable luxury and, supposedly, debauch. Hollywood production methods became streamlined, gaining in size and efficiency what they sacrificed in substance and quality. Eventually, the enormous economic power of the film industry was concentrated in the hands of a few company heads who dominated dictatorially not only the production but also the distribution —an unbeatable monopoly. To counter the risk of protest, rejection, or censure, after having invested a fortune in a new production, the producers took the precaution of establishing a system of self-regulatory precensorship, the so-called Hays office, that, trying absurdly to codify morality, did more harm than good.

The United States became an island unto itself, although one disturbed by ominous stirrings under the shiny surface of prosperity, exuberance, and relaxed morality. Women were allowed unprecedented freedom in dress and manners, independence, and living style, a change that furnished appealing story material and attractive settings. Prohibition, organized crime, and gangster warfare occupied the headlines and provided sensational film fare. The Hollywood ambition for "colossal" productions found its master in Cecil B. DeMille, creator of biblical epics, as well as other specialized talent for staging the equally popular, elaborate musicals. Chaplin's *A Woman of Paris,* a sophisticated comedy of manners, was followed by equally elegant comedies, superbly directed by

Ernst Lubitsch. The Western became established as a very popular genre, developing its own typical story pattern, its special hero prototype, and its own stars. With Buster Keaton appeared a comic of a stature resembling Chaplin's, and Harold Lloyd and Laurel and Hardy were close behind. *Goldrush* was the first typical Chaplin feature in a long line of masterpieces following in quick succession. John Ford began his by now legendary career. Griffith's prestige, too exclusively based on the success of his two great epics, suffered an unjustified neglect in the chronicle of the twenties. It is evident that the Hollywood system did frustrate but not wholly destroy the creativity of some distinguished and some promising directors. However, the sheer number of notable productions, new directors, prominent stars, and the diversity of genres put the American contribution far above that of the rest of the world.

Gradually, as production resumed in Europe, foreign films were imported, acquainting the American audience with new ideas, new styles, and new personalities, though neither with sufficient regularity nor in sufficient quantity to reach large masses. But, as Arthur Knight points out, the success of E. A. Dupont's *Variety* was followed by a veritable "Germanization" of the Hollywood studios. There is one significant gap in this volume in the film documentation of the twenties: the Soviet cinema, and it is not the reviewers' fault. Due mostly to political reasons, the import of films from the Soviet Union was much delayed and not remotely representative. Little was known in this country of the enormous productivity and the vital experimentation of such prominent directors as Kuleshof, Vertov, Eisenstein, Pudovkin, and Dovzhenko.

At the end of this prosperous decade, the advent of sound fell like a deadly blow, creating utter chaos in the movie industry; it was never to be the same again.

DR. JEKYLL AND MR. HYDE

John Barrymore as Dr. Jekyll and Mr. Hyde came to the screen of the Rivoli yesterday afternoon.

This statement must be the outstanding and joyfully heralded feature of any report on the motion picture version of the story that Robert Louis Stevenson wrote and the play in which Richard Mansfield appeared—for the excellence of the photoplay, everything that distinguishes it from the pictures that come and go from day to day marks it as something special and extraordinary—is centered in Mr. Barrymore's flawless performance. He receives some aid from the camera, of course, but those who go to the Rivoli this week will be impressed more by his independence of cinematic trickery than by the skilful and wholly legitimate use he makes of it. Those who expect the photoplay to be good because "it's just the thing for the movies" will find that it is good because it's just the thing for John Barrymore. It is true that the screen lends itself peculiarly to the story, but it can be only a sufficient medium for Mr. Barrymore's unique ability. It is what Mr. Barrymore himself does that makes the dual character of Jekyll and Hyde tremendous. His performance is one of pure motion-picture pantomime on as high a level as has ever been attained by anyone. In a story that was written as a "shocker" and a play that is always a melodrama, he creates such a genuinely beautiful Jekyll and compellingly hideous Hyde, and emphasizes the contrast between the two with such a sure eye for essentials, that one must believe, in both while he sees them and afterwards admire a work of art.

But all of this may seem trivial to some. While Mr. Barrymore is achieving greatness as Richard III on the stage, anything he does in "the movies" must be totally unimportant to many, and serious applause of his effort on the screen will probably be put on a par with lauding the idle limericks of a great poet. But there is no real support for such an attitude. Even if one waive the contention that Mr. Barrymore's Dr. Jekyll and Mr. Hyde is not reduced to present insignificance by his contemporary Richard III, he may fall back on the fact that a great many more people will see the former than the latter, and have through it their only opportunity of knowing anything about what Mr. Barrymore can do. This is true for today and more importantly true for the future. Coming generations—there's H. 3d, for example—will hear of John Barrymore's Richard III, and, only hearing, may be skeptical or indifferent, as are many today of reports about Booth and Garrick, but they may see Dr. Jekyll and

Mr. Hyde and, in addition to enjoying something of Mr. Barrymore's art, they will receive a personal impression of the actor that will enable them to know and appreciate him as his predecessors are not now known and appreciated. And, anyhow, it is contended that Dr. Jekyll and Mr. Hyde is a work well worth while in itself for all time. So no apologies are offered for consideration of it.

High praise of the photoplay, however, must be limited to what Mr. Barrymore does in it. The production, aside from his performance, is uninspired. It is usual. The story has been movie-molded almost to the obliteration of its individual character, and those who were led to hope that it would escape the moral monger will be disappointed. It bears the unmistakable stamp of the motion-picture mill.

John Barrymore's acting, though, more than offsets everything else. It places the picture high up among screen accomplishments.

Also at the Rivoli is a frisky little comedy, entitled "Uneasy Feet," in which pantomimic legs and feet amusingly tell a story without the aid of words. It is a most agreeable departure from prevalent slapstick and horseplay.

Mr 29, 1920

THE MARK OF ZORRO

Douglas Fairbanks's latest motion picture, "The Mark of Zorro," is at the Capitol this week. The program says that it is "from" a story by Johnston McCulley, called "The Curse of Capistrano," but one who has not read Mr. McCulley's story imagines that it is pretty far from it. There's too much Fairbanks in it for any one to have written it without the athletic comedian definitely in mind. What is on the screen is probably "The Curse of Capistrano" spiced and speeded up to suit the taste of Douglas Fairbanks and the many who enjoy his gay and lively style of playing. This means that whatever plausibility there was in the original has been sacrificed for headlong action, that whatever consistency there was has given place to intermittent fun and thrills, that whatever of sentiment there was has become romantic nonsense. All of which may mean that "The Mark of Zorro" is more enjoyable than "The Curse of Capistrano" could ever hope to be.

Certainly there are moments in the motion picture which must delight anyone, no matter how preposterous they are. There is a duel scene, for example, which is something distinctly original in the history of mortal combat on the stage or screen, and there are spirited races and pursuits, sudden appearances, quick changes and flashes of tempestuous love-making that are typically, and entertaingly, Fairbanksian.

But "The Mark of Zorro" is also different in some respects from the usual Fairbanks picture. It is somewhat tamer, for one thing, the scenary especially having more of the quality of inertia. There are no mountain slides or floods in it, and the hero himself actually appears sometimes as a constitutionally languid individual, wearied by the exertions of a carriage ride.

He is one Don Diego Vega, an aristocrat of Spanish California, who seems content to loaf through life in fancy clothes and rich surroundings, but is really so moved by the tyranny of his country's rulers that he originates for himself another role, that of Senor Zorro, an alert and mysterious avenger of the people's wrongs, who appears suddenly when least expected by the authorities, and disappears as suddenly when most desired by them, always in black mask and costume, with a sure sword, a swift horse and a sense of humor.

There may be those who will find "The Mark of Zorro" a little tedious in places because Fairbanks is not frolicking through every scene of it and, as he never creates a character and will not confine himself to any possible plot or plan, his pictures must depend almost entirely upon his own athletics and absurdities, supplemented by those of scenery and cast. So, whenever, "The Mark of Zorro" calms down, something seems to be missing.

The settings of the picture are picturesquely, and some of them magnificently, Spanish, and they often contrast amusingly with the emphatically non-Spanish appearance of some of the players, including, of course, Fairbanks himself. Still, the cast does what is expected of it, and, as no one cares whether the story is consistently Spanish or just outlandish, there's no fault to find. Those who do the principal work are Noah Berry, Marguerite De LaMotte and Robert McKim. The production was well-directed by Fred Niblo.

N 29, 1920

PASSION

One of the pre-eminent motion pictures of the present cinematographic age is at the Capitol this week. It is most inappropriately entitled "Passion," and has been imported from Europe, having originated in Northern Germany, by Associated First National Pictures, Inc. The Polish actress, Pola Negri, plays its leading rôle, and its director was Ernst Lubitch, who is said to have a reputation as a cinematician of the first rank abroad.

According to report, the Continental name of the picture was "du Barry," and this title might well have been retained, for it comes as close to giving a key to the story as any that comes to mind. The story is that of Louis XV.'s mistress in her environment, and this environment, the life of the day, with its individual figures and its human masses, at least as they are popularly imagined, is the real material of the narrative. u Barry herself is only a part of it all, and so are the others, especially the King and Armand de Foix, who, with the woman between them, form the three principals of the plot. It is about these three, the toy of erratic destiny, the mad King, and the humble first love of the du Barry when she was only Jeanne, the milliner's apprentice, that the action centres, but they are merely the centre of action that radiates in all directions and reaches through the Court of Louis and the seething life of Paris, from the omnipotence of the fat Bourbon tyrant to the overwhelming might of the frenzied revolutionary mob.

It is in building this story of prerevolutionary France, reaching its peak in the revolution, that Mr. Lubitch has done something notable. The affairs of Mme. du Barry, Louis and Armand by themselves are simply sordid, with Armand's part in them dignified somewhat by a touch of tragedy, and any director who let them stand out from their background would have had merely a sordid tale to tell. But Mr. Lubitch has had the skill to weave them into their setting, make them a part of all that is going on, and, while keeping them in the centre as objects of focused interest, he has never permitted them to hold the interest exclusively. So his picture has dramatic sweep as well as localized intensity; it lives as a human document; and it satisfies historic curiosity. How far it departs from actual history is immaterial. So far as the present writer is able to judge it has caught the atmosphere and meaning of its time, and historical fiction has accomplished its object when it does this.

It is also as a cinematician that Mr. Lubitch and whoever may have been responsible with him have won distinction. The settings seem truly of the Paris of the latter eighteenth century, and the costuming and habits of the people portrayed are harmonious with them. And few spectacles, if any, have surpassed the scenes of the street crowds and revolutionary mobs, which increase in number and importance as the story hurries to its final scene—du Barry at the guillotine. The French Revolution has never been so vividly pictured, probably, as in this photoplay. What is was, as ugly as it was, and as human, is forcefully presented, which means dramatically.

But all that Mr. Lubitch and his associates behind the camera did could not have made "Passion" the living thing it is without its cast. Seldom has a photoplay been as excellently acted. First among the players is Pola Negri.

Here is one of those rare persons with screen personality. Her moving photograph is stamped with individuality. And largely because of her definite pantomimic ability, or whatever distinctive motion picture acting may be called. It is not physical beauty that wins for her. She is lovely in many scenes, it is true, but some of her features are not beautiful, and she makes no apparent effort to pose becomingly without regard to the meaning of her performance. She is expressive. That is her charm. She makes du Barry real, as fascinating as she has to be, with as much of the appearance of dignity as she must have on occasion, and as contemptible and cowardly as she was. She actually wins sympathy for a woman who cannot at any time be admired. This is an accomplishment.

The other players in the cast are not named, but whoever they are they play right up to Pola Negri, especially those who impersonate Louis XV., Armand de Foix, the Duc de Choiseul, the Comte Jean du Barry, and Paillet, the cobbler. Also many in the large assemblage of people brought into the picture contribute importantly to its success.

"Passion," therefore, may be written down as one of the pre-eminent pictures of the day. Its shortcomings are the shortcomings of the photoplay of the current period, with its lack of color, its subjection to the literal rather than the imaginative camera, and its dependence upon "words, words, words." In "Passion" the photoplay about reaches its limit of excellence, and reveals its limitations. And the excellence and the limitations are together a guarantee of something greater than the photoplay to come. Meanwhile, let "Du Barry," as it must be thought of, be enjoyed.

D 13, 1920

THE KID

Charlie Chaplin is himself again—at his best, in some ways better than his previous best, and also, it is to be regretted, at his worst, only not with so much of his worst as has spoiled some of his earlier pictures. His return to the screen after more than a year's absence is in "The Kid," which was shown last night at Carnegie Hall as the feature of an entertainment for the benefit of the Children's Fund of the National Board of Review of Motion Pictures. In the near future the picture will come to the Strand Theatre for its regular Broadway run.

"The Kid" is not only the longest comedy in which Chaplin has appeared since becoming the best-known figure of the film world, but it is real comedy. That is, it has something of a plot, its people are characters, and the fun of it is balanced with sadness. And Chaplin is more of a comedian than a clown. It is the comedy that has been foreshadowed by the former shorter Chaplin works.

Also, although the screen's unequaled comedian is in no danger of losing his laurels to any one, haste must be made to mention a new individual in his company, as much of an individual as Chaplin himself, and a source of immense delight. This person is a wonderful youngster by the name of Jack Coogan, surely not more than 6 or 7 years old, and as finished, even if unconscious, an actor as the whole screen aggregation of players is likely to show. He is The Kid, and he will be remembered in the same image with Chaplin. They have many scenes together, and every one of them belongs to both of them. Come on, Jack Coogan, there must be more of you.

The blemish on "The Kid" is the same that has marred many of Chaplin's other pictures—vulgarity, or coarseness. There is only a little of it in the present work, just two scenes that will be found particularly offensive by some. They are funny. That cannot be denied. One laughs at them, but many try not to, and are provoked with themselves and Chaplin for their laughing. This is not good. The laugh that offends good taste doesn't win. And these scenes would never be missed from "The Kid." It has plenty of unadulterated fun to go far and long without them. Why can't Chaplin leave out such stuff? Why don't the exhibitors delete it?

There is less pure horse-play in "The Kid" than in the other Chaplins. The comedian depends chiefly upon his inimitable pantomime, and it scores every time. He also gets many laughs from the ludicrous situations which he concocts. There's nothing clumsy about the picture's continuity. Its "comedy relief" actually comes as a well-timed relief.

The story is simply about a curious derelict who has an abandoned baby thrust upon him. His life with the child fills most of the six reels, and comes to happy issue after a dream of heaven, which for burlesque stands alone.

The competent cast also includes Edna Purviance and Tom Wilson, Chaplin's reliable leading woman and favorite policeman.

Ja 22, 1921

THE FOUR HORSEMEN OF THE APOCALYPSE

The motion-picture version of Vicente Belasco Ibañez's impassioned novel of the war, "The Four Horsemen of the Apocalypse," was presented for an indefinite run, under the direction of Dr. Hugo Riesenfeld, at the Lyric Theatre last night. A large number of spectators, many of them invited for the occasion, gave it hearty approval.

It is as a work in kinetic photography the screened "Four Horsemen" should first be considered, because its standing as a photoplay depends upon its pictorial properties and not upon its relation to a widely read novel. The most important fact about the production, then, is that, although it has a good deal of the wordiness, erratic tempo and illogical emphasis common to screen adaptations of printed stories, it is nevertheless distinguished from many other works of its kind by genuine cinematographic qualities. It is made, if not entirely, at least in large part, of telling moving pictures. Many of its scenes are the result of fine photography, and, better still, fine cinematography. Rex Ingram, the director of the production, is among those who believe that principles of painting and sculpture should be applied to motion pictures, and scenes in "The Four Horsemen" are concrete illustrations of what the application of these principles means. Evidently Mr. Ingram's expressed ideas are not merely subjects of idle conversation with him. He tries to do what he says ought to be done. His pictures, for example, are smooth and soft, and yet as distinct as the sharpest photography could make them; they are effectively lighted; and their dramatic, as well as purely pictorial, value has been moving and still objects. Mr. Ingram must have devoted much time and thought to composition, and in a number of instances he has achieved something different and better than materials at the disposal of other directors and frequently used by them in the last few years. For example, there is a scene of troops marching through a French village, which is scarcely a new subject at this post-war date, yet Mr. Ingram has presented it with new effectiveness by breaking the main line of march of the troops and occasionally diverting from it companies and squads of men. Thus he has given fluidity and unity to his whole scene instead of dividing it into two still pictures as a continuous column of men moving in a straight line or simple curve would do—and often has done in other photoplays.

Mr. Ingram has made many eloquent motion pictures. This means that, although the spectator now and then has the impression that the photoplay is simply the novel splendidly illustrated, this impression is dissipated as often as it is formed by scenes and successions of scenes which speak for themselves, tell their part of the narrative in their own language without the aid of words. The execution of the citizens of Ville-blanche, for example, is done in pure cinematography, and is one of the most impressive incidents of the story. In bringing the symbolic Four Horsemen into the photoplay Mr. Ingram again has done his work cinematographically, and with such a discerning sense of the unreal in reality that what might easily have been banal or incongruous has become a pervading and leavening part of the picture.

The photoplay has been cast with a clear eye for types and acting ability. The characters used primarily to give color to the picture—South American na-

tives, Spanish, French and German specimens—are all strikingly individualized, and those who have the more extensive roles not only look their parts but act them intelligibly, especially Rudolph Valentine as the young Julio Joseph Swickard as old Don Marcelo Alice Terry as Marguerite, Alan Hal as Karl von Hartrott, and Nigel D Brulier as Tchernoff, the Russian mystic.

Many will want to know, of course, how closely the photoplay resembles e book, and they may be assured that it is, on the whole, a faithful and appreciative translation of what Blasco Ibañez wrote. There have been changes, some necessary or wise, others capricious, but June Mathis, who made the scenario, has followed the main trend and thought of the novel. All things considered, she has done a difficult job well. There have been omissions, of course, as all of the book could not be put into a film of reasonable length, but the part of the story that is its reason for existence, the latter section dealing with the war, has been treated adequately and in the intense spirit of the original. The section dealing with South American life has been only sketched, though vividly in spots, and its chief character, the old centaur, Madariaga, has just been mentioned in passing, so to speak. The love affair between Julio and Marguerite and the character of Tchernoff have been considerably idealized, and the death of Julio has been made more melodramatic than it was in the novel. Also the spiritistic element, absent from the book, has been introduced into the photoplay, and another innovation, much less justifiable, is the bringing in of a pet monkey which has been made to act as if he definitely understands and sympathizes with the moods and situations of the human beings around him. Of course, trained animals do not do this, and the tricks of the monkey are simply broad comedy, entirely out of harmony with the rest of the story. It was felt, no doubt, that "comic relief" was desirable in so serious a work, and accordingly the incongruous animal was dragged in to supply the missing ingredient, but the added stuff does not accomplish the first business of an ingredient, which is to mix with the other ingredients of a compound. It is too bad that the adapters felt called upon to monkey with their material.

When all is said about "The Four Horsemen," however, the central fact remains that it is an exceptionally well done adaption of a novel, and an extraordinary motion picture work to boot.

Mr 7, 1921

THE CABINET OF DR. CALIGARI

FEW motion pictures have excited more interest, advance and accompanying, than the latest German production to reach this country, the cubistic photoplay, "The Cabinet of Dr. Caligari," which the Goldwyn Company has bought and will show at the Capitol

Theatre week after next. The picture was first reviewed for American readers in an article in The Freeman by Herman George Scheffauer, which was reprinted in part in these columns on Nov. 28 last. Mr. Scheffauer, who saw the photoplay in Berlin, noted its "bizarre expressionistic form" and described its action as taking place in a "cubistic world of intense relief and depth." He considered it important, however, not so much because of its cubism as because in it space had been "given a voice," had "become a presence."

The picture was also seen in Berlin by Arthur Ziehm, a dealer in foreign films, who has written the following account of it:

"From the viewpoint of effect on their audience, the authors of ' The Cabinet of Dr. Caligari ' had the advantage of treating the subject of madness. Granting their mad premise, the story works itself out logically and remorselessly to the final sane ending. While original both in inspiration and interpretation, ' The Cabinet of Dr. Caligari ' strikes a pitch akin to that heard in the stories of Hoffmann, Poe, Fitz James O'Brien and Ambrose Bierce. It should be said that while the interpretation has added immeasurably to the photoplay, yet the profounder reason for the thrill which it awakens lies in the actual story of Dr. Caligari.

"That story is told through the lips of a madman, and it is in catching his twisted conceptions that the scenic artists have done notable things. The sets are a little mad. Everything is awry, somewhere; and, because it is almost impossible just to lay your fingers on the place, the sets add to the atmosphere of mystery and terror which permeates the picture. Recently I saw Mr. Jones's ' Macbeth '; the difference between his work in that play and the work done in Caligari is simply that Mr. Jones failed —this time—and the artists in the photoplay succeeded. The sets in the picture do not blacken your eye with their aggression or box your ears with their abruptness. They are subtly woven into the tale of Dr. Caligari."

"Since the picture is to be shown in New York, it would not be right to give away the secret behind it, thus robbing it, for those who read this article, of its element of surprise. However, a few general outlines can be given. The picture opens in a garden, with two men talking. One of them remarks that he feels the presence in the air of evil things from the past. A woman, pale, and dressed completely in white, passes; the other man tells the first speaker that the woman is his fiancée, and assures him that, whatever his experiences in the past, they cannot equal those endured by himself and his sweetheart. The scene fades out in old-time movie fashion and fades into the story which is being told in the garden.

"This story within the story is laid in a little provincial town with a half-medieval aspect. Everything has an air of old worldliness, from the student who throws away his book when he hears of the fair to the fair itself and the old men and young men and old women and young women who throng it. Furthermore, everything has an air of exaggeration which makes the characters seem unreal as human beings, but extraordinarily real as embodying qualities of goodness and evil, peace and terror.

"Dr. Caligari, who embodies sheer wickedness, is a masterly conception, and the work of Mr. Krauss in this rôle will, undoubtedly, arouse as much comment and enthusiasm in America as it did in Europe. The doctor is an elderly man who wears a cape and a battered top hat, while behind his eyeglasses are strange, roving eyes. In the conception of the man who is telling the tale he does evil for the sheer delight that it affords him. This monster reaches the town when the fair is being held and solicits from the town clerk permission to exhibit a somnambulist on the ground. The permission is granted, but not without rudeness on the part of the clerk. That night the unfortunate man is murdered in his bed.

"This is the beginning of a mysterious sequence of crimes. The hero—the story-teller—tells of how he visited the doctor's booth with a friend when the doctor, opening a huge, standing cabinet, revealed an immensely tall and skinny man, fast asleep. This creature is completely under the domination of the doctor. He sleeps until awakened by Caligari, and when awake obeys his master implicitly.

"The showman invites the audience to have their fortunes told by the awakened sleeper and the creature predicts to the friend of the story-teller that he will not live beyond tomorrow's dawn. Next day he is found murdered in his bed. In all the murders a strange, dagger-like weapon is used, so that there is no doubt that they are all the work of one man. Eventually the sweetheart of the hero is threatened with the hatred of the old wretch and from this point onward the story moves to an unguessed-at climax.

"It is obvious that a synopsis of such a story cannot convey the flavor of the actual vehicle. ' The Cabinet of Dr. Caligari ' represents to me something very real and terrible. Do you remember the fear that you felt when you were a guest in ' The House of Usher '? The story of Caligari is entirely dissimilar, yet awakens the same kind of fear— that fear of things having no reason and loving evil instinctively."

"The Cabinet of Dr. Caligari " was written by Carl Mayer and Hans Janowitz; it was directed by Robert Wien,

and its scenic designers were H. Worm.
Walter Reimen and Walter Rork, according to the announcement from the Capitol. Mr. Scheffauer, in his article in The Freeman, credited it chiefly to "Walter Reiman, Walther Röhrig and Hermann Warm."

Mr 20, 1921

THE CABINET OF DR. CALIGARI

Opinions about "The Cabinet of Dr. Caligari," at the Capitol this week, will probably be sharply divided—and that's the first thing that recommends the picture, for, although individuality so pronounced that it breeds active disagreement does not necessarily denote peculiar excellence, it is bound to have a strong appeal for habitual motion-picture spectators depressed by stock stuff.

The most conspicuous individual characteristic of the photoplay is that it is cubistic, or expressionistic. Its settings bear a somewhat closer resemblance to reality than, say the famous "Nude Descending a Staircase," but they are sufficiently unlike anything ever done on the screen before to belong to a separate scenic species. A house, for instance, is recognized as a house, but, with its leaning, trapezoidal walls, its triangular doors and its bizarre floor patterns, it does not look like any house anybody ever lived in—likewise the irregular alleyways between inclined buildings, the crazy corridors and the erratic roofs.

Doubtless these expressionistic scenes are full of meaning for the specialist in the form of art they represent, but the uninitiated, though they will now and then get a definite suggestion from some touch here or there, and enjoy it, are not asked to understand cubism, for the settings are the background, or rather an inseparable part, of a fantastic story of murder and madness such as Edgar Allan Poe might have written. This story is coherent, logical, a genuine and legitimate thriller, and after one has followed it through several scenes the weird settings seem to be of its substance and no longer call disturbing attention to themselves.

The two principal characters in this horrific story are Dr. Caligari, an uncanny old wizard, and Cesare, an unearthly somnambulist completely in his power, who is his agent in the commission of crime for crime's sake. Werner Krauss as the doctor gives one of the most vivid performances recorded on the screen, and Conrad Veidt is no less the embodiment of the ghostly, ghastly sleep-walker. The others in the cast are also effective, and if they all act with exaggerated gestures and facial contortions, this, too, is in keeping with the story and its settings. Everything is unreal in "The Cabinet of Dr. Caligari." There is nothing of normalcy

about it.

So the film, then, is a shocker for those who like such to revel in. It is a feast for those who want their fiction strong and straight.

But none of this bears directly on the importance of "Dr. Caligari" as a motion picture, for it is not likely that it will establish a vogue of cubistic films, unless, indeed, it is commercially successful, as it may be, and the enterprising "fillum" men, accustomed to making "mother-love," "homespun" and "religious" pictures in pursuit of the popularity of other successes so catalogued, suddenly discover that "the public wants cubistic stuff" and grind out terrible imitations of this original work. The picture is significant, though, not because it is expressionistic in any special sense, but because it is expressionistic in the general sense that all of its elements, its settings, its plot, its people, are expressive, eloquent, and, for the most part, harmoniously so. Sometimes the more nearly normal characters in their unnatural surroundings give an impression of incongruity, but this wears off after a time, and in most of the scenes there is unity and vitality. Hermann George Scheffauer, who saw the picture in Berlin, wrote about it in "The Freeman" under the caption, "The Vivifying of Space," and this indicates its importance as a work of cinematography. It gives dimensions and meaning to space, making it an active part of the story, instead of merely the conventional and inert background for the performance of puppets. It leaves literalness behind, and leaps into the field of creative imagination.

The picture has been skillfully titled by Katherine Hilliker, who has not only inserted well-selected words where they are needed, but, with restraint rare among expert title writers, has not stuck in words where they are not needed, though she has used "fakir" when, apparently, she means "faker."

As presented at the Capitol by S. L. Rothafel, with a prologue and epilogue calculated to supply an atmosphere of usualness and a happy ending for those who demand them, and with stirring interpretative music by the orchestra, the picture's effectiveness is materially increased.

It should be stated further, perhaps, for the benefit of those who have not yet added the word "European" in its new sense to their motion-picture vocabulary, that the film comes from Germany, where it attracted considerable attention before it was brought to this country.

Ap 4, 1921

ANNE BOLEYN

"Anne Boleyn," the second Ernst Lubitsch production to reach this country from Germany, is at the Rivoli this week. It has been renamed "Deception," as Mr. Lubitsch's "DuBarry" was renamed "Passion" for American consumption, it being the opinion of the distributers, apparently, that such titles as "Passion" and "Deception" are more suited to the American spectator, who, Mr. Griffith is reported to have said, has "the mind of a child nine years old," than are "DuBarry" and "Anne Boleyn."

But though names may be changed, moving pictures may not, and therefore "Anne Boleyn," or "Deception," in its substance, remains as Mr. Lubitsch made it. And he did not make it for anyone with the mind of a child nine years old. That is the most important distinction of the picture, as it was of "DuBarry"; therein lies its fundamental difference from most of the American productions. While there is excellent photography in both "DuBarry" and "Anne Boleyn," there is better photography in many of the films made in America, and though the settings of the former are impressive and the scenes skillfully composed, they sometimes seem less genuine than the settings in many American pictures.

The dramatic material of most of the American pictures, however, is puerile, and their treatment is mechanical, compared to the material and treatment of a photoplay like "Deception"—it has to be called that sooner or later, so let it go. Here is a real story told so that intelligent people can enjoy it. Here is sturdy evidence that the screen is for adults as well as children, although a number of parents had their babies at the Rivoli yesterday to see the bestiality of Henry VIII and his court. Here is a work that holds the alert interest almost continuously, despite the fact that it is historical. Many people shy at the historical in entertainment, fearing either that they will be bored again or may be accidentally educated, but they needn't avoid "Deception," unless they object to a real story of real people, with an impressive tragic ending. Those who don't will probably be entertained as they have seldom been entertained in a motion picture theatre.

Exactly how accurate the history of "Deception" is one who has not made a specialty of England in the time of the Tudors cannot say, but it seems authentic, on the whole, except, perhaps, in the idealization of the character of Anne Boleyn, who is represented as quite a saint. Surely the Henry VIII. of Emil Jannings, as was his Louis XV., is one of the finest pieces of character work ever done on the screen. The licentious old king lives before your eyes. Who says they can't portray character in moving pictures merely because they use mechanical dolls instead of actors as a rule? Go to see His Most Christian Majesty, Henry VIII., and some of the others of his court at the Rivoli this week.

The Anne Boleyn of Henny Porten is also convincing most of the time, though it is to be regretted that Miss Porten seems so heavy sometimes, and is not as personable as she seemed in Henry's eyes. There's no doubt that in some scenes she does finished acting, becoming truly impressive at times, especially

in the scenes preceding her execution, but when she tries to be young and gay she misses her mark. As photographed, at least, she is too old and too ponderous, possibly too Teptonic, for "sweet Anne," if not for the tragic Queen.

The others in the cast, discreetly unnamed, are well enough suited to their parts, and persuasive in their acting, though in some of them that methodical ponderosity commonly attributed to the Germans is too evident.

There is nothing to suggest the quality of heaviness about Mr. Lubitsch, however. He has a Continental touch. Did he ever work in Paris or Vienna? Anyhow, his continuity and his separate scenes are handled with deftness. There is eloquence in almost every picture and in succession the scenes compose a climactic story that marches straight to its ending and stops when the end comes, which it does with Anne Boleyn going to the executioner's block in one of the most effective scenes ever put upon the screen. Mr. Lubitsch is a cinematician, too. He has to be to make such expressive moving pictures. Thank heaven, they have not been overloaded with subtitles, and they do not need as many as they have. Rich, colorful, dramatic, "Deception" is a photoplay for those who want genuine realism and can do without simpering heroines, pretty heroes, mechanical plots, and sentimental happy endings.

Ap 18, 1921

THE BIRTH OF A NATION

D. W. Griffith's motion picture classic, "The Birth of a Nation," has been revived for a week at the Capitol Theatre. A good many photoplays have been made and the dramatic screen has progressed importantly in a number of directions since this picture opened at the Liberty Theatre on March 3, 1915, six whole years ago—only six years ago, but the production that was sensationally pre-eminent then remains one of the pre-eminent works of today.

It has rivals now, and in some things they surpass it. Several of them have photographic subtleties and other cinematographic qualities that it does not possess. It lacks the unity and coherence of later motion picture masterpieces, and free imitation of its melodramatic devices has weakened their effectiveness. But when all of this is admitted, "The Birth of a Nation" still needs no apology. It stands today a triumphant achievement of the screen.

As melodrama, it is one of the most genuine thrillers ever made, and it shows some of the best acting, some of the most vivid, if sketchy, characterization, to be found on the screen. As a spectacle it still has power to stir the imagination notwithstanding the fact that there are other pictures built on a larger scale and more finished in detail. If it seems crude in places, and is in the last analysis chiefly a glorified melodrama, it has, nevertheless, a glory of its own.

Considered as a historical work, "The Birth of a Nation" is a thing of contradictions. Some of its scenes are truly flash-backs to the period of civil war and reconstruction in America. Sometimes it is almost epic in quality. But in many scenes it is falsely romantic and as blindly partisan as the most violent sectional tradition. It may be said that, as a rule, it comes closest to historical truth when it is furthest from Thomas Dixon. It has always been a great pity that, in undertaking to build a photoplay on the struggle between the North and South, Mr. Griffith went for material to so garbled and prejudice-feeding an account as "The Clansman." He permanently impaired his work by doing so.

"The Birth of a Nation" takes on a new interest in comparison with Mr. Griffith's later productions. It gives evidence that its maker has advanced in some ways since 1914-15, while retrograding in others. Apparently, for example, he has become more sure in putting character on the screen and has developed a more competet idea of dramatic unity, but he seems, on the other hand, to have lost something of the sense of restraint in telling a story and to be more addicted to shallow and platitudinous preaching. There are actually cinematographic bits in "The Birth of a Nation" which are not shouted down by subtitles, and there are intense scenes cut quickly, when they should be cut, and many illuminating flashes on details of action and character that leave them bright in the imagination, not dulled by overemphasis. One cannot suppress the hope that, in some respects, Mr. Griffith will soon return to his earlier style.

It is a pleasure of course to renew acquaintance with the now prominent players in "The Birth of a Nation." Henry Walthall, Mae Marsh, Miriam Cooper, Lillian Gish, Mary Alden, George Siegmann and the others in the cast have seldom been better, and often much worse, than they were six years ago. And the brief but clear-cut performance of Robert Harron reminds the spectator afresh that the screen suffered a real loss in his death.

The picture has a new musical accompaniment at the Capitol, adapted by S. L. Rothafel and arranged by Erno Rapee, William Axt and Hermann Hand, which, though effective now and then, is much too noisy most of the time.

THE GOLEM

The black magic of the Middle Ages, sorcery, astrology and all of the superstitious realities of people so legendary in appearance and manners that the unnatural seems natural among them have been brought to the screen of the Criterion in "The Golem," the latest motion picture to come from the explorative innovators of Germany. The photoplay gives the impression of some fabulous old tale of strange people in a strange world, fascinating, exciting to the imagination, and yet so unfamiliar in all of its aspects that it always seems remote, elusive even, when one would like to get closer to its meaning.

Paul Wegener, who directed the production, has shown his greatest artistry, perhaps, in maintaining the consistency of his production. Even his method of telling the story without the usual directness and coherence of modern narration seems a part of the age and subject with which he deals. It will doubtless be disconcerting to some; it will be said that the photoplay does not develop climactically, and in places its lack of direction does leave the mind somewhat at sea, but this is not to say that it is ever dull, for one cannot lose interest in a work so strangely engrossing and with such power as "The Golem" has in many of its scenes.

This power is derived mainly from a combination of exceptional acting and the most expressive settings yet seen in this country. Resembling somewhat the curious constructions of "The Cabinet of Dr. Caligari," the settings may be called expressionistic, but to the common man they are best described as expressive, for it is their eloquence that characterizes them. They give impressions of distance, of compactness, of massiveness, of old-world unearthliness that could not be conveyed in any other way. They are as active a part of the story as any of its characters, and afford another striking illustration of how much constructed scenery, furniture, buildings and the like may mean in a photodramatic composition. It is not because they are weird, but because they vivify the action of the story, that they are cinematographic works of art.

The acting of the players, too, is of that pantomimic quality essential to the motion picture if it is to be a living thing. None of the players is named, except Mr. Wegener, so individual credit cannot be distributed, but the old Rabbi Loew, his daughter, her betrothed, Rudolph Habsburg, and the others in the cast, including many who are only vital figures of the crowds, all define their characters clearly. None of them is simply a silenced chatter-box, as are so many supposed screen actors in this country.

The most impressive performance is that of Mr. Wegener as the Golem. This is the name for a huge figure of clay fashioned by Rabbi Loew and brought to life by the insertion of a magic word in a receptacle in his chest. The rabbi employs the monster to propitiate Rudolph, who has ordered the banishment of the Jews from Prague, but, like the creature of Frankenstein's creation, the Golem does not remain obedient and seeks its own dumb satisfaction to the threatened havoc of the Ghetto. He is reduced to the impotence of inanimate clay only when a Christian child whom he picks up playfully unscrews the bright star in his chest which holds the magic word.

The story is said to be based on an old Jewish legend, but it is no part of orthodox Jewish tradition surely. It is, however, an absorbing Old World story, most effectively told.

Its effect is heightened by Dr. Hugo Riesenfeld's presentation of it with appropriate accompanying music, an inspiring musical prologue and motion picture views of the still ancient-seeming City of Prague.

By way of light relief the picture is followed by a dance by May Kitchen Cory in Benda masks, another of Tony Sarg's delightful chapters on the merry men of prehistoric times, and a mirthful Keaton comedy called "Hard Luck."

Je 20, 1921

CABIRIA

When Gabriele d'Annunzio's "Cabiria rose like a cinematographic sun on the motion picture world in 1914 great was the brightness thereof. It was luminous and spread its light over wide areas of the public then lying far beyond the screen's horizon. People who had never deigned to go to the movies before went to see it, and came away saying it was the greatest picture they had ever seen. And others who had seen several other productions said the same thing. For seven years "Cabiria" has lived in the memory of many as, to them at least, the greatest motion picture ever made. And now it is revived this week at the Strand and must stand the test of comparison with the screen's achievements since 1914.

It will come through the test with its colors unlowered. To say that it really is the greatest picture ever made would be going too far. In a number of ways the screen has advanced since it was produced, while it, apparently, has slipped back, upsetting, in a way, the common assumption that a motion picture once made is forever and always the same. Visual memory is not perfect, but it seems safe to say that the pictures in the "Cabiria" of 1914 were clearer, in better relief as to details,

than those to be seen now at the Strand. On the assumption that the print used is new, the conclusion must be that the negative, for some reason, has faded a little. Whatever the cause, many who see the picture are likely to complain of its dimness, not because they are really unable to distinguish its important details or to get the effect of its magnificent scenes, but because it is so much less clear than the finely distinct pictures of today.

But the less finished photography of seven years ago, or the fading of the negative, whichever it is, cannot obscure the enduring greatness of "Cabiria." It remains a great motion picture, one which any one can well afford to see twice and which no one who wants to follow the screen can afford to miss. In some of its particulars it has never been equalled and in others it has never been surpassed.

Only the recent German productions, for example, approach it in the richness and authenticity of its historical setting. As is generally known, its period is that of the Punic Wars, and those qualified to know have testified that it brilliantly reproduced much of the atmosphere and appearance of the world of Rome and Carthage. There are no scenes of Rome, but Carthage has been reconstructed, while the Roman fleet and methods of fighting, as well as the Romans themselves, are restored. The picture, in fact, brings rather a vague part of history vividly to life. It is absorbingly interesting.

In this setting is a melodrama. A shrewd person who had never heard of "Cabiria" might approximate the date of its production by the loose, episodic nature of its continuity and the amount of running about, jumping, pursuing and fleeing indulged in by its characters. Clearly it belongs to the perpetual-motion age of motion pictures. But, whereas in an ordinary work of this age, the motion would seem confusing and crazy-wild, in "Cabiria" it is employed so efficiently, it is so well directed toward its end without, overflow of aimless activity, that it serves to animate for all what otherwise would be a purely historical work of restricted appeal.

The figure that stands out most, of course, is that of Maciste, whose real name, it is said, is Ernesto Pagani. This towering but well-formed and graceful giant fascinates the eye. He is an extraordinary physical specimen, and yet not a mere exhibit. He acts, he is a part of the story, he is convincing. Next to his, the most graphic characterization is that of the wineshop keeper by Antonio Branioni. This miserable little man is placed opposite Maciste in a number of scenes and the effect is striking.

But, though "Cabiria" is full of details, many of them of really dramatic or melodramatic quality, it is as a spectacle, as a pageant, that it holds its own with the best pictures of today, and so the chief credit for its production must go to Gabriele d'Annunzio, the poet, who conceived it, and to Giovanni Pastrone, who directed it. Through their labors, Italy reached a peak of motion picture accomplishment. Now that the war is over, she should go still higher.

JI 4, 1921

"HAMLET," with Asta Nielsen in the title role; directed by Sven Gade; produced by a Copenhagen company in Denmark and Berlin. At the Lexington Theatre.

In order to enjoy the foreign screen version of "Hamlet," which opened an engagement at the Lexington Theatre Monday evening, the spectator should first of all get Shakespeare out of his mind as much as possible. The picture is not, and does not pretend to be, an adaptation of the famous tragedy. As every one knows, there was a legend of Hamlet before Shakespeare ever wrote, and there is also a book called "The Mystery of Hamlet," written in comparatively recent years by the late Dr. Edward P. Vining, and it is upon this legend and the book that the photoplay at the Lexington is based. As may be expected, then, although it follows the Shakespearean narrative in many particulars, it also departs from it in many others, the most important of which is likely to prove a startling innovation to many. Dr. Vining sought to explain the character of Hamlet on the ground that the Prince was a woman who, for reasons of State, had been raised as a man, and it is this theory that the photoplay accepts and seeks to make plausible.

Now the spectator who goes to see this motion picture "Hamlet" with his mind not too much set against this unusual theory and who can also refrain from anticipating various details of action by his knowledge of Shakespeare, has an evening or an afternoon of rare screen entertainment before him. For the Nielsen-Gade "Hamlet" is an extraordinary work. It does not need to apologize to any production that has come from a foreign or domestic studio since the invention of motion pictures. It holds a secure place in the class with the best.

First of all, it is a human story. Even those who approach anything labeled classic or highbrow with apprehension are likely to find it as thrilling, as gripping, as their favorite melodrama—or so it surely seems, for it is hard to imagine any one not held by its intenser scenes at least. And there are many fine points about it, little bits of byplay, touches of action, flashes of significant pantomimic and pictorial expressiveness that the discerning will delight in.

One cannot speak of the work of Miss Asta Nielsen without enthusiasm. There will be discussion as to her physical charms. Some undoubtedly will call her beautiful, while others, preferring a different type of wife or sweetheart or sister, will say she is merely striking in appearance. But what does all this matter? The woman can act. She acts. That's the thing. She does not just pose before the camera, nor does she rant and tear around violently. She impersonates a character, she makes it live and have a meaning, a hundred meanings. Her mouth is not simply something to paint a cupid's bow on. It is an organ to express the thoughts and feelings of the woman within. And her other features are not merely facial adornments or fixtures to be adorned, but human parts that reveal a human being. Miss Nielsen has grace, too, and the control of her body that permits her to use it to beautify her character and make its movements and postures significant.

But still Miss Nielsen is not the whole picture. The other rôles are exceedingly well done and the settings, even when the photography is not what this country would have given them the benefit of, are expressive. They have a depth seldom seen in American pictures and immeasurably heighten every dramatic crisis of the story. The composition of the scenes throughout, with relatively few exceptions, is such as to give each its greatest strength. Mr. Gade, the director, also deserves his honors for the production.

The most serious fault with the American version of the picture is that it is overtitled. Scenes which can stimulate the imagination are made explicit by words. Also occasional quotations from Shakespeare not only do not fit, but keep in mind the play which the spectator should put out of his mind to enjoy the motion picture fully.

N 9, 1921

SIR ARNE'S TREASURE

ONE of the regrets of the motion picture reviewer's life is that circumstances compel him to see so many photoplays that he doesn't want to see and to miss others that he would really like to look at. It is especially regrettable when conflicting engagements prevent his attending the exhibition of a worthwhile production, and this is the case with respect to the present writer and the Swedish Biograph Company's photoplay, "Sir Arne's Treasure." This picture has been shown several times hereabout in recent weeks, and reports have indicated that it is a work of special merit, but the present writer has not yet found himself free to go to see it. There has been no account of it in these columns, therefore.

Now, however, an account may be given, for Mrs. Frances Taylor Patterson, instructor in photoplay composition at Columbia University, having seen the picture and having noticed that it has not been reviewed here, has written concerning it, as follows:

The Swedish Biograph Company has produced a picture called 'Sir Arne's Treasure' which seems to me to be a revelation in motion picture production. Since it is based upon a story by Selma Lagerlof, it cannot be said to be a photoplay in the purest sense of the word—it was not composed in the language of the screen as were 'The Golem,' 'The Cabinet of Dr. Caligari' and 'Passion.' It is an adaptation rather than an original photoplay. Nevertheless, I have never seen a production which approaches more nearly to consummate art. Pictorial beauty, histrionic beauty and dramatic beauty are consistently sustained through all its scenes. The lights and shadows in some of the interiors are reminiscent of Rembrandt. This picture is fluid art. The scenes move with a smoothness and harmony of motion that are admirable. There is an air of quietude, of dignity, in the sequence, with never a note of exaggeration, or of over-sustained repose. The characters are not puppets, not mere marionettes who dance as the director pulls the strings. They are living people; they are personalities created in pantomime, which is the language of the screen.

"The play dramatizes the snowy wastes and icy fastnesses of the north country. The ice-locked firths and bays are used symbolically and bring about the unraveling of the plot. Beauty which we usually associate upon the screen with the scenics and nature pictures is here used to dramatic purpose. The play is frankly a tragedy built along the lines of the Greek tragedies, moving inevitably toward catastrophe. But the tragedy is logical; it satisfies our sense of dramatic justice. There could be no marriage between Elsa and Sir Halmar, who is the murderer of her little sister. Little Elsa, thrown over her lover's shoulder, receives the bayonet thrusts of the men-at-arms and gives her life for her lover. But he after his long vigils with her dead body in the hold of the ship, gives himself up, and the ice breaks and the bays and firths open wide to the sea.

"The picture is a period picture set in a kingdom of the north 350 years ago. The attention to detail in settings, costumes, customs and properties is remarkable.

"I first saw this picture at the Town Hall and was so struck with its beauty that I secured a print to exhibit and analyze before my classes in photoplay composition here at Columbia. A second viewing bears out the impression of the first. I have not seen the picture reviewed in your columns or elsewhere. In fear lest such outstanding artistry go unnoticed, I take this occasion to call the picture to your attention. It embodies the Swedish contribution to the gallery of Italian, German, French and Norwegian pictures now being exhibited in our theatres."

D 25, 1921

TOL'ABLE DAVID, with Richard Barthelmess, directed by Henry King, adapted from a story by Joseph Hergesheimer; "The Fast Male," with Joe Rock, a comedy; New Year Song Tableau, with male quartette. At the Strand.

As if to show what may be done with stock stuff Director Henry King and his associates have taken Joseph Hergesheimer's story "Tol'able David," and, with a realistic cast headed by Richard Barthelmess, converted it into a generally persuasive and culminatingly exciting photoplay, which may be seen at the Strand this week. This is not to say that Mr. Hergesheimer's story was stock stuff, but that the basic material taken from it for the picture has been used time and time again on the screen and is familiar in the "filium" world as homespun melodrama. Fundamentally that's all that "Tol'able David" is, rural romance, employing the usual properties, a young and intrepid hero, a generously built and generous-hearted mother, a sweet little country girl and an assortment of villains for the hero to overcome. How often it has been done, and how unconvincing it all is—usually.

But not this time. This time you believe it. It seems real. In most of its scenes it gets you. For Mr. King and those responsible with him have eliminated most of the slush. "Tol'able David" is sentimental in places, but not sloppy. It is bucolic, but its rusticity is not rubbed in. In all things, except, possibly, the fight between David and the three hyenish mountaineers, it is restrained, imaginatively suggestive when not briefly literal. For this reason it is stimulating. Dealing in well-known scenes and actions, it

28

merely introduces them. As each appears the mind of the spectator takes it in and completes it, and the story moves on to the next detail, which the mind immediately picks up and carries on. Thus there is a constant spontaneity of response on the part of the spectators. They are always telling part of the story to themselves, so they are always actively interested. Nothing is so tiresome as a story in which familiar details are dwelt upon and drawn out until there is nothing left for the spectator or the listener to imagine. And most motion picture directors seem to think they have a monopoly of the world's imagination, which shows they have no imagination at all. But Mr. King, apparently, has an imagination, and has therefore left much for any one who sees "Tol'able David" to imagine. As a result, his photoplay is sharply pointed in its more intensified scenes, whether humorous, sentimental or dramatic, and continuously illuminating and promising, which means interesting, in its more moderate intermediary scenes.

And Mr. King has accomplished this result in the only way in which it can be accomplished on the screen—that is, in the medium of motion pictures. Not only did he and his company go to the Southern mountains where suitable natural settings abounded, but they took advantage of the ability of the camera to produce certain effects not inherent in any natural setting, and they applied principles of pictorial composition and cinematography to make their scenes expressive and pleasing to the eye. "Tol'able David" has vitality, therefore. It lives as a motion picture.

Largely, of course, because of the acting. Mr. Barthelmess, for instance, does the best work of his screen life. In a rôle somewhat similar to the one he had in "Way Down East," he has dropped most of the mannerisms and exaggerated poses that marred his performance in that picture. He doesn't grin foolishly any more, and he seems to be under better control in his intenser moments. His work, on the whole, is more finished and promising. He ought to go on to still better things. The others in the cast are also adequate, and more. Gladys Hulette, as the heroine, is a country girl whom you may call genuinely sweet, in the sense in which Barrie, and not the press agents, use the word, and she does a good deal more than pose her part. To a pleasing degree, she acts it, giving it meaning, making it real. So also Ernest Torrence, Warner Richmond, Marion Abbott, Patterson Dial and the others.

Although "Tol'able David" remains a homespun melodrama, then, which at times is too melodramatic, it is much more than that. It has characters whom you are willing to accept as real people, in whom you take an active interest, and it does not always leave you asking yourself whether it ever has happened or even could happen in actual life. It happens for you while you are watching it, and that's all you care about.

Ja 2, 1922

FOOLISH WIVES, directed and written by Erich von Stroheim, with Mr. von Stroheim, Rudolph Christians, Maude George, Mae Busch, Miss Dupont, Dale Fuller, Caesare Gravina and others in the cast. At the Central Theatre.

Erich von Stroheim's "Foolish Wives," which has been on the way for more than a year, and is said to be one of the most costly motion pictures ever made, finally arrived at the Central Theatre last night. More than is the case with most other photoplays attributed to an individual, this production is the work of Mr. von Stroheim, for he not only wrote and directed it, but is by far the most conspicuous figure in its cast. So to him, therefore, must go the bulk of whatever approval and disapproval the picture wins. And, from different people, with varying ideas—and powers of endurance—he is likely to receive much of both.

"Foolish Wives," first of all, but not most importantly, is an expensive picture. It is said to have cost, exactly $1,103,736.38, and although a good deal of this cost was probably due to delays and other misfortunes that beset the production of the film, no inconsiderable sum was actually spent in the things that show on the screen, especially the settings. The action takes place in Monte Carlo, and Mr. von Stroheim seems to have reproduced the chief city of Monaco on the coast of California. The settings cannot be even mentioned in detail. But they are as rich and splendid as one who thinks of Monte Carlo can imagine, though in some instances it must be confessed photographic effects that might have been obtained with them have been missed, principally because of faulty lighting. This is not generally true. Many of the photographs are strikingly effective. It is only that some are not.

However, splendid settings never made a dramatic photoplay, and "Foolish Wives" could have been made with much less architecture without losing its essential dramatic quality. It does possess this quality, in many separate scenes and in frequent sequences of scenes, because, most importantly, it is largely composed of dynamic, expressive motion pictures. Mr. von Stroheim is a maker of motion pictures. He has a keen sense of the dramatic and a pictorial point of view, and the result is that "Foolish Wives" teems with scenes that mean something, that throw light on character and action, that strike the spectator fairly between the eyes and make him sit up and read pictures. This is the chief value of the film.

The picture is thus vitalized through Mr. von Stroheim's own cinematographic skill, and through the acting of himself and the others in the cast. His role is that of a human beast of prey, an unbelievably contemptible animal whose vocation and avocation is preying on women—without scruple and indiscriminately. He takes their money and their honor, whether they are serving maids, half-witted gir's or the wives of men in high station. And Mr. von Stroheim makes this character most repellantly realistic. All of the polish of such a villain, all of the cruelty, all of the cowardice, are portrayed in his finished, fiendish acting.

Posing as a Russian Count, he works with two accomplices, a pair of women who pose as Countesses, his cousins, played by Maude George and Mae Bush in his own style of sharp emphasis, only now and then becoming too exaggerated. Miss Dupont has the rôle of the principal " foolish wife," and, without giving it any particular individuality, makes it sufficiently clear to serve the purpose of the story. Her husband, who is a special envoy of the United States to the Principality of Monaco, is programed as Rudolph Christians, although it is reported that, when Mr. Christians died during the production of the picture, Robert Edeson was drafted for the part. If both do appear in different scenes of the photoplay as presented, any attempt to identify them separately would become a guessing contest.

The character, Andrew J. Hughes, is consistently presented, and is, as presented by Mr. Christians or Mr. Edeson or both, an adequately forceful figure. Dale Fuller, as a maid and one of the victims of the bogus Count, does telling work, as does also Caesare Gravina, as the father of a half-witted girl whom the beast destroys. It is through this father's vengeance that the monster finally meets a horrible end. The wife of the American envoy narrowly escapes him.

From all of which you may gather the main idea of the story. It is not pleasant. In many places it is decidedly repulsive. It is what is generally called " continental," and as such is exceedingly well done.

But whether you like that kind of a story is a question and whether you like it for fourteen reels of film, or three hours and a half on a stretch, with only five minutes' intermission, is another question. Surely, no matter how well done the picture is, and no matter how absorbing the story may be, the film is too long. It achieves its effects by its illuminating details, but it is too detailed to hold the attention for so long. You don't read a book written on such a subject as " Foolish Wives," in its style, for three hour and a half at a sitting. You couldn't. And it is wearying to sit through the film. Yet it was cut from 390 reels!

As the picture approaches its end it stirs the interest with an exciting fire scene, which comes as if to show that Mr. von Storcheim can be spectacular, too. It is as good as anything of its kind yet seen on the screen, except that the flames sometimes appear white and sometimes red, with disconcerting effect.

Ja 12, 1922

ORPHANS OF THE STORM

D. W. Griffith has been approached by representatives of two South American nations who want him to make historical films dealing with their respective countries, it is reported, but note this:

" One of the conditions provided," adds the announcement, " is that Mr. Griffith shall make two versions, one suitable for the South American eye, and the other tamed to the standard of the North American censor."

It is said that the South Americans were impressed with Mr. Griffith's treatment of a historical subject in the current " Orphans of the Storm," at the Apollo Theatre, and perhaps they were aware of how little incentive Mr. Griffith needs to indulge his love of the spectacular in history. It is interesting to note here, therefore, just how slight was the trace of the French Revolution in the original stage version of " The Two Orphans," from which Mr. Griffith started. The action of the play occurred about two years before the storming of the Bastile, and its only direct reference to the Revolution, according to a witness who has examined the old melodrama, came when de Vaudry remarked that he had seen a play containing expressions of revolutionary sentiments forbidden by the police, which, however, had not been suppressed, the King finding himself forced to yield to the people, who insisted that the play be let alone. Then the following dialogue took place:

De Presles—The King compelled to yield? If that is true, royalty has lowered its dignity.

Vaudrey—No, Marquis. It is the people who are asserting theirs.

De Presles—Why, if this goes on, they will not be satisfied until they suppress one's titles and privileges.

Vaudrey—That would not at all surprise me.

Picard—Excuse me, sir, but that is as ridiculous as though you were to say that one of these days the Parisiens would arise and demolish the Bastile!

Vaudrey—Who knows?

And from that came the idea of all the revolutionary scenes and Danton's ride in " Orphans of the Storm."

Incidentally, " Orphans of the Storm " affords an interesting illustration of how a photoplay, commonly supposed to be much less fluid than a stage production, may be revised after its formal presentation. It is well known, of course, that film may be cut and pasted almost indefinitely, so that scenes shown originally may be eliminated, and others at first held out inserted wherever an exhibitor chooses, but Mr. Griffith has gone further than this. Since the opening of " Orphans of the Storm " at the Apollo he has himself observed, and has engaged others to observe, the reactions of spectators, and as a result he has not only deleted certain scenes, but has made others at his studio in Mamaroneck and put them into the photoplay. Frank Puglia as Pierre, for instance, has been brought to life and kept alive for the happy ending; Creighton Hale has been given additional space as the amusing Picard; the Carmagnole dancers now have more to do, and the scene at the guillotine has been made less horrifically detailed, according to reports from the front of the house.

Ja 29, 1922

THE GLORIOUS ADVENTURE, with Lady Diana Manners, produced in England under the direction of J. Stuart Blackton, from a scenario by Felix Orman; "The Deluge," fourth episode of the Bible serial; Rubinstein's "Concerto in D Minor," played by Edna Baldwick. At the Capitol.

Viewed as a motion picture, J. Stuart Blackton's English-made film "The Glorious Adventure," which is at the Capitol this week, is chiefly interesting as the first full-length photoplay entirely in colors. Although there is no likelihood of the abandonment of black-and-white photography, in which effects not otherwise obtainable can be produced, the future will undoubtedly bring a perfection of color photography and an extension of its use that will greatly enrich the screen. "The Glorious Adventure" may be regarded, therefore, as significant of a new day, and, in a measure, as a definite approach to it. This means that, while much has been done with colors in the film, the pictures give evidence that much remains to be done before color photography may be said to have been satisfactorily developed. The process used in the present instance is said to have been worked out by William Van Doren Kelley for the Prizma Company. According to report, its chief feature is the use of two lenses, which permit the simultaneous exposure of two frames of the film, one through a red filter and the other through a green. This simultaneous exposure of two frames has resulted in the elimination of the fringes which used to mar all colored pictures, so in this particular, anyhow, "The Glorious Adventure" marks a definite improvement over most of the old color work. The colors, however, still run to strong hues, with harsh reds predominating, which displeasing effect is heightened by what seems a needless use of red in costumes and settings. The answer to this may be that red materials are the best subjects for the color camera, but the fact remains that there are scenes in "The Glorious Adventure" with little or no red intentionally in them and they are among the most pleasing in the photoplay. There are also other scenes in which the strong colors seem suitable

and tellingly contrasted, and these are good, too. So the photoplay is not without impressiveness. At times it is strikingly effective. But more often it seems crude, with the chromatic intensity of a cheap postcard and the indistinctness of a poorly lighted photograph. And some of the scenes are excellent examples of exceptionally bad composition, too.

In addition to its colors, the film offers Lady Diana Manners in its leading rôle. According to report, she is considered quite a beauty in England, and she may be approved here by those who like the cold, blond type. But, surely, no one will say that she does any acting.

The story of "The Glorious Adventure" is set, and elaborately set, in the time of Charles II. It is pure melodrama, and is often less plausible than even melodrama should be. Also, it seems to take unlicensed liberties with history sometimes. But its costumes, its characters, and quite a little of its action, especially that connected with the great fire of London, frequently make it entertaining. Most of its players are English, apparently, and little known in this country, and, besides, they are types, rather than actors impersonating their characters. This, perhaps, is not altogether their fault, the direction of the film and the obscuring effect of the colors in many scenes being partly responsible. But it remains true that there is little real acting in the photoplay. On the whole, however, and for a number of reasons, the production is well worth seeing.

Ap 24, 1922

NANOOK OF THE NORTH, produced by Robert J. Flaherty, F. R. G. S., for Revillon Freres; "My Country," one of Robert C. Bruce's "Wilderness Tales," held for a second week. At the Capitol.

If a man goes among a strange people whose life is reduced to an elemental struggle for existence, if he has the disposition to photograph these people sympathetically, and the discernment to select his particular subjects so that their life in its relation to their opposed environment is illumined, the motion picture which he brings back may be called "non-dramatic" only by the acceptance of the trade's arbitrary use of the term. Such a picture has the true dramatic essentials—and such a picture is Robert J. Flaherty's "Nanook of the North," which is at the Capitol this week.

Beside this film the usual photoplay, the so-called "dramatic" work of the screen, becomes as thin and blank as the celluloid on which it is printed. And the photoplay cannot avoid the comparison that exposes its lack of substance. It is just as literal as the "travel" picture. Its settings, whether the backgrounds of nature or the constructions of a studio, merely duplicate the settings of ordinary human experience—or try to. And its people try to

From The New York Times Film Reviews

31

persuade spectators that they are just ordinary people, ordinary, that is, for the environment in which they happen to be placed. So the whole purpose of the photoplay, as a rule, is to reproduce life literally. And this is the purpose of the travel film. But the average photoplay does not reproduce life. Through the obvious artificialities of its treatment, through the unconcealed mechanics of its operation, through its reflection of a distorted or incomplete conception of life, rather than of life itself, it usually fails to be true to any aspect of human existence. It is not realistic in any sense. It remains fiction, something fabricated. It never achieves the illusion of reality.

But "Nanook of the North," also seeking to give an impression of reality, is real on the screen. Its people as they appear to the spectator, are not acting, but living. The struggles they have are real struggles. There is no make-believe about the conflict between them and the ice and snow and wind and water that surround them. When Nanook, the master hunter and a real Eskimo, matches himself against the walrus, there is no pretense about the contest. Nanook's life depends upon his killing the walrus, and it is by no means certain that he will kill him. Some day he may not. And then Nanook will die. So the spectator watches Nanook as a man engaged in a real life-and-death struggle. And how much more thrilling the sight is than that of a "battle" between two well-paid actors firing blank cartridges at each other!

And people want character in their hero, courage and strength, quick and sure resourcefulness and, for them, a friendly disposition. They have all these things in Nonook when he faces a Northern blizzard, when he harpoons a giant seal, when he builds an igloo, when he stands on a peak of ice directing the movements of his followers. He is emphatically a leader, a man who does things, a man who wins. but who, at any moment, may lose. He is a genuine hero then, one who is watched with alert interest and suspense and far-reaching imagination. What "dramatic" photoplay can show such a one!

Nor is he alone. His family, his wife, his children, his dogs, and the paraphernalia of his life are around him. So he is not isolated. The picture of his life is filled out, humanized, touched with the humor and other high points of a recognizably human existence. Thus there is body, as well as dramatic vitality, to Nanook's story. And it is therefore far more interesting, far more compelling purely as entertainment, than any except the rare exceptions among photoplays. No matter how intelligent a spectator may be, no matter how stubbornly he may refuse to make concessions to the screen because its pictures are "only the movies," he can enjoy "Nanook of the North."

And this is because of the intelligence and skill and patience with which Mr. Flaherty has made his motion picture. It took more than just a man with a camera to make "Nanook of the North."

Mr. Flaherty had to wait for his light, he had to select his shots, he had to compose his scenes; he had to direct his people, in order that Nanook's story might develop its full force of realism and drama on the screen. So it is due to Mr. Flaherty that Nanook, who lives his life by Hudson Bay, also lives it at the Capitol.

Je 12, 1922

The Third Dimension.

BACK HOME AND BROKE, written for the screen by George Ade, directed by Alfred E. Green, with Thomas Meighan, Lila Lee, Laurence Wheat, James Marlowe and others; "Movies of the Future," a Plasticon stereoscopic picture; "Toddling Tots," a music film; "Felix Turns the Tide," a Pat Sullivan cartoon comedy; "Around the Christmas Tree," sung by Gladys Rice, Barbara Rawle, Inga Wank and Fred Jagel. At the Rivoli.

The most significant, if, at the same time the most modest, film on Broadway this week, is, perhaps, the Plasticon stereoscopic picture at the Rivoli, prophetically, rather than boastfully, entitled "Movies of the Future." The process by which this film was made was worked out by William Van Doren Kelley, inventor of the Prizma color pictures, who does not assert that the pictures are perfect, but that they do give an illusion of depth and can be improved in the future. And the pictures bear him out, at least so far as the illusion of depth is concerned. That they can be improved seems highly probable too.

These stereoscopic pictures have to be seen to be appreciated. Persons accustomed to viewing ordinary flat pictures cannot easily anticipate the effect of seeing every object in a scene stand out with length, breadth and thickness as it does in real life. They do just this, in Mr. Kelley's short film, which is composed of scenes in and about New York City. You see trees in the foreground as close to you as they were to the camera, and objects further back as far away as they were from the lens. Everything is distinct and separate and solid. It is not perfectly clear, however. The main fault with the process is that it requires the use of colored glasses by the spectators, which cut down the illumination. This is probably one of the directions in which Mr. Kelley hopes for improvement.

To make these stereoscopic pictures Mr. Kelley uses two negatives exposed through red and green color filters from slightly different angles. These negatives are superimposed on a single strip of positive film from which the projections on the screen are made. Looked at with the naked eye the pictures thus projected seem blurred, but looked at through red and green glasses, which are passed out in the theatre, the colors are neutralized, the "green" picture being seen through the red filter in front of the spectator's right eye and "red" picture being seen through the green. A black and white picture in three dimensions is the result.

It should be added that these pictures are not those made by the Teleview process, which will be presented for the first time publicly at the Selwyn Theatre next Wednesday evening.

But, though interesting, the movies of the future do not provide the chief entertainment at the Rivoli this week. That is supplied by the photoplay, "Back Home and Broke," which was written for the screen by George Ade, brightly directed by Alfred E. Green, and acted with spirit by Thomas Meighan, Lila Lee, Laurence Wheat, James Marlowe and a number of others. If you are in the Rivoli when this picture begins—and you ought to be to enjoy the last part of it fully—don't walk out. You may be tempted to do so, for the opening reel or two is dull. It doesn't seem possible that George Ade could do anything so flat. There's simply an overdrawn, uninspired picturization of small town life—as it is lived in the movies. A supposedly rich man dies and it is found out that he wasn't rich. His widow and son have nothing and the whole town, with the exception of the heroine and a few others, turns against them. Finally the son goes West to work an oil well in which his father had sunk part of his fortune—and you know, of course, that he is going to strike a gusher. But wait, you don't know the half of it—and it's a shame to tell you, because it's so much more fun to get it from the screen, yet it's impossible to say how good the picture is without giving away the main idea. Here's as much as must be, and not more than need be, said, then.

Did you ever feel that you were not properly appreciated in your home town, and did you ever dream of coming into an immense fortune some day and going back to the old place to reward your few real friends, confound your many enemies and amaze everybody? Well, as the hero of this beautiful fairy story at the Rivoli, Thomas Meighan visualizes your dream for you. He does everything that you have dreamed of doing and in just the way you would love to do it. Talk about the psychological participation of the spectator, talk about his identification of himself with the hero—it's there. That, undoubtedly, is the real reason why the picture is so enjoyable, that and the fact that it is brightly done for the most part in a light comedy manner that relieves one of the necessity for taking it seriously.

But once more a subtitle writer has done everything in his power to spoil a film. There must be a conspiracy of title writers bent upon saving the screen for words, words, words. Their object apparently is to make pictures unnecessary. For let the director, his actors, his scene designer and his camera man express any idea in pictures, let them make a scene that has a point to it, and immediately a title writer rushes in to tell you all about it in screaming words before you can have the fun of getting it from the pictures. If a man's a villain, or a hero or a comedy character you are not allowed to discover the fact for yourself from the way he looks and acts, but must sit like a dummy and read a subtitle which says, "This fellow's a mean one," or "This boy's noble," or "This guy's funny," and then, if you like, you may watch the character in question giving a demonstration of the title writer's perspicacity. The only thing they overlooked in "Back Home and Broke" is a scene in which one of the characters shows by pantomime that he is bragging of having known the hero since he was "so high." It's a wonder this got by. The title writer must have been loafing on his job. The union will probably fine him a day's pay for it.

But he didn't succeed in spoiling the picture entirely. He couldn't do that. It's too good.

D 25, 1922

SALOME, with Mme. Nazimova, Mitchell Lewis, Nigel de Bruller, Rose Dione and others. Directed by Charles Bryant. Settings and costumes designed by Natacha Rambova after the Aubrey Beardsley drawings in the first edition of the Oscar Wilde play, on which the picture is based. At the Criterion.

The costumes, settings and photography of Nazimova "Salome," which began an engagement at the Criterion Theatre last night, is an unusual and, at the same time, a visually satisfying spectacle. It is different but does not depend upon mere difference for its attraction. The eye looks upon it and finds it good.

Consistently fantastic, making no effort at literalism in investiture, the picture appeals at once as a work of free imagination. Natacha Rambova, who designed the settings and costumes after the Aubrey Beardsley drawings in the first edition of the Wilde play, has used only black, white, silver and gold in her materials and has sought her effects in the masses and lines for which the camera is always crying. And in every instance, it would seem, she has made the pictorial point desired, with, of course, the appreciative co-operation of Charles Bryant, the Director of the production, and his photographer. It is true that some may take exception to this or that detail of setting of costuming —to Mme. Nazimova's head dress of bouncing white balls, perhaps—but most of those who accept the fanciful treatment of the production as a whole probably will not be disturbed by any particular feature of it.

But, in addition to this pictorial treatment, there is the story, the story of Oscar Wilde's "Salome," and its treatment as a dramatic narrative. And this is another matter, in which questions and objections arise. It can be reported that the acting is excellent, as a rule; it is admitted that at different points in the action there is true dramatic intensity; and Mme. Nazimova's representation of Salome as young and innocent and yearning may even be accepted by those willing to get altogether away from logic and reality; but after this is said there remains the story itself, and it is disappointing. It runs out in an anti-climax. And the reason is evident.

Mme. Nazimova's Salome is satisfactory to the censors. She takes pride, it is reported, in the fact that she was able to make a screen version of the famous story that would win official sanction—which, it must be granted, is an accomplishment. But can an approvad Salome be interesting, can she be a genuinely dramatic figure? Take the dance, for instance. This is the climax of the drama. The way is prepared for it by words and action that unmistakably indicate its character. The spectators know what to expect as well as Herod himself. And when it comes it has the approval of the cenors! The moral monitors of New York permit the dance that Herod thinks is worth half a kingdom! Can you imagine it? You cannot. Nor do you see the dance. You see an exceedingly tame and not remarkably graceful performance that Herod wouldn't have given standing room in his kingdom for. Yet on the faces of Herod and the other onlookers you see expressions intended to indicate that such a dance as you have been led to imagine is being performed. It shows you part of it and in what you see there is nothing to account for the gross eagerness in the faces of the men. So the whole scene collapses—and it is supposed to be the high climax of the story. But some one may reply that the real dance wouldn't be allowed, and that if it were decent people wouldn't want to look at it. Exactly. The real "Salome" is impossible on both counts. Why, then, does any one attempt it at all? And isn't it overrated as a drama, anyhow?

Ja 1, 1923

THE PILGRIM, written and directed by Charles Chaplin, with Mr. Chaplin, Edna Purviance, Mack Swain, Sydney Chaplin, Dinky Dean and others; "Colonel Heeza Liar, Detective," a Bray cartoon comedy; "Odds and Ends," a Pathe split reel; "I Know a Garden," a Prizma picture. At the Strand.

Charlie Chaplin is at the Strand again. That's enough for most people. Those who stand apart from the crowd may talk of Mr. Chaplin's "art," and those who stop to measure one thing by another may put his latest comedy beside "Shoulder Arms" and "The Kid" and tell you how far short it falls of the mark set by these classics, but, meanwhile, they are showing "The Pilgrim" eight times a day, and eight times a

day the crowd will laugh at it.

And not from habit, either. If Chaplin had never made another comedy, if he had never been heard of before, "The Pilgrim" would be a hit. That's the test, and no one can doubt, surely, that "The Pilgrim" meets it.

No, this picture is not the equal of "The Kid." It lacks that comedy's subtleties, it isn't as sharply pointed with humanity, it isn't as finely characterized, but it's a genuine Chaplin, nevertheless. It has subtleties of its own, it is human in flashes and its characters are a good deal more than stage clowns. Furthermore, if it is broader than "The Kid," it is also more direct as a burlesque. It has its own field. It is neither aimless buffoonery nor an imitation. And this is to Chaplin's credit. He has not copied himself nor has he played low to the mob with haphazard slapstick. He has aimed at something in his new work and hit it.

The object of his jesting is Main Street, small-town life, the small-town congregation, little people who look large to themselves—and are afraid to have any fun. And what fun Chaplin has with them! He isn't vicious, his ridicule is general rather than specific, and it does not seem likely that any one will be offended by his mockery—except, of course, those who are too much like the people in the picture to enjoy its jibes. It's a rare man, you know, who can look into a mirror and laugh. But, though good natured, the fun is pointed with an idea and it does hit something. When you see Chaplin as an escaped convict masquerading in a preacher's clothes, delivering a most earnest sermon at a hard-shelled congregation, familiar scenes are recolored for you, and when, at the end of the performance, a boy in the audience begins to applaud enthusiastically you feel the unconventional appropriateness of the preacher's smiling bows as he takes the curtain call. It is a darned good sermon, too.

Chaplin passes through the town. For a day and a half he is accepted as its new parson, and then a kind-hearted Sheriff leaves him straddling the international boundary line between the United States and Mexico, with the dangerous lawlessness of the latter counry to the right and the dangerous law of the former to the left. He must choose between them—but before he is driven to either terrifying alternative the picture mercifully fades out, with the meek little clerical convict still astride the boundary line. It's a neat ending—and, incidentally, a good beginning for another comic tragedy.

What goes on in the town while Chaplin is there forms, of course, the main part of the comedy, but it would dull the edge of it to supply details here. Pure 'arce, pointed satire, sentimental touches and bounding horseplay are mixed up together, all, as the saying goes, for your delight. And the peculiar joy of the picture is that it is a motion picture. It's what happens in the scenes that makes the story; it is the expressiveness of the pictures, and most of all of Chaplin's own exclusive pantomime, that gives "The Pilgrim" and all its predecessors a true cinematographic character of their own. And to those who believe that a motion picture above all things should be a composition of pictures that move and mean something, this is the film's most important and significant recommendation—and the chief reason why the Chaplin comedies are so popular, whether those who laugh at them know it or not.

Also on the varied and evenly excellent bill at the Strand is one of those skillful Bray cartoon comedies, " Colonel Heeza Liar, Detective "; an interesting split reel called " Odds and Ends," a Prizma color work, " I Know a Garden," and " Robert Louis Stevenson," a Kineto picture.

F 26, 1923

THE SCREEN

The Valet's Initiation.

RUGGLES OF RED GAP, with Edward Horton, Ernest Torrence, Lois Wilson, Fritzi Ridgeway, Charles Ogle, Louise Dresser, Anna Lehr, William Austin, Lillian Leighton, Thomas Holding, Frank Elliott and others, adapted from Harry Leon Wilson's story, directed by James Cruze. At the Rivoli.

Our old friend, Ruggles, and Cousin Egbert came to the screen again yesterday when James Cruze's production of Harry Leon Wilson's intensely amusing story, " Ruggles of Red Gap," was presented at the Rivoli. This narrative was filmed once before, about five years ago. The present version is an entertaining one with many humorous twists, but it has been approached from an angle that robs the tale of much of its charm. The story is told by the scenario writer and not by Ruggles, and instead of opening up in Paris it unfolds in Red Gap, to which it returns after a brief stay in the French capital.

Edward Horton does well as Ruggles, but there are a number of actors who could have obtained a great deal more out of this character. Ernest Torrence buffoons Cousin Egbert, failing to sense the actual character of the Westerner who will " go just so fur and no further." As might be expected, the best

sequences in this production are those pictured in a Hollywood Paris. There one sees to a certain degree the man who rebelled against the stiffer sartorial effects and all social events. The women in the cast are convincing and the Honorable George is efficiently portrayed by Frank Elliott. He is always accompanied by his monocle, which, after securing in his eye to gaze upon something or somebody, he always lets it fall before it could serve as an aid to his vision.

The best series of scenes is where Ruggles is elevated to a Colonelcy by Cousin Egbert after having superintended the arraying of the Westerner in a tail coat and top hat. Accompanied by Ruggles, dressed in all his new glory, Cousin Egbert, feeling in need of a drink, is about to enter the Café de la Paix when he sees Jeff Tuttle, and forthwith Jeff, Cousin Egbert and Ruggles take seats at a table. Tuttle orders, with three fingers as a sign, "visky sodee," and Cousin Egbert enthuses over his friend's knowledge of French. After having tried the same signal and patter a second and third time Jeff decides that the taxi chauffeur must be thirsty and they invite him to join them, overruling the protestations of Ruggles, who declares the man to be socially impossible. It is not long before the chauffeur is wearing the topper, and Ruggles has the Western hat of " Old Sourdough," with Jeff in a derby, and the incorrigible Egbert under the taxi driver's peaked cap—a delicate contrast to the morning coat.

A compelling quartet filled with good cheer, mixing French and English, they swing along until they come to a carousel. They approach one of the wooden steeds of the merry-go-round as they would a fractious broncho, springing back lest it buck or kick.

" Let the Colonel ride her. He knows how," shouts Cousin Egbert, and with much fuss the valet is lifted into the saddle of the inanimate horse.

Returning home in a fearsome condition they are met by Mrs. Effie, very well acted by Louise Dresser. She is shocked at their appearance, and especially at the condition of the faultless servant. Equal to the occasion, Cousin Egbert explains that Ruggles is to blame as he pawned his watch and threatened them with death unless they drank drink for drink with him. They give " three rousing cheers " in the midst of this talk.

In Red Gap Belknap Jackson of the North Side, trying to put Ruggles in his place, kicks him, whereupon Cousin Egbert says:

" Ask him if it is Tuesday, and if he answers ' yes,' punch him in the eye.
" But it is Tuesday," says Ruggles. Cousin Egbert declares that that makes it certain. The Colonel is interviewed in the Red Gap newspaper, eventually opens the United States Grill, and the Earl of Brinstead hies there to put at an end the attention the Honorable George is paying to a girl. But the Earl becomes infatuated with the girl

himself.

This is a good picture, but it might have been infinitely better if other tactics had been adopted by the scenario writer.

S 10, 1923

THE SCREEN

Paris and Parisites.

A WOMAN OF PARIS, with Edna Purviance, Clarence Geldert, Carl Miller, Lydia Knott, Charles French, Adolphe Menjou, Betty Morrissey, Malvina Polo and others, written and directed by Charles Spencer Chaplin.

Our old friend Charlie Chaplin, the world's screen clown, has flung aside temporarily his shapeless trousers and his tiny derby, plucked off his eyebrow mustache, and in a well-tailored suit has graduated into Charles Spencer Chaplin, director par excellence. His first production, in which he does not appear, fascinated an interesting and curious throng last night in the Lyric Theatre.

As a film director Chaplin reveals himself as a bold, resourceful, imaginative, ingenious, careful, studious and daring artist. This effort is called "A Woman of Paris," not an especially original title considering the brilliance displayed in so many sequences of this photoplay. The story is not an unusual one, but the handling of it gives it a marvelous depth of charm, for in this film, which runs for about two hours, Chaplin, the director, has not permitted a scene to be made in a hasty or thoughtless manner. He shows something a little different from the work of other directors throughout the photoplay. Close-ups are denied the players, and the production also is devoid of the aggravating flash-backs. These eliminations are such a relief. Under Chaplin's astute guidance the acting of the players is stripped of what might be termed "standardized motion-picture acting."

Where there is a café scene—as there are in several sequences in this production—Chaplin has studied his sets and the human possibilities. There is nothing too extravagant, and in his contrasts Chaplin has obtained wonderful effects.

The first scenes of this picture show a dismal little French village, and Marie St. Clair, played by Edna Purviance, turned out of her cottage by her angry father. She goes to the home of her sweetheart, but his father will not permit her to remain there. Hence they go to the little railway station, meaning to take the train for Paris. She waits for Jean Millet, the sweetheart (Carl Miller), who goes back for a bag, and finally telephones to him. His father has been taken ill, so the girl in desperation boards the train for Paris

alone.

A year later in the French capital Marie's beauty has won for her all the comforts money can buy. Adolphe Menjou plays Pierre Revel, the wealthiest bachelor in Paris, who furnishes the luxuries for the girl, who dines nightly with him. There are many captivating scenes in the French restaurant, and excellent light comedy is worked out by the head waiter.

The gay life in a studio is shown—where a woman of the Latin Quarter, covered in nothing but folds of silk, is gradually uncovered—the wrapping being wound around a fat old gentleman. And so that the censors will not be offended, the girl only shows her bare feet and ankles, and pokes her head from behind a screen. In another sequence the daring Chaplin shows a Swedish masseuse busy on Marie, who is covered with a sheet. When the sheet is lifted one sees the masseuse at her labors, but Marie is out of the picture.

Marie, sick of the continued gayety, refuses to dine with Pierre. Afterward other friends in the Latin Quarter insist upon her joining them. She knocks on the wrong door and finds herself confronted by her old sweetheart. From then on Marie is torn between poverty and love or luxury and gayety. Jean's mother opposes her son marrying Marie, and this begets a tragic ending, handled so skillfully that happiness beams in the last scenes. One sees the smiling Marie sitting on a farmer's cart and passing at the rate of fifty miles an hour in his automobile is the lascivious Pierre. They do not see each other.

There is a picturesque prologue to this film—a scene showing a studio with the artists and women singing.

Chaplin shows himself by this production to be a sort of O. Henry of the silent drama. The interesting and pleasing touches in the various scenes are like simple words used by an author to give spark and life to his story. This film lives, and the more directors emulate Mr. Chaplin the better will it be for the producing of pictures.

O 2, 1923

THE TEN COMMANDMENTS, with Theodore Roberts, Charles de Roche, Estelle Taylor, Julia Faye, Terrence Moore, James Neill, Lawson Butt, Clarence Burton, Noble Johnson, in the great spectacle; in the modern story are Edyth Chapman, Richard Dix, Rod La Roque, Leatrice Joy, Nita Naldi, Robert Edeson, Charles Ogle and Agnes Ayres.

It is probable that no more wonderful spectacle has ever been put before the public in shadow-form than the greatly heralded prelude to Cecil B. DeMille's costly film, which opened last night to a brilliant and eager gathering in the George M. Cohan Theatre. It is called, and it hardly seems necessary to mention the title "The Ten

Commandments." It is built in two sections, the spectacle and the melodrama. Two men might have directed this feature, as it goes from the sublime to the out-and-out movie. Not that the latter part is bad, but that almost any melodramatic picture would have fitted into the second section of this photodrama.

But the sight of the Israelites in bondage in Egypt, their slaving before the chariots, their treatment by the despots of the day, the swiftly drawn chariots and their steeds, and the great bas-reliefs of figures whose shin-bones would have made two big men. All this was obviously directed by a genius who held in his hand the cost. There are many impressive colorful scenes of the Israelites in the desert, some of them appearing better and more natural than other such effects we have witnessed on the screen.

Charles de Roche, whom we first met in a minor part of "The Spanish Jade," who recently was seen as a Hindu with Pola Negri in "The Cheat," impersonated the terrible Rameses. He was impressive, and like all the other players in this section of the picture, wore his raiment of cloth and metal as if it were comfortable.

There was the death of all the first borns of the Egyptians, and the great and so-called magnificent Rameses praying to his god throughout the night to put life into his boy's body, and no life came. His god had no power like the God of the Israelites.

Coupled with the orchestration there has been nothing on the film so utterly impressive as the thundering and belching forth of one commandment after another, and the titling and photography of this particular effect was remarkable. It was the quivering, crashing, resounding blare from the string and wind instruments that did much to assist in the desired effect. The sky clouds, and then seems to burst, and from the ball of smoke appears golden lettering with one or another of the commandments, stress being laid upon those that are considered the most important, if one may say such a thing.

The costumes in this million dollars' worth of prelude are splendidly created, and not in a single instance is there a jarring note in this regard. Theodore Roberts, who recently was seen in the character of a business man with a cigar in his mouth, gave an excellent portrayal of Moses, the Lawgiver. His make-up was faultless, and the sincerity with which he acted this part made the whole affair doubly effective. Undoubtedly it was a series of sequences that made one think, that carried a message, that was done with meticulous precision, and boomed forth so well that it would have needed an unusually perfect modern drama to stand up in comparison with it. In this spectacle, with a good photographic and scenic effect, the crossing through a water flanked path of the Red Sea was shown, and it drew applause from the packed theatre. Prior to that there was the Pillar of Fire which confused and halted the Egyptians hastening after the slaves they had released through fear of the God of the Israelites.

But—and unfortunately we have to say but—the strain on Mr. De Mille told, and as soon as he swept on to his modern drama he was back to the ordinary and certainly uninspired movie, one in which the direction at times had "business" apparently intended to appeal to the very young. Too many "inserts" were shown. In one case there was a letter which was put on the screen three different times, and from what we now remember once would have been sufficient. The cracking walls of a cathedral being constructed by the hapless man in this portion of the film are brought out so many times that it is extremely tedious, and we would also like to say that if an old mother reads her Bible it is no reason why a motion picture director should have her carrying around a volume that weighs about a hundredweight. Also, why have her pictured after death with the same huge Bible? This is a story of two sons, one bad and the other good, a woman from a leper island, and the breaking of all the Commandments by the conscienceless love making, unfaithful and plotting weakling.

At the same time it must be admitted that in this melodrama there are also some excellent and well-thought out ideas, and some eye-smiting shots. There is considerable suspense where the wife of the wicked brother ascends to the top of the scaffolding of the rickety structure, constructed with rotten cement. It is the catching of her heel on a corner that uncovers the cheap and rotten concrete, as she nearly falls. And Mr. De Mille has not forgotten to give his spectators an impression of height in the full sequence. You see the woman ascending, you see her looking down, and although a car appears insignificantly small upon the roadway this young lady can detect her husband out with another woman in an automobile.

Whatever has been done in the second instalment of this picture—which in all is said to have cost a million and one-half dollars and classed by Mr. De Mille as "the cheapest picture ever made," because of the reward in sheckels it will reap—one must say that great heights of costuming and direction have been attained in the prelude.

The actors are capable throughout, and the performance in the modern portion of Rod LaRoque, as the wicked son, was particularly commendable. Richard Dix was good as the faithful and law-abiding son.

D 22, 1923

THE MARRIAGE CIRCLE, with Adolphe Menjou, Marie Prevost, Creighton Hale, Florence Vidor, Monte Blue and Harry Myers, based upon Lothar Schmidt's "Only a Dream," directed by Ernst Lubitsch; "Sea Fantasie," orchestral overture; special prologue. At the Strand.

It is unalloyed bliss to watch "The Marriage Circle," Ernst Lubitsch's latest film, which is being revealed this week at the Strand. Beginning with a hole in a sock and culminating with a characteristic twist, this picture is filled with surprises and moves along with a hitherto unknown rapidity of action. In direction it is not unlike Chaplin's "A Woman of Paris," but the story based on Lothar Schmidt's "Only a Dream" is far more amusing than the narrative contained in the Chaplin feature.

"The Marriage Circle" has its locale in Vienna, and it possesses, in spite of being made in California, a distinct European flavor, with the result that one finds oneself chuckling over the misfortunes of two married couples. This is due to the direction of the story and the thoroughly competent acting by the cast of six players.

Simplicity is the kenote of this production, in which suspense and exposure are constantly being unfurled without any waste of time. The direction is original and subtle, and it is easy to perceive that Mr. Lubitsch handled this film without interference, with the result that one is really regretful when the last scene appears, as no seven and a half reels ever seemed so short. Chaplin's background was more fertile in contrasts, as in "A Woman of Paris" there was the dreary little French village and then the splendors of Paris, the luxurious flat of the girl and the humble apartment of the sweetheart and mother. In "The Marriage Circle" there are two homes, one of a careless couple and the other of a physician and his loving wife. The contrast appears in the lives of the persons in these two homes, and the story mocks the weakness of men.

Lubitsch reduces furnishings to the barest necessities, believing that too much furniture detracts attention from the players. Frequently in this picture he shows a medium shot with one of the characters posed against an unpaneled door for a background.

As in the Chaplin production, Adolphe Menjou is splendid, and he does much to prove the value of true screen acting in helping to tell the story. Monte Blue rises to every possibility in a rôle that requires an abundance of expression. One moment he is laughing, the next surprised, then angry and finally fearful. His wonderful elasticity of countenance and ability to give a real idea of his feelings is a feature of this amusing and intensely interesting photoplay.

No time is lost in getting the audience in a good humor, as we first see Professor Stock (Adolphe Menjou) arising in the morning and pulling on a sock in which he discovers an inconvenient hole. In his drawer there are no more socks, but in his wife's drawer there are scores of folded stockings. He goes to the window, attaching a small mirror,

but is pushed aside by his selfish wife, Mizzie Stock, played by Marie Prevost. Soon after she leaves the house Professor Stock resumes his shaving operation, suddenly observing, through the window, his wife getting into a taxicab with a strange man. He is not aware that Mizzie had taken a taxicab that was engaged, and that the real owner suddenly turned up. She had offered to release the driver, but they decide to ride on together, Mrs. Stock to drop the man at his office.

After a mild flirtation the man gets out and Mizzie drives on to see an old friend who has been married recently. It is soon divulged that her morning companion is none other than her old friend's husband. And Mizzie had given Mrs. Braun the flowers Dr. Braun had left in the taxicab!

One of the best parts of this picture is where Mrs. Stock is loath to seat her husband next to a stunning blonde. She is seen arranging the dinner table, placing Dr. Braun's card by that of Mizzie, incidentally the last person he wants as a dinner companion. Dr. Braun stealthily approaches the table and changes the cards, putting the blonde's card—Miss Hofer—next to his chair. Mrs. Stock's quick eye takes in this change, and she petulently returns the cards to their original places. When Mizzie arrives Mrs. Stock whispers something about the blond, with the result that the artful Mrs. Stock goes to the table, and, unseen, puts Miss Hofer's card in her own place, which is to disarm suspicion concerning herself. Mizzie is tired of her own husband and he is bored with her, so much so that the Professor does not come to the dinner.

After dinner Braun dances with Miss Hofer, and Mrs. Stock, angry and jealous, solicits Mizzie's help. There is nothing Mizzie wanted more. Quick as a flash she gives Miss Hofer to believe that her dress is unhooked, and steps into Braun's arms and glides over the floor.

Complication follows complication, and to assist in this, Stock engages a detective to follow his wife. Harry Myers plays the part of the sleuth, and although he does not have as much to do as the other players, he is efficient in the character.

Miss Prevost is just the girl for the part of the flirt, who never loses an instant to lay a trap for the man with whom she is infatuated. Creighton Hale is seen as Dr. Braun's partner, Dr. Mueller. He is quite enamored of Mrs. Braun, and steals in one night, believing that the affection is slightly requited, and while her eyes are closed, kisses her, she believing that it is her husband—until she opens her eyes. This is food for a further complication and a most amusing scene.

The various ways in which Mr. Lubitsch has taken his characters is very interesting, and he even photographs some of the scenes through the window curtains. He has inspired his players with vivaciousness, and although all are good usually in their screen work, they are much better under his artistic and astute instruction. Mr. Hale is just as well suited to his rôle as Mr. Menjou and Monte Blue are to theirs. In fact a careful study has evidently been made to have the respective player in the most suitable part, something which is rarely done in films.

This is a delightfully entertaining picture of sousd, artistic merit, which may inspire other producers to do something along the same line.

F 4, 1924

Arabian Nights Satire.

THE THIEF OF BAGDAD, with Douglas Fairbanks, Snitz Edwards, Charles Belcher, Julanne Johnston, Anna May Wong, Winter Blossom, Etta Lee, Brandon Hurst, Tote Du Crow, So-Jin, K. Nambu, Sadakichi Hartmann and Noble Johnson; written for the screen by Elton Thomas, directed by Raoul Walsh, photographed by Arthur Edson, presented by Comstock & Gest. At the Liberty.

Imagine a clever satire on the "Arabian Nights" with marvelous photography and you have an inkling of Douglas Fairbanks's new picture, "The Thief of Bagdad," which was presented last night in the Liberty Theatre to an audience which one might see at the opening of a favorite opera with a great tenor and a famous prima donna. Seeing that this film (the word hardly seems to fit such a wonderful picture) treated of scenes in Bagdad, Morris Gest, that Prince of Miracles in O. Henry's "Bagdad on the Subway," saw fit to give the theatre a thoroughly Oriental atmosphere, with drums, ululating vocal offerings, odiferous incense, perfume from Bagdad, magic carpets and ushers in Arabian attire, who during the intermission made a brave effort to bear cups of Turkish coffee to the women in the audience.

It is a picture which reminds one of Barrie, of Kipling, of Hans Andersen, and for the time that one is beholding the miraculous feats of the photographer, the remarkable sets and costumes that are a feast for the eye, one forgets all about the humming, buzzing, brilliantly lighted Broadway, and for the time being, if you will, becomes a child again.

Douglas Fairbanks is his happy-go-lucky self throughout the picture, in which he shows his dexterity and agility, but not to an extent to destroy any illusion the photoplay sheds on the audience. In most of this production Fairbanks is bronzed and naked to his waist line, showing a fine depth of chest and impressively muscular arms.

There are mammoth scenes in this effort, which add to the splendidly told story with a remarkably perfect

atmosphere of "The Thousand and One Arabian Nights." One sees the City of Bagdad, with polished paving lending a reflection that causes one to look upon it as a city suspended in mid-air. There are desert scenes, and a wonderful Crystal City, supposed to be under the sea, which was actually built out of glass.

To reach the Crystal City, Fairbanks has to dive to a great depth into the sea, and this effect is obtained through the aid of the slow motion camera and glass. The Thief, who is enamored of a fascinating Princess whose errand he is attempting to accomplish, is attacked by a brontosaurus of the seas, and with a sharp knife the tiny man—as he seems on the screen—like St. George of old, slays the monster.

He has numerous other escapades with dreadful-looking beasts, and then he goes through the Cavern of Fire, and in course of time discovers the famed Flying Horse. This white steed with wings was the cause of uproarious laughter as, with Fairbanks on its back, it sped across the screen.

He is actually a young man in search of his birthright—true manhood and power over men—who has discovered that happiness cannot be stolen. Once he has found his quest he is able to give birth to armies, and to use a cloth that makes him disappear, leaving only triangular reflection showing where he is. The trick photography is in no place better than where the magic carpet is introduced. It was discovered by a plethoric Prince, eager for the Princess's hand. This carpet is seen flying from the floor of the palace, up stairways, through doors and out into the skies. It is wonderfully effective and inspiring. There are Buddhas that have fingers about twelve feet long, doors with teeth that open from the sides, top and bottom and close in the middle, that look as if they were thirty feet high, great gates that dwarf dozens of men, and a magic rope, which the thief steals, and on which he is able to climb at will. You see him sling this rope into the air and in a second the agile star of this picture is clambering up it.

Julanne Johnston makes a stunning Princess, lethargic but beautiful. Her bed is in the midst of a room that looks like one of the "Robin Hood" sets. Anna May Wong impersonates the Mongol slave and So-Jin enacts the Mongol Prince. So-Jin is remarkable for his undemonstrative countenance, cruel and comfortable, with just a scintillation of a smile when dirty work is to be done. Snitz Edwards, with an excellent make-up, has the rôle of the Thief's Evil Associate. Noble Johnson figures as the Indian Prince. He is effective and true to type, with a splendid imitation of an Indian beast.

The Thief only has to toss powder to the floor to make an army. No sooner has the powder turned to smoke than up come a dozen men, and soon one sees what looks like an army of more than a thousand aiding the one-time Thief of Bagdad. Never has an audience shown its appreciation of such an entertainment as the one in the Liberty did last night. This film is filled with brilliant ideas that caught the sympathy of the audience, so that they were actually thrilled when the Thief arrived in time to aid the Princess.

There are some wonderfully well-worked-out double exposure photographic effects, and even to an experienced eye the illusion is in nearly every instance kept up to a state of perfection. It is something that could only be accomplished by means of the camera and the screen, something that one could never see upon a stage.

It is an entrancing picture, wholesome and beautiful, deliberate but compelling, a feat of motion picture art which has never been equaled and one which itself will enthrall persons time and again. You can see this film and look forward to seeing it a second time.

Mr 19, 1924

THE IRON HORSE, with Winston Miller, Peggy Cartwright, Charles Edward Bull, James Gordon, Will Walling, George O'Brien, Madge Bellamy, Fred Kohler, Cyril Chadwick, Gladys Hulette, James Marcus, Francis Powers, J. Farrell MacDonald, James Welch, Colin Chase, Jack O'Brien, Walter Rogers, George Wagner, John Padjan, Charles O'Malley, Delbert Mann, Jack Ganzhorn, Chief Big Tree, Chief White Spear, Frances Teague, Stanhope Wheatcroft and Edward Piel, written by Charles Kenyon and John Russell, directed by John Ford. Special music score by Erno Rapee. At the Lyric.

Another stirring chapter in American history was told last night when a picture entitled "The Iron Horse" was presented at the Lyric Theatre by William Fox, before a gathering that included persons prominent in the film firmamen and men who are powers in the railroad world. This ambitious production dwelt trenchantly upon the indomitable energy, resourcefoulness and courage of those who spanned the continent with steel. Little does one realize in these days of modern comforts, the tirelessness of those Americans who shed their life's blood with a smile in the race to get first to the goal with rails and ties.

Gray-haired men, whose fathers had constructed railroads in the pioneer days, were much moved by the spectacle in shadows that passed before their eyes. And some of them wept, not so much at the story interspersing this gigantic accomplishment of the '60s as at the sight of the men working with sledge hammers on the spike nails, as tie after tie and rail after rail were laid down. They wept also when they saw the slow moving old engine with its ungainly funnel, which to the folk of the olden days ran so smoothly on its quickly constructed path of iron.

As one watches this film one is impressed by the fact that Americans have had more to battle against than any other nation. In the first place they had miles by the thousand to conquer, then they had the difficulties of the terrain, and finally they had literally to fight their way along as they were working, for they were attacked night and day by hostile Indians who could not and would not understand the white man's ways. Their arrows pierced the hearts of those who carried on in their almost impossible task, and knowing the limited numbers of the invaders of their soil, the redmen charged and charged again and again in an effort to weaken the energy of the railroad pioneers.

In this picture is shown with true dramatic emphasis the welding together of two great points with steel. One sees the Indians bearing down on those working at a job, which in all conscience is bad enough even in these days, without having to believe that their lives are in danger from an energetic enemy. One might just as well imagine men constructing a steel skyscraper being shot at when they have just above finished the framework of their great structure.

Yet with all their discomforts amid the great risk, it is shown, and truthfully, in this picture that these pioneers had a keen sense of humor. They were sports, and as sports they had to settle disputes even among themselves. For no chapter of history in a film can be told without a heroine, a hero and a villain, and the chances are that this is a more or less accurate description.

As scene after scene passes in shadows and lights upon the screen one cannot help thinking of that remarkable production, "The Covered Wagon," to which "The Iron Horse" is a sort of sequel. Sometimes people in the audience wondered why cattle figured so often in the picture, forgetting that these railroad builders had to eat. One is also impressed by the fact that in every halt of any consequence they founded towns as they went along, and usually the first sign painted was that for a saloon.

There are herds of buffalo, with that famous old scout, Buffalo Bill, firing into the animals to feed those who must live. It was incidentally through the efficiency with which he accomplished this work that Colonel William Frederick Cody derived his nickname of Buffalo Bill.

The outstanding actor in this production is not the good-looking hero, nor even the comely girl, but the man who officiates in the comedy character, that of Sergeant Slattery. Francis Powers plays this part beautifully, making one think of many characters in American history, of Kipling's "Soldiers Three," and also of Marryat's "Masterman Ready." When things are dull and men are gloomy it is Sergeant Slattery who takes upon himself to lighten up matters with a joke or a laugh, and even when he is gripping his gun against the Indians there is a twinkle in his eye.

Of the many scenes which drew applause last night were those on the desert, where hosts of men were scampering along with a will in laying their ties, while others equally handy wielded their sledge hammers and riveted the rails to the wood. It looked like a slow job even if it were merely a score of miles, but to realize the immense distance that had to be covered almost made one cover one's eyes with one's hands.

John Ford, the director of this film, has done his share of the work with thoroughness and with pleasing imagination. There are certain stretches in the production that are long and at times tedious, but this is due to the cutting and is a fault which can be remedied. While George O'Brien, who impersonates the heroic Davy Brandon, is quite good in most of his acting, the producers have permitted him to have too much of the show at certain junctures, especially where he heaves his manly chest. In the fights with Cyril Chadwick, who plays Peter Jesson, he is capable, although at times too theatric. He seems to remember that he is a fine young specimen of manhood. His shirt sleeves are tucked up high enough to give one a good view of his biceps, which appear to be frequently strained for effect.

The climax to this production is where the Union Pacific and Central Pacific engines touch headlights at Promontory Point, Utah—which happened on May 10, 1869. After this happens the stalwart Davy Brandon is seen standing with a foot on each rail, surveying the accomplishment started by his father.

Madge Bellamy is seen as Miriam Marsh, the sweet young heroine, who is really very pretty and sympathetic. Charles Edward Bull has the rôle of Abraham Lincoln, and his make-up as the martyred President is so good that the mere sight of him brought volleys of applause from the spectators. Chadwick is splendid as the despicable Jesson, making the most of every situation, but nevertheless leaving one with the impression that his mustache and collar are rather up to date.

The real villain, the man with two fingers off his right hand who is always concealing this fact by keeping his hand in his coat pocket, is Deroux, who slew Brandon's father. Fred Kohler handles this rôle with restraint and full effect.

This is an instructive and inspiring film, one which should make every American proud of the manner of men who were responsible for great achievements in the face of danger, sickness and fatigue. They were, as we said, true sports, who worked with a vim and got satisfaction and even fun out of the hazardous labors.

Ag 29, 1924

FEET OF CLAY, with Vera Reynolds, Rod La Rocque, Victor Varconi, Ricardo Cortez, Julia Faye, Theodore Kosloff and Robert Edeson, adapted from a novel by Margaretta Tuttle, directed by Cecil B. De Mille; Phonofilm of "Three Presidential" nominees; "Famous Music Master Films," Stephen Foster; "Lunacy," third dimension stereoscopic film. At the Rivoli.

Wild and weird ideas are to be seen in "Feet of Clay," Cecil B. De Mille's new picture now holding forth at the Rivoli. We are informed that it was adapted from a novel by Margaretta Tuttle, except for one long sequence which is attributed to a literary effort called "Across the Border." One beholds the average scenario writer's conception of the diversions of the wealthy, the sight of young people in a Harlem flat in which they eventually attempt suicide by turning on the gas, and, as a grand finale, there is a Hollywood idea of the Great Beyond. To us the flow of fleeting scenes seemed like a nightmare one might have experienced following an afternoon at Long Beach, a lobster dinner and cramming into the same evening a flamboyant cabaret show and that inspiring play "Outward Bound."

The acting and the direction of this very strange affair are in keeping with the exaggerations of the narrative, the incidents of which are both improbable and implausible. Some of the scenes depicting aquamarine sports are interesting so long as one does not bother about the subtitles or the story. But after Kerry Harlan (Rod La Rocque) is bitten by a shark and his consequent lameness is seen in his Harlem flat and also at a glaring garden party, one is apt to presume that Mr. De Mille was indulging himself in making this production. He is not content with the ordinary triangle muddle, as he makes this a quintet affair.

The characters in this picture have alarming experiences thrust upon them, for besides picturing a man attacked by a shark, there is a sequence devoted to an erring wife hiding from her elderly husband on a narrow ledge about six stories high. After clinging to telegraph wires for what seems to be an eternity, she finally falls and is killed. Then Mrs. Harlan enters her unpretentious abode in Harlem and discovers her husband unconscious from the flow of gas. Believing him dead, she decides to commit suicide also. This is followed by a long sequence in which the couple are seen in about the same plight as the Halfways in "Outward Bound." The shattering of a window by a boot, thrown by the girl we presumed to be unconscious, results in the young couple being saved.

The sequence dealing with the Hereafter depicts scores of persons slowly threading their way to the desk of the Bookkeeper, who decides on which side they are to continue. The Harlans are turned back, not having completed their life's experiences.

The story is built around the shark's bite. Harlan manages to keep his lameness a secret from his bride, but she will dance, and finally in a jealous fit he decides that he is going to cut in and be her partner. He stumbles several times and eventually falls, bringing down a string of colored lanterns.

Summed up—if it is possible to do so with such a series of incidents—this is a love affair of a young couple disturbed on one side by the beautiful wife of an elderly surgeon and on the other by a good-looking young bachelor.

There is a wide difference between some of the subtitles. One reads: "When the air is charged with tempest, trifles can breed tragedy." A spoken title reads: "Snap into it, Sapho! This is no refuge for society dames with broken arches." And another says: "I must beat it, as Benedick will dock me again if I'm late."

One of the ridiculous scenes, and ther are not a few of them, shows Dr. Fergus Lansell (Robert Edeson) entering Harlan's flat. After a perfunctory glance at Harlan's foot—which it is said must be kept off the ground for a year or gangrene will set in—Dr. Lansell sniffs the air, having obviously detected the perfume used by his wife. She is hiding in one of the rooms, the last to be opened.

It seems strange that the hero of this story should be so friendly with people whose wealth "is in the seven figures." He has $80 a week and the sad-looking Harlem flat.

The Harlans are married aboard a yacht, and at a giddy social function it is decided that the young couple shall pay the penalty by a kiss for every person of the opposite sex. So one has a scene of men lined up waiting for the bride's kisses and the girls waiting like a corporal's guard for a kiss from Harlan.

It is not necessary to go into the individual acting of the principals in this production, as none of them excels in any particular scene nor seems especially fitted to the rôle allotted to him or her.

An interesting Phonofilm in which President Coolidge, John W. Davis and Robert M. La Follette are seen and heard is a feature on the program at the Rivoli and at the Rialto.

S 22, 1924

THE NAVIGATOR, with Buster Keaton, Kathryn McGuire, Frederick Vroom, Noble Johnson, Clarence Burton and H. M. Clugston, written by Jean Havez, Clyde Bruckman and Joe Mitchell, directed by Mr. Keaton and Donald Crisp; overture, "Orpheus"; "Bohemia," a camera tour; "In a Song Shop"; special prologue. At the Capitol.

By MORDAUNT HALL

Buster Keaton's sphynx-like face is to be seen at the Capitol this week in a nautical film-farce, called "The Navigator," wherein his wildest emotions are reflected by an occasional upward turn of his right eyebrow. Now and again the Keaton eyes evince a suggestion of life, but his lips barely budge. To have a contrast to this comedian's placidity of countenance, we had only to look at those wat᎒᎒ this picture. Mouths

were wide open in explosions of laughter and eyes sparkled with merriment. "The Navigator" is an excellent panacea for melancholia or lethargy, as it is filled with ludicrous and intensely humorous situations. It even strikes one as being astonishing that this comedian can keep such perfect control over his physiognomy during the action of this parcel of mirth. While it took three writers to pen the narrative and two directors to produce it, the actual players are limited to Mr. Keaton and Kathryn McGuire.

It is funny enough to see this indefatigable stoic as a pampered young man in a wonderful mansion, but, as might be gathered, it is even more absurd to view his actions when he and the heroine are alone aboard a drifting steamship.

This time Mr. Keaton is seen as Rollo Treadway, a young man who is helpless without servants and who even rides in his expensive automobile to cross the street. Being bored, he announces to his butler that he thinks that it is a good thing to be married. Without further ado he goes over to Betsy O'Brien and proposes. Betsy, who never pictured herself as Rollo's wife, promptly spurns his offer of marriage. Anticipating his honeymoon, Rollo had bought two steamship tickets for Honolulu, to which spot he decides to travel alone. As early rising is distasteful to him he decides to board the vessel that night, and while doing so his tickets are blown away by a sudden strong gust of wind. He gets on the wrong ship, but goes to bed in one the staterooms. Betsy, in seeking her father, who had been held up and gagged by spies, rushes aboard the same steamship, not knowing that the hawsers have been cut.

For out at sea next morning Rollo discovers there is nobody at the helm or in the engine room, and, what is more important to him, not a steward to serve him breakfast. Suddenly he hears gentle footfalls, and there is an amusing chase around the decks of the vessel. Betsy runs away from the sound of Rollo, and Rollo is keenly anxious to get away from what he imagines to be some terrible ghost. Their subsequent meeting is the cause of much hilarity, especially when Rollo makes coffee with sea water.

Later he is seen as a diver, the vessel having gone ashore off an island inhabited by countless cannibals. Under water he is prodded by a swordfish and caught by the arm of a ravenous octopus. Above the cannibals have boarded the vessel and captured Betsy, to whom Rollo tries to signal that he wants to come to the surface. Finally he frightens the savages by strolling out of the water onto the beach.

While there is no denying the jocular and farcical action of this picture, there are stretches which should be cut, as some of the humor is just a bit overdone. Nevertheless, Mr. Keaton deserves untold credit for his originality in thinking up most of the funny scenes.

O 13, 1924

THE SCREEN

Frank Norris's "McTeague."

GREED, with Gibson Gowland, Jean Hersholt, Chester Conklin, Sylvia Ashton, ZaSu Pitts, Austin Jewell, Oscar and Otto Gottel, Jan Standing, Max Tyron, Frank Hayes, Fanny Midgley, Dale Fuller, Cesare Gravina, Hughie Mack, Tiny Jones, J. Aldrich Libbey, Rita Revela, Lon Poff, William Barlow, Edward Gaffney, S. S. Simonx and others; adapted from Frank Norris's "McTeague," directed by Erich von Stroheim. At the Cosmopolitan.

The sour crême de la sour crême de la bourgoisie, and what might be its utterly ultra habits, were set forth last night before an expectant gathering in the Cosmopolitan Theatre in the fleeting shadows of the picturized version of Frank Norris's "McTeague," which emphasized its film title of "Greed." The spectators laughed, and laughed heartily, at the audacity of the director, Erich von Stroheim, the producer of "Foolish Wives," and the director who was responsible for part of "Merry Go Round." Last January this picture was thought by its director to be perfect in forty-two reels, which took nine hours to view. He capitulated to its being cut down to about 30,000 feet, and is said to have declared that any audience would be content to sit through six hours of this picture. However, it was cut to less than half that length.

It is undeniably a dramatic story, filled with the spirit of its film title, without a hero or a heroine. The three principals, however, deliver splendid performances in their respective rôles. Gibson Gowland is unusually fine as McTeague; but from beginning to end this affair is sordid, and deals only with the excrescences of life such as would flabbergast even those dwelling in lodging houses on the waterfront.

Mr. von Stroheim has not missed a vulgar point, but on the other hand his direction of the effort is cunningly dramatic. There is McTeague, who graduates from a worker in the Big Dipper Gold Mine to being a dentist without a diploma. He hails his new work with silent satisfaction, and when Trina Sieppe, Marcus Schouler's sweetheart, comes to his "painless parlors," he examines her teeth, informing her in due time that she must have three of them extracted and a bridge. The cost immediately enters her mind, but finally there is acquiescence, and she succumbs to the ether. McTeague gazes upon her quiescent countenance, and then, after fighting against his desire, he kisses her.

Sometime afterward he tells Marcus that he is in love with Trina, and the latter surrenders his sweetheart, who on the morning she went to McTeague's parlors had bought a chance in a lottery, the high prize of which was $5,000.

Soon after this one hears that Trina has won the $5,000, and Marcus's countenance is black and ominous. Then follows an obnoxious wedding scene with grotesque comedy. Hans Sieppe, the bride's father, insisting on drilling the figurantes, even to chalking marks on spots for them to stand on. Mr. von Stroheim outdoes himself in the wedding breakfast sequence, as the participants at the meal all attack the edibles in a most ravenous manner, the male element being protected from their ignorance of etiquette by napkins tucked around their necks.

In the struggle for existence Mrs. McTeague clings to her $5,000 even after McTeague is forbidden to practice dentistry and is forced to seek his livelihood as best he can. She gradually becomes a miser, counting her gold on her bed and concealing it in her trunk as fast as she can when she hears her husband's heavy tread. Then she grows eager for every penny she can extort from him, going through his pockets when she knows by his breathing that he is asleep. It all ends as might be anticipated—in the murder of the woman by McTeague, who escapes to Death Valley with the sack of golden coins, which his wife had polished with such meticulous care night after night.

Marcus, who, in spite of protestations of friendship had never forgiven McTeague for depriving him of the $5,000, is one of the first to read of the reward offered for the murderer. It is not long before he and a posse are plunging forth into the sun-scorched desert in search of their quarry. The Death Valley scenes are stark reflections of what happen in such circumstances and true to Frank Norris's story. Mr. Gowland gives a realistic portrayal of a man struggling along on the hot sands with the blazing sun overhead. He has the gold. He has killed his wife. And Marcus is after him! The climax is not only mindful of Frank Norris's story, but also of Jack London's "Love of Life." Mr. von Stroheim has introduced situations which make the fight for existence still stronger in its appeal than one would have imagined. Fancy two men struggling in the desert suddenly seeing the only possible chance of life—water—being carried away by a frightened mule.

Irving Thalberg and Harry Rapf, two expert producers, clipped this production as much as they dared and still have a dramatic story. They are to be congratulated on their efforts, and the only pity is that they did not use the scissors more generously in the beginning.

Mr. Gowland slides into the character and stays with it, and in spite of McTeague's aggressiveness and obvious hot temper, he and his wife are the only characters with whom one really would care to shake hands. Mr. Gowland is clever in his exhibition of temper and wonderfully effective in the desert scenes with his sweaty arms and bleary eyes.

Marcus Schouler is impersonated by Jean Hersholt, an efficient screen actor, but in this film he is occasionally overdressed for such a part. His rôle also calls for demonstrations which are not always pleasant. ZaSu Pitt portrays the rôle of Trina, into which she throws herself with vehemence. She is natural as the woman counting her golden hoard, and makes the character live when she robs her husband of trifling amounts. The other members of the cast are capable.

D 5, 1924

THE SCREEN
By MORDAUNT HALL.

"THE LAST MAN"
&
"COMIN' THRO' THE RYE"

IN the last ten days we have taken the opportunity to view two foreign productions, one of which is a masterpiece and the other an old-fashioned story produced in an old-fashioned way. The first is the German production called "The Last Man," and the second is Cecil Hepworth's "Comin' Thro' the Rye," a British picture.

"The Last Man" is a story told without titles, except for two or three inserts, and yet one is never in doubt as to what the director wishes to convey. While subtitles are not necessary, there is no doubt but a caption here and there would have done no harm. It seems to us to be rather straining the point to avoid subtitles altogether, even if the picture is clever and one is not actually conscious of the lack of titles. Some of the lines from a play from which a pictorial effort has been adapted never detract from the production. The captions are interesting, but this does not mean we think that each sequence should be boomed by text which is practically only repeating what has been told in pantomime.

Whether producers who have an eagle eye on box-office returns will look with enthusiasm on "The Last Man" is problematical. The French production, "Crainquebille," an excellent character sketch, was not received with open arms by the theatre owners. It was the story

of an old man, without love, and the comedy it contained was whimsical and delicate. It was very much like O. Henry's "The Cop and the Anthem."

There is real art both in the acting and in the camera work of "The Last Man." It has no love story, and the heart interest, like "Crainquebille" deals with an old man. The present German production has the advantage of more modern ideas in photography and in producing technique. The story grips one from beginning to end and, owing to the author "taking pity on his chief character" and giving him another act, there is a jubilant finish.

Natural Scenes.

None of the scenes in "The Last Man" causes one to think of studios, and the action is so natural in many of the sequences that one is quite stirred without words of explanation. Pride and its fall is one idea that can be gleaned from the story, while another is the ingratitude toward old age. One can also look upon it as a story unfolding the theme of the vanity of mortals.

In a striking bit of photography in which the rain seems to be real, one perceives a tall and hefty old porter, with carefully combed hair and mustache, standing at the main entrance of the important Atlantic Hotel, helping persons from taxis and lugging great trunks to the mat in front of the building. His greatcoat is the pride of his existence. It is lavishly trimmed with wide gold braid and set off by a cap. The whole effect would make an Admiral's uniform look like that of a First Lieutenant.

After hauling a trunk in the rain from one vehicle, the old porter enters the hotel for a breathing spell. He settles on a seat. Just at that instant the imposing hotel manager appears, and after observing a conveyance arriving while the porter is resting he makes a note of it in his little book. The porter eventually goes out and again and late that night as usual forges his way to his humble abode in a tenement quarter, where his glittering braid is looked upon as something which gives tone to the whole neighborhood. Women bow to him and men salute to him, each receiving a military touch of the cap from the proud old porter. He is rather pleased with himself.

His Amazement.

Next day when he goes down to work

he observes with amazement that there is a younger man, also robed in a great-coat covered in gold braid, whistling for taxis and escorting persons into the hotel. Emil Jannings gives a wonderful exhibition of the old man's feelings when confronted with the surprise of his life. Soon he is seen in the manager's office, where he is told that he is to take the aged menial's place in the washroom, as that veteran has been pensioned. The porter crumples up with the news, but takes advantage of an opportunity to steal the key of the cupboard, in which he is told to hang his glorious coat.

When the time comes for him to go home he remembers that his daughter is to be married that night. He cannot think of appearing at the wedding with-out his gold-bedecked overcoat, so he stealthily crawls along the corridor, keeping close to the wall, and finally sneaks into the manager's office. Soon he issues forth, bent and much aged by his humiliation, but wearing the treasured uniform.

He is no longer his esteemed self on reaching home, but with the aid of wine he holds himself together. A little too much wine sends him into the land of dreams where the whole story comes be-fore him. This section of the story is particularly impressive. One sees the old porter as he had been a couple of days before—straight, strong and filled with honest pride.

It is raining and four or five men are seen trying to lift a trunk. In his dream the porter waves them aside and with-out any apparent exertion with one brawny arm lifts up the trunk. He pitches it up in the air, exchanges a word with one of the men and then catches the trunk with one hand.

The Porter's Dream.

Next morning the dream was only a dream. Demotion had really happened! He was no longer entitled to the uni-form. He sneaks out of the house, gets to the usual road crossing and hurries over toward the hotel, but, being fearful lest he be caught with his coat, he final-ly checks it at the near-by railroad sta-tion. After that one sees him in the shab-by clothes which the glorious coat had covered for so long, stealing into the washroom to attend to his new duties.

Mr. Jannings is perhaps a trifle off his guard in one or two places in this picture. He appears too bowed and bent after the humiliation, hardly able to walk, and yet he has sufficient energy to dash across the street like a youth catching a train. His facial expressions are wonderfully indicative of moods, conveying every atom of feeling flowing through the old man's mind, changing here with a glimmer of hope and then to tragic despair at the thought of the horrible humiliation. To serve in the hotel as a humble washroom attendant in a mere white coat was bad enough, but to have to go home night after night and emerge morning after morning in the shoddy clothes, emphasizing his ro-tundity, was more than he could bear. The cackling females in the tenement quarter are seen delivering the news when one of their ilk has discovered ac-cidentally that the porter, the man of gold braid and pomp, is nothing but a white-coated attendant.

In the picturing of several scenes the director has obtained great effect by the wheeling up of the camera, once actu-ally passing the main objective on the screen; it gives the effect of traveling from one's seat and following the per-sons on the screen.

We will not dwell upon the happy de-velopment in the last act, as the author has decided that this is merely given to the porter in pity, and that the story ought to end with the disappointed old man in his white jacket. Nevertheless, fiction readers will delight in this addi-tional chapter, and in the way it is told it is just as clever as the preceding ones. "The Last Man" is a master-piece on which it is hoped New York will have the opportunity of delivering its verdict.

"The Last Man" was filmed in the Ufa studio in Neubabelsberg, near Berlin, F. W. Murnau being responsible for the direction. Karl Mayer, author of "The Cabinet of Dr. Caligari," wrote the scenario of the current photoplay.

On the other hand, "Comin' Thro' the Rye" is a frayed and clumsy produc-tion, in which the players appear to em-ulate old tragedians rather than persons in real life. Time and again the char-acters start when it appeared to us that they ought to have heard the footsteps on the grass before the approaching player really appeared in the picture. There is a lot of slow, tedious action, with painful expressions that do not re-flect emotions of real life. The heroine might just as well be suffering from the toothache as from the pangs of love. Yet this production has been highly praised in England—which is strange, for it is hardly comparable with ordinary features produced in this country. We had hoped for much in this picture—which is a sweet, old-fashioned love story—with its beautiful English background.

D 21, 1924

THE SCREEN

By MORDAUNT HALL.

THE LAST LAUGH, with Emil Jannings, Mary Delschaft, Kurt Hiller, Emilie Kurz, Hans Unterkircher and George John, written by Carl Mayer, author of "Dr. Caligari," directed by F. W. Murnau; MISS BLUEBEARD, with Bebe Daniels, Robert Frazier, Kenneth MacKenna, Raymond Griffith, Martha Madison, Diana Kane, Lawrence d'Orsay, Florence Billings and Ivan Simpson; "Beautiful Galatea," a dramatization of von Suppe's overture, by Josiah Zuro, with dancers and the ensemble. At the Rivoli.

Although we have already reviewed the Ufa production, "The Last Laugh," which was originally known as "The Last Man," seeing it again prompted us to write a few more words about this highly artistic film masterpiece. Emil Jannings, who will be remembered for his performances in "Passion" and "Peter the Great," officiates as an old hotel doorman who is proud of his great coat, bedecked with gold lace, his cap and also his position. Going home at night is a formality with him. He salutes the people who live in his tenement district, and does likewise when leaving for work in the morning. His salute is much like an Admiral would give to a midshipman.

He finds himself rather exhausted one day after handling a heavy trunk and is discovered by the manager, who decides that the doorman is getting old and should be replaced. The doorman comes to work next day, and to his utter amazement he sees another doorman wearing just such a coat as his own. Eventually the old man finds himself sentenced to take the place of the washroom attendant, who wears only a plain white coat.

There are no titles in this film—merely a few inserts to guide the viewer. And yet one is never in doubt as to the action of this admirable picture, which is a remarkable piece of direction, with exquisite lighting effects. In one sequence one sees the doorman returning home. An elderly caretaker puts out the light in the dismal hall of the building in which he lives. Other lights are gradually extinguished, until the only glimmer is that in the old man's apartment. Soon this goes out. Later the dawn is shown, coming gradually, with men and women arising, the sweepers and cleaners busy, and finally the pompous old doorman emerging from his abode, saluting to right and left as he stalks on to the hotel, with which he is so proud to be connected.

The author inserts one title between acts in this picture. In this caption he tells the audience that the story ought really to end in the tragic way. But he says he has taken pity on the character and therefore has decided to give it another ending. This part is comedy, but it is singularly well done.

Mr. Jannings tells the story with amazing strength by his actions and his expressions. There were tears to the right of us, tears to the left of us and tears in our own eyes as we looked at this production a second time. Major Geoffrey Moss, who wrote "Isn't Life Wonderful?" told us that he had a great regret on leaving for England, and that was that he had not seen "The Last Laugh" once again.

"Miss Bluebeard" is another picture showing at the Rivoli. It is a clever farce, which is capably acted. Bebe Daniels, Robert Frazer and Raymond Griffith have perhaps the principal rôles. There are scenes in France and London, the initial scenes being exceedingly adroit. Colette Girard, played by Miss Daniels, is seen flirting with one man, then hiding him under the sofa to attend to another admirer, who also takes a place under the same piece of furniture. The audience is then informed that the scene takes place on the stage of a Paris theatre.

Larry Charters wants to keep away from women, and Colette is eager to deprive herself of male company. She finds herself at a small French railroad station, where she and a young man miss the train. They go to the Mayor, who occasionally rents rooms, to find shelter. He is fond of cognac and had been expecting a couple who wanted to be married. Colette and Hawley sign what they think is a hotel register, which turns out to be a marriage license. The Mayor declares them to be man and wife, and then flops over in a drunken coma. And what adds to the complications is that Hawley had been posing as Charters.

Mr. Griffith has the comedy rôle of the Hon. Bertie Bird, who loves to sleep, and is constantly being drawn into other persons' affairs and made very uncomfortable. He makes the spectators roar with laughter when he tries to imitate a cat. Ivan Simpson is splendid in the rôle of a butler.

Of course, this is a frivolous affair, amusing and at times lacking in suspense, but never in action. It was directed by Frank Tuttle, having been adapted from Avery Hopwood's play, "Little Miss Bluebeard."

Ja 28, 1925

Charlie Chaplin's New Comedy.

THE GOLD RUSH, with Charlie Chaplin, Mack Swain, Tom Murray, Georgia Hale, Malcolm Waite and Henry Bergman, written and directed by Charlie Chaplin; special prologue with singing arranged by Joseph Plunkett. At the Mark Strand.

By MORDAUNT HALL

The great host of spectators that attended the midnight presentation on Saturday at the Mark Strand of Charlie Chaplin's delightful comedy, "The Gold Rush," was convincing proof that a large contingent of New Yorkers is never too tired or too hot to laugh. Quite a number of persons in the interesting gathering had deserted the cool of the country and not a few of them had already been to one show that night.

Just before the curtain went up on the prologue there was a wave of applause and people stood up to behold the little film fun-maker struggling along the aisle, greeting old friends and being introduced to scores of people. He was a little nervous and appeared to be much relieved when he reached his seat in the body of the theatre. No sooner were the lights switched on after the finish of the picture—at twenty minutes past 2 o'clock yesterday morning—than the enthusiastic assembly appealed vociferously for a speech from the author-actor, and Mr. Chaplin, escorted by two friends, went to the stage and thanked the audience, ending his brief talk by saying that he was very emotional.

It was a proud night for Chaplin, as while he sat looking at the picture and listening to Carl Edouarde's orchestra he was not insensible to the chuckles and shrieks of laughter provoked by his own antics on the screen. The joy of the spectators testified to the worth of the picture, on which he had worked for more than eighteen months.

There is more than mere laughter in "The Gold Rush." Back of it, masked by ludicrous situations, is something of the comedian's early life—the hungry days in London, the times when he was depressed by disappointments, the hopes, his loneliness and the adulation he felt for successful actors. It is told with a background of the Klondike, and one can only appreciate the true meaning of some of the incidents by translating them mentally from the various plights in which the pathetic little Lone Prospector continually finds himself. It is as much a dramatic story as a comedy. Throughout this effort there runs a love story, and one is often moved to mirth with a lump in one's throat. Chaplin takes strange situations and stirs up tears and smiles. He accomplishes this with art and simplicity, and in his more boisterous moments he engineers incidents that at this presentation provoked shrieks of laughter. You may analyze some of them and think them absurd. They are, but it does not alter the fact that you find yourself stirred by the story, gripped by its swing and filled with compassion for the pathetic little hero. You forget the ridiculous garb of the Lone Prospector and he grows upon you as something real.

Chaplin obtains the maximum effect out of every scene, and a fine example of this is where he stands with his back to the audience. He is watching the throng in a Klondike dancing hall, garbed in his ridiculous loose trousers, his little derby, his big shoes and his cane. He is lonely, and with a hunch of the shoulders and a gesture of his left hand he tells more than many a player can do with his eyes and mouth. He is just thinking of the girl Georgia, the dancing hall queen, who is not even conscious of the presence of the little man who adores her.

Later Georgia and some other girls visit the funny little tramp in his comfortless shack. She learns that this strange little person loves her when she finds a torn photograph of herself and a faded rose under the pillow of his bunk. Georgia and her friends, in a mocking way, chat with the Lone Prospector, but to his great joy they agree to be his guests at supper on New Year's Eve in the shack. He is in such an ecstasy of delight when they leave that he leaps about the tiny place, hurling pillows into the air and literally making the feathers fly. He sobers down when Georgia returns for her gloves, but is oblivious to his ridiculous appearance. His life is one of ups and downs, but he goes forth with a will to earn what he can to make his New Year's Eve party a success.

This Lone Prospector shovels snow, which sequence is reminiscent of the breaking of the windows in "The Kid." Finally the night of nights comes, and the Lone Prospector lays the table for the supper. On Georgia's plate he places a heart-shaped souvenir on which is inscribed, "I love you." A newspaper fancifully torn to make a pattern serves as the tablecloth. There are snappers, presents, but above all, a roast chicken. The tender little tramp looks at the clock as he sits waiting at the head of the table, and finally he falls asleep. There follows a dream sequence of rare charm. The girls have arrived and the host is bubbling with high spirits as he observes Georgia's pleasure over the gifts. He has thought up something to amuse his guests and at the psychological moment he tells the girls that he will demonstrate the "Oceana Roll." The ragged tramp, who incidentally at this juncture has only one shoe, his right foot being wrapped in burlap, digs two forks into two bread rolls and then proceeds to give an amazing conception of a dance, using the rolls as feet, the solemnity of his countenance suiting the dancing action; it reminds one of a caricature with a huge head and a tiny body. Eventually the little prospector awakens from his wonderful dream to realize that Georgia and her friends have disappointed him.

In a preceding chapter our friend is quartered with Big Jim McKay. They are both so hungry that the little man suggests making a meal out of one of his shoes. It may sound utterly absurd, but Chaplin extracts unexpected comedy out of this idea. He boils the shoe, and serves it as carefully as if it were a wonderful chicken. He puts the shoe on a plate and gives Big Jim the sole with the protruding nails, taking the upper for himself. Big Jim gazes upon the portion put before him and decides that he would sooner have the upper. Thereupon Charlie treats the laces as if they were spaghetti, and when he comes to eating the sole, he goes about it as if the dish were a duck or a chicken. He eats the "meat" from the nails, and the audience roared with laughter when Chaplin finds a bent nail and offers it as a wishbone to Big Jim.

Then there is the part where Big Jim becomes half mad with hunger, and in his delirious moments his little companion fades out into a huge turkey. Big Jim is about to slay what he takes to be a tempting bird, when the image fades into Charlie. It happens again, and the supposed bird runs out into the snow, and just as the big man is about to shoot the bird dissolves into his little friend.

In a subsequent struggle with the starved Jim, the little prospector suddenly finds that his companion has fled and that he is hanging on to the hind leg of a bear. Quick as a wink Charlie seeks the gun he had hidden in the snow and forthwith takes aim, fires. Then, instead of going out to see if the bear is dead, he gleefully lays the table.

Mr. Chaplin's acting in this film is more sympathetic than in any of his other productions. Some persons may think that he looks older in this picture, but this idea is caused by the fact that as a hungry prospector Chaplin puts black under his eyes to make them appear hollow. He does not lose a single opportunity to impress a situation upon the audience. It may only be the raising of an eyebrow, the touching of his little derby, or the longing look at the girl. The scenic effects are splendidly portrayed.

Under his astute and imaginative direction Georgia Hale gives a most natural performance as Georgia. Mack Swain is remarkable as Big Jim McKay and Malcolm Waite is convincing as the sneering villain.

Here is a comedy with streaks of poetry, pathos, tenderness, linked with brusqueness and boisterousness. It is the outstanding gem of all Chaplin's pictures, as it has more thought and originality than even such masterpieces of mirth as "The Kid" and "Shoulder Arms."

Ag 17, 1925

THE SCREEN
By MORDAUNT HALL.

Miss Gould's New Theatre.

THE MERRY WIDOW, with Mae Murray, John Gilbert, Roy d'Arcy, Josephine Crowell, George Fawcett, Tully Marshall, Cont Conti, Sidney Bracy, Don Ryan, Hugh Mack, Ida Moore, Lucille Van Lent, Charles Margelis, Harvey Karels, Edna Tichenor, Gertrude Bennett, Zalla Zarana, Jacqeline Gadsdon, Estelle Clark, d'Arcy Corrigan, Clara Wallcks, Frances Primm, Zack Williams, Eugene Pouget and others. Adapted from the musical comedy of the same name. Directed by Erich von Stroheim. At the Embassy.

It was just before 8 o'clock last night when the finishing touches had been put on the new Embassy motion-picture theatre, of which Miss Gloria Gould is managing director. Nevertheless, fifteen minutes later the audience, composed of society people, film magnates, novelists and stage and screen favorites, began to arrive. Miss Gould stood in the foyer receiving congratulations from many of the persons who were there to witness Erich von Stroheim's production of "The Merry Widow," the photoplay which inaugurated the new theatre's career.

It is a chummy little theatre, with comfortable seats, artistically lighted and decorated. It seats about 400 and is the latest toy of Marcus Loew. It was a sweltering night and therefore no time to judge of the efficiency of the ventilating system. Along the rows of seats one saw sweltering men and women waving their hats, fans, programs and mopping their faces with handkerchiefs. The price of tickets for the opening was $5.50, but most of the spectators were guests of the management. Outside two great arc lights threw a glare upon the little building; not that it was needed, but obviously to draw a crowd, so that many of the passersby would be aware that something not quite usual was going on at Forty-sixth Street and Broadway. There was, therefore, quite a struggle when the throng poured out of the building and had to fight its way through the crowd that had gathered before the doors. This is a weakness motion picture producers have; their motto seems to be "Look—and go and tell the world."

Mr. von Stroheim's last pictorial effort was "Greed," which was based on Frank Norris's story, "McTeague." prior to that he was chiefly remembered for "Foolish Wives," a film on which Carl Laemmle is said to have spent $1,-000,000. In this current mileage of celluloid Mr. von Stroheim at times evinces a tendency to what might be termed an

48

Emile Zola-Elinor Glyn complex. He is strong for violent love, but delights in having a little convenient mud somewhere in the vicinity. He has also a weakness for Prussian heads, well shaved, and for men who use monocles when inquisitive about the appearance of a lady with light feet. There are close-ups of ankles, of booted feet, and of Mae Murray with a tear-stained countenance.

This picture is one of strong passions, and it is in many respects ably directed. There are points where it would have been better for Mr. von Stroheim to have an iron hand over him. You see the arrival of Monteblanc's royalty, and the next scene shows you a few pigs. This is a true Stroheim touch. He wishes to give you continual contrasts, and should a splendidly uniformed Prince in white, red and gold fall, it is not on a dry pavement but in some convenient pool of the blackest mire. If the hero, the younger Prince, falls by the wayside after much wine, dancing and song, he is discovered a huddled heap on the bridle path, still very much inebriated. These two Princes were accustomed to stealing kisses from every girl they encountered, and much is their amazement when the royal osculation meets with a rebuff.

The Widow is, of course, impersonated by Mae Murray, who demonstrates true acting ability in this effort. Hitherto she was like a top, and one seldom caught much more than a flash of her face. Here she stands still; she wears her costumes with a full realization of their splendor. She is a poor dancing girl, with cubistic lips, when she is introduced. The two Princes think that she is wonderful, even in her ugly, plaid skirt, and they sit her between them at a table. There is then the time-worn display of conversational feet, and the comedy of the two men touching each other's boots, believing them for an instant to be Sally's tiny slippers.

No such picture would be complete without one or two scenes of life in Paris, and in this instance we stay for a while in Maxim's, where, according to this man with the Zola-Glyn complex, Princes come in their full regalia—cloaks, decorations, topboots, and collars three and a half inches high.

There is a beautiful duel scene—not that the conflict is especially wonderful, but the location on which the duel is held is admirable, almost like an etching. One thinks, after viewing it, that it is just the place for a pistol fight. There are fine, leafless trees flanking a carpet-like meadow, and overhanging the scene is a mist that might belong to the dawn. The Princes arrive, for these brothers are to fight. Our hero, played by John Gilbert, listens to the instructions, and when the count comes he aims his pistol in the air. He turns his breast to his brother's pistol and that scoundrel takes full advantage of it and proves that he can shoot moderately well—straight enough to wound

badly and cause a lot of worry to the heroine.

Both Mr. Gilbert and Roy d'Arcy as the two Princes, acquit themselves with distinction, especially Mr. d'Arcy, who is seen in the rôle of the Crown Prince. He perhaps makes it too patent that he is not accustomed to wearing a monocle, through his constant fingering of this bit of glass. But he has a leer, a wicked-looking open mouth filled with perfect teeth, and a nasty stoop to his shoulders. His is really a fine stretch of acting, a little exaggerated in spots, but nevertheless something to make one think about, and which brings back memories of Guy de Maupassant's "Mademoiselle Fifi."

Before closing this criticism we must mention the skillful performance rendered by Tully Marshall, who comes into his own in the part of the old roué who sought the hand of the fair Sally, and then made her a wealthy widow.

This is not a production to which one ought to take those who have finer sensibilities. It is meant for a riotous love story, and as such it is cleverly pictured. And the closing scenes made in color are beautiful, as one perceives the colored uniforms, the glittering gems, the pearls and the ermine in the gold crown.

And we might add that "The Merry Widow" waltz has lost none of its charm.

Ag 27, 1925

By MORDAUNT HALL

THE FRESHMAN, with Harold Lloyd, Jobyna Ralston, Brooks Benedict, James Anderson, Hazel Keener, Joe Harrington and Pat Harmon, written by Sam Taylor, John Grey, Ted Wilde and Tim Whelan, directed by Sam Taylor and Fred Newmeyer; Colony Melody Masters; "Campus Capers," a special prologue to the feature. At the Colony.

If laughter really is a panacea for some ills, one might hazard that a host of healthy persons were sent away from the Colony yesterday after regaling themselves in wild and rollicking explosions of mirth over Harold Lloyd's comic antics in his latest hilarious effusion, "The Freshman." Judging from what happened in the packed theatre in the afternoon, when old folks down to youngsters volleyed their hearty approval of the bespectacled comedian, the only possible hindrance to the physical well-being of the throngs was an attack of aching sides.

In this new production Mr. Lloyd burlesques a young college student with athletic aspirations. While it is a decidedly boisterous affair, it is evident that Mr. Lloyd knows his public. He gives them something easy to laugh at, a film in which the authors could not be accused of dodging slapstick or of flirting with subtlety. It is a story which deserved more gentle handling, but there's no gainsaying that the buffoonery gained its end in its popular appeal. Occasionally this jazz jester rubs in the fun by repeating his action, and he also anticipates laughter.

Harold Lamb (Mr. Lloyd) first is introduced as a deserving youth who idolizes the past year's most popular student at Tate College. Harold's father is a rampant radio enthusiast, and in one sequence is deluded into the belief that he has reached some far-distant country, only to discover that what he hears are the odd yells of his college-mad son, who is practicing as a cheer-leader in a room above.

We see Harold prancing around a ballroom in a basted dinner jacket, the tailor not having had time to finish the job. Subsequently the sleeves part company with the jacket and the trousers streak open at the sides. He is a gullible young man and heeds the flattery of the College Cad, with the result that his first appearance in the institution of learning is made unexpectedly on a stage, which incidentally was intended to be ready for the hehead of the Faculty. A kitten disturbs him in his speech and crawls up his sweater, finally squeezing itself out of the collar of that garment, while the mother-cat, quite concerned about its offspring, takes her stand at Harold's feet.

The most amusing chapter in this stretch of fun is where Harold succumbs to the notion that he is a possible candidate for the football team. He permits himself to be tackled and bowled about by the husky students, and is eventually permitted to sit on the players' bench at the most important contest of the season. Tate's team fares badly, one after another being put hors de combat. The coach observes the ridiculous Harold aching for his chance, but has no faith in the young man who wears his spectacles under his rubber nose protector. Harold's insistence, however, gives him his chances and all sorts of laughable gags follow, one of them being introduced when Harold is warned by the umpire that he must release the ball when the official whistles. Later one perceives Harold clutching the ball, dashing toward the opponent's goal. Suddenly there is a factory whistle. He is five yards from his destination when he halts and throws down the ball.

A number of the subtitles in this picture are quite witty. The football field is alluded to as a place where "men are men and necks are nothing." The coach is described as being so tough that he shaves with a blow torch. The college President is said to be so aloof that he won't marry for fear of hearing his wife call him by his first name.

This is a regular Harold Lloyd strip of fun, which is made all the more hilarious by introducing something like suspense in the sequences on the football field. It is not quite so good as "Why Worry," and not really as sharp in its humor as "Safety Last."

S 21, 1925

THE SCREEN
By MORDAUNT HALL.

A Superlative War Picture.

THE BIG PARADE, with John Gilbert, Renee Adoree, Hobart Bosworth, Claire McDowell, Claire Adams, Robert Ober, Tom O'Brien, Karl Dane and Rosita Marstini, adapted from a story by Laurence Stallings, directed by King Vidor; special music score. At the Astor Theatre.

An eloquent pictorial epic of the World War was presented last night at the Astor Theatre before a sophisticated gathering that was intermittently stirred to laughter and tears. This powerful photodrama is entitled "The Big Parade," having been converted to the screen from a story by Laurence Stallings, co-author of "What Price Glory," and directed by King Vidor. It is a subject so compelling and realistic that one feels impelled to approach a review of it with all the respect it deserves, for as a motion picture it is something beyond the fondest dreams of most people. The thunderous belching of guns follows on the heels of a delightful romance between a Yankee doughboy and a fascinating French farm girl. There are humor, sadness and love, and the suspense is maintained so well that blasé men last night actually were hoping that a German machine gun would not "get" one of the three buddies in this story.

At the outset there is as much fun as there is in a book of Bairnsfather drawings, and yet there is no borrowing from that artist. It is the natural comedy that came to the American troops in France, men who landed in a foreign country without the slightest idea of the lingo. The incidents have been painted skilfully, from the blowing of the whistles as the signal that America had entered the war to the skirmishing attack in a forest. And even in a large shell hole the three pals find something to joke about.

There are incidents in this film which obviously came from experience, as they are totally different from the usual jumble of war scenes in films. It is because of the realism that the details ring true and it grips the spectator. At this presentation there were men who were not easily moved, men who had seen many pictures and were familiar with all the tricks in making them. Yet these men in the lobby during the intermission spoke with loud enthusiasm about this, a production of one of their rivals.

Just as the scenes are as perfect as human imagination and intelligence could produce them, so the acting is flawless throughout. Nothing could be more true to life than the actions and the expressions of the three buddies in khaki. They are just ordinary United States citizens, one the son of a millionaire, another a rivetter and the third a bartender. John Gilbert enacts the part of the hero. Jim Apperson, the scion of a wealthy family. Tom O'Brien figures as Bull, the jovial Irishman who served drinks across a bar, and Karl Dane is seen as Slim, the fearless rivetter. Renée Adorée impersonates Melisande, the bewitching French girl, who falls in love with Jim, her affection, being surely and certainly reciprocated by that young gentleman, in spite of the fact that he had left a sweetheart in America.

Possibly the scenes where Jim enjoys his flirtation are more delightful than any other part of the story, because it seems so natural for the couple to be fond of each other. They sit together. Jim, proud of his dexterity with his chewing gum, while Melisande, being ignorant of this jaw-exercising concoction. In endeavoring to imitate Jim swallows her piece of gum. When Jim wants to tell Melisande of the trouble that affects his capacious heart, he has to resort to a dictionary, and often he inserts English words to emphasize his utterances, as the foreign tongue strikes him as being so inadequate.

Bull and Slim decide that Melisande is too serious minded, too much infatuated with Jim, so they dodge the idea of romance and become extraordinarily practical. While Jim is upstairs with the French family, pretending to listen to the letters that have come from poilus at the front, Slim and Bull are enjoying themselves in the wine cellar, expressing surprise that any man who has such a wonderful cellar should be content to spend any time elsewhere.

Then comes the time when the call of battle tears Jim away from Melisande. There is a big parade—a parade of lorries filled with American doughboys bound for the fighting lines. Melisande clings to the vehicle carrying her Jim, until she falls in the street, pressing a shoe, he has given to her, to her bosom. Mr. Vidor is painstaking in putting forth the best work possible, with all the artistry of which the camera is capable, and it is a touch worthy of any artist where Melisande is seen crouched on the straight French road.

Guns, guns and guns roar during most of the second part of this picture, and yet these chapters are flavored with touches that create laughter, coupled as they are with clever captions. For instance: Word is sent to the three buddies while they are in a great shell-hole that one of them must go out and silence that "toy gun." Who will go is the question. This is smartly settled by Slim, the champion tobacco chewer and spitter of his contingent. He draws a circle on the wall of the hole and says that the one who spits nearest the centre will have the chance to go and put an end to the men with the "toy gun." Slim wins easily, as he knew he would, and he drags himself over the top and along the undulating ground, torn with high explosives.

The very lights rend the heavens and he has to duck to save himself from being spotted. Eventually he is seen with gun-butt uplifted and later he crawls out from the mess with two German helmets. The machine guns are popping at him, making noise like a giant tearing calico, and he is wounded. Jim and Bull have to stay where they are, as it is declared that orders are orders. Eventually the two pals go after their friend, and they find he has been "done in."

Jim sees red as he plunges toward the enemy lines, and there follows a striking human incident. He would kill one of the enemy, who is half gone. He is rough with him, but the German asks for a cigarette. Jim has one, only one, in his tin hat. He gives it to the German, who before he has a chance to take a puff breathes his last. Jim looks at the man, and, with that indifference that is bred by war, he takes the cigarette from the man's lips and smokes it himself.

There is the big parade of hospital ambulances, the long stretches of cots in a church, the unending line of lorries, and all that breathes of the war as it was. The battle scenes excel anything that has been pictured on the screen, and Mr. Vidor and his assistants have ever seen fit to have the atmospheric effects as true as possible.

This is a pictorial effort of which the screen can well boast. It carries one from America to France, then back to America and finally to France again. And one feels as if a lot had happened in a single evening.

N 20, 1925

THE SCREEN

By MORDAUNT HALL.

Nanook of the South.

MOANA, Robert J. Flaherty's picture of life and romance on a South Sea island; overture, selections from "Martha"; "The Moonlight Sonata," a glimpse of Beethoven; Vess Ossman and Rex Schepp, banjoists; Doris Vinton, danseuse. At the Rialto.

Robert J. Flaherty's second production was presented yesterday at the Rialto. This idyll of the South Seas is called "Moana," and not even the unfortunate rasping introduction by hardy banjoists and an energetic dancer would rob this picture of any of its beauty, its good nature, its fervent appeal, its wonderful trees and glorious sunshine. In Mr. Flaherty's former effort, "Nanook of the North," there was the drama of stoics in grim weather amid stark surroundings. The people were courageous, true sports who made the most of everything, and those sitting in a picture theatre on Broadway were not apt to envy the existence of Nanook and his friends. In "Moana" Mr. Flaherty has captured the spirit of the Polynesians and reflected their blissful content in their own surroundings. Here we have a poem which is filled with charm, without any makeshift villain to interfere with the effort—which was produced in the small village of Safune on the Island of Savau—and the consequence is that it is a joyful and at the same time a thoroughly artistic contribution to motion pictures.

Even in the tense sequence in which Moana—which incidentally means "The Sea," and also is the name of the leading character in this effort—undergoes the ordeal of being tattooed, the producer proves that this marking on the young hero's flesh is real. Mr. Flaherty's players, all Polynesians, are natural in every expression and gesture, and there are playful incidents, such as the participants might indulge in without a camera before them. Sometimes it seems that Mr. Flaherty does so well that it is hard that a camera was near the characters.

The remarkable clearness of the water is something upon which Mr. Flaherty dilates, and it is pleasing to the viewer. You see the hardy young Polynesians darting after fish, snaring wild boars and catching a huge tortoise. In all these chapters there is a cheerful note, and therefore it all happens as one might expect. One is not surprised that Mr. Flaherty introduces his film with a quotation from Robert Louis Stevenson, in which the author wrote that three great things in life were the first love, the first sunrise and the first sight of a Samoan Island. When one recalls Stevenson's scathing description of Edinburgh one can readily appreciate what he means by his tribute to the South Seas after seeing Mr. Flaherty's picture. Mr. Flaherty looks at his little dot of land in the South Seas through Stevenson's eyes, and in all probability this producer could make a telling production of life in bleak Edinburgh, which would have contended Mr. Stevenson.

To say that this pictorial effort is informing or educational rather than dramatic is quite true, but the life on this island is pictured so captivatingly that one feels like shouting with glee that it is not just another movie.

In this gently running Polynesian etching Mr. Flaherty shows some astounding feats performed by the natives, aided, of course, by the mother of invention. They flatten out the inner layer of the bark of a mulberry tree until it reminds one of gold-leaf. He depicts them getting the cocoanuts, then squeezing the milk from the cores; it is done so naturally, with a smile or a pat from one of the players, that one might think that this island was the land of milk and honey and a spot where the only villain was a storm. They do have wild boars at Savau, but it happens, Mr. Flaherty tells us, that this is the only dangerous beast on this pin-point of a place.

The tattooing chapter deals with the ordeal through which a young male has to go to become a full-fledged man. It is peculiarly interesting. The needle used by the tattooing experts, known as Tufungas, which at first looks like a modern implement, turns out to be made of bone. The Tufunga has a light hammer with which he taps the needle. His work is to tattoo a certain pattern on a man from the waist to the knees, and we are reminded in this picture that the most painful period of this operation is when the Tufungas are decorating the knees.

Not only is Mr. Flaherty to be congratulated on what he has put into this film, but he deserves a great deal of praise for having kept it free from sham.

F 8, 1926

THE SCREEN
By MORDAUNT HALL.

Mr. Fairbanks's New Picture.

THE BLACK PIRATE, with Douglas Fairbanks, Billie Dove, Tempe Piggott, Donald Crisp, Sam de Grasse, Anders Randolf, Charles Stevens, John Wallace, Fred Becker, Charles Belcher and E. J. Ratcliffe, adapted from a story by Elton Thomas, directed by Albert Parker. At the Selwyn Theatre.

Douglas Fairbanks's glorious chromatic production, "The Black Pirate," was presented last night at the Selwyn Theatre before a gathering that included a host of celebrities from various walks of life. The audience was ushered into the realm of piracy by the singing of "Fifteen Men on a Dead Man's Chest" and afterward by a ghost-like voice that asked every one to go back to the days of bloodthirsty sea robbers.

With its excellent titles and wondrous colored scenes this picture seems to have a Barrieque motif that has been aged in Stevensonian wood. Just as Albert Parker, its director, said, the grouping of the characters, the artistic lighting and the prismatic shades make one think that it is something that had been discovered in a dark cellar, and after being polished and varnished to give it a satin gloss, it was shown to the public. The unrivalled beauty of the different episodes is mindful of the paintings of old masters, which is not so astonishing considering that Mr. Fairbanks had on his staff Carl Oscar Borg, the Swedish artist and other experts, including Dwight Franklin, an authority on pirates, and Robert Nichols, an Oxford poet, who is an intimate friend of Sir James M. Barrie. Three other important film features were previously produced wholly in natural colors. They were "The Glorious Adventure," "The Toll of the Sea," and "The Wanderer of the Wasteland." The latter was by all odds the best of the trio, but even that Western subject could not be included in the same class with this marvelous current offering.

Mr. Fairbanks realized that color must be subordinated to the action of the episodes, and therefore, although the telling prismatic effects occasionally reap their full reward, they are put forth with deliberation and restraint. In this photoplay, which was made by the Technicolor process, there is no sudden fringing or sparking of colors, the outlines being always clearly defined without a single instance of the dreaded trembling "rainbow" impinging itself on the picture. For the most part modulated shades are employed, such as sepia, the dominating tone which is far more effective than a lavish scattering of reds and greens. In fact, decisive red is only depicted to show the blood on the hands of a man or on his sword.

The picture is a series of robust scenes slung on a slender thread of a story. In it there are many clever ideas that will assuredly appeal to every reader of "Treasure Island," or the man who as a youngster felt his heart throb on listening to the accounts of the terrifying Blackbeard and brutal Morgan, those English marauders of the Spanish Main. There is the buried treasure, the blowing up of vessels, the romance involving a beautiful girl, the nonchalant use of cutlasses and knives, the dramatic episode of the handsome hero walking the plank and the subsequent capture of the greedy robbers.

Aware that audiences will at first be engrossed with the natural colors, Mr. Fairbanks begins his narrative slowly, and does not appear himself until nearly ten minutes after the film has started. In the meantime a bald-headed, picturesque brute with a knife in his teeth does his best to steal the interest of the spectators by snatching rings from dead victims that are brought before him, and giving bloody orders that are carried out unhesitatingly. He had just caused a vessel to be blown up. Aboard was the man who is subsequently known as the Black Pirate (Mr. Fairbanks) and his father.

The father dies and the son vows vengeance. On the desert island where the sea robbers have buried their treasure the bald-headed brute and his cohorts encounter the young man. It is the pirate leader's idea that "Dead men tell no tales," but he eventually is won over to fighting a duel with the stranger, who defeats this chief of the pirate crew. The successful and handsome young antagonist soon afterward goes forth to capture a ship single-handed. After severing the rudder ropes the Black Pirate climbs up the stern of the vessel and in a series of sudden onslaughts he makes short shrift of men who are in his way. His method of descending from the dizzy heights of the ship's rigging is to dig a knife into the sails and rip them from top to bottom as he comes down.

An unforgettable sequence is where the Black Pirate, after outwitting the scheming villain, returns with husky, deep-chested men to rout the sea-robbers. They are in a huge boat manned by oars, and in the course of the attack the boat is sunk, another idea such as might streak through a boy's imagination. But all is not lost for the crafty and agile Black Pirate arranges to have his horde of followers swim under water in squadrons formed like birds or the airplanes of today. Scores of these swimmers, armed with cutlasses and knives, make their way to the ship that flies the skull and cross-bones.

Donald Crisp gives a splendid portrait of an old Scot who is faithful to the Black Pirate. Mr. Crisp's make-up is as true as steel, and he furnishes some good comedy by putting a cutlass under his chin so that when he dozes off to sleep, his face drops and he is rudely awakened by a prod from the weapon. Billie Dove figures in the rôle of the willowy heroine who is to be slain if the ransom is not forthcoming by noon. Sam de Grasse's impersonation of the "No honor among thieves" villain is capital. Anders Randorf and Fred Becker reflect cunning and brutality in their respective rôles.

As for Mr. Fairbanks, he seems more active than ever. He goes through his fighting stunts with the same cheerfulness he did in other productions. He is ever in keeping with the character and reflects a smiling mood in most of the sequences. This is a production which marks another forward stride for the screen, one that the boy and his mother will enjoy and one that is a healthy entertainment for men of all ages. It has been Mr. Fairbanks's dream for several years to make such a picture and last night he and Mary Pickford saw it again from a theatre box.

Mr 9, 1926

THE SCREEN
By MORDAUNT HALL.

A German Masterpiece.

VARIETY, with Emil Jannings, Lya de Putti and Warwick Ward, adapted from a story entitled "The Oath of Stephen Huller; directed by E. A. Dupont; overture, "Martha"; special prologue to the feature. At the Rialto.

The strongest and most inspiring drama that has ever been told by the evanescent shadows is at the Rialto. It is a German film known as "Variety" and was produced by the Ufa concern in Berlin about a year ago under the direction of E. A. Dupont. In this picture there is a marvelous wealth of detail; the lighting effects and camera work cause one to reflect that occasionally the screen may be connected with art. While there may be some speculation concerning the appeal of this striking piece of work, because of the tragic climax of the actual story, there is no doubt regarding its merit. Scene after scene unlocks a flood of thoughts, and although the nature of the principal characters is far from pleasing; the glimpses one obtains are so true to life that they are not repellent.

Emil Jannings, who is best remembered for his acting in "The Last Laugh" and "Passion," fills the principal rôle. He is theatric at times, but his performance is a masterly one. He is not alone in this feature, and it may be a matter of opinion as to whether Lya de Putti and Warwick Ward, an English actor, are not even better than Mr. Jannings in their portrayals. Certainly Jannings has the

least conventional rôle and more to tell by his expressions. However, Miss de Putti and Mr. Ward give an extraordinarily brilliant account of themselves and they rise to the occasion in episodes that are by no means easy to handle.

Benjamin Christianson's picture, "The Devil's Circus," was much the same sort of story, but where that production missed the mark "Variety" supplies the interest and booms where the Hollywood photodrama spluttered.

It is the story of the mésalliances in the lives of three trapeze performers, the locale being Berlin. The first scenes depict a convict, who hitherto had been unwilling to disclose the reason for the murder he had committed, suddenly unfolding the tale to the warden of the prison. He is impelled to do so by the mention of his wife, whom he had deserted for a girl with a comely face. This girl at first enjoys the life with the man, who is much older than she, but when a handsome English trapeze performer appears she falls in love with him. It is through a sketch on a marble top table in a café poking fun at him that the older man discovers the duplicity of the girl. He meditates how he will revenge himself on the Englishman. His first thought is to let the Englishman drop when he is doing his usual triple somersault, but he eventually decides that he will end the British performer's life with a knife. The chronicle is pictured as the convict tells it.

The picture is unfolded with unusual care, points being made when new characters are introduced. The director shows the Boss, as the hefty older man is called, a domesticated individual, who had given up his trapeze work because he had broken both legs. Then the Girl is introduced, and the Boss sways in his attentions to his baby and his wife to the arched eyebrows and brown eyes of the Girl. He finds admiration for youth and beauty too strong and soon he decamps with the Girl, going back to his old vocation, working in a carnival.

The introduction of the English performer is distinctly lucid and clever, for first one perceives all the performers reporting for the opening of the Wintergarten, and then a Continental express is seen entering the Friedrichstrasse Station. The famous Artinelli, known in all the capitals of Europe for his daring as a trapeze performer, alights from the train and informs the Wintergarten manager that he can't put on his act because his brother fell during a show at the London Coliseum. Here one perceives Artinelli, as the Englishman is known, watching the Wintergarten show as one of the audience. He is spoken of as an artist in

54

his line, and it irritates him to be on the wrong side of the stage. You see what he is looking at—the comic dwarfs, the dancing girls, the Japanese jugglers, the dazzling girl who does the light fantastic with her brawny partner and other scenes, every one of which is tellingly portrayed. The girl in shimmering rhinestones and white tights elicits marked attention, which fact is brought out through the opera glasses held by several men and women. Her form is shown in the lenses of the glasses. Artinelli joins up with the Boss and the Girl.

The Boss, before the Girl's eyes fascinated Artinelli, had not lost his domestic trait, for when the Girl extends her stockinged foot and shows the Boss a hole in the toe of her stocking, he calmly takes the stocking, picks up a needle and proceeds methodically to darn the hole.

Artinelli's surrender to the attractive girl is gradual and natural. The Boss, who had to go and see an old friend one night, leaves the two to enjoy the evening together. He wakes up at 3 in the morning and the Girl has not returned. Then an hour later. The Girl had crept into the room in the meantime.

Miss de Putti, as the Girl, gives a marvelous portrayal of the deceitful little minx.

Mr. Ward is glib and easy, just the type for a successful trapeze performer who is meticulous about his make-up, using rouges on his lips and penciling his eyebrows.

This is a production which not only shows the way in which a story should be unfurled, but impresses one with the magic of the camera in picturing effects, such as the torrent of thoughts rushing through a maddened mind and the views of the audience from the eyes of a hurtling trapeze performer.

Je 28, 1926

NELL GWYN, with Dorothy Gish, Sidney Fairbrother, Randle Ayrton, Juliette Compton, Judd Green and Edward Sorley; by Marjorie Brown; scenario and direction by Herbert Wilcox. At the Rivoli.

"Nell Gwyn," said to be the first British feature picture presented here, is one which British National Pictures, Ltd., may well be glad to sponsor. It is entirely English in production and cast, with the exception of the lead, which is happily played by Dorothy Gish. The faults of most historical pictures, cluttered up as they usually are with scenery which producers seem to think the audience should see because it existed at the time in which the story is placed, is conspicuously absent, and "Nell Gwyn" is a smoothly developed and charming presentation of one of the most picturesque persons who ever intrigued the British court.

The brattish, lovable, whimsical and generous nature of Nell, mistress of the King and idol of all London, gives the picture its flavor. It is impossible to think harshly of her. She found her way out of an alley to the theatre, where her droll humor made the city laugh, by the only means at her command. She never forgot her friends. her charities were boundless, she loved her royal patron and, if history is to be credited, remained faithful to his memory after his death. It is this Nell which the picture shows, a delightful hoyden, even in Whitehall. Majesty never had any terrors for her; she retained her fascination by being herself.

With such a character it was possible to produce a picture full of whimsy and drollery. Nell meets the King at the door of the theatre in Drury Lane, that quaint old street full of pushcarts and theatrical history, and presents him with an orange "to sweeten the company he keeps." Her vivacity attracts him, and when the audience is driven from the unroofed building by the rain he invites her to the inn opposite. Nell dines sumptuously, waving a chicken bone under the nose of her royal companion or poking him in the ribs with her elbow with a frank camaraderie which appeals to his weary senses.

And when his companions have not sufficient money to pay the bill, Nell does so with an amusing appreciation of her position, which is infinitely attractive to Charles. He promises that she shall have her chance to be an actress, and sends her silken substitutes for her torn stocking, and buckled shoes to take the place of her shabby footgear.

Whether Nell entered the theatre through Charles, or received her opportunity through earlier admirers, hardly matters. Once in the theatre her fortune was made, for her fame as a comedienne is fully as great as her fame as the King's favorite. She used the stage as the means to discountenance her rivals, and one of the most amusing scenes in the picture is the way in which she subjects Lady Castlemaine, her chief antagonist, to the ridicule which no favorite can withstand. Nell has been forgotten at a reception in Whitehall, where she had been lately installed, embarrassed and unhappy, while her royal lover hastens to the side of Castlemaine.

gorgeous in a huge hat which is the centre of attraction. Nell pouts and then laughs, and the next night at the play comes on dressed in a hat so huge it might be an umbrella, under which her antics reduce her rival to impotent anger.

But that is not all of Nell. When two of her old friends visit her at the palace she drags in the King to make him promise that he would give the palace he was building for her at Chelsea to the disabled soldiers of his kingdom. Tradition has it that that is the origin of Chelsea Hospital. And on Charles's deathbed, when with a wry smile he apologizes to his brother for taking so long to die, it is Nell who hurries to him and comforts him.

"Don't let poor Nell starve," he tells his brother, and then asks her, as the tears stream down her cheeks, to laugh one of her gay laughs for him, and to that laugh, joining in its infectious merriment, he dies.

That was the end of Nell's career. For although King James obeyed his brother's wish and provided for her, she did not long survive her lover. But the picture of Nell ends with her scornfully disdaining King James's outstretched hand, and blowing a kiss to the bust of Charles.

Whatever may be the shortcomings of English motion picture producers, if they can put together other pictures as simply and with as much dramatic effect as this story of Nell Gwyn they should have no difficulty obtaining a showing for them anywhere. The story moves quickly and surely, with nothing to strain one's credulity, and the acting of Miss Gish and Randle Ayrton, who takes the part of Charles, is excellent. So is that of Juliette Compton as Lady Castlemaine. The immorality of the period is suggested without being offensive, and for the second time this Summer a good picture has not been spoiled by prudery. The titles are unusually good and frequently amusing, that dear old gossip Pepys being resorted to for purposes of verisimilitude.

Jl 19, 1926

By MORDAUNT HALL

THE VITAPHONE, a new invention synchronizing sound with motion pictures; DON JUAN, with John Barrymore, Mary Astor, Willard Louis, Estelle Taylor, Warner Oland, Montagu Love, Helene Costello, Jane Winton, Myrna Loy, John Roche, June Marlowe, Yvonne Day, Phillipe de Lacy, Josef Swickard, Lionel Braham, Phyllis Haver, Nigel de Brulier and Hedda Hopper, inspired by the legends of "Don Juan," written for the screen by Bess Meredyth, directed by Alan Crosland; Vitaphone music score. At Warners' Theatre.

A marvelous device known as the vitaphone, which synchronizes sound with motion pictures, stirred a distinguished audience in Warners' Theatre to unusual enthusiasm at its initial presentation last Thursday evening. The natural reproduction of voices, the tonal qualities of musical instruments and the timing of the sound to the movements of the lips of singers and the actions of musicians was almost uncanny. This "living sound" invention, without a musician being present, also furnished the orchestral accompaniment to an ambitious photoplay entitled "Don Juan," in which John Barrymore plays the title rôle.

The future of this new contrivance is boundless, for inhabitants of small and remote places will have the opportunity of listening to and seeing grand opera as it is given in New York, and through the picturing of the vocalists and small groups of musicians, or instrumental choirs of orchestras, the vitaphone will give its patrons an excellent idea of a singer's acting and an intelligent conception of the efforts of musicians and their instruments. Operatic favorites will be able to be seen and heard, and the genius of singers and musicians who have passed will still live.

The introductory Vitaphone feature, which incidentally prefaced the program, was that of Will H. Hays delivering a speech congratulating the Warner Brothers, the Western Electric Company, the Bell Telephone laboratories and Walter J. Rich on this remarkable achievement. There was no muffled utterance nor lisping in the course of the talk; it was the voice of Hays, and had any of his friends closed their eyes to his picture on the screen they would have immediately recognized the voice. Every syllable was audible and clear.

This was followed by a vitaphone of the Philharmonic Orchestra under the direction of Henry Hadley, in which one was not only impressed by the clarity of the tonal colors and softer interludes, but also by the thrilling volume of the full orchestra. During the exhibition of this subject the screen scenes swayed from those of the whole body of musicians to small groups as each instrumental choir took up its work.

Elman Heard in "Humoresque."

Mischa Elman, the noted violinist, was seen and heard playing Dvorak's "Humoresque," with Josef Bonimo at the piano, and every note that came to one's ears synchronized with the gliding bow and the movements of the musician's fingers. It seemed at times that the sound was so distinct that

56

during a pause had a pin been dropped in the studio it would have been heard.

The "Caro nome" aria from "Rigoletto," rendered by Marion Talley, gave one an excellent idea of the qualities of the singer's voice and also of her acting. As she retreated from the front of the stage her voice became modulated, and then there were times when one heard her as if from a front seat in the Metropolitan Opera.

"An Evening on the Don," delivered by Russian dancers and singers, contained a wealth of charm. Then the seductive twanging of a guitar manipulated by Roy Smeck captured the audience. Every note appeared to come straight from the instrument and one almost forgot that the Vitaphone was responsible for the realistic effect.

There was a decided opulence about the entertainment, for next on the list was Efrem Zimbalist, violinist, accompanied by Harold Bauer. Mr. Zimbalist played variations of Beethoven's "Kreutzer Sonata," and whether it was a note from the piano or the plucking of the violin strings, it was audible throughout the theatre and just as inspiring as if Mr. Zimbalist and Mr. Bauer had themselves been before the audience.

The powerful voice of Giovanni Martinelli then came from the screen, singing in an enthralling fashion "Vesta la giubba" from "Pagliacci," accompanied by the Philharmonic Orchestra. Nothing like it had ever been heard in a motion picture theatre, and the invited gathering burst into applause such as is seldom heard in any place of amusement. The singer's tones appeared to echo in the body of the theatre as they tore from a shadow on the screen—a shadow that appeared earnest and intense in the delivery of Leoncavallo's well-known composition.

The final special Vitaphone feature was of Anna Case, supported by a dance divertissement of the Cansinos, accompanied by the Metropolitan Opera chorus and Herman Heller's orchestra. This was also pleasing and extraordinarily effective in delivering the singer's glib and quickly turning tones.

And so one came to the picture, "Don Juan," and it can readily be appreciated that only a cleverly produced film could hold its own against the entertainment that had preceded it. Messrs. Warner were sufficiently astute to screen the prologue, or the first chapter of the photoplay, before announcing an intermission. By the time the first stretch of "Don Juan" faded out the spectators were in the mood of a person who does not wish to leave an interesting novel. Don Juan then was a child and his father, impersonated by Mr. Barrymore in an excellent make-up, had become a sort of misogynist.

In a subsequent chapter Don Juan, grown up, rises to the conception of the character of "Donny Johnny." He has his flights of fancy for beauty, and no sooner does he gaze upon one pair of eyes after having left a fair creature in another room than he finds some new charm, some fresh temptation. It is a difficult position that Pedrillo (Willard Lewis) has, for when the insincere Don Juan is in a fix Pedrillo, his faithful attendant, has to risk the spear or the sword of a jealous man. Don Juan scatters kisses through this production and he appears to know that he is irresistible, even to Lucretia Borgia. He plays with her admiration as he would with a pretty maid's, and a mere subordinate in the Borgia Palace unwittingly tempts the susceptible Don just when he has an appointment to meet the lovely Lucretia, who, be it known, is not slow to use her power for revenge.

Mr. Barrymore leaps through the scenes of this production in a captivating manner, and sometimes the principal character and the story remind one of a Fairbanks film, and in the amorous moments one is impelled to think of Valentino.

The players, arrayed in fifteenth century costumes, conduct themselves with marked ability, appearing to sense that restrained action demanded of them in a period picture. And this aids materially in making the film interesting. It was directed by Alan Crosland, who also produced "Enemies of Women," and one perceives in the current offering scenes that are reminiscent of the former film in which Lionel Barrymore played the principal part.

John Barrymore is as lithe as ever, and his attire in many of the episodes of this photoplay set off his slender form. Naturally as the Spanish Don, he is heroic. No sword can ever defeat his, and no walls are sound enough to hold him in prison. That this Don Juan is handsome is as true as he is fickle; until, of course, he experiences a heart thrust from Adriana della Varnese's soulful eyes. When the Don disarms his antagonist and that individual is at his mercy, the gallant Spaniard flings his swords aside and springs from the top of a flight of stairs on to his panting opponent, which performance was greeted with a hearty outburst of applause from the audience.

Here we have a number of lavishly filmed scenes, in which the feminine element is not clad for wintry blasts, and as a contrast to the pictured orgies there are glimpses of Don Juan in a prison cell by the Tiber. Through a wild demented individual who is incarcerated in the adjoining cell Don Juan discovers that a granite block is loose, and thereupon he and the madman, who incidentally has a reason for hating Don Juan, labor together to draw away the great stone, neither knowing the identity of the other. Then come scenes of a struggle in the river and dexterous and resourceful performances by the Great Lover, who rescues and fights his way to the bliss of devoting attention to one woman—Adriana.

Lucretia Borgia is impersonated by Estelle Taylor, who in private life is Mrs. Jack Dempsey. She betrays imagination in handling her rôle, which is by no means an easy one, for Lucretia is proud, but the Don is surrounded by the glamour of a thousand loves, and therefore she has at first to be merely mildly interested in the Spaniard, then vindictive, then sure of her own unrivaled attractiveness, and finally she gives the idea of nonchalant revenge, as if the whole matter had really never meant very much to her.

Mary Astor is charming as Adriana, and that capital actor, Willard Louis, who played the part of the Prince Regent to John Barrymore's "Beau Brummel," gives a stanch conception of perplexed loyalty. Caesar Borgia, to whom the blood of another is but a trifling incident, is played by that reliable performer, Warner Oland, who never steps out of character.

Hence, in this film, there are the playing with feminine hearts, dazzling heroics, a brown-eyed maid, love—and an optimistic fade-out.

Ag 7, 1926

THE SCREEN
By MORDAUNT HALL.

A Nathaniel Hawthorne Classic.

THE SCARLET LETTER, with Lillian Gish, Lars Hanson, Henry B. Whitehall, Karl Dane, William H. Tooker, Marceline Corday, Fred Herzog, Jules Cowles, Mary Hawkes, Joyce Coad and James A. Marcus, adapted from Nathaniel Hawthorne's classic, directed by Victor Seastrom; presentation and music score arranged by Major Edward Bowes, David Mendoza and William Axt. At the Central Theatre.

The prudery of the ignoble bigots in Puritanical days is adroitly put forth in the picturization of Nathaniel Hawthorne's story, "The Scarlet Letter," which was presented at the Central Theatre last night. No attempt has been made to render this a movie, for it is as faithful a transcription of the narrative as one could well imagine. The producer has not sparred for a happy ending, and in portraying the conduct of the scandalmongers he has found a way to include a little comedy here and there without exaggerating the characters.

"The Scarlet Letter" was directed by Victor Seastrom, an earnest Swedish director who gained no little fame through his production "The Stroke of Midnight," a picture which has never been exhibited publicly in this country. Mr. Seastrom also made the film version of "He Who Gets Slapped." The adaptation of Hawthorne's classic was entrusted to Frances Marion, whose clever script for "The Dramatic Life of Abraham Lincoln" assisted materially in the production of that masterful study of the martyred President.

Louis B. Mayer, head of the Metro-Goldwyn-Mayer studio, could not have chosen a better director than Seastrom for Nathaniel Hawthorne's narrative. He is painstaking in studying his characters, and it was to his advantage to have Lillian Gish in the principal rôle, that of Hester Prynne. Miss Gish has a strong inclination for such parts, and in this vehicle she gives an excellent conception of the courage of a young woman in the face of sneering, scorn and tittle-tattle. It causes one to contrast those days with the present time; the fashions of the past with the feminine creations of our generation. She is charming. She falls from grace, and after the perfunctory trial she is condemned to bear the letter "A," to tell the world that she has sinned.

After the preliminary scenes near Boston, the director loses no time in depicting the shameless bigotry of the people, by first showing Hester Prynne's canary escaping from its cage and then having the young woman locked in the stocks for unseemly merriment and prancing through the lanes on the Sabbath. Actually she had only run after her bird, and this caused her to be late for the church service. A splendid idea of the little it took to start wagging tongues is obtained through the glimpes one has of the congregation, who look at Hester with the eyes of Pharisees eager to be present at her punishment.

In those good old days it was the law that no engaged couples should be permitted to kiss until they were married. Hence they are pictured talking through a long tube. No feminine underwear was permitted to be hung on a clothesline, where it might meet the eyes of the men, and through this edict Mr. Seastrom displays a touch of comedy.

It was with not a little pleasure that one perceived Mistress Hibbins rudely delivered into the hands of the mighty by the cunning of the loquacious Giles. He enters the gossiper's home, puts on her bonnet while she is asleep; and, while standing near an open window, delivers a nasty opinion of the Governor and the Beadle, just as those serious-minded gentlemen are passing. Mistress Hibbins's protestations of innocence fall on deaf ears, and she is sentenced to be ducked by means of a primitive implement which causes the punishment to be quite an excellent entertainment to others, especially to those who had suffered by the good lady's constant babble. And the hefty Giles decides that he is unusually fortunate because he has to officiate at the ceremony of ducking the scandalmonger.

The Rev. Dimmesdale strikes one as being a peculiarly spineless person, wavering between a confession of his sin and clinging to his position as minister. He is the father of Hester's child, and he punishes himself one night by branding the letter "A" on his own chest. This rôle is acted by Lars Hanson, who, while he is indubitably sincere in his performance, occasionally appears to be too optimistic in his expression.

Henry B. Walthall figures as Roger Prynne, who is supposed to have been a prisoner of the Indians for seven years, which accounts for a beard and expression mindful of Svengali. There is a stirring scene when he appears, for he is a physician who had deserted Hester soon after they were wed. He knows that her sick child is not his, but he finally concocts medicine that saves the little girl, hoping for a later vengeance on the father of the child and Hester. Here one thinks that he has little to say in the matter, considering his treatment of Hester.

Karl Dane, who won his screen spurs by his performance as Slim in "The Big Parade," officiates in this new picture as Giles. He does exceedingly well with the rôle.

There are some cleverly pictured scenes in the church and the sights of crowds betray imaginative direction, both in the handling of the players and in their arrangement according to the shades of their costumes.

Ag 10, 1926

BEAU GESTE, with Ronald Colman, Noah Beery, Neil Hamilton, Ralph Forbes, Alice Joyce, Mary Brian, Norman Trevor, William Powell, Victor McLaglen and Donald Stuart, adapted from Major Percival Christopher Wren's novel of the same name, by John Russell and Paul Schofield. Music score arranged by Dr. Hugo Riesenfeld. At the Criterion.

By MORDAUNT HALL

Adventure, romance, mystery and brotherly affection are skillfully linked in the pictorial translation of Percival Christopher Wren's absorbing novel, 'Beau Geste," which was presented last night at the Criterion Theatre before an audience in which were represented society, literature, art, motion picture magnates, stage and screen celebrities. It is a film in which there is something different and one wherein Herbert Brenon, producer of the screen versions of "Peter Pan" and "A Kiss for Cinderella," has succeeded in maintaining a remarkable degree of suspense. It is the first photodrama that gives one a true conception of life in the French Foreign Legion—its heterogeneous mass, its paucity of pay, the brutality of a non-commissioned officer, the double dealings of a lickspittle and the courage of a small band who remained faithful to the tricolor. It gives you an idea of the grilling sun, of the value of water and of that gift—liberty.

Without striving for any extraneous smart photographic effects, Mr. Brenon clings as closely as possible to the story. He expatiates upon the unique defense of the desert fortress, and while he adroitly pictures the brutality of Sergeant Lejaune he at the same time depicts the courage and the strategy of this tyrant.

Immediately after reading "Beau Geste" Mr. Brenon was eager to picture the story, explaining that he considered the central figure of this narrative an idol. It was not long afterward that Messrs. Zukor and Lasky acquiesced to the purchase of the film rights to the novel and to its direction by Mr. Brenon. He was to have produced it in Algeria, but the Riffian conflict interfered. Hence, it was decided to make the film in a stretch of the desert east of Burlingame, Cal., and southwest of Yuma, Ariz., and those who know Yuma will appreciate that the perspiration running down the faces of the players in this production is not always the result of make-up.

There are spectacular scenes on the baked sands, with hordes of players costumed to represent Arabs and, in other episodes, a contingent of the Foreign Legion. There is an excellent reproduction of a fort, supposed to be in the African desert, the walls of which tower above the smooth, windswept sands. It is a structure that needs no caption to tell one that it is hot, and the few comforts supposed to be inside awaken sympathy for the men of many nations who bury themselves in the Foreign Legion to escape prison, to forget love affairs or for the mere sake of hoped-for adventure. The chance of an attack by the Arabs is almost a welcome piece of news, because of the bitter ennui of life in the fort.

Dr. Hugo Riesenfeld arranged the music score for this picture, and his orchestra thrills one with its fine rendering of French marches that are played at appropriate moments. There is the "Sambre et Meuse," and as the perspiring fighters are seen one is impelled to hum—"Le regiment de Sambre et Meuse * * * avec leurs sur l'epaules. And subsequently the musicians play the stirring music of the Foreign Legion.

The pictorial narrative begins with Major de Beaujolais's discovery of the fort, with the strange dead men at the embrasures, one with a pipe between his teeth, another with his gun at his shoulder and so forth. Following that the story reverts to the boyhood days of the three brothers—Michael, who is known as Beau Geste; Digby and John. The youthful activities of this trio at a country home in England are pleasantly portrayed, and then comes the sale by the aunt, Lady Brandon, of the famous "Blue Water" sapphire to an Indian potentate. You perceive Beau Geste, as a boy behind a suit of armor, hearing of the whispered sale, and then the tale goes forth several years to the enlistment of Beau in the Foreign Legion, because he does not wish his aunt to be blamed for the loss of the valuable stone. He wants his relatives to think that he stole it.

Then comes the coincidental meeting of the brothers in the Foreign Legion, which is tersely but effectively filmed, with the varied types of recruits and their abandon, the first stoic reception of brutal treatment and the punishment meted out to a night prowler. Eventually, John is separated from his brothers, and the chief background, the fort, is introduced as it was before Beaujolais discovered it in its sinister state.

Noah Beery, who has on many occasions demonstrated his talent for acting before the camera, here gives an unforgettable performance as the tyrant, Sergeant Lejaune. His work is quick, vivid, natural and virile. He blackguards his men and instantly takes advantage of the death of his superior officer. When he hears, through Boldini, of the threat of mutiny he takes the bull by the horns at night and surprises the rebellious clique. He is alert during the attack on the fort and shows his imagination when he lugs dead soldiers on his broad shoulders and props them up at the structure's embrasures. It is he who is killed by Digby, who resents Lejaune's touching his dying brother Beau Geste. Time and again, through

Lejaune's deception, the Arabs are forced to retreat. Boldini, the stool-pigeon, is ordered to the tower to take the place of a man who has toppled over with a bullet through his heart.

Ronald Colman is easy and sympathetic in the title rôle. His acting in this production is only equaled by his impersonations in "The White Sister" and "The Dark Angel." Alice Joyce is charming as Lady Brandon. Norman Trevor is effective as Beaujolais, and William Powell gives an excellent character study of Boldini, especially when he depicts the rascal's last stages of fear.

Ag 26, 1926

THE SCREEN

By MORDAUNT HALL.

The Vitaphone and "The Better 'Ole."

VITAPHONE subjects, including Elsie Janis, Al Jolson, Reinald Werrenrath, Willie and Eugene Howard, George Jessel and an orchestral overture; THE BETTER 'OLE, with Sydney Chaplin, Doris Hill, Harold Goodwin, Theodore Lorch, Ed Kennedy, Charles Gerrard, Tom McGuire, Jack Ackroyd, Tom Kennedy and others, based on Captain Bruce Bairnsfather's drawings and play, directed by Charles F. Reisner. At the Colony.

Additional Vitaphone features and an uproariously funny but thoroughly farcical conception of "The Better 'Ole" were presented last night at the Colony Theatre by Warner Brothers before an enthusiastic audience that included many notable persons. One might mention that among those whose laughter was heard were Condé Nast, Will H. Hays and Jack Dempsey, the latter still bearing the marks of Gene Tunney's fists. It was a wonderfully successful evening, in which the Vitaphone provided stirring entertainment for the first half of the performance and Sydney Chaplin, as Captain Bruce Bairnsfather's Oild Bill in a truly Hollywood notion of "The Better 'Ole" provoked many an outburst of hilarity after the intermission.

The Vitaphone program proved just as absorbing as that which was offered some time ago at Warners' Theatre, where, incidentally, it is still running. The series of "living sound" subjects are, in this present instance, in a far lighter vein, but none the less remarkable, even though there was occasionally the suggestion of a lisp and a noticeable scratching sound in one or two of the numbers. The overture, a Vitaphone orchestral number, was slightly marred by a whistling undertone.

In some of the singing numbers there was not a sign of a flaw and the performers were not only able to gain the full attention of the audience but, during the exhibition of most of these numbers, despite the lack of color, one was impressed by the personality of the singers, especially in the renditions of Al Jolson, Elsie Janis, Willie and Eugene Howard and George Jessel.

In a special setting Reinald Werrenrath is heard and seen singing "The Long, Long Trail" and other melodies. The program is ably balanced, for when Elsie Janis appeared on the screen the persons that packed the theatre to the doors were soon applauding as one individual. In fact, not since the initial offering of the wonderful Vitaphone has such spontaneous applause been heard in a cinema theatre. Miss Janis is brilliant in a song entitled "When Yankee Doodle Learned to Parlez Vous," and her dancing on a motor lorry adds to the effectiveness of the pictorial side of the number. She also sings "Madelon," "In the Army," "The Good Old War" and "Good Bye-ee."

Whatever slight defects there were, the audience did not consider them, and it was, in most instances, just as if Miss Janis were on the stage. One forgot all about the Vitaphone in listening to the distinct words of the songs, which to many must have brought back the days of the fighting in France.

In Willie and Eugene Howard's offerings, sounds like a starter's whistle and a taxicab horn were heard. This feature is called "Between the Acts at the Opera," and it is just as funny at the Colony as it is on any stage.

Al Jolson is seen, and of course heard, in three songs: "The Red, Red Robin," "April Showers" and "Rock-a-Bye Baby," with a Dixie melody. This Vitaphone assuredly destroys the old silent tradition of the screen. This time it was the audience that was silent, so keen was everybody to catch every word and note of the popular entertainer, and when each number was ended it was obvious that there was not a still pair of hands in the house.

After delivering a funny monologue that caused the audience to laugh longer than they were expected to, George Jessel's shadow is heard singing Irving Berlin's song, "At Peace with the World and You."

Immediately the word "Intermission" was flashed upon the screen many of the persons left their seats and the conversation in the lobby was wholly devoted to a eulogy of the Vitaphone.

Charlie Chaplin's brother, Sydney, then had his fling at fun. His comedy, "The Better 'Ole" relies only on the characters of Old Bill, Alf and Bert and that unforgettable drawing, "If yer knows a better' ole, go to it." Aside from that, Old Bill goes through war experiences such as Captain Bairnsfather at least never put into the original stage version of this comedy or in his drawings. Mr Chaplin is partial to the farmyard in this production, which has many side-splitting incidents. He does a great deal with an egg, after having milked a cow, and then discovers that the egg has hatched in his pocket.

The longest period of hefty comedy is delivered through a dummy horse, with the Vitaphone orchestral accompaniment rendering that popular song, "Horses, Horses, Horses." Sydney Chaplin and Alf are respectively the front and rear legs of the animal. It is seen, or these characters are, in many an awkward dilemma. The dummy horse even drinks from a trough with some German horses and the look in the real horse's eye as he gazes at the dummy is enough to make a cynic chuckle. This dummy horse has a charmed life, for he is shot at by drunken German soldiers, but eludes all the bullets.

There are moments when this comedy drags, but this failing will undoubtedly be remedied, for it merely means the curtailing of some of the scenes.

The performance did not finish until after midnight.

O 8, 1926

WIDE VISION PICTURES

By MORDAUNT HALL

At the Cameo this week, besides the D. W. Griffith featured production, there is an extraordinarily interesting exhibition of what are called "natural vision" pictures. In a caption it is set forth that the usual screen picture is limited to a vision angle of about 30 degrees, or the sight of one eye. The new process claims to give an angle of 60 degrees, to accomplish which a screen virtually twice the ordinary size is necessary.

In projecting these films at the Cameo, the screen is widened, and, incidentally, the process under which these pictures are made is termed the "Widescope." It is a distinct advantage over the ordinary screen image, inasmuch as it gives one something like the width and height of a stage. It also assists in the lengthening of scenes in photoplays, and you have an opportunity of seeing persons approaching from the background and of following their activities far better than on the average screen.

This "Widescope" avoids the constant changing of scenes, as the spectator is apt to become interested in a group, more than in the long-shots, medium-shots and close-ups. Of course, it does not kill the idea of the actor's cherished close-up. The other shots are also needed, but it is obvious that one can become interested for a relatively prolonged period in the action of a scene which is not changed, except for the sake of contrast or dramatic effect.

The scenes projected yesterday were exteriors, and the lighting could not be a test necessarily of the efficacy of the lens. Some of the detail of the scenes was not as good as the average outdoor picture. There were scenes of skiing and other snow "shots."

This series of pictures was obtained through a process perfected by John Elms after nine years of effort. He first attempted to synchronize three cameras to obtain pictures of the width and height of the present "natural vision." This failed and he tried two cameras, which also proved unsuccessful. Finally by means of a series of lenses and prisms in a single camera he has obtained the effect he wanted.

The film is twice the width of the ordinary strip of film, and the "frame" is 25 per cent. higher than the picture on the standard film. It was explained by a representative of the process that by means of an attachment that costs only a nominal sum the wide-vision pictures can be projected in any theatre. To take them, however, the special camera is necessary.

N 9, 1926

By MORDAUNT HALL

WHAT PRICE GLORY, with Victor McLaglan, Edmund Lowe, Dolores Del Rio, William V. Mong, Phyllis Haver, Elena Jurado, Leslie Fenton, Barry Norton, Sammy Cohen, Ted McNamara and August Tollaire, adapted from the play by Maxwell Anderson and Laurence Stallings, directed by Raoul Walsh; special music score by Erno Rapee. At the Sam H. Harris Theatre.

Often humorous, sometimes grim, with a sentimental strain here and there, the film translation of "What Price Glory," the play by Maxwell Anderson and Laurence Stallings, which was presented last night at the Sam H. Harris Theatre, is a powerful screen effort. The blazing jealousy of Captain Flagg and Sergeant Quirt is vividly pictured in those scenes behind the lines, and these same soldiers are depicted as brothers in arms, as marines who forget everything in loyalty to their flag, once they step out of their billets to fight. Both are shown to be men who under fire are touched by the very weakness of others that they sneered at back of the trenches.

As in the play, war is stripped of its glamour, and there are moments when Kipling's lines,

"Where there ain't no Ten Commandments,

"An' a man can raise a thirst,"

fit this subject. It is a story of wine, woman and war, in which the estaminet keeper's daughter plays a significant part.

Taking advantage of the scope offered by the screen, the bickering and recriminations between Flagg and Quirt are first shown in China, where a Sadie Thompson type of girl—described as having divorced one regiment to be married to the Marines—first steps in between the two professional soldiers. How Quirt outwits Flagg is brought out in these scenes, as it is later in others in the Philippines and in France. So successfully has this been accomplished by Raoul Walsh, the director, that not only was there many an explosion of laughter last night, but two or three times the audience reached such a high pitch of enthusiasm that they applauded loudly.

The rôle of Captain Flagg is played by Victor McLaglan, who is thoroughly in his element. He does not lose an opportunity to portray the mood of Flagg, whether it is when he is drinking, flirting, sneering or fighting. He is a giant in stature, with a uniform that looks as if it really belonged to him. He is brutal at times, a man who takes his food when it comes. snatching at it with his great hands. When pushing his way through the lines of fighters in the trenches his one thought is to fight, with a hope of victory. He enjoys his moments back of the fighting front. He loves wine and women. He is no beauty, but his very strength and courage elicit admiration.

Edmund Lowe, who hitherto has been seen in so-called leading man parts, officiates as Sergeant Quirt, the non-commissioned officer who has the temerity to say what he thinks to Flagg, and who once says to the Captain when that officer is in a quandry: "Think fast, Captain Flagg!"

Mr. Lowe has given himself whole-heartedly to the character he fills. He, too, sneers, especially at Flagg. Fear is unknown to him, and he has a way with women that always puts Flagg in the shade. Just when things appear to be going relatively quietly for Flagg, Quirt appears and threats and denunciations tear through the air. No profanity is seen in the text of this picture, but one can readily tell from the movements of their lips what these two Marines are calling each other.

The charmer of the Marne, Charmaine, is impersonated by Dolores Del Rio, who, with no little abandon, gives an excellent characterization of Cognac Pete's daughter. She looks the part, with her dark hair parted in the centre and her portrayal of ineffable delight when she sees Quirt, to whom she gives the garters Flagg had presented to her, is true to the Mademoiselle d'Armentieres type.

Some idea of the comedy in this production can be gathered from the scene wherein Flagg first observes Charmaine's fickleness. He comes into the estaminet, his billet, having "taken Bar le Duc by storm," which, being interpreted, means that he had learned about women in Bar le Duc. He glares at Quirt, the top sergeant he had left in charge, and then is boiling mad when Quirt slips off his coat and is seen to be wearing those garters on his shirt sleeves.

There are some very realistic fighting scenes in this production, with cannon booming. Very lights tearing through the air and poison gas being wafted from the enemy lines. These periods are thrilling, being pictured with an unusually faithful conception of war as it was in France. The "Trench of Death," a short scene, is one of the tragic notes. Here a whole line of men is buried through the explosion of a mine and after the disaster the bayonet points are beheld sticking up through the earth.

A boy who knew nothing of war, who spent most of his leisure time writing to his mother, is splendidly played by Leslie Fenton. It is a difficult part, but Mr. Fenton clings with effective sincerity to the mood of the youngster.

And the last episode is superb. It is that in which Quirt, after stealing back to Charmaine, with a colonel's overcoat covering his pajamas, shouts after Flagg, who is "moving on" again:

"Flagg, wait for baby."

THE ARMORED CRUISER POTEMKIN, with a cast from the Moscow Art Theatre; "Moussorgskyana;" "Roaming Over Russia," a scenic feature; "Potemkin" chorus. At the Biltmore Theatre.

By MORDAUNT HALL

The widely discussed Soviet film, "The Armored Cruiser Prince Potemkin," received its initial public screening last night before an audience that packed the Biltmore Theatre. The narrative purports to be an accurate picturization of the events connected with the mutiny of the crew aboard the Prince Potemkin, on Black Monday, June 13, 1905. Whether or no one is disposed to accept all the details as a faithful record, the fact remains that it is a production in which the director displays a vivid imagination and an artistic appreciation of motion picture values.

Last night it was obvious that the applause came from prejudiced persons, for the admirable features of this film passed without a murmur, while an officer being thrown into the sea, the rescue of the ringleader of the insurrectionists and a title reading, "Down with the Czar," stirred some spectators to a high pitch of enthusiasm. This picture is being offered by what is now known as Amkino, a new name for the Sovkino, as the Russian film affiliation is known.

S. M. Eisenstein, who is said to be less than 30 years old, directed this picture, a relatively short film. He obviously received the cooperation he wanted from the Soviet Government, and it is furthermore apparent that among his advisers were men who were thoroughly familiar with battleships.

There are in some land scenes hundreds of persons who are at first depicted manifesting their sympathy for a dead sailor, and later these "extras" figure as the targets for Cossacks, running wildly to get under cover from the Romanoff bullets.

Mr. Eisenstein reveals in the warship scenes an excellent conception of rhythm. There is a sort of purr to this picture as it is unfurled. But there are some scenes where the director wanders too far to elicit sympathy for the sailors who are objecting to the rotton meat. It is also questionable whether any commander of a warship would have wrestled with his men, which is shown in this picture just before the actual mutiny.

Then, too, Mr. Eisenstein fails to take into consideration human instincts in the face of a score of rifles. The order is given for the sail-cloth with which to cover the first group of insubordinate sailors. It is thrown over the men without one of them struggling, and finally when the order comes to fire they either seem stunned at what has happened or they show tremendous faith in their comrades, for not one of them budges. At this moment one anticipates that some of these men would struggle from under the sailcloth and leap into the sea.

In the scenes on land in Odessa, Mr. Eisenstein pictures his villain as black as he can make him and stresses the shooting of women, working up to a climax where he depicts a mother killed and the perambulator, in which is her child, rolling down the great flights of stone steps.

One of the bits of real art in this feature is where the producer comes to the early morning of the day following the mutiny. Here there are glimpses of the Port of Odessa—fishing smacks in a mist, and other scenes which truly impress one with the inactivity of dawn. Then it becomes gradually lighter and things begin stirring.

Mr. Eisenstein's portrayal of the Potemkin under way is another inspiring episode, for here he first shows the mutineers asleep, some in corners of the ship where before they were probably never permitted to slumber, and others making themselves comfortable in the officers' quarters. The look-out then gives the alarm that the other Russian warships are approaching. The engine dials are shown, then the men scurrying along the decks and up and down gangways, and finally in due course, after the men on the Potemkin discover that the other vessels are gaining fast upon them, there is the order to load the guns.

Amunition hoists are busy and the Potemkin's men lay out the shells, some of which, judging by the ease with which they were carried, were not real thing. The guns are sighted, and one perceives the great branches of steel moving slowly. The producer gives a glimpse of the water and the guns, which tells of the speed the ship is making.

The scenes excluded from this film are one showing the squirming maggots in a piece of meat and another concerned with a scene on land. A touch of quasi-comedy is offered when the ship's surgeon—who insisted that the meat would be all right when it was washed with salt and water—is flung into the sea after a struggle and his spectacles are left behind dangling on a hawser.

No undue attention is called to any particular actor in this film, aside from giving one or two of the players a chance to register their personality. There is the ring-leader of the mutineers, the Commander of the Potemkin, and one or two other officers. These rôles were portrayed by members of the Moscow Art Theatre.

This production was prefaced by a Russian scenic feature and the "Potemkin Chorus" which rendered several Russian songs. "The Armored Cruiser Potemkin" was not thrown upon the screen until after the intermission and the entertainment was ended about half past ten.

D 6, 1926

THE SCREEN
By MORDAUNT HALL.

FLESH AND THE DEVIL, with Greta Garbo, John Gilbert, Lars Hanson, Barbara Kent, William Orlamond, George Fawcett and others, based on Hermann Sudermann's novel, "The Undying Past," directed by Clarence Brown; Caroline Andrews, soprano; "Chester Hal Girls"; Julia Glass, pianist. At the Capitol.

Produced with admirable artistry, both in the unfurling of the chronicle and in the character delineation, "Flesh and the Devil," a picture based on Hermann Sudermann's novel, "The Undying Past," is a compelling piece of work in which there are but few conventional movie notes. There is, it is true, a flood of sunshine and a wealth of flowers for the final sequence, but in the previous chapter tragedy had stalked into the picture.

In this photoplay Clarence Brown has mingled adroitly hard and fast realism with soft and poetic glimpses. Sometimes he appears to have given just a little too much consideration to doing something different, but his ideas are eminently successful most of the time.

It is a story of passionate love for a

64

woman and the friendship of two men who, as boys, like the knights of old had mixed their blood; their friendship is the conquering power over their blazing affection for a conscienceless creature. There are scenes in this film which one will not readily forget, for Mr. Brown, who has several worthy pictures to his credit, has really analyzed the feelings of the characters and flashed an idea of their thoughts upon the screen.

There is a distinguished cast in this production. The three principals are Lars Hanson, John Gilbert and Greta Garbo. They are ably supported by Barbara Kent and George Fawcett.

The first scene of this production immediately captures the attention. It is in a German barracks with the student soldiers being awakened by a gruff officer. Ulrich von Kletzingk, one of the troopers, discovers that his chum has not returned to the barracks, and he therefore makes the bed look as if Leo von Sellenthin were in it and then hastens to answer to his name. When Leo's name is called, Ulrich steps out of line and reports that Leo is ill. The Captain tells Ulrich to fall out, and the student and the officer go to the sleeping quarters. Ulrich is fearful lest the officer discover that Leo's bed is empty, but suddenly, just as the Captain is about to pull off the clothes, Leo's head arises, and great is Ulrich's relief.

Not long after this Felicitas, impersonated by Greta Garbo, attracts Leo's searching eyes. She steps into her carriage and speeds off, Leo wondering who is this lithe, attractive woman. Then he hears that she is going to be at the ball that night, and after one dance with his face near the charmer Leo is no longer heart-whole and fancy free. Subsequently the unexpected appearance of Felicitas's husband, Count Rhaden, brings a bout a duel between Leo and the Count.

Mr. Brown gives a most impressive idea of the duel, moving his camera back so that the two figures are silhouetted against the skyline. There are a couple of puffs of smoke, and all that denotes the result of the pistol shots is the next scene, wherein Felicitas is looking at herself in a mirror as she tries on a mourning veil.

As a penalty for having engaged in a duel, Leo is sent to Africa for three years. When he returns he discovers that Ulrich has married Felicitas, the girl for whom Leo had spent three years under the scorching African sun and whom he had been racing for thousands of miles to see again.

This brings about a conflict between Leo and Ulrich, for Felicitas fawns upon Leo and entices him to come to see her when Ulrich is absent.

Miss Garbo is undeniably alluring as Felicitas. Mr. Gilbert and Mr. Hansen give sound performances in their respective rôles.

Ja 10, 1927

By MORDAUNT HALL

THE GENERAL, with Buster Keaton, Glenn Cavender, Jim Farley, Frederick Vroom, Marian Mack, Charles Smith and Frank Barnes, written and directed by Buster Keaton and Clyde Bruckman; overture, "Northern Rhapsody"; "Soaring Wings," a Ufa film; Celia Turrill and Westell Gordon in a rendering of Irving Berlin's new song, "What Does It Matter"; "Milady's Boudoir," with Jose Coles and the Capitol ballet corps. At the Capitol Theatre.

In spite of his bursts of speed and flashes of ingenuity, Johnnie Gray, the hero of "The General," the new picture at the Capitol, is hardly the person who would be trusted with a locomotive. This rôle is played by Buster Keaton, who appears to have bitten off more than he can chew in this farcical affair concerned with the days of the Civil War. Mr. Keaton still preserves his inscrutable expression; he looks like a clergyman and acts like a vaudeville tumbler.

The production itself is singularly well mounted, but the fun is not exactly plentiful. Sometimes laughter yesterday afternoon was stirred up by slapstick ideas, and at other junctures the mere stupidity of the principal character had the desired effect.

During a few chapters in the beginning there was more or less interest in this feature. It happens when the preoccupied Johnny Gray is driving his dear old locomotive, known as the General, through the Northern lines. He is chased by other locomotives equally speedy and graceful. The other love of Gray's life, Annabelle Lee (not a locomotive but an attractive girl) spends part of her time putting anything from toothpicks to great logs into the locomotive fire. Together, hero and heroine throw out timber and crates to hinder their pursuers. One wonders that the man who has sense enough to defeat his enemies is so utterly brainless when he throws wood on the tender.

This is by no means so good as Mr. Keaton's previous efforts. Here he is more the acrobat than the clown, and his vehicle might be described as a mixture of cast iron and jelly.

The Broadway cinemas are exhibiting this week some excellent scenes of the riots in Hankow, China. This strip of film was taken by International News

From The New York Times Film Reviews

Reel's cameraman Ariel L. Varges. It was shipped by boat from Hankow down the Yangtse River and then, when it eventually reached Vancouver, it was brought by airplane to New York.

An absorbing subject is "Soaring Wings," a Ufa production. Through slowed-down motion it reveals the grace of birds flying, and even shows a hawk's attack on a pigeon.

The dance and song offering is a creditable one. "What Does It Matter?" Irving Berlin's latest composition, is rendered by Celia Turrill and Westell Gordon.

F 8, 1927

By MORDAUNT HALL

METROPOLIS, with Alfred Abel, Gustav Froelich, Rudolph Klein-Rogge, Theodor Loos, Heinrich George and Brigitte Helm, adapted from the novel by Thea von Harbou, directed by Fritz Lang; "Steamer Days," a scenic; "The Silhouette," with Madelaine King, Mimi Martini and Julia Parker. At the Rialto.

Nothing like "Metropolis," the ambitious Ufa production that has created wide international comment, has been seen on the screen. It, therefore, stands alone, in some respects, as a remarkable achievement. It is a technical marvel with feet of clay, a picture as soulless as the manufactured woman of its story. Its scenes bristle with cinematic imagination, with hordes of men and women and astounding stage settings. It is hardly a film to be judged by its narrative, for despite the fantastic nature of the story, it is, on the whole, unconvincing, lacking in suspense and at times extravagantly theatric. It suggests a combination of a preachment on capital and labor in a city of the future, an R. U. R. idea and something of Mrs. Shelley's "Frankenstein." Its moral is that the brains and the hands fail when the heart (love) does not work with them. The brains represent capital, and the hands, labor.

The production itself appears to have been a Frankenstein model to the story. Fritz Lang, the famous German director who was responsible for the "Siegfried" film, handled the making of the photodrama. Occasionally it strikes one that he wanted to include too much and then that all one anticipates does not appear. But at the same time the various ideas have been spliced together quite adroitly. It is a subject on which an adverse comment has to be taken from the perspective of the enormity of the task, as most other pictures would fade into insignificance if compared to it. When one criticizes the halting steps of workmen, their stagy efforts to demonstrate fatigue and even the lacking details of life in this metropolis, one realizes that there is in this screen effort much that borders on symbolism.

The narrative is based on a novel by Mr. Lang's wife, Thea von Harbou, who also supplied the manuscripts for "The Indian Mausoleum" and "Siegfried." Roughly, it concerns an inventor who makes a woman from a real woman, without injuring the latter. This manufactured Mary at first is employed to quell the dissatisfied workers, but by some queer freak she eventually incites the men and women laborers to rebel against the wealthiest man in Metropolis.

Here the producer shows the laborers living in tall buildings underground, while the families of the wealthy enjoy the fresh air and sunshine atop a great skyscraper. Metropolis is ruled by John Masterman, a man of great brain and whose only soft spot in his heart is for his son, Eric. This son falls in love with Mary, one of the workers, and he, in sympathy for those who work and dwell far under the ground, becomes one of the underlings, much against his father's wishes.

Mr. Lang introduces the up-to-date appliances in Masterman's office, including a giant board with push buttons and the television means of communication, whereby he can see the man to whom he is talking but himself can't be seen. You see a quailing man going to the telephone to talk with Masterman. This ruler of Metropolis also has his secretaries, who stand in abject fear of him, and one of these, a bloodless, square-headed individual in whom bone predominates, is delegated to watch Eric. This secretary has a slanting forehead and a receding chin, an excellent type for the heartless Masterman.

Some idea of the prodigious work in this production can be imagined when it is said that about 37,000 extras were engaged in some of the episodes. Eleven thousand of the men have shaven heads. These workers are perceived storming the gates of the underground tunnel, and are also beheld going to and from their daily toil. The relief watch walks with easy step, while the others, tired after their hours of monotonous work, are halting in their gait and bent of back.

The sequence in which Rotwang, the inventor, manufactures a double of Mary is put forth in a startling fashion. Rotwang first gives chase to the real Mary, and then puts her in a glass cylinder, around which appear circles of radium lights. To add to the impression, there are boiling liquids in glass globes, and finally the Mary without a soul is produced with the help of an iron Robotlike woman Rotwang had made previously. The artificial Mary, the "woman" who could walk and talk but possessed no soul, has queer drooping underlids to her eyes. She leers at those who approach her. In one sequence she stirs the multitude of workers with her arguments in favor of Masterman, and in another she is seen as a dancing queen. Meanwhile the real Mary has been shut up in a chamber in Rotwang's house of many doors.

In the last chapter of this picture, after the artificial Mary has turned traitor to Rotwang and Masterman, the "woman" is discovered and burned. During this scene the manufactured Mary suddenly changes into the form of the metal creature. There is a flood underground, and it is through the fact that Eric and the real Mary save the workers' children that Masterman himself is spared.

Brigitte Helm is extraordinarily fine in the rôles of the real and the artificial Mary. Alfred Abel gives a vivid portrayal of Masterman, and Gustav Froelich is excellent as Eric. Rudolf Klein-Rogge is splendid as the inventor. The cast is remarkably well chosen.

Mr 7, 1927

THE SCREEN
By MORDAUNT HALL.

Jesus of Nazareth.

THE KING OF KINGS, with H. B. Warner, Dorothy Cumming, Ernest Torrence, Joseph Schildkraut, James Neill, Joseph Striker, Robert Edeson, Sidney D'Albrook, David Imboden, Charles Belcher, Clayton Packara, Robert Ellsworth, Charles Requa, John T. Prince, Jacqueline Logan, Rudolph Schildkraut, Sam De Grasse, Casson Ferguson, Victor Varconi, Mabel Coleman, Montague Love, William Boyd, M. Moore, Theodore Kosloff, George Siegmann, Julia Faye, Josephine Norman, Kenneth Thomson, Alan Brooks, Viola Louis, Muriel MacCormac, Clarence Burton, James Mason, May Robson and others, adapted for the screen by Jeanie Macpherson, directed by Cecil B. DeMille. At the Gaiety Theatre.

So reverential is the spirit of Cecil B. DeMille's ambitious pictorial transcription of the life of Jesus of Nazareth, the Man, that during its initial screening at the Gaiety Theatre last Monday evening, hardly a whispered word was uttered among the audience. This production is entitled, "The King of Kings," and it is, in fact, the most impressive of all motion pictures. To anybody, whether familiar or not with the making of shadow stories, this long series of animated scenes, with its fine settings, adequate costumes and uniforms and its host of players, is an extraordinary and unprecedented film undertaking. Mr. DeMille has not satisfied himself with the mere action of the story, but he has endeavored in various ways to depict the characteristics of the Twelve Apostles and others, and in more than one instance he has set forth incidents in an inspired fashion. Mr. DeMille errs, however, in not leaving more to the imagination and in emphasizing far too vividly all the harrowing details of the Crucifixion.

Even though the introduction of Christ is accomplished in a fashion so gentle that it is masterful, the presence of Jesus on the screen creates a feeling akin to resentment, largely because Mr. DeMille has insisted on having his camera too close to the player. Mr. DeMille might better have bowed to distance in many of his scenes, especially that in which the three crosses are shown.

With admirable dignity and sympathy, H. B. Warner acts the part of Christ. Mr. Warner's countenance is not the general conception of that of Jesus; Mr. Warner's expression is a little severe, and his smile, despite his obvious earnestness and sincerity, is more mundane than spiritual; it is not a smile of sympathy or pity.

The first appearance of the Saviour comes as though through the eyes of a little blind girl as she gradually recovers her sight. There are blurred circles on the screen and these become clearer and clearer until, through Jesus's miracle, the little one perceives Christ before her.

The story opens in a startling and strange way. Instead of gazing upon something gentle, such as Christ delivering the Sermon on the Mount of Olives, one sees in prismatic colors the gilded abode of Mary Magdalene. On leaving this episode, Mr. DeMille takes the spectators to Jesus of Nazareth and soon afterward Christ is seen raising Lazarus from the tomb. A memorable sequence is that in which the boy Mark is made to walk.

The question of paying tribute to Caesar is expertly photographed. Here Mr. DeMille takes full advantage of the incident with the wide scope of the camera. Peter is sent forth to catch a fish, in the mouth of which, as he was told, he finds the silver piece. Roman Centurions, who had been watching the disciple, immediately after Peter leaves, throw lines into the sea, and when they look into the mouths of the fish they catch their feelings are mingled with disappointment and wonder. During this chapter, Mr. DeMille avails himself of the opportunity to give an idea of the wisdom of Christ in answering Caiaphas, the High Priest.

Not the least effective of the scenes is that in which Christ turns the money-lenders out of the Temple. Jesus is shown going from one money-lender's table to another, overturning them.

In the second half of this production Jesus appears before Caiaphas and subsequently before Pontius Pilate. Up to the time the director reveals the scourging of Christ, this part is excellent. But in lieu of merely showing a Roman wielding a thong, Mr. DeMille persists in stressing all the terrible pain. A centurion, who pricks his hand against a thorn, cuts down the twigs and makes the crown to be placed on Christ's head. Here again the agony is dilated upon.

The scenes in which Pontius Pilate discourages further punishment of Christ and where he eventually washes his hands of the trial, after asking the multitude whether they chose Jesus or Barabbas shall be freed, are inspiringly pictured. And so is the incident dealing with Peter thrice denying Christ "before the cock crows." Ernest Torrence figures as Peter, and, although he is just a trifle extravagant at times, the pathos of Peter's plight and mental anguish is skillfully portrayed.

One of the most beautiful scenes in this production is that of the Last Supper. It is strikingly like the old paintings of this subject, but here the figures come to life. Christ is seen passing the water and the wine and eventually the anxious eleven Apostles question Him as to who is the one who "shall betray Him."

Those scenes dealing with the carrying of the Cross to Calvary are remarkable, but even they might have been no less effective by having the figures further away from the camera. The incident wherein Simon of Cyrene offers to bear Christ's cross is filmed with reverence, solemnity and sympathy.

After the crucifixion there is a wonderful storm effect, with the "rending of rocks." The cross on which is Christ stands, while everything else is blown away, and the throngs are filled with terror.

The cast of this production is an imposing one, for a number of well-known actors have been content to appear in minor parts. Caiaphas is portrayed with marked ability by Rudolph Schildkraut, and his son, Joseph Schildkraut, impersonates Judas Iscariot. Robert Edeson is splendid as Matthew. Mary, the Mother, is impersonated by Dorothy Cumming. Jacqueline Logan appears as Mary Magdalene. Victor Varconi is excellent as Pontias Pilate. One could, in fact, go down the long list of players and commend one after the other.

Dr. Hugo Riesenfeld's music score, with the introduction of many well known hymns, including "Lead, Kindly Light," is a distinct asset to the production.

Ap 20, 1927

A German Film.

STREETS OF SORROW, with Greta Garbo, Asta Nielsen, Einar Hanson, Werner Krauss, Jaro Furth, Silvia Torf, Countess Agnes Esterhazy, Countess Tolstoi and others, based on the novel by Hugo Bettauer, directed by G. W. Pabst; overture, Rachmaninoff's Prelude, with a motion picture conceived by Castleton Knight; "Aesop Fable"; "Heels Over Heads in Love." At the Cameo.

A gray squirrel coat, a butcher whose haircut is a cross between a Bowery bartender and an old-time Tommy Atkins, an overcrowded cabaret, a murder confession, sordid slices from life and a number of other things are mixed up together in a German film called "Streets of Sorrow." It ends in being about as coherent as the first attempts at futuristic painting were to the ordinary gallery visitor.

There are moments when this picture doesn't seem so bad, but then these are killed by some preposterous exhibitions of agony. Greta Garbo, who has since become a finished screen actress, at the time this picture was produced did not know the elementary rudiments of make-up. She has spoiled her own attractive features through her efforts to add to the languidness of her eyes. She is, however, the most interesting personality in this picture, even more so than Werner Krauss, who is just as unnatural in this queer piece of work as he has been natural in others.

"Streets of Sorrow" is a Sofar-film production, which prompts one to think that it is about as far from being an entertainment as it is possible to get. It would really be quite enough to say that "Streets of Sorrow" is too pathetic for words and let it go at that.

"Heels Over Heads in Love," a French novelty film on the order of "Knee-Deep in Love," is quite an interesting feature.

JI 6, 1927

of the diamond and dressing room. It's rough-house stuff, but full of fun and go. Mr. Ruth himself makes a pleasing screen figure, and is abetted in comicality by Louise Fazenda and others. Anna Q. Nilsson supplies the scenic quality, and quite a bit of vivid acting, too. The plot is all about baseball, with, of course, a timely home run in the end, but it's all tied together with a gay romance and promises to show audience-holding strength. The Babe is his own hero, too. Last night's crowd approved him as a screen actor as well as a home-run king.

The Vocafilm numbers which preceded the photoplay were varied and some of them seemed to make promises for the machine by which sounds and pictures are synchronized, but the performance, apart from the actual synchronization, was something short of perfect. There was a quite audible scrape in the sounds, and sometimes a screech that sounded like static startled the audience. The voices, too, had a metallic sound and the instrumental music seemed harsh. The Vocafilm accompaniment to Ruth's picture, while too loud in places, was effective in reproducing the shouts of crowds and comic noises.

JI 26, 1927

THE SCREEN

Seen and Heard.

VOCAFILM PROGRAM, diversified motion pictures synchronized with music and voices; "Babe Comes Home," with George Herman Ruth, Vocafilm accompaniment. At the Longacre.

The Vocafilm experiment at the Longacre Theatre last night didn't go so well, but Babe Ruth's picture, 'Babe Comes Home," proved a merry thing. It came to the spectators after they had sat through more than an hour of phonetic films that went more or less askew, yet it genially overcame this handicap and sent the people out laughing at midnight.

The story, based on one of Gerald Beaumont's baseball yarns, is broad comedy, but with a real atmosphere

The Crooked Hypnotist.

DR. MABUSE, with Rudolph Klein-Rogge, Aude Egede Nissen, Gertrude Welcker, Alfred Abel and others, directed by Fritz Lang; a Chaplin comedy. At the Fifth Avenue Playhouse.

A Ufa production made about five years ago is holding forth at the Fifth Avenue Playhouse. It looks to be about ten years old when one considers the acting and the verbose titles, which, incidentally, were written in England. Eighty-six of these captions were eliminated for exhibition here, but there still remain about 150, the usual number for a feature film. Here and there this picture is interesting, for there are scenes of queer gambling clubs, where if you breathe the word "Pineapple" you are permitted to enter after you have explained that you want "cards" and not "cocaine." According to this narrative there were in this town quite a number of secret clubs, and it is in these organization that Dr. Mabuse, hypnotist and so-called psychoanalyst, engaged in his nefarious activities. Money was what he wanted and what he got, until in the end he received the sentence the police had waiting for him.

This queer Dr. Mabuse is able to carry on a conversation at one end of a room and hypnotize a person at the other. Nobody is safe from him and even the stupid old police chief is cast under Mabuse's spell, which, of course, is very apt to cause any ordinary police official to lose his job. But not in this picture, for Chief De Witt carries on to the bitter end. It may be persistence, but as the film unfurls one does wish he had used his brains more in the fifth or sixth reel instead of waiting until the tenth.

Dr. Mabuse is supposed to be clever in his disguises. He mystifies everybody with whiskers, beards, mustaches and aquiline noses.

One can hardly allude to "Dr. Mabuse" as an old master, for the works of artists of past ages are something to enjoy. "Dr. Mabuse" is far too long even as it is, and it has been cut down several reels. It is something like a serial posing as a mystery play. It was one of Fritz Lang's first pictures. Since that time Mr. Lang has earned wide praise by his direction of "Siegfried." He is also responsible for "Metropolis," but that's another story, as Kipling would say.

Ag 9, 1927

Fifty-fifth Street Cinema. It is nicely produced, for nobody can complain about the acting, the photography, the lighting effects or the costumes. But the producer defies you to fathom what the characters are up to. This production has no titles, and after viewing it one concludes that captions, exasperating though they may be in some pictures, would be a blessing in this case. It is not long before this picture begins to create a desire to yawn, and half an hour after it has been cavorting across the screen you may become fidgety, for with all its artistic bent one gleans less about the photoplay than one would in viewing an ordinary Hollywood production stripped of its titles.

It is like a good-looking woman who is a deaf mute or a stage play in which the actors permit only one word in a hundred to be heard. On the program it is described as "a drama of jealousy in six acts, unaided by the literary subtitle." Art or no art, it was quite pleasing to descend from the pinacles of highbrowism to the valley of comedy and once again enjoy some of the episodes in Charlie Chaplin's old burlesque of "Carmen," which is hailed on the program as "a sure cure for any one's operatic aspirations."

Ag 10, 1927

THE SCREEN
By MORDAUNT HALL

A Puzzling Picture.

WARNING SHADOWS, a German production directed by Dr. Arthur Robison, with Fritz Kortner and Alexander Granach in featured roles; Charlie Chaplin in his o'd comedy, "Carmen"; "Rachmaninoff's Prelude in C Sharp Minor." At the Fifty-fifth Street Cinema.

A German picture called "Warning Shadows," which met with some success in London about three years ago, is to be seen this week at the

THE SCREEN
By MORDAUNT HALL.

The Strong and the Meek.

UNDERWORLD, with George Bancroft, Clive Brook, Evelyn Brent, Larry Semon, Fred Kohler, Helen Lynch, Jerry Mandy and Karl Morse, based on a story by Ben Hecht, directed by Josef von Sternberg; Jesse Crawford's organ concert; "Sealing Whacks," a "Krazy Kat" cartoon; "Tokio Blues," with Joseph Sargent, John Barney, Rose Low, Helen Kim, Katsu Kuma, Willie Slar Solar and others, devised and staged by John Murray Anderson. At the Paramount Theatre.

Two sterling character studies are to be seen in "Underworld," the present film offering at the Paramount Theatre. The players who contribute the outstanding performances in this yarn of robbery, murder and the death cell are George

Bancroft and Clive Brook. Mr. Bancroft portrays the fearless burglar and killer, "Bull" Weed, and Mr. Brook impersonates a grateful derelict, a man humbled through his steadfast association with John Barleycorn.

Although there are several episodes in this picture that could have been improved upon by a little more thought and study, it is a compelling subject, one that has a distinctly original vein. It was directed by Josef von Sternberg, who gained notoriety by his work on that disagreeable production "The Salvation Hunters." Here, however, largely through the competent work of Messrs. Bancroft and Brook, Mr. von Sternberg gives a better idea of his powers as a director. While Mr. Bancroft's acting is possibly not quite as intriguing as it was in James Cruze's film "The Pony Express," this stalwart player is nevertheless so well suited to his part that one does not care so much about his guffawing when a smile would be more effective.

"Bull" Weed is feared by all who know him, especially by "Buck" Mulligan, the oily rascal who camouflages his nefarious activities by spending some of his time in a florist's shop. "Bull," one can imagine, has a voice like thunder and a temper like the animal from which he derived his sobriquet. To flirt with "Bull's" girl is just asking for a bullet through the heart, for "Bull," a well-dressed crook, like "Wild Bill" Hickok, is wont to shoot from the hip. He is a burglar with a sense of humor who smiles when others might frown, but his smile may be caused by the pleasure anticipated over the idea of snuffing out a life, robbing a bank or grabbing a diamond necklace.

You see him in one scene smiling meaningly as he gazes at an electric sign of the "A. B. C. Investment Company," over which flash the words:

"The world is yours."

It is to "Bull" that "Rolls Royce" (Mr. Brook), the drink-sodden ex-lawyer, is grateful. When "Rolls" was shuffling about without a nickel, "Bull" pressed a good, thick roll of bills into the astonished derelict's hand. In this part Mr. Brook is always restrained and natural; his make-up, whether his stubby beard in the initial scenes or an idea of a blotchy countenance in others, is most effective. "Rolls" is as true as steel to "Bull," but "Feathers,"

"Bull's" girl, has eyes for "Rolls," that is, after he has pulled himself together. And "Rolls" is by no means indifferent to "Feathers."

When "Bull" puts a bullet through "Buck" Mulligan and is sentenced to be hanged, "Feathers" and "Rolls'" scheme to help him to escape. The police get an inkling of what's going to happen and they are prepared, which causes "Bull" to believe that he has been double-crossed by "Rolls" and "Feathers." In the end "Bull" is satisfied that they have both done their best to help him.

There are a few strained incidents, including one where "Rolls" dashes across the street when a house is surrounded by police, and another where "Feathers" publicly wears the diamond necklace that "Bull" had that afternoon stolen with other valuables from a jeweler's. The story, however, contains a good deal of sound drama.

Evelyn Brent is very attractive and she gives a capable performance as "Feathers." Sometimes Mr. von Sternberg shows that he is too fond of posing her looking away from the persons with whom she is supposed to be conversing, but that is his fault. Larry Semon springs into this story as a comic character, but his efforts are a monkey wrench in the machinery.

John Murray Anderson's stage presentation, "Tokio Blues," is an exceptionally artistic piece of work.

Ag 22, 1927

THE SCREEN
By MORDAUNT HALL

Mme. Duse's Only Picture.

"MADRE," with Eleanora Duse; "The Rink," an old Chaplin comedy; "Twang," a comicality; "Life's Greatest Thrills"; Singers' Enemy." At the Fifth Avenue Playhouse.

Through the medium of two old motion pictures at the Fifth Avenue Playhouse this week the past is being flashed into the present. One of these subjects is an Italian drama known as "Madre," the only film to which the late Eleanora Duse lent her talent, and the other is "The Rink," an early comedy in which Charlie Chaplin displayed his wonderful faculty for creating laughter.

"Madre" is only interesting because of Mme. Duse's presence. Her efforts in this gloomy feature are confined to depicting the sacrifice of a mother for her illegitimate son. Yet every gesture and movement made by the great actress awakens thoughts of her illustrious career. She obviously understood the technique of acting before the camera far better than many of her more experienced contemporaries, for her actions are never too studied and always rhythmic. She was averse to make-up, and therefore in the early episodes of this picture, when she is supposed to be a young woman, her hair is covered with a cloth. Fifteen years (according to the story) then elapse, and Mme. Duse appears as she was, shortly before her death. You see her fine features, crowned by her white hair.

There are quite a number of scenes in this production that might have been excluded to its advantage, as the narrative is never stirring.

Chaplin's comedy soon aroused laughter from the audience that had been silent. His antics in "The Rink" are not without originality. Where you would expect to see the comedian flounder all over the place when he is on roller skates, he turns out to be a master at gliding over the floor. His little cane comes in as useful as d'Artagnan's sword, for it needs but a touch at the bulky man on skates to send him to the floor.

A comical parody on "Chang," called "Twang," treats New York as if it were a jungle and anything from cats to ferryboats, something to be dreaded. It was devised and titled by Joseph Fleisler.

S 21, 1927

SUNRISE, with Janet Gaynor, George O'Brien, Bedil Rosing, Margaret Livingston, J. Farrell Macdonald, Ralph Sipperly, Jane Winton, Arthur Housman, Eddie Boland and others; based on Hermann Sudermann's "Trip to Tilsit"; directed by F. W. Murnau. Movietone features, including Mussolini making an address and the Vatican Choir. At the Times Square Theatre.

A remarkable program revealing in two different phases the enormous potentialities of the screen was presented last night at the Times Square Theatre by William Fox. The main attraction, "Sunrise," the first film to be made in America by F. W. Murnau, director of "The Last

Laugh" and "Faust," was prefaced by several excellent Movietone features, in which the figurantes were heard as well as seen. It was distinctly impressive to look upon the physiognomy of Henry P. Fletcher, the United States Ambassador to Italy, and hear him present, while standing on Italian soil, Benito Mussolini. It was also wonderful to hear and see the Duce come from a building and reply to the introduction. In the course of this brief address Mussolini referred to the energy of the American people.

"I salute the noble Government of the United States," the Duce was heard to say. "I salute the Italians of America, who unite in a single love our two nations."

Mussolini also made a Movietone talk in Italian. Other synchronizations of sound and sight were the Vatican Choir, the renditions of which were stirring. Then there were the Italian troops on parade with their bands, and not only were the officers' commands heard, but also the stamping of their horses' hoofs. Actually, this was as perfect a series of screen views combined with sound as could well be imagined.

The other phase of the entertainment was the new picture, which cost a staggering sum of money; and as it is unfurled one appreciates the tremendous task that confronted the producers in turning it out.

"Sunrise" was adapted from Hermann Sudermann's story "A Trip to Tilsit," and, although Tilsit is actually a town in East Prussia, it is set forth in one of the very few subtitles that the locale of this story might be in any country. As it threads its way across the screen this narrative gathers impetus. It is filled with intense feeling and in it is embodied an underlying subtlety. Mr. Murnau shows himself to be an artist in camera studies, bringing forth marvelous results from lights, shadows and settings. He also proves himself to be a true story teller, and, incidentally, here is a narrative wherein the happy ending is welcome.

The principals in this gripping subject are George O'Brien and Janet Gaynor, who both give inspired performances. It is a slowly told tale, and sometimes Mr. O'Brien appears to be just a little lethargic in his movements, but this is explained by the nature of the character he is portraying—a susceptible, thick-headed country lout, a man who never gives a thought to his appearance and who is utterly ignorant of anything approaching social amenities. Miss Gaynor impersonates his faithful.

trustful wife and mother of his baby. At the outset there is a bedizened girl from the city, who delights in gazing down at her shiny patent-leather shoes. She entrances the Man (Mr. O'Brien), and after he slips away from his home she caresses him and then suggests that he sell his farm and come to the city and live with her. The Man, who is unshorn and wears a flannel shirt, asks what about his wife, and the City Girl whispers to him to take his wife out and drown her.

She tells him that by capsizing the boat he can make it appear to be an accident. Thereupon the Man is seen bidding his wife to come to her doom, but when he is about to throw the poor little creature overboard, he thinks better of it. He rows over to the other side of the lake, but once the Wife sets foot on shore she flees in fear, followed by her lumbering husband. Mr. Murnau then goes on to depict the joy of the Man in having discovered how greatly he loves his wife.

In a remarkable series of scenes one is taken through the city on a tram car, and then follow the adventures in an amusement park, in which a straying pig affords some of the comedy. Mr. Murnau does all his work quite differently from any other director and when he stoops to somewhat hilarious fun it does not matter, for it is filmed with astuteness and originality.

In an early chapter there are a flood of flashes concerned with people going on a holiday, and you perceive a steamboat's nose shot up mystically on the sands of the seashore. To show the city, an immense set was constructed, and on it there were two surface car lines and countless vehicles. You perceive a whirring disk and then this gradually dissolves into the joyous sight of the amusement park.

Mr. Murnau uses a moon, and he evidently likes its reflection on the water. He fashions a storm on a lake, and keeps the spectators on the edge of their seats until the finale of the production. He makes you hope that the characters won't do such and such a thing, and you trust that the Man and his Wife will get back safely to their picturesque little farmhouse.

This picture is exotic in many ways for it is a mixture of Russian gloom and Berlin brightness.

Miss Gaynor, guided by the genius of Mr. Murnau, gives a strangely sympathetic portrait of the Wife. Her hair is braided into a coil at the back of her head, and her big, bright eyes are never like those of the usual Hollywood actress. Margaret Livingston impersonates the City Girl with felinelike watchfulness and purring caresses. There is not a weak spot in any of the performances and the incidents are stamped with genuineness and simplicity. You find yourself thinking now and again that it is just the sort of thing farm people might do on going to Tilsit.

Mr. Murnau proves by "Sunrise" that he can do just as fine work in Hollywood as he ever did in Germany.

S 24, 1927

Al Jolson and the Vitaphone.

THE JAZZ SINGER, with Al Jolson, May McAvoy, Warner Orland, Eugenie Besserer, Cantor Josef Rosenblatt, Otto Lederer, Bobbie Gordon, Richard Tucker, Natt Carr, William Demarest, Anders Randolf and Will Walling; based on the play by Samson Raphaelson; directed by Alan Crosland; Vitaphone interpolations of Mr. Jolson's songs and orchestral accompaniment by Vitaphone. At Warners' Theatre.

By MORDAUNT HALL

In a story that is very much like that of his own life, Al Jolson at Warners' Theatre last night made his screen début in the picturization of Samson Raphaelson's play "The Jazz Singer," and through the interpolation of the Vitaphone and the audience had the rare opportunity of hearing Mr. Jolson sing several of his own songs and also render most effectively the Jewish hymn "Kol Nidre."

Mr. Jolson's persuasive vocal efforts were received with rousing applause. In fact, not since the first presentation of Vitaphone features, more than a year ago at the same playhouse, has anything like the ovation been heard in a motion-picture theatre. And when the film came to an end Mr. Jolson himself expressed his sincere appreciation of the Vitaphoned film, declaring that he was so happy that he could not stop the tears.

The Vitaphoned songs and some dialogue have been introduced most adroitly. This in itself is an ambitious move, for in the expression of song the Vitaphone vitalizes the production enormously. The dialogue is not so effective, for it does not always catch the nuances of speech or inflections of the voice so that one is not aware of the mechanical features.

The Warner Brothers astutely realized that a film conception of "The Jazz Singer" was one of the few subjects that would lend itself to the use of the Vitaphone. It was also a happy idea to persuade Mr. Jolson to play the leading rôle, for few men could have approached the task of singing and acting so well as he does in this photoplay. His "voice with a tear" compelled silence, and possibly all that disappointed the people in the packed theatre was the fact that they could not call upon him or his image at least for an encore. They had to content themselves with clapping and whistling after Mr. Jolson's shadow finished a realistic song. It was also the voice of Jolson, with its dramatic sweep, its pathos and soft slurring tones.

One of the most interesting sequences of the picture itself is where Mr. Jolson as Jack Robin (formerly Jakie Rabbinowitz) is perceived talking to Mary Dale (May McAvoy) as he smears his face with black. It is done gradually, and yet the dexterity with which Mr. Jolson outlines his mouth is readily appreciated. You see Jack Robin, the young man who at last has his big opportunity, with a couple of smudges of black on his features, and then his cheeks, his nose, his forehead and the back of his neck are blackened. It is also an engaging scene where Jack's mother comes to the Winter Garden and sees him for the first time as a black-face entertainer.

There is naturally a good deal of sentiment attached to the narrative, which is one wherein Cantor Rabinowitz is eager that his son Jakie shall become a cantor to keep up the traditions of the family. The old man's anger is aroused when one night he hears that Jakie has been singing jazz songs in a saloon. The boy's heart and soul are with the modern music. He runs away from home and tours the country until through a friend he is engaged by a New York producer to sing in the Winter Garden. His début is to be made on the Day of Atonement, and, incidentally, when his father is dying. Toward the end, however, the old cantor on his deathbed hears his son canting the "Kol Nidre."

Some time afterward Jack Robin is perceived and heard singing "Mammy," while his old mother occupies a seat in the front row. Here Mr. Jolson puts all the force of his personality into the song as he walks out beyond the footlights and, some times with clasped hands, he sings as if to his own mother.

The success of this production is due to a large degree to Mr. Jolson's Vitaphoned renditions. There are quite a few moments when the picture drags, because Alan Crosland, the director, has given too much footage to discussion and to the attempts of the theatrical manager (in character) to prevail upon Jack Robin not to permit sentiment to sway him (Jack) when his great opportunity is at hand. There are also times when one would expect the Vitaphoned portion to be either more subdued or stopped as the camera swings to other scenes. The voice is usually just the same whether the image of the singer is close to the camera or quite far away.

Warner Oland does capable work as Cantor Rabinowitz. May McAvoy is attractive, but has little to do as Mary Dale. In most of her scenes Eugenie Besserer acts with sympathetic restraint.

Cantor Josef Rosenblatt contributes an excellent Vitaphoned concert number in the course of the narrative.

O 7, 1927

REVOLUTION FILM THRILLS MOSCOW

Crowded Opera House Cheers Vivid Depiction of Red Victory of Ten Years Ago.

Row of Silent Cannon Suddenly Open Up With Shells Bursting Over Kremlin and Turn Tide.

By WALTER DURANTY.

By Wireless to THE NEW YORK TIMES.

MOSCOW, Oct. 31.—A crowded audience of Soviet leaders and hundreds of foreign delegates to the anniversary celebrations went wild with enthusiasm at the Grand Opera House tonight as "Moscow in October," the first of the "refighting of the Revolution" films was shown publicly.

The movie ended amidst the boom of cannon with the victorious attack of the Red Guards upon the Kremlin Fortress. The film had no plot or love theme, but the events portrayed were sufficiently dramatic to maintain interest.

Unlike the Leningrad overturn, where the attack of the cruiser Aurora on the Winter Palace put the power into Bolshevist hands, almost from the outset the Moscow revolution opened with a temporary victory of the Whites, who recovered the Kremlin from the rebellious Fifty-sixth Regiment commanded by the Bolshevik Berstin.

Then we saw the White Guards marching through the streets to attack the Bolshevist centre and to meet there an immense outpouring of workers and soldiers from the factory districts.

The young director of the film, M. Barnet, used typically Russian impressionism in showing the hurrying clouds of huge billows of smoke from the factory chimneys to heighten the effect of Russian excitement. Then followed the whirlwind street fighting, with the superior arms and discipline of the Whites gradually prevailing against the revolutionary numbers.

Meanwhile an artillery regiment on the outskirts of Moscow remained undecided with its silent guns trained on the city. Repeated views of the long row of lonely cannon made a striking contrast to the storm and stress of the battle scenes where rifle and machine-gun fire were pouring and grenades were bursting and men were fighting and dying.

Then a Revolutionary addresses the artillerymen and in a furious speech tells them of the Bolshevist victory at Petrograd. In a wave of enthusiasm they rush to their guns. Shells burst in Red Square, crash down on the Kremlin towers and send up immense waterspouts from the river at the foot of the fortress.

Then as the Whites are seized with panic and, hotly pursued, flee from the Kremlin, the band played the "International," the drums boomed the thunder of the cannon, and the audience leaped to its feet in a tumult of cheering.

Judged by critical standards the film may have defects—the early scenes dragged and there were far too many captions. But the latter part of the picture had a fury tempo which might well carry off its feet a less sympathetic audience than this, many of whom had partaken in the grim, earnest struggle which they watched in make-believe. And it is still recent enough to rouse the ready Russian emotions.

When the Whites celebrated their temporary success by a religious ceremony at the Shrine of the Iberian Virgin at the entrance to Red Square, there was an extraordinary low sound in the theatre—an accumulated "ugrrr" of hatred, like a bulldog's growl.

N 1, 1927

By MORDAUNT HALL

LOVE, with Greta Garbo, John Gilbert, George Fawcett, Emily Fitzroy, Brandon Hurst, Phillipe de Lacy and others, based on Tolstoy's novel, "Anna Karenina," directed by Edmund Goulding. At the Embassy Theatre.

Greta Garbo, the Swedish actress, in a picture called "Love," an adaptation of Tolstoy's "Anna Karenina," outshines any other performance she has given to the screen. This production was presented last night at the Embassy Theatre, and Miss Garbo's singularly fine acting as Anna held the audience in unusual silence. It can be said that Miss Garbo is ably supported by John Gilbert, but throughout this photodrama it is the portrait of Anna that is the absorbing feature. Other characterizations and even the story take second place when compared to the work of this Nordic player.

Miss Garbo is elusive. Her heavy-lidded eyes, the cold whiteness of her face and her svelte figure compel interest in her actions. Sometimes she reminds one of a blond Mona Lisa and on other occasions she is gentle and lovely. Only in one sequence does she seem to be a little out of character and that is probably due to obedience to the director's instructions.

Possibly the most sympathetic chapter in this tragic tale is where Anna, after a prolonged absence with Count Vronsky, returns to her husband's home to see her little boy. Unknown to her husband she creeps upstairs and discovers the youngster asleep. He gradually awakens and, as he had been told that his mother was dead, he believes that he is dreaming when he beholds his beautiful mother sitting on his bed. Then joy spreads over the boy's face as he throws his arms around Anna's neck. Phillipe de Lacy, a bright-ates the boy. This episode also gives Miss Garbo a great opportunity of which she takes full advantage.

The producers have been coura-geous enough to give this highly satis-factory screen offering a tragic end-ing, and although it comes abruptly, it is nevertheless dramatic and logi-cal.

Edmund Goulding, who has been through the picture mill as an actor, a scenario writer, and a director, handled this subject. His share of the work is commendable, except in one or two stretches when he mani-fests a penchant for musical comedy ideas.

Mr. Goulding should be highly con-gratulated, however, on the excel-lence of the steeplechase scene, in which the Russian officers take their horses over the hurdles. Here, rider after rider falls, and although it is anticipated that Count Vronsky is going to come to grief, there is a good deal of sustained suspense be-fore his mount goes down.

This story of illicit love begins with a snowstorm in which, through an accident to her sleigh, Anna first meets Vronsky. He is so infatuated later by her magnetic charm that he takes her in his arms, an action for which he apologizes. Karenin, Anna's elderly husband, resents the attention that Count Vronsky pays to his wife, chiefly because he be-lieves that it will interfere with his diplomatic career. Eventually, fol-lowing the horse race accident, Vronsky and Anna decide to run away together.

The way in which Anna is re-minded of her little son is somewhat conventional, but, nevertheless, graciously depicted.

In the last chapter Mr. Goulding portrays the Grand Duke pardoning Vronsky for having had the affair with Anna. Then one perceives the woman, the fine outline of her coun-tenance shrouded by a veil, standing on the platform of a railroad station. The headlights of an engine are seen approaching and then a shadow leaps in front of the oncoming locomotive.

Mr. Gilbert's part in this picture is cleverly done, but it might have been even better if he had controlled his stare and his smile. George Faw-cett is admirable as the Grand Duke and Emily Fitzroy is splendid as the Grand Duchess. Brandon Hurst con-tributes an excellent character study as Anna's husband.

N 30, 1927

SOVIET FILM 'MOTHER' ACCLAIMED IN VIENNA

IN a review of "Mother," one of the latest productions of the So-viet Russian Film Producing Company going the rounds of Eu-rope, the Vienna Arbeiter-Zeitung's critic, after summarizing the novel by Maxim Gorky upon which the film is based, says:

"This very dramatic film was done by a lyrical director, V. Pudovkin. He interpolated many landscape pic-tures among the scenes of action, reflected the unrest of humanity and of nature, made the dawning of free-dom coincide with the coming of Spring and linked the parade of the May Day demonstrants with the breaking up of the ice in the river.

"Most poetic are the scenes where the prisoners are dreaming of their meadows, of their horses, of their plows. Here the film becomes a great poem in pictures. The same thing is true of the mighty closing scenes, where from the palaces of old Russia there gradually arise the monuments of the new over which waves the red flag. The heroic death scene of the mother and the little symphony in pictures at the end wipe out the feeling of depression that dominates four-fifths of its action. Individuals have fallen, the son, the mother. But the revolution marches on and its victims are not forgotten.

"The director's lyrical attitude to-ward the material determines the tempo, which is somewhat slower than one might wish. The numerous views of the breaking up of the ice and some other passages materially hamper the course of events. In his photographic work, Pudovkin makes the best of the Russians' previous experiences. The figures developed from below have an especially powerful, impressive and threatening effect. The individuals are characterized by cleverly thought-out details.

"A beetle has laboriously worked his way out of a spoon filled with mush. The soldier who pushes him in again must be a rough fellow, delighting in evil-doing. The scenes of the revolt in the prison and the great death scene of the mother are excellent. Here Pudovkin's work equals that in the directing of 'Engineer Ukhtomsky' and 'Ivan the Terrible.' It is idle to compare 'Mother' with 'Armored Cruiser Potemkin.' The exceptional case of 'Potemkin' cannot remain for all time the standard by which to measure Russian films. 'Potemkin' was a supreme piece of work which cannot be duplicated even by the Russian film art every day.

"V. Baranovskaya, in her simple, convincing rôle of the mother, carries the burden of all proletarian mothers on her shoulders. M. Batalof, the son, is a good type, as are the other players. In general, this film makes slight demands upon the actors. Its revolutionary artistic effect depends upon the material, the good dramatic continuity and its visual interpretation by the director."

Ja 8, 1928

THE LOVES OF JEANNE NEY

A Post-War Yarn

A PARTICULAR disappointment to me was another Ufa picture, "The Love of Jeanne Ney." Its director, G. W. Pabst, has been a favorite of mine for years and I was glad to see his talent come to fruition in the brilliant Freud film "Secrets of the Soul." In this last film, however, he has missed the mark by half a house. The novel by Ilya Ehrenburg from which the picture was taken is, I am told, an excellent and suggestive piece of work, but the scenario is lacking in concentration and consistency.

It begins in the Crimea just after the close of the World War. Jeanne, the daughter of a French journalist, and Andreas, a Soviet leader, are attracted to each other. The Soviets take the city and Jeanne's father is killed. But she herself is helped by her lover to escape to Paris. There she takes a position as secretary to her uncle, a callous private detective. His daughter is blind and Chalybieff, a swindler who has been partially responsible for the death of Jeanne's father, is making love to the blind girl in order to get her dowry. Andreas is sent to Paris on a secret mission and he and Jeanne meet often. The uncle has a very valuable diamond in his safe and is murdered by Chalybieff while he is stealing the jewel. The swindler is able to throw suspicion on Andreas, who is unwilling to tell his whereabouts as he had spent the night with Jeanne. Jeanne, however, remembers that Chalybieff had seen them together on the night of the murder and goes to ask help. He believes that she knows the truth and gives up the jewel.

The scenes in Russia are promising in their melancholy drabness, but so soon as the action shifts to Paris all atmosphere is lost. The uncle is handled in a cheaply humorous style and the blind daughter is such a side issue as never to awaken our interest or sympathy. Also, Chalybieff is overplayed in the most exaggerated manner, a typical ten-twenty-thirty villain and one can almost hear his "Ha! Ha! Ha! Foiled again!" And then the two young lovers: Uno Henning was satisfying from a Continental viewpoint, but Edith Jehanne is one of those film beauties with two expressions, of which one is "dumb." Why did Pabst choose this French player when he could have any number of German actresses who would have been far better in the rôle? For instance, Brigitte Helm, who is sentenced to the thankless part of the blind girl. I suppose the idea is to make the picture more salable in

France—an attempt to put into practice the much discussed Franco-German alliance against America. If this is going to be typical of the results (as I am afraid it will be), Hollywood will be able to sleep nights again.

Of course, the season is hardly half over and all my gloomy prognostications may be refuted in the Spring. Surely nothing could be more desirable, as Hollywood without European stimulation is unthinkable. And several of the promised Ufa releases read most encouragingly. Fritz Lang of "Metropolis" has completed "Spione," Elisabet Bergner will star in "Donna Diana," "The Mysterious Mirror" is said to bring entirely novel technical effects. And Erich Pommer is back again with a series of three films in view.

Ja 15, 1928

By MORDAUNT HALL

THE LAST COMMAND, with Emil Jannings, Evelyn Brent, William Powell, Nocholas Soussanin and Michael Visaroff, based on a story by Lajos Biros, directed by Josef von Sternberg; Miriam Lax, soprano; "Have a Drink!" a Pathe novelty scenic. At the Rialto Theatre.

From the standpoint of its narrative, Emil Jannings's latest picture, "The Last Command," now at the Rialto Theatre, is one of the most satisfactory of shadow stories. It is logical throughout. It was inspired by the experiences of a Russian General, who fled to this country after the revolution in his own land. This production has its forced moments, its sluggish incidents, but the chronicle is equipped with a double strain of suspense. It strikes one as a good short story turned to excellent account in film form. It is a far more plausible account than that of "The Way of All Flesh," but in the older picture the detail was more carefully filmed than that of "The Last Command."

This current offering has a clever finish, an ending that is particularly skillfully devised, and one that is most effective. And if there are moments when Mr. Jannings holds the same expression and pose too long, you are rewarded for the most part with a brilliant performance in which there is a wealth of imagination. In the closing scenes Mr. Jannings gives a highly gifted and gripping portrayal of the last moments of the bent and bowed czarist generalissimo working as an extra in a motion picture studio. You see General Dolgorucki meet his death in the same uniform he wore with pomp and confidence of his high office before the red flag flew from Moscow's Kremlin, and the fiddle, a piano and a 'cello are rendering the old Russian National anthem.

Just before the General crumples up on the salt-covered barbed-wire battleground of the studio, he hears his militant hymn and the director, a Russian who had no reason to love the General, gave the old man the words of comfort that caused the extra, in his unbalanced mental state, to believe that the Russia that was had come into power again.

Mr. Jannings does not wear a cap in this scene, as he realized that it would conceal to a certain extent his various expressions. He is magnificent as he straightens up at the sound of his militant hymn and then drops to the studio "snow."

"He was a great actor, that old guy," observes the casting director.

"And a great man, which is more," adds the picture director, who incidentally in Russia had felt the General's riding crop on his cheek.

The motion picture end of this feature is wonderfully good, even to the selection of the players. There are the "yes men," the light experts, the electric wires like eels around the studio floor. The instructions are done to a T, without anything being too extravagant. The story opens up with the choosing of a General for the battle scene, and Dolgorucki's photograph is brought out. It results in his selection and soon the casting director's assistant is on the wire calling Dolgorucki on the telephone at his shabby abode. He is told to report at 6:30 the next morning.

As the broken Russian military commander, Jannings gives a hint of the man's sufferings. He wears a beard. His face is that of an aristocrat, but every half second he shakes his head, like a man suffering from shell shock. They gibe him about this in the studio and scoff at him when he tells them, the other extras, that the Czar gave him his military cross. Jannings is perceived gazing at his make-up box, the cover of which is a mirror. He looks, every so often shaking his head.

Then comes a fade-out and soon one sees the General as he had been before the Kerensky or Soviet days. He is a man of courage, one who may use his riding crop occasionally, but who is not cruel. He loves his fatherland and even sneers at the Czar for taking a division of troops from the battle front to satisfy the Little Father's vanity.

More might have been accomplished with these Russian scenes to give a better idea of the General. His style appears to be cramped at times, for while one is told that he is a cousin of the Czar and commander of the Russian armies, he does not appear to be doing much more than the work of a captain.

There is pictured the flaring up of the rabble, and Jannings is shown with swollen lips, blood-smeared, standing against a wall of a railway station. In some of these flashes Mr. Jannings—who, as the General, admittedly has suffered frightful punishment— could nevertheless have shown in his eyes some fire when the men and women goad him and spit water in his face. His strength may have been ebbing, but he now and again lifts some coal to the locomotive's fire, and subsequently he musters up enough strength to bang the locomotive driver over the head with a shovel, and then to leap from the locomotive to the snow. But it is Mr. Jannings's splendid work that causes one to want just a bit more. He lives the character and the most trifling shortcoming makes one wonder at it.

After the chapters in Russia, wherein there is qute a good portrait of the last Czar, the story goes back to the studio.

Evelyn Brent is pleasing as a girl who helps the General. William Powell gives a sterling portrait of a motion picture director and also as one of the ringleaders of the infuriated mob.

Ja 23, 1928

TENDERLOIN, with Dolores Costello, Conrad Nagel, Mitchell Lewis, Georgie Stone, Dan Wollheim, Pat Hartigan, Fred Kelsey, G. Raymond Nye, Dorothy Vernon and Evelyn Pierce, written by Melville Crosman, directed by Michael Curtiz; with vitaphoned episodes; other vitaphone subjects include overture, "Orpheus": "Cugat and His Gigolos"; Adele Rowland; Beniamino Gigli and Giuseppi De Luca; Abe Lyman and his orchestra. At the Warners' Theatre.

By MORDAUNT HALL.

No better illustration of going from the sublime to the ridiculous could be imagined than that afforded at Warners' Theatre last night through the medium of the Vitaphone. After having listened to the silver tones of Beniamino Gigli and Giuseppi DeLuca, one's ear drums were jarred periodically by resounding threats, jeers and protestations in a ruddy melodrama, the first film subject to be presented with any great degree of dialogue. The vitaphone performed its task admirably, for it reproduced faithfully the sounds of the contrasting subjects, and the synchronization of the voices with the lips of the shadows images was excellent.

The first part of this Vitaphone program is as good as anything that has been heard, especially the operatic stars and a violinist. Their efforts aroused genuine applause. Other subjects with dancing and orchestral music also delighted the audience. Messrs. Gigli and De Luca rendered a duet from "The Pearl Fishers." Lighter offerings also won their way to the hearts of those in the packed theatre.

Eventually the curtains parted and the silent screen announced the presentation of "Tenderloin," which is, as one might anticipate, a crook story. It has its shadings, for you go from the muddy puddles of east side streets to silver-sheathed lakes in the country, from dingy hovels to flowered meadows. Then there is also always the entrancing presence of Dolores Costello, who impersonates Rose Shannon, a dancer. Miss Costello's gowns are rather beyond a dancing girl and Michael Curtiz, the director of this film, is determined that beauty shall have its place on the screen. Every possible angle of Miss Costello's face is beheld in the course of this contribution. She is seen in smiles and tears, and eventually there comes a scene where this Rose is persecuted by the artists of the Third Degree. This section of the film is the first that is accompanied by sound, so that after reading the melodramatic phrases in the subtitles, one is startled by the thundering voice of a sleuth trying to make our dainty heroine confess that she stole the bag containing $50,000. The other minions of the law join in brow-beating the girl, who, bless her heart, still sticks to her story, which happens to be the truth.

Chuck, a notorious gangster, who wears well-cut clothes, is at first attracted to Rose by her beauty, but subsequently he learns to love her. All through the story, however, until the exceptionally artificial storm strikes the screen, there is a doubt in Chuck's mind as to whether Rose is not the possessor of the $50,000, which had been taken out of the bag and replaced by poker chips and newspapers. Chuck's colleagues suspect him, and they decide in their own way to make him pay the piper. So one comes to a sequence wherein Rose and the "Professor," a lame, but immensely powerful man, are left alone in a country house. For this episode it was thought that the Vitaphone was necessary and therefore one again hears the blasts from the shadows on the screen.

The "Professor" enters the room, locks the door, puts the key in his pocket, and then looks at Rose, who is in her prettiest negligé with her fair hair showered over her shoulders. The "Professor" thunders that he knows all about women and he virtually tells Rose that it is a case of the money or her life. Not having the money, Rose shrinks with fear, and the "Professor" approaches her with due respect for all the old melodramatic ideas. Rose pleads that if he knows all about women, he ought to let her alone, or something of the sort. It looks black for Rose, but suddenly the door is heard to smash and soon Chuck beats the portal to splinters and leaps to Rose's rescue. Ah, it is not too late!

"I love her," insists Chuck.

Rose tells Chuck that she loves him, it being uttered according to the the most shrieking conception of movie subtitles. The villain chuckles at Chuck and the latter perceiving that this "Professor" is going to do something dangerous with a lamp promptly pulls the trigger of his revolver and for an instant the villain knows that his pursuit of the heroine is off—that he is a bleeding giant cowed by a few inches of cold steel. Suddenly the "Professor" seizes his opportunity and you know that there is something else to come, besides the solving of the mystery as to who took the money out of the bag.

Thunder and lightening help out the dreadful night, and Rose finds it expedient for her to dash from the house and go back to her city room. Then there are further threats, this time from the other gangsters, and Rose changes her mind and decides to return to warn Chuck. The storm tears down trees and the flood makes its appearance. But believe it or not, Rose reaches her hero in time to save him!

Conrad Nagel is hardly suited to the rôle of the gangster, Chuck. It was he, who incidentally did admirably as the hero in Sir James M Barrie's "Quality Street." Mitchel Lewis is capable as the "Professor."

but words such as he has to utter would destroy the value of any acting.

It looks very much as if the title writer had supplied the words for the actors, and it is therefore easy to appreciate the result. At any rate the spectators were moved to loud mirth during the spoken episodes of this lurid film.

Mr 15, 1928

BERLIN, A SYMPHONY OF A BIG CITY, produced by Carl Mayer, Walter Ruttmann and Karl Freund; "The Bridegroom," with Harry Langdon; "The Nightingale." At the Fifth Avenue Playhouse.

"Berlin, A Symphony of a Big City" is an exceptionally clever production in which there are flashes of a variety of activities in a metropolis from dawn one day to dawn the next. It was conceived by Carl Mayer and executed by Karl Freund, the cameraman who was responsible for the remarkable photographic feats in "Variety" and "The Last Laugh." It is much the best picture of his type that has been made, and while it, of course, has no story it is always interesting. As the scenes pass on one realizes the diligent, resourceful and imaginative task in the making of this subject. There is nothing haphazard about it, for the sparks of life are filmed with serious continuity and a keen sense of the artistic.

The first "shot" is that of a slothful body of water at daybreak. From that the producer takes his audience to trains coming from the suburbs, to street cars and buses, and then the empty city streets are depicted. Finally stragglers come along, then an increasing number of people are beheld pursuing their daily goal. The various occupations of the hosts are brought out by crisp scenes of factories, turning out electric light bulbs and other articles.

An excellent episode is that dealing with the luncheon hour. Not only are the shopgirls, the clerks and their employers depicted feeding the inner man, but there are scenes in a zoo, showing that eating is popular on all sides.

Toward evening the picture-makers have shrewdly decided to add to the effect by showing the streets after a gentle rain. The reflections of the lights on the asphalt paving are really beautiful. Gradually the workers are perceived leaving their

80

toil and lights are turned on in houses, hotels and stores. This follows a fair conception of sports on water and land.

Then the theatres are shown and subsequently cabarets, and in the end sleep conquers the life of the metropolis.

Other interesting features at the Fifth Avenue Playhouse include that charming prize color production "The Nightingale," also a Langdon comedy called "The Bridegroom" and a very old Mary Pickford film.

My 14, 1928

THE END OF ST. PETERSBURG, with Alexis Davor, Peter Petrovich, Olga Korjoff, Anna Baranowska, Paul Petroff, Katrina Kaja, Natan Golow, W. Obelensky, Serge Alexandroski and Feodor Varvarow; scenario by Natan Zarchi; directed by Vyesolod Pudovkin; special music score by Herbert Stothart. At Hammerstein's Theatre.

A rich vein of imagination rushes through "The End of St. Petersburg," a Soviet picture presented last night by Arthur Hammerstein at the Hammerstein Theatre. It was directed by Vyesolod Pudovkin, a Russian chemist, who reflects the same genius for camera angles and a selection of types as S. M. Eisenstein, producer of "Potemkin." Mr. Pudovkin has a striking faculty for pictorial expression, and while he may leap from men and machinery to the Stock Exchange and thence to the water-ridden trenches, he succeeds in keeping to the thread of his story.

The narrative is eminently satisfactory Soviet propaganda, for it shows the hardships of the proletariat and the money-mad capitalists. A few of the spectators in the upper reaches of the theatre and those behind the orchestra seats last night applauded the victorious Russian hordes, especially when the Czar's Winter Palace was supposed to be demolished. Mr. Pudovkin evinces a fondness for destructionists, for he appears to bear a grudge against works of art erected by a Czarist administration. He constantly returns in the course of this chronicle to a bronze horse, which he occasionally succeeds in picturing from an angle so that the shadow of the monument is ridiculous.

In the scenes dealing with the man

of money Mr. Pudovkin, in a none too gentle fashion, swings from the comforts of the financier's office to the battle zone, and he also delights in depicting the gamblers on the Stock Exchange, and then, in a fraction of a second, returning to the soldiers wallowing under fire in mud and water.

This picture is interesting because of its peculiarly fine conception of camera flashes. Only a few feet, a very few, are used in some scenes and yet they are filmed so well that they make an indelible impression. The close-ups are exceptionally clever, for not only are the players singularly well suited to the rôle they act but their expressions in the gigantic close-ups are true to the mood.

The story runs from before the World War to the establishment of the Soviet system. It has little to do with the latter, but it attempts to show the reason for the disapproval of Kerensky. This leader is beheld in an immense amphitheatre making one of the magnetic addresses for which he was famous.

In the opening episodes there is a peasant youth, rough, clear-eyed, who comes to St. Petersburg. Before he appreciates what's happening to him he finds himself a strikebreaker. Eventually he is depicted realizing the wrong he has done to his brother workers and he decides to remedy it. He plunges into the office of the factory manager and, to the horror of the other employes, he rains blows on the man. Then, with a secretary fainting, he forges into the inner office of the capitalist, whom he treats in the same way he had the factory manager. The police arrive and the young peasant is locked up, but when war breaks out he is hauled from prison to be a fighter.

Mr. Pudovkin is the producer of a film called "Mother," and Mme. Baranowska, who figures as the peasant's mother in "The End of St. Petersburg," also played in that previous production. Aside from her there are no professional players in this current offering, yet, through the comprehensive direction, the persons who act the different parts are true to life in their actions and expressions. In fact one feels sometimes as though this film were a remarkable news reel of the Russian Revolution.

The cinematic effort is accompanied by a most useful musical score with excellent effects.

My 31, 1928

G. BERNARD SHAW ACTS IN MOVIETONE

In Norfolk Jacket and Knee Breeches He Impersonates Mussolini, With Frown.

THEN HIS ENGAGING SELF

"Happy to Be Here," He Says in Voice Clearly Heard—A Remarkable Achievement by Fox.

GEORGE BERNARD SHAW in a Movietone Feature; also THE RED DANCE, a silent motion picture, with Dolores Del Rio, Charles Farrell, Ivan Linow, Boris Charsky, Dorothy Revier, Andre de Segurola and Dimitri Alexis, directed by Raoul Walsh; other Movietone features include Richard Bonnelli's rendition of the "Prologue" from "Pagliacci" and "The Family Picnic." At the Globe Theatre.

By MORDAUNT HALL.

Under the auspices of William Fox the voice of George Bernard Shaw was heard last night for the first time publicly in this country. It happened through the Movietone at the Globe Theatre and even the celebrated literary light might have enjoyed his own mimicry of Mussolini. There was in it a suggestion of embarrassment, as he sparred with "well, well," and then remembered that when he was saying "good night," there might be occasions when there were afternoon audiences, so he added "good afternoon," and "good luck."

This Shaw talking picture is a remarkable achievement for besides bringing to this country the utterances of the playwright and author, it also brought his actual voice, with his indubitable charm of intonation. It gave the audience an indelible conception of Shaw as he is, with his ever delightful tongue-in-the-cheek manner. He had evidently viewed the Movietone of Mussolini, wherein that Italian Dictator emerged from his palatial domain in Rome with

the tread of a cavalry officer and the bearing of a Napoleon. Mr. Shaw issues forth from an English bush, and, as his shadow becomes more distinct, it is perceived that he was wearing a Norfolk jacket and knee breeches. He looked to be in excellent health, vigorous and ready for a battle of wits.

As Mr. Shaw hesitates about his speech, perhaps just a little awed by the machinery before him, he suddenly strikes a familiar pose of Il Duce, with a frown that causes his eyebrows to make almost a horizontal line with the bridge of his nose. The expression is one that is instantly reminiscent of the pictures of Mussolini. The author of "Plays Pleasant and Unpleasant," "Saint Joan" and many other works then proceeds to explain that while Mussolini invariably appears with a frown, he (Shaw) can throw off the mask of severity and be his engaging self. Here Mr. Shaw raises his eyebrows, opens his eyes wide and appears in a jocular mood, addressing his imaginary audience with evident relish, apparently appreciating that quite a few hundred thousand persons are going to sit watching his Movietone talk.

Mr. Shaw says that he is "very happy to be here," as people who have only read his books and never seen him have fancied that he is a curious individual, whereas they can now see for themselves that he is an affable and pleasant person.

The first Movietone comedy, "The Family Picnic," was then presented, and although the voices were a little loud during some passages, the subject was one that afforded a heap of amusement. It depicts a family going out on a picnic in an automobile and not a little consternation was created last night when it was revealed that after all the trouble of preparing things the all-important food basket had been left on the curbstone outside the dwelling. This meant an abrupt return and a new start on the trip.

Richard Bonelli, the opera singer, in another Movietone subject, is seen and heard rendering the "prologue" from "Pagliacci." With all its splendid vocal quality, this feature is a trifle too loud, rather like a giant singing in stentorian tones.

There are also several Movietone news reel subjects, which give one a conception of the potential possibilities of this device, which not only takes the animated shadow to the four corners of the earth but also the voice.

Following the sound and shadow

entertainment there was presented "The Red Dance," a pictorial drama of Russia, before and after the revolution. There is a good deal of lethargy about the opening chapters of this offering, but interest picks up in the latter passages, those concerned with the overthrow of the Romanoffs and the triumph of the proleteriat. These incidents are pictured entertainingly, with a mingling of satire and burlesque.

The subtitles of this production rather make Tasia, a peasant girl, talk like an educated settlement worker. Nearly all the characters argue too much and there is often hardly the faintest suggestion of peasant parlance, but rather that of the slang or phraseology of America.

Nevertheless, it is quite amusing to perceive that the burly beef-eating giant, Ivan Petroff, played by Ivan Linow, appreciates the humor of the change in the government. He says that it is strange that he is now a General; Tasia, a dancer at the Moscow Theatre, and the village barber a Minister of Education—that is when he can read the appointment.

There are some good scenes in this somewhat wild piece of work, but it is often incoherent. It has evidently been cut before being screened.

Charles Farrell plays the part of a Russian Grand Duke, a personage who is to marry the Princess Varvara. He is quite becoming in his long cloak. A number of the characters usually dodged in Russian film stories are pictured in this chronicle. There are occasional flashes of Rasputin and Trotzky, and the former is held to blame for the conditions of the soldiers. Masses of prisoners are depicted in a queer circular prison and in the latter sequences these captives are liberated.

Je 26, 1928

THE LOVES OF JEANNE NEY, with Edith Jehanne, Brigitte Helm, Hertha von Walter, Uno Henning, Fritz Rasp, A. E. Liche, Eugen Jensen, Hans Jaray and Wladimir Sokoloff; news reel, "The Skating Carnival at St. Moritz," and Chaplin revival, "The Vagabond." At the Cameo.

The scene of Jeanne shifts meekly and without much purpose from the Russia of the so-well-known revolution to the boulevards of Paris. As it goes it takes in fighting, sorrow, happiness and a robbery of sections of the Romanoff crown jewels.

Nevertheless, there are times when the acting of various persons in the cast swings the picture into something more valuable than the story itself can give. There is also a bit of good camera work doing its part to raise the level of the tale.

Edith Jehanne, as Jeanne, runs up against the unfortunate situation of having to face the greater number of impassable barriers, and hence she glides, rather than acts, her way through. At the same time she does not overact—a temptation which under the circumstances might easily be overwhelming.

A. E. Liche, as Jeanne's uncle, gives a good performance. The character he takes is a miserly detective, and the scene in which he is portrayed as counting the money he expects to realize from the sale of a diamond is most able, both as acting and photography.

The rest of the program includes a good hot-weather picture of ice skating, and the old Chaplin picture "The Vagabond."

Jl 10, 1928

THE PASSION OF JOAN OF ARC

By W. L. MIDDLETON.

PARIS.

IN "The Passing of Joan of Arc" M. Carl Dreyer has produced a singularly arresting and original film, which will certainly be much discussed. He presents the heroine in the new realistic manner as an inspired peasant girl, without the gaudy trappings of legend, and the figure he makes of her is no unworthy companion to the stage picture drawn by Bernard Shaw.

M. Dreyer's method is not to embellish or embroider his theme, but to concentrate it within its simplest essentials. He does not elaborate; he intensifies. The story of the film can be told in a few sentences. As its title implies, it has to do only with the final scenes of Joan's life—the trial, the recantation and its withdrawal, the burning in the marketplace at Rouen. We see her before the ecclesiastical judges (with Warwick and the English soldiery in the background), assailed with threats and exhortations, argument and wheedling, all directed to convincing her that her simple but terrific faith is a blasphemous heresy. After this first encounter the girl, back in prison, almost escapes her fate by dying. Another appearance before the tribunal in the cemetery of Saint Ouen and Joan, momentarily shaken, signs her recantation. Immediately afterward, horror-stricken at what she regards as her betrayal of herself, she calls Bishop Cauchon and his fellow-judges to the prison and retracts the confession of guilt which she had made to save her life. She is told that she is to be burned at the stake. Then follows the journey across the crowded market-place and the supreme agony of martyrdom.

Cinematic Art.

This plain story, which goes little beyond the historical facts, is the frame of a poignant picture of suffering. There is no attempt to create the splendor of pageantry. The whole interest is psychological. Mlle. Falconetti, whose miming in "L'Enfant Prodigue" and other pieces has made her well known on the Parisian stage, takes the part of Joan with an artistic sincerity which stands the test of a series of close photographic studies of intense emotional expression. Naively heroic, pathetically girlish, strong as a soldier, wavering humanly under her ordeal, a visionary, she strikes the true note constantly. If Mlle. Falconetti can repeat impersonations on this level cinema-goers will see a great deal more of her. M. Dreyer has made full use of the special advantage of the cinematographic art, which permits a permanent record to be taken slowly, scene by scene, until the parts can be brought together to compose a picture of feeling apparently sustained continuously at the highest pitch.

It is a quality of the film that the spectator retains so many clearly defined memories of faces and figures. There is the admirable study of Bishop Cauchon by M. Sylvain, the doyen of the Comédie Française.

The judges stand out as so many examples of distinct and faithful characterization. Even the crowd is a subject for psychological study; it is scarcely ever seen in the mass, but sections of it pass before us, with individuals clear and conspicuous like sculptures in a Greek frieze. M. Dreyer's method shows that he has the courage of his convictions. He carries simplicity to the extent of having only four sets of stage scenery. A great many effects in the film depend on the movement of buildings relatively to the spectator, so that a castle, apparently descending from the sky, shoots disconcertingly into its place on the solid earth. A striking use is made of the device of photographing persons in the drama from unusual angles. The judges, for instance, are frequently photographed from below, while the marching troops—whose uniforms, by the way, curiously and unnecessarily resemble those of British soldiers in the late European war—are seen from above. Some may think that there are too many of these impressionist flashes, but they seize the attention. M. Dreyer has made an impressive film.

Ag 12, 1928

THE DOCKS OF NEW YORK, with George Bancroft, Betty Compson, Baclanova, Clyde Cook, Mitchell Lewis, Gustav von Seyffertitz, Guy Oliver, May Foster and Lillian Worth; news reel, Paul Ash and the Paramount Stage Orchestra in "Blossoms." At the Paramount.

Nine-tenths of the persons seeing the Paramount's offering this week will like it. Perhaps the most serious objections the other tenth will have are that "The Docks of New York" is a little too long and that it has an anti-climax. The picture as a whole is good, however, with able acting and occasional bits of exceptional directing.

The story, briefly, deals with a stoker who has just one night in town before sailing. He saves a girl who tries to commit suicide, then visits a saloon. Later in the evening the girl whom he has rescued and he discuss love, finally deciding that they may as well get married. The next morning he goes away on his ship; the girl is arrested for stealing. However, the stoker has a fight with his chief, and as the ship passes the waterfront he jumps off and swims ashore. He goes to jail; the girl promises to wait for him.

Were it not for the preposterous ending, "The Docks of New York" would take a higher rank. Had its conclusion been the stoker's leaving in the morning it would have been much better than it is. But the desire for a happy ending has survived.

Josef von Sternberg has directed the play with tact and with an eye to minute details. There are few spots which do not ring true. When the girl jumps into the water the camera catches it all by reflection. She leaps from the pier and a second or so later the splash ruffles the surface of the water.

George Bancroft gives a good performance as a blustering, carefree stoker with but one night on shore. Betty Compson plays the part of Sadie well. Baclanova, of course, is the villainess—or at least as near an approach to it as there is in the picture. Gustav von Seyffertitz has only the small part of Hymn Book Harry.

On the stage Paul Ash glorifies "Blossoms." There are elaborate springtime sets, and such persons as Arthur Ball, the Foster Girls, Sammy Lewis, Patty Moore and George Dewey Washington take part.

S 17, 1928

OUR DANCING DAUGHTERS, with Joan Crawford, John Mack Brown, Dorothy Sebastian, Anita Page, Kathlyn Williams, Nils Asther, Edward Nugent, Dorothy Cummings, Huntly Gordon, Evelyn Hall and Sam de Grasse, written by Josephine Lovett, directed by Harry Beaumont; Fox Movietone News; Van and Schenck via the movietone; "Under the Sea," a stage spectacle, with Walters and Ellis, Mario Naldi and the Chester Hale dancing girls. At the Capitol Theatre.

Hundreds of girls and young women were attracted yesterday to the Capitol Theatre and their presence probably was due chiefly to the title of the film feature, "Our Dancing Daughters," a chronicle concerned with the wild young people of this generation. The Capitol now is equipped for the reproduction of sounds, which fact was only too patent yesterday, for while "Our Dancing Daughters" is not furnished with dialogue, it has a musical accompaniment, several love songs, stentorian cheering and, at the end, a chorus of shrieks.

Whether this audible mixture adds to the entertainment value of the picture is a matter of opinion. It assuredly detracts from the action of the picture in some of the sequences. The romantic melodies that accompany the love-sick looks and the violent embraces of the principal characters are reminiscent of the old-time singing to lantern slides. The enthusiastic cheering impresses one as though the producers wanted to make the most of sound, and the shrieks in the closing scenes come from mute figures to whom terror has suddenly given tongues.

There is nothing startlingly novel about "Our Dancing Daughters," for while there is an undeniable vivacity to many of the scenes, the action is not particularly well portrayed and it is frequently anything but conservative. Cocktails, flasks and mad dancing appear in quite a number of episodes. It is quite unnecessary to depict an intoxicated girl, as is done for considerable length in this film. Presumably it is to point a moral, for the young woman falls to her death down a flight of stairs.

The wide-eyed Joan Crawford, who is attractive in many of the scenes, figures as one of the dancing daughters. After an unusually violent terpsichorean performance, this young woman, known as Diana, suddenly takes an interest in Ben Blain, a stranger to the hectic life but the son and heir of a multi-millionaire.

Harry Beaumont, the director, has among his worthy sequences in this film, one in which the fractious Diana tells her companion, Beatrice, that she is in love. This incident is quite appealing and it caused great glee yesterday afternoon.

But Diana is doomed to be disappointed, for a little blonde, the daughter of a mercenary mother, succeeds in capturing the heart of the peculiarly susceptible Mr. Blain. This fair-haired minx, named Anne, soon leads Mr. Blain to the altar and poor Diana is left to brood over a blighted life. Josephine Lovett, who wrote "Our Dancing Daughters," cannot be accused of much subtlety in ridding Mr. Blain of his tempestuous bride.

John Mack Brown is sympathetic as Mr. Blain. Dorothy Sebastian is appealing as Beatrice. Anita Page gives a fairly good portrayal of her idea of a dancing daughter.

"Under the Sea," an elaborate and effective stage contribution and a movietone of Van and Schenck are among other numbers on the program.

O 8, 1928

An Old Swedish Film.

THE LEGEND OF GOSTA BERLING, with Greta Garbo and Lars Hanson; based on Selma Lagerlof's novel, directed by Mauritz Stiller; "Nature's Wizardry," "Fiddlesticks," an old Harry Langdon comedy. At the Fifth Avenue Playhouse.

It is, to say the least, almost impossible to obtain a clear idea of the hysterical incidents in the old Swedish picturization of Selma Lagerlof's prize novel, "The Legend of Gosta Berling." Sometimes it is reminiscent of "The Scarlet Letter," chiefly because it has a clergyman who is unfrocked, and then of "The Miracle of the Wolves," because it has a few animals supposed to be of the unpopular breed.

There is an endless fire in this film, which gives one little opportunity of gazing upon Greta Garbo, who officiates as Countess Dohna. Miss Garbo, in this film, made several years ago, is striking in her appearance. She has a suggestion of the same languid eyes she now lends to Hollywood productions. While Miss Garbo is anywhere around in this film one is interested in it, even though the whole state of affairs is terribly muddled.

Some people pass out of sight while others appear to change their features. There are huge parties and then when one would like to have a half dozen seconds with a scene, off it goes and on comes something that does not appear even to belong to the same tale.

Lars Hanson acts the part of Gosta Berling. He does it moderately well, but his actions cannot be said to be informative. He might love the Countess and he might not.

There is quite an absurd scene on the ice when the Countess goes forth, one knows not where, but finds Berling. He puts her on his sled and starts in the opposite direction to that which the Countess pretends she wishes to go. But they cannot turn back, for they are followed by wolves. This gives the director, Mauritz Stiller, a chance to flash to the faces of Berling and the Countess, then to the horse's hoofs, then to the ice and then to the wolves and back again.

The really interesting study at the Fifth Avenue Playhouse is the Ufa short film, "Nature's Wizardry."

O 29, 1928

THE SCREEN

By MORDAUNT HALL

New Little Cinema Opens.

TEN DAYS THAT SHOOK THE WORLD, a Soviet production, directed by S. M. Eisenstein, a story of the overthrow of the Kerensky Government; "Queen Elizabeth," with Sarah Bernhardt, the first real feature film; overture, Rachmaninoff "Prelude in C Minor"; "Blackmail," an old Pickford picture. At the Little Carnegie Playhouse.

The Little Carnegie Playhouse, the newest cinema in the Broadway realm, situated a few yards from Carnegie Hall, opened its doors last night to a fashionable audience. Part of this theatre was at one time Roger Wolfe Kahn's Le Perroquet Club de Paris. It has since been enlarged, and the entrance instead of being on Fifty-sixth Street is now on Fifty-seventh.

This elegant small theatre can boast of almost as much lobby as it has auditorium. Its capacity is 409 silver and black seats and the other decorations are also most modern. It believes in satisfying people who come there, for if they are not partial to the screen offerings they can go into one of the small rooms giving off the lobby and there engage in dancing, a game or bridge, a mah-jong contest or even ping-pong. In addition there are cigarettes and coffee. This theatre's carpets are thick, soft and new and the place has quite a Parisian air.

Those who went there last night gathered in the game rooms and in the lobby until past 9 o'clock, when that first old feature picture, "Queen Elizabeth," with Sarah Bernhardt, was screened after a nonsensicality in which Maurice Cass officiated as the "Voice of Bernard Shaw," while Shaw was perceived on the screen in an old film. But the main offering is the Soviet film, "Ten Days

86

That Shook the World," produced by S. M. Eisenstein, director of "Potemkin."

And so to the film. It is clever, but a bore. It is kaleidoscopic, so much so that when months seem to have passed since one saw a man with a flag of truce, you find he is still sitting in the same position awaiting an answer. Mr. Eisenstein is too fond of picking out statues and then giving you the mental activities of a crude-visaged fighting man. He has the wonderful advantage of being able to use hordes of people; the palaces of Petrograd, Moscow or other cities. He need have no fear of the cost. In fact it may be that he has such an abundance of material that he needs almost as much time to picture that with which he is dealing as the events took. He gives one day and it seems a week, even though it may not be actually more than ten minutes.

His masters, the Soviet, being ever wishful of seeing the Bolsheviks get their due in a picture, Mr. Eisenstein does not neglect to show the fight of Right against the Mailed Fist even in the clash with Kerensky. He makes Kerensky a frightfully nervous individual. In fact, he looks more nervous than ill. Mr. Eisenstein gives far too many details in the sweep of events, for in addition to covering an enormous amount of detail he thinks up cinematic angles that add to the mélée. It comes to one, therefore, like a superb nightmare. A little of it would be wonderfully interesting, a little more becomes quite enough. But, as it is shown, there is a great deal too much.

Yet it must be admitted that in the course of the wanderings from queer-looking faces, fixed eyes, women in uniforms, brass heads on great gates, statues with and without harps, one is every now and again confronted with a flash that is fired with imagination, and then on other occasions a bit of photography that is as soft and seductive as a Turner study.

There is crammed into this film enough for half a dozen productions, but most of the episodes are unfinished. Mr. Eisenstein revels in showing the pillaging of Bolshevik troops as they found their hobnailed boots for the first time on the waxed floors of a palace. He gives some striking scenes in a wine cellar, first showing the joy of a woman and some men at finding the bottles, and later the soldiers battering the bottles with the butts of their rifles until they are knee deep in Burgundy, claret, champagne, sauterne and, mayhap, brandy. The search of the

soldiers reveals a photograph of the late Czar, forks, spoons—a heap of silverware.

A few crates of St. George's Crosses come in for rough treatment, as they are scattered about a room. And then there is a title setting forth:

"And this is what we fought for."

Some of the action is a little muddled, but where Eisenstein does masterful work is in those scenes with hundreds and hundreds of people. It really seems as if they were part of the Revolution, as if the scenes belonged to a news reel. The faces look scared and others are grim. There are "shots" looking down upon the Winter Palace that are remarkable in their pace. Eisenstein appears to have a General at his elbow, to give orders that the men know must be obeyed.

This film was originally released abroad under the title of "October."

N 3, 1928

THE SCREEN
By MORDAUNT HALL.

Lillian Gish.

THE WIND, with Lillian Gish, Lars Hanson, Montague Love, Dorothy Cummings, Edward Earle, William Orlamond, Leon Ramon and others, adapted from a story by Dorothy Scarborough, directed by Victor Seastrom; "Jewels," a Mort Harris stage offering, with Walt Roesner, Harry Rose and others; Odette Myrtil in a Metro-Goldwyn-Mayer Movietone feature. At the Capitol Theatre.

Yesterday afternoon's rain was far more interesting than the Capitol Theatre's current screen offering, "The Wind," an adaptation of a story by Dorothy Scarborough. The rain was real, and in spite of the lowering skies there was life and color around you. In the picture, the wind, whether it is a breeze or a cyclone, invariably seems a sham, and Lillian Gish, the stellar light in this new film, frequently poses where the wind is strongest; during one of the early episodes she does her bit to accentuate the artificiality of this tale by wearing the worst kind of hat for a wind.

Victor Seastrom hammers home his points until one longs for just a suggestion of subtlety. The villain's sinister smile appears to last until his dying breath. Mr. Seastrom's wind is like some of the vocal effects in sound pictures, for nobody can deny its power, but it comes in a strict continuity, with seldom the impression of a gust. And instead of getting along with the story, Mr. Seastrom makes his production very tedious by constantly calling attention to the result of the wind. If it were realistic, it would be all very well, but it isn't. Sand and dust are discovered on the bread, on the dishes, on the sheets, and wherever Letty (Miss Gish), a spiritual young Virginian, turns.

In the desert home of Letty's cousin, Beverly, other hard sights greet this young Southern girl. Cora, Beverly's wife, is perceived cutting the heart out of the carcass of a steer, and Mr. Seastrom takes pains that you will be impressed by Letty's nice white hands and the gory fingers of the housewife.

Roddy, the callous scoundrel, pursues the fair Letty in the old-fashioned way. He is the type who would carry out his evil desires if he had to go through fire and brimstone. As a matter of fact, he turns up smiling during a fearful wind, obviously with one purpose in mind. And during the scenes that follow Miss Gish acts in very much the same way she did in the haphazard days of films. She rolls her eyes, stares, twitches, and then notices the revolver placed nicely on a table.

Letty had been told by Cora that her room was preferable to her company, and seeing the fuss made over Letty by Beverly, one is rather tempted to feel more than a slight sympathy for the adamant wife. Letty is driven off to a shack and soon she is married to Lige, impersonated by Lars Hanson. It is during Lige's absence on a round-up that Roddy intrudes upon Letty's loneliness, and this ends in Letty pulling the trigger of a pistol (by accident) and Roddy meeting his doom. There is a fade-out and soon it looks as though Letty were digging a grave in the desert, but it develops that she has already covered up the body—and so there is the idea here that "dead men tell no tales."

In some of the sequences Miss Gish is dainty and charming and she succeeds in giving one the impression of repressed hysteria. Mr. Hanson's acting is excellent throughout. He makes Lige wholesome, but, at times, a trifle too light-hearted. There is the suggestion that he and William Orlamond, as Sourdough, are endeavoring to give a twin performance similar to the work of Ernest Torrence and Tully

Marshall in "The Covered Wagon." The sound effects with this production are not calculated to increase the demand for such ideas. There are a couple of songs which come forth as if they were being sung by somebody behind the screen, and then there is an Airedale which emits a few barks and a howl, and a train conductor who quite nervously ejaculates, " 'Board!' ".

This week being the ninth anniversary of the Capitol, Major Edward Bowes, the managing director, appears in a Movietone subject, talking to the ("Capitol family") and telling them of the good things in store for them. He introduces while a shadow on the screen, Walt Roesner, the master of ceremonies, and then out comes the flesh and blood Mr. Roesner, who looks up at his fourteen-oot shadow and argues with it as to who shall continue the program. Quite clever.

The stage show is glistening and colorful and Harry Rose won laughter and applause.

N 5, 1928

THE SCREEN
By MORDAUNT HALL.

A Picture in Colors.

THE VIKING, with Donald Crisp, Pauline Starke, Le Roy Mason, Anders Randolph, Richard Alexander, Harry Lewis Woods, Albert MacQuarrie, Roy Stewart, Toben Meyer, Claire MacDowell and Julia Swayne Gordon, based on Ottilie A. Liljencrantz's novel, "The Thrall of Lief the Lucky," directed by R. William Neill; "Phipps," a talking film sketch, with Lowell Sherman, Cyril Chadwick and Betty Francisco; Cliff Edwards on the spoken screen. At the Embassy Theatre.

Although the figures often look as if they had stepped out of an opera comique, there is something compelling about "The Viking," an all-Technicolor production launched last evening in the cozy Embassy Theatre. The story is based on Ottilie A. Liljencrantz's novel "The Trail of Lief the Lucky," which concerns the hardy Norsemen who are supposed to have crossed the Atlantic one thousand-odd years ago and landed on this country's soil.

The prismatic effects in this production may not always be the desired quality, especially when it concerns fire and water, but they are none the less agreeable. There is the glint of metal and the flashing of semi-precious stones on the wristbands of the horned or wing helmeted, flaxen-haired warriors of bygone ages. Occasionally there are scenes that are like beautiful paintings, but here and there the colors, while they do not fringe or mix, are not quite true.

The make-up of the players is often more than a trifle overdone, especially when the villain reveals on close inspection his mouse-colored eyelids. Most of the men appear to have had excellent razors and to have been most punctilious even on this auspicious voyage in indulging their fancy for a morning shave.

It will also be remarked by most people who witness this production that for a girl of the North in the year 926 Helga has been most careful regarding her wardrobe. Pauline Starke, who with a long, fair wig impersonates Helga, sees to it that the maid had quite a few changes aboard Lief's little craft. She is perceived in various colors, which come out extremely well, but sometimes her costumes are just a wee bit too reminiscent of the far-famed bathing beauty of 1928. Latterly she appears in a snow-white plain wedding gown, which comes as quite a surprise, for one never for a moment imagines that she is thus prepared for the wedding ceremony, especially considering she is virtually a stowaway aboard the vessel after it slips away from the murderous Eric's stronghold in Greenland. Miss Starke, however, succeeds in looking very attractive and in doing a great deal to call attention to her figure.

Donald Crisp, who played the pugilist in D. W. Griffith's "Broken Blossoms" and who directed Douglas Fairbanks's picture, "Don Q," here figures as the hardy Lief. He does very well with the rôle, especially during some of the sequences aboard his boat. He has a blonde mustache that is carefully curled and which never seems to have a hair out of place. Quite often you expect Mr. Crisp, and also some of the other players, to burst forth into song as they stand face to face in anger or love.

Lief appears to have been somewhat dull-witted for it seems strange that he should have countenanced the presence of Egil, a dark-haired villain, aboard his boat after it turned its nose westward from Greenland. It is this Egil who is always popping up and causing trouble. He fills the slaves and others aboard the vessel with the notion that sooner or later the boat is going to drop over the edge of the world and that they all are going to be devoured by monster dragons.

There is a none too convincing scene of England's cliffs, but who knows but that they were not so white in those days? Greenland's icy mountains have not been omitted, but they look far from real, despite the natural color. This is, however, a picture where lips are red and when the hardy Vikings shed a little blood they let the red gore be seen on their blades.

Anders Randolph, who portrays the axe-throwing Eric the Red, gives a sterling account of himself. His pallid countenance bespeaks the anger that stirs him. Le Roy Mason fills the part of the English nobleman who is captured in his own castle and taken as a slave by the dreaded Vikings.

Three Metro-Goldwyn-Mayer Movietone productions were exhibited before the feature was screened. A playlet called "Phipps," with Cyril Chadwick, Lowell Sherman and Betty Francisco, was amusing in its lines, but the technical end of the production is very poor.

N 29, 1928

THE SCREEN

By MORDAUNT HALL.

Jeanne d'Arc's Trial.

THE PASSION OF JOAN OF ARC, with Maria Falconetti, Maurice Schutz, Ravet, Andre Berley, Antonin Artaud, A. Lurville, Jacques Arnna, Mihalesco, R. Narlay, Henry Maillard, Michel Simon, Jean Ayme. Jean d'Yd, L. Larive, Henry Gaultier, Paul Jorge and others; adapted from a scenario by Joseph Delteil, directed by Carl Dreyer, setting and costumes designed by Jean Victor Hugo and d'Hermann Warm. At the Little Carnegie Playhouse.

By a strikingly original method, in which facial expressions virtually tell the story, Carl Dreyer, a Danish director, has brought to the screen, with a cast from the Comédie Française, a most poignant study of the last eight hours of the life of Jeanne d'Arc. This remarkable example of cinematic work, which was exhibited publicly for the first time in this country last night at the Little Carnegie Playhouse, is called "The Passion of Jeanne d'Arc, the narrative being confined to the dramatic episodes of the trial of the Maid of Orleans and burning her at the stake in Rouen's Place du Vieux Marché.

It is a production of unequaled artistry, for its technique, so different from other films, grows on one until thoughts are only for the story. This series of queer camera angles is admirably suited to this particular subject, but it is questionable whether the same idea would fit in with the demands of other stories. The backgrounds are light in shade, so that the heads and faces of the participants are all the more clear. The effects of these scene designs are exotic but never bizarre.

But in spite of Mr. Dreyer's imaginative camera work and direction, it is the acting of Maria Falconetti as Jeanne that is the paramount feature of this production. It is true that she has been guided by Dreyer's genius, but it is doubtful whether any other actress could have given such an inspired performance. On leaving this little theatre it is not of the scenes or the camera work that one thinks, but of the touching peasant countenance of Mlle. Falconetti, who to play this part suffered her luxuriant hair to be shorn like the felons of old.

Mlle. Falconetti's face as she appears in this picture is at first startling, for she resembles in no way the conception of the Maid of Orleans. She is clad in a man's uniform, one that might be a prisoner's garb. There is a flash that reveals that her ankles are shackled. Her face is brown and there are thin wrinkles on her forehead. She is at first not prepossessing, but as time goes on, her face, due to the faint changes of expression, appeals to one as something far more beautiful than one is accustomed to behold on the screen. Her lips are untouched with rouge. They seem dry, and through these parted lips one observes the whiteness of her teeth. Her nose is straight and small. Her eyes, often welling with tears that seem real, do most of the acting for this production.

Even during the pitiless questioning of Bishop Cauchon and her other inquisitors, this Jeanne d'Arc never tightens the muscles of her face. She is defiant in a pacific manner. When she signs her abjuration she is resigned to life in prison, but soon afterward she repudiates this document and accepts her tragic fate. There is no sign of hysteria at any point of this picture. It is all as if told in hushed tones. The girl herself inspires reverence and pity.

At first she stares at her judges with wonderment. Then as the questioning goes on, tears come from her eyes and roll down her tanned cheeks. She is the personification of faith. She makes admissions: that she beheld the vision of St. Michael and that she expects the salvation of her soul from God. She declares, quietly, one perceives, that she will only wear woman's clothes again when she has fulfilled the mission God gave her.

While these telling scenes are screened, one perceives the wrinkled faces and shorn heads of the priests. Mr. Dreyer focuses his camera so that there are huge heads in the foreground, others smaller, then others still smaller, until the eye catches the face of Jeanne. Sometimes she is in a corner of the screen and the rest is vacant. Mr. Dreyer uses the lines of the garments of the prelates for effect in a subsequent episode. On one side there is the procession of the clergy, and huddled against the wall of the building are several pathetic specimens of humanity. On the other side of the screen in the foreground is the big wheel of a barrow.

Each man's face always appears to be thinking of the trial, of what he is saying.

Jeanne is asked whether this St. Michael she says appeared to her had hair. Her reply is:

"Why not?"

There is Houppevelle, who pitied Jeanne and was sentenced to death. There are d'Estivet and Jean de Maître. On the faces of some of the inquisitors there are expressions that belie their utterances. The lenses used for this production seem to show one the very eyeballs of these brainy, cruel, hard men of 500 years ago who are concentrating to convict one poor girl from the soil.

The production ends with the agony of Jeanne, bound to the stake with blazing faggots around her. Her lips mutter:

"Where shall I be this evening, Father?"

There is Warwick and his band of men, all wearing steel hats curiously like those the Americans wore in the World War. He is ever alert to see that this girl, then 19, shall not escape him, and when death comes to the figure seen through the smoke, one voice shouts: "You have killed a saint!''

Above, the birds are perceived in the sky.

Mr 29, 1929

FRENCH FILM

THE PASSION OF JOAN OF ARC

By MORDAUNT HALL.

FRANCE can well be proud of that great picture, "The Passion of Jeanne d'Arc," for while Carl Dreyer, a Dane, is responsible for the conspicuously fine and imaginative use of the camera, it is the gifted performance of Maria Falconetti as the Maid of Orleans that rises above everything in this artistic achievement. Like the others in the cast, Mlle. Falconetti is a member of the Comédie Française. She, it is true, has been guided with veritable genius by Mr. Dreyer, but as one witnesses her eyes filling with tears or perceives a faint grateful smile crossing her appealing countenance, one feels that it would be difficult indeed to elicit from any other actress such an eloquent interpretation as she gives in this production, which deals only with the trial of Jeanne d'Arc and her terrible fate.

Mlle. Falconetti's portrayal actually reveals that faith that guided the girl knight of France. Her sadness seems very real and sometimes, as a ear courses down her cheek, her eyes widen at hearing something from the aged, erudite men who question her pitilessly. It all happened 500 years ago, but nevertheless as one sits in the Little Carnegie Theatre, gazing upon this remarkable motion picture, one is constantly torn between pity and hate.

The face of this French actress with her closely cropped hair is at first compelling but startling. Her eyes are staring; her lips, untouched by rouge, seem dry and her skin is brown, like that of a girl of the soil. But as the picture continues one finds in the sensitive features something truly magnetic, especially the occasional glance of hope. When the startled eyes fill with tears, this Maid of Orleans permits only the merest suggestion of expression from her features slightly quivering lips. Her expression never tightens a feature, and while she is unswerving in her faith, it is not portrayed by any movement of the jaws, but invariably by the eyes. She is not bitter or vengeful, but she is sure of herself in her replies to her inquisitors.

The Questioning.

This girl is clad in a military uniform, on which not even a button glistens. It is like that of a private who has been neglected. Her boots are clumsy, and as she staggers in to face Bishop Cauchon and the others one notices that her ankles are shackled.

She admits she was born to save France. Not only one question is put to her at a time, but several by different prelates. They come to the vision of St. Michael and ask her for a description of the angel. She is asked whether the apparition had hair and her reply is:

"Why not?"

"Why does she wear men's clothes?" and "Would she like a gown?" She replies that she will wear women's clothes only when she has fulfilled her God-given mission. What does she expect from God? Her answer:

"The salvation of my soul."

She is told that she blasphemes and the aged heads and wrinkled faces shake as some of them mumble "Shame."

"Has God made a promise to you?"

"It is not for you to judge me," says the girl, "lead me before the Pope."

Original Direction.

Mlle. Falconetti is superb during this questioning and Mr. Dreyer darts here and there with his camera, sometimes revealing Jeanne in a corner of the room with the big heads and smaller heads in the foreground. He reminds one of something that is occurring and then flashes elsewhere to other heads. And all this is accomplished without dissolves or fadeouts in such an effective way that no matter what the angle from which the scenes are pictured it is always satisfying and not, as one might suppose, tricky or impressionistic. It is, as a matter of fact, a curious feat, for while the manner in which this film is pictured, with its many close-ups, is so thoroughly suited to this particular subject, it is doubtful whether this screen technique would be as effective for any other story.

Mr. Dreyer makes the most of the long lines of the priest's garments; in the foreground on one side is the wheel of a barrow. There is sycophancy written on one face, on another there is admiration in the eyes, which is however denied by the sneer on the lips. For a second there may be a close-up of a shorn priest who is evidently not at all sure of himself, and then Mr. Dreyer turns his lens on another visage, on which is a contrasting expression.

There are the English soldiers with "tin hats," which are curiously like those the Americans and British wore in the World War.

If exception could be taken at any sequence it is where the English soldiers are perceived tormenting Jeanne, by snatching a ring from her finger, putting a straw crown she had made in prison on her head and by sticking their arrows in her arms. This seems too brutal at this stage of the proceedings for even a callous warrior of that day.

A Wonderful Face.

This picture, which shows Warwick watchful that the girl shall not escape her tragic fate, gives a sane impression of the trial.

The scenes where Jeanne is finally led to the stake in the Place du Vieux Marché, Rouen, are agonizing in their remarkable realism, and this is, of course, one of the reasons that Britain has banned "The Passion of Jeane d'Arc." America benefits where Britain loses, for as a film work of art this takes precedence over anything that has so far been produced. It makes worthy pictures of the past look like tinsel shams. It fills one with such intense admiration that other pictures appear but trivial in comparison.

When one leaves the theatre the face of that peasant girl with all its soulfulness appears to leap from one to another in a throng. Long afterward you think of the tears welling from the eyes, of the faith that seemed to stay any suggestion of irritation. Then comes the return of that scene where the nineteen-year-old girl who saved France is bound to the stake and surrounded by a pile of faggots and as the smoke streaks up birds are seen in the heavens.

Mlle. Falconetti is now appearing in scenes of a picture called "Catacombs," which is also being directed by Mr. Dreyer. In order to meet the demands of the part of Jeanne d'Arc, Miss Falconetti agreed to have her luxuriant hair shorn, and when she is returned to a prison cell, before she repudiates her abjuration, she submits to having part of her hair clipped even shorter.

Bishop Cauchon is acted with marked intelligence and appreciation by M. Sylvain. Others in the cast are Maurice Schutz, Ravet, Andre Berley, Antonin Artaud, A. Lurville, Jacques Arnna, Mihalesco, R. Narlay, Henry Maillard, Michel Simon, Jean Ayme, Jean d'Yd, L. Larive, Henry Gaultier and Paul George. The work of these skilled players is true, restrained and earnest.

"The Passion of Jeanne d'Arc" was filmed in Clamait studio in France. The scenario is based on a book on the Maid of Orleans by

92

Joseph Delteil, who also assisted in the direction. The settings were designed by Jean Victor Hugo and d'Hermann Warm. Mr. Warm is responsible for the weird backgrounds of "The Cabinet of Dr. Caligari."

When this production was first released in Paris the Archbishop asked for a startling number of eliminations, but eventually the film was permitted to be circulated without any exclusions.

Mr 31, 1929

THE SCREEN
By MORDAUNT HALL.

A Vitaphone Operetta.

THE DESERT SONG, a Vitaphone singing and talking production, with Joan Boles, Carlotta King, Louise Fazenda, Johnny Arthur, Edward Martindel, Jack Pratt, Otto Hoffman, Robert E. Guzmab, Marie Wells, John Miljan, Del Elliott and Myrna Loy, based on the operetta, "The Desert Song," directed by Roy Del Ruth. At Warners' Theatre.

With colorful settings, impressive scenes of Riffs ahorse on the undulating sands and some well-recorded singing, the first audible film operatta came to the screen of Warners Theatre last night under the auspices of the Warner Brothers and through the medium of the Vitaphone. It is an interesting experiment but one wherein the story even allowing for the peculiar license necessary for such offerings, lays itself open to chuckles rather than sympathy or concern regarding the events.

The initial scenes promise a good deal, for some of the flashes are in Technicolor. The characters, however, seem to seize upon song at inopportune moments, which fact might be all very well on the stage but it is a weakness in a picture, for it causes sudden fluctuations of moods, of the persons involved, that are conducive to merriment. The characters in this tale of the French and the Riffians are so easily hoodwinked by the individual known as the Red Shadow that it becomes ludicrous, and added to this there are lines of dialogue that cannot be listened to with a straight face.

The comedy offered by a society reported of the Paris newspaper is really of too low an order to fit in with this type of musical offering, even though it did create laughter.

The singing, however, is good, and it would be a great deal better if the theatre reproducing device was tuned down a little, for the vocal tones are invariably far louder than the human voice. This is a shortcoming that can be corrected, and some of the interludes of melody are truly effective. John Boles, who plays the Red Shadow, the masked head of a band of daring Riffians, has a voice that is quite pleasing. Carlotta King as Margot, the French girl who seeks adventure, is rather overwhelming during a number of passages in which she is called upon to sing. There are other agreeable voices and an imposing chorus. It is somewhat disquieting, however, when during a dramatic juncture the Ouled Nail dancing girls and the French officers and the Riffs relieve their feelings in an outburst of song.

In one sequence, General Birbeau is supposed to be so engrossed in his conversation that he does not observe that the whole place is overrun with Riffs. One presumes that a shadow in the doorway would have been seen by this white-haired military leader. But there are none so blind as those who must not see and none so deaf as those who must not hear!

The Red Shadow is the General's son, who poses as somewhat weak-minded when he is unmasked, but so soon as he goes to a wooden trunk and pulls forth (as he does countless times during this yarn) his Red Shadow costume, he becomes an intrepid leader, a man of unflinching courage, a wit who dares to be in love with the bored Margot. One might imagine that Margot would have suspected the Red Shadow and Pierre Birbeau were one and the same person, but she never for an instant reveals that she thinks so. It is with marvelous ease that Pierre pulls the wool over the eyes of all his companions and toward the end he is challenged by his father to a sword duel. Of course, rather than fight with his father, he undergoes temporary disgrace at the hands of his band of Riffs.

The prismatic effects during the Technicolor stretches are beautiful and Roy Del Ruth, the director, has photographed some of these scenes so that the long shadows enhance the sight of Arab figures riding on the wind-swept sands.

Johnny Arthur tries hard to be

funny and sometimes succeeds. Louise Fazenda is his mate in the picture and she endeavors to help along the lighter vein. Edward Martindel is none too military in his bearing as the old general. John Miljan is acceptable as a Captain Fontaine, who is as credulous as the rest of the characters.

"The Desert Song" music is by Sigmund Romberg, while the book is by Oscar Hammerstein 2d, Otto Harbach and Frank Mandel. It is an adaptation of the stage offering that was presented at the Casino Theatre in December, 1926.

My 2, 1929

THE SCREEN
By MORDAUNT HALL.

Dialogue and Color.

ON WITH THE SHOW, with Betty Compson, Arthur Lake, Sally O'Neill, Joe E. Brown, Louise Fazenda, Ethel Waters. William Bakewell, Sam Hardy, Lee Moran, Wheeler Oakman, Harry Gribbon, Thomas Jefferson, the Fairbanks twins, Josephine Houston and others, based on a story by Humphrey Pearson, directed by Alan Crosland. At the Winter Garden.

Those enterprising pioneers of the talking films, the Warner Brothers, who less than three years ago startled the world with their Vitaphone productions and only recently tried their luck with an audible operetta, last night took another forward step by launching at the Winter Garden the first dialogue motion picture in natural colors.

This presentation, known as "On With the Show," is to be felicitated on the beauty of its pastel shades, which were obtained by the Technicolor process, but little praise can be accorded its story or to the raucous voices. The dialogue, so jarring on one's nerves, sometimes comes from cherry-red lips on faces in which the lily and the rose seem to be struggling for supremacy. It is like hearing Eliza Doolittle's argot in "Pygmalion," when she is arrayed in all her Mayfair glory.

Nobody in the course of this picture speaks with anything but harsh notes, and therefore one looks upon the prismatic effects as the heroine of the production, and not the little

blonde, whose hair shimmers like new wheat. One almost imagines the lovely hues writhing in agony at being called upon to decorate such a story. And yet the colors belong to the people and the properties of this yarn.

Some of the utterances cause one to ponder on what might happen if the works of old masters were suddenly gifted with speech. It would have been better if this film had no story and no sound, for it is like a clumsy person arrayed in Fifth Avenue finery.

From the prismatic angle, however, it is immensely interesting and the producers have resourcefully presented scenes in colors which have never before decorated the screen. There are several flashes of an audience in a theatre in which one observes the variety of hues worn by the women and the black and white of the men. The lights are a natural shade, and sequences back stage always keep to a fairly true reflection of colors, especially when it comes to the complexions of the players.

There are amusing moments in the story when the incidents are concerned with what is going on in front of the footlights. But even this comedy is buffoonery that is none too novel. The note of pathos toward the end is pathetic enough in all conscience, but whether one is apt to pity the poor old man who held up the person in the theatre box office and stole the money is a matter of opinion.

Sam Hardy, the manager of the theatrical troupe that is in hard straits, is forced on one occasion to impersonate a butler on the stage. While one might fancy Mr. Hardy stammering a bit over a long sentence, the sight of this individual being unable to say three words without getting his tongue twisted is far from funny.

The narrative is one of the girl who went before the audience and sang when the leading woman rebelled because a goodly sum in salary was owing to her. The heroine impersonates a phantom sweetheart and therefore wears a veil. She is supposed to sing a refrain on the stage.

There are times when other songs are not particularly well synchronized, but as this feature is equipped with color one becomes intrigued by the variety of charming shades at the cost of the actions of the players. It is better to please the eye with reds, greens and other colors than to listen attentively to the squabbling of a group of players who are impersonating fourth-rate theatrical troupers.

The players fit in with the scheme of things, but none of them delivers an outstanding characterization.

My 29, 1929

"Blackmail."
By ERNEST MARSHALL.

LONDON.

Just at the moment British spirits have been raised by the production of the first full-length talking subject made in a British film studio. "Blackmail" is the name of the piece and Alfred Hitchcock is the director. Claim is advanced that "Blackmail" is the "best talk-film yet," and that it will "give a shock to the Americans." As it has yet only been shown privately, to an audience composed of experts, it may not be certain that the public verdict will be in accord with all the eulogies that have been uttered about it. It is announced, however, that the directors of the Gaumont-British circuit of cinemas were so impressed by it that they have booked it for all their houses at a fee running into many thousands of pounds. "Blackmail" is to have its London première early in August at the Capitol.

That "Blackmail" has merits is admitted by all who have seen it, but not all the critics are in agreement as to the degree of its merits. Alfred Hitchcock had already won a high reputation as a master of technique. One writer says that in "Blackmail" he has succeeded "in translating into vocal terms the doctrines of expressionism which the great Germans like Pabst and Lubitsch have exploited in pictorial values." Another critic, while not so enthusiastic, states that the director should be well pleased with his work, "which easily surpasses its forerunners in the peculiar gifts which the sound film is acquiring for itself. From the first Mr. Hitchcock has held firmly to the principles of movement which underlie his craft. 'Blackmail' is a true motion picture and frees us from the idea that the camera must be transfixed and the pictorial flow of the film arrested merely for the pleasure of recording a variety of strange noises." Yet another critic is forced to disclaim any disrespect for the production which he thinks is "the most intelligent compromise between talk and pictures that has yet been found, and, as one would expect from Mr. Hitchcock, it is a blaze of pictorial cleverness and technical skill." It has, however, adds this pundit, "the defects of Mr. Hitchcock's virtues" and "most of the sequences are too long."

Altogether, one gathers the impression that "Blackmail" may possibly not make such a strong appeal to the general public as it deserves to because of its artistic qualities.

Its Vocal Qualities.

"Blackmail" is a crime story, with the "flying squad" of Scotland Yard portrayed in a fashion which will rejoice the heart of Lord Byng. London is the scene of their exploits, and there are glimpses of many of the best known landmarks of the British metropolis. The story begins in a famous West End café, where a girl meets an artist who induces her to go to his studio in Chelsea, with disastrous results, and closes at the British Museum, where the blackmailer only escapes falling into the hands of the pursuing detectives by falling through the celebrated glass dome of that institution.

One feature of "Blackmail" which is especially singled out for approval is that "after the nasal noises imported from America, the English voices are like music." Here, however, comes in the vexed question as to the use of "doubles" for the stars whose pictured presentments are more pleasing than their vocal efforts. The leading feminine rôle in "Blackmail" is played by Miss Anny Ondra, but the voice heard is not hers but that of Miss Joan Barry. Miss Ondra is a Czechoslovakian;

Miss Barry is one of the most promising of the younger school of British actresses. That Miss Ondra was being "doubled" as to the voice by Miss Barry, who does not appear on the screen, was not mentioned at the time of the "trade show" on the program; but that two people contributed to the making of one part was speedily detected. It is suggested that the film requires one "final shot, in which Alfred Hitchcock should be seen introducing Joan Ondra to Anny Barry." It is also asked whether it was Joan or Anny who received the bigger salary, and whether it is fitting that a face should be more remunerative than a voice, or a voice than a face. And also whether the public should be deluded into believing that a pleasing voice necessarily goes with a pleasing face; and half a dozen other similar questions.

Jl 14, 1929

THE SCREEN
By MORDAUNT HALL.

A Negro Talking Picture.

HALLELUJAH, with Daniel L. Haynes, Nina Mae McKinney, William Fountaine, Harry Gray, Fannie Belle De Knight, Everett McGarrity, Victoria Spivey, Milton Dickerson, Robert Couch and Walter Tait, based on a scenario by Wanda Tuchock, directed by King Vidor. At the Embassy Theatre.

That Texan, King Vidor, producer of "The Big Parade" and other outstanding cinematic achievements, is responsible for "Hallelujah," a most impressive audible film with a negro cast. This production was offered last night by Metro-Goldwyn-Mayer at the Embassy Theatre. It has a prosaic beginning, one with negroes picking cotton and chanting "The Suwanne River," but so soon as Mr. Vidor strikes his stride he spins his tale with gradually growing emphasis, until in the closing chapters there is a pursuit through a swampy forest that brings to mind Eugene O'Neil's "Emperor Jones."

Throughout this talking and spasmodically singing study one appreciates that Mr. Vidor knows his subject, and it seems as though he permits some periods to drag just to add strength by contrast to his stirring episodes. Perhaps a few of the passages are a trifle dull, but in portraying the peculiarly typical religious hysteria of the darkies and their gullibility, Mr. Vidor atones for any sloth in preceding scenes.

The humor that issues from "Hallelujah" is natural unto the negro, whether it deals with a hankering after salvation, the dread of water in baptism, the lure of the "come seven, come 'leven" or the belated marital ceremonies. It is brought out with a knowledgeful hand, and in the more serious turns of the subject the same familiarity with the ways of the dusky sons of Ham is revealed.

Although it is a talking venture, Mr. Vidor has not permitted sound to interfere with chances for telling photography, and several of the sequences are set forth with flashes of uplifted hands and magnified shadows. The dying gasp of Chick, the wayward wench, is accomplished by realistic horror.

As for the vocal tones, they are splendid and the dialogue contributed by Ransom Rideout is free from forced phrases or superfluous words. It tells the story succinctly, in most cases, and the actions and expressions of the players are suited to their utterances.

When the story gets under way, Zeke, a fine-looking negro, who has sold his cotton for nearly a hundred dollars, is seen in a dance hall crowded with darkies. Chick, the temptress, employs her feminine wiles and soon Zeke is lured into a dice game with a loudly dressed person known as Hot Shot. Of course Zeke loses his money and there ensues a struggle in which Zeke grabs Hot Shot's revolver and fires point-blank at the crowd. He mortally wounds his own brother, who dies in the cart Zeke drives back to his home.

Why he wasn't punished for this shooting is not explained, but soon this Zeke becomes a rabid preacher, who talks of cannon-ball expresses to hell, while made up as a locomotive driver. The scene where Zeke calls upon a throng of darkies to mend their ways is extraordinarily gripping. Mr. Vidor turns his camera intermittently to Chick, who at first sneers at Zeke but afterward capitulates to salvation until she suffers from religious hysteria.

When Chick returns from the revival meeting to her insalubrious home she finds Hot Shot, who at first endeavors to cajole her to come with him, but Chick won't listen, and then the wild Hot Shot attacks the girl and is met with an unexpected retaliation. When Hot Shot is on the floor, Chick picks up a poker and strikes her antagonist in a frenzied fashion, saying as she does so:

"Ain't no one goin' to stand in my path to glory!"

This onslaught on Hot Shot is exaggerated, so much so that one does not expect to see him again. But Mr. Vidor not only brings him back to the story whole, hearty and impertinent, but keeps him going as a menace until the end.

The audience was much amused by the scenes dealing with the baptism of the darkies, especially the first and second immersions.

These stretches are pictured with thoroughness, with a host of the white-clad hallelujah-raving blacks standing on the side of the water ready to go through the baptism but evidently somewhat fearful of the ducking. Mr. Vidor stresses the hysteria of those who claim salvation, even to showing a woman who confesses after her immersion that she has been a "bad woman."

The religiously inclined Chick is, however, soon as dangerous to Zeke as ever, and he finally succumbs to her peculiar fascination, jilting a girl, as black as coal, for the chocolate-colored Chick, who once again leads him a pretty dance by accepting a proposal to elope with Hot Shot.

Chick, having whispered promises to Hot Shot before Zeke returns home one night, prepares to flee with her loudly dressed amour, who is to return to drive her away in his buggy. She makes fun of Zeke's suspicions regarding having seen a buggy outside his home and then starts to cook food for him. Suddenly Zeke becomes drowsy and the sly Chick chants to him and coaxes his head until Zeke is snoring.

This is all capitally pictured, but even better are those scenes where Zeke gives chase to Hot Shot and Chick, especially the passages following Chick's death, when Zeke grimly pursues Hot Shot through the swamp, proceeding with sure and determined steps, while his quarry dashes excitedly by trees, through water and stumbling, always realizing that the avenger is gaining on him.

Some of the spirituals enhanced the proceedings, and Daniel Haynes, who acts the part of Zeke, sings, among other melodies, Irving Ber-

lin's composition, "The End of the Road." There are other tunes, such as "Swing Low, Sweet Chariot," and "Going Home," that were effectively rendered.

Mr. Haynes does capital work as Zeke. Nina Mae McKinney also gives a clever performance as Chick. William Fountaine makes the most of the rôle of Hot Shot. Harry Gray plays the part of a white-bearded parson.

Ag 21, 1929

THE SCREEN
By MORDAUNT HALL.

Floating Glimpses of Russia.

LIVING RUSSIA OR THE MAN WITH THE CAMERA, a Soviet film conceived and directed by Dziga Vertoff; "When Moscow Laughs," an Amkino comedy, with Anna Sten and others. At the Film Guild Cinema.

Around the clock in a Soviet city is depicted by camera flashes in a film known as "Living Russia or the Man With the Camera," which is now at the Film Guild Cinema. It is much like "Berlin, a Symphony of a Big City," only it hardly matches its German rival in interest, principally because its glimpses are too fleeting. It is a disjointed array of scenes in which the producer, Dziga Vertoff, does not take into consideration the fact that the human eye fixes for a certain space of time that which holds the attention. In the German film there was a suggestion of poetry, but in the Russian offering there is only originality to redeem it. As a matter of fact it becomes quite tedious and the hour that it lasts seems at least an hour and a half.

It is also somewhat confusing. The individual who pops up every now and then with his camera has really little if anything to do with the picture, for what he photographs is not shown. One sees him at work, it is true, but he is no more interesting than a number of other persons in this kaleidoscopic stream.

Another muddled notion is that of beginning the twenty-four hours with the night before, and where the Germans would have pictured a variety of persons partaking of their meals, dancing, or enjoying a theatrical entertainment, this Russian producer contents himself by depicting a throng of persons sitting in a small motion picture theatre. The screen is set and one hopes for some denouement, but it does not come.

There are undoubtedly clever stretches in this picture, which was photographed in Odessa, Kharkov and Kieff. The notion of having everything come to a sudden stop is ingenious, especially when one discovers that the reason is that a motion picture film joiner is pausing at her work. The slow-motion passages of athletes diving, throwing the shot and other physical exercises are well conceived. The wheels of business and industry being set in motion is another laudable phase of this feature. But often one would like to dwell upon some of the doings.

M. Vertoff, however, is in a hurry, and he may show a traffic policeman, and while one is studying his smock, off goes the minion of the law and on comes something else. Glimpses of a poster come on the heels of living persons.

At the end of the day's work the director shows one factory machine after another coming to a stop, and this is followed by the hour or so of recreation.

On the same program is another Russian film called "When Moscow Laughs." It is evidently typical of Russian humor and nothing that is likely to stir an American to any great degree of mirth.

S 17, 1929

THE SCREEN
By MORDAUNT HALL.

Britain's First Talking Film.

BLACKMAIL, with Anny Ondra, Sara Allgood, Donald Calthrop, Charles Paton, John Longden, Cyril Ritchard, Hannah Jones. Harvey Braban and former Detective Sergeant Bishop of Scotland Yards, based on the play of the same name by Charles Bennett, directed by Alfred Hitchcock. "Jazz Time," with Jack Payne's Band; "Odd Numbers," with Gwen Farrar and Billy Mayerl; "In an Old World Garden," with Paul England and Mimi Crawford. At the Selwyn Theatre.

"Blackmail," Britain's first talking picture, which was wildly acclaimed by London critics, is now on view at the Selwyn Theatre. It is a murder story based on a play by Charles Bennett, and in spite of its

many artificial situations and convenient ideas it possesses a dramatic value that holds the attention. It has the advantage of authentic backgrounds, even to an episode for which the British Museum serves as a setting. Its vocal delivery is nicely modulated. The diction of the players is very English but none the less pleasing and suitable to the chronicle. Its continuity is smooth, the narrative being told without any extravagant flourishes, and the performances of the players reveal that two or three of them could do even better work.

The characters impress one as always being far too obedient to the director's iron will. They do the wrong thing to set the story right. An artist who is murdered is more natural in life than any of the other persons. The photography is seldom up to American standards, for the director, Alfred Hitchcock, frequently fails to see that his scenes are adequately lighted and more often than not the images do not stand out as distinctly as they might if more attention had been paid to the shading of the interior walls.

This drama, which the producers describe as a romance of Scotland Yard, tells of a girl named Alice White stabbing to death an artist in defense of her honor. Her sweetheart, a Scotland Yard detective, is assigned to the case. Through finding Miss White's glove in the murdered man's studio, and also because he had seen her the previous night in company with the artist, this sleuth draws his own conclusions. He is eager to shield Miss White, but a blackmailer, impersonated by Donald Calthrop, turns up in the store kept by the girl's father.

This Blackmailer is gifted with the eye of a hawk. The detective and Miss White behave so queerly that if any one had heard of the murder they would at once have suspected the two of knowing something about it. The climax is arranged through silencing the blackmailer's tongue by death.

During the sequence leading up to the killing of the Artist, Miss White is shown to be a chameleon-like type of girl. At first she is reluctant to accompany the Artist to his studio, but subsequently she accepts the invitation. Once there, the Artist mixes a drink and soon the supposedly modest Miss White, who is not in the least affected by the concoction she has imbibed, notices a sort of circus gown hanging over a screen. She is tempted to see how she looks in it and soon is perceived donning the costume behind a screen, while the artist plays the piano. The Artist admires her in the fancy frock and forthwith embraces her, which the girl resents. The artist is not to be discouraged and one perceives the girl's hand come from behind a curtain and snatch up a convenient bread knife.

This stretch has its strong and its weak aspects, but the weak ones predominate, for the girl's character is too vacillating.

The dialogue in this film is frequently so staccato that it reminds one of the speech of Dickens's Alfred Jingle. Three words are uttered and then follows a curious and artificial silence. Then there may be either four or five words with another hushed period. This talking matches the action of the players, for Mr. Hitchcock, to heighten the dramatic effect, often calls upon his actors to move with exasperating slowness.

Anny Ondra, a Czechoslovakian actress who does not speak with any noticeable foreign accent, officiates as Miss White. She has a well-defined personality and does creditable work. The failing in her acting in some scenes is due to the direction. Cyril Ritchard gives a natural performance as the artist. Sara Allgood does well as Mrs. White and so does Charles Paton as the father. Donald Calthrop in most of his scenes is excellent. John Longden does fairly well as the girl's sweetheart.

There are on the surrounding program some interesting British short subjects which are capitally recorded.

O 7, 1929

THE SCREEN
By MORDAUNT HALL.

Russian Symbolism.

ARSENAL, a Soviet production produced by Alexander Dovzhenko; "The Soviet Fliers in America;" "Wine," a Harold Lachman production. At the Film Guild Cinema.

Imaginatively conceived and cleverly photographed though the scenes undoubtedly are in "Arsenal," a Soviet symbolic argument against war which is now holding forth at the Film Guild Cinema, a little of this sort of thing goes a long way.

Before it is half over, it becomes more than slightly wearisome, except possibly to those who have spent part of their lives in Russia. Yesterday afternoon the little theatre was filled with Bolshevist sympathizers, who applauded loudly references to "a worker" and also sequences satirizing the Ukrainian bourgeois.

This picture, a silent one, of course, is presumed to deal in a more or less vague way with the struggle in the Ukraine between the Bolsheviki and Petlura's forces, but it has no real drama as it makes no pretense of telling a story. It is a sketch penciled by the director and there are patches which only those concerned in the making of this production could explain.

So far as the dead are concerned, little is left to the imagination. The director revels in calling attention to a lifeless soldier with a grin on his countenance and on several occasions he swings his camera on the physiognomy of a supposedly dead soldier, calling special attention to the man's glazed eyes. These glimpses of victims of war strike one as being far too real to show on a screen in a place where one hopes to find entertainment.

In an early episode there is an old woman who is forced to stagger over the ground, sowing the soil with seeds. She drops exhausted and then the director, who is Alexander Dovzhenko, turns to a scene of a man in uniform, evidently intended to resemble the late Czar, who is in the throes of writing a letter announcing that he has killed a crow.

These are some excellent examples of camera angles, but at the same time M. Dovzhenko tries too often to make his scenes on a slant for effect, possibly to show the "cockeyed" state of the world in that quarter.

M. Dovzhenko, himself an Ukrainian, pokes fun at the bourgeois of his own locality and in one episode depicts the cowardice of the bourgeois and the courage of a worker, by portraying the former afraid to pull the trigger of a pistol on a proletarian and then showing the proletarian snatching the weapon from the bourgeois and killing him. This part of the offering is shrewdly done, for the bourgeois is made to appear so dazed that he does not know that the pistol has been taken from him, and with an empty hand he makes a motion of pulling a trigger with his forefinger.

In the last passage the Man, who goes through the horrors and deprivations of war, is to be shot as a deserter. The soldiers fire without effect and then the Man, a symbol of bolshevism, bares his chest and declares that "there is something there that bullets cannot kill."

It is a film that defies criticism in many respects, for if one writes that the actions of some of the participants are woefully exaggerated, the director would naturally argue that it is symbolism. At the same time, although one is impelled to be in thorough sympathy with its argument against war, one cannot but help feeling that one-fourth of the footage of this production would be ample for one sitting.

N 11, 1929

"Storm Over Asia"

By MORRIS GILBERT.

PARIS.

The critics hailed Poudovkine, director of "Tempête sur l'Asie," as a new genius who has discovered how to reproduce the most exact "rhythm of life" out of an apparent confusion and disorder. The result is contrasted with the "routine American presentations," to the considerable detriment of the latter. More conservative eyes draw a different conclusion. To them it seems, without making any comparisons, that Poudovkine has merely touched the edge of an excellent cinematographic idea and has somehow let it escape without ever quite getting hold of the vital drama which is concealed somewhere at the centre.

"Tempête sur l'Asie" does serve, however, to present to Western eyes an actor of unmistakable talent and power, Inkijinoff, a Tartar Valentino, as it seems. Young, striking in appearance, playing with much restraint, he is able to portray a character, originally of utmost primitive simplicity but growing when thrust into a foreign world, to a complexity and force which, apparently, only the construction of the picture limits. If one piece of work can be taken as a test, Inkijinoff has a bright future.

The story deals with a coup d'état of a foot-loose Russian General cast adrift by the revolutionary muddle of 1918 and wandering with his troops over the face of Asia. He turns up in Mongolia, with the intention of making himself ruler there, and seeks to further his plan by setting up a peasant lad reputed to be a descendant of the great Ghengis Khan as a native Emperor. The young peasant, Timour, played by Inkijinoff, is docile and considerably bewildered by these events. But when a last atrocity is committed before his eyes Timour runs amuck, stirs up the peasantry and starts to sweep Petroff away. This development, broached only in the last five minutes of the picture, is actually accomplished by a frightful windstorm, which overthrows Petroff, his horses and his men, while Timour and his Mongolians ride before the storm, in brief, confused, "modernistic" flashes.

The character of Timour, as Inkijinoff first pictures him, is strangely likable. He is first discovered in his father's wattled tent on the bleak Manchurian plains starting off for the annual fur market, his father being ill, with the family's most valuable possession, a silver fox fur. The sale of this fur for a proper price—put at 500 taels—would insure a year's comfort for Timour's people, but it is not to be. A thieving fur dealer seizes the fox, Timour runs foul of Petroff's guards in trying to recapture it and takes to the mountains.

There he joins a band of guerrillas and is eventually captured by Petroff's men. He is ordered shot, and the command is carried out. But the bullet is not fatal, and when Petroff discovers among Timour's effects a talisman indicating that the lad is of the blood of the ancient conquerors he orders the young peasant salvaged. Timour convalesces. Presently, growing accustomed to his new position as a cherished hostage, a means of holding the country for Petroff, Timour perceives his silver fur about the neck of the General's daughter. The thieving dealer has given it to her. The discovery helps to bring about the climax which actually occurs when Timour finds a young Mongolian about to undergo execution.

Inkijinoff succeeds in imparting a quiet and simple steadfastness to the rôle of Timour. His stubborn peasant refusal to sell the fur cheap is skillfully filmed. His willingness to join any comrades in the work at hand and his trustfulness of others make several brilliant passages. Notable is the sequence in which a corporal of Petroff's army takes Timour out to shoot him. The youth has no knowledge of what is before him, and strides along, his arms bound, but with a happy faith in the corporal, whom he takes for a friend. At the last, the corporal agonizingly orders Timour to turn his back, as one would order a friendly, eager puppy to go home, and fires. It is a poignant scene.

The next time Timour appears on the screen he is convalescing. But something else has happened to him besides his wounds. He has grown suspicious. His whole character has deepened, as shown by the capable Inkijinoff. The General's daughter offers him a drink of water. He takes the glass and holds it until his visitors leave the room. Then, though sick with thirst, he pours the water on the floor.

Out of minor episodes such as that Poudovkine has built a picture sometimes very gripping, sometimes merely distraught. A minor character, a brigand chief, is finely conceived. There are a number of excellent battle passages, and the wild Asian landscape is beautifully photographed.

There are indications that the producers have sought to render a true reproduction of manners, customs and mood of the land where their story is laid. One remarkable sequence shows the ceremonious reincarnation of a Grand Llama, with devil horns, clappers, bells, curious head dresses and religious dances featured.

In his declared purpose of abandoning "outworn" forms, the producer has only partially succeeded. The effect as a whole is disjointed and a little clumsy. At the start the picture is far too sluggish, and the entire later development of the plot is crowded into the last few minutes of the action. But it is creating a furor here.

N 17, 1929

A New Dimension: Sound

Sound arrived with shocking suddenness, throwing the whole movie industry into total disarray. The event that established sound in the history of the cinema, was the première of *The Jazz Singer* in 1927, with synchronous music, dialogue, and sound effects. The tremendous impact of the new invention on both the world of business and entertainment is not appropriately echoed in the reviews of the time. There were some good reasons for this lack of response. The first sound films were of no artistic consequence. Compared with the richness, beauty and, technical perfection of the late silents, the first sound film productions were clumsy, stiff, and self-conscious, obviously inhibited by technical problems. (It should not be forgotten that one of the supreme accomplishments of the silent era was Carl-Theodor Dreyer's *The Passion of Joan of Arc*, in 1928). The consequences of the introduction of sound were incalculable. All the studios and, as fast as possible, all the movie theatres had to install sound equipment at enormous cost. Countless actors and actresses who had been successful in the silent movies did not have the required voice quality or speaking ability and lost their jobs overnight. The international exchange of performers from different countries encountered insurmountable language barriers. Instead of merely photogenic people of the right type, well-trained actors were lured to Hollywood, causing a shortage in the theatres. There was also a great demand for stage plays that could be adapted to the screen as well as for writers who could write screen plays with dialogue. Editing for sound turned out to be much less flexible than editing for visual emphasis, and it took some time until the effectiveness of planned silence was discovered. The once all-powerful image was reduced to a functional background for the spoken word. The marvelous fluidity of silent shooting and editing was sacrificed to technical exigencies. The camera, encased in a soundproof cabin, was virtually stationary, as were the performers who had to keep within the limited range and direction of the microphones.

The new situation required not only sound experts but also directors of vision and imagination in order to control the complexities of the recalcitrant invention and put it to creative use. To begin with, the excessive demand for "100 percent all-talking" pictures had to be reduced to reasonable proportions, although the uncinematic practice of the photographed stage play survived tenaciously, and is with us even today.

101

For the sound film was neither a silent film with sound added nor a spoken play with images added, but an entirely new species whose particular language had yet to be developed and refined. So long as the spoken word dominated the action, it was almost inevitably at the expense of the visual autonomy; the images became merely illustrations or, at best, elaborations of the words. There were, of course, also music and natural sound (and, much later, synthetic sound) to vary and color the range of aural effects and to create a fuller sound orchestration. But in spite of the producers' and directors' ingenuity, the ultimate development of the sound dimension depended decisively on technical advances. Within a short time, new camera designs allowed for greater mobility; new, highly sensitive, directional microphones liberated the actors from the shackles of the sound equipment; most importantly, the technique of postsynchronization made the performance independent of synchronous, on-the-spot recording. Thus the sound film slowly regained some of the lost virtues of the silents. With modern dubbing techniques, the speaking or singing voice or any sound effect whatever could be afterwards inserted wherever needed. It had again become possible to shoot films with a cosmopolitan cast. On the other hand, though, many films derived authentic effects from the deliberate use of the language of their origin.

The natural genre to triumph in the world of sound was the Broadway musical, easily transplanted onto the sound stage, much elaborated and magnified in the process. Over the years, the supermusical became one of the unequaled specialties of Hollywood, although the more sophisticated, personal style of Fred Astaire's dance musicals competed successfully with the overblown decorativeness of the Broadway adaptations. It was a bad period for the once popular silent comedians and a great time for such vaudeville-trained comics as the Marx Brothers and W. C. Fields. Chaplin, virtually alone, made the transition not only without break or diminution of his established character but actually with increased stature. The prevailing problem throughout this time was still the dominance of the literary model, based on the mistaken belief that a good novel or play would automatically make a good film. It is true that the thirties progressively perfected new ways of using sound, music, and the spoken word. Yet, in spite of the phenomenal studio activity, some fine films, the contributions of some great directors, and the refinement of the technique the decade represents a period of transition rather than of consolidation.

A FRAGMENT OF AN EMPIRE, with Yacov Goodkin, Feodor Nikitkin Ludmila Semenova and Valery Solovtzev, written by L. Vinogradsky and F. Ermler, directed by M. Ermler; "Springtime," a Disney cartoon; "Barbers' College," a Pathe comedy. At the Cameo.

In "A Fragment of an Empire," the Soviet producer, Frederick Ermler, gives a vivid conception of a shell-shocked Russian soldier who regains his mental equilibrium some time after the Bolsheviki dispatched the Romanoffs and turned St. Petersburg into Leningrad. ·

In certain respects this film is a trifle sketchy, but it is nevertheless impressive and imaginative. It is grim, sometimes unnecessarily morbid, for in the initial sequence there are scores of dead bodies being loaded on a train. One of them moves. The man is alive, and he becomes one of the characters in the tale that is unfurled in a heliographic fashion.

The fragment of the empire is a harsh, cruel person, who happens to have married the shell-shocked soldier's wife, she thinking she was a widow at the time. The motion picture, a silent one, winds up with a caption setting forth:

"We have still much work to do, comrades."

Judging by the story, a part of this work is the eradicating of such men as the unsavory specimen in this film. Very cleverly has the director solved the way in which Sergeant Filimonov becomes rational. Before going to war he had worked with machines in a factory as a hosier and it is the whirring sound of a sewing machine that gradually mends his mind. This is capitally pictured, as is also a later passage in which the sergeant is told of the new master. These flashes dart from factory to factory, to offices and even to the ships on sea, showing that the worker is the master.

When this Sergeant Filimonov reaches Russia's capital, he wonders at the changes. Familiar statues have disappeared. Nothing is the same. He finds his old employer, who explains matters to some extent and tells him to go to the Fabcom, the factory committee. The sergeant, dazed and bewildered, asks for Mr. Fabcom, and even long afterward he imagines that the individual who is considerate and kind to him is Mr. Fabcom. This young man, now highly successful, is, incidentally, the one who was found alive among the dead.

The sergeant has an unkempt beard. He needs a bath, and in the brief space allotted to his ablutions there is reflected the relief of the man. His head and face are a mass of white soap lather. It looks funny, but soon it is anything but comic, for after the preliminary flash, it is real. How he is enjoying the bath!

Perhaps the director is a trifle too severe with his "fragment," for this man, who is an educational teacher, seems to overstep the mark of truth. He is too hard with his wife, having her attend to him like a valet and then, when he teaches his class, with a microphone before him so that unseen pupils can profit by his knowledge, he refers to the necessity of kindness toward wives. It rather looks as if the producer was taking a poke at Trotsky, for this individual, while heavier, often has an expression similar to the former Bolshevik War Commissioner.

Feodor Nikitin gives a remarkable portrayal of the shell-shocked soldier. Yacov Goodkin is capital as the soldier saved from a frightful death. Valery Solovtzev makes the instructor thoroughly disagreeable. M. H.

Ja 27, 1930

HAPPY DAYS, with Janet Gaynor, Will Rogers, Charles Farrell, Warner Baxter, Victor McLaglen, Edmund Lowe, Frank Albertson, El Brendel, Walter Catlett, William Collier, Dixie Lee, Sharon Lynn, George MacFarlane, J. Harold Murray, Paul Page, Tom Patricola, Ann Pennington, Frank Richardson, David Rollins, Marjorie White, "Whispering" Jack Smith, James J. Corbett, Richard Keene, George Olsen and others, based on a story by Sidney Lanfield and Edwin Burke, directed by Benjamin Stoloff; "Niagara Falls," a Grandeur scenic; "Rhapsody," with Von Grona and the Roxy ballet corps; Movietone News; "La Grande Jardiniere," with Beatrice Belkin, Patricia Bowman and others. At the Roxy Theatre.

By MORDAUNT HALL.

William Fox's first Grandeur audible picture to have had the studio advantages of special settings and illumination is now at the Roxy, which, besides being the largest cinema theatre in the world, can for the time being also boast of having the largest screen ever constructed. It is 42 feet wide and 20 feet high, the standard screen of this house being 24 by 18 feet. The single Grandeur film frame is twice that of the standard picture and a trifle higher. An additional advantage of the Grandeur film is that it permits the sound track to be three times as wide as that of the standard film. This increased space results in the voices being more modulated and in the incidental sounds being more natural.

This enlarged picture is called "Happy Days," most of it being a minstrel show with a host of the Fox stars and feature players.

Full opportunity is taken of the imposing screen in the matter of enormous stage settings and large groups of players, but while this production is enlightening concerning the benefits of the Grandeur film, it is not one that gives as full a conception of the possibilities as future films of this type will probably do. That is to say, those offerings on the same scale with a definite dramatic story accompanied by indoor and out-of-doors scenes will perhaps prove still more impressive than the actions of players in a minstrel show with a haphazard undercurrent narrative. Also at the first showing about noon yesterday the device behind the screen for reproducing the sound was not always arranged so that the voices came directly from the person whose lips were moving. This, it is true, was only apparent in semi-close-up "shots," and doubtless this theatre reproduction fault will be corrected. On the other hand, this Grandeur film has the attribute of permitting from three to half a dozen persons to appear, in the foreground, quite large enough to carry out the dialogue, without flashing to one person while the others are left off the screen, as is done in the ordinary films.

"Happy Days" may not be highly exciting, but through the medium of its presentation it affords a really good and impressive entertainment, which at a second showing to a packed theatre yesterday afternoon was roundly applauded. There are songs from several of the Fox favorites, including J. Harold Murray, Victor McLaglen, George MacFarlane, Frank Richardson, "Whispering" Jack Smith, Marjorie White, Dixie Lee and others.

An amusing number is one contributed by Mr. McLaglen and Mr. Lowe in which the former goes his partner in the vicissitudes of pictorial stories one better by singing while Mr. Lowe contents himself with reciting. They tell what good friends they really are in spite of their animosity in other films. Judging by what happens, this assertion can be taken with a grain of salt.

This Grandeur film is not only imaginatively staged but beautifully photographed. When one of the minstrels is called upon to do his stunt, the burnt cork suddenly vanishes from his face and his physiognomy is white.

In one of the features a bevy of dancing girls suddenly appears from two huge shoes. In another there is a giant baby carriage with about a dozen crying infants, and in a third a wedding cake that makes the players look like Lilliputians. James J. Corbett comes forth as one of the victims of interlocutors, and Charles Farrell and Janet Gaynor chant a melody as they put a tiny house together.

Will Rogers, Walter Catlett and William Collier contribute to the fund of gayety, and Ann Pennington delights with an exhibition of the light fantastic.

All the scenes in sweeping nearly across a proscenium such as the Roxy's are wonderfully effective, for through the increased stature of the characters portrayed it makes this stage seem no larger than that of an ordinary theatre. Giant shadows are performing, but through the comparative size of everything they do not strike one as being too big, not even when they are drawn into a semi-close-up.

In some of the early scenes there are exterior views which are also striking.

The story deals with the energetic and comic efforts of Marjorie White to help Colonel Billy Batcher, the reigning genius of the "Mammoth Minstrels," who is stranded somewhere along the Mississippi. Miss White is an enterprising little person who enlists the support of the players mentioned to give a benefit performance in Memphis for Colonel Batcher. Part of the time Miss White finds it necessary to masquerade as a page boy in the Screen and Stage Club, but one day through gruff treatment, her long hair betrays her sex and then everybody is eager to dash to Memphis to aid Billy Batcher. And so there is the special minstrel show on the screen in Grandeur form.

F 14, 1930

THE SCREEN
By MORDAUNT HALL.

Miss Garbo's First Talker.

ANNA CHRISTIE, with Greta Garbo, Charles Bickford, George F. Marion, Marie Dressler, James T. Mack and Lee Phelps, based on Eugene O'Neill's drama, directed by Clarence Brown; "Zip! Zip!" a stage contribution arranged by Arthur Knorr, with Danzi Goodall, Lillian Shade, the Royal Philipino Orchestra, the Chester Hale dancers and others. At the Capitol.

In her first talking picture, an adaptation of Eugene O'Neill's "Anna Christie," the immensely popular Greta Garbo is even more interesting through being heard than she was in her mute portrayals. She reveals no nervousness before the microphone and her careful interpretation of Anna can scarcely be disputed. She is of the same nationality as Anna is supposed to be and she brings Anna to life all the more impressively through her foreign accent being natural, because it is something for which she does not have to strive.

Miss Garbo's voice from the screen is deep toned, somewhat deeper than when one hears her in real life. The low enunciation of her initial lines, with a packed theatre waiting expectantly to hear her first utterance, came somewhat as a surprise yesterday afternoon in the Capitol, for her delivery is almost masculine. And although the low-toned voice is not what is expected from the alluring actress, one becomes accustomed to it, for it is a voice undeniably suited to the unfortunate Anna.

Uunlike most of the film actresses in their débuts in talking films, Miss Garbo suits her actions to the words. She thinks about what she is saying and accompanies the lines with suitable gestures and expressions. There is no hesitancy in her speech, for she evidently memorized her lines thoroughly before going before the camera, and not in a single instance does she seem to be thinking about what she must say next, which has been the case in the first audible efforts of many of the male and female performers.

In her opening scene she enters the "ladies' entrance" of a wharf saloon in New York. Marthe, her father's mistress, a drink-sodden creature well on in years, is seated at a table endeavoring to satisfy an almost unquenchable thirst with a large glass of ale and lager. Marthe quickly realizes that the girl, who orders whisky and lights a cigarette, is Chris's daughter, from whom he had just received a letter. Chris knows nothing of his daughter's crimson career, and at that moment he has gone to eat soup and drink coffee to sober up for the meeting with the girl, whom he has not seen since she was 5 years old.

"You're me, forty years from now," says Anna to Marthe. The older woman lets the girl know that Chris believes his Anna to be an example of purity. When Chris, played by George Marion, who figured in the same rôle on the stage and in the excellent silent pictorial version of several years ago, enters the bar section of the saloon, he is heard and Marthe decides to go and collect her belongings from Chris's barge and make herself scarce.

Marie Dressler, who plays Marthe, may overact occasionally, but most of her performance is exceptionally clever. She, with all Marthe's bibulous nature, elicits sympathy for the dissolute woman and often she relieves the sordid atmosphere with effective comedy. Miss Dressler has done good work in audible screen offerings, but her speech, expressions and her general gesticulations make this far and away her outstanding film characterization.

The nervous Chris is told that the girl he was expecting is in the room set apart for women. He enters and gazes upon the daughter he has not seen for fifteen years. After the preliminary greeting and explanations, he says that he thinks that it is a suitable occasion to be celebrated with a glass of port. So the girl who had imbibed spirits sips the glass of wine and subsequently is seen living on her father's coal barge.

Clarence Brown, who has directed a number of Miss Garbo's silent films, is also responsible for this audible picture. He depicts with marked ability the girl and the father renewing relations, without the old man ever suspecting his daughter's wayward life in the middle West. Then Matt, the stoker, is washed up with others on a stormy sea and Chris resents this man's attentions to his daughter. Matt, impersonated by Charles Bickford, is a powerful physical specimen of humanity, who scoffs at Chris's interference. He falls in love with Anna, and during one interlude they are seen at Coney Island, where Matt has an opportunity of demonstrating his strength and his prodigious lung-power.

The reproduction of the voices was often much too loud yesterday afternoon, but the scenes of the altercation between Chris and Matt and those wherein Anna confesses to her florid past are a compliment to the screen, for these players make the most of their respective opportunities, especially Miss Garbo. Anna's scorching tirade against her father and her revelations of her scarlet days are delivered in a highly dramatic fashion. Matt's disappointment, his eventual return and his satisfaction in knowing that Anna had at least never loved any other man but himself are equally satisfying.

Mr. Bickford succeeds splendidly with his portrayal of Matt. Mr. Marion's familiarity with the rôle does not diminish the importance of his present interpretation of the man who shakes his fist at that "Ole Devil Sea."

Mr 15, 1930

ALL QUIET ON THE WESTERN FRONT, with Louis Wolheim, Lewis Ayres, John Wray, Raymona Griffith. George Summerville, Russell Gleason, William Bakewell, Scott Kolk, Walter Browne Rogers, Ben Alexander, Owen Davis Jr., Beryl Mercer, Edwin Maxwell, Marion Clayton, Richard Alexander, Pat Collins, Yola D'Avril, Arnold Lucy, Bill Irving, Renee Damonde, Poupee Andriot, Edmund Breese, Heinie Conklin, Bertha Mann, Bodil Rosing, Joan Marsh and others, based on Erich Maria Remarque's book, directed by Lewis Milestone, with dialogue by Maxwell Anderson and George Abbott. At the Central Theatre.

From the pages of Erich Maria Remarque's widely read book of young Germany in the World War, "All Quiet on the Western Front," Carl Laemmle's Universal Pictures Corporation has produced a trenchant and imaginative audible picture, in which the producers adhere with remarkable fidelity to the spirit and events of the original stirring novel. It was presented last night at the Central Theatre before an audience that most of the time was held to silence by its realistic scenes. It is a notable achievement, sincere and earnest, with glimpses that are vivid and graphic. Like the original, it does not mince matters concerning the horrors of battle. It is a vocalized screen offering that is pulsating and harrowing, one in which the fighting flashes are photographed in an amazingly effective fashion.

Lewis Milestone, who has several good films to his credit, was entrusted with the direction of this production. And Mr. Laemmle had the foresight to employ those well-known playwrights, George Abbott and Maxwell Anderson, to make the adaptation and write the dialogue. Some of the scenes are not a little too long, and one might also say that a few members of the cast are not Teutonic in appearance; but this means but little when one considers the picture as a whole, for wherever possible, Mr. Milestone has used his fecund imagination, still clinging loyally to the incidents of the book. In fact, one is just as gripped by witnessing the picture as one was by reading the printed pages, and in most instances it seems as though the very impressions written in ink by Herr Remarque had become animated on the screen.

In nearly all the sequences, fulsomeness is avoided. Truth comes to the fore, when the young soldiers are elated at the idea of joining up, when they are disillusioned, when they are hungry, when they are killing rats in a dugout, when they are shaken with fear and when they, or one of them, becomes fed up with the conception of war held by the elderly man back home.

Often the scenes are of such excellence that if they were not audible one might believe that they were actual motion pictures of activities behind the lines, in the trenches and in No Man's Land. It is an expansive production with views that never appear to be cramped. In looking at a dugout one readily imagines a long line of such earthy abodes. When shells demolish these underground quarters, the shrieks of fear, coupled with the rat-tat-tat of machine guns, the bang-ziz of the trench mortars and the whining of the shells, it tells the story of the terrors of fighting better than anything so far has done in animated photography coupled with the microphone.

There are heartrending glimpses in a hospital, where one youngster has had his leg amputated and still believes that he has a pain in his toes. Just as he complains of his, he remembers another soldier who had complained of the same pain in the identical words. He then realizes what has happened to him, and he shrieks and cries out that he does not want to go through life a cripple. There is the death room from which nobody is said to come out, and Paul, admirably acted by Lewis Ayres, is taken to this chamber shouting, as he is wheeled away, that he will come back. And he does. The agony in this hospital reflects that of the details given by Herr Remarque.

In an early sequence there is the introduction of the tyrant corporal, Himmelstoss, who has no end of ideas to keep young soldiers on the alert, sometimes amusing himself by making them crawl under tables and then, during the day, ordering them to fall on their faces in the mud. Just as by reading the book, one learns, while looking at this animated work, to hate Himmelstoss. And one occasion when the audience broke their wrapt stillness last night was with an outburst of laughter. This happened when Paul and his comrades lay in wait for the detested non-commissioned officer, and, after thrashing him, left him in a stagnant pool with a sack tied over his head.

Soldiers are perceived being taken like cattle to the firing line and then having to wait for food. There is the cook, who finds that he has enough rations for twice the number of the men left in the company, and when he hears that many have been killed and others wounded he still insists that these soldiers will only receive their ordinary rations. Here that amiable war veteran, Katczinsky, splendidly acted by Louis Wolheim, grabs the culinary expert by the throat and finally a sergeant intervenes and instructs the cook to give the company the full rations intended for the survivors and those who have either died or been wounded.

Now and again songs are heard, genuine melody that comes from the soldiers, and as time goes on Paul and his comrades begin to look upon the warfare with the same philosophic demeanor that Katczinsky reveals. But when the big guns begin to boom there are further terrors for the soldiers and in one of these Paul has his encounter with a Frenchman in a shell hole. Paul stabs the Frenchman to death and as he observes life ebbing from the man with whom he had struggled, he fetches water from the bottom of the shell hole and moistens the Frenchman's lips. It is to Paul a frightening and nerve-racking experience, especially when he eventually pulls from a pocket a photograph of the wife and child of the man he had slain.

Raymond Griffith, the erstwhile comedian who, years before acting in film comedies, lost his voice through shrieking in a stage melodrama, gives a marvelous performance as the dying Frenchman. It may be a little too long for one's peace of mind, but this does not detract from Mr. Griffith's sterling portrayal.

Another comedian, none other than George (Slim) Summerville, also distinguishes himself in a light but very telling rôle, that of Tjaden. It is he who talks about the Kaiser and himself both having no reason to go to war—the only difference, according to the soldier in the trenches, being that the Kaiser is at home. It is Tjaden who is left behind when the youngsters swim over to the farmhouse and visit the French girls.

Much has been made of the pair of boots and the soldier who wanted them and declared, when he got them from the man who passed on, that they would make fighting almost agreeable for anybody. Mr. Milestone has done wonders with this passage, showing the boots on the man and soon depicting that while they may have been comfortable and watertight, boots don't matter much when a shell with a man's name written on it comes his way.

The episodes are unfolded with excellent continuity and one of the outstanding ones is where Paul goes home and finds everything changed, including himself. He is asked by the same professor who had taught him, to talk to the new batch of pupils about the war. He remembers his enthusiasm for it when he enlisted in 1914 and he now knows how different are his impressions since he has been stringing barbed wire under the dangerous glare of Very lights in No Man's Land. He knows what a uniform means, and believes that there is no glory at the front; all he has to say to the boys is hard and terse. He tires of the gray heads who think that they know something about war and prefers to cut his leave short and go back to the fighting area rather than listen to the arguments of those who have not been disillusioned by shells, mud, rats and vermin.

During the intermission a curtain is lowered with "poppies, row on row," a glimpse of Flanders field. After that comes more grim battle episodes and more suffering of the men in the gray-green tunics.

All the players do capital work, but Beryl Mercer does not seem to be a good choice for the rôle of Paul's mother. This may be due, however, to having seen her relatively recently in the picturization of Sir James M. Barrie's playlet, "The Old Lady Shows Her Medals."

Messrs. Milestone, Abbott and Anderson in this film have contributed a memorable piece of work to the screen.

Ap 30, 1930

OLD AND NEW, a Soviet production directed by S. M. Eisenstein and George V. Alexandrov; Russian news reel; Pathe sound news; Charlie Chaplin's old comedy, "Shoulder Arms." At the Cameo.

S. M. Eistenstein, the young Russian who produced "Potemkin" and whom Douglas Fairbanks hopes to engage to direct his next picture, is responsible for an enlightening cinematic study called "Old and New," which is to be seen now at the Cameo. In this film, a silent one, Mr. Eisenstein ridicules the Greek Church and also pokes fun at the Soviet bureaucracy. It is another production in which Bolsheviks blow their own horn for their efforts in introducing modern agricultural and other machinery in the near and remote areas of Russia.

Although this picture possesses in most of its scenes a fund of interest, there are times when Mr. Eistenstein dilates too long on some of his sequences, and consequently they become a trifle tedious. Throughout this film, however, this producer reveals his keen observation and his marvelous faculty of stressing his points by means of photography.

In quite a number of instances he delights in extravagances, either in portrayinig the abject poverty of the people or in depicting the greed and laziness of the more fortunate farmer. One is impelled to think as these scenes are shown that Mr. Eisenstein has selected isolated cases to make his film impressive.

His ability to show the expanse of country on a relatively small screen is marvelous, and so is his work in close-ups. As in "Potemkin," which was infinitely more dramatic, the director in this current work is usually careful in the choosing of his types. There are never two persons alike among those who appear in this film. The woman, Martha, who, following starvation and disappointment because she cannot borrow a horse to work on her tract of land, turns out to be a kind of Joan of Arc of the soil, one who urges revolution against the prevailing conditions during the Romanoff régime. She encourages the acceptance of new inventions, the first of which is

a separator. There are some remarkable views portraying the hopeful persons and the doubting ones watching the working of this machine.

It is during a stretch in which the priests and peasants are praying for rain that Mr. Eisenstein makes a target of the Church. There are the men and women on their knees with their heads bent low and the priests holding ecclesiastical banners leading the populace in prayer. Rain is expected after the service, but disappointed persons raise their eyes to the skies and perceive no welcome clouds. The priests mop their perspiring faces and eventually leave the spot.

Mr. Eisenstein goes on to show the wonderful improvement wrought by the agricultural machinery, and finally brings his production to a close with the performance of a tractor pulling a long train of carts. much to the wonder of many of the peasants, who had fancied that no machinery could take the place of the horse in the work on the soil.

In directing this film Mr. Eisenstein was assisted by George V. Alexandrov.

My 3, 1930

THE SCREEN
By MORDAUNT HALL.

The Silver Fox Skin.

STORM OVER ASIA, with V. Inkizhinov, A. Tchistiakov, L. Dediseff, L. Belinskaya and A. Sudakevich, produced by the Sovkino, directed by Vsevolod Pudovkin; "Honolulu Wiles," a "Krazy Kat" cartoon; Clark and McCullough in a short talker called, "A Peep on the Deep." At the Cameo.

Excellent photography and sterling work by the eminently suitable cast are the conspicuous assets of Vsevolod Pudovkin's silent cinematic contribution, "Storm Over Asia," which was produced under the auspices of the Soviet Government some three years ago and is now on exhibition at the Cameo. As for the narrative it is the same old theme which the Bolsheviks delight in presenting with prejudice. This time the noble angle is portrayed by Mongol trappers and the evil side by representatives of the White Army of 1918 and any prosperous persons, and, as one might presume, the Mongols are triumphant.

There is, however, much that is compelling in this production in the early scenes, but in the closing episodes it becomes hysterical and absurd incidents occur, including a man, who, through injuries, is hardly able to move around, suddenly becoming a veritable Samson.

Yesterday afternoon whenever anything ill befell the officers or soldiery of the White Army, or the Mongols met with success, there was a hearty round of applause, which happens here invariably during the screening of a Russian picture.

M. Pudovkin has a remarkable eye for pictorial views and he also succeeds in eliciting marvelously expressive acting from those under his guidance. The glimpse of L. Dediseff's interpretation of a bearded district commander of the White Troops, of V. Inkizhinov's portrayal of a Mongol trapper, of A. Tchistiakov's performance as a rebel leader, make an indelible impression on the spectator. Their facial expressions and their gestures are extraordinarily lifelike.

The climactic moment of the chronicle is somewhat reminiscent of Frankenstein's experience with his monster, except that in this case the Monster chances to be a Mongol who has been chosen by the White Army commander to rule the rebellious tribesmen. He is the trapper, who is supposed to be a descendant of the redoubtable Genghis Khan of old. Just when the elderly commander is patting himself on the back for his idea in picking the new ruler, the trapper, in some mysterious manner, becomes a tower of strength, hurling furniture and bric-a-brac about the house and doing it just at the psychological moment—when the rebels make a successful drive.

The pith of the story lies in the idea of a dealer refusing to pay the just price for a silver fox skin. Much is made of this skin, its rich fur and the scarcity of the animal. This Pudovkin emphasizes most ably. The trapper is seen until the purchase of the skin as a good-natured stolid person, but thereafter he is sullen. He has reason to be, for he has been captured while wearing the rebel uniform and sent out to be shot. The White soldier who takes him out into the outlying hills to put a bullet through him is against such methods, but he obeys his commander. No sooner does the soldier return than he is ordered to go back to find his victim, who is said to be either dead

or dying. It happens that a professor in looking over belongings of the trapper gleans information concerning the Mongol's ancestry. The soldiers discover their victim and the authorities proceed to give him the best of medical attention. The commander is delighted when the trapper is well on the road to recovery. Then this injured Mongol turns the tables on the White Army's commander.

"Storm Over Asia" is presented with a most pleasing Vitaphone musical accompaniment.

S 8, 1930

THE SCREEN
By MORDAUNT HALL.

"Earth."

SOIL, with S. Swashenko, S. Shkurat, P. Masokha and others. Directed by Alexander Dovjenko and produced by the Soviet. At the Eighth Street Playhouse.

Although there are many beautifully photographed views in the Soviet silent film, "Soil," which is now on exhibition at the Eighth Street Playhouse, it is far from being an entertaining study. The theme—the triumph of modern farm machinery over primitive methods—is virtually the same as that of Sergei Eisenstein's last picture, "Old and New," but Alexander Dovjenko, the young Ukrainian producer who made "Arsenal," in this current offering fails either to match his rival's direction or his ability as a storyteller.

In its present form it seems surprising that such a cinema work should have created the fuss this picture did when it was first exhibited last March in Moscow under the title of "Earth." The attack on the Church is not particularly effective; it is lacking in the subtlety with which Eisenstein ridiculed the priests in "Old and New." In his production, M. Eisenstein in a climactic sequence showed a long train of caterpillar farm machines, but in this present film Dovjenko shows only one farm machine by which he gives an idea of the speed with which work can be accomplished by up-to-date appliances.

Like M. Eisenstein, M. Dovjenko has an eye for landscape photography. He gives some compelling

110

flashes of undulating wheat fields and close-ups of wheat swaying in a breeze. There are also some effective glimpses of still life, but one might be justified in surmising that this picture has received a generous pruning before it reached the American public. There is a lack of clarity even in those harmless stretches where M. Dovjenko waxes poetic.

The expressions on the faces of those who portray the principal characters are true to the mood, but the work of these persons is never as telling as those in the Eisenstein production.

In one sequence a farmer is so resentful against those who favor modern machinery that he has to be stayed from slaughtering an old horse so that the animal cannot be taken from him.

Much of this film is chaotic, especially during the church episode and some of the closing scenes.

O 21, 1930

MOROCCO, with Marlene Dietrich, Adolphe Menjou, Ullrich Haupt, Gary Cooper, Juliette Compton, Francis McDonald, Albert Conti, Eve Southern, Michael Visaroff and Paul Porcasi, based on a play by Benno Vigny, directed by Josef von Sternberg. At the Rivoli.

Strange things happen in most Foreign Legion stories after they have undergone a major operation in a film studio, and "Morocco," an audible pictorial adaptation of "Amy Jolly," a play by Benno Vigny, is no exception. Aside from some expertly directed scenes and effective staging, this production is chiefly interesting because it served to introduce the attractive German film favorite, Marlene Dietrich. This player won favor abroad in a picture called "The Blue Angel," which was directed by Josef von Sternberg, who is also responsible for this current presentation.

Miss Dietrich bears a resemblance to Greta Garbo, but her acting hardly rivals that of the Swedish star. She has, however, an ingratiating personality and one might be justified in presuming that if she had been given more rein by Mr. von Sternberg her work might have been more satisfactory, for her gamut of emotions here consists only of gazing intently, smiling and looking languid. She, like the other players in this film, is handicapped by the economy in dialogue, which results in many an uncomfortable pause between two performers.

Mr. von Sternberg evidently knows his camera, and he has done very well so far as the recording of voices is concerned, but he is far from efficient in directing the spoken lines. He accepts absurdly improbable situations, and he is often guilty of extraordinarily abrupt happenings and inconsistent characterizations.

Adolphe Menjou is one of the actors in this film, and he also appears at a disadvantage. He impersonates Mr. Kennington, who falls in love with Amy Jolly (Miss Dietrich). During one stage of the proceedings Mr. Kennington presents Amy, a notorious person, with an emerald and diamond bracelet, and she, probably for the first time in her life, refuses the gift. This is one of those things that could only happen in Northern Africa when such a girl is in love with a private in the Foreign Legion! Amy is evidently a woman who makes up her mind on the spur of the moment, if the way she becomes infatuated with Legionaire Tom Brown is any criterion. She offers to give him one of her apples that fetch big prices from the civilians in the cabaret audience, and Tom Brown, impersonated by Gary Cooper, decides to part with 20 francs for it. Amy gives him one of her languid looks and then hands him the key to her apartment, saying as she does so, "Here's your change."

Tom Brown tells Amy that he will desert if she will accompany him to Europe and Amy agrees to do so. Then, a little later, Tom writes on a mirror in Amy's room that he has changed his mind. Amy is thus left to forget her infatuation by promising to marry Kennington; but she also changes her mind and in the closing scene she decides to "follow the drum," going forth on the scorching sands with other women in the wake of the troops. She takes off her shoes and plods along, it being evident that, if she lasts an hour, it will be all.

Paul Porcasi is clever as the music hall manager. Ullrich Haupt plays quite well the part of an officer and husband of a faithless wife whose life is conveniently snuffed out by Riffian bullets. Mr. Cooper is efficient, but, admitting his good looks, it is doubtful if a woman of Amy's stripe would fall in love so suddenly with him or decide to abandon luxury and comfort for this private in the Foreign Legion.

N 17, 1930

Mr. Jannings and Miss Dietrich.

THE BLUE ANGEL, with Emil Jannings, Marlene Dietrich, Kurt Gerron, Rosa Valetti, Hans Albers, Eduard V. Winterstein,

Reinhold Bernt, Hans Roth, Karl Huszar-Puffy, Wilhelm Diegelmann and others, based on a novel by Heinrich Mann, directed by Josef von Sternberg and supervised by Erich Pommer; Paramount news; "Go Ahead and Eat," an audible film comedy. At the Rialto.

In a film tragedy titled "The Blue Angel," which was directed by Josef von Sternberg in Berlin for Ufa, that talented German screen player Emil Jannings, who left Hollywood because of the vocalizing of pictures, makes his first appearance in a talking production. Marlene Dietrich, the attractive Teutonic actress who is to be seen at the Rivoli in Mr. Sternberg's "Morocco," shares honors with Mr. Jannings in this foreign work.

The plot of "The Blue Angel" recalls that of "The Way of All Flesh," Mr. Jannings's first American silent film, but in this current chronicle, instead of being a bank employe, Mr. Jannings impersonates a professor of English literature in a German boys' high school. The story is cleverly told in most of the sequences, while penultimate scenes would be all the better if they were curtailed or modified, as the actual ending is quite impressive.

The fall from grace of an elderly man is a favorite theme with Mr. Jannings, one that has served him in most of his films since the making of "The Last Laugh." As the characters here are different, however, the interest is rekindled and the broken English of the persons involved is accounted for with a certain crafty logic.

As an actor who speaks his lines, Mr. Jannings is perhaps even better than he was in his mute productions, for the speech to a great extent governs his actions and it stays him from his penchant for unnaturally slow movements. There are times here when no words pass the lips of the characters for uncomfortable seconds, but the final analysis is that it is a decidedly interesting picture with exceptionally fine performances contributed by Mr. Jannings and Miss Dietrich, the latter being much more. the actress than she is in "Morocco."

Professor Immanuel Rath's (Mr. Jannings) humdrum existence is ably stressed. The landlady where he lives knocks on his door at the same time every morning and announces that his breakfast is served. As the hour of 8 rings out from the old clock tower the professor always is crossing the street or entering the school building. He, for some reason or other, omits the greeting of "Good morning" to his pupils, who stand when he enters the classroom and only at his bidding take their seats. As a professor of English he insists on English being spoken. He is a man without a sense of humor, careful about his attire and stolidly opposed to the students betraying any mirth or glee. His curiosity concerning the youngsters who frequent the cabaret, "The Blue Angel," is aroused by finding in his classroom picture postcards of the stellar feminine performer at that gay resort. She is known as Lola Frohlich (Miss Dietrich), who is supposed to be an English singer.

Lola is a rather taciturn creature, but occasionally she reveals subdued enthusiasm, coupled with a dry sense of humor. It is not unfunny to her to have the professor looking for his students in her dressing room, particularly when three or four of them flee after being warned that the pedagogue is in the offing. One evening, however, when the youths are hiding in a cellar, Lola, after the professor has resented the conduct of another man toward her, hears that the police are on the scene, and the urbane Rath also takes refuge in the retreat afforded his pupils, who incidentally have lifted the cellar covering and have been watching with keen amusement the professor's admiration of Lola.

Once in the cellar with the young scapegraces, the professor is a target for ridicule and blows. The result is that when he, following a night away from his own abode, arrives late at his classroom, the pupils revolt and the noise they make is heard throughout the building, with the consequence that Professor Immanuel Rath is asked by the school principal for his resignation.

But all is not lost for the disgraced professor, for Lola becomes his wife. There follow time lapses in which one perceives the professor turned into a clown, wearing a false nose and a ridiculously large collar. This goes on until he eventually becomes insane, imitating the crowing of a rooster, which he had once done for a laugh in his rational days. While the professor is on the stage as the foil for a conjurer, Lola is enjoying the attentions of a lover, and she is observed by her elderly spouse. It is then that his senses leave him, and he eventually staggers over to his old classroom and dies at his desk as the bell in the old clock tower is striking the hour.

Not only is Mr. Jannings's and Miss Dietrich's acting excellent, but

112

they are supported by an unusually competent cast.

Having quite a good story, Mr. von Sternberg's direction is infinitely superior to that of "Morocco," and the settings for this film are very effective.

D 6, 1930

THE SCREEN
By MORDAUNT HALL.

A French Audible Production.

SOUS LES TOITS DE PARIS (Under the Roofs of Paris), with Albert Prejean, Pola Illery, Edmond Greville, Gaston Modot, Bill Bocket and Paul Ollivier, directed by Rene Clair, produced by Tobis in Paris; "Fire Fighters," a "Mickey Mouse" cartoon; "A Night in Paris." At the Little Carnegie Playhouse.

Prefaced by the playing of "The Star-Spangled Banner" and the singing of "La Marseillaise" by Miss Dorothy Johnson of the American Opera Company, there was offered last night before a brilliant gathering in the Little Carnegie Playhouse a French film, called "Sous Les Toits de Paris," which is a curious combination of clever cinematic work, silent episodes with music, others with dialogue and some with singing. The naïveté of this subject is rather appealing, but Rene Clair, the director, is more of a camera expert than a director of talking sequences.

Even with the competent acting of some of the players—notably Albert Prejean, who has a most ingratiating personality—this picture becomes somewhat tedious after the first half. The introductory scenes, however, are highly satisfactory, particularly when M. Clair has a fancy for a little irony. He also shows in captivating fashion how a catchy tune is repeated by persons in their tenement abodes after having heard it rendered by a street singer. Although there is little that is convincing in the muddled narrative, a good deal of artistry shines forth in many of the episodes. It is, for instance, rather amusing to observe a pickpocket trying to snatch purses while Albert (M. Prejean) is singing and selling copies of his song.

The audience was moved to laugh-ter when a fat woman suddenly ceases her humming and singing on discovering that her purse had been stolen. And on the floor below an enraged man, who is averse to the fat woman's melody, is surprised when she stops. He, at the time, is bathing his feet.

The story is concerned with Albert and Louis, two fast friends, who quarrel and make up a dozen times a day. Albert falls in love with a vacillating creature named Pola. The bully of the district, Fred, fawns upon Pola, but she is just a little too crafty for him. In the end, quite unexpectedly, Louis walks off with this girl.

M. Prejean sings agreeably and his acting is splendid. He expresses sincerity and he has a charming smile. Pola Illery impersonates the girl and her performance is not without merit. Gaston Modot does quite well as the good-looking rogue, Fred. Edmond Greville is clever as Louis. The dialogue sequences are the weakest, for M. Clair has a habit of setting two characters on the screen, having them talk for a few seconds, and then dismissing them to take up the talking of other individuals. This film was produced in Paris by the Tobis sound system. Although efforts have been made to give perspective to the musical sounds, there are times when the volume is much too strong, or it was last night. M. Clair covers the absence of speech in several stretches with music, and no matter where his scenes happen to be, there is always a convenient unseen orchestra.

D 16, 1930

LITTLE CAESAR, with Edward G. Robinson, Douglas Fairbanks Jr., Glenda Farrell, Sidney Blackmer, Thomas Jackson, Ralph Ince, William Collier Jr., Maurice Black, Stanley Fields and George E. Stone; from the novel by W. R. Burnett, directed by Mervyn LeRoy; newsreel and Vitaphone short features. At the Strand.

"Little Caesar," based on W. R. Burnett's novel of Chicago gangdom, was welcomed to the Strand yesterday by unusual crowds. The story deals with the career of Cesare Bandello, alias Rico, alias Little Caesar, a disagreeable lad who started by robbing gasoline stations and soared to startling heights in his "profession" by reason of his belief in his high destiny.

The production is ordinary and would rank as just one more gangster film but for two things. One is the excellence of Mr. Burnett's credible and compact story. The other is Edward G. Robinson's wonderfully effective performance. Little Caesar becomes at Mr. Robinson's hands a figure out of Greek epic tragedy, a cold, ignorant, merciless killer, driven on and on by an insatiable lust for power, the plaything of a force that is greater than himself.

Douglas Fairbanks Jr. as Rico's **pal, who brings about his friend's downfall by trying to live a decent life away from his old haunts, is miscast,** and in addition suffers by comparison with the reality of Mr. Robinson's portrayal. At times Mr. Fairbanks talks and acts like the cheap Italian thug he is supposed to represent, but more often he is the pleasant, sincere youth who has been seen to so much better advantage elsewhere.

Little Caesar comes to the big town and joins Sam Vettori's gang, one of the two principal "mobs" in that city. Both gangs are under the supervision of Pete Montana, who in turn owes his allegiance to a mysterious "Big Boy," the king of the underworld. Early in his career Little Caesar plans and executes a raid on a cabaret protected by the rival gang, and in so doing kills a crime commissioner. Thereafter, step by step, he ousts Vettori, Pete Montana and the rival gang leader, and soon only "Big Boy" bars his way to complete mastery of the city's underworld.

His pal, Joe Massara, is threatened with the fatal "spot" because he knows too much, and that young man's sweetheart turns State's evidence. The "mob" is broken and scattered, and Little Caesar is cornered and killed by a crafty detective's appeal to the gangster's vanity.

Glenda Farrell is excellently authentic as Massara's "moll," and William Collier Jr. contributes a moving performance in a minor rôle. Thomas Jackson as the detective is also noteworthy.

Ja 10, 1931

By MORDAUNT HALL.

CITY LIGHTS, with Charlie Chaplin, Virginia Cherrill, Florence Lee, Harry Myers, Allan Garcia, Hank Mann and others, written and directed by Mr. Chaplin. At the George M. Cohan Theatre.

Charlie Chaplin, master of screen mirth and pathos, presented at the George M. Cohan last night before a brilliant gathering his long-awaited non-dialogue picture, "City Lights," and proved so far as he is concerned the eloquence of silence. Many of the spectators either rocking in their seats with mirth, mumbling as their sides ached, "Oh, dear, oh, dear," or they were stilled with sighs and furtive tears. And during a closing episode, when the Little Tramp sees through the window of a flower shop the girl who has recovered her sight through his persistence, one woman could not restrain a cry.

Mr. Chaplin arrived in the theatre with a police guard, and after greeting some of his many friends in the house he took an aisle seat beside Miss Constance Collier. When the picture came to an end he went to the stage and thanked those present for the enthusiasm with which they had received his work.

It is a film worked out with admirable artistry, and while Chaplin stoops to conquer, as he has invariably done, he achieves success. Although the Little Tramp in this "City Lights" in some sequences is more respectable than usual, owing to circumstances in the story, he begins and ends with the same old clothes, looking, in fact, a trifle more bedraggled in the last scene than in most others of his comedies. He has the same antics, the same flip of the heel, the same little cane, mustache, derby hat and baggy trousers.

Here one comes to the conclusion that Chaplin is in many respects the O. Henry of the screen, for he has twists to his sequences that are just as unexpected as those of the famous short story writer.

This tale happens in any city. It seems to be a mixture of Philadelphia, London, New York and Hollywood. And in the beginning the comedian takes a fling at the talking pictures, revealing by incoherent sounds that one can understand what is meant and also that these sounds are quite unnecessary. He wastes no time in getting down to comedy, for right at the outset is the episode wherein the Little Tramp is discovered in the arms of a central figure of a group of statuary that has just been unveiled.

Not long after that he meets the flower girl and with gentle suggestion it is conveyed to the spectator

114

that she is sightless. This girl is impersonated by Virginia Cherrill, who by accident one night before the comedian had cast his picture sat next to him at a pugilistic encounter in Hollywood. Under Chaplin's unfailing guidance, Miss Cherrill gives a charmingly impressive performance.

Then there is the meeting of the Little Tramp and the Eccentric Millionaire, played by Harry Myers, who did so well in the old picture of Mark Twain's "Connecticut Yankee at the Court of King Arthur." This Millionaire loves the Little Tramp as a brother when he is in his cups, but when he is sober he does not recognize him, which naturally makes it most awkward at times for the Tramp, whose one aim in life is to get enough money together to pay a specialist to perform an operation on the blind girl's eyes.

The first meeting between the Millionaire and the Tramp is when the Millionaire goes to a river embankment, bent on suicide, with a stone and a noosed rope in a suit case. The Tramp endeavors to persuade the Millionaire to abandon the idea of taking his life and the chapter of accidents ends in the Little Tramp being hurled into the water with the noose around his neck and the Millionaire having to officiate as the rescuer.

Perhaps the stretch that caused most merriment is where the Little Tramp finds himself in the prize ring facing a real pugilist. He darts about, always keeping, so far as is possible, behind the referee, and during some of the scenes the Tramp separates the referee and his antagonist. In any ordinary comedy the Tramp would have won the contest, but Chaplin wills otherwise.

The Millionaire gives the Tramp his expensive car. Thus the little fellow discovers himself thrown out of the house by the sober Millionaire but he has a glistening car. Without a penny in his pocket and eager for a smoke he drives the automobile slowly along the curb and observes a man throw away a half-smoked cigar. Quick as a flash the Tramp leaps out of the car and, as he does so another tatterdemalion stoops to pick up the cigar. The Little Tramp however, pushes the other man aside looks at him as much as to say, ". saw it first," then he picks up the butt and enters his lovely runabout.

After the Millionaire has taken back his automobile, the Tramp, in his efforts to get money for the blind girl, has his worries as a street clean-er. Then he has the great satisfaction of again falling into the arms of the Millionaire, happily intoxicated. The Tramp unfolds the pathetic story of the blind girl and the Millionaire in a most generous mood peels off more than a thousand dollars in bills. Burglars are in the house and in the course of the excitement the Millionaire sobers up, with the consequence that the Little Tramp has to scoot away. He succeeds in giving the flower girl the money, but cannot evade spending a few months in prison.

At the film's end is a beautifully poetic bit, with the little fellow peering in at the window of a flower shop and recognizing the hitherto blind girl who has recovered her sight and does not, of course, know him. She laughs at him, and through another masculine figure, well dressed, one realizes that she imagines that her hero must look like this individual. A touch of the hand, however, reveals that the humble, little chap with the torn trousers and odd mustache, is her benefactor.

The synchronized music score helps the movement of this comedy. It was composed by Chaplin and arranged by Arthur Johnston. There are times when the notes serve almost for words and so far as sound effects go, Chaplin won gales of laughter last night when the Tramp swallows a whistle and every time he breathes **he whistles. This sound interlude was made the most of, for the whistle calls cabs and dogs and angers a host of people.**

It was a joyous evening. Mr. Chaplin's shadow has grown no less.

F 7, 1931

FILM NEWS

THE MURDERER DIMITRI KARAMASOFF

BERLIN.

Art Dominates.

Then at the Capitol we had "The Murderer Dimitri Karamasoff," a film whose merits lie in quite another direction. Here art, not nature, has the upper hand. Its inspiration was one of the richest of novels, Dostoyevsky's "The Brothers Karamasoff." But wisely enough there was no attempt made to squeeze the epic fullness of the book into the scenario. Leonhard Frank, himself one of Germany's best modern novelists and dramatists, has concentrated only on Dimitri and left the rest of the figures, with the exception of Grushenka, merely background and casual undertone. The weakness of Dimitri is made clear to us. We feel his vacillation between the pure sweet girl to whom he is betrothed and the fiery sensuousness of the coquette Grushenka. Although his commitment to Siberia for the murder of his father is a judicial crime, we feel, as Dostoyevsky meant us to, that it is a fit atonement for his life of uncontrolled passion. This is a scenario with a will to consequences, with an artistic conscience — how many of them can you recall?

And what a splendid "collective" the Terra assembled to bring it to life. The novelist Leonhard Frank I have already mentioned, but the film director Fedor Ozep, the stage director Erich Engel, the composer Karol Rathaus and the players Anna Steen and Fritz Kortner have all an equal share in the achievement. Ozep is perhaps the best of the younger Russian directors—his "Yellow Ticket" and "Living Corpse" (Redemption). Here he has brought to bear all the camera technique of the Russian film and added sound to the pictorial. Erich Engel, after Max Reinhardt the leading German stage director (and that is saying a great deal), was responsible for the dialogue and again showed his ability to characterize through the color and tone of voice. Rathaus is known in the musical world as one of the solidest talents among the younger generation and here proves that he can write music that expresses and underlines the mood without forcing itself into the foreground. Fritz Kortner gives as Dimitri his best performance in the talker. Evidently, owing to the curbing hand of Erich Engel, who has often been his director on the stage, his work is reserved and simple.   C. HOOPER TRASK

Mr 1, 1931

An Old Griffith Film.

WAY DOWN EAST, a revival of the D. W. Griffith film, with synchronized musical score and sound; with Lillian Gish, Mrs. David Landau, Josephine Bernard, Mrs. Morgan Belmont, Patricia Fruen, Florence Short, Lowell Sherman, Burr McIntosh, Kate Bruce, Richard Barthelmess, Vivia Ogden, Porter Strong, George Neville, Edgar Nelson, Mary Hay, Creighton Hale and Emily Fitzroy. At the Cameo Theatre.

The D. W. Griffith melodrama, "Way Down East," which won great favor ten years ago, is being revived at the Cameo. What it proves is that the motion picture is least able to weather the flight of time. An outstanding picture of its day, "Way Down East" offers not a tear in a thousand feet of film to this generation, although still retaining a pleasant sentimental interest. Lillian Gish in her more tempestuous bursts of grief may bring a reminiscent smile to the spectator.

The most interesting feature of the revival is the work of two promising members of Miss Gish's supporting cast who have since made their mark in Hollywood—Lowell Sherman and Richard Barthelmess. Mr. Sherman is without the mustache which has come to be an indispensable factor in his latter-day villainies, and his manner with the ladies is not what it is today. Mr. Barthelmess, the rustic knight-errant of the piece, has not changed noticeably with the years, except for a general maturing.

As a tragedy of small-town bigotry, "Way Down East" loses much of its force today because the cards are too carefully stacked against winsome Anna Moore. Trapped by a vicious scoundrel into a fake marriage, thrown on her own resources by the death of her mother, scorned by the world because she is an unwed mother and finally sent out into a New England blizzard when her identity is discovered, the poor girl continues to be kicked about long after she has lost her frail footing in this contest of The Universe vs. Anna Moore.

The audience yesterday sniggered appreciatively as Mr. Barthelmess, leaping desperately from one ice floe to the other, snatched Miss Gish from the edge of the raging falls.

A. D. S.

Mr 16, 1931

116

By MORDAUNT HALL.

The last motion picture made by F. W. Murnau, the German director of that famous film, "The Last Laugh," who died last Thursday from injuries received in an automobile accident near Santa Barbara, Cal., was presented last night at the Central Park Theatre. It is called "Tabu" and the story, which is based on a Polynesian legend, was written by Mr. Murnau in collaboration with Robert J. Flaherty, producer of "Nanook" and "Moana." It was filmed in the South Seas, on the islands of Bora Bora and Takapota.

It is an enchanting piece of photography synchronized with a most pleasing music score arranged by Dr. Hugo Riesenfeld. It is otherwise a silent film, with unobtrusive titles or "inserts" to explain the incidents where it is necessary. The first part comes under the heading of "Paradise" and the latter half is described as "Paradise Lost." It is like a picture poem, with its sunshine and happiness in the beginning and its stormy drama in the end. The cast includes six principals, three of whom are Polynesians, two half-castes and a Chinese. Mr. Murnau spent the first three months of his long stay in the South Seas selecting his players, none of whom had acted before.

A handsome, stalwart native named Matahi impersonates the Boy; Reri, a good-looking native, figures as the Girl. Hitu is the Old Warrior. The other characters are the Policeman, the ship's captain and a Chinese trader.

In the opening scenes of this photographic gem, the Boy is perceived enjoying the sport of spearing fish. After he and others tire of this they run to a waterfall, shaded by heavy foliage. The Boy relishes the shower bath under the silver spray, and soon he espies the girls bathing in a pool below, and with that spirit of joyous youth that permeates these first chapters, the Boy uses the waterfall as a chute and plunges down it to the deep, clear water below. In all that is filmed in these Bora Bora

scenes there is up to a certain point the love of life of the natives. One feels it as the scenes flash by, for nothing mars the pleasure of the admiration the Boy has for the Girl and the Girl for the Boy. Nothing, one thinks, can interfere with the happiness of these young people. For all one knows, they might be without houses or huts, just living in the open, near the shallow inlets of crystal clear water.

Then the menace appears in the form of Hitu, the Old Warrior, who arrives aboard a sailing vessel to select a girl to be the Sacred Maiden who intermediates between the gods and the people. It is the proclamation of the Lord of all the Isles that a girl must be chosen from Bora Bora, and Hitu's choice is Reri, the Girl. Perhaps Matahi might have been shrewd enough to hide Reri, but he is impelled to go back for his little brother, and when he boards the vessel Reri already has been chosen, and it is an unpardonable sin for any man to look at her.

Under a noticably artificial moon, Matahi swims out to the sailing craft that night and succeeds in kidnapping his Reri and, forthwith, fearing the wrath of Hitu, they go to the Island of Takapota, where things are vastly different to the peaceful state of affairs in Bora Bora. There are shops. Men dive for a living. There are traders, half castes, and some of them delight in modern dancing and wearing American clothes.

It is necessary to work so as to live, and therefore Matahi becomes a pearl diver. Soon he is the best diver of them all. He is forced to celebrate the finding of a valuable pearl, and wine is drunk by everybody, poor Matahi not knowing that wine costs money and that sooner or later he will have to pay. Then there is the Policeman who has orders to arrest Reri and Matahi, the Girl and the Boy, and to be free from the law's clutches Matahi gives the Policeman his valuable pearl.

The title "Tabu" applies to an area of water in which it is forbidden to dive for pearls because a giant shark guards this spot below. A native is killed by this shark, and although the spot is rich with pearls the shark becomes more terrifying than the law.

But when Matahi discovers that he and Reri have not enough money to go still further away from the pursuing Hitu he gets up one night and decides to risk his life in the forbidden area to bring up a pearl. He returns with a pearl, all they need for their happiness, but when he reaches his shack Hitu has stolen Reri and on the moon-lit water one perceives the old warrior's sailing craft.

Realizing what has happened, Matahi leaps into the sea and swims swiftly in the direction of the ship. He seems likely to reach his goal, when suddenly the sailing ship gets under way, but the native still keeps on, until in the last fade-out he sinks, as his sweetheart is taken away by Hitu.

These natives give remarkable performances. Their expressions and actions are as natural as the players in Russian pictures.

Mr 19, 1931

THE FRONT PAGE, based on the play by Ben Hecht and Charles MacArthur; directed by Lewis Milestone; produced by Howard Hughes. At the Rivoli Theatre.
Walter Burns..................Adolphe Menjou
Hildy Johnson...................Pat O'Brien
Peggy............................Mary Brian
Bensinger...........Edward Everett Horton
Murphy.......................Walter Catlett
Earl Williams...............George E. Stone
Molly..........................Mae Clarke
Pincus.......................Slim Summerville
Kruger..........................Matt Moore
McCue.........................Frank McHugh
Sheriff Hartman.........Clarence H. Wilson
Schwartz.........................Fred Howard
Wilson.............................Phil Tead
Endicott.......................Eugene Strong
Woodenshoes................Spencer Charters
Diamond Louie................Maurice Black
Mrs. Grant......................Effie Ellsler
The Mayor.....................James Gordon
Jacobi.........................Dick Alexander

By MORDAUNT HALL.

A witty and virile talking picture has been wrought from "The Front Page," the play of Chicago newspaper life by Ben Hecht and Charles MacArthur. This film, which is now at the Rivoli, differs but little in construction from the parent work. It is a fast-paced entertainment and, while its humor is frequently harsh, it assuredly won favor with the audience yesterday afternoon.

Adolphe Menjou, who has hitherto confined himself to the impersonation of suave philanderers, steps outside those bounds and portrays Walter Burns, the keen managing editor of a Chicago daily, a rôle that was acted on the stage by Osgood Perkins. Under the direction of Lewis Milestone, producer of "All Quiet on the Western Front," Mr. Menjou does excellent work. He may be a little too gentle occasionally, but

in most of his scenes he is true to the character, even to digging his hands in his trouser pockets, raving about news leads and spouting expletives.

Pat O'Brien, a newcomer to the screen, is entrusted with the impersonation of Hildy Johnson, played on the stage by Lee Tracy. Mr. O'Brien gives quite a good account of himself as the reporter who, when he is about to abandon newspaper work, harkens to the call of a good story.

Although some of the minor characters are not quite as effective as they were on the stage, there is as good an impression of them as film footage permits. They indulge in their argot and have their own interpretations of the news of a story, this being set forth chiefly by the descriptions used by them in telephoning their news bulletins from the press room of the Criminal Courts Building in the Windy City.

In the course of this sturdy melodrama, Earle Williams, a convict who was to be executed, escapes, and general excitement reigns in the Criminal Courts Building. Sheriff Hartman is thoroughly humiliated, for the prisoner got away through having borrowed Hartman's pistol while demonstrating where he (Williams) stood during the moment of the crime of which he was convicted. Politics is mixed with newspaper activities when the Mayor and Hartman try to bribe a messenger who brings word of Williams's reprieve by the Governor.

It is emphatically humorous when Williams is hidden in a roll-top desk in the press room by Johnson and Burns, whose sole desire is to have a news scoop. And eventually there comes Hartman's discovery of the prisoner and the handcuffing of Johnson and Burns for helping a criminal to escape.

In a clever manner the producers have succeeded in retaining many more of the lines of the play than was anticipated. The censor is in more than one instance virtually defied through ingenious ideas.

Edward Everett Horton plays the dreamy, poetic reporter, Bensinger, in which rôle he is quite successful. Mary Brian is Peggy. Clarence H. Wilson gives a sterling performance as Hartman. Matt Moore, Slim Summerville, Spencer Charters and Walter Catlett do their share to make this a rousing entertainment.

Mr 20, 1931

THE PUBLIC ENEMY, based on a story by Kubec Glasmon and John Bright. Directed by William A. Wellman. Produced by Warner Brothers. At the Strand.

Matt	Edward Woods
Tom	James Cagney
Mike	Donald Cook
Mamie	Joan Blondell
Gwen Allen	Jean Harlow
Tom's mother	Beryl Mercer
Bu Moran	Ben Hendricks Jr.
Paddy Ryan	Robert Emmett O'Connor
Nails Nathan	Leslie Fenton
Bess	Louise Brooks
Putty Nose	Murray Kinnell
Kitty	Mae Clark

It is just another gangster film at the Strand, weaker than most in its story, stronger than most in its acting, and like most maintaining · a certain level of interest through the last burst of machine-gun fire. That was not the intention of the Warners, whose laudable motive it was to have "The Public Enemy" say the very last word on the subject of gang pictures. There is a prologue apprising the audience that the hoodlums and terrorists of the underworld must be exposed and the glamour ripped from them. There is an epilogue pointing the moral that civilization is on her knees and inquiring loudly as to what is to be done. And before the prologue there is a brief stage tableau, with sinuous green lighting, which shows a puppet gangster shooting another puppet gangster in the back.

"The Public Enemy" does not, as its title so eloquently suggests, present a picture of the war between the underworld and the upperworld. Instead the war is one of gangsters among themselves; of sensational and sometimes sensationally incoherent murders. The motivation is lost in the general slaughter at the end, when Matt and Tom, the hoodlums with whose career of outlawry the picture is concerned, die violently.

Edward Woods and James Cagney, as Matt and Tom respectively, give remarkably lifelike portraits of young hoodlums. The story follows their careers from boyhood, through the war period and into the early days of prohibition, when the public thirst made their peculiar talents profitable. Slugging disloyal bartenders, shooting down rival beermen, slapping their women crudely across the face, strutting with a vast self-satisfaction through their little world, they contribute · a hard and true picture of the unheroic gangster.

The audiences yesterday laughed frequently and with gusto as the swaggering Matt and Tom went through their paces, and this rather took the edge off the brutal picture the producers appeared to be trying to serve up. The laughter was loudest and most deserved when the two put a horse "on the spot," the reason being that the animal had had the temerity to throw Nails Nathan, the gang leader.

There is a reminder of newspaper headlines toward the close when Tom, lying wounded in a hospital, is kidnapped and murdered. The acting throughout is interesting, with the exception of Jean Harlow, who essays the rôle of a gangster's mistress. Beryl Mercer as Tom's mother, Robert Emmett O'Connor as a gang chief, and Donald Cook as Tom's brother, do splendidly.

A. D. S.
Ap 24, 1931

THE SCREEN

A German "Beggar's Opera."

DIE DREIGROSCHENOPER ("The Beggar's Opera"), based on a story by Bert Brecht; directed by G. W. Pabst; a Warner-Tobis Berlin production. At the Warner Theatre.

Mickie Messer	Rudolf Forster
Polly Peachum	Carola Neher
Peachum	Fritz Rasp
Mrs. Peachum	Valeska Gert
Tiger Brown	Reinhold Schunzel
Jenny	Lottie Lenje
A Jailor	Vladimir Sokolof
A Ballad Singer	Ernst Busch

By MORDAUNT HALL.

At the Warners' Theatre is a German language film known as "Die Driegroschenoper" ("The Three Groats Opera"), which was inspired by John Gay's celebrated work of 200 years ago, "The Beggar's Opera." For those familiar with the Teutonic tongue, it is a moderately entertaining offering, but persons who anticipate enjoying the original combination of sharp satire and pleasing melody will be disappointed.

The story is not credited to Gay, but to Bert Brecht, and the musical compositions, of which there are only a few, to Kurt Weil. Both Brecht and Weil were so dissatisfied with the pictorial result that they protested to the producers. A general compromise was, however, effected and the production was presented in Berlin about three months ago.

G. W. Pabst, who has won distinction with several of his pictures, is responsible for the direction, and the Russian André Andreyeff, designed the settings, which are admirable, even though one may differ with his conception of London of olden days. Herr Pabst's direction reveals occasional brilliant moments, but his characters in their attire look more German than English. Even the police chief and the uniformed policemen never for an instant impress one as being from the "tight little isle."

It is a production filled with anachronisms. Herr Brecht evidently tried to bring the story forward a hundred years or so, and Herr Pabst goes so far as to show one of the characters writing on a typewriter.

What purports to be Newgate Prison looks to be almost an up-to-date jail. In fact, the scenes constantly change in their atmospheric aspect in a bewildering fashion.

In this narrative the host of beggars decide to march down upon a coronation procession, in which there is a queen who bears some resemblance to Queen Mary. It is one of the most amusing incidents, for at one point all the bewigged jurists, lifting their gowns to give their limbs freedom, are perceived fleeing for their lives from the vast horde of mendicants.

Here the principal character, a sort of racketeer, is named Mickie Messer. He wears white tops to his shoes, black stitching on his white gloves and a check suit, and now and again lifts his voice to a pleasant melody. If the girl with whom he is infatuated wants a bridal gown, it is stolen from a shop window by one of Messer's underlings, who please to pose as beggars.

The stream of beggars returning from the day's "work" is expertly depicted. The halt and the lame walk, and the blind decide to open their eyes.

The chief of police, Tiger Brown, wears a monocle that makes the eye in which it is look twice as large as the other. He has his worries with these tatterdemalions, for it is a case of hands off at one moment, and when Messer is taken into custody and shackled to the bars of the modern-looking prison cell he, through the cunning of his mistress, succeeds in escaping after turning the key on the keeper.

There is the forbidding old Peachum with his queer beard, who is driven almost hysterical by the various happenings. He would call off the army of beggars from their descent on the coronation procession when he learns that his daughter, Polly, is head of a bank. And so it goes, with the times varying from a hundred years ago to what might be looked upon as almost the present day.

Rudolf Forster, who plays Messer, gives quite a clever performance, considering the circumstances. Carola Neher also does well in this conception of Polly Peachum. Reinhold Schunzel's portrayal of Tiger Brown likewise has a certain merit.

The melodies are quite agreeable and one would not complain if there were more of the singing and less of some of the action. It is, however, a fantastic affair which has none of the charm, vitality and bitter satire of Gay's "Beggar's Opera."

The vocal recording is for the most part exceedingly good, except when those players with penetrating voices were obviously too close to the microphone.

My 18, 1931

THE SCREEN
By MORDAUNT HALL.

A French Musical Farce.

LE MILLION, a French dialogue film, inspired by a play by G. Berr and M. Guillemaud; directed by Rene Clair. At the Little Carnegie Playhouse.

Beatrice ....Annabella
Michel ....Rene Lefebvre
Crochard ....Paul Olivier
Prosper ....Louis Alibert
Sopranelli ....Constantin Stroesco
La Chanteuse...............Odetta Talazac
Vanda ....Vanda Creville

René Clair, producer of "Sous les Toits de Paris," is responsible for an infinitely more brilliant French language film which was presented last night before a distinguished gathering in the Little Carnegie Playhouse. It is called "Le Million" and as it skips merrily on its way the characters frequently burst into song. In it M. Clair has avoided the errors he made in "Sous les Toits de Paris," for here when he darts from one scene to another, he permits the persons involved to finish what they are saying, or, at least, to impart the desired information.

This picture, which has been warmly acclaimed in London and on the Continent, may be referred to as a musical farce or tuneful operetta. But no matter what it is called, it is a scintillating entertainment which pleased the first night audience immensely. M. Clair's agile mind is revealed in most of the scenes. Added to his spoofing of crooks, the police and opera singers, there are compelling camera effects and a constant series of surprises and, even though it is rather overdone, some excellent suspense.

For the benefit of those who do not understand French, there are several scenes in which two Britishers on a roof, peeping in at the doings in an atelier below, tell in English of what has happened and is at the moment taking place. This clever idea does not spoil the frolic, for each one of these interruptions only takes a few seconds and they are so adroitly conceived that they become part and parcel of the tale.

This glittering production breezes all over Paris, with a chase after a coat in the pocket of which is a lottery ticket for 1,000,000 florins. In the early scenes, a young artist named Michel, who is in debt up to his ears, is caught by his butcher, grocer, landlord and others, and while they are venting their wrath on him, a news vendor arrives with the announcement of the winning lottery number. Michel and his comrade, Prosper, have two tickets, and the former looks in his note book and discovers that he is the owner of the ticket with the lucky number. But the ticket is in his coat that he left upstairs in Beatrice's room when he was mistaken for a thief who had taken refuge in Beatrice's apartment. With the creditors chorusing, "Le Millionaire," Michel darts upstairs, not knowing, as the audience does, that Beatrice, in her desire to aid the thief to escape, had given the coat to him. And, what adds to the artist's anxiety, is that Beatrice has left for the opera, where she is a dancer.

These scenes are splendidly filmed, even to the nervousness of poor Michel while awaiting Beatrice and his pretending to enjoy the festivities that the creditors insist upon.

The grocer, landlord, butcher and others are so elated over the fact that Michel is a millionaire that they consider that it is a mere matter of time before he produces the lottery ticket. Little do they know that the much-wanted coat has been sold to an opera singer, who, of course, knows naught of there being a million florins in the pocket. He only wanted the old coat for a scene in his production.

The attempts to find the garment are invariably farcical, and until the end Michel, Prosper, Beatrice and a blond girl named Vanda are often within touch of the garment, but unable to get it. The pursuit takes them to the place of Père la Tulipe, who, under cover of a second-hand clothing store, runs a resort for crooks. Later, the coat is sought behind the scenes of the opera and also on the stage while the opera singer is performing.

Meanwhile, there is the sequence where Michel, who had agreed to share his million with Prosper, is held by the police under suspicion of being the notorious Père la Tulipe. Prosper turns up at the police station, but when he is asked whether he can identify Michel, he says that he has never seen the artist before. And on he goes, hoping to find the precious coat before Michel is released.

Père la Tulipe's gang have their melodious drill and likewise the police. While the opera singer, Sopranelli, is singing a duet with a stout female, M. Clair turns to the property man above who is tossing paper snow on the stage. This picture is filled with unexpected ideas, apart from the doings of the characters, and while the feverish activities are stretched to the snapping point the dénouement, when it does come, is accomplished astutely.

In some of his opera scenes, M. Clair has his fun with the audience. There are those who are impressed by the singing, others who are relieved that the duet is finally ended and a man who might pass for a well-dressed pugilist is in tears. It is a combination of farce, burlesque, travesty and satire, all of which is sharpened with keen wit.

An actress enjoying the single name of Annabella gives a pleasing performance as Beatrice. René Lefebvre lives up to the fast pace of this film by his portrayal of Michel. Louis Alibert is excellent as Prosper. Constantin Stroesco is wonderfully good as the tempermental Sopranelli, who in one sequence is forced by the crooks to sing to prove that he is really a tenor. Vanda Greville, who hardly talks like a French girl, officiates as Vanda. Paul Ollivier is splendid as Pere La Tulipe, or Crochard as he is called in the program.

My 21, 1931

"À Nous La Liberté,"
PARIS.

AFTER slumbering for several months, the native motion-picture producers awakened one morning last week to find

Paris the centre of all cinematographic attention in Europe. Directors from every city, with their stars, came to the Champs-Elysées for the première of René Clair's third talking film, "A Nous la Liberté."

The vogue for the work of this director, created by his previous "Sous les Toits de Paris" and "Le Million," is at its height, so that expectation for the new film was great. Tout Paris came out for the event which was widely ballyhooed.

Preliminary press reports had stated that the young director was still searching for a new form in "A Nous la Liberté." They also said that, dissatisfied with the distended effects of his first two productions in sound, he was now embarking on a trail which might lead to a definite pattern for his future work.

Small wonder it is, then, that during the hour following the last scene, the lobby was jammed with excited representatives of film companies from various parts of the world who were sending detailed telegrams that evening of what new ideas Clair had brought to the screen.

Just as at the crowded press showing of a week previous, however, no two persons had a similar impression of the film. Having been the only American journalist invited to the trade showing, I had listened with interest to the critical comments evoked. If he had done nothing else, the director had mystified the critics. So he bewildered the first-night audience.

Writers Are Puzzled.

On all sides one hears the question of what did Clair mean by his film. Is he poking fun at the films? Is he embittered against life? Has he let his sense of fantasy get out of hand? Or is he still groping for a medium by which he can compress his dreams into the demands of the motion picture?

His tale, from his own pen, is simple. The opening of the film finds Emile and Louis as convicts. The entire life of the prison is given a definite tempo, such as Clair gave "Le Million" by monotonous hammering effects. Louis escapes and eight years later is found as the director of a large phonograph factory. The prison is changed into an industrial enterprise. The monotonous effects continue and the former prisoners are now laborers. Emile enters the factory as a workman and soon discovers his former cellmate. They again become cronies. But other of the convicts discover the director and reveal his identity to the police as he is inaugurating a new factory and being proclaimed one of the leading citizens of the country. He abandons his business and together with his friend takes to the open road singing "A Nous la Liberté."

The public cheers portions of the film, such as the capture of Emile by factory foremen, who insist that he must work even though he prefers to tramp the countryside; or when the orators are eulogizing Louis's career as the police are assembling to arrest him. But the glimpses which still bring Clair nearest to the cinema public are those when he allows his sense of humor to run loose. Two such scenes, although prolonged as they were in "Le Million," throw the house into hysterics at every performance.

A long bench in the factory is shown where every laborer has his dull task of placing one rivet into a phonograph panel. Attracted by a girl, Emile misses his chore and then scrambles madly through the line to place his rivet. The whole factory is thrown into confusion as every workman tries to make up for the gap.

There are the chase flashes such as Clair has always employed. And one of his most ironical moments comes when prominent government and civic officials forget their sense of ceremony to pursue a myriad of 1,000 franc notes which are blown off the roof of the factory by a strong wind.

The Principals.

The director has chosen a cast of unknowns whose work is virtually the visualization of his ideas. Rolla France, Germaine Aussey, Raymond Cordy, Henri Marchand, Paul Olivier and Jacques Shelly have the principal rôles.

JOHN CAMPBELL.

Ja 10, 1932

THE MAN I KILLED, an adaptation of a play by Maurice Rostand; directed by Ernst Lubitsch; produced by Paramount Publix. At the Criterion Theatre.

Dr. Holderlin	Lionel Barrymore
Elsa	Nancy Carroll
Paul	Phillips Holmes
Walter Holderlin	Tom Douglas
Anna	Zasu Pitts
Schultz	Lucien Littlefield
Mrs. Holderlin	Louise Carter
Priest	Frank Sheridan
Bresslauer	George Bickel
Mrs. Miller	Emma Dunn
Grave-digger	Tully Marshall
Mrs. Bresslauer	Lillian Elliott
Fritz	Marvin Stephens
Fritz's father	Reginald Pasch
Flower-shop girl	Joan Standing
War Veteran	Rodney McLennon

By MORDAUNT HALL.

Ernst Lubitsch, the masterful German director, has turned his attention from frivolous comedies to an ironic, sentimental post-war film drama, called "The Man I Killed," an adaptation of a play by Maurice Rostand. This picture, which was offered last night before a distinguished gathering in the Criterion, is further evidence of Mr. Lubitsch's genius, for, while it is tearful, its story is unfurled in a poetic fashion, with an unexcelled performance by Lionel Barrymore and fine acting by Phillips Holmes and Nancy Carroll. It has its moral—a pacifistic one that affected the audience—and if the pathos is stressed, there is no denying the human and truthful qualities of the simple tale.

Each sequence is fashioned with sincerity and great care. The different scenes are all photographed with admirable artistry. It even has its moments of light humor. One episode dealing with small-town gossipers brings to mind something along the same line in the late F. W. Murnau's old silent classic, "The Last Laugh." But aided by the microphone, Lubitsch goes his colleague one better, by adding to the prattling group the sound of tinkling door bells.

"The Man I Killed" is one of those narratives that might be told in a very few words, but under Mr. Lubitsch's guidance, with a script written by Ernest Vajda and Samuel Raphaelson, each scene becomes more and more stirring. First, one realizes that Paul, a sensitive French soldier, has killed a German, named Walter Holderlin. He sees the dying man struggle to finish half his signature to his sweetheart, Elsa.

There are scenes in which church bells are heard between the booming of guns and other glimpses of soldiers in a church with scabbarded swords lining the aisles. When the uniformed men go down on their knees one's eyes become riveted on the spurred boots. All of this is typical of Mr. Lubitsch.

Eventually Paul is perceived in a church. He approaches a priest and the camera invades the privacy of the confessional. Paul tells of the man he killed, and the cleric grants him absolution. After that the mournful young Frenchman journeys to Falsberg, as the place where the Holderlins live is known. Old Dr. Holderlin, Walter's father, does not conceal his hatred of Frenchmen. He is if anything more vindictive than any of his friends. But after he hears that Paul has come to put flowers on the grave of his son, he relents in his bitterness and becomes philosophical. Then there is Elsa, who hoped to be Walter's bride. She becomes interested in Paul, chiefly because he is so affected by any mention of young Holderlin.

Not being able to bear his secret any longer, Paul tells Elsa that he killed Walter on the field of battle. By that time Dr. and Mrs. Holderlin look upon Paul with such great affection that they dread the very idea of his leaving. The old German argues that he and his ilk were too old to fight, but they were not too old to hate. He emphasizes the fact that when his son left for the war he cheered.

Elsa insists that Paul must not let the old people know that he killed Walter.

Irony courses through the tale to the last, when the old doctor hands his dead son's violin to Paul, who plays a serenade while Elsa accompanies him on the piano.

The magic of the Lubitsch mind is not only reflected in the artistry of the production and the direction, but also in the habiliments of the players and their make-up. It is quite a different Lionel Barrymore in this picture. And Mr. Barrymore lives up to Mr. Lubitsch's ideas. Mr.

Barrymore appears as quite an old man. His step is uncertain and his hand shakes a bit. Mr. Holmes is splendid as the saddened Frenchman. He moves as if dazed, and one appreciates that night after night he sees the figure of the dying German. **Miss Carroll is particularly well suited to her rôle. Zasu Pitts, Lucien Littlefield and Tom Douglas also serve this production capably.**

Ja 20, 1932

GRAND HOTEL, an adaptation of Vicki Baum's play; directed by Edmund Goulding; produced by Metro-Goldwyn-Mayer. At the Astor Theatre.

Grusinskaya, the Dancer	Greta Garbo
The Baron	John Barrymore
Flaemmchen, the Stenographer	Joan Crawford
Preysing	Wallace Beery
Otto Kringelein	Lionel Barrymore
Senf	Jean Hersholt
Meierheim	Robert McWade
Zinnowitz	Purnell B. Pratt
Pimenov	Ferdinand Gottschalk
Suzette	Rafaela Ottiano
Chauffeur	Morgan Wallace
Gerstenkorn	Tully Marshall
Rohna	Frank Conroy
Schweimann	Murray Kinnell
Dr. Waitz	Edwin Maxwell

By MORDAUNT HALL.

For the first showing last night of the film of Vicki Baum's stage work, "Grand Hotel," those worshipers of the stars of the Hollywood firmament choked the sidewalk outside the Astor and also the theatre lobby while policemen afoot and on horse urged the throng to keep moving. And from across Broadway blinding beams of light added to the general excitement.

Inside the theatre it was for a time difficult to move but very slowly, for many of those who had tickets pressed into the aisles and behind the orchestra seats with the evident hope of catching a glimpse of one or another cinema celebrity. But once microphone music came from the stage the spectators hastened to their places and soon the introductory scene of the much talked of motion picture was emblazoned on the screen. It was that of the telephone operators in the Grand Hotel and then the pushing and shouting was a thing of the past.

It is a production thoroughly worthy of all the talk it has created and the several motion-picture luminaries deserve to feel very proud of their performances, particularly

Greta Garbo and Lionel Barrymore. So far as the direction is concerned, Edmund Goulding has done an excellent piece of work, but occasionally it seems as though he relies too much on close-ups. Nevertheless he has sustained a steady momentum in darting here and there in the busy hostelry and working up to an effective dramatic pitch at the psychological moment. In all, the picture adheres faithfully to the original and while it undoubtedly lacks the life and depth and color of the play, by means of excellent characterizations it keeps the audience on the qui vive.

It is indubitably a capital subject to bring to the screen, for it benefits by the sweeping scope of the camera and in swaying from room to room and from the lobby to the telephone switchboard, Mr. Goulding gives some markedly fine photographic effects. But it should be stated that in one scene he permits an extremely gruesome idea to creep in. This will probably be eliminated at some of the future exhibitions.

Miss Garbo, of course, impersonates the dancer, Grusinskaya, played on the stage by Eugénie Leontovich. Miss Garbo, possibly appreciating that she was supported by a galaxy of efficient performers, decided that she would do her utmost to make her rôle shine. And she succeeds admirably. She is stunning in her early scenes and charming in the love scene with Baron Geigern, portrayed by John Barrymore with his usual savoir faire. And later, wearing a chinchilla coat, she is gay and lighthearted, for love has beckoned to the temperamental dancer. Grusinskaya leaves the screen hopeful of meeting the Baron at the railroad station, but the audience knows that the good-natured and sympathetic thief has met his doom at the hands of the ignoble Preysing, a part acted by Wallace Beery.

It fell to Lionel Barrymore's lot to play Otto Kringelein, the humble bookkeeper who decides in an introductory scene that, as he has not long to live, he will go out of this world in a blaze of glory. Mr. Barrymore brings out every possible note of this sensitive person, who talks with bated breath to the Baron, entertains with champagne and caviar; loathes his employer, the hard-fisted, sensual Preysing, for whom he has worked for a pittance. He is going to die and therefore what cares he if Preysing discharges him? But, instead of passing away, he entrains for Paris with the attractive stenographer, Flaemmchen, who is seen in the person of Joan Crawford.

Through Mr. Barrymore's skilful interpretation one gleans the satisfaction of this obsequious human adding machine has in hobnobbing with people of the world and in living in the corner suite of the Grand Hotel. Mr. Barrymore is superb when he as Kringelein finds himself tipsy, tipsy but elated. If ever an actor got under the skin of a character Mr. Barrymore does here.

And, although Miss Garbo and Lionel Barrymore deliver talented portrayals, it does not mean that any aspersion is to be cast at the work of others in the cast. Miss Crawford, for instance, is splendid as Flaemmchen. She, too, does all that is possible to vie with the others in the cast. Then there is John Barrymore as the Baron. Nobody could hope to see such a type better acted. This Baron is handsome, a little sly, eager for money, but always thoughtful and friendly when it comes to his association with Kringelein. He steals Kringelein's wallet, but, when he hears Kringelein bewailing his loss, he "finds" the wallet, and how glad is Kringelein!

As for Mr. Beery, it may seem that while his performance does not quite compare with that of Siegfried Rumann, the stage Preysing, it is nevertheless a very worthy characterization. Mr. Beery is sufficiently ponderous and forbidding as Preysing, but in having to assume a German accent he is not quite in his element. But those who did not see Mr. Rumann will undoubtedly decide that Mr. Beery's performance is good enough.

No review of this picture would be complete without a mention of the genuinely pleasing work of Ferdinand Gottschalk, who acts the loyal underling of Grusinskaya. Lewis Stone also does well as Dr. Otternschlag and Jean Hersholt is up to his usual high standard as the porter, Senf, whose chief interest during the running of the story is the condition of his wife, who finally gives birth to a child as the story comes to a close. And it is Dr. Otternschlag who is given to saying that "people come and people go, and nothing ever happens in the Grand Hotel."

And the audience has seen manslaughter, gambling, a baron bent on stealing pearls, love affairs, a business deal and various other doings. And "nothing ever happens!"

Ap 13, 1932

HORSE FEATHERS, a story by Bert Kalmar, Harry Ruby and S. J. Perelman; directed by Norman McLeod; music by Bert Kalmar and Harry Ruby; presented by Paramount Publix Corporation. At the Rialto Theatre.
Professor Wagstaff ....Groucho Marx
Harpo ....Harpo Marx
Chico ....Chico Marx
Zeppo ....Zeppo Marx
Connie Bailey ....Thelma Todd
Jennings ....David Landau
Peggy Carrington.......Florine McKinney
Mullens ....James Pierce
McCarthy ....Nat Pendleton
President of College.......Reginald Barlow
Professor Hornsvogel.........Robert Greig
Policeman ....Ben Taggart

By MORDAUNT HALL.

The Four Marx Brothers score again in "Horse Feathers," a picture which came to the Rialto last night. Groucho's characteristic corkscrew humor, Chico's distortions of English and Harpo's pantomime aroused riotous laughter from those who packed the theatre for this first performance. Some of the fun is even more reprehensible than the doings of these clowns in previous films, but there is no denying that their antics and their patter are helped along by originality and ready wit.

Harpo does his usual turn with the harp, looking like an angel in disguise. Chico plays the piano in his facile fashion and Groucho essays a little in the way of singing. It falls to Groucho's lot to be chosen as president of Huxley College at the outset of this bundle of mirth. Chico is a bootlegger masquerading as a more or less peaceful ice man and Harpo is a dog catcher. As for Zeppo, the sedate member of the family, he is a Huxley student, who is infatuated with the College Widow, Connie Bailey, played by the handsome Thelma Todd.

After being introduced by the retiring college president, Groucho, who is scarcely neat in his attire, begins his little talk by saying that he thought his razor was dull, until he heard the speech of his predecessor. Soon after that Groucho renders a song, each verse of which ends with "I'm against it." This gradually turns into another ballad, a stanza of which runs:
"I soon dispose of all those,
  Who put me on the pan.
Like Shakespeare said to Nathan Hale,
  I always get my man."
The retiring president and the faculty join in with "He always gets his man."

When Groucho is surprised flirting with Connie Bailey, he is told by her guardian, Mr. Jennings, that he (Jennings) will teach Groucho to pay attention to the girl and Groucho replies that he does not need any teaching as he is getting along splendidly.

There are glimpses of this college president searching for two football players in a speakeasy and Groucho and Chico furnish much hilarity by their entrances and exits and the password, which happens to be "swordwish." Harpo, being mute, makes sure that he will gain entrance to the place, so he carries with him a fish with a sword in its mouth.

Harpo as the dog catcher is busy during several of the scenes, but he has some of his most trying moments when he and Chico are locked up in a room by the two football players, whom they hoped to kidnap to prevent their playing for a rival college. Their only way to escape is to saw a circle in the floor and when this is done they drop into the room below. They escape from that room by the same idea and drop on four women playing bridge, Chico boasting of having at least made a grand slam.

The football game receives most attention in this offering. Poor old Huxley might have been defeated had not Chico, Groucho and Harpo used their wits. Harpo may be silent but during this hectic gridiron performance he apparently does a great deal of thinking. Nothing escapes him whereby he can help Huxley to down the other college. And Groucho is not idle, not by any means. He dives into the game with football headgear and morning coat, ready to cheat and foul for his alma mater. At one time the ball is on a lusty elastic rope so that the Huxley opponents never know where it is. They dash madly at one player and in one instance discover the apparently gentle Harpo sitting on the ball enjoying a sandwich.

The futility of struggling to get a ball down the field evidently strikes Harpo, who thinks that the best way to make goals in time is to get enough footballs, and he succeeds in bringing four or five to make the necessary touchdowns.

Although this game is the highlight of the picture, there are several other sequences which provide their full share of laughter, notably when Groucho goes boating on a lake with the fair Connie, who, at the behest of Jennings is eager to ascertain the signals of the Huxley team. Groucho becomes slightly exasperated when Connie tries to wheedle the signals out of him by baby talk and it is not long before the lovely college widow is forced to swim for her life. Behind the boat is a duck who quacks at Groucho, or, as he put it, "smart quacks."

Then there is the time when Chico tells Groucho that the college owes him $2,000 for ice. He asks Chico what he charges for a cake and the ice-man answers that Scotch ice is $7 a cake, rye ice is $9 and champagne ice, $13.20. When Groucho wants to know what the 20 cents is for, Chico replies: "For the ice."

There is also the amusement provided during a lecture on anatomy, which is interrupted by both Groucho and Harpo, the former desiring to know whether the lecturer's stuff is on the level or whether he is just making it up as he goes along.

Although no little laughter is stirred up by Harpo and Chico, the life of this little party is Groucho. Miss Todd is effective as the College Widow. David Landau is gruff enough as Jennings and Nat Pendleton, a former Olympic wrestler, is impressive as a football player.

Ag 11, 1932

MAEDCHEN IN UNIFORM, a German language picture, an adaptation of Christa Winsloe's play, "Gestern und Heute"; directed by Leontine Sagan. At the Criterion Theatre.

The Principal ....Emilia Unda
Fraulein von Bernburg ......Dorothea Wieck
Fraulein von Kesten ......Hedwig Schlichter
Manuela von Meinhardis........Hertha Thiele
Ilse von Westhagen ......Ellen Schwannecke

By MORDAUNT HALL.

The widely-discussed German language picture, "Maedchen in Uniform" ("Girls in Uniform"), which won glowing praise and enjoyed remarkable success in Berlin, Paris and London, finally was presented, with subtitles in English, at the Criterion last night. The New York State Board of Censors at first frowned upon the suggestion in this film of the "Captive" theme, but recently they reconsidered their refusal to grant it a license.

It is a beautiful, tender, and really artistic cinematic work. The story is an adaptation of Christa Winsloe's play, "Gestern und Heute" ("Yesterday and Today"), and the girls in uniform are the pupils in a Potsdam school for daughters of aristocratic families. It was produced by Leontine Sagan, under the experienced eye of Karl Froelich, one of Germany's most distinguished directors. From the moment its scenes appear on the screen, one cannot help but sense its unusual quality, for where it might be ordinary or flat, the fine photography and the assembling of the glimpses give a conception of space and depth: Every opportunity is taken to make the most of pleasing shadows and high-lights, and yet it is never exotic.

Just as the story is told with admirable simplicity, so are the scenes pictured. It is a film which pleases the eye constantly, for one envisions not only the characters, but also their surroundings, whether they are in halls, rooms or in a garden. It is a production in which the background counts for much, and added to this aspect there are the players who are so well suited to their respective rôles. It is not a film in which there is any evil intent, provided one analyzes the conditions of such students. The suspicions of the severe principal of the institution are approached subtly, with a gesture of "Honi soit qui mal y pense." It is actually more of a rap on the knuckles for the militaristic notions than an exposition of unnatural affection.

To this Potsdam school there comes the sensitive Manuela von Meinhardis, who happens to be motherless. Her frock is taken from her and she receives in its place an ill-fitting, ugly striped dress. It is her uniform while she is in the school and, coupled with the coiffure the students are forced to adopt, it standardizes them to a great extent, giving them all virtually the same degree of plainness. The encounter with the Uriah Heep-like Assistant Principal does not cause Manuela to feel any happier, for the bowed, elderly woman, always most sycophantic to the Principal and rubbing her hands together, is cold and dismal, her every move dominated by her superior.

Fraülein von Bernburg, one of the teachers, however, with her heavy eyelids and aristocratic features, is sympathetic. Manuela is motherless, and that is the reason given for Fraülein von Bernburg paying more attention to this girl than she does to the others. She inspires Manuela's devotion to her.

The antithesis to Fraülein von Bernburg is the Principal, a devotee of the militaristic notions. She walks with a cane and as she passes the other teachers or the pupils, all bow low to her. It is her right, she apparently thinks, for she never appears to give anybody so much as a nod. If she happens to enter one of the rooms where the girls are laughing or chatting, all of them at once become silent, without so much as a hushed whisper, and if she addresses one of the girls, the pupil almost trembles as she replies.

There comes a breath of joy to this school when the pupils are rehearsing Schiller's play, "Don Carlos," in which Manuela plays the title rôle. Then there is the grand night when the play is given and Manuela excels anything expected of her. As a reward for their histrionic efforts the girl players, still in costume, receive a sip or so of punch and so delighted are they all that they pour their punch into Manuela's glass and she drinks it. It has an effect on her, not much, but she is flushed and talkative and standing on a balcony she tells loudly of her great affection for Fräulein von Bernburg.

The Principal on hearing of this suspects something evil and Manuela finds herself in the miserable plight of having to sit alone, without speaking to anybody. When a Princess comes to visit the school, the Principal gives orders for Manuela to join the other scholars and the visitor asks, first for one girl and then for Manuela.

There is a dramatic sequence toward the end in which the students all reveal their great affection for Manuela.

It is a film in which all the characters fasten themselves in one's mind, not as actors, but as real persons. The performances of all are deserving of the highest praise.

This film. of which last night was a showing for the press and which is open to the public from now on, is offered over here by John Krimsky and Gifford Cochran, who after seeing it in Paris took an airplane to Berlin and contracted with the German producers for the American rights. Mr. Krimsky is president of Playchoice and Mr. Cochran is an artist with a studio in Munich.

S 21, 1932

TROUBLE IN PARADISE, adapted from Laszlo Aladar's play, "The Honest Finder"; directed by Ernst. Lubitsch; produced by Paramount Publix. At the Rivoli Theatre.

Lily..........................Miriam Hopkins
Marianne Colet...................Kay Francis
Gaston Monescu.............Herbert Marshall
The Major..................Charles Ruggles
Francois...............Edward Everett Horton
Giron.....................C. Aubrey Smith
Jaques........................Robert Greig

By MORDAUNT HALL.

Surely "Trouble in Paradise," a picture which was presented at the Rivoli yesterday, points no moral and the tale it tells is scant and innocuous, yet, because it was fashioned by the alert-minded Ernst Lubitsch, it is a shimmering, engaging piece of work. In virtually every scene the lively imagination of the German producer shines forth and it seems as though he were the only person in Hollywood who could have turned out such an effective entertainment from such a feathery story.

Mr. Lubitsch has drawn heavily upon Paramount's resources for his scenic designs, which are an important adjunct to this flippant film. Here the director has a flair for beautiful clocks of various types and in one sequence, while the voices of two players are heard carrying on their bantering, all one sees is a clock on a table. When the characters pass into another room, there is still another clock. Upstairs there is a modernistic grandfather clock and outside a window there is the tower from which chimes tell the hour. The settings are lovely and spacious with meticuluous attention to furnishings. No more inviting example of 1932 decorations has been offered on the screen.

This merry trifle, which was first spun as a play by Laszlo Aladar and arranged for a motion picture by Grover Jones and Samson Raphaelson, deals, if you please, with those light-fingered gentry who rob and pick pockets. Imagine the charming Miriam Hopkins impersonating an ingratiating, capable thief! Then try to visualize Herbert Marshall as a delightful scoundrel who might look upon Alias Jimmy Valentine as a posing blunderer! They are such an interesting pair of crooks that it is not altogether astonishing that the other characters find them companionable.

First one has a glimpse of Venice with a refuse collector singing "O Sole Mio" as he steers his craft through the canals. The camera then introduces Gaston Monescu posing as a baron, and later Lily, whom Gaston calls his "little shoplifter" and "sweet little pickpocket."

This pair eventually turn their attention to Paris and Mme. Marianne Colet, the widow of a wealthy perfumery manufacturer. Marianne, impersonated by Kay Francis, has two suitors, neither of whom finds much favor with her. One is the Major, played by Charles Ruggles, who stays quite sober throughout the proceedings, and the other is François, who has been an easy victim for Gaston in the City of the Doges.

Through returning Mme. Colet's precious bag, which he had stolen, Gaston, after accepting the 20,000 francs' reward and explaining that he is one of the new poor, soon is ensconced in Marianne Colet's mansion as her secretary, and Lily, not long afterward, is employed as a typist. She has to sit on her hands when talking to Marianne Colet, for fear she might hurt the chances of stealing 100,000 francs in cash—cash being always better than jewelry—by pilfering one of the pieces of jewelry in a box.

As for Marianne Colet, one might say that her interest in Gaston is keener than most women who employ secretaries, and it prompts the fair but reprehensible Lily to tell Gaston that she admires him as a burglar and a thief, but she warns him not to sink to the low level of a gigolo.

After their fashion, they have a romantic and busy time at Marianne Colet's. There are moments when it looks as though Mr. Lubitsch were going to let fly a few ideas like René Clair's, but he stops himself and never for an instant can it be said that Lubitsch ever copies another director. Time and again in this feature he offers ideas which will undoubtedly be well imitated in Hollywood. He does not take this fable seriously at all, but he leaves nothing undone to make it the sort of thing that will keep audiences in a constant state of chuckles.

Mr. Marshall is as smooth and easy as ever. He looks more the baron than the thief Gaston. It is not surprising that Marianne thinks of promoting him from secretary to husband. Miss Hopkins makes Lily a very interesting person, who steals as another girl might sing. Lily even steals her way out of the last scene in the film. Kay Francis is attractive and able as Marianne, whose sins consist of being too credulous and in being very fond of romantic adventures.

N 9, 1932

A Mine Disaster.

KAMERADSCHAFT, a German language picture; story by Karl Otten; directed by G.-W. Pabst; a Nero Production. At the Europa.

Emile..........................George Challa
Jean..........................Daniel Mendaille
Wittkopp..........................Ernst Busch
His Wife..................Elisabeth Wendt
Kasper.................Alexander Granach
Wilderer....................Fritz Kampers
Kaplan.......,...........Gustav Puettjer
An Old French Miner..........Alex Bernard
His Grandson...................Pierre Louis

The little Europa is now harboring one of the finest examples of realism that has come to the screen. It is a German production called "Kameradschaft" and the dialogue, which is sparse, is in both German and French, with superimposed sub-titles in English. The inspiration for this impressive production was the coal mine disaster at Courrieres in 1906, in which nearly 1,200 lives were lost. In the picture the narrative has been set forward, making it post-World War, and its theme is that the sympathy existing between the German and French miners knows no boundaries.

G. W. Pabst, the director, has placed the action of his picture in a place referred to as Courbiere, on the Franco-German border. After the preliminary scenes sketching the Germans going over to the French side to a dance hall and the introduction of several characters, Herr Pabst concerns himself first with the fire in the mine, then with the series of explosions, the shock to the town, the volunteers going to the rescue and a lorry filled with German miners tearing across the border to go to the rescue of the imprisoned Frenchmen. Shots are fired over the heads of the Germans, but a sensible officer orders his men not to shoot.

The scenes in the mine are so real that one never thinks of them as being staged. When a hole is battered through a wall, the wall looks as if it had been built to stay. Throughout the length of this tale of horror one feels as though one were permitted through some uncanny force to look into all parts of the mine. There is the old man who insists on going to the rescue of a youngster. The elevator does not function and the old man, instead of waiting, crawls down ladder after ladder. There is the plight of some of the trapped men who are up to their armpits in water, and their demeanor is contrasted with that of a mule.

Above there are the hysterical wives and daughters clamoring at the iron gates, as though they might be able to help. Shadows though they are, it is a sequence filled with telling pathos. All the noises and sounds are wonderfully natural. There is the gurgle of water, the rush of coal and the final crumbling of the black mass and men beating on iron pipes to signal to the rescuers. Like sailors caught in a sunken submarine, the miners watch and hope, looking for a chance to get through to another part of the mine.

And on the surface the dead and unconscious are being brought up on stretchers, some being worked upon with pulmotors and others recovering through the effects of the fresh air.

There is the gate labeled "Frontiere 1919," which is torn down, and in one of the closing scenes of this film, as it was first shown in Berlin, the gate was depicted being put up again. The derisive howls and hisses from audiences, however, caused the producers to omit this idea. The friendship between the miners is cemented in this version of the film by not having the gate.

This "Kameradschaft" has been enormously successful in England and on the Continent.   M. H.

N 9, 1932

A FAREWELL TO ARMS, an adaptation of the novel by Ernest Hemingway; directed by Frank Borzage; produced by Paramount Publix. At the Criterion Theatre.

Catherine Barkley	Helen Hayes
Lieut. Frederic Henry	Gary Cooper
Major Rinaldi	Adolphe Menjou
Helen Ferguson	Mary Phillips
The Priest	Jack La Rue
Head Nurse	Blanche Friderici
Bonello	Henry Armetta
Piani	George Humbert
Manera	Fred Malatesta
Miss Van Campen	Mary Forbes
Count Greffi	Tom Ricketts
Gordoni	Robert Cauterio
British Major	Gilbert Emery

By MORDAUNT HALL.

Bravely as it is produced for the most part, there is too much sentiment and not enough strength in the pictorial conception of Ernest Hemingway's novel, "A Farewell to Arms," which came to the Criterion last night. Notwithstanding the undeniable artistry of the photography, the fine recording of voices and Frank Borzage's occasional excellent directorial ideas, one misses the author's vivid descriptions and the telling dialogue between Lieutenant Frederic Henry and the Italian officers. It is Mr. Borzage rather than Mr. Hemingway who prevails in this film and the incidents frequently are unfurled in a jerky fashion.

To be true it was an extremely difficult task to tackle, a rather hopeless one in fact, considering that the story is told in the first person. Possibly if any one has not read Mr. Hemingway's book, the picture will appeal as a rather interesting if tragic romance. In some of the scenes, however, the producers appear to take it for granted that the spectators have read the book.

The film account skips too quickly from one episode to another and the hardships and other experiences of Lieutenant Henry are passed over too abruptly, being suggested rather than told. Here and there Mr. Borzage has some sterling sequences, such as after Lieutenant Henry is wounded and is being carried on a stretcher to the ambulance and from the ambulance to the hospital. In some scenes he does not show the wounded man, but contents himself by depicting what the wounded man sees—the faces from above him, the temporary hospital ceiling and so forth.

In this tale of love and war on the Italian front, Gary Cooper gives an earnest and splendid portrayal of Lieutenant Henry, an American, serving with the Italian ambulance corps, who falls in love with an English nurse named Catherine Barkley. Helen Hayes is admirable as Catherine and beside the tall, gaunt Mr. Cooper she looks a very tiny person. When he puts his cape over her she is almost hidden, and the contrasting figures elicited one of the few laughs from the audience. Another clever characterization is contributed by Adolphe Menjou as Major Rinaldi, the surgeon. It is unfortunate that these three players, serving the picture so well, do not have the opportunity to figure in more really dramatic interludes.

Often one is confused as to where the players are, and when Henry decides to escape from Italy to Switzerland the glimpse of his getting into a boat is much too like many another Hollywood scene. Then, too, Mr. Borzage is too partial to a deluge of rain instead of a drizzle.

The first meeting of Catherine and Henry is set forth satisfactorily, but subsequently the picture appears to gather speed, as though the director feared he could not get in all the details he wished. There is the time when Henry leaves for the front and Catherine gives him the little St. Anthony charm, and then there is the moment when Henry is the victim of a high explosive shell.

They have not omitted the discovery in the hospital of Henry's empty liquor bottles, and Helen Ferguson, another nurse and a genuine friend of Catherine's, tells the Lieutenant that she will report the matter. The coolness of the ambulance corps officer is neatly brought out here, for no sooner has Helen, who dislikes

Henry, left the ward, than he goes to the head of the bed and uncovers a full bottle, out of which he takes a drink.

After Catherine goes to Switzerland to give birth to her baby, Henry writes many letters to her, but they are held up by the censor. Eventually these missives are all mailed together and when Catherine receives them she realizes what has happened and faints.

Several of the strong dramatic incidents of the novel are not included in the film, obviously because the producers did not wish to offend Italians. Here there is a note of victory coupled with the presumed death of Catherine, for Henry carries Catherine's inert form from her cot to a window as the throngs outside are celebrating the armistice.

Aside from the players mentioned, Mary Phillips gives an easy and natural interpretation of Helen Ferguson. Jack LaRue is satisfactory as the priest. Blanche Friderici is capital as the head nurse. Henry Armetta does his usual good work in the role of an ambulance driver, and Gilbert Emery is persuasive as a British Major.

D 9, 1932

CAVALCADE, an adaptation of the play by Noel Coward; directed by Frank Lloyd; a Fox production. At the Gaiety Theatre.

Jane Marryot	Diana Wynyard
Robert Marryot	Clive Brook
Fanny Bridges	Ursula Jeans
Alfred Bridges	Herbert Mundin
Ellen Bridges	Una O'Connor
Annie	Merle Tottenham
Margaret Harris	Irene Browne
Cook	Beryl Mercer
Edward Marryot	John Warburton
Joe Marryot	Frank Lawton
Edith Harris	Margaret Lindsay
Mrs. Snapper	Tempe Piggott
George Granger	Billy Bevan
Ronnie James	Desmond Roberts
Uncle Dick	Frank Atkinson
Mirabelle	Ann Shaw
Tommy Jolly	William Stanton
Lieutenant Edgar	Stuart Hall
Duchess of Churt	Mary Forbes
Edward (age 12)	Dick Henderson Jr.
Joey (age 8)	Douglas Scott

By MORDAUNT HALL.

It is a most affecting and impressive picture that the Fox studios have produced from Noel Coward's stage panorama, "Cavalcade." It reached the Gaiety last night and, without having seen the original, one senses the genuine quality of the film and also the advantages that have been taken of the camera's far-seeing eye. Never for an instant is the story, which takes one through three decades of life in England, lost sight of, notwithstanding the inclusion of remarkable scenes of throngs in war and peace, and it is a relief to observe that the obvious is left to the spectator's imagination.

One sees England, merry and sad, belligerent and peaceful, an England with the characters speaking their minds. The atmosphere of London and elsewhere has been reproduced in a masterful fashion, from the days of the Boer War to the present time. In the early episodes one hears occasionally the sound of horses' hoofs on the streets and now and again an old four-wheeler puts in an appearance. Then there are familiar sights, including the pillar boxes, the lamp posts, flashes of the East End and Mayfair, including a distant view of the Houses of Parliament with Big Ben booming the hour.

This production was directed by Frank Lloyd, under the experienced supervision of Winfield Sheehan, who knows his London. In all its scenes there is a meticulous attention to detail, not only in the settings, which include one of Trafalgar Square during the armistice celebrations, but also in the selection of players. The principals are English and Clive Brook, Diana Wynyard and Frank Lawton give conspicuously fine performances. Then there are also highly pleasing portrayals in lighter roles by Herbert Mundin, Una O'Connor, Beryl Mercer and others.

It is a tale of joy and woe, chiefly concerned with the experiences of Robert Marryot and his wife, Jane, and embracing what happens to their children and their servants. It is unfurled with such marked good taste and restraint that many an eye will be misty after witnessing this production.

It begins with New Year's Eve

in 1899, with the Marryots drinking their customary toast. Robert is to leave the following day for South Africa as an officer in the City Imperial Volunteers. Their butler, Alfred Bridges, impersonated by Mr. Mundin, who has joined up as a private, is leaving on the same troop ship. Mafeking is being besieged and it is questionable whether it can hold out much longer. Jane Marryot's brother is one of the officers in Mafeking.

Jane hates war and she dislikes even to see her two little boys playing with toy cannon and soldiers. The music of martial bands, with the inevitable "Soldiers of the Queen," gets on Jane's nerves. Months afterward, however, she is jubilant when her husband returns. There is some excellent comedy at this time afforded by Bridges and his wife, Ellen. All are glad the war is over. The next stirring moment happens when the news comes that Queen Victoria is dying. Subsequently the film is concerned with the Queen's funeral, seen by the characters (but not by the spectators) from a window in their home. The funeral march is heard and Jane comments on five kings being in one group of the procession.

The years roll by and Bridges and his wife are running a "pub," which is none too successful, due to the landlord imbibing too freely himself and being too generous to his customers. It ends with Bridges being fatally injured by being run over by a horse-drawn vehicle. One also hears from Fanny Bridges, his daughter, who later distinguishes herself as a dancer and eventually takes up singing the "blues."

Edward Marryot, one of the Marryots' sons, and Edith Harris go on their honeymoon as passengers aboard the Titanic and just a glimpse of a life-belt tells of their untimely ends. Without ever a hasty word between them, the Marryots console themselves that they still have one son, Joe.

Then comes 1914, with the first shock of the World War, its Zeppelins dropping bombs and the wounded being brought in by ambulance trains. Joe goes forth to fight and he returns on leave, after being the only remaining officer of his original battalion. It is just after he returns to the front that he is killed, but Jane and Robert Marryot are beheld drinking to each other's health when 1930, or is it 1932, is welcomed by the usual throngs singing "Auld Lang Syne." With its discordant and peaceful notes life goes on.

Miss Wynyard is excellent as Jane Marryot. She portrays her rôle with such sympathy and feeling that one scarcely thinks of her as an actress. Mr. Brook is at his best as Robert Marryot. Mr. Lawton is capital as Joe Marryot. In fact all in the large cast give a good account of themselves.

Ja 6, 1933

KING KONG, based on a story by the late Edgar Wallace and Merian C. Cooper; directed by Mr. Cooper; presented by RKO Radio Pictures. At the Radio City Music Hall and RKO Roxy.

Ann Redman	Fay Wray
Denham	Robert Armstrong
Driscoll	Bruce Cabot
Englehorn	Frank Reicher
Weston	Sam Hardy
Native Chief	Noble Johnson
Second Mate	James Flavin
Witch King	Steve Clemento
Lumpy	Victor Long

By MORDAUNT HALL.

At both the Radio City Music Hall and the RKO Roxy, which have a combined seating capacity of 10,000, the main attraction now is a fantastic film known as "King Kong." The story of this feature was begun by the late Edgar Wallace and finished by Merian C. Cooper, who with his old associate, Ernest B. Schoedsack, is responsible for the production. It essays to give the spectator a vivid conception of the terrifying experiences of a producer of jungle pictures and his colleagues, who capture a gigantic ape, something like fifty feet tall, and bring it to New York. The narrative is worked out in a decidedly compelling fashion, which is mindful of what was done in the old silent film "The Lost World."

Through multiple exposures, processed "shots" and a variety of angles of camera wizardry the producers set forth an adequate story and furnish enough thrills for any devotee of such tales.

Although there are vivid battles between prehistoric monsters on the island which Denham, the picture maker, insists on visiting, it is when the enormous ape, called Kong, is brought to this city that the excitement reaches its highest pitch. Imagine a 50-foot beast with a girl in one paw climbing up the outside of the Empire State Building, and after putting the girl on a ledge, clutching at airplanes, the pilots of which are pouring bullets from machine guns into the monster's body.

It often seems as though Ann Redman, who goes through more terror than any of the other characters in the film, would faint, but she always appears to be able to scream. Her body is like a doll in the claw of the gigantic beast, who in the course of his wanderings through Manhattan tears down a section of the elevated railroad and tosses a car filled with passengers to the street. Automobiles are mere missiles for this Kong, who occasionally reveals that he relishes his invincibility by patting his chest.

Denham is an intrepid person but it is presumed that when the ape is killed he has had quite enough of searching for places with strange monsters. In the opening episode he is about to leave on the freighter for the island supposed to have been discovered by some sailor, when he goes ashore to find a girl whom he wants to act in his picture. In course of time he espies Ann, played by the attractive Fay Wray, and there ensues a happy voyage. Finally through the fog the island is sighted and Denham, the ship's officers and sailors, all armed, go ashore. It soon develops that the savages, who offer up sacrifices in the form of human beings to Kong, their super-king, keep him in an area surrounded by a great wall. Kong has miles in which to roam and fight with brontosauri and dinosauri and other huge creatures.

There is a door to the wall. After Denham and the others from the ship have had quite enough of the island, Kong succeeds in bursting open the door, but he is captured through gas bombs hurled at him by the white men. How they ever get him on the vessel is not explained, for the next thing you know is that Kong is on exhibition in Gotham, presumably in Madison Square Garden.

During certain episodes in this film Kong, with Ann in his paw, goes about his battles, sometimes putting her on a fifty-foot high tree branch while he polishes off an adversary. When he is perceived on exhibition in New York he is a frightening spectacle, but Denham thinks that he has the beast safely shackled. The newspaper photographers irritate even him with their flashlights, and after several efforts he breaks the steel bands and eventually gets away. He looks for Ann on the highways and byways of New York. He climbs up hotel façades and his head fills a whole window, his white teeth and red mouth adding to the terror of the spectacle.

Everywhere he moves he crushes out lives. He finally discovers Ann and being a perspicacious ape, he decides that the safest place for himself and Ann is the tower of the Empire State structure.

Needless to say that this picture was received by many a giggle to cover up fright. Constant exclamations issued from the Radio City Music Hall yesterday. "What a man!" observed one youth when the ape forced down the great oaken door on the island. Human beings seem so small that one is reminded of Defoe's "Gulliver's Travels." One step and this beast traverses half a block. If buildings hinder his progress, he pushes them down, and below him the people look like Lilliputians.

Miss Wray goes through her ordeal with great courage. Robert Armstrong gives a vigorous and compelling impersonation of Denham. Bruce Cabot, Frank Reicher, Sam Hardy, Noble Johnson and James Flavin add to the interest of this weird tale.

Mr 3, 1933

The Duesseldorf Murders.

M. based on a story by Thea von Harbou; directed by Fritz Lang; a Nerofilm production; distributed by Foremco Pictures Corporation. At the Mayfair.

The Murderer..................Peter Lorre
The Mother.................Ellen Widmann
The Child...................Inge Landgut
The Safebreaker........Gustaf Grundgens
The Burglar...................Fritz Gnass
The Card-Sharper.............Fritz Odemal
The Pickpocket................Paul Kemp
The Confidence Trickster......Theo Lingen
The President of Police,
.......................Ernst Stahl-Nachbaur
The Minister.................Franz Stein
Superintendent Lohman......Otto Wernicke
Superintendent Groeber......Theodor Loos
The Blind Beggar.........Georg John
Counsel for the Defense...Rudolf Blumner
The Watchman...............Karl Platen
The Criminal Chief.......Gerhard Bienert
The Landlady...............Rosa Valetti

Based on the fiendish killings which spread terror among the inhabitants of Düsseldorf in 1929, there is at the Mayfair a German-language pictorial drama with captions in English bearing the succinct title "M," which, of course, stands for murder. It was produced in 1931 by Fritz Lang and, as a strong cinematic work with, remarkably fine acting, it is extraordinarily effective, but its narrative, which is concerned with a vague conception of the activities of a demented slayer and his final capture, is shocking and morbid. Yet Mr. Lang has left to the spectator's imagination the actual commission of the crimes.

Peter Lorre portrays the Murderer in a most convincing manner. The Murderer is a repellent spectacle, a pudgy-faced, pop-eyed individual, who slouches along the pavements and has a Jekyll-and-Hyde nature. Little girls are his victims. The instant he lays eyes on a child homeward bound from school, he tempts her by buying her a toy balloon or a ball. This thought is quite sufficient to make even the clever direction and performances in the film more horrible than anything else that has so far come to the screen. Why so much fervor and intelligent work was concentrated on such a revolting idea is surprising.

It is unfurled in a way that reveals Mr. Lang and Thea von Harbou, his wife, evidently studied what happened in Düsseldorf during the score of atrocious murders, which incidentally caused young women to go about armed with pepper in case they were picked out by the slayer as possible victims. In the film the Commissioner of Police gives all his attention to trying to track the murderer down. He goes about his work in a systematic fashion, but when another crime is perpetrated he is talked to heatedly over the telephone by his superior.

So far as the film spectator is concerned, there is no mystery concerning the criminal. He is perceived looking into a mirror, making grimaces at himself, and later dawdling along the street, looking into shop windows. He has a habit of whistling a few bars of a tune, and apparently it is something he has little control over, for this whistling is actually responsible for his capture.

Mr. Lang has the adroit idea of having thugs, pickpockets, burglars and highwaymen eventually setting about to apprehend the Murderer.

His crimes are making things too hot for them and, bad as they are, they are depicted as being almost sympathetic characters compared to the Murderer. Every criminal in the town is told by the chief crook to be on the lookout for anybody who looks suspicious. Beggars and peddlers, as well as the thieves and swindlers, are all eager to catch the Murderer.

It is not astonishing that anybody doing a kindly turn for a child is suspected of being the criminal. A harmless individual is almost mobbed by hysterical women and enraged men. Meanwhile the Murderer is at large and has boastfully written of his last crime to the newspapers. The letter is analyzed. It was written evidently on a rough wooden table, and the sleuths draw circles about the map of the town as they widen their search.

But his capture does not come about through the minions of the law. It is a blind man, a peddler of toy balloons, who gives the alarm. He had sold a balloon a few days before to the man who had whistled the notes of an operatic tune. Suddenly the blind man several days later hears the melody whistled again, and it dawns upon him in a few seconds that the Murderer is passing. He gives the alarm, and in the course of the chase a youth, who had marked in chalk the letter "M" on his hand, slaps the suspect on the back.

There is a wild chase, the crooks being eager to get their man. They are willing to risk being held for crimes, and when the Police Commissioner understands from a prisoner that he and others were following the Murderer, the official is so stunned that he lets the cigar he is smoking drop from his mouth. One perceives the panting Murderer trying to get the lock off a door, his eyes wilder than ever, and perspiration dripping from his forehead. But the frantic, shrieking man is finally captured by the thieves, and a most interesting series of scenes is devoted to his trial. He bleats that he is a murderer against his will, whereas those before him commit crime because they want to. A thief presides at the trial. The Murderer has counsel, who says that the Murderer needs a doctor more than punishment. Then the Murdered is handed over to the police and a mother of one of the fiend's little victims declares that the death of the man will not give her back her child.

It is regrettable that such a wealth of talent and imaginative direction was not put into some other story, for the actions of this Murderer, even though they are left to the imagination, are too hideous to contemplate.　M. H.

Ap 3, 1933

GOLD DIGGERS OF 1933, based on the late Avery Hopwood's play, "The Gold Diggers"; music and lyrics by Harry Warren and Al Dubin; directed by Mervyn LeRoy; a Warner Brothers production. At the Strand.

J. Lawrence Bradford......Warren William
Carol........................Joan Blondell
Trixie Lorraine............Aline MacMahon
Polly Parker................Ruby Keeler
Brad..........................Dick Powell
Faneuil H. Peabody.............Guy Kibbee
Barney Hopkins................Ned Sparks
Fay..........................Ginger Rogers
Don.....................Clarence Nordstrom
Dance Director.............Robert Agnew
Gigolo Eddie..............Tammany Young
Messenger Boy...........Sterling Holloway
Clubman............Ferdinand Gottschalk

By MORDAUNT HALL.

To the accompaniment of tuneful melodies and flying sparks from the jokesmith's shop, Mammon apparently bows to Cupid in "Gold Diggers of 1933,' the new Warner Brothers' musical film, which was greeted by a throng at the Strand last night. It is an imaginatively staged, breezy show, with a story of no greater consequence than is to be found in this type of picture. But it has several humorous episodes and more than once the audience that filled the theatre to the doors applauded the excellent camera work and the artistry of the scenic effects.

In the early stages of this contribution the Gold Diggers are suffering from the economic depression. Gone are the good old days when their bewitching smiles brought bracelets, necklaces and fat checks. Soon, however, there is an unexpected turn in their fortunes, and the Gold Diggers are quick to prove that they have lost none of their business acumen. Trixie Lorraine, played by Aline MacMahon, is the most heartless of the girls of '33, but even she in the end becomes the bride of Faneuil H. Peabody, who in everyday life is none other than the comic Guy Kibbee.

On several occasions there were roars of mirth, and once this outburst was due to Mr. Peabody going to the mirror and comparing his likeness to a Pekinese. The romantic and unmercenary girl of this tale is Polly Parker, who is portrayed by Ruby Keeler. Polly is in love and she wants no hats or checks. One is sure she is sincere, from the expression on her attractive face when she looks at the young musical composer, temporarily known as Brad. This musical genius is acted by Dick Powell, the young man who attracted attention by his occasional songs in the film of "Blessed Event."

Brad happens to be a scion of a good family, and he comes to the rescue of the chorus girls and eventually is called upon to play the leading male rôle in his own musical comedy.

It falls to the lot of Warren William to appear as J. Lawrence Bradford, Brad's older brother, who of course, is very much averse to Brad's idea of marrying Polly. He might just as well have saved himself the trouble of objecting, for he, like Peabody, is ensnared by Carol (Joan Blondell), who, after she has received from J. Lawrence a check for $10,000 as hush money, merely frames it. Incidentally when he is making out the check, he first offers Carol $5,000 and she asks him whether he thinks that he is in the Mills Hotel.

Harry Warren and Al Dubin are responsible for the music and lyrics of the film. The songs include "Shadow Waltz," "Pettin' in the Park," "We're in the Money," "I've Got to Sing a Torch Song" and "Remember My Forgotten Man. The last named is particularly cleverly presented, with striking costumes and impressive staging. The "Forgotten Man" is the World War Veteran.

Miss MacMahon adds another fine performance to her list of Hollywood efforts. Miss Blondell is lively as the temporarily distressed Carol. Ruby Keeler does quite well as the heroine. Mr. Powell pleased the audience enormously with his singing and also his acting. Mr. William is capital in his rôle. Guy Kibbee rings the bell again with his work as the love-smitten elderly aristocrat. Ginger Rogers makes her numbers count for their full worth and Ned Sparks is thoroughly in his element as the producer of the musical comedy within a musical comedy.

Je 8, 1933

DINNER AT EIGHT, an adapatation of the play by George S. Kaufman and Edna Ferber; directed by George Cukor; a Metro-Goldwyn-Mayer production. At the Astor.

Carlotta Vance	Marie Dressler
Larry Renault	John Barrymore
Dan Packard	Wallace Beery
Kitty Packard	Jean Harlow
Oliver Jordan	Lionel Barrymore
Max Kane	Lee Tracy
Dr. Wayne Talbot	Edmund Lowe
Mrs. Oliver Jordan	Billie Burke
Paula Jordan	Madge Evans
Jo Stengel	Jean Harsholt
Mrs. Wayne Talbot	Karen Morley
Hattie Loomis	Louise Closser Hale
Ernest DeGraff	Phillips Holmes
Mrs. Wendel	May Robson
Ed Loomis	Grant Mitchell
Miss Alden	Phoebe Foster
Miss Copeland	Elizabeth Patterson
Tina	Hilda Vaughn
Fosdick	Harry Beresford
Mr. Fitch	Edwin Maxwell
Mr. Hatfield	John Davidson
Eddie	Edward Woods
Gustave	George Baxter
The Waiter	Herman Bing
Dora	Anna Duncan

By MORDAUNT HALL.

With its remarkable array of histrionic talent and with George Cukor at the helm, the film adaption of the play, "Dinner at Eight," which was offered last night by Metro-Goldwyn-Mayer at the Astor, could scarcely help being successful. And it lives up to every expectation, even though a few of the unforgettable lines penned by George S. Kaufman and Edna Ferber have been lost in the general shuffle. The picture clings as closely as possible to the original, and the many opportunities along cinematic lines have been fully appreciated by Mr. Cukor and others responsible for the offering.

This "Dinner at Eight" has a cast of twenty-five, and among the players are most of the stellar lights of the Metro-Goldwyn-Mayer studios, besides a few borrowed from other companies. It is one of those rare pictures which keeps you in your seat until the final fade-out, for nobody wants to miss one of the scintillating lines.

It is a fast-moving narrative with its humor and tragedy, one that offers a greater variety of characterizations than have been witnessed in any other picture. Some are polished and others decidedly rough and ready. They range from Mrs. Oliver Jordan, the snobbish hostess, who is wrapped up in the dinner she is giving for Lord and Lady Ferncliffe, to the scheming Dan Packard and his wife, Kitty, who in the play was said to talk "pure spearmint." But there is a reason in all cases for inviting the guests.

A strong line of drama courses through the story notwithstanding the flip dialogue. The picture runs along with a steady flow of unusually well knit incidents, which are woven together most expertly toward the end. This is owing to the fine writing of Mr. Kaufman and Miss Ferber, and it might easily be said that the wonder would be that anybody could go askew in turning such a play into pictorial form.

Veteran players of the stage, who have since been won over to talking pictures, are the principal assets in this film. It is a great pleasure to behold Marie Dressler away from her usual rôles, dressed in the height of fashion and given lines that aroused gales of mirth from the first-night audience.

Miss Dressler acts Carlotta Vance, the stage beauty of the mauve decade. Carlotta is a woman of much common sense who has a retort for every quip made to her. When one woman, obviously well on in years, hints that she was a child when she first saw Carlotta, the former actress ends the conversation by suggesting that they talk about the Civil War. Carlotta has her Pekingese dogs, one of which boasts of the name of Tarzan.

Another stage favorite of old is Billie Burke, who appears as the handsome Mrs. Oliver Jordan. A week before the dinner in honor of the Ferncliffes, she is worrying about the affair, making sure that there will not be the slightest hitch. An orchestra is ordered, extra servants hired and, when the morning of the dinner comes around, an aspic in the form of a lion is made. Little does Mrs. Jordan think that her dinner is going to be a memorable fiasco.

Lionel Barrymore fills the part of Mr. Jordan, whose mind is more concerned about money matters and his steamship line than his wife's dinner. His brother John is cast as Larry Renauld, the motion picture actor who brags of having earned $8,000 a week at one time, while he has only 7 cents to his name.

The scenes depicting Dan Packard, played by Wallace Beery, and Kitty, his ash-blonde wife, acted by Jean Harlow, are filled with gruff fun. There is hardly a moment while they are at home when the air is not filled with acrimonious accusations and retorts. Kitty rather likes the idea of blossoming out in society, while Dan's heart is set on being a big gun in politics. Edmund Lowe impersonates Dr. Wayne Talbot, who is infatuated with Kitty, one of his patients.

Mrs. Jordan's state of mind can well be imagined when she hears over the telephone that the Ferncliffes are unable to attend the dinner as they are on their way to Florida. Added to this are other troubles, including the tragic end of Larry Renault, who, unknown to Mrs. Jordan, had had an affair with her daughter, Paula.

Miss Dressler is splendid as the wise Carlotta. Miss Burke's contribution to the story is all one could wish. She is the personification of an anxious hostess at one moment and subsequently a deeply disappointed woman. John Barrymore tackles his rôle with his usual artistry. His acting during Larry's last moments is most effective. Mr. Beery fits into the rôle of Dan Packard as though it were written especially for him and Miss Harlow makes the most of the part of Kitty. Lionel Barrymore is suave and sympathetic. Edmund Lowe does quite well as Dr. Talbot.

It was a grand evening, an entertainment that caused one to forget about the deluge outside.

Ag 24,1933

In Old Mexico.

THUNDER OVER MEXICO, an abridgement of the film, "Que Viva Mexico," which was directed by Sergei M. Eisenstein and photographed by Edward Tisse, with an anonymous cast of native Mexicans; distributed by Sol Lesser; presented by Upton Sinclair. At the Rialto.

Even though "Thunder Over Mexico," a film which is now at the Rialto, may fall short of what it might have been had its director, Sergei M. Eisenstein, himself supervised the assembling and cutting of the mass of scenes he photographed in Mexico, it is, until the latter stages, a testimonial to its producer's imagination, skill and artistry.

According to authoritative sources, M. Eisenstein, the Soviet producer of "Potemkin" and "Ten Days That Shook the World," photographed no less than 285,000 feet of film in Mexico, and it is dubious whether he could have done much better by the picture if it were to be exhibited at one sitting, for in its present form it is only a little over 7,000 feet. Nevertheless, it has stirred up a great many protests from persons who maintain that Eisenstein's work has been massacred. Sol Lesser is responsible for the arranging and cutting of the scenes as the film stands now. He culled first 40,000 feet from the fifty-four miles of film and then went to work to turn that into a commercial length feature. It is true that the picture is absurdly abrupt in the closing interludes, but for fully three-quarters of its length it shows Eisenstein, the stylist, at his best.

"Thunder Over Mexico" is being presented by Upton Sinclair, who was instrumental in getting the capital for Eisenstein to make the film after the Russian severed his connection with Paramount Publix, because the studio heads of that concern did not see eye to eye with him in the proposed picturization of Theodore Dreiser's "An American Tragedy." As Eisenstein was refused permission to re-enter the United States after he had been working on the picture in Mexico, the 2,850 cans of film were shipped to Hollywood, and it is reported that executives from all the major studios looked at the bewildering mileage of pictures and declared that it was not possible to put the mass into coherent form.

Be that as it may, "Thunder Over Mexico," thanks to Messrs. Sinclair and Lesser, is now here. Its characters are played for the most part by Mexicans who had no experience in acting. Yet, under the tutelage of M. Eisenstein, they acquit themselves with no little distinction. The drama in which they figure concerns the days of twenty-seven years ago, but the actual story is prefaced by glimpses of Aztec ruins on the Anahuac plateau, the Mayan relics on the Yucatan plains and other suggestive views. The director points to the rugged monuments of the Aztecs and compares the profiles with those of the individuals who serve in the narrative.

There are flashes of compelling beauty, skies that are angry and others that smile. Throughout the work there are lovely highlights and deep shadows, virtually all the scenes having been made in the open. It is a story of a peon who accompanies the girl he intends to marry on a visit to his master, the wealthy man who owns the hacienda. The master's daughter is about to celebrate her own engagement. The peon, incidentally named Sebastian, is refused permission to enter his master's home. The girl, Maria, enters alone and in the course of time she is insulted by one of the master's guests. Trouble follows for Sebastian when he resents the insult and it culminates with Sebastian and two of his friends being bound, put into holes in the ground and trampled to death by horses going back and forth.

The climax to the film is horribly realistic. To accentuate the sadistic effect the sole sounds one hears—except for the music accompaniment in this otherwise silent production are the agonized cries of one of the victims.

In one or two scenes M. Eisenstein derides religion, but later the title writer does the reverse, for one gathers that present conditions in Mexico come, in the film, as an answer to a girl's prayer.

At the opening performance of the film on Friday Mr. Sinclair declared that the picture followed Eisenstein's own scenario and that the scenes had been selected in proper proportion to make practicable footage.

The musical accompaniment to the picture was arranged by Dr. Hugo Riesenfeld.   M. H.

S 25, 1933

THE PRIVATE LIFE OF HENRY VIII, written by Lajos Biro and Arthur Wimperis; directed by Alexander Korda; produced by London Film Productions; released by United Artists. At the Radio City Music Hall.
Henry VIII...............Charles Laughton

Thomas Culpeper.............Robert Donat
Henry's old nurse................Lady Tree
Catherine Howard............Binnie Barnes
Anne of Cleves............Elsa Lanchester
Anne Boleyn.................Merle Oberon
Thomas Cromwell..........Franklin Dyall
Wriothesly ....Miles Mander
Jane Seymour.................Wendy Barrie
Cornell ....Claud Allister
Thomas Peynell.................John Loder
Catherine Parr..............Everley Gregg
Archbishop Cranmer ....Laurence Hanray
Duke of Cleves..............William Austin
Holbein ....John Turnbull
Duke of Norfolk............Frederick Cully
French executioner........Gibb McLaughlin
English executioner............Sam Livesey

By MORDAUNT HALL.

Charles Laughton, whose shadow is scurrying around the country in several pictures, including "The Sign of the Cross," in which he gave his clever conception of Nero, is at the top of his form in the title rôle of "The Private Life of Henry VIII," which was directed in London by the Hungarian Alexander Korda . The current work, which is now at the Radio City Music Hall, was not always received with unstinted praise on the other side of the Atlantic, because, although it was admittedly a clever production, some of the critics resented the buffooning of the fiery and amorous monarch. But in this country it probably will be enjoyed heartily without any such reservations, for it is a really brilliant if suggestive comedy.

Mr. Laughton not only reveals his genius as an actor, but also shows himself to be a past master in the art of make-up. In this offering he sometimes looks as if he had stepped from the frame of Holbein's painting of Henry. He appears to have the massive shoulders and true bearded physignomy of the marrying ruler. Mr. Laughton may be guilty of caricaturing the rôle, but occasionally truths shine in the midst of the hilarity. He gives an admirable idea of Henry's vanity and also of his impetuousness, his sense of humor, his courage and fear. There is Laughton's amusing twist of his mouth and nose when he outwits, as Henry thinks, other persons in his entourage. This Henry is seldom able to conceal his actual thoughts. If he admires a woman, not only she knows, but everybody else. If he dislikes anything, as he does the appearance of Anne of Cleves, he almost groans.

He has a distinctive gait and glories in his strength. He also lays

138

claim to being the best card player in England. When he laughs the laughter of others is heard, gradually increasing in volume, until all subordinates are laughing with their respective superiors. The wives who lose their heads apparently cause him concern only until the execution is over.

Catherine Howard is the real beauty of his mates. She appears at a banquet and is about to sing, when Henry asks her if she knows "What Shall I Do For Love?"—one of his own compositions. Fortunately she is able to sing the ballad and it is quite evident that Henry has lost his heart. But it chances that the frightful Anne of Cleves is about to leave the Continent for England. Henry trusts that she will not risk the Channel crossing, but she turns up with her very plain maids-in-waiting. Her English is broken and her face scarcely prepossessing. But it is not her desire to please Henry. All she wants is not love, but money—two palaces and a generous income for life. She plays cards with Henry, and, boast as he may of his ability at the game, he loses. And the rapacious Anne refuses to trust him for a hand or two. He has to go forth and borrow crowns from his courtiers.

Before Anne reaches England, Henry thinks that he will visit the apartment of the dainty Catherine Howard. He walks stealthily along the corridors, but his silhouette is beheld and there roars forth the command "The King's Guard!" He takes another direction and again the order is heard. Just as a soldier is about to shout it a third time Henry puts his hand over the man's mouth and then succeeds in knocking on Catherine's door.

"Who's there?" asks Catherine.

"Henry," answers the man of many moods nervously.

"Henry who?" comes from the inside.

"The King," replies the visitor, meekly.

It is a great relief to Henry when Anne consents to a divorce and he is exuberant when he finds the way clear to make Catherine Howard his wife.

It is a remarkably well-produced film, both in the matter of direction and in the settings and selection of exterior scenes. There are several lovely glimpses of old structures, including the Tower of London. No knives and forks were used in that day and therefore the always scrupulously dressed monarch thinks nothing of devouring a chicken in his hands and tossing the bones to the floor.

The performances of the supporting players are uniformly good, especially the portrayals of Elsa Lanchester, who in private life is Mrs. Laughton. She is excellent as the fine little business woman, Anne of Cleves. Binnie Barnes is able and charming as Catherine Howard.

O 13, 1933

Fun in French.

QUATOREZ JUILLET, a dialogue film in French with Annabella, Georges Rigaud, Raymond Cordy, Paul Olivier, Thomy Bourdelle, Raymond Aimos and Pola Illery; directed by Rene Clair: a Tobis-Klangfilm production At the Little Carnegie Playhouse.

Rene Clair's latest French dialogue film, "Quatorze Juillet," which has reached the screen of the Little Carnegie Playhouse, may not in some respects be up to the high standard set by his other productions, but it will satisfy those who delight in this Gallic director's gifted technique. It also has alluring melodies and not a few of the incidents recall some of those in his first picture, "Sous Les Toits de Paris."

If "Quatorze Juillet" is not as engrossing in its story as M. Clair's "Le Million," theer is no denying that it has one episode that is as clever as any he has put before the public. This particular phase of the tale is concerned with an intoxicated individual in evening attire, who is beheld suddenly toying with a revolver. He polishes the weapon with his handkerchief and, much to the consternation of waiters, musicians and patrons, points the firearm in their direction. It is a question of getting the revolver from the inebriated man, and finally a headwaiter musters up sufficient courage to approach the drunk's table. Understanding that his weapon is desired, the intemperate one, much to the relief of all, willingly parts with it. The musicians emerge from their hiding place behind a grand piano, the waiters resume work ànd the diners continue their converstaion. Then our friend cooly produces another revolver from his hip pocket and proceeds to cause further excitement, until Anna, a flower girl, succeeds in gaining possession of the dangerous plaything.

M. Clair constantly shows his keen sense of humor. There is true poetry in this recital, too, and the performances of all concerned are most efficient. M. Clair gives suspense and then virtually laughs at the spectator, for what is anticipated seldom occurs.

In the section of Paris with which the story is concerned one first sees the poor people adorning their windows with flags and lanterns for the Quatorze Juillet. M. Clair is, as always, careful about details, even to showing, when a lantern is blown away by a gust of wind, how the gamins scramble to get the precious object. There is Jean, a happy-go-lucky taxicab driver, who encounters, the dainty Anna. Evidently they fall in love, but it happens that Jean has a persistent mistress named Pola, who declines to leave his unpretentious abode. When Anna discovers that Pola is living with Jean, there is a breach, and, for one reason and another, Jean falls into bad company until he aids two thugs who are about to rob the café where Anna happens to have found employment.

The thugs enter the place and Jean keeps watch outside, little knowing that Anna will be blamed by her employer in the event of money being stolen from the cash register But all ends well, except that the restaurant discharges Anna for being careless.

M. Clair has his fun with another taxicab driver besides Jean. Then the inebriated old man, always genial, turns up at various parts of the tale. There are artistic flashes of the neighborhood, the gathering of crowds attracted by an automobile accident, a dash of gossip and eavesdropping.

"A Nous La Liberté" was a kaleidoscopic work, but this current venture glides along at a leisurely pace, frequently accompanied by pleasing music. Even the threat-

ening scenes are touched up with M. Clair's impudent fun. There are the celebrations of the Quatorze Juillet, with hosts of gay péople, the deluges of Summer rains, the flashes of life in restaurants and cafés.

The delightful Annabella gives an ingratiating portrayal of Anna. Among the other excellent performers are Georges Rigaud, Raymond Cordy, Paul Oliver and Pola Illery.   M. H.

O 20, 1933

More 'Thunder Over Mexico.'

EISENSTEIN IN MEXICO, a collection of views of Mexico taken by S. M. Eisenstein; presented in connection with "Thunder Over Mexico." At the Fifty-fifth Street Playhouse.

The return to New York last night of Sergei M. Eisenstein's much-discussed silent film "Thunder Over Mexico" was signalized by the presentation at the little Fifty-fifth Street Playhouse of a collection of views labeled "Eisenstein in Mexico."

According to the program, this haphazard string of scenes from various parts of the republic is a representative selection "from all material photographed by Eisenstein which contains political or social criticism." If such is the case, the average American spectator is likely to classify the controversy over the Soviet director's Mexican adventure as "much ado about nothing." The travelogue type of pictures of modern machines and rather snappy Mexican troops and firemen, contrasted with scenes of medieval superstition at the shrine of the Virgin of Guadalupe and in Yucatan, possesses a certain amount of interest, but is a long way from what one had been led to expect.

One of the most attractive bits shows a fête at Xochimilco, the famous Mexican flower Venice a few miles from the capital city. As in other parts of the Eisenstein Mexican film the photography is excellent.   H. T. S.

N 1, 1933

140

A Cocteau Concoction.

LE SANG D'UN POETE, a silent French
film, with Enrique Rivero and Elizabeth
Lee Miller; directed by Jean Cocteau;
presented by Edward T. Ricci. At the
Fifth Avenue Playhouse.

Jean Cocteau's "futurist" film,
"Le Sang d'un Poete" (The Blood
of a Poet), has arrived at the Fifth
Avenue Playhouse. Although reports from Paris in the Winter of
1931-32 told of the violent disputes
aroused by this eccentric production in the ranks of the film "in-
telligentsia," there seems slight
chance of anything like that happening in New York.

While the various imaginery episodes shown on the screen, to the
accompaniment of microphone comment by M. Cocteau himself, rein-
forced by English titles for those
unfamiliar with French, have a certain fascination, especially for persons interested in film technique,
they are hardly calculated to set the
Hudson River on fire.

The main idea would seem to consist in showing how easy it is for
artists to go crazy over their own
creations. When the young hero
(M. Rivero) is working on a crayon
sketch (during the battle of Fon-
tenoy, in 1745, according to the running comment) he apparently cuts
the palm of his hand severely. The
sight of his own blood drives him
mad and furnishes the excuse for a
series of disjointed and not over-
exciting incidents.

An attractive part of the picture
is that acted by Mlle. Miller, who
appears as a statue, a muse and the
personification of humanity. M.
Cocteau's hero pursues his check-
ered career from the middle of the
eighteenth century to the present
time, without being any the worse
for wear. Some of the photographic
effects are unusual. The music by
George Auric is classified as "interpretative," but the task of clar-
ifying M. Cocteau's thoughts (if
there really are any in the film) is
scarcely one that affords much in
the way of entertainment. H. T. S.

N 3, 1933

The Four Marx Brothers.

DUCK SOUP, based on a story by Bert
Kalmar and Harry Ruby; directed by
Leo McCarey; a Paramount production.
At the Rivoli.

Rufus T. Firefly ....Groucho Marx
Chicolini ....Chico Marx
Brownie ....Harpo Marx
Bob Rolland ....Zeppo Marx
Vera Marcal ....Racquel Torres
Ambassador Trentino ......Louis Calhern
Mrs. Teasdale ....Margaret Dumont
Secretary ....Verna Hillie
Agitator ....Leonid Kinsky
Zander ....Edmund Breese
Secretary of War ....Edwin Maxwell

Those mad clowns, the Marx
brothers, are now holding forth on
the Rivoli screen in their latest concoction, "Duck Soup," a production in which the bludgeon is employed more often than the gimlet.
The result is that this production
is, for the most part, extremely
noisy without being nearly as mirthful as their other films. There
are, however, one or two ideas in
this sea of puns that are welcome,
and Groucho, Chico, Harpo and
Zeppo reveal their customary zeal
in striving to get as much as possible out of these incidents.

Groucho is the latest of the performers to indulge in a mythical
kingdom story, for he, as the more
or less illustrious Rufus T. Firefly,
after being referred to as possess-
ing the statesmanship of Gladstone,
the humility of Lincoln and the
wisdom of Pericles, is made the
dictator of Freedonia. Slapping the
face of Ambassador Trentino, Sylvania's representative, means little
to Firefly, even though it may result in war. As one might imagine,
there is not only friction between
Freedonia and Sylvania during most
of this story, but also among other
persons in the country ruled over
by Groucho, or Mr. Firefly. Mrs.
Teasdale, whose husband was a serious thinker who once held Firefly's job, is keen to see that Firefly
gets full support from other
worthies.

During one important juncture
for Freedonia, one discovers that
two of the brothers Marx—Chico
and Harpo—have decorated their
faces with black mustaches and
spectacles, so that they look like
doubles of Groucho. This gives the
performers a chance for many
stunts, including the idea that one
of them is the reflection of the
other in a mirror. The insanity
persists until a third, or the real
Groucho, appears on the scene,
which yesterday aroused a torrent

of laughter.

Another equally hilarious morsel is where the dumb Harpo does a Paul Revere ride for Freedonia's sake. It happens, however, that Harpo, unlike the original, has an eye for a pretty face, and therefore when he perceives a girl in the window the ride comes to an abrupt end. Wild activities ensue, however, for the husband of the young blonde turns up and Revere's imitator has to hide under the water in a bathtub. Subsequently, when the frightened husband has made himself scarce, Harpo thinks that it would be a good idea to bring his horse into the house.

In another episode Groucho works himself up into a state of frenzy over a supposed insult, and when Ambassador Trentino appears with a hope of avoiding war, Groucho again slaps Sylvania's envoy. A certain amount of fun is furnished by Harpo's being constantly busy with a pair of scissors. He cuts the tails off Trentino's well-tailored coat and also uses his shears to cut a panama hat in half and to despoil other articles of clothing.

Now and again the governmental activities in Freedonia are interrupted with music and song. Besides the characteristic work of the Marx brothers, Louis Calhern gives an adequate interpretation as Trentino. Margaret Dumont is satisfactory as the eminent Mrs. Teasdale and Edwin Maxwell officiates as Secretary of War.   M. H.

N 23, 1933

QUEEN CHRISTINA, based on a story by Salka Vierted and Margaret P. Levino; directed by Rouben Mamoulian; a Metro-Goldwyn-Mayer production. At the Astor.
Queen Christina..............Greta Garbo
Don Antonio de la Prada......John Gilbert
Magnus ....Ian Keith
Chancellor Oxenstierna.......Lewis Stone
Ebba.......................Elizabeth Young
Aage.......................C. Aubrey Smith
Prince Palatine Charles Gustavus,
               Reginald Owen
French Ambassador......Georges Renevent
Archbishop................David Torrence
General.............Gustav von Seyffertitz
Inn Keeper ....Ferdinand Munier

By MORDAUNT HALL.

Soon after entering the Astor Theatre last night for the presentation of Greta Garbo's first picture in eighteen months, the spectators were transported by the evanescent shadows from the snow of New York in 1933 to the snows of Sweden in 1650. The current offering, known as "Queen Christina," is a skillful blend of history and fiction in which the Nordic star, looking as alluring as ever, gives a performance which merits nothing but the highest praise. She appears every inch a queen.

S. N. Behrman, the playwright, is responsible for the dialogue, which is a bright and smooth piece of writing, and Rouben Mamoulian did the direction. Mr. Mamoulian still has a penchant for asking the audience to fasten their gaze on his work with lights and shades rather than continuing the story, but here he does it less frequently than hitherto, and his scenes are, without a doubt, entrancing compositions.

It is an easy flowing romance in which there are several pleasingly humorous situations. As Queen Christina, Miss Garbo reveals her sense of humor and she handles some of the reticent levity in a superb fashion. She is forceful as Her Majesty and charming as Christina the woman. She is effectively supported in the romance by John Gilbert, who acts Don Antonio, an emissary from the King of Spain.

When Christina was born one is informed that her father Gustavus Adolphus regretted that she was not a boy. He persuaded her as a child to wear knickerbockers and it can be assumed that Oxenstierna, Chancellor of Sweden, insisted that she continue dressing as a boy after she was crowned Queen. This penchant for male attire is the result of a beguiling incident and the producers take the opportunity of giving Christina an elderly valet instead of a maid.

Christina has a dominant personality and, in the film she is beloved of her people. She goes dashing on horseback over the snow-covered countryside escorted only by her valet Aage, who is played by C. Aubrey Smith. They do not spare their horses in riding and it chances that some miles distant from town they come across a coach, the front wheels of which are caught in the deep snow. Christina tells the driver how to get the vehicle freed and one of the passengers is so relieved at being able to continue his journey that he presents to the Queen a silver piece, one adorned by her own profile. This passenger, who is none other than Don Antonio, thinks the Queen is quite an intelligent young man.

It is in a lovely wayside inn a few hours later that Don Antonio next sets eyes on the "intelligent young man," who, to digress for an instant, insists to one member of her court that she will not die an old maid, but "a bachelor." Christina has reserved for herself the last room at the inn. By this time Don Antonio appreciates that the "intelligent young man" is evidently well born and wealthy. They chat together and become unusually interested in each other. Eventually, Don Antonio suggests that they share the room and—after some hesitation—Christina agrees.

In course of time Don Antonio realizes that his companion is a woman. It is a case of love and—they spend the night together. Subsequently it is an abashed and bewildered Spaniard who presents his credentials to the Queen and discovers in the gorgeously clad creature on the throne his companion of the wayside inn. The fact that he comes to the Swedish ruler with a proposal of marriage from the King of Spain adds considerably to the emissary's confusion.

How the film ends is best left untold here. And if history has been gilded it is accomplished neatly and intelligently. Mr. Mamoulian's glimpses and vistas of the Queen's palace are extraordinarily striking and as a contrast to them there is the rugged simplicity of the tap room in the inn.

The conflict of the narrative is simple but effective. Besides the fascinating Swedish performer, there are several players who contribute good work. Mr. Gilbert is far more restrained than he was in his silent films. Ian Keith is splendid as the artful Magnus. Lewis Stone is admirable as sensible old Oxenstierna. C. Aubrey Smith is splendid as Aage. The other performers also acquit themselves favorably.

D 27, 1933

IT HAPPENED ONE NIGHT, based on a story by Samuel Hopkins Adams; directed by Frank Capra; a Columbia production. At the Radio City Music Hall.
Peter Warne ....Clark Gable
Ellie Andrews ....Claudette Colbert
Alexander Andrews ....Walter Connolly
Mr. Shapeley ....Roscoe Karns
King Westley ....Jameson Thomas
Danker .... Alan Hale
Lovington ....Wallis Clark
Henderson ....Harry Bradley
Zeke ....Arthur Hoyt
Zeke's wife ....Blanche Frederici

By MORDAUNT HALL.

There are few serious moments in "It Happened One Night," a screen feast which awaits visitors to the Radio City, and if there is a welter of improbable incidents these hectic doings serve to generate plenty of laughter. The pseudo suspense is kept on the wing until a few seconds before the picture ends, but it is a foregone conclusion that the producers would never dare to have the characters acted by Clark Gable and Claudette Colbert separated when the curtain falls.

In this merry romance, which is an adaptation of a magazine story by Samuel Hopkins Adams, Peter Warne (Mr. Gable) and Ellie Andrews (Miss Colbert) enjoy the discomforts of a long-distance bus ride; they also experience the pain of hitch-hiking and the joys of tourist camps. Besides these glimpses, one beholds Alexander Andrews searching for his daughter in an airplane, expostulating with secretaries and sleuths because he is unable to find the missing girl, incidentally an heiress.

Warne is one of those crack newspaper men frequently discovered in Hollywood's spacious studios. He does not hesitate to tell his superiors in outbursts of slang precisely what he thinks of them, even though his finances at the time are at a low ebb. Ellie is an obstinate young person, who to spite her father has become the wife (in name only) of a dashing young man named King Westley. She finds herself virtually a prisoner on her father's yacht and, in the introductory scenes, she is on a hunger strike. Soon afterward she darts from her cabin to the deck, leaps overboard and swims for Florida and freedom.

It is while she is on her way from Miami to New York that she encounters Warne, an audacious person. To make matters more interesting, the producers or the author decide that the fiery Ellie must have her suitcase stolen. As days go by, Warne and Ellie experience the pangs of hunger and, at one period, they have to content themselves with a meal of raw carrots.

"It Happened One Night" is a good piece of fiction, which, with all its feverish stunts, is blessed with bright dialogue and a good quota of relatively restrained scenes. Although there are such flighty notions as that of having Ellie running away from a marriage ceremony when the guests—and particularly King Westley—had expected to hear her say "I will"; or those depicting Warne volleying vituperation over the telephone at his city editor; there are also more sober sequences wherein Warne and Ellie spread cheer to the audience, notwithstanding their sorry adventures with little or no money.

Miss Colbert gives an engaging and lively performance. Mr. Gable is excellent in his rôle. Roscoe Karns affords no little fun by his flirtatious conduct on board a bus. Walter Connolly is in his element as Ellie's father and Alan Hale gives a robust portrayal of an artful owner of a flivver.

F 23, 1934

Gorky's 'Mother.'

MOTHER, 1905, a silent Soviet film, with Vera Baranovskaya, Nikolai Batalof and A. Tchistyakof; directed by V. I. Pudovkin; a Mezhrabpomfilm production. At the Acme Theatre.

Perhaps New York motion-picture enthusiasts ought to be thankful that "Mother, 1905," the Soviet production now at the little Acme Theatre in Union Square, had to wait so long before being approved by the board of censors. Because, after having seen a multitude of good, and indifferent, Russian dialogue films during the last few years, the spectators again have a chance to enjoy a silent work of the type that made S. M. Eisenstein and V. I. Pudovkin famous the world over as masters of direction.

Based on Maxim Gorky's novel, "Mother," the gripping story of a Russian working woman turned into a revolutionary strike leader through oppression, this screen effort brings back memories of "Potemkin," "The End of St. Petersburg" and similar examples of Russian film technique. From the moment the drunken husband and father (A. Tchistyakof) is seen reeling home until the mother (Vera Baranovskaya) and the son (Nikolai Batalof) fall victims to the Czar's troops, there is no let-up in interest. While many of the scenes of violence growing out of the struggle between capital and labor are far from being peculiarly Russian or outdated, the director naturally has given them a special Czarist flavor, emphasized by the spoken comment in English that takes the place of titles.

The production is brought up to date by a series of scenes showing revolutionary incidents of 1917, the building of the great Dnieprostroy Dam and the May Day parade in Moscow in 1933. The acting of the principals is first rate and the support is excellent.   H. T. S.

My 30, 1934

OF HUMAN BONDAGE, adapted from Somerset Maugham's novel; directed by John Cromwell; an RKO Radio production. At the Radio City Music Hall.
Philip Carey ....Leslie Howard
Mildred Rogers ....Bette Davis
Sally Athelny ....Frances Dee
Nora ....Kay Johnson
Griffiths ....Reginald Denny
Emil Miller ....Alan Hale
Mr. Athelny ....Reginald Owen
Dunsford ....Reginald Sheffield
Dr. Jacobs ....Desmond Roberts

By MORDAUNT HALL.

W. Somerset Maugham's widely circulated novel, "Of Human Bondage," has come through the operation of being transferred to the screen in an unexpectedly healthy fashion. It may not possess any great dramatic strength, but the very lifelike quality of the story and the marked authenticity of its atmosphere cause the spectators to hang on every word uttered by the interesting group of characters. If one did not remember Leslie Howard's clever acting in "Outward Bound" and "Berkeley Square," one might be tempted to say that his portrait of Philip Carey, in this current Radio City Music Hall feature, excels any performance he has given before the camera. No more expert illustration of getting under the skin of the character has been done in motion pictures. Mr. Howard suffers seemingly all the woe and cheer experienced by Carey.

Another enormously effective portrayal is that of Bette Davis as Mildred Rogers, the waitress who continually accepts Carey's generosity and hospitality and reveals herself as a heartless little ingrate. In a climactic episode, which recalls an incident in Kipling's "The Light That Failed," this sorry specimen of humanity slashes Carey's efforts at art, destroys his medical books and furniture and, in the film, even burns his bonds and private papers, leaving the apartment as though it had been struck by a tornado.

At the first showing yesterday of this picture the audience was so wrought up over the conduct of this vixen that when Carey finally expressed his contempt for Mildred's behavior applause was heard from all sides. There was a further outburst of applause when the film came to an end.

John Cromwell, the director, has given many a subtle and imaginative touch to his scenes. Now and again he makes use of staccato bits of music to emphasize Carey's clubfoot limp. It is pathetic, but strong, to observe this young man, always aware of his affliction. He studies painting in Paris, but is soon discouraged and eventually goes in for medicine and does not prove to be as bright as the majority of his colleagues.

It is genuinely affecting when Carey encounters old Athelny, a generous but odd individual, who when Carey is penniless not only invites the young man to stay at his house, but insists on his invitation being accepted. By that time Carey has elicited much sympathy, and therefore it is somewhat of a relief to see him in a home. One has more than a vague notion that Athelny's attractive daughter, Sally, will eventually become Mrs. Carey.

There is nothing stereotyped about this film, and even the closing scenes are set forth with a pleasing naturalness and a note of cheer. Just as Mr. Howard and Miss Davis submerge their own personalities in those of the parts they act, so does Reginald Owen, who appears as Athelny. Mr. Owen keeps within rational bounds in his portrayal, but nevertheless by his speech and actions causes Athelny to stand out. Frances Dee is charming as Sally, and Alan Dale does well as Mildred's first lover. Reginald Denny guffaws a little too much, but he otherwise does quite well by the part of the double-faced Griffiths, who is the father of Mildred's child. Kay Johnson gives an intelligent performance as Nora, a writer in whom Carey becomes interested after Mildred goes away, apparently to get married.

Je 29, 1934

THE SCARLET EMPRESS, adapted from a diary of Catherine the Great; arranged by Manuel Komroff; directed by Josef von Sternberg; a Paramount production. At the Capitol.

Sophia Frederica ?
Catherine II } ...... Marlene Dietrich
Count Alexei.....................John Lodge
Grand Duke Peter...............Sam Jaffe
Empress Elizabeth..........Louise Dresser
Catherine as child............Maria Sieber
Prince August............C. Aubrey Smith
Countess Elisabeth.......Ruthelma Stevens
Princess Johanna.................Olive Tell
Gregory Orloff...............Gavin Gordon
Mons. Lieut. Ovtsyn......Jameson Thomas
Chancellor Bestuchef.......Erville Alderson
Marie ....Marie Wells
Herr Wagner...........Edward Van Sloan

Scorning to employ the humdrum laws of dramatic development, Josef von Sternberg has created a bizarre and fantastic historical carnival in "The Scarlet Empress," which began an engagement at the Capitol yesterday. By ordinary standards Mr. von Sternberg outrages even the cinema cognoscenti who have continued, in the face of his excesses, to preserve their faith in him as one of Hollywood's most interesting and original directors. A ponderous, strangely beautiful, lengthy and frequently wearying production, his new work is strictly not a dramatic photoplay at all, but a succession of overelaborated scenes, dramatized emotional moods and gaudily plotted visual excitements.

Its players, with the twin exceptions of Sam Jaffe as the crazy Peter and Louise Dresser as the Empress Elizabeth, seem to lose their hold on humanity under Mr. von Sternberg's narcotic influence, and become like people struggling helplessly in a dream. Mr. von Sternberg has even accomplished the improbable feat of smothering the enchanting Marlene Dietrich under his technique, although his fine camera work never does her less than justice.

Since the verdict has to be in the negative, let it be pronounced quickly. For Mr. von Sternberg, having sacrificed story, characterization and life itself to his own hungry and unreasonable dreams of cinema greatness, has at the same time created a barbaric pageant of eighteenth century Russia, which is frequently exciting. His scenes are like the vast, tortured world of another William Blake. In the great halls and chambers of the the imperial palace, weird figures of enormous height stand sculptured in attitudes of suffering. Gargoyles with nightmare faces and twisted bodies support mirrors and candelabra. There are panels of saints and martyrs in what is evidently the Byzantine style, and ikons, gigantic iron doors and clusters of candles. Five emaciated martyrs of tremendous size guard Elizabeth's bed. The imperial treasure chests bear the sculptured bodies of saints in high relief on their covers. The imperial throne is shaped in the form of the avenging double-eagle of the Russias. There is a mirror curved into a horned and winged gargoyle and a chair formed in the image of a martyred saint, to accommodate the sitter in the saint's lap.

These are examples of how Mr. von Sternberg has reconstructed the coarse and primitive Russian court of Elizabeth. Against these settings he arranges violence, cruelty and lewdness in a procession of mobile tableaux which describe much the same events in young Catherine's life as those described in the British film, "Cath-

erine the Great." Men die on the wheel and the rack, women are crucified in picturesque attitudes for the von Sternberg cameras, and the imbecile Peter arranges individual and mass slaughters to amuse himself. Meanwhile the innocent Catherine, transported to Russia to be the bride of Peter and provide the throne with a potential ruler, is shocked by the barbarism of the court. Gradually she adapts herself to its immoral standards, taking lovers first cautiously and then with open abandon. Finally, when the murderous Peter succeeds his aunt and threatens to assassinate Catherine in order to make a place on the throne for his mistress, the handsome girl wins the army and seizes the throne for herself.

Running a solid hundred minutes, the film first shocks and stimulates the imagination, and then, lacking the dramatic skill to refresh its audiences, becomes steadily duller. A superb musical score has been synchronized beautifully with the picture.

A. D. S.

S 15, 1934

MAN OF ARAN, produced by Robert Flaherty, with a musical score by John Greenwood; a Gainsborough production; presented by Gaumont-British. At the Criterion.
The Man..............Colman (Tiger) King
His wife....................Maggie Dirrane
Their son...................Michael Dillane

By ANDRE SENNWALD.

Robert Flaherty, the mellow wanderer with a camera, has made a memorable film out of the tragic and beautiful fundamentals of human behavior in his "Man of Aran," which British Gaumont presented at the Criterion last evening. With the fervor of a poet and the skill of a magnificent cameraman he once more examines the theme which lies close to his heart, the grim and ceaseless struggles of primitive beings to preserve their lives against the crushing assaults of their environment. As in his "Nanook of the North," he strips his new work of dramatic artifice and plunges it to the heart of earthy and basic experience. It is bare, cruel and authentically real; it is ardent with life, and it represents the pure cinema at its best. Expelling everything which is artistically alien to the camera, Mr. Flaherty employs only one ally, and that is music.

The Aran Islands, he tells us in his foreword, are three naked wastes of rock off the western coast of Ireland. Empty of trees or soil or any natural gifts for the sustenance of man, they are exposed to the blind fury of the open Atlantic. In the Winter storms, the islands are almost smothered by the boiling sea, which piles up on the bare and unfriendly cliffs in endless and terrible cataclysms. On the Aran Islands, the negation of fruitfulness, man fights bitterly for the privilege of life. "It is a fight," says Mr. Flaherty, after two years on the islands, "from which he will have no respite until the end of his indomitable days.

Here is a splendid theme for a man of Mr. Flaherty's imagination and he utilizes it to make a motion picture of consummate beauty. With the raging seas for a symphonic accompaniment, he describes the daily life of the Man of Aran and his wife and child. He shows them at their pitiful daily tasks, braving the seas in a small boat for fish, laying seaweed and handfulls of dirt on the bare rocks for their potato planting. The endless tread-mill monotony of their struggle for existence is written without words in the faces of the native Aranites who compose Mr. Flaherty's cast of actors—rugged, honest faces, divorced from all the fruits of living but those of family, friendship and the sense of meager conquest that they get as they come to grips with life. There are some excellent scenes of the men in a tiny curragh harpooning a whale to obtain oil for the lamps in their thatched cottages. On their journey back from one of these trips they are caught in a wild Atlantic storm. From the cliffs the Man's wife and child watch the small boat and pray for its safety. Miraculously the battered curragh makes the shore and the men crawl up on the rocky ledge, leaving the boat to be broken to bits by the waves.

That is all the story Mr. Flaherty has to tell. Yet he gives it a remarkable vigor and impact by his constant use of contrast. First the plodding, bowed and pathetic humans, snatching their pittance from the rocks and the water; then their magnificent opponent, the sea, smashing eternally against the

rocks in a resistless and cruel barrage of sound and fury.

In the overwhelming climax the mad assault of the sea as it climbs hundreds of feet up the cliffs and sweeps its tons of white-spumed water over the top accomplishes a sense of terror and emotional exhaustion in the spectator, leaving him with the feeling that it is useless to continue the struggle against such odds. The musical score is excellently blended with the screen in a fine emotional composition. Although the first impression is that the synchronized sound and voices are an obtrusive element in the pure flow of the camera, one gradually becomes accustomed to them. "Man of Aran" immediately joins the great tradition of "Grass," "Tabu" and Mr. Flaherty's own "Nanook."

O 19, 1934

THE LIVES OF A BENGAL LANCER, as adapted by Grover Jones and William Slavens McNutt, from Francis Yeats-Brown's book; screenplay by Waldemar Young, John L. Balderston and Achmed Abdullah; directed by Henry Hathaway and produced for Paramount by Louis D. Lighton. At the Paramount.

Captain McGregor	Gary Cooper
Lieutenant Forsythe	Franchot Tone
Lieutenant Stone	Richard Cromwell
Colonel Stone	Sir Guy Standing
Major Hamilton	C. Aubrey Smith
Hamzulla Khan	Monte Blue
Tania Volkanskaya	Kathleen Burke
Lieutenant Barrett	Colin Tapley
Mohammed Khan	Douglas Dumbrille
Emir	Akim Tamiroff
Hendrickson	Jameson Thomas
Ram Singh	Noble Johnson
Major General Woodley	Lumsden Hare
Grand Vizier	J. Carrol Naish
The Ghazi (prisoner)	Rollo Lloyd
McGregor's Servant	Charles Stevens
Afridi	Mischa Auer
Solo Dancer	Myra Kinch

By ANDRE SENNWALD.

Borrowing the title of Mr. Yeats-Brown's Indian odyssey of four or five years ago, the film-makers have invented a heroic narrative of Kiplingesque adventure around Khyber Pass, which began an engagement yesterday at the Paramount. The cinema "Lives of a Bengal Lancer" is as joyous in its gunplay as it is splendid and picturesque in its manufacture, and it proves to be consistently lively despite its great length. Anticipating the kind of upper-crust sneers which a free screen adaptation of a literary work is is sure to suffer, its makers are careful and even eager to clarify their intentions, although they slightly diminish the effect of their apologies by referring to the book as a novel.

In its exciting and somewhat blood-chilling account of the gallant band of fighting men who guard the Northern frontier of England's empire in India, the work is in the vigorously romantic tradition of Kipling and Talbot Mundy. While it usually manages to avoid Kipling's fatally objectionable preoccupation with the white man's burden, it is so sympathetic in its discussion of England's colonial management that it ought to prove a great blessing to Downing Street. Mr. Yeats-Brown himself may be a trifle astonished to discover that a ravishing Russian spy has found her way into the story. Happily, though, the photoplay ignores her most of the time. With an adventurous delight which is tempered by a grim respect for the fighting qualities of the Afridi, it plunges into the dashing stuff of border patrols, guerilla warfare, Afghan torture methods and the honor of the regiment. Henry Hathaway, the director, executes a skillful and convincing blend of the studio scenes and the authentic atmospheric films made in India several years ago by a Paramount expedition headed by Ernest Schoedsack.

Not with the Kipling roughneck does "The Lives of a Bengal Lancer" deal, but with the well-bred Englishmen who are gentlemen as well as officers of the king. Thus you find Sir Guy Standing being superbly cold as the colonel who preserves his detachment toward the ordinary human emotions even when his son is in hourly danger of having his eyes put out by the ingenious Afghans who have captured him. In the same spirit Gary Cooper and Franchot Tone, rather than betray the route of the ammunition train to their captors, submit with cool nonchalance to the curious Afghan custom of shoving lighted slivers under the finger nails of tightlipped captives. The tale tells of Lieutenant Stone (Richard Cromwell), the unseasoned son of the commander of the Bengal Lancers, who is so angered by his father's cool passion for discipline that when he is captured by the Afghans he decides to give away military secrets rather than uphold the honors of the corps in the torture chamber. In the great battle in the fortress, though, he acquits himself heroically.

Since all this may give you the impression that the film is overly insistent upon the military phases of life among the lancers, you ought to be informed that it is equally successful in its humor. There are first-rate performances by Sir Guy Standing as the stern disciplinarian, by Gary Cooper as the dour and surly Scotsman, by Franchot Tone as his flippant comrade, and by young Mr. Cromwell as the weakling of the outfit. A number of skillful actors lurk behind turbans and Afghan beards. "Lives of a Bengal Lancer" is a superb adventure story and easily the liveliest film in town.

Ja 12, 1935

THE SCREEN

A Russian Civil War Film.

TCHAPAYEF, a dialogue film in Russian; directed by Sergei and Georgi Vasilyef; a Lenfilm production. At the Cameo Theatre.
Tchapayef.................Boris Bobotchkin
Furmanof......................Boris Blinof
Anka...................Barbara Myasnikof
Pyetka.........................Leonid Kmit
Colonel Borozdin.............I. N. Pevtsof
Petrovitch......................S. Shkurat

While American audiences hardly can be expected to become as enthusiastic over "Tchapayef," the latest Russian visitor to the screen of the Cameo Theatre, as their fellow film patrons in the Soviet Union, they are almost certain to enjoy what is probably the best talking picture turned out in the U. S. S. R.

From the very beginning, when Tchapayef, the heroic leader of a band of Red partisans fighting against a section of the White Guards in the Urals in 1919, is seen capturing a bridge and routing the enemy, until the final reel, where he sinks beneath the waters of a river under the bullets of the reactionary troops and the film ends with the Red cavalry avenging his death, there is action, action, action. This doesn't mean that

148

machine guns are rattling and blood flowing all the time, as there really are only three scenes of fighting, all of them highly effective. But the interest of the spectators is held every minute by the development of the story, which conforms closely to the actual historical episodes upon which it is based, and the dramatic and comic incidents scattered with a liberal hand throughout the scenario.

Even hardened observers are likely to find themselves seriously following the course of the unobtrusive love affair between Anka, a textile worker serving a machine gun in the Red army, and Petkya, Tchapayef's favorite lieutenant, and to be thrilled by her devotion and skill. Then there are all sorts of humorous situations, involving peasants, Red partisans and the leader himself, and Furmanof, the political commissar attached to Tchapayef's force by the Soviet High Command. At first the rough-and-ready partisan chief mistrusts the educated young man from Moscow, but soon the latter wins his confidence and undying friendship. Many of the flashes of wit are at the expense of the partisans' and muzhiki's ignorance of what the war is all about, but there is an undercurrent of earnestness that keeps the humor from descending to the slapstick variety.

This time the Bolshevist filmmakers allow the White Guard leaders and their followers to act like persons not much worse than the usual run of human kind. In fact, about the only piece of brutality charged to the colonel in command of the White troops is the allowing of the brother of his faithful old orderly, Petrovitch, to be beaten to death for attempted desertion to the Reds. One of the most impressive scenes in the whole film is when a detachment of White Guards made up of former officers charges in parade formation in an almost successful effort to break down their adversaries' morale. The young directors of the picture were fortunate in having such a fine type of actor as Boris Bobotchkin to fill the exacting rôle of Tchapayef. Despite his heroism, he remains a human being, with lots of weaknesses, but with a dash and sincerity that are winning in the extreme. Every one of the principal players is excellent and the ensemble work hardly can be excelled. The photography is at all times up to the high Russian standard and the sound reproduction is clear. Plenty of English super-imposed titles explain the action to persons ignorant of Russian. **H. T. S.**

Ja 15, 1935

THE DEVIL IS A WOMAN, adapted from a story, "The Woman and the Puppet," by Pierre Louys; adaptation by John Dos Passos; continuity by S. K. Winston; music and lyrics by Ralph Rainger and Leo Robin; directed by Josef von Sternberg; a Paramount production. At the Paramount.

Concha Perez	Marlene Dietrich
Antonio Galvan	Cesar Romero
Don Pasqual	Lionel Atwill
Don Paquito	Edward Everett Horton
Senora Perez	Alison Skipworth
Morenito	Don Alvarado
Dr. Mendez	Morgan Wallace
Tuerta	Tempe Pigott
Maria	Jil Dennett
Conductor	Lawrence Grant

By ANDRE SENNWALD.

It is not hard to understand why Hollywood expressed such violent distaste for Josef von Sternberg's new film. For the talented director-photographer, in "The Devil Is a Woman," makes a cruel and mocking assault upon the romantic sex motif which Hollywood has been gravely celebrating all these years. His success is also his failure. Having composed one of the most sophisticated films ever produced in America, he makes it inevitable that it will be misunderstood and disliked by nine-tenths of the normal motion picture public. The uninformed will be bored by "The Devil Is a Woman." The cultivated filmgoer will be delighted by the sly urbanity which is implicit in Mr. von Sternberg's direction, as well as excited by the striking beauty of his settings and photography.

Based upon Pierre Louys's novel, "The Woman and the Puppet," the film also is an atmospheric expression of Rimsky-Korsakoff's "Caprice Espagñole," which has been woven into the musical score. On the surface it is the Carmenesque tale of a Spanish fille de joie who wrecks the life of an influential middle-aged politician. Recited chiefly in flashbacks rather than in a straightforward narrative style, it is revealed against the

From The New York Times Film Reviews

sensuous background of the Spanish fiesta. Always a master of light and shadow, Mr. von Sternberg achieves a delicate and sinister beauty, shot through with laughter and song and the confetti madness of the festival.

In Mr. von Sternberg's hands a story which is deceptively conventional on the surface becomes a heartless parable of man's eternal humiliation in the sex struggle. As Don Pasqual dances foolishly at the bidding of the young woman who has him biologically trapped, we begin by laughing with the director at the ludicrous spectacle and end by suspecting that the joke has been a grisly one. For Don Pasqual's downfall is complete. An intelligent and self-respecting gentleman, he is always conscious of what is happening to him in this absurd pursuit of a woman who can never give him anything to compensate for what he is losing. Tragically aware of Concha's contempt for him, he is nevertheless helpless to free himself from the narcotic effect of her physical beauty. It is the particular triumph of the picture that Concha, instead of running off finally with the young man who has caught her fancy—the conventional movie fade-out—remains a consistent character by returning to her middle-aged lover.

This column regards "The Devil Is a Woman" as the best product of the Sternberg-Dietrich alliance since "The Blue Angel." Miss Dietrich herself, under the director's knowing guidance, provides, in addition to her vast personal allure, a series of highly effective panels in the career of a talented fancy lady. Lionel Atwill is at his best as the pathetic Pasqual. His performance elicits not only the ironic laughter which Mr. von Sternberg expects you to produce toward him, but also an emotion that almost but never quite becomes sympathy. These two are the symbols of the endless futility of passion. Cesar Romero personifies the third verity as the virile young man who almost defeats the woman at her own game. There are excellent minor performances by Edward Everett Horton as the provincial governor and Alison Skipworth as the girl's scheming guardian.

My 4, 1935

THE INFORMER, as adapted by Dudley Nichols from Liam O'Flaherty's novel; directed by John Ford; an RKO Radio production. At the Radio City Music Hall.
Gypo Nolan	Victor McLaglen
Mary McPhillip	Heather Angel
Dan Gallagher	Preston Foster
Katie Madden	Margot Grahame
Frankie McPhillip	Wallace Ford
Mrs. McPhillip	Una O'Connor
Terry	J. M. Kerrigan
Mulholland	Joseph Sauers
Tommy Connor	Neil Fitzgerald
Rat Mulligan	Donald Meek
The Blind Man	D'Arcy Corrigan
Donahue	Leo McCabe
Daly	Gaylord Pendleton
Flynn	Francis Ford
Madame Betty	May Boley
The Lady	Grizelda Harvey

By ANDRE SENNWALD.

John Ford, who earned our gratitude last season with "The Lost Patrol," has made an astonishing screen drama out of Liam O'Flaherty's novel "The Informer." Having no patience with the childlike rigmarole of routine film manufacture, he recites Mr. O'Flaherty's realistic drama of the Dublin slums with bold and smashing skill. In his hands "The Informer" becomes at the same time a striking psychological study of a gutter Judas and a rawly impressive picture of the Dublin underworld during the Black and Tan terror. It would not be strictly accurate to say that the photoplay unlooses the O'Flaherty work on the Music Hall's screen without compromise. But within his obvious limitations, Mr. Ford has achieved one of the finest dramas of the year.

There is something just a bit sinister about the way Victor McLaglen becomes brilliant under Mr. Ford's guidance. If you remember Mr. McLaglen in "The Lost Patrol," you may not be surprised to learn that he makes something stark and memorable out of the stupid giant in "The Informer," who betrays his best friend to the Black and Tans for £20. The animal cunning of the man, his transparent deceits and his naïve belief in his powers of deception are woven into the fabric of a character that is worthy the pen of a Dostoievski. Amid the murk and drizzly mists in which the drama is played out, he becomes some dreadful and pathetic creature of darkness. Although the photoplay makes you understand why informer is the ugliest word

150

in an Irishman's vocabulary, there is a tragic quality in this man's bewildered terror.

The cycle of Gypo Nolan's torment, from his betrayal, through his frantic spree with the blood money, to his death under the revolutionary guns, is enclosed within the twelve hours of a rainy night. When Frankie McPhillip comes down from the hills to visit his mother, it is partly hunger and partly a vague notion to flee with his sweetheart to America that makes Gypo walk into Black and Tan headquarters and claim the price that is on his friend's head. From that time until his death he is scourged by conscience and fear. He goes to the McPhillip home intending to divert suspicion from himself by attending the wake, and there he begins the strange behavior which finally betrays him to the organization. He numbs his tortured nerves with liquor and surrounds himself with underworld sycophants. He cannot drink too much or spend his money too quickly. At the court of inquiry he bears false witness against an innocent man, not knowing that he himself is on trial for his life. He dies at last, an abject coward, after he has been routed from his sweetheart's house.

It is one of the minor faults of "The Informer" that Katie, Gypo's companion, has been made into a conventional motion picture sweetie who pleads for his life as he lies hidden in her room. That is dramatically false, since Mr. O'Flaherty emphasizes the utter loneliness of an Irishman who has betrayed the cause, the traitor whom nobody will shield. It also struck this column that some judicious slicing in the middle section of the film would improve its tempo.

Under Mr. Ford's shrewd and sensitive direction there are excellent performances by Wallace Ford as the hunted Frankie McPhillip, by Una O'Connor as his sorrowing mother, by Donald Meek as the man whom Gypo accuses, and by May Boley as the Madame Betty of the establishment where Gypo carouses. J. M. Kerrigan is amusing as a crafty tout, and Preston Foster, as the revolutionary commandant, does what he can with a rôle which was richer in the novel than it is on the screen.

My 10, 1935

BECKY SHARP, an adaptation of the Langdon Mitchell play, which was based on Thackeray's "Vanity Fair"; screen play by Francis Edward Faragoh; color designs by Robert Edmond Jones; directed by Rouben Mamoulian; a Pioneer Pictures production; presented by RKO Radio. At the Radio City Music Hall.

Becky Sharp	Miriam Hopkins
Amelia Sedley	Frances Dee
Marquis of Steyne	Sir Cedric Hardwicke
Lady Bareacres	Billie Burke
Miss Crawley	Alison Skipworth
Joseph Sedley	Nigel Bruce
Rawdon Crawley	Alan Mowbray
William Dobbin	Colin Tapley
George Osborne	G. P. Huntley Jr.
Pitt Crawley	William Stack
Sir Pitt Crawley	George Hassell
Duke of Wellington	William Faversham
General Tufto	Charles Richman
Duchess of Richmond	Doris Lloyd
Tarquin	Leonard Mudie
Lady Blanche	Bunny Beatty
Bowles	Charles Coleman
Briggs	May Beatty
Miss Flowery	Finis Barton
The Prince Regent	Olaf Hytten
Fifine	Pauline Garon
Page	James Robinson
Miss Pinkerton	Elspeth Dudgeon
Charwoman	Tempe Pigott
Lady Jane Crawley	Ottola Nesmith

By ANDRE SENNWALD.

Science and art, the handmaidens of the cinema, have joined hands to endow the screen with a miraculous new element in "Becky Sharp," the first full-length photoplay produced in the three-component color process of Technicolor. Presented at the Radio City Music Hall yesterday for its first public showing, it was both incredibly disappointing and incredibly thrilling. Although its faults are too numerous to earn it distinction as a screen drama, it produces in the spectator all the excitement of standing upon a peak in Darien and glimpsing a strange, beautiful and unexpected new world. As an experiment, it is a momentous event, and it may be that in a few years it will be regarded as the equal in historical importance of the first crude and wretched talking pictures. Although it is dramatically tedious, it is a gallant and distinguished outpost in an almost uncharted domain, and it probably is the most significant event of the 1935 cinema.

Certainly the photoplay, coloristically speaking, is the most successful that has ever reached the screen. Vastly improved over the gaudy two-color process of four and five years ago, it possesses an extraordinary variety of tints, ranging from placid and lovely grays to hues which are vibrant with warmth and richness. This is not the coloration of natural life, but a vividly pigmented dream world of the artistic imagination. Rouben Mamoulian and Robert Edmond Jones have employed the new process in a deliberately stylized form, so that "Becky Sharp" becomes an animate procession of cunningly designed canvases. Some of the color combinations make excessive demands upon the eye. Many of them are as soothing as black and white. The most glaring technical fault, and it is a comparatively minor one, is the poor definition in the long shots, which convert faces into blurred masses. In close-ups where scarlet is the dominant motif, there is also a tendency to provoke an after-image when the scene shifts abruptly to a quieter color combination.

The major problem, from the spectator's point of view, is the necessity for accustoming the eye to this new screen element in much the same way that we were obliged to accustom the ear to the first talkies. The psychological problem is to reduce this new and spectacular element to a position, in relation to the film as a whole, where color will impinge no more violently upon the basic photographic image than sound does today. This is chiefly a question of time and usage. At the moment it is impossible to view "Becky Sharp" without crowding the imagination so completely with color that the photoplay as a whole is almost meaningless. That is partly the fault of the production and partly the inevitable consequence of a phenomenon. We shall know more about the future of color when its sponsors employ it in a better screen play than "Becky Sharp."

The real secret of the film resides not in the general feeling of dissatisfaction which the spectator suffers when he leaves the Music Hall, but in the active excitement which he experiences during its scenes. It is important and even necessary to judge the work in terms of its best—not its worst or even its average. "Becky Sharp" becomes prophetically significant, for example, in the magnificent color-dramatization of the British ball in Brussels on the eve of Waterloo.

Here the Messrs. Mamoulian and Jones have accomplished the miracle of using color as a constructive dramatic device, of using it for such peculiarly original emotional effects that it would be almost impossible to visualize the same scene in conventional black and white. From the pastel serenity of the opening scenes at the ball, the color deepens into somber hues as the rumble of Napoleon's cannon is heard in the ballroom. Thenceforward it mounts in excitement as pandemonium seizes the dancers, until at last the blues, greens and scarlets of the running officers have become an active contributing factor in the overwhelming climax of sound and photography.

If this review seems completely out of focus, it is because the film is so much more significant as an experiment in the advanced use of color than as a straightforward dramatic entertainment. Based upon Langdon Mitchell's old dramatization of "Vanity Fair," it is gravely defective. Ordinarily Mr. Mamoulian is a master of filmic mobility, but here his experimental preoccupation with color becomes an obstacle to his usual fluid style of screen narration. Thus a great deal of "Becky Sharp" seems static and land-locked, an unvarying procession of long shots, medium shots and close-ups. It is endlessly talkative, as well, which is equally a departure from Mr. Mamoulian's ordinary style.

Perhaps it was inevitable that Thackeray's classic tale of the ambitious Becky and her spangled career in English society would be reduced on the screen to a halting and episodic narrative. But the film is unconscionably jerky in its development and achieves only a minor success in capturing the spirit of the original. In many of the screened episodes, Thackeray's satirical portraits come perilously close to burlesque, and they barge over the line in several places. Miriam Hopkins is an indifferently successful Becky, who shares some excellent scenes with many others in which she is strident and even nerve-racking. Frances Dee makes an effective Amelia, and photographs beautifully in addition There are fine performances in the celebrated rôles by Sir Cedric Hardwicke, Alison Skipworth, Nigel Bruce and Alan Mowbray.

But one thing is certain about "Becky Sharp." Its best is so good that it becomes a prophecy of the future of color on the screen. It forced this column to the conclusion that color will become an integral motion picture element in the next few years. If Mr. Mamoulian and Pioneer Pictures can be persuaded to film a modern story for their next venture, striving to repress their use of color to the more sombre hues of our twentieth century civilization, "Becky Sharp" will have fulfilled its great promise.

Je 14, 1935

TOP HAT, from a play by Alexander Farago; screen play by Dwight Taylor and Allan Scott; adapted by Karl Noti; lyrics and music by Irving Berlin; directed by Mark Sandrich; produced by Pandro S. Berman for RKO Radio. At the Radio City Music Hall.

Jerry Travers	Fred Astaire
Dale Tremont	Ginger Rogers
Horace Hardwick	Edward Everett Horton
Madge Hardwick	Helen Broderick
Alberto	Erik Rhodes
Bates	Eric Blore
Curate	Donald Meek
Curate's Wife	Florence Roberts
Hotel Manager	Gino Corrado
Call Boy	Peter Hobbs

By ANDRE SENNWALD.

Fred Astaire, the dancing master, and Miss Rogers, his ideal partner, bring all their joyous gifts to the new song and dance show at the Radio City Music Hall. Irving Berlin has written some charming melodies for the photoplay and the best of the current cinema teams does them agile justice on the dance floor. When "Top Hat" is letting Mr. Astaire perform his incomparable magic or teaming him with the increasingly dexterous Miss Rogers it is providing the most urbane fun that you will find anywhere on the screen. If the comedy itself is a little on the thin side, it is sprightly enough to plug those inevitable gaps between the shimmeringly gay dances.

Last year this column suggested that Miss Jessie Matthews would make a better partner for the debonair star than our own home girl. Please consider the matter dropped.

Miss Rogers, improving magnificently from picture to picture, collaborates perfectly with Mr. Astaire in "Top Hat" and is entitled to keep the job for life. Their comic duet in the band stand, danced to the lyric music of "Isn't This a Lovely Day," and their romantic adagio in the beautiful "Cheek to Cheek" song are among the major contributions of the show. In his solo flights, when he is abandoning his feet to the strains of "Fancy Free" or lulling Miss Rogers to sleep with the overpowering opiate of his sandman arrangement, Mr. Astaire is at his impeccable best. Then there is the "Top Hat, White Tie and Tails" number, which fortifies the star with a chorus of gentlemen of the evening and makes for a highly satisfying time.

The narrative complication which keeps the lovers apart for ninety minutes will have to go down as one of the most flimsily prolonged romantic misunderstandings of the season. Mr. Astaire, star of a London show, is occupying a hotel suite with his manager, the jittery Edward Everett Horton, at the time he falls in love with Miss Rogers. Somehow the lady becomes convinced, as ladies will, that Mr. Astaire is the one who is married to her friend, Helen Broderick, when all the time it is Mr. Horton. By a miracle of attenuation this mistaken identity persists in complicating matters all through the picture, causing Miss Rogers to slap Mr. Astaire's face vigorously every time he catches up with her, Miss Broderick to poke the unfortunate Mr. Horton in the eye, and the passionate Latin, Erik Rhodes, to make terrifying lunges in all direction with a bared rapier. An amusing but largely undevelopel secondary theme in the film concerns Mr. Horton's feud with his man servant, Erik Rhodes, whereby the two manage not to be on speaking terms despite the intimacy of their life.

All the minor players are such skilled comedians that they are able to extract merriment from this none too original comedy of errors. Miss Broderick, that infamously funny lady, has too little support, though, from the script. "Top Hat," after running almost its entire course with admirable restraint, collapses into one of those mammoth choral arrangements toward the end. It isn't worth ten seconds of the delightful Astaire-Rogers duet during the thunderstorm. Anyway, "Top Hat" is worth standing in line for. From the appearance of the lobby yesterday afternoon, you probably will have to.

Ag 30, 1935

ANNA KARENINA, from the novel by Count Leo Tolstoy; screen play by Clemence Dane and Salka Viertel; directed by Clarence Brown; produced by David O. Selznick for Metro-Goldwyn-Mayer. At the Capitol.

Anna Karenina	Greta Garbo
Vronsky	Fredric March
Sergei	Freddie Bartholomew
Kitty	Maureen O'Sullivan
Countess Vronsky	May Robson
Karenin	Basil Rathbone
Stiva	Reginald Owen
Yashvin	Reginald Denny
Dolly	Phoebe Foster
Levin	Gyles Isham
Grisha	Buster Phelps
Anna's Maid	Ella Ethridge
Lili	Joan Marsh
Vronsky's Valet	Sidney Bracey
Tania	Cora Sue Collins
Butler	Joe E. Tozer
Tutor	Guy D'Ennery
Cord	Harry Allen
Princess Sorokino	Mary Forbes
Mme. Kartasoff	Ethel Griffies
Matve	Harry Beresford
Governess	Sarah Padden

By ANDRE SENNWALD

Miss Garbo, the first lady of the screen, sins, suffers and perishes illustriously in the new, ably produced and comparatively mature version of the Tolstoy classic at the Capitol Theatre. Having put on a couple of mental years since the 1927 version of "Anna Karenina," which called itself "Love" and meant it, the cinema now is able to stab tentatively below the surface of Tolstoy's passion tales and hint at the social criticism which is implicit in them. Samuel Goldwyn's screen edition of "Resurrection" last year discussed Tolstoy's theories of social reform, and now

"Anna Karenina" widens the iris of the camera so as to link the plight of the lovers to the decadent and hypocritical society which doomed them. The photoplay is a dignified and effective drama which becomes significant because of that tragic, lonely and glamorous blend which is the Garbo personality.

The producers shrewdly relieve the sober drama of Anna's ill-starred romance with the dashing Count Vronsky by including one episode of hearty merriment. The officers of Vronsky's regiment, about to embark on one of their imperial orgies, begin the evening by playing an alcoholic variation of follow the leader. Standing at attention at the banquet board, they drain three glasses in rapid succession, march to the head of the table, crawl under it to the foot, then snap back to attention again and repeat the process until only one man is left standing. Fredric March, the Vronsky of the photoplay, wins the contest handsomely.

Familiar as "Anna Karenina" is in outline, it is freshly touching in its description of a great romance which is slain by the very elements which give it birth. Anna, devotedly attached to her son and serenely resigned to a loveless marriage bargain, finds her great romance after eight years of married life when she meets Vronsky. It sweeps everything else away: "Not to think, only to live, only to feel." Her husband, subscribing to the code of exterior respectability which governs Muscovite society, is content to let her engage in an illicit amour. But when the affair becomes an open scandal he bars Anna from his home.

She has sensed the dark shadow from the beginning and is willing to make the sacrifice. But Vronsky, more impetuous, less mature, only grasps the penalty of their sin when it is upon them, and soon rebels against the social exile to which he and Anna are condemned. Anna, herself, having given and lost everything for a love which was too fragile to survive the cruelty of society, finds the end of the way under the wheels of a locomotive.

Miss Garbo, always superbly the apex of the drama, suggests the inevitability of her doom from the beginning, streaking her first happiness with undertones of anguish, later trying futilely to mend the broken pieces, and at last standing regally alone as she approaches the end. Bouncing with less determination than is his custom, Mr. Marsh gets by handsomely as Vronsky. "Anna Karenina," in fact, suffers in performance only at the hands of young David Bartholomew, the child star of "David Copperfield." The lad renders the part of Anna's son wtih a terrifying, and assured maturity that makes his emotional scenes with Miss Garbo seem helplessly phony. Basil Rathbone is excellent as the husband and there are good performances by Reginald Owen, Maureen O'Sullivan and Phoebe Foster.

Ag 31, 1935

THE THIRTY-NINE STEPS, as adapted by Charles Bennett from John Buchan's novel; continuity by Alma Reville, with dialogue by Ian Hay; directed by Alfred Hitchcock; a Gaumont British production. At the Roxy.

Hannay	Robert Donat
Pamela	Madeleine Carroll
Professor Jordan	Godfrey Tearle
Mrs. Jordan	Helen Haye
Miss Smith	Lucie Mannheim
Crofter's Wife	Peggy Ashcroft
Crofter	John Laurie
The Sheriff	Frank Cellier
Mr. Memory	Wylie Watson
Maid	Peggy Simpson

By ANDRE SENNWALD.

Alfred Hitchcock, the gifted English screen director, has made one of the fascinating pictures of the year in "The Thirty-nine Steps," his new film at the Roxy Theatre. If the work has any single rival as the most original, literate and entertaining melodrama of 1935, then it must be "The Man Who Knew Too Much," which is also out of Mr. Hitchcock's workshop. A master of shock and suspense, of cold horror and slyly incongruous wit, he uses his camera the way a painter uses his brush, stylizing his story and giving it values which the scenarists could hardly have suspected. By comparison with the sinister delicacy and urbane understatement of "The Thirty-nine Steps," the best of our melodramas seem crude and brawling.

If you can imagine Anatole France writing a detective story, you will have some notion of the artistry that Mr. Hitchcock brings

to this screen version of John Buchan's novel. Like "The Man Who Knew Too Much," the photoplay immerses a quite normal human being in an incredible dilemma where his life is suddenly at stake and his enemies are mysterious, cruel and desperate. Richard Hannay, a young Canadian, is sitting in a London music hall when a man is killed, whereupon a young woman confesses the murder to him and begs him for sanctuary. In his rooms she explains that she is playing a lone game of counterespionage against foreign spies who have stolen a valuable military secret and are preparing to take it out of the country. Then the enigmatic lady is herself murdered, leaving Hannay with the meager information that his own life is now in danger, that he will learn the secret of the Thirty-Nine Steps in a certain Scottish hamlet, and that he must beware of a man whose little finger is amputated at the first joint.

That is the situation, and for the next four days Hannay finds himself in the most fantastic predicament of his life. The police are hunting him for the murder of the young woman and the spies are hunting him because he knows too much. His career is a murderous nightmare of chase and pursuit, in which he continually escapes by inches from the hangman's noose and the assassin's bullet. Mr. Hitchcock describes the remarkable chain of events in Hannay's flight across England and Scotland with a blend of unexpected comedy and breathless terror that is strikingly effective.

Perhaps the identifying hallmark of his method is its apparent absence of accent in the climaxes, which are upon the spectator like a slap in the face before he has set himself for the blow. In such episodes as the murder of the woman in Hannay's apartment, the icy ferocity of the man with the missing finger when he casually shoots Hannay, or the brilliantly managed sequences on the train, the action progresses through seeming indifference to whip-like revelations. There is a subtle feeling of menace on the screen all the time in Mr. Hitchcock's low-slung, angled use of the camera. But the participants, both Hannay and his pursuers, move with a repressed excitement that adds significance to every detail of their behavior.

Robert Donat as the suavely desperate hero of the adventure is. excellent both in the comic and the tragic phases of his plight. The lovely Madeleine Carroll, who begins by betraying him and believes his story when it is almost too late, is charming and skillful. All the players preserve that sureness of mood and that understanding of the director's intention which distinguished "The Man Who Knew Too Much." There are especially fine performances by John Laurie as the treacherous Scot who harbors the fugitive, Peggy Ashcroft as his sympathetic wife, Godfrey Tearle as the man with the missing finger, and Wylie Watson as the memory expert of the music halls, who proves to be the hub of the mystery.

S 14, 1935

THE SCREEN

MUTINY ON THE BOUNTY, from the novels by Charles Nordhoff and James Norman Hall; screen play by Talbot Jennings, Jules Furthman and Carey Wilson; musical score by Herbert Stothart; directed by Frank Lloyd; a Metro-Goldwyn-Mayer production. At the Capitol.

Bligh	Charles Laughton
Christian	Clark Gable
Byam	Franchot Tone
Smith	Herbert Mundin
Ellison	Eddie Quillan
Bacchus	Dudley Digges
Burkitt	Donald Crisp
Sir Joseph Banks	Henry Stephenson
Captain Nelson	Francis Lister
Mrs. Byam	Spring Byington
Tehani	Movita
Maimiti	Mamo
Maggs	Ian Wolfe
Morgan	Ivan Simpson
Fryer	De Witt Jennings
Muspratt	Stanley Fields
Morrison	Wallace Clark
Hayward	Vernon Downing
Tinkler	Dick Winslow

By ANDRE SENNWALD.

The weird and wonderful history of H. M. S. Bounty is magnificently transferred to the screen in "Mutiny on the Bounty," which opened at the Capitol Theatre yesterday. Grim, brutal, sturdily romantic, made out of horror and desperate courage, it is as savagely exciting and rousingly dramatic a photoplay as has come out of Hollywood in recent years. The Nordhoff-

Hall trilogy was, of course, born to be filmed, and Metro-Goldwyn-Mayer has given it the kind of production a great story deserves. As the sadistic master of the Bounty, the barbarous madman who was half god and half devil, Charles Laughton has the perfect rôle, and he plays it perfectly. Frank Lloyd, well remembered for "The Sea Hawk" and "Cavalcade," has performed a distinguished job of direction. For all its great length, this is just about the perfect adventure picture.

The film concentrates on the first two volumes of the trilogy, "Mutiny on the Bounty" and "Men Against the Sea," and touches only slightly on the fate of the mutineers as they prepare to face permanent exile with their Tahitian women on the uncharted Pitcairn's Island. If the work has a flaw, it stems from Metro's characteristic prodigality. This is a crowded and fascinating canvas, but the film tends to become slack and dissipate some of its terrifying power because of the sheer burden it imposes on the spectator of watching the screen for more than two hours.

The history of the celebrated naval case will not suffer if I summarize it briefly. In 1787 H. M. S. Bounty, commanded by the able but intolerably savage Lieutenant Bligh, left England bound for Tahiti. The spirit of revolt grew among both officers and men during the voyage as Bligh's mania for discipline increased in fury. Discharging her cargo at Tahiti, the Bounty was sailing for home when Christian, the second in command, led the mutinous sailors and seized the ship. Bligh and eighteen loyal men were set adrift with the ship's launch in mid-Pacific, while the triumphant mutineers put back to Tahiti.

Miraculously Bligh took his open boat 3,600 miles across the ocean to the Dutch East Indies, a feat that is almost unparalleled for skill and courage in nautical annals. In the photoplay, though not in fact, Bligh commands the second British ship which pursues the mutineers and is wrecked in the futile search. Midshipman Byam and several other loyal seamen who were forced to accompany the rebels were returned to England for trial. Condemned with the rest, Byam, in the film, is pardoned after an eloquent speech in which he informs the court-martial of the conditions which drove Christian and the crew to mutiny.

Mr. Laughton's performance as the incredible Bligh is a fascinating and almost unbearable portrait of a sadist who took rapturous delight in watching men in pain. We get the full horror of his personality early in the film when a seaman, convicted of striking an officer, is ordered to be lashed on every vessel in the fleet. Brought to the Bounty, he is discovered to be already dead from his previous floggings, but Bligh, observing the cold letter of the regulations, insists that the corpse receive the appointed forty lashes in full view of his officers and men. His penalties for minor offenses are the judgments of a maniac. From the swish of the lash he derives a lewd joy.

Bligh's reign of terror on the Bounty is described with such relish that in time you discover yourself wincing under the lash and biting your mouth to keep from crying out. Yet, on the astounding odyssey in the small boat, Bligh becomes a man of heroic stature, fiercely guiding the rudder through the ocean wastes while his men lose their senses from thirst and hunger. I could have wished that these superb sequences telling of Bligh's indomitable will to live and find vengeance had been extended at the expense of the romantic business on Tahiti. At the court-martial the film punishes Bligh by submitting him to the contempt of his fellow-officers. History, kinder to this amazing man, discloses that he rose to be an admiral in the King's navy.

There are numerous performances of excellence under the relentless eye of Mr. Laughton, notably Clark Gable as the rebellious second-in-command, Franchot Tone as the humane Midshipman Byam, Dudley Digges as the magnificently drunk ship's doctor, Herbert Mundin as a timorous mess boy, Eddie Quillan as a victim of the press gang and a dozen others. "Mutiny on the Bounty" contains the stuff of half a dozen adventure pictures. It is superlatively thrilling.

THE SCREEN

Groucho Marx and His Brothers

A NIGHT AT THE OPERA, based on a story by James Kevin McGuinness; screen play by George S. Kaufman and Morrie Ryskind; musical score by Herbert Stothart; music and lyrics by Nacio Herb Brown and Arthur Freed, and Kaper, Jurmann and Ned Washington; directed by Sam Wood; a Metro-Goldwyn-Mayer production. At the Capitol.

Otis B. Driftwood	Groucho Marx
Fiorello	Chico Marx
Tomasso	Harpo Marx
Rosa	Kitty Carlisle
Ricardo	Allan Jones
Lassparri	Walter King
Gottlieb	Siegfried Rumann
Mrs. Claypool	Margaret Dumont
Captain	Edward Keane
Henderson	Robert Emmet O'Connor

By ANDRE SENNWALD.

The merry Marx boys, whittled down from a quartet to a trio, have arrived in town with the loudest and funniest screen comedy of the Winter season. If "A Night at the Opera" is a trifle below their best, it is also considerably above the standard of laughter that has been our portion since they quit the screen. George S. Kaufman and Morrie Ryskind have given them a resounding slapstick to play with and they wield it with maniacal delight.

Even when their gags sound as if they were carved out of Wheeler and Woolsey with an axe, the boys continue to be rapturously mad. You may have wondered what the trouble has been with the operatic films. You will discover the answer at the Capitol: the Marx Brothers weren't in them.

The Marxist assault on grand opera makes a shambles of that comparatively sacred institution. Groucho, you see, is a phony musical impresario who has attached himself to a dignified lady in the hope of separating her from a portion of her $8,000,000. Chico is managing an ambitious Italian tenor against the tenor's will and better judgment. Harpo, the mischievous pixie, is up to his old habit of getting in everybody's way. Their adventures as impostors, stowaways and hunted madmen progress to a delirious climax at a performance of "Il Trovatore" in what is evidently intended to be the Metropolitan. Here the comedy bursts its shackles and spatters into magnificent fragments as the brothers, with the police and the opera management hard on their heels, pop in and out of the performance and transform Verdi into low buffoonery.

Among other things "A Night at the Opera" finally does justice to Harpo, whose pantomimic genius sometimes has a habit of getting lost behind Groucho's machine-gun patter. The whimsical little fellow, half pagan and half innocent child, manages to be in the approximate centre of all the film's best moments. There is his superbly demoniac pantomime at the breakfast table, where he puts the food and crockery to curious uses and winds up by making a sandwich with Groucho's cigar. At one point the sly authors arrange a situation around him that threatens to bludgeon him into breaking his golden silence. That occurs when the brothers are being fêted at City Hall in the guise of three eminent Italian aviators whose beards and uniforms they have borrowed. But Harpo wriggles out of the obligation to make a speech by a device that you will have to see to believe.

It would be pleasant to report that the omission of Zeppo, the romantic juvenile of the gang, also means the elimination of the conventional musical comedy romance. That isn't quite so, although the boys do keep the amorous business from becoming too tiresome. "A Night at the Opera" is especially fortunate in its straight people. Margaret Dumont, that fine and gracious stooge in all the Marx Brothers pictures, is proficient once again as the dignified art patroness who falls under Groucho's baleful eye. Siegfried Rumann is an excellent exponent of outraged respectability as the opera impresario. Robert Emmet O'Connor also is an asset as a cynical Irish detective who finds the boys a little too formidable for him.

D 7, 1935

THE GHOST GOES WEST, from a story by Eric Keown; screen play by Robert E. Sherwood; directed by Rene Clair; produced by Alexander Korda for London Films; released by United Artists. At the Rivoli.

Murdoch Glourie, Donald Glourie	Robert Donat
Mr. Martin	Eugene Pallette
Peggy Martin	Jean Parker
Mrs. Martin	Everly Gregg
Lady Shepperton	Elsa Lanchester
The MacLaggan	Hay Petrie
Old Glourie	Morton Selten
Mrs. MacNiff	Elliot Mason
Shepherdess	Patricia Hilliard

Sons of MacLaggan—Jack Lambert, Colin Leslie, Richard Mackie, J. Neil More, Neil Lester.
Creditors—Herbert Lomas, Quentin McPherson, Arthur Seaton, David Keir.

By ANDRE SENNWALD.

This review seems to require a preamble. Faced with an event of such imposing interest as René Clair's first English-speaking film, it is a grave temptation to go in for comparisons. That is distinctly the wrong approach to "The Ghost Goes West," which M. Clair made in England for Alexander Korda. The film is not pure Clair, or even characteristic Clair, because for the first time he is working in a strange language and from a script that is not his own. Robert Sherwood, who wrote the screen play, is as much a part of the film as the director himself. Consequently, the new film at the Rivoli Theatre reveals little stylistic relation to the precious handful of French films which bear his name. Nor does it possess, except in isolated scenes and details, any such distinct form as might identify it immediately with the cinema's finest master of comedy.

This is an unhappily pompous way to introduce such a gay, urbane and brilliantly funny film as "The Ghost Goes West." The Messrs. Sherwood and Clair are toying a gracefully long, loud laugh at the expense of American millionaire art lovers and European tradition. Their ghost, very solidly played by Robert Donat, is of the Scotch persuasion, he is a handsome devil, and even after 200 years he has an eye for the ladies. His adventures with the castle that is dismantled and transported to America are always merry and sometimes sharply satirical.

How Murdoch Glourie of the proud Glourie clan became a ghost in the first place is quite a story in itself. The lad was better at love than war, and when his dying father sent him out to avenge an insult the rival MacLaggans had flung at the clan, Murdoch was ignominiously killed. His father thereupon died of humiliation and, meeting his son in the limbo that is between heaven and earth, condemned him to haunt Glourie Castle until such time as he found an opportunity to bring the insolent MacLaggans to their knees. Poor Murdoch hadn't much luck and only gave the castle a bad name with his midnight prowlings until the happy day when his modern counterpart sold the castle to an American chain-store king. Then he began to go places.

Although the film is not cast in the fluid, rapidly paced style of Clair's typical work, it has a sly wit and an adroitness of manner that make it delightful. His signature is clearly marked in the episodes telling of the ghost's arrival in America, when the spook becomes a newspaper sensation and gets a civic welcome. The film jibes skillfully at the bad taste of the American nouveau riche. When, for example, the grocery king has moved the castle, stone by stone, to his estate in Florida, he proceeds to put in modern improvements and even installs gondolas in the moat. The rivalry of the modern Glourie and his ghostly ancestor for the kisses of the badly confused daughter of the millionaire makes the romantic theme a constructively comic element in the film instead of a necessary evil.

Mr. Donat, who revealed his brilliant talent for romantic comedy in "The Thirty-nine Steps," plays his two rôles with fine zest and even manages a Scottish burr with fair success. Eugene Pallette is uproariously solemn as the millionaire and Jean Parker plays the daughter engagingly. It would be criminal not to single out Morten Selten for special mention. As the proud old head of the Glourie clan he makes such an indelible impression during his brief appearance on this earth that his ghostly dialogues with his son acquire an added hilarity. "The Ghost Goes West" is the first important film of the new year, and a joyous one. It is the cream of an ebullient jest.

THE SCREEN

MODERN TIMES, written, directed and produced by Charles Chaplin; musical score by Mr. Chaplin; settings by Charles D. Hall; released through United Artists, At the Rivoli.

A Tramp ....Charles Chaplin
A Gamin..................Paulette Goddard
A Cafe Proprietor.........Henry Bergman
A Mechanic ....Chester Conklin
The Burglars .... { Stanley Sandford
                         { Hank Mann
                         { Louis Natheux
President of a Steel Corporation.
                              Allen Garcia

By FRANK S. NUGENT.

The hands of the cinema clock were set back five years last night when a funny little man with a microscopic mustache, a battered derby hat, turned up shoes and a flexible bamboo cane returned to the Broadway screen to resume his place in the affections of the film-going public. The little man—it scarcely needs be said—is Charlie Chaplin, whose "Modern Times," opening at the Rivoli, restores him to a following that has waited patiently, burning incense in his temple of comedy, during the long years since his last picture was produced.

That was five years ago almost to the day. "City Lights" was its name and in it Mr. Chaplin refused to talk. He still refuses. But in "Modern Times" he has raised the ban against dialogue for other members of the cast, raised it, but not completely. A few sentences here and there, excused because they come by television, phonograph, the radio. And once—just once—Mr. Chaplin permits himself to be heard, singing some jabberwocky of his own to the tune of a Spanish fandango.

Those are the answers to the practical questions. They do not tell of Mr. Chaplin's picture, or of Chaplin himself, or of the comic feast that he has been preparing for almost two years in the guarded cloister in Hollywood known as the Chaplin studio.

But there is no cause for alarm and no reason to delay the verdict further: "Modern Times" has still the same old Charlie, the lovable little fellow whose hands and feet and prankish eyebrows can beat in irresistible tattoo· upon an audience's funnybone or hold it still, taut beneath the spell of human tragedy. A flick of his cane, a quirk of a brow, an impish lift of his toe and the mood is off; a droop of his mouth, a sag of his shoulder, a quick blink of his eye and you are his again, a companion in suffering. Or do you have to be reminded that Chaplin is a master of pantomime? Time has not changed his genius.

Speak then, of the picture, and of its story. Rumor said that "Modern Times" was preoccupied with social themes, that Chaplin—being something of a liberal himself—had decided to dramatize the class struggle, that no less an authority than Shumiatsky, head of the Soviet film industry, had counseled him about the ending and that Chaplin, accepting that advice, had made significant changes.

Mr. Chaplin's foreword to his picture was dangerously meaningful. " 'Modern Times,' " it reads, "is a story of industry, of individual enterprise—humanity crusading in the pursuit of happiness." Verily, a strange prelude to an antic.

Happily for comedy, Mr. Chaplin's description is only part of the truth and we suspect he meant it to be that way. Hollywood has quoted him as saying, "There are those who always attach social significance to my work. It has none. I leave such subjects to the lecture platform. To entertain is my first consideration."

We should prefer to describe "Modern Times" as the story of the little clown, temporarily caught up in the cogs of an industry geared to mass production, spun through a three-ring circus and out into a world as remote from industrial and class problems as a comedy can make it.

It finds Charlie as a worker on an assembly line in a huge factory. A sneeze or a momentary raise of his head is all that is needed to disrupt the steady processional of tiny gadgets whose nuts he must tighten with one swooping twist. At lunch hour his boss places him in an experimental automatic feeding machine. Like Charlie, the device goes berserk. Bowls of soup are tossed in his face, a corn-on-the-cob self-feeder throws moderation to the winds and kernels to the floor. The machine alternately grinds corn into his face and wipes his mouth with a solicitous, but entirely ineffectual, self-wiper. Charlie recovers in a hospital. When he returns, discharged as cured, he runs into the unemployment problem.

So much for the industrial crisis. Finished with it for the time, the picture involves its hero in a radical demonstration, a prison riot, several police patrol wagons, a gamin (Paulette Goddard, his new leading lady), who is homeless and helpless as he; a job as night watchman in a department store, more trouble with the law, a new job as a singing waiter in a restaurant and still more trouble with the law. There is, for good measure, a return to the factory, but no longer as a piece of human machinery on the assembly line.

Sociological concept? Maybe. But a rousing, rib-tickling, gag-bestrewn jest for all that and in the best Chaplin manner. If you remember his two-reeler, "The Skating Rink," you will be pleased to hear that Mr. Chaplin has not forgotten it either, and has found a place somewhere in his story for a more modern companion piece. You have seen him as a waiter years before, and you should be delighted to learn that he has not forgotten his tray-juggling technique. You should know, of old, his facility for dodging the Keystone cops and he clatters away just as nimbly now even though his pursuers wear more modern uniforms.

So it goes, and mighty pleasantly, too, with Charlie keeping faith with his old public by bringing back the tricks he used so well when the cinema was very young, and by extending his following among the moderns by employing devices new to the clown dynasty. If you need more encouragement than this, be informed then that Miss Goddard is a winsome waif and a fitting recipient of the great Charlot's championship, and that there are in the cast several players who have adorned the Chaplin films since first the little fellow kicked up his heels and scampered into our hearts. This morning there is good news: Chaplin is back again.

THE TRAIL OF THE LONESOME PINE,
as adapted by Harvey Threw and
Horace McCoy from the story by John
Fox Jr.; screen play by Grover Jones;
filmed in Technicolor under the direction
of Natalie Kalmus; directed by Henry
Hathaway; a Walter Wanger production;
released by Paramount. At the Paramount.

June Tolliver	Sylvia Sidney
Jack Hale	Fred MacMurray
Dave Tolliver	Henry Fonda
Judd Tolliver	Fred Stone
Tater	Fuzzy Knight
Melissa Tolliver	Beulah Bondi
Falin	Robert Barrat
Buddie	Spanky McFarland
Major Thurber	Nigel Bruce
Clayt's Wife	Ricca Allen
Ezra's Wife	Margaret Armstrong
Dave Tolliver at 5	Powell Clayton
Dave Tolliver at 10	George Ernest
Old Dave	Frank McGlynn Jr.
The Tolliver Clan	Alan Baxter, Ed Le Saint, Hank Bell, Fred Burns, Richard Carle, Bud Geary, Jim Welch and John Beck.
The Falin Clan	Bob Cortman, Jim Corey and William McCormick.

By FRANK S. NUGENT.

Color has traveled far since first
it exploded on the screen last June
in "Becky Sharp." Demonstrating
increased mastery of the new element, Walter Wanger's producing
unit proves in "The Trail of the
Lonesome Pine," which opened yesterday at the Paramount, that
Technicolor is not restricted to a
studio's stages, but can record quite
handsomely the rich, natural coloring of the outside world and whatever dramatic action may be encountered in it.

The significance of this achievement is not to be minimized. It
means that color need not shackle
the cinema, but may give it fuller
expression. It means that we can
doubt no longer the inevitability of
the color film or scoff at those who
believe that black-and-white photography is tottering on the brink
of that limbo of forgotten things
which already has swallowed the
silent picture.

Chromatically, "Trail of the
Lonesome Pine" is far less impressive than its pioneer in the field.
"Becky Sharp" employed color as
a stylistic accentuation of dramatic
effect. It sought to imprison the
rainbow in a series of carefully
planned canvases that were radi-
antly startling, visually magnificent, attuned carefully to the mood

of the picture and to the changing
tempo of its action.

The new picture attempts none of
this. Paradoxically, it improves the
case for color by lessening its importance. It accepts the spectrum
as a complementary attribute of the
picture, not its raison d'être. In
place of the vivid reds and scarlets,
the brilliant purples and dazzling
greens and yellows of "Becky," it
employs sober browns and blacks
and deep greens. It may not be
natural color, but, at least, it is
used more naturally. The eye, accustomed to the shadings of black
and white, has less difficulty meeting the demands of the new element; the color is not a distraction, but an attraction—as valuable
and little more obtrusive than the
musical score.

Lest this be interpreted as a completely eulogistic bulletin, let it be
known that the Paramount's new
film is far from perfect, either as
a photoplay or as an instrument for
the use of the new three-component
Technicolor process. Again speaking of the color, it would appear
that blue still baffles the camera;
that light browns have a tendency
to run to green, that red is either
extremely red or hopelessly orange.
These are remediable defects, we
feel, and ones that Hollywood's
skill will overcome.

Of the story, John Fox Jr.'s well-
known novel speaks for itself. Published in 1908 and twice before used
as a basis for a film—once with
Charlotte Walker and once with
Mary Miles Minter—it tells of the
feud between the Tollivers and the
Falins of Kentucky, of John Hale,
the young "furriner" who comes
into the mountains to build a railroad, and of June Tolliver, the un-
tamed young savage who sheds her
newly acquired coat of civilization
when the Falins kill chubby little
Buddy Tolliver during their guerrilla warfare against Hale and his
railroad crew.

Unlike "Becky," this is no turgid,
drawing room drama with a super-
abundance of dialogue and a minimum of action. Like "Becky," it
is none too generously endowed
with story values. For all its gunplay and fist-swinging, its plot—
considered alone—would be unimpressive and little more meaningful
than the elemental fodder on which
most Class B melodramas feed. But

when, to that story, is added a cast of unusual merit and a richly beautiful color production, then it becomes a distinguished and worthwhile picture, commanding attention no less for its intrinsic entertainment value than as another significant milestone in the development of the cinema.

Of the performances there should be special mention for Fred Stone's portrayal of the grizzled Judd Tolliver; for Henry Fonda's Dave Tolliver, the youth who accepts the "kill a Falin" dictum as one of the eternal verities; for Robert Barrat's Falin; for Fred MacMurray's personification of the "furriner"; for Beulah Bondi's Melissa, the mountain woman who lives under the terrorizing grip of feud; for Spanky McFarland, the pudgy-faced little Buddy, whose death is the tragedy of the film; for Sylvia Sidney, who is a lovely — if not completely authentic — hill billy, for Nigel Bruce as an engineer.

But the real credit for "Trail of the Lonesome Pine" belongs not to John Fox Jr., nor to the cast, but to Natalie Kalmus, who supervised the color photography; to Alexander Toluboff, who was responsible for the art direction, and to Henry Hathaway, its director, who adhered steadfastly, in the face of what must have been great temptation, to his avowed intention of keeping color under control.

F 20, 1936

DESIRE, from a comedy by Hans Szekely and R. A. Stemmle; screen play by Edwin Justus Mayer, Waldemar Young and Samuel Hoffenstein; music and lyrics by Frederick Hollander and Leo Robin; directed by Frank Borzage; produced for Paramount by Ernst Lubitsch. At the Paramount.

Madeleine de Beaupre......Marlene Dietrich
Tom Bradley................Gary Cooper
Carlos Margoli.............John Halliday
Mr. Gibson................William Frawley
Aristide Duval............Ernest Cossart
Police Official...........Akim Tamaroff
Dr. Edouard Pauquet.......Alan Mowbray
Aunt Olga.................Effie Tilbury
Pedro....................Enrique Acosta
Pepi.....................Alice Feliz
Customs Inspector........Stanley Andrews

By FRANK S. NUGENT

Ernst Lubitsch, the Gay Emancipator, has freed Marlene Dietrich from Josef von Sternberg's artistic bondage, and has brought her vibrantly alive in "Desire," which is the Paramount Theatre's generous contribution to this festive season. Permitted to walk, breathe, smile and shrug as a human being instead of a canvas for the Louvre, Miss Dietrich recaptures, in her new film, some of the freshness and gayety of spirit that was hers in "The Blue Angel" and other of her early successes. The change is delightful, and so is the picture.

You will not, in "Desire," find a great story, but you will discover one that has been splendidly told. If it is a Lubitsch production, constantly highlighted by those indefinable touches of his, still one should not overlook the skill of its director, Frank Borzage; its excellent camera work, or the performances not only of Miss Dietrich, but of Gary Cooper, John Halliday, Ernest Cossart, Alan Mowbray and Akim Tamaroff. All were in the best comedy mood, and all contributed importantly to one of the most engaging pictures of the season.

Known, and rather more aptly, as "The Pearl Necklace" during its incubation period in the Paramount studios, the film is set briskly in motion when Miss Dietrich brazenly filches a pearl necklace from a Parisian jeweler and races for the Spanish border. Driving more leisurely in the same direction happens to be Mr. Cooper, cheerfully representing a Detroit engineer on vacation.

When the customs officials begin inspecting their baggage, Miss Dietrich slips the necklace into Mr. Cooper's coat pocket, he tosses the coat into his suitcase and, from then on, Miss Dietrich is compelled to flirt outrageously—but to the engineer's wholly understandable delight—until an opportunity is presented to recover the bauble. By that time—unless you have anticipated the story—the lovely jewel thief has decided to leave her criminal associates and become a housewife in Detroit.

Familiar as the yarn may be, it sparkles and twinkles under the Lubitsch touch, moves with the proper suspense and has an unbeatable combination, Cooper and Dietrich, to carry the light romantic interest. If the picture proves anything beyond the genius of its producer, it is that Miss Dietrich is not dependent upon stylized photography and direction, but has a proper talent of her own; it proves, too, that Mr. Cooper, who has had comparatively few comic opportunities heretofore, can be as engaging a light comedian as the screen has found.

His scenes with Miss Dietrich and with Mr. Halliday, her partner in crime, are fully as merry as those between Ernest Cossart (as the duped jeweler) and Alan Mowbray (the unwitting instrument by which the theft was accomplished). And when that is said, Mr. Cooper has received a full meed of praise. "Desire," clearly, was one of the nicest gifts from the Easter rabbit.

Ap 13, 1936

MR. DEEDS GOES TO TOWN, from a story by Clarence Budington Kelland; screen play by Robert Riskin; directed by Frank Capra; a Columbia production. At the Radio City Music Hall.

Longfellow Deeds	Gary Cooper
Babe Bennett	Jean Arthur
MacWade	George Bancroft
Cornelius Cobb	Lionel Stander
John Cedar	Douglass Dumbrille
Walter	Raymond Walburn
Judge Walker	H. B. Warner
Mme. Pomponi	Margaret Matzenauer
Bodyguard	Warren Hymer
Theresa	Muriel Evans
Mabel Dawson	Ruth Donnelly
Mal	Spencer Charters
Mrs. Meredith	Emma Dunn
Psychiatrist	Wyrley Birch
Budington	Arthur Hoyt
Farmer	John Wray
Mr. Semple	Jameson Thomas
Mrs. Semple	Mayo Methot
Waiter	Gene Morgan
Morrow	Walter Catlett
Jane Faulkner	Margaret Seddon

By FRANK S. NUGENT

Frank Capra and Robert Riskin, who are a complete production staff in themselves, have turned out another shrewd and lively comedy for Columbia Pictures in "Mr. Deeds Goes to Town," which opened yesterday at the Radio City Music Hall. The directing-writing combination which functioned so successfully in "It Happened One Night," and "Broadway Bill" has spiced Clarence Budington Kelland's story with wit, novelty and ingenuity. And, spurred along by the capital performance of Gary Cooper, Jean Arthur, Lionel Stander, Douglass Dumbrille and the rest, the picture moves easily into the pleasant realm reserved for the season's most entertaining films.

Longfellow Deeds is the hero of the occasion and Longfellow Deeds becomes one of our favorite characters under the attentive handling of Mr. Cooper, who is proving himself one of the best light comedians in Hollywood. Mr. Deeds is the poet laureate of Mandrake Falls, Vt. He writes greeting-day verses, limericks and Edgar Guestian jingles with equal facility, and he plays the tuba in the town band. Then an uncle dies, leaving his $20,000,000 estate to the Vermont innocent, and Mr. Deeds, slightly dazed but unimpressed by his sudden riches, is tossed willynilly and tuba into scheming New York.

Crooked lawyers beset him, the board of the opera elects him chairman, a girl reporter gains his confidence and then headlines him as the "Cinderella Man." Crushed, derided, deceived and disillusioned, the lean Longfellow prepares to share the wealth by establishing a collective farm colony and then, cruelest jest of all, he is haled before a lunacy commission and only by the narrowest of margins and the love of Miss Arthur, the repentant sob sister, escapes being adjudged a manic depressive.

If this is the story in outline, it does not attempt to capture the gay, harebrained but entirely ingratiating quality of the picture. To appreciate that, you will have to watch Mr. Cooper struggling with the tuba, Mr. Stander fighting off apoplexy, Raymond Walburn (that most perfect gentleman's gentleman) raising his voice against an echo, and, ultimately, the scene of the lunacy commission's hearing which is as perfect a spoof of alienists and expert testimony as the screen has presented. It is on this rousingly comic note that the picture ends, and the memory of it should be enough to erase the vague impression we got that the film had bogged down for a time in mid-career.

Ap 17, 1936

THE GREEN PASTURES, an adaptation of Marc Connelly's play which was suggested by Roark Bradford's stories, "Ol' Man Adam An' His Chillun' "; screen play by Mr. Connelly and Sheridan Gibney; choral music arranged and conducted by Hall Johnson; directed by Marc Connelly and William Keighley; a Warner Brothers production. At the Radio City Music Hall.

De Lawd	Rex Ingram
Gabriel	Oscar Polk
Noah	Eddie Anderson
Moses	Frank Wilson
Mr. Deshee	George Reed
Archangel	Abraham Gleaves
Adam	Rex Ingram
Eve	Myrtle Anderson
Cain	Al Stokes
Zeba	Edna M. Harris
Cain the Sixth	James Fuller
High Priest	George Randol
Noah's Wife	Ida Forsyne
Shem	Ray Martin
Flatfoot	Charles Andrews
Ham	Dudley Dickerson
Japheth	Jimmy Burress
Abraham	William Cumby
Isaac	George Reed
Jacob	Ivory Williams
Aaron	David Bethea
Pharoah	Ernest Whitman
Head Magician	William Cumby
Joshua	Reginald Fenderson
Master of Ceremonies	Slim Thompson
King of Babylon	William Cumby
Prophet	Clinton Rosamond
Hezdrel	Rex Ingram
Hall Johnson Choir.	

That disturbance in and around the Music Hall yesterday was the noise of shuffling queues in Sixth Avenue and the sound of motion-picture critics dancing in the street. The occasion was the coming at last to the screen of Marc Connelly's naïve, ludicrous, sublime and heartbreaking masterpiece of American folk drama, "The Green Pastures." And the direct exciting cause was the fact that no profane hands have been allowed, in the words of the Second Cleaning Angel, to "gold up" its marvelous and unforgettable felicities. It still has the rough beauty of homespun, the irresistible compulsion of simple faith.

And if all this were not enough, however, there are a few amusing touches of pure cinema, such as the luxurious overstuffed clouds in mid-empyrean that the angels fish from, and an exhaustive circus menagerie of animals caught in the historical act of being loaded into an absurdly inadequate, picture-bookish Noah's Ark. The film also has the advantage of being able to open with a long shot of a peaceful, churchgoing Negro community, and there could be no pleasanter music to clear the imagination for the experience of Mr. Deshee's Sunday School class than the lonesome bell of a little back-country church-house, and the sight of pious townsfolk going along to meeting.

Needless to add, it is a surprise and a joy to hear again that there are fish-frys in heaven, and naughty cherubs (Augustine seems to have been misinformed); that the channel-cats never fail to bite there and that the stock of ten-cent see-gars never runs out.

It is reassuring to be reminded that in the days before the flood when de Lawd, walking the earth like a natchel man, asked the flowers how they were makin' out, the flowers used to reply in reedy child-like voices: "We'se O. K., Lawd." We had forgotten that heaven's gate resembles the carriage entrance of an old Southern plantation house, but it does in the picture, so it suits us perfectly.

Of course, as Mr. Deshee tells Myrtle and Randolph and Carlisle, and the other Negro children in his Sunday School class, "You gotta git your minds fixed." But that will be easy once you recover from the shock of seeing all the a-dult angels wearing straw hats at rakish angles, in a heavenly grove of live-aks and cypresses hung with Spanish moss, or Fitzhugh, the cherub, riding a docile cloud overhead and whooping like an Indian. "Now, you hear'd me. You want me to fly up there and slap you down?" shouts a Mammy Angel. It won't be hard to get your minds fixed.

We have to thank Oscar Polk for an interesting personification of the Angel Gabriel—not only for the tall, Afro-Gothic of his figure, with its robe of monumental descending folds—but for the fact that he is a pretty subtle Gabriel who depends for his efforts on a sort of cumulative understatement —a Gabriel who grows on you. Oscar's main stylistic device seems to be an epic fatigue—the result, apparently, of contemplating for aeon after aeon the ageless unresting energy of de Lawd, and of trying to keep up with him. Any actor who could deliberately underplay the famous line, "Gangway for de Lawd God Jehovah," as though it were merely another chore in an eternity of such annunciation, is a formidable artist. You can hear a mild agrarian enthusiasm in his voice only when he leans over and contempltes the newly created earth: "Dat'd make mighty nice farming country, Lawd. Just look at dat South Forty over dere."

Perhaps a confirmed monotheist can only accept one Lawd in his time, and that is why—in a vague,

164

self-reproachful sort of way—we are of two minds about Rex Ingram's interpretation of this most gradiose of contemporary rôles. Perhaps the memory of the late Richard B. Harrison is too recent to be effaced altogether by a Lawd, however beautifully made up, however luminous of physiognomy and imbued with the mystical consciousness of his diestic heritage, as the obviously younger, springier Lawd of Rex Ingram. We've tried a hundred ways to forget the strength of character combined with native dignity and sweetness of the septuagenarian Lawd of the stage play, but we just can't. He's still de Lawd, as far as we are concerned.

Barring this purely sentimental reservation, we feel that inasmuch as Ingram was also asked to play Adam and "Hezdrel" he has done infinitely better than anyone had the right to expect, even of a one-man stock company. He commands a physical presence to which Harrison never pretended and there are scenes which he plays in so exquisite a manner that not even Harrison could excel them. He never stems to be spiritually or emotionally out of touch with any of his rôles, and he has the technical advantage, when he decides to r'ar back and past a miracle, that we are permitted to see the miraclt—the churning cosmos, the new world spinning in the void. In cases like this the experts are allowed to pull a few inoffensive rabbits out of the hat.

But not enough to become a bore. When de Lawd decides to visit the earth, for instance, he simply takes his hat and cane, informs Gabe that he will be back Saddy, and dignifiedly walks as though down a little staircase out of sight. This is as satisfactory a transition from eternity into time as any. Similarly, the moment of thunder and the play of revelatory lightning on the face of Noah at the dinner table when de Lawd makes himself known was already the most dramatic incident in the play, just as the speech, "I shoulda known you, Lawd; I shoulda seen de glory," is the most profoundly moving bit of text. In the main, there was nothing the camera could do to intensify the play's great moments, and it is encouraging enough to realize that it has done nothing to lessen them, either.

It ought not to be necessary to repeat the high-lights of a story which is changeless and eternal. A few chosen at random would be the scene when Eddie Anderson's superb Noah feels a twitch of his "buck auger" and sure enough it turns out to be a sign of rain; when de Lawd tenderly leads the aged and dynig Moses upward into a land "a million times nicer dan de land of Cane-yan," and when, after renouncing his people in wrath, he is won back by the wheedling of "de Delegation" (Abraham, Isaac, Jacob and Moses) combined with the strange prayers of the apochryphal Hezdrel addressed to the new God of Mercy.

Of such stuff is compounded not only the "divine comedy of the modern theatre" but something of the faith that moves mountains. It is, indeed, hard not to like the simple and gratifying theology of "The Green Pastures" as much as anything about it. It has concreteness and gives one a nostalgic feeling that it ought to be true and that if it isn't we are all, somehow, obscurely the worst for it. Rex Ingram, Oscar Polk, Eddie Anderson, Hank Wilson, Ernest Whitman, George Reed and the others, move against a rich background of spirituals sung by the Hall Johnson choir.   B. R. C.

Jl 17, 1936

CAMILLE,, as adapted by Zoe Akins, Frances Marion and James Hilton from Alexandre Dumas's "La Dame Aux Camelias"; directed by George Cukor; produced by Metro-Goldwyn-Mayer. At the Capitol.
Marguerite....................Greta Garbo
Armand.....................Robert Taylor
Monsieur Duval..........Lionel Barrymore
Nichette................Elizabeth Allan
Nanine....................Jessie Ralph
Baron de Varville..........Henry Daniell
Olympe....................Lenore Ulric
Prudence.............Laura Hope Crews
Gaston.....................Rex O'Malley
Gustave.................Russell Hardie
Saint Gaudens...............E. E. Clive
Henri.....................Douglas Walton
Corinne....................Marion Ballou
Marie Jeanette..............Joan Brodel
Louise......................June Wilkins
Valentin.................Fritz Leiber Jr.
Mme. Duval...............Elsie Esmonds

By FRANK S. NUGENT

Having passed its fiftieth anniversary, "Camille" is less a play than an institution. Just as "Hamlet" is the measure of the great actor, so has the Dumas fils' classic become the ultimate test of the dramatic actress. Greta Garbo's performance in the new Metro-Goldwyn-Mayer version at the Capitol is in the finest tradition: eloquent, tragic, yet restrained. She is as incomparable in the rôle as legend tells us that Bernhardt was. Through the perfect artistry of her portrayal, a hackneyed theme is made new again, poignantly sad, hauntingly lovely.

George Cukor, the classicist of the Metro studios, has retained the full flavor of the period—France in the middle of the last century—without drenching his film with the cloying scent of a hothouse. "Camille," under his benign handling and the understanding adaptation by Zoe Akins, Frances Marion and James Hilton, is not the reverentially treated museum piece we half expected to see. Its speech has been modernized, but not jarringly; its characters, beneath the frill and ruffles of the Fifties, have the contemporary point of view; its tragedy is still compelling, for the Lady of the Camellias must eternally be a tragic figure.

Miss Garbo has interpreted Marguerite Gautier with the subtlety that has earned for her the title, "first lady of the screen." Even as the impish demi-mondaine of the early sequences, she has managed to convey the impression of maturity, of a certain etherialism and spiritual integrity which raise her above her surroundings and mark her as one apart. Her love for Armand, dictating her flight from Paris and the protection of the Baron de Varville, becomes, then, less a process of reformation and regeneration than it is the natural realization of her true character; less a variation of life than a discovery of life.

To appreciate her complete command of the rôle, one need only study her approach to the key scenes of the drama. Where the less sentient Camille bides her time until the moment comes for her to tear her passions and the scenery to tatters, Garbo waits and then understates. It is her dignity that gives strength to her scene with M. Duval when he asks her to give up his son. It is because her emotions do not slip their leash—when you feel that any second they might—that saves her parting scene with Armand from being a cliché of renunciation. And, above all, it is her performance in the death scene—so simply, delicately and movingly played—which convinces me that Camille is Garbo's best performance.

Robert Taylor is surprisingly good as Armand, a bit on the juvenile side at times, perhaps, but certainly not guilty of the traditional sin of the many Armands of the past—callowness. As the Baron de Varville, Henry Daniell is suavely perfect. It is a matter for rejoicing that a character, so clearly stamped for villainy, should receive, belatedly, some of the sympathy he deserved: Camille did, you know, treat him shamefully. From Jessie Ralph as Nanine, Lionel Barrymore as M. Duval, Lenore Ulric as Olympe, Laura Hope Crews as Prudence and Rex O'Malley as Gaston we have received what we had every right to expect—good, sound, supporting performances. That they should have been noted at all, in view of Miss Garbo's brilliant domination of the picture, is high praise indeed.

Ja 23, 1937

A STAR IS BORN, from a story by William A. Wellman and Robert Carson; screen play by Dorothy Parker, Alan Campbell and Mr. Carson; musical score by Max Steiner; directed by Mr. Wellman; produced by David O. Selznick for Selznick International; released by United Artists. At the Radio City Music Hall.

Esther Blodgett—Vicki Lester..Janet Gaynor
Norman Maine ....Fredric March
Oliver Niles................Adolphe Menjou
Lettie ....A..May Robson
Danny McGuire..............Andy Devine
Libby ....Lionel Stander
Anita Regis................Elizabeth Jenns
Pop Randall................Edgar Kennedy
Casey Burke.................Owen Moore
Theodore Smythe............J. C. Nugent
Aunt Mattie...............Clara Blandick
Esther's brother...........A. W. Sweatt
Miss Phillips (clerk).........Peggy Wood
Harris ....Adrian Rosely
Ward ....Arthur Hoyt
Posture Coach..Guinn (Big Boy) Williams
Otto Friedl.................Vince Barnett
Academy Awards Speaker....Paul Stanton
Billy Moon... ....Franklin Pangborn

By FRANK S. NUGENT

It is not as dull a Spring as we had thought. Selznick International came to April's defense yesterday with one of the year's best shows, "A Star Is Born," which probably will find the Music Hall's treasurer turning cartwheels in the streets this morning. For here, at least, is good entertainment by any standards, including the artistic, and convincing proof that Hollywood need not travel to Ruritania for its plots: there is drama a-plenty in its own backyard.

"A Star Is Born" is a Hollywood story of, by and for its people. It has the usual preface, attesting to the fictional quality of the characters and incidents depicted, but it is nonetheless the most accurate mirror ever held before the glittering, tinseled, trivial, generous, cruel and ecstatic world that is Hollywood. That, in itself, guarantees its dramatic interest, for there is no place on this twentieth-century earth more fascinating—not even that enchanting make-believe republic which James Hilton called Shangri-La.

Looking at it objectively, one might argue that William Wellman, Robert Carson, Dorothy Parker and Alan Campbell (who coined the plot) have been passing Confederate money. Their thesis is the old one about the rising star and the falling star in the theatrical firmament whose paths cross, create a pyrotechnic glow where they meet, then flame out tragically as one soars onward in her flight as the other dips sadly and dies. If this were all, then "A Star Is Born" would be no more than commonplace, a jaded repetition of a basic theatrical formula.

But there are vibrance and understanding in their writing, a feeling for telling detail and a sympathy for the people they are touching. It is not a maudlin picture—not nearly so heroic let us say, as its dramatic corollary, "Stage Door." Janet Gaynor's movie-struck Esther Blodgett is not a caricature; Fred-ric March's waning Norman Maine is not an outrageous "ham"; Adolphe Menjou's Oliver Niles (of Oliver Niles Productions) is no more—and no less—human than many producers are. They are honest, normal, well-intentioned folk; different, of course, for Hollywood would make them so; but we can believe in them and understand them and be moved by their tragedy. Conviction can bring any formula to life.

So then. we have the story of little Esther Blodgett who came to Hollywood and stood beatifically in the concrete footprints of Norman Maine outside Grauman's Chinese Theatre; who somehow—by one of those 100,000-to-1 chances—became the sensational Vicki Lester and Mrs. Norman Maine; who could not arrest her husband's swift descent, nor protect him from being called Mr. Vicki Lester, nor stay him when he stepped gallantly from the scene. Little Esther Blodgett had her success in Hollywood, but she paid for it. "Stage Door" never took that into account.

It is, as we said before, a good picture. It has been capitally played all down the line. Its script is bright, inventive and forceful. Mr. Wellman's direction is expert. Its color—we almost forgot to mention it, so casually was it used—proves Technicolor's value in a modern story, demonstrates that it need not, should not, be restricted to the gaudy costume dramas. Not even its three climaxes, one right after the other, are enough to alter our verdict. The Music Hall, after a long famine, is spreading a feast again.

Ap 23, 1937

CAPTAINS COURAGEOUS, as adapted from Rudyard Kipling's novel by John Lee Mahin, Marc Connelly and Dale Van Every; musical score by Franz Waxman, with lyrics by Gus Kahn; directed by Victor Fleming; produced by Louis D. Lighton for Metro-Goldwyn-Mayer. At the Astor.

Harvey Cheyne	Freddie Bartholomew
Manuel	Spencer Tracy
Disko	Lionel Barrymore
Mr. Cheyne	Melvyn Douglas
Uncle Salters	Charley Grapewin
Dan	Mickey Rooney
"Long Jack"	John Carradine
Cushman	Oscar O'Shea
Priest	Jack La Rue
Dr. Finley	Walter Kingsford
Tyler	Donald Briggs.
"Doc"	Sam McDaniels
Charles	Billie Burrud

By FRANK S. NUGENT

Metro's "Captains Courageous," which had its première at the Astor last night and will be shown henceforth on a two-a-day basis, is another of those grand jobs of moviemaking we have come to expect of Hollywood's most prodigal studio. With its rich production, magnificent marine photography, admirable direction and performances, the film brings vividly to life every page of Kipling's novel and even adds an exciting chapter or two of its own.

In tailoring the narrative to the starring dimensions of Freddie Bartholomew, the trio of adapters (John Lee Mahin, Marc Connelly and Dale Van Every) had to trim several years from the age of Harvey Cheyne, changing him from a spoiled 19-year-old to a spoiled 12-year-old. Except for that and a few pardonable additions, they have steadfastly followed the Kipling tale of an imperious and detestable young scamp who toppled from a liner's rail off the Grand Banks, was picked up by a Portuguese doryman from the schooner We're Here and became a regular fellow during an enforced three-months fishing cruise.

Interesting as the early sequences are, with their telling revelation of Harvey's character, the picture does not really come alive until the cameras turn upon the We're Here. Then, in its depiction of the men and methods of the old Gloucester fleet, it takes on almost the quality of a documentary film, enriched by poetic photography of schooners spanking along under full sail, of dories being lowered into a running sea and shading in, quite deftly, the human portraits of the fishermen with their quiet heroism and resignation, their Down East humor and their stern code of decency.

The picture's character gallery is happily served. Young Master Bartholomew, who, frankly, never has been one of this corner's favorites, plays Harvey faultlessly, presenting at first as reptilian a lad as a miniature Basil Rathbone might have managed and bringing him around eventually to the grieving, bewildered small boy who has lost the one person he loved and cannot readily admit his father into the desolate sanctuary of his heart.

Spencer Tracy, as Manuel, the boy's idol, seemed curiously unconvincing in the beginning, probably because the accent does not become him—but made the part his in time. Then there is Lionel Barrymore, who is a flawless Captain Disko, and Melvyn Douglas giving an understanding interpretation of the elder Cheyne, and John Carradine as Long Jack, Mickey Rooney as Dan, Charles Grapewin as Uncle Salters and others equally assured. Victor Fleming's direction has kept the tale flowing, Hal Rosson's photography has given it beauty and excellent characterization has lent to it poignance. Metro can take pride in its production.

My 12, 1937

STAGE DOOR, an adaptation of the play by Edna Ferber and George S. Kaufman; screen play by Morrie Ryskind and Anthony Veiller; directed by Gregory La Cava; produced by Pandro S. Berman for RKO Radio. At the Radio City Music Hall.

Jean Maitland	Ginger Rogers
Terry Randall	Katharine Hepburn
Anthony Powell	Adolphe Menjou
Linda Shaw	Gail Patrick
Catherine Luther	Constance Collier
Kaye Hamilton	Andrea Leeds
Henry Sims	Samuel S. Hinds
Judith Canfield	Lucille Ball
Harcourt	Franklin Pangborn
Bill	William Corson
Richard Carmichael	Pierre Watkin
Butch	Grady Sutton
Stage Director	Frank Reicher
Hattie	Phyllis Kennedy
Eve	Eve Arden
Annie	Ann Miller
Mary Lou	Margaret Early
Dizzy	Jean Rouverol
Mrs. Orcutt	Elizabeth Dunne
Olga Brent	Norma Drury
Ann Braddock	Jane Rhodes
Susan	Peggy O'Donnell
Madeline	Harriett Brandon
Cast of Stage Play	Katharine Alexander
	Ralph Forbes
	Mary Forbes
	Huntley Gordon

By FRANK S. NUGENT

The RKO-Radio version of "Stage Door," which was opened at the Music Hall yesterday, is not merely a brilliant picture (although that should be enough), but happens as well to be a magnificently devastating reply on Hollywood's behalf to all the catty little remarks that George Kaufman and Edna Ferber had made about it in their play.

Those impolite playwrights, you

remember, had filled the mouths of the aspirant Bernhardts of their Footlights Club with gall and wormwood whenever the Hollywood topic arose, which was fairly constantly. It was, we were told, a factory and a graveyard of art, a place of complete untalent and all-pervading witlessness, of sables for the body and starvation for the soul, etc.—all very wittily expressed and neatly packaged (through the courtesy of Metro-Goldwyn-Mayer which had backed the show).

For a factory and a graveyard and other unpleasant institutions, Hollywood has done some rather incredible things with the Kaufman-Ferber contribution, not the least of them being the transformation of a fragile piece of theatrical wishful-willing into a far more soundly contrived comedy drama. Script-writers Morrie Ryskind and Anthony Veiller have taken the play's name, its setting and part of its theme and have built a whole new structure which is wittier than the original, more dramatic than the original, more meaningful than the original, more cogent than the original.

Where the team of K & F (who really should have been ashamed) drew Hollywood as the leering man with the waxed black mustache, RKO has countered by showing that the villain of all serious acting fledglings is the Broadway producer who is too busy to look and listen. But with this premise, which was the whole sum of the stage's "Stage Door," the film edition had only begun its narrative. Back it goes to the Footlights Club where the stagestruck maidens nurse their disappointments and sharpen their claws (on whatever victim is handy) and gossip betimes over the triangular sham battle being fought by Ginger Rogers, Katharine Hepburn and Gail Patrick over and around Adolphe Menjou.

Miss Hepburn (to put this outburst into some sort of order) is the wealthy girl with stage notions and a serious outlook. Miss Rogers is the more realistic type. Miss Patrick has decided to play her producers offstage. Mr. Menjou is the rake who has his better side. Miss Andrea Leeds, the real discovery of the picture, is the tortured young woman who has waited a year for the One Role. There are the other young ladies of the ensemble, and a cleverly individualized bevy they are, whose several destinies tragically or comically counterpoint those of the primary four.

The twists and turns of the narrative are sensibly motivated, the direction of Gregory La Cava has given it zest and pace and photographic eloquence, and the performances are amazingly good—considering that Mr. Kaufman's Hollywood is just a canning factory. Miss Hepburn and Miss Rogers, in particular, seemed to be acting so far above their usual heads that, frankly, we hardly recognized them. A round of curtain calls would demand a bow and smile from Constance Collier, Lucille Ball, Franklin Pangborn, Eve Arden, Ann Miller, Margaret Early and Phyllis Kennedy, among the many others. And now, do we hear a retraction from Mr. Kaufman?

O 8, 1937

SNOW WHITE AND THE SEVEN DWARFS, a feature-length cartoon based on Grimms' fairy tale; adapted by Ted Sears, Otto Englander, Earl Hurd, Dorothy Ann Blank, Richard Creedon, Dick Rickard, Merrill De Maris and Webb Smith; music by Frank Churchill, Leigh Harline and Paul Smith; supervising director, David Hand; produced in Technicolor by Walt Disney for release by RKO-Radio. At the Radio City Music Hall.

By FRANK S. NUGENT

Sheer fantasy, delightful, gay and altogether captivating, touched the screen yesterday when Walt Disney's long-awaited feature-length cartoon of the Grimm fairy tale, "Snow White and the Seven Dwarfs," had its local première at the Radio City Music Hall. Let your fears be quieted at once: Mr. Disney and his amazing technical crew have outdone themselves. The picture more than matches expectations. It is a classic, as important cinematically as "The Birth of a Nation" or the birth of Mickey Mouse. Nothing quite like it has been done before; and already we have grown impolite enough to clamor for an encore. Another helping, please!

You can visualize it best if you imagine a child, with a wondrous, Puckish imagination, nodding over his favorite fairy tale and dreaming a dream in which his story would come true. He would see Snow White, victim of the wicked Queen's jealousy, dressed in rags, singing at her work quite unmindful of the Magic Mirror's warning to the Queen that the Princess, not she, was now the "fairest in the land." Then he would see Snow White's banishment from the castle, her fearful flight from the hobgoblins of the forest, her adoption by all the friendly little creatures of the wood and her refuge at the home of the seven dwarfs.

And then, if this child had a truly marvelous imagination—the kind of impish imagination that Mr. Disney and his men possess—, he might have seen the seven dwarfs as the picture sees them. There are Doc, who sputters and twists his words, and Happy, who is a rollicking little elf, and Grumpy, who is terribly grumpy—at first—, and Sleepy, who drowses, and Sneezy, who acts like a volcano with hay fever, and Bashful, who blushes to the roots of his long white beard, and Dopey. Dopey really deserves a sentence all by himself. No, we'll make it a paragraph, because Dopey is here to stay.

Dopey is the youngest of the seven dwarfs. He is beardless, with a buttony nose, a wide mouth, Gable ears, cross-purpose eyes and the most disarming, winning, helpless, puppy-dog expression that creature ever had. If we had to dissect him, we'd say he was one part little Benny of the comic strips, one part Worry-Wart of the same and one part Pluto, of the Mickey Mouse Plutos. There may, too, be just a dash of Harpo Marx. But he's all Dopey, forever out of step in the dwarfs' processions, doomed to carry the red tail-light when they go to their jewel mines, and speechless. As Doc explains, "he never tried to talk."

So there they are, all seven of them, to protect the little Princess from her evil stepmother, the Queen, to dance and frolic and cavort—with the woodland creatures—in comic Disneyesque patterns, and ultimately to keep vigil at Snow White's glass-and-gold coffin until Prince Charming imprints "love's first kiss" upon her lips and so releases her from the sleeping death that claimed her after she ate the witch's poisoned apple. For this, you know, is partly the story of Sleeping Beauty.

But no child, of course, could dream a dream like this. For Mr. Disney's humor has the simplicity of extreme sophistication. The little bluebird who overreaches itself and hits a flat note to the horror of its parents; the way the animals help Snow White clean house, with the squirrels using their tails as dusters, the swallows scalloping pies with their feet, the fawns licking the plates clean, the chipmunks twirling cobwebs about their tails and pulling free; or the ticklish tortoise when the rabbits use his ribbed underside as a scrubbing board—all these are beyond a youngster's imagination, but not beyond his delight.

And technically it is superb. In some of the early sequences there may be an uncertainty of line, a jerkiness in the movements of the Princess; but it is corrected later and hand and lip movements assume an uncanny reality. The dwarfs and animals are flawless from the start. Chromatically, it is far and away the best Technicolor to date, achieving effects possible only to the cartoon, obtaining—through the multi-plane camera—an effortless third dimension. You'll not, most of the time, realize you are watching animated cartoons. And if you do, it will be only with a sense of amazement.

Nor can any description overlook so important a Disney element as the score. There are eight songs—solos, duets, choruses—which perfectly counterpoint the action. In the traditional ballad manner are "The Wishing Well Song," "Some Day My Prince Will Come" and "One Song." Livelier is the dwarfs' theme, "Hi-Ho," "Whistle While You Work," "The Washing Song" and "Isn't This a Silly Song." We've lost one or two, but no great matter. They're gay and friendly and pleasant, all of them, and so is the picture. If you miss it, you'll be missing the ten best pictures of 1938. Thank you very much, Mr. Disney, and come again soon.

Ja 14, 1938

THE RIVER, written and directed by Pare Lorentz; narrated by Thomas Chalmers; musical score by Virgil Thomson; photography by Stacy Woodard, Floyd Crosby and Willard Van Dyke; produced by the Farm Security Administration; released by Paramount Pictures Corporation. At the Criterion.

By FRANK S. NUGENT

"This is the story of a river, a record of the Mississippi, where it comes from, where it goes, what it has meant to us and what it has cost us."

That is Pare Lorentz's prologue to "The River," the documentary film he produced for the Farm Security Administration and which had its first public Broadway screening at the Criterion yesterday. It is a simple statement of purpose, a simple statement of theme. In its simplicity and in the artful simplicity of its production, it is a poetic, stirring and majestic picture. The old words have been too freely used; to call it "epic" in Hollywood's presence implies an ignorance of laudable superlatives. But we employ the word in the pre-Goldwyn sense, and "The River" is an epic—an epic of the great brown giant that served man and rose against him when he betrayed it.

It is the story of neglect and ignorance and greed, of cotton land milked dry, of ruthless timber cutting, of earth scarred by the miners of coal and iron. It is the story of the river's rebellion, of floods and erosion and the desolate wasting of the land. And it is the story, still in its first chapters, of reforestation, scientific land cultivation, of dams and power plants and model homes. It is the story of the Mississippi as told by a modern realist, not by an Edna Ferber in romantic salute to a romantic past.

And Mr. Lorentz has told its story well. His film is more impressive photographically than his "Plow That Broke the Plains" of last year. Virgil Thomson's score, a symphonic blend of old spirituals, folk ballads and original music, has matched the images perfectly. Mr. Lorentz's narrative, spoken by Thomas Chalmers, has the rhythmic cadence of flowing water. We cannot resist quoting one of its passages:

From as far West as Idaho,
Down from the glacier peaks of the Rockies;
From as far East as Pennsylvania,
Down from the turkey ridges of the Alleghanies;
Down from Minnesota, twenty-five hundred miles,
The Mississippi River runs to the Gulf.
Carrying every drop of water that flows down two-thirds of the continent;
Carrying every brook and rill,
Rivulet and creek—
Carrying all the rivers that run down two-thirds of the continent—
The Mississippi runs to the Gulf of Mexico.
Down the Yellowstone, the Milk, the White and the Cheyenne;
The Cannonball, the Musselshell, the James and the Sioux;
Down the Judith, the Grand, the Osage and the Platte;
The Skunk, the Salt, the Black and Minnesota;
Down the Rock, the Illinois and the Kankakee,
The Allegheny, the Monongahela, Kanawha and Muskingum;
Down the Miami, the Wabash, the Licking and the Green,
The Cumberland, the Kentucky and the Tennessee;
Down the Ouchita, the Wichita, the Red and Yazoo;
Down the Missouri three thousand miles from the Rockies;
Down the Ohio a thousand miles from the Alleghenies;
Down the Arkansas fifteen hundred miles from the Great Divide;
Down the Red, a thousand miles from Texas;
Down the great Valley, twenty-five hundred miles from Minnesota,
Carrying every rivulet and brook, creek and rill,
Carrying all the rivers that run down two-thirds of the continent,
The Mississippi runs to the Gulf.

Prose like that, accompanied by pictures like those his camera crew have obtained and by Mr. Thomson's eloquent score, places "The River" at the top of American documentaries; challenges the best the international documentarians have done. Not even a Supreme Court decision could stay us from calling this New Deal venture one of the finest films ever made.

F 5, 1938

YOU CAN'T TAKE IT WITH YOU, as adapted by Robert Riskin from the play of that name by George S. Kaufman and Moss Hart; directed and produced by Frank Capra for Columbia Pictures. At the Radio City Music Hall.
Alice Sycamore ....Jean Arthur
Martin Vanderhof.......Lionel Barrymore
Tony Kirby ....James Stewart
Anthony P. Kirby..........Edward Arnold
Kolenkhov ....Mischa Auer
Essie Carmichael ....Ann Miller
Penny Sycamore ....Spring Byington
Paul Sycamore ....Samuel S. Hinds
Poppins ....Donald Meek
Ramsey ....H. B. Warner

DePinna ....Halliwell Hobbes
Ed Carmichael.................Dub Taylor
Mrs. Anthony Kirby.........Mary Forbes
Rheba ....Lillian Yarbo
Donald ....Eddie Anderson
John Blakely ....Clarence Wilson
Professor ....Josef Swickard
Maggie O'Neill ....Ann Doran
Schmidt ....Christian Rub
Mrs. Schmidt ....Bodil Rosing
Henderson ....Charles Lane
Judge ....Harry Davenport

By FRANK S. NUGENT

Pulitzer Prize plays do not grow on bushes, a circumstance which is bound to complicate their grafting to the cinema. "You Can't Take It with You" was a tremendously amusing play. George Kaufman and Moss Hart, who wrote it, had just three curtains to make, one set to cover them all and an irresistably comic panel of characters. Brevity was not merely the spice of their wit, but the salvation of it. Everything happened so quickly, and so humorously, that only postmortem reflections suggested that the dramatists might have been raising a towering, but essentially fragile, structure. Grandpa Vanderhof himself was an inexcusably anachronistic figure: no one, these days, can afford not to pay an income tax.

Columbia's film of the play, which moved into the Music Hall yesterday, has had to justify that Pulitzer award. Simply because it is a motion picture, and not a play, it has had to explore the Kaufman-Hart characters more thoroughly than the playwrights had need to. Instead of three curtains, there had to be a flowing narrative; instead of one set, there had to be a dozen (or more); instead of seeing things always through the direct, but nonetheless distorted, eyes of the amazing Vanderhofs and Sycamores, there had to bea certain respect for the viewpoint of the abused and ultra-rich Kirbys.

Frank Capra, its directors, and Robert Riskin, its adapter, have vindicated that Pulitzer award, even at the expense of comedy. The characters Messrs. Kaufman and Hart invented were not unidimensional after all. When you look them through, as the picture does, you discover they were people, not caricatures. The playwrights drew their outlines; the picture has filled them in. Vanderhofs, Sycamores and Kirbys all have substance now. Beyond doubt, none of them is quite so funny—except possibly the hungry Russian, the lit'ry Mrs. Sycamore, the ballet-dancing Essie—but they are far more likeable, far more human.

Humans, of course, are not as laughable as caricatures of humans. "You Can't Take It With You" isn't as comic on the screen as it was on the stage. At least, not in its total effect. When it chooses to be funny it can be funny as the dickens. But it chooses, too, on the screen, to be serious and, at times, moral and sentimental. Grandpa Vanderhof's philosophy was in defense of simple enjoyment of life. On the stage, its application was pretty comic; in reality, even in the reality of the screen, it can become pretty serious.

Mr. Riskin has done a lot with the story, chiefly in deference to the feelings of the Kirbys of the world, but it remains the high-spirited fable of the Sycamore girl and the Kirby boy who had to introduce their families to each other. The Kirby Srs. were from Wall Street and Park Avenue. The Sycamores and Vanderhofs were of a long line of amiable lunatics: Grandpa, who quit work one day thirty-five years before because it wasn't fun; Mrs. Sycamore, who wrote endless plays because some one left a typewriter on her doorstep; Mr. Sycamore and Mr. De Pinna, who made their own fireworks; Essie, who danced, and Ed, who fooled around with a homemade printing press and revolutionary circulars. The Sycamores and Vanderhofs always were sitting on gunpowder kegs. There were bound to be sparks when the flinty Kirbys came to call.

It's a grand picture, which will disappoint only the most superficial admirers of the play. Columbia, besides contributing the services of its famous writing-directing team, has chosen its cast with miraculous wisdom. Lionel Barrymore's Grandpa is the least bit of a let-down after Henry Travers's playing of the role on Broadway, but we're willing to admit our dissatisfaction may be due to the fact that Mr. Travers's Grandpa came first. Beyond that prejudicial doubt we enthusiastically admire every one and everything—Jean Arthur's Alice Sycamore, James Stewart's honest young Kirby, Edward Arnold's badgered tycoon, Spring Byington's delightful Penny, Donald Meek's Mr. Poppins (a new one on Mr. Kaufman) and all the other names on the long cast sheet. And, before we forget it, "You Can't Take It With You" jumps smack into the list of the year's best.

S 2, 1938

GRAND ILLUSION, based on a story by Jean Renoir; screen play by Mr. Renoir and Charles Spaak; music by Jerome Kosma; directed by Mr. Renoir; an R. C. A. production; released by World Pictures Corporation. At the Filmarte.

Marechal	Jean Gabin
De Boeldieu	Pierre Fresnay
Von Rauffenstein	Eric von Stroheim
Rosenthal	Dalio
Peasant Woman	Dita Parlo
An Actor	Carette
A Surveyor	Gaston Modot
A Soldier	Georges Peclet
A Teacher	Edouard Daste

By FRANK S. NUGENT

Surprisingly enough, in these combustible times, the French have produced a war film under the title "Grand Illusion." It served to re-open the Filmarte last night and it serves to warn the British that they no longer have a monopoly upon that valuable dramatic device known as understatement. Jean Renoir, the film's author and director, has chosen consistently to underplay his hand. Time after time he permits his drama to inch up to the brink of melodrama: one waits for the explosion and the tumult. Time after time he resists the temptation and lets the picture go its calmer course.

For a war film it is astonishingly lacking in hullabaloo. There may have been four shots fired, but there are no screaming shells, no brave speeches, no gallant toasts to the fallen. War is the grand illusion and Renoir proceeds with his disillusioning task by studying it, not in the front line, but in the prison camps, where captors and captives alike are condemned to the dry rot of inaction. War is not reality; prison camp is. Only the real may survive it.

Renoir cynically places a decadent aristocrat, a German career officer, in command of the camp; he places his French counterpart among the prisoners. There is an affinity bred of mutual self-contempt, of the realization of being part of an outgrown era. The other prisoners are less heroic, but more human. They are officers, of course, but officers of a republic, not an aristocracy. One is Marechal, ex-machinist; another is Rosenthal, a wealthy Jew. Von Rauffenstein, the German commandant, held them both in contempt. The elegant Captain de Boeldieu respected them as soldiers, admired them as men, faintly regretted he could not endure them as fellow-beings.

So it becomes a story of escape, a metaphysical escape on de Boeldieu's part, a tremendously exciting flesh and bone escape on the part of Marechal and Rosenthal. Renoir's narrative links the two adventures for a while, but ultimately resolves itself into a saga of flight. As an afterthought, but a brilliantly executed one, he adds a romance as one of his French fugitives finds shelter in the home of a young German widow. The story ends sharply, with no attempt to weave its threads together. It is probably the way such a story would have ended in life.

Renoir has created a strange and interesting film, but he owes much to his cast. Eric von Stroheim's appearance as von Rauffenstein reminds us again of Hollywood's folly in permitting so fine an actor to remain idle and unwanted. Pierre Fresnay's de Boeldieu is a model of gentlemanly decadence. Jean Gabin and Dalio as the fugitives; Dita Parlo as the German girl, and all the others are thoroughly right. The Filmarte is off to a good beginning.

S 13, 1938

CHILDHOOD OF MAXIM GORKY, from a scenario by I. Gruzdev based on Maxim Gorky's autobiography, "My Childhood"; directed by Mark Donskoi; produced by Soyuzdetfilm in the U.S.S.R.; released by Amkino. At the Cameo.

Alexel Peshkov (Gorky)	Alyosha Lyarsky
Grandmother	V. O. Massalitinova
Grandfather	M. G. Troyanovsky
Varvara	E. Alexeyeva
Uncle Yakov	V. Novikof
Uncle Mikhail	A. Zhukof
Grigori	K. Ziubkof
Gypsy	D. Sagal
The Lodger	S. Tikhonravof
Lenka	Igor Smirnof

By FRANK S. NUGENT

Obviously designed as the first volume of a trilogy, "Childhood of Maxim Gorky," the new Russian film at the Cameo must be regarded not as a complete dramatic unit, but as a preface and an introduction to nebulous Volumes Two and Three. To consider it any other way would be to discredit a work which, at some future date, may properly be considered the brilliant first chapters of a biographical masterpiece. And yet, should those later chapters develop badly, Volume One—or "Childhood"—would have to be called no great work after all. Here is a bewildering critical problem, for how can one evaluate something of the present in terms of something of the mysterious future?

Gorky's childhood, as the film realistically describes it, might have many meanings, or none. A program note calls it the story "of the blossoming of a genius." With a change of scene it might as easily have been the story of a Horatio Alger hero, with half its pages missing. Gorky, or Alexei Peshkov, was orphaned, sent to board with his semi-human grandfather and savage brood of uncles and cousins, was beaten, kicked and made to find his true friends on the garbage dumps and in the hovels of Nizhni-Novgorod. The picture ends with his flight, a small boy bravely trudging across the open fields.

Alexei Peshkov has not, as you can see, begun to develop into Maxim Gorky, although it is entirely possible that the misery to which he had been subjected already had begun to mold the character that was to become Gorky. But, here again, one is compelled to speculate, to predicate an opinion upon known and unknown future fact. "Childhood" is not good biography, for it presents only the superficials of its hero, the things that happened to him, not what he thought of them. On the other hand, it might be the best kind of cinema biography, for it may lead in its later volumes to a surer revelation of character through this very objectivity.

But this much is certain: "Childhood" is splendid social reportage. Director Donskoi and his cast have breathed vigorous life into Russia of the Seventies and, with unfailing courage, have created scene after scene of bold, uncompromising realism. Although it is not without its humor, its tenderness and kindness, most of it is ugly and violent. Amid such surroundings one may surmise how an Alexei Peshkov came to call himself Maxim Gorky—Maxim the Bitter. But that is sheer speculation; we would prefer to reserve judgment until the rest of the trilogy has been screened.

S 28, 1938

PYGMALION, as adapted by W. P. Lipscombe and Cecil Lewis from the play by George Bernard Shaw; screen play and dialogue by Mr. Shaw; musical score by Arthur Honegger; directed by Anthony Asquith and Leslie Howard; produced in England by Gabriel Pascal and released by Metro-Goldwyn-Mayer. At the Astor.

Henry Higgins	Leslie Howard
Eliza Doolittle	Wendy Hiller
Alfred Doolittle	Wilfrid Lawson
Mrs. Huggins	Marie Lohr
Colonel Pickering	Scott Sunderland
Mrs. Pearce	Jean Cadell
Freddy	David Tree
Mrs. Eynsford Hill	Everley Gregg
Clara Hill	Leueen MacGrath
Count Aristid Karpathy	Esme Percy
Ambassadress	Violet Vanbrugh
Vicar	O. B. Clarence
Duchess	Irene Brown
Grand Old Lady	Kate Cutler

By FRANK S. NUGENT

To put a completely straight face upon the matter, "Pygmalion," which had its première at the Astor last night, marks the debut of a promising screen writer, George Bernard Shaw. This Mr. Shaw, for many years identified with the legitimate theatre, the rotogravure section and the Letters-to-the-Editor columns, appears to have had little difficulty adapting himself to the strange new medium of the cinema. The difficulty, in fact, may be in the cinema's adapting itself to Mr. Shaw. His jocular boast, in the jocular preface to his picture, is that he intends to teach America what a "film should be like." But that sounds more revolutionary than it is; it is as optimistic as his wish that every one see "Pygmalion" at least twenty times.

Mr. Shaw is not revolutionizing the cinema in "Pygmalion" any more than he revolutionized the theatre when he first put his comedy on in London in 1914. It caused a "bloody" scandal then, but Mrs. Pat Campbell and Sir Herbert Beerbohm Tree were able to ride over it. The film version is no more startling, providing you keep a straight face upon the matter, for the camera is frequently flushing a covey of actors from a conversational thicket and Mr. Shaw sometimes is caught chuckling so hard behind his whiskers that it isn't quite clear what has been making him laugh. All this, of course, providing one keeps a straight face upon the matter.

Film Version Happily Sewed

But "Pygmalion" is not a comedy for straight faces, and any one who puts one on at the Astor should have his theatre-going credentials examined and his sense of humor sent off for repairs. In the Shaw repertory, it is not one of the major items, so need not be taken too seriously. Taken lightly, as befits it, the comedy trips light from the tongue of any troupe—stage or screen—which has the grace to memorize its lines, to say them well and with appropriate gesture while a good director clears or clutters up his sets and adds the precious element of timing.

In each of these rather statistical particulars, Mr. Shaw's first film has been most happily served—although we reserve the right to enter a qualifier or two later. His story of a modern Pygmalion, a phonetics expert named Henry Higgins, who molds the common clay of Eliza Doolittle, cockney flower girl, into a personage fit to meet an Archduchess at an embassy ball, has been deftly, joyously told upon the screen. That instinct for comedy might have been expected of a Higgins by Leslie Howard, or a dustman by Wilfre dLawson, or a Mrs. Higins by Marie Lohr. It comes almost more satisfyingly, since unexpected, in the magnificent Eliza of Wendy Hiller.

Miss Hiller is a Discovery. (She deserves the capital.) We cannot believe that even Mr. Shaw could find a flaw in her performance of Pygmalion's guttersnipe Galatea. Eliza is the bedraggled cabbage leaf gruff Professor Higgins takes into his home, feeds, clothes, batches (by proxy, of course) and teaches so that she can pass for a gentlewoman at the embassy ball and thereby win his wager. And as Eliza, who progresses from the "Garn, I'm a good girl, I am" days

to those poignant ones when she is cat-clawing at her creator's eyes, Miss Hiller is so perfectly right that we wonder how either Mrs. Pat Campbell or Lynn Fontanne (of the Theatre Guild production) could have touched her.

The picture has rung a few changes on the play. The embassy ball is a new sequence, instead of an off-stage incident, and has been worked with suspense, comedy and fresh dramatic interest. The Dustman is not entirely the towering comic figure he was. His plaintive speech about being the victim of middle class morality has been retained, naturally; but they lopped him off a trifle at the end. Professor Higgins's methods of phonetics instruction are added comic devices, and the scene at the Higgins tea party, when Eliza is getting a dress rehearsal for her social debut, has been enriched by some added Shavian dialogue.

"In Hampshire, Hereford and Hartford, hurricanes rarely ever happen," says Eliza dutifully, hitting her "h's" carefully. That is just before she starts telling about her aunt who drank gin like mother's milk and was "done in" by the fond folks at 'ome.

Mr. Shaw truly has taught the American film-makers something. He is showing them how valuable a writer can be, how unnecessary it is to drape romantic cupids over a theatre's marquee, how wise it is to permit a leading man an occasional session of cruelly masculine ranting. But he must learn, too, not to let his cameras freeze too often upon a static scene. And he might have improved upon the film's conclusion—just as he might have bettered that of the play. But that's beside the point, which is that "Pygmalion" is good Shaw and a grand show.

D 8, 1938

THE LADY VANISHES, from a screen play by Sidney Gillatt and Frank Launder, based on Ethel Lina White's story, "The Wheel Spins"; directed by Alfred Hitchcock and produced by Gaumont-British. At the Globe.

Iris Henderson ....Margaret Lockwood
Gilbert ....Michael Redgrave
Dr. Harz ....Paul Lukas
Miss Froy ....Dame May Whitty
Mr. Todhunter ....Cecil Parker
Mrs. Todhunter ....Linden Travers
Caldicott ....Naughton Wayne

By FRANK S. NUGENT

Just in under the wire to challenge for a place on the year's best ten is "The Lady Vanishes" (at the Globe), latest of the melodramatic classics made by England's greatest director, Alfred Hitchcock. If it were not so brilliant a melodrama, we should class it as a brilliant comedy. Seeing it imposes a double, a blessedly double, strain: when your sides are not aching from laughter your brain is throbbing in its attempts to outguess the director. Hitch occasionally relents with his rib-tickling, but his professional honor would not brook your catching up with his plot.

A lady vanishes on a train. One moment she was sitting there, plump, matronly, reading a needlework magazine, answering to the name and description of Miss Froy, governess, London-bound from the Tyrol. The next, she was gone. And the young woman in the compartment, awakening from her doze, was solemnly assured by her neighbors that they had seen no Miss Froy. A brain specialist aboard suggests that Miss Froy was a hallucination induced by the blow she had received when a flower box fell on her head at the station.

The young man, who had been one of the avalanche-bound guests at the inn was skeptical, too, but offered to help. The two Englishmen aboard didn't want to be involved; they were eager to reach England in time for the cricket finals. The pacifist was afraid his reputation might suffer; he obviously was traveling with a woman not his wife.

Still, there was something about Miss Froy. When we first saw her she was being serenaded (odd for a woman her age) by an elderly porter in the Tyrolean inn. And then, although she didn't know it, a pair of shadowy hands knotted about the porter's neck and he died. Besides, she was standing beside the young woman at the station when some one pushed the flower pot off the roof. Could that have been meant for Miss Froy? Yet it doesn't seem quite credible for every one in the train to enter a conspiracy about her—conductors, dining room stewards, a countess, a noted surgeon, a music hall performer, a nun, two cricket-mad Englishmen, a woman in tweeds. (Mr. Hitchcock, a very old Nick of a St. Nich, is laughing fit to kill.)

Well, there's the puzzle, and we cannot conceal our admiration over the manner in which Mr. Hitchcock and his staff have pieced it together. There isn't an incident, be it as trivial as an old woman's chatter about her favorite brand of tea, that hasn't a pertinent bearing on the plot. Everything that happens is a clue. And, having given you fair warning, we still defy you to outguess that rotund spider, Hitch. The man is diabolical; his film is devilishly clever.

His casts are always neglected by reviewers, which isn't fair, especially since he has so perfect a one here. Honors belong, of course, to his priceless cricketers, Caldicott and Charters—or Naughton Wayne and Basil Radford—whose running temperature about "how England is doing" makes the most hilarious running gag of the year. Margaret Lockwood and Michael Redgrave as the puzzled young woman and her ally are just the sort of pleasant, intelligent young people we should expect to find going through a casual Hitchcock gesture to boy-meets-girl.

The others are equally right—Dame May Whitty as the surprising Miss Froy, Paul Lukas as the specialist, Cecil Parker, Linden Travers—in fact, all the others. Did we say "The Lady Vanishes" was challenging the best ten? Let's amend it: the bid has been accepted.

D 26, 1938

LA BÊTE HUMAINE

With admirable realism, the French have concentrated in putting la vie romancée on the screen without noticeable embellishment. The producers have no use for the happy ending when the happy ending was unnatural (as it is at least half of the time). They have been free, of course, of the Will Hays office pressure, and although the church lists its preferences, its influence is not so profound as it is in the United States. When the French have wished to be honest, there has been no power but public taste to temper the desire.

Of such integral honesty is the latest great French film, "La Bête Humaine." For more than a month it has played to packed houses at the Madeleine, one of the largest cinema houses in Paris. It will probably run for a month more. This picture, adapted from Emile Zola's story, is woven of the deepest tragedy of life—the story of a man whose parents and grandparents were drunkards. He cannot escape the curse they bequeathed him—the urge, on certain occasions, to kill. This Jacques, a railroad engineer, falls in love with a young girl, already married. His happiness is short-lived. In one of these sudden attacks of madness he murders her. The next day he leaps from his speeding locomotive to death.

It is strong stuff—two violent deaths, one suicide. The suicide ends the picture. It is truth at its shocking best (or worst) and it is played to the hilt by Jean Gabin and Simone Simon. Gabin never played in a role with more simplicity and understanding. Back in her native land Mlle. Simon displays the talent which Hollywood never gave her an opportunity to show. And, as no person has succeeded before, Jean Renoir, the director, has seen the romance and the paradoxes of railroad life—the smoke and the speed, the dirt and the freshness of the country air through which the train flashes momentarily.

It is a challenge to the American cinema to produce more films of the character of "Algiers," "Three Comrades" and "The Citadel." It is also a challenge to the French cinema. For the critic of "Le Canard Enchaîné" plaintively voiced last week what many French moviegoers are wondering: the world of spies, guns, drunkards, prostitutes and violent deaths certainly does exist, but is there not also one in which people take time off to chuckle and laugh?

F 26, 1939

STAGECOACH, based on the story "Stage to Lordsburg," by Ernest Haycox; screen play by Dudley Nichols; directed by John Ford; a Walter Wanger production; released by United Artists. At the Radio City Music Hall.

Dallas	Claire Trevor
Ringo Kid	John Wayne
Buck	Andy Devine
Hatfield	John Carradine
Doc Boone	Thomas Mitchell
Lucy Mallory	Louise Platt
Curly Wilcox	George Bancroft
Lieutenant Blanchard	Tim Holt
Gatewood	Berton Churchill
Peacock	Donald Meek
Chris	Chris Martin
Captain Whitney	Cornelius Keefe
Chris's wife	Elvira Rios
Billy Pickett	Francis Ford
Mrs. Whitney	Florence Lake

By FRANK S. NUGENT

In one superbly expansive gesture, which we (and the Music Hall) can call "Stagecoach," John Ford has swept aside ten years of artifice and talkie compromise and has made a motion picture that sings a song of camera. It moves, and how beautifully it moves, across the plains of Arizona, skirting the sky-reaching mesas of Monument Valley, beneath the piled-up cloud banks which every photographer dreams about, and through all the old-fashioned, but never really outdated, periods of prairie travel in the scalp-raising Seventies, when Geronimo's Apaches were on the warpath. Here, in a sentence, is a movie of the grand old school, a genuine rib-thumper and a beautiful sight to see.

Mr. Ford is not one of your subtle directors, suspending sequences on the wink of an eye or the precisely calculated gleam of a candle in a mirror. He prefers the broadest canvas, the brightest colors, the widest brush and the boldest possible strokes. He hews to the straight narrative line with the well-reasoned confidence of a man who has seen that narrative succeed before. He takes no shadings from his characters: either they play it straight or they don't play at all. He likes his language simple and he doesn't want too much of it. When his Redskins bite the dust, he expects to hear the thud and see the dirt spurt up. Above all, he likes to have things happen out in the open, where his camera can keep them in view.

He has had his way in "Stagecoach" with Walter Wanger's benison, the writing assistance of Dudley Nichols and the complete cooperation of a cast which had the sense to appreciate the protection of being stereotyped. You should know, almost without being told, the station in life (and in frontier melodrama) of the eight passengers on the Overland stage from Tonto to Lordsburg.

To save time, though, here they are: "Doc" Boone, a tipsy man of medicine; Major Hatfield, professional gambler, once a Southern gentleman and a gentleman still; Dallas, a lady of such transparently dubious virtue that she was leaving Tonto by popular request; Mrs. Mallory, who, considering her condition, had every reason to be hastening to her army husband's side; Mr. Gatewood, an absconding banker and windbag; Mr. Peacock, a small and timid whisky salesman destined by Bacchus to be Doc Boone's traveling companion; Sheriff Wilcox and his prisoner, the Ringo Kid. The driver, according to the rules, had to be Slim Summerville or Andy Devine; Mr. Devine got the call.

So onward rolls the stage, nobly sped by its six stout-hearted bays, and out there, somewhere behind the buttes and crags, Geronimo is lurking with his savage band, the United States Cavalry is biding its time to charge to the rescue and the Ringo Kid is impatiently awaiting his cue to stalk down the frontier-town street and blast it out with the three Plummer boys. But foreknowledge doesn't cheat Mr. Ford of his thrills. His attitude, if it spoke its mind, would be: "All right, you know what's coming, but have you ever seen it done like this?" And once you've swallowed

your heart again, you'll have to say: "No, sir! Not like this!"

His players have taken easily to their chores, all the way down the list from Claire Trevor's Dallas to Tom Tyler's Hank Plummer. But the cutest coach-rider in the wagon, to our mind, was little Donald Meek as Mr. Peacock, the whisky-drummer. That, of course, is not meant as a slight to Thomas Mitchell as the toping Dr. Boone, to Louise Platt as the wan Mrs. Mallory, George Bancroft as the sheriff or John Wayne as the Ringo Kid. They've all done nobly by a noble horse opera, but none so nobly as its director. This is one stagecoach that's powered by a Ford.

Mr 3, 1939

ALEXANDER NEVSKY, from a story by Sergei Eisenstein and D. I. Vassiliev; directed by Eisenstein and Peter A. Pavlenko; musical score by Sergei Prokofiev; produced by Mosfilm Studios in the U. S. S. R.; released here by Amkino. At the Cameo.

Prince Alexander Nevsky	Nikolai Cherkassov
Vassily Buslai	N. P. Okhlopkov
Gavrilo Olexich	A. L. Abrikossov
Master Armorer	D. N. Orlov
Governor of Pskov	V. K. Novikov
Nobleman of Novgorod	N. N. Arski
Mother of Buslai	V. O. Massalitinova
Olga, a Novgorod girl	V. S. Ivasheva
Vassilissa	A. S. Danilova
Master of the Teutonic Order	V. L. Ershov
Tverdillo, mayor of Pskov	S. K. Blinnikov
Anani, a monk	I. I. Lagutin
The Bishop	L. A. Fenin
The Black-robed Monk	N. A. Rogozhin

By FRANK S. NUGENT

After more than six years of unproductivity, not all of it voluntary, Sergei Einsenstein, the D. W. Griffith of the Russian screen, has returned to party favor and to public honors with "Alexander Nevsky," a rough-hewn monument to national heroism which had its New World unveiling at the Cameo last night. This is the picture which saved Eisenstein's face, and possibly his hide, after his "Bezhun Lug" was halted after two years' shooting because of its allegedly unsympathetic treatment of the Communist revolution. It is the picture which prompted Josef Stalin to slap its maker on the back and exclaim, "Sergei, you are a true Bolshevik." And it is a picture, moreover, which sets up this morning an unusual problem in reviewing.

For Eisenstein's work can no more withstand the ordinary critical scrutiny, a judgment based on the refinement and subtlety of its execution than, say, the hydraulic sculpture and rock-blasting that Gutzon Borglum is dashing off on Mount Rushmore. Eisenstein is sublimely indifferent to détail, whether narrative or pictorial. His minor characters are as outrageously uni-dimensional as those Griffith created for "Intolerance" and "Birth of a Nation." He is patently unconcerned about a change from night to day to night again during the space of a two-minute sequence, and if it pleases him to bring on torchbearers at midday, simply because the smoke smudge is photographically interesting, he is not deterred by any thoughts of their illogic.

His concern, obvious from the start, is only with the broad outline of his film, its most general narrative and scenic contours and with a dramatic conflict arising, not out of the clash of ideas or ideologies (although these have been unsubtly appended), but from the impact of great bodies of men and horse. His picture, whatever its modern political connotation, is primarily a picture of a battle and it must stand, or fall, solely upon Eisenstein's generalship in marshaling his martial array. And of his magnificent pictorial strategy there does not appear to be any question: it is a stunning battle, this re-enactment of his of the beautiful butchery that occurred one Winter's day in 1242, when the invading Teutonic knights and the serfs, mujhiks and warriors of Novgorod met on the ice of Lake Peipus and fought it out with mace and axe, with pike and spear and broadsword.

The Russians won by might and strategy and the collapse of the ice under the weight of German armor, and Prince Alexander rings out the defiant charge, "Go home and tell all in foreign lands that Russia lives. Let them come to us as guests and they will be welcome. But if any one comes to us with the sword he shall perish by the sword. On this the Russian land stands and will stand." So has Eisenstein discharged his party duty; and so the comrades at the Cameo cheered last night and outthrust their chins at Hitler. Which is all right, too, since it pleases them.

But no propagandistic drum-beating is more than a muffled thump against the surge of Eisenstein's battle. Nor are his people much more than specks upon the bloody ice. Nikolai Cherkassov's Alexander is an exception, since both the role and its player are cast in the heroic mold. But the others, simply through their creator's indifference to their needs, are caricatures (like the Teuton priests), or gargoyles (like the traitors, spies and enemy knights), or simpering nothings (like the little heroine) or mere focal points for watching the display of medieval arms (like the rival Russian soldiers). It is impossible not to admire Eisenstein's colossal unconcern with these refinements of film-making, not to marvel at his stylistic insistence that all people walk along a skyline, and not to wish, in the same breath, that more directors had his talent for doing great things so well and little things so badly.

Mr 23, 1939

WUTHERING HEIGHTS, as adapted by Ben Hecht and Charles MacArthur from the Emily Bronte novel; directed by William Wyler; a Samuel Goldwyn production; released by United Artists. At the Rivoli.

Cathy	Merle Oberon
Heathcliff	Laurence Olivier
Edgar	David Niven
Ellen Dean	Flora Robson
Dr. Kenneth	Donald Crisp
Hindley	Hugh Williams
Isabella	Geraldine Fitzgerald
Joseph	Leo G. Carroll
Judge Linton	Cecil Humphreys
Lockwood	Miles Mander
Robert	Romaine Callender
Earnshaw	Cecil Kellaway
Heathcliff (as a child)	Rex Downing
Cathy (as a child)	Sarita Wooton
Hindley (as a child)	Douglas Scott

By FRANK S. NUGENT

After a long recess, Samuel Goldwyn has returned to serious screen business again with his film "Wuthering Heights," which had its première at the Rivoli last night. It is Goldwyn at his best, and better still, Emily Brontë at hers. Out of her strange tale of a tortured romance Mr. Goldwyn and his troupe have fashioned a strong and somber film, poetically written as the novel not always was, sinister and wild as it was meant to be, far more compact dramatically than Miss

Brontë had made it. During December's dusty researches we expect to be filing it away among the year's best ten; in April it is a living thing, vibrant as the wind that swept Times Square last night.

One of the most incredible aspects of it is the circumstance that the story has reached the screen through the agency of Ben Hecht and Charles MacArthur, as un-Brontian a pair of infidels as ever danced a rigadoon upon a classicist's grave. But be assured: as Alexander Wollcott was saying last week, they've done right by our Emily. It isn't exactly the faithful transcription, which would have served neither Miss Brontë nor the screen—whatever the Brontë societies may think about it. But it is a faithful adaptation, written reverently and well, which goes straight to the heart of the book, explores its shadows and draws dramatic fire from the savage flints of scene and character hidden there.

And it has been brilliantly played. Laurence Olivier's Heathcliff is the man. He has Heathcliff's broad lowering brow, his scowl, the churlishness, the wild tenderness, the bearing, speech and manner of the demon-possessed. Charlotte Brontë, in her preface to her sister's novel, said Heathcliff never loved Cathy; the only claim he might have had to humanity was his lukewarm regard for Hareton Earnshaw; take that away, she said, and Heathcliff is demon, ghoul or Afreet. Hecht and MacArthur have taken Hareton away. In fact, they have removed the novel's entire second generation, have limited the story to Heathcliff and Cathy, to Edgar and Isabella Linton and their servants, dogs and the desolate moor where their drama is played. But Heathcliff is no demon and he loved Cathy, in the film as in the novel.

To the sheltered Brontës, it must have seemed that a passion so consuming, violent and destructive—of itself and what it touched—must have been diabolic. Even now on the Rivoli's screen there is something overwhelming in the tumult of the drama's pulse, the sweep and surge of Heathcliff's love and hate, their crushing before them of all the softness of that Yorkshire world a century ago, their brave defiance of heaven and hell and death itself. No wonder Charlotte

recoiled in holy horror and exclaimed "Afreet!" and that Emily, like Mrs. Shelley with her "Frankenstein," only dimly sensed the potent force she was wielding.

So Mr. Olivier has played Heathcliff, and Merle Oberon, as Cathy, has matched the brilliance of his characterization with hers. She has perfectly caught the restless, changeling spirit of the Brontë heroine who knew she was not meant for heaven and broke her heart and Heathcliff's in the synthetic paradise of her marriage with gentle Edgar Linton. The Lintons, so pallid, so namby-pamby in the novel, have been more charitably reflected in the picture. David Nivens's Edgar, Geraldine Fitzgerald's Isabella are dignified and poignant characterizations of two young people whose tragedy was not in being weak themselves but in being weaker than the abnormal pair whose destinies involved their destruction. And, in Flora Robson's Ellen (Nellie in the novel), in Miles Mander's Mr. Lockwood, Hugh Williams's sottish Hindley, and the others, Mr. Goldwyn has provided a flawless supporting cast.

William Wyler has directed it magnificently, surcharging even his lighter scenes with an atmosphere of suspense and foreboding, keeping his horror-shadowed narrative moving at a steadily accelerating pace, building absorbingly to its tragic climax. It is, unquestionably, one of the most distinguished pictures of the year, one of the finest ever produced by Mr. Goldwyn, and one you should decide to see.   Ap 14, 1939

THE CITY

We finally caught up with two of the pictures for the Fair: "Pete-Roleum and His Cousins," produced as an "institutional film"—whatever that may mean—for the petroleum industry exhibition; and "The City," a four-reel documentary on city planning made possible by a grant from the Carnegie Corporation and sponsored by the American Institute of Planners. "Pete-Roleum" is interesting technically, since it employs little rubber puppets, but the dialogue is of-

180

fensively banal—"Oh, dear! Dearie me! My gracious!" exclaims the Heckler when Pete and his Globular Cousins go into retreat—and we see no threat to Walt Disney in this new method of animation.

* * *

"THE CITY," however, is one you should not miss. It is not merely excellent as a documentary on housing, with its graphic depiction of planless squalor and planned comfort, but it contains one of the most bitterly hilarious sequences of the year—a deft montage of city life as millions of uncomplaining ⁓ ∾ York cliff-dwellers know it. The flashing images pass almost too swiftly to be recalled, but we remember faces caught in the midstream of traffic, subway-shovers, automatic pancake lifters, sandwich cutters, taxicab jams in the side streets, Sunday drivers, roadside picnics, Wall Street on a Sabbath morning, the Bronx express Thursday night. The impression is almost painfully comic and comically painful. If any of your out-of-town visitors want to know what New York is like, "The City" would be the perfect, the complete answer. It will be shown publicly at the Fair beginning on Friday in the Little Theatre of the Science and Education Building.

My 21, 1939

BEAU GESTE, screen play by Robert Carson based on the novel by Percival Christopher Wren; directed and produced by William A. Wellman for Paramount. At the Paramount.
Beau Geste ....Gary Cooper
John ....Ray Milland
Digby ....Robert Preston
Sgt. Markoff ....Brian Donlevy
Isobel Rivers ....Susan Hayward
Rasinoff ....J. Carrol Naish
Michael Geste (age 12)..Donald O'Connor
Major de Beaujolais.....James Stevenson
Renoir ....Harry Woods
Dufour ....James Burke
Schwartz ....Albert Dekker
Hank Miller ....Broderick Crawford

Originals are always better than imitations, and in view of all the depressing copies of "Beau Geste" which the cinema has suffered during the last thirteen years (take

any picture about the French Foreign Legion at random) the prototype of them all seems eminently worth repeating, for a change. It should also prove encouraging to persons with faith in the continuing validity of the screen's most gallant gestures to note that "Beau Geste," in the Paramount's current re-make, is still good cinema—that the absurd nobility, brotherly devotion and self-sacrifice of the Geste tribe are still unflagging ingredients for action melodrama.

On the other hand, the law of diminishing returns has got in its dirty work over the years: since 1926 the Foreign Legion motif has been so sadly overworked, so cruelly abused, that today the original may itself take on some of the irritatingly reminiscent quality of an imitation. In a sense, it is an imitation—an imitation in talk and sound effects of what was admittedly a classic in silence, and romantics with a too glowingly nostalgic recollection of Herbert Brenon's magnum opus may even be disappointed in the present exhibit. It must be acknowledged that the suspense and the timing are less torturing, less conducive to sweaty palms, than in the early epic, but then, it is now possible to hear the bugles and the wicked spatter of Arab gunfire, not to mention the shrieks of the poor devils beaten or maimed forever by that beast in human guise, Sergeant Markoff.

There is, of course, something a little nightmarish about the heroics of the Geste brothers, with their somewhat stagy, "Let me be the first to die" competition, something unreal about their eternal Britishness, which is not improved by the fact that "Beau" is now Gary Cooper, with unimpaired Texan accent, instead of Ronald Colman, that John, the survivor of all this touching fustian at last, is Ray Milland, and that Digby is the capable but curiously un-Anglican Robert Preston. These are niggling faults, but they mar what should be a poem of pure action, as do the children who play so stiffly the Geste brothers and Isobel Rivers in their chivalrous and storybook haunted youth.

On the whole, it is perhaps an unfortunate thing for Beau Geste the Second that Beau Geste the First was so distinguished, for Mr. Wellman's film seems dominated by the tremendous shadow of its predecessor. But it would be a mistake on that account to assume that the current generation will not find the current "Beau" a stirring piece of cinema, worth more than all the combined photostatic copies which followed the first and, alas! preceded the second. Those dead legionnaires, staring down from the gun embrasures of the desert fort, can still give one the creeps. The mystery of the disappearing bugler, of the two vanishing corpses, of the immense funeral pyre romantically burning in the desert, are still matters for shuddery speculation. Who stole that unparalleled sapphire, the "Blue Water"? The question is still a gripping one.

As for that earlier, perhaps blessedly silent, "Beau Geste"—what the present generation doesn't know, it will certainly never miss.

B. R. C.

Ag 3, 1939

MR. SMITH GOES TO WASHINGTON, screen play by Sidney Buchman based on a story by Lewis R. Foster; directed and produced by Frank Capra for Columbia Pictures. At the Radio City Music Hall.

Saunders	Jean Arthur
Jefferson Smith	James Stewart
Senator Joseph Paine	Claude Rains
Jim Taylor	Edward Arnold
Governor Hopper	Guy Kibbee
Diz Moore	Thomas Mitchell
Chick McGann	Eugene Pallette
Ma Smith	Beulah Bondi
Senate Majority Leader	H. B. Warner
President of the Senate	Harry Carey
Susan Paine	Astrid Allwyn
Mrs. Hopper	Ruth Donnelly
Senator MacPherson	Grant Mitchell
Senator Monroe	Porter Hall
Senate Minority Leader	Pierre Watkin
Nosey	Charles Lane
Bill Griffith	William Demarest
Carl Cook	Dick Elliott

By FRANK S. NUGENT

Scorning such cinemacerated branches of the government as the FBI, the Army, Coast Guard and Department of State which, by usage, have become Warner exclusives any way, Columbia's Frank Capra has gone after the greatest game of all, the Senate, in "Mr. Smith Goes to Washington," his new comedy at the Music Hall. In doing so, he is operating, of course, under the protection of that unwritten clause in the Bill of Rights entitling every voting citizen to at least one free swing at the Senate.

Mr. Capra's swing is from the floor and in the best of humor; if it fails to rock that august body to its heels—from laughter as much as injured dignity—it won't be his fault but the Senate's and we should really begin to worry about the upper house.

For Mr. Capra is a believer in democracy as well as a stout-hearted humorist. Although he is subjecting the Capitol's bill-collectors to a deal of quizzing and to a scrutiny which is not always tender, he still regards them with affection and hope as the implements, however imperfect they may be, of our kind of government. Most directors would not have attempted to express that faith otherwise than in terms of drama or melodrama. Capra, like the juggler who performed at the Virgin's shrine, has had to employ the only medium he knows. And his comedy has become, in consequence, not merely a brilliant jest, but a stirring and even inspiring testament to liberty and freedom, to simplicity and honesty and to the innate dignity of just the average man.

That may seem altogether too profound a way of looking at Mr. Capra's Mr. Smith, who is blood brother of our old friend, Mr. Deeds. Jefferson Smith came to Washington as a short-term Senator. He came with his eyes and mouth open, with the blessing of the Boy Rangers and a party boss's prayer that he won't tumble to the graft clause in the bill the senior Senator was sneaking into law. But Senator Smith tumbled; dazedly, because he couldn't quite believe the senior Senator was less than godlike; helplessly, because the aroused political machine framed him four ways from Sunday and had him up for expulsion before he could say Jack Garner. But the fight somehow triumphs, especially when there's a canny young secretary on Senator Smith's side to instruct him in the ungentle art of the filibuster and preserve his faith, and ours, in democracy.

If that synopsis is balder than the Capitol's dome, it is because there is not space here for all the story detail, the character touches, the lightning flashes of humor and poignance that have gone into Mr. Capra's two-hour show. He has paced it beautifully and held it in perfect balance, weaving his romance lightly through the political phases of his comedy, flicking a sardonic eye over the Washington scene, racing out to the hinterland to watch public opinion being made and returning miraculously in time to tie all the story threads together into a serious and meaningful dramatic pattern. Sidney Buchman, who wrote the script, has his claim on this credit, too, for his is a cogent and workmanlike script, with lines worthy of its cast.

And there, finally, Mr. Capra has been really fortunate. As Jefferson Smith, James Stewart is a joy for this season, if not forever. He has too many good scenes, but we like to remember the way his voice cracked when he got up to read his bill, and the way he dropped his hat when he met the senior Senator's daughter, and the way he whistled at the Senators when they turned their backs on him in the filibuster. (He just wanted them to turn around so he could be sure they still had faces.) Jean Arthur, as the secretary—lucky girl being secretary to both Deeds and Smith—tosses a line and bats an eye with delightful drollery. Claude Rains, as the senior Senator, Edward Arnold, as the party steam-roller, Thomas Mitchell, as a roguish correspondent, are splendid all.

Have we forgotten to mention it? "Mr. Smith" is one of the best shows of the year. More fun, even, than the Senate itself.

O 20, 1939

NINOTCHKA, adapted by Charles Brackett, Billy Wilder and Walter Reisch from an original screen story by Melchior Lengyel; directed by Ernst Lubitsch for Metro-Goldwyn-Mayer. At the Radio City Music Hall.

Ninotchka.....................Greta Garbo
Count Leon d'Algout.......Melvyn Douglas
Duchess Swana...................Ina Claire
Iranoff...................... Sig Rumann
Buljanoff.................... Felix Bressart
Kopalski ....Alexander Granach
Commissar Razinin............Bela Lugosi
Count Rakonin..............Gregory Gaye
Hotel Manager.................Rolfe Sedan
Mercier.................... Edwin Maxwell
Gaston.................... Richard Carle

By FRANK S. NUGENT

Stalin won't like it. Molotoff may even recall his envoy from Metro-Goldwyn-Mayer. We still will say Garbo's "Ninotchka" is one of the sprightliest comedies of the year, a gay and impertinent and malicious show which never pulls its punch lines (no matter how far below the belt they may land) and finds the screen's austere first lady of drama playing a dead-pan comedy role with the assurance of a Buster Keaton. Nothing quite so astonishing has come to the Music Hall since the Rockefellers landed on Fiftieth Street. And not even the Rockefellers could have imagined M-G-M getting a laugh out of Garbo at the U.S.S.R.'s expense.

Ernst Lubitsch, who directed it, finally has brought the screen around to a humorist's view of those sober-sided folk who have read Marx but never the funny page, who refuse to employ the word "love" to describe an elementary chemico-biological process, who reduce a Spring morning to an item in a weather chart and who never, never drink champagne without reminding its buyer that goat's milk is richer in vitamins. In poking a derisive finger into these sobersides, Mr. Lubitsch hasn't been entirely honest. But, then, what humorist is? He has created, instead, an amusing panel of caricatures, has read them a jocular script, has expressed — through it all—the philosophy that people are much the same wherever you find them and decent enough at heart. What more could any one ask?

Certainly we ask for little more, in the way of thoroughly entertaining screen fare, than the tale of his Ninotchka, the flat-heeled, Five-Year-Plannish, unromantically mannish comrade who was sent to Paris by her commissar to take over the duties of a comically floundering three-man mission entrusted with the sale of the former Duchess Swana's court jewels. Paris in the Spring being what it is and Melvyn Douglas, as an insidious capitalistic meddler, being what he is, Comrade Ninotchka so far forgot Marx, in Mr. Lubitsch's fable, as to buy a completely frivolous hat, to fall in love and, after her retreat to Moscow, to march in the May Day parade without caring much whether she was in step or not.

If that seems a dullish way of phrasing it, we can only take refıge in the adventitious Chinese argument that one picture is worth a million words. Mr. Lubitsch's picture is worth at least a few thousand more words than we have room for here. To do justice to it we should have to spend a few hundred describing the arrival of the Soviet delegation in Paris where they debate the merits of the Hotel Terminus (a shoddy place) and the Hotel Clarence where one need push a button once for hot water, twice for a waiter, thrice for a French maid. Would Lenin really have said, as Comrade Kopalski insisted, "Buljanoff, don't be a fool! Go in there and ring three times."

We should need a few hundred more to describe the Paris tour of Ninotchka, under Mr. Douglas's stunned capitalistic guidance; the typically Lubitsch treatment of a stag dinner party, with the camera focussed on a door and only the microphone capable of distinguishing between the arrival of a cold meat platter and that of three cigarette girls on the hoof; the Moscow roommate's elaboration of the effect of a laundered Parisian chemise upon the becottoned feminine population of an entirely too-cooperative apartment house.

For these are matters so cinematic, so strictly limited to the screen, that news print cannot be expected to do justice to them, any more than it could do full justice to Miss Garbo's delightful debut as a comedienne. It must be monotonous, this superb rightness of Garbo's playing. We almost wish she would handle a scene badly once in a while just to provide us with an opportunity to show we are not a member of a fan club. But she remains infallible and Garbo, always exactly what the situation demands, always as fine as her script and director permit her to be. We did not like her "drunk" scene here, but, in disliking it, we knew it was the writer's fault and Mr. Lubitsch's. They made her carry it too far.

We objected, out of charity, to some of the lines in the script: to that when Ninotchka reports: "The last mass trials were a great success. There are going to be fewer but better Russians"; and to that when the passport official assures the worried traveler she need not fret about the towel situation in Moscow hotels because "we change the towel every week." But that is almost all. The comedy, through Mr. Douglas's debonair performance and those of Ina Claire as the duchess and Sig Rumann, Felix Bressart and Alexander Grannach as the unholy three emissaries; through Mr. Lubitsch's facile direction; and through the cleverly written script of Walter Reisch, Charles Brackett and Billy Wilder, has come off brilliantly. Stalin, we repeat, won't like it; but, unless your tastes hew too closely to the party line, we think you will, immensely.

N 10, 1939

GONE WITH THE WIND, as adapted by the late Sidney Howard from Margaret Mitchell's novel; directed by Victor Fleming, musical score by Max Steiner; production designer, William Cameron Menzies; special effects by Jack Cosgrove; fire scenes staged by Lee Zavitz; costumes designed by Walter Plunkett; photography by Ernest Haller, supervised for Technicolor Company by Natalie Kalmus; technical advisers, Susan Myrick and Will Price; historian, Wilbur G. Kurtz; produced by David O. Selznick and released by Metro-Goldwyn-Mayer. At the Capitol and Astor Theatres.

Scarlett O'Hara	Vivien Leigh
Rhett Butler	Clark Gable
Ashley Wilkes	Leslie Howard
Melanie Hamilton	Olivia de Havilland
Mammy	Hattie McDaniel
Gerald O'Hara	Thomas Mitchell
Ellen O'Hara	Barbara O'Neil
Frank Kennedy	Caroll Nye
Aunt Pittypat Hamilton	Laura Hope Crews
Doctor Meade	Harry Davenport
Charles Hamilton	Rand Brooks
Belle Watling	Ona Munson
Carreen O'Hara	Ann Rutherford
Brent Tarleton	George Reeves
Stuart Tarleton	Fred Crane
Pork	Oscar Polk
Prissy	Butterfly McQueen
Suellen O'Hara	Evelyn Keyes
Mrs. Merriwether	Jane Darwell
Mrs. Meade	Leona Roberts
Big Sam	Everett Brown
Uncle Peter	Eddie Anderson
Tom a Yankee Captain	Ward Bond
Bonnie Blue Butler	Cammie King
Johnny Gallegher	J. M. Kerrigan
Emmy Slattery	Isabel Jewell
India Wilkes	Alicia Rhett
Jonas Wilkerson	Victor Jory
John Wilkes	Howard Hickman
Maybelle Merriwether	Mary Anderson
A Yankee Looter	Paul Hurst
Cathleen Calvert	Marcella Martin
Beau Wilkes	Mickey Kuhn
Bonnie's Nurse	Lillian Kemble Cooper
Reminiscent Soldier	Cliff Edwards
Elijah	Zack Williams

By FRANK S. NUGENT

Understatement has its uses too, so this morning's report on the event of last night will begin with the casual notation that it was a great show. It ran, and will continue to run, for about 3 hours and 45 minutes, which still is a few days and hours less than its reading time and is a period the spine may protest sooner than the eye or ear. It is pure narrative, as the novel was, rather than great drama, as the novel was not. By that we would imply you will leave it, not with the feeling you have undergone a profound emotional experience, but with the warm and grateful remembrance of an interesting story beautifully told. Is it the greatest motion picture ever made? Probably not, although it is the greatest motion mural we have seen and the most ambitious film-making venture in Hollywood's spectacular history.

It—as you must be aware—is "Gone With the Wind," the gargantuan Selznick edition of the Margaret Mitchell novel which swept the country like Charlie McCarthy, the "Music Goes 'Round" and similar inexplicable phenomena; which created the national emergency over the selection of a Scarlett O'Hara and which, ultimately, led to the $4,000,000 production that faced the New York public on two Times Square fronts last night, the Astor and the Capitol. It is the picture for which Mr. Gallup's American Institute of Public Opinion has reported a palpitantly waiting audience of 56,500,000 persons, a few of whom may find encouragement in our opinion that they won't be disappointed in Vivien Leigh's Scarlett, Clark Gable's Rhett Butler or, for that matter, in Mr. Selznick's Miss Mitchell.

For, by any and all standards, Mr. Selznick's film is a handsome, scrupulous and unstinting version of the 1,037-page novel, matching it almost scene for scene with a literalness that not even Shakespeare or Dickens were accorded in Hollywood, casting it so brilliantly one would have to know the history of the production not to suspect that Miss Mitchell had written her story just to provide a vehicle for the stars already assembled under Mr. Selznick's hospitable roof. To have treated so long a book with such astonishing fidelity required courage—the courage of a producer's convictions and of his pocketbook, and yet, so great a hold has Miss Mitchell on her public, it might have taken more courage still to have changed a line or scene of it. But if Selznick has made a virtue

of necessity, it does not follow, of necessity, that his transcription be expertly made as well. And yet, on the whole, it has been. Through stunning design, costume and peopling, his film has skillfully and absorbingly recreated Miss Mitchell's mural of the South in that bitter decade when secession, civil war and reconstruction ripped wide the graceful fabric of the plantation age and confronted the men and women who had adorned it with the stern alternative of meeting the new era or dying with the old. It was a large panel she painted, with sections devoted to plantation life, to the siege and the burning of Atlanta, to carpetbaggers and the Ku Klux Klan and, of course, to the Scarlett O'Hara about whom all this changing world was spinning and to whom nothing was important except as it affected her.

Some parts of this extended account have suffered a little in their screen telling, just as others have profited by it. Mr. Selznick's picture-postcard Tara and Twelve Oaks, with a few-score actors posturing on the premises, is scarcely our notion of doing complete justice to an age that had "a glamour to it, a perfection, a symmetry like Grecian art." The siege of Atlanta was splendid and the fire that followed magnificently pyrotechnic, but we do not endorse the superimposed melodramatics of the crates of explosives scorching in the fugitives' path; and we felt cheated, so ungrateful are we, when the battles outside Atlanta were dismissed in a subtitle and Sherman's march to the sea was summed up in a montage shot. We grin understandingly over Mr. Selznick's romantic omission of Scarlett's first two "birthings," and we regret more comic capital was not made of Rhett's scampish trick on the Old Guard of Atlanta when the army men were rounding up the Klansmen.

But if there are faults, they do not extend to the cast. Miss Leigh's Scarlett has vindicated the absurd talent quest that indirectly turned her up. She is so perfectly designed for the part by art and nature that any other actress in the role would be inconceivable. Technicolor finds her beautiful, but Sidney Howard, who wrote the script, and Victor Fleming, who directed it, have found in her something more: the very embodiment of the selfish, hoydenish, slant-eyed miss who tackled life with both claws and a creamy complexion, asked no odds of any one or anything—least of all her conscience—and faced at last a defeat which, by her very unconquerability, neither she nor we can recognize as final.

Miss Leigh's Scarlett is the pivot of the picture, as she was of the novel, and it is a column of strength in a film that is part history, part spectacle and all biography. Yet there are performances around her fully as valid, for all their lesser prominence. Olivia de Havilland's Melanie is a gracious, dignified, tender gem of characterization. Mr. Gable's Rhett Butler (although there is the fine flavor of the smokehouse in a scene or two) is almost as perfect as the grandstand quarterbacks thought he would be. Leslie Howard's Ashley Wilkes is anything but a pallid characterization of a pallid character. Best of all, perhaps, next to Miss Leigh, is Hattie McDaniel's Mammy, who must be personally absolved of responsibility for that most "unfittin'" scene in which she scolds Scarlett from an upstairs window. She played even that one right, however wrong it was.

We haven't time or space for the others, beyond to wave an approving hand at Butterfly McQueen as Prissy, Thomas Mitchell as Gerald, Ona Munson as Belle Watling, Alicia Rhett as India Wilkes, Rand Brooks as Charles Hamilton, Harry Davenport as Doctor Meade, Carroll Nye as Frank Kennedy. And not so approvingly at Laura Hope Crews's Aunt Pitty, Oscar Polk's Pork (bad casting) and Eddie Anderson's Uncle Peter (oversight). Had we space we'd talk about the tragic scene at the Atlanta terminal, where the wounded are lying, about the dramatic use to which Mr. Fleming has placed his Technicolor — although we still feel that color is hard on the eyes for so long a picture—and about pictures of this length in general. Anyway, "it" has arrived at last, and we cannot get over the shock of not being disappointed; we had almost been looking forward to that.

D 20, 1939

HOLLYWOOD: THE BEGINNING OF THE END

The decade of the forties delineates a fairly consistent picture: an ascent to the highest peak of success and the beginning decline of Hollywood's might and glory. Up to the mid-forties, the American film industry seemed unassailably secure and, in the international trade, far ahead of any other country in the world; by the end of the decade, domestic trouble of unsuspected magnitude and the shrinking of the foreign markets had reached the proportions of a crisis. Up till the late thirties, some of the most blatantly propagandistic Nazi films had been screened and reviewed in New York. This was characteristic of the peculiar detachment of the United States from the events across the Atlantic—at least in the cinema. In the movies, World War Two remained remote until Pearl Harbor. It is interesting to compare the British productions, revealing the immediate impact of the enemy attacks on their country, with the relatively disengaged American films of the same period. On the other hand, Hollywood's non-cinematic contributions to the war effort, the support of the morale of the armed forces by personal appearance tours of the leading stars in the battle areas overseas, were enormously generous as well as effective. The return to peacetime production turned out to be more difficult than had been the adaptation to the war conditions. There were severe labor troubles in the mid-forties; long overdue trials resulting in the condemnation of the industry's monopolistic practices; high import duties abroad and, in 1947, the notorious hearings by the House Committee on Un-American Activities for alleged Communist infiltration into the studios, followed by the rapid spread of the so-called "blacklisting" of "unfriendly" witnesses and other people rightly or wrongly suspected of subversive political activities. In a climate of fear and suspicion, a wave of anticommunism swept the country at large and Hollywood in particular. The vicious "witch-hunting" in the wake of the trials deprived the industry of a sizable number of first-rate people, and there was an appreciable decline in quality in almost every branch of the production process. And, as a final blow, television began to affect the box office at an accelerating pace.

During this time significant changes occurred in both content and style of the Hollywood productions. One can easily deduce the prevailing climate of opinion from the film "villains" representing the enemy or the evil principle. As already

187

mentioned, it was first the Nazis, after Pearl Harbor the Japanese, and, during the "red scare," the Russians who figured as the natural enemies of everything America stood for. Although musicals and comedies continued to flourish, the general tendency was toward greater realism and less romantic escape. *The March of Time*, "a new kind of screen journalism," had been popular since 1935, demonstrating the effectiveness of factual, documentary reportage. Now Hollywood adopted this principle, with modifications, for many fictional films. These films were shot in natural locations, with emphasis on the documentary accuracy of subject, setting, and characterization; among the new subjects were crime, drug addiction, dipsomania, mental illness, and other subjects that had been taboo before. There were also some timid attempts to deal with race problems and anti-Semitism. This new, realistic tendency had its precedents in such substantial productions as *The Grapes of Wrath* (1940) and *Of Mice and Men* (1940), but the wave of semidocumentary films started only after the end of the war. Independent of trends and fashions, Orson Welles created the strikingly unorthodox, innovative film *Citizen Kane* (1941), which is generally considered a landmark in the history of the cinema.

In the meantime, Europe began to recover from the ravages of war and occupation. Foreign productions of genuine artistic merit were imported in growing numbers, especially from England, France, and Italy, while the once powerful German cinema subsided completely, not to recover to this day. Perhaps the most pervasive European influence in the midcentury originated in Italy, under the name of "Neo-realism." Its basic rationale was the representation of unstylized, unidealized reality. Several major directors emerged out of this environment, among them Rossellini, Visconti, de Sica, Fellini. It was the creative power and conviction of those artists that validated their philosophy; it was the outstanding quality of their films that accounts for the prestige of the postwar Italian cinema.

OF MICE AND MEN, screen play by Eugene Solow adapted from the John Steinbeck play; directed and produced by Lewis Milestone; a Hal Roach presentation; released by United Artists. At the Roxy.

George.....................Burgess Meredith
Mae..........................Betty Field
Lennie.....................Lon Chaney Jr.
Slim.......................Charles Bickford
Candy......................Roman Bohnen
Curley.....................Bob Steele
Whit.......................Noah Beery Jr.
Jackson....................Oscar O'Shea
Carlson....................Granville Bates
Crooks.....................Leigh Whipper

By FRANK S. NUGENT

His biographers report that John Steinbeck's pet aversions are Hollywood and New York. Happily the feeling is not reciprocated. Hollywood, which brought his "Grapes of Wrath" so magificently to the screen, has been no less reverent toward the strangely dramatic and compassionate tale that Steinbeck called "Of Mice and Men." And New York, unless we have miscalculated again, will endorse its film version, at the Roxy, as heartily as it has endorsed the film of the Joads. The pictures have little in common as narrative, but they have much in common as art: the same deft handling of their material, the same understanding of people, the same ability to focus interest sharply and reward it with honest craftsmanship and skill.

"Of Mice and Men" is news no longer. It has the familiarity of a widely sold novelette, of a successful play that won the New York Drama Critics Circle award as the best American contribution to the 1937-38 season. It would be idle, we think, to say that it has found new meaning, new depth, new significance as a film. Nor should such added value be required. Lewis Milestone, who directed it; Eugene Solow, who adapted it, and Burgess Meredith, Lon Chaney Jr., Betty Field and the others who have performed it, have done more than well in simply realizing the drama's established values. "Of Mice and Men" need not have been better as a play than it was as a novelette; it need not be better as a picture, so long as it is just as good.

Book and play have been followed as literally as the screen demands and the Hays office permits. There is a short prologue; the camera enlarges the play's vista to include the fields where the barley-buckers worked, the messroom, the town cafe where the hands might spend their wages; but nothing has been added that does not belong, nothing has been removed that was important to the proper telling of the story. If we must be reduced to comparisons we should say the film has been better cast in almost every role: Young Mr. Chaney does not quite erase the memory of Broderick Crawford's Lennie, but Mr. Meredith's George is an improvement on the flat, recitative interpretation by the play's Wallace Ford, and Miss Field is superb (an abused but useful word) as Mae.

Mr. Steinbeck wrote, as you probably are aware, the pathetic, fate-ridden drama of two bundle stiffs who dreamed, and kindled other men's dreams, of owning their own little ranch and living off "the fatta the lan'." George used to talk about it to Lennie, and Lennie, whose mind wasn't clear "on accounta he'd been kicked in the head by a horse," used to crow with delight at the notion of having to tend the rabbits and be permitted to stroke their soft fur. Lennie liked the feel of smooth things, but he was so strong his touch killed them —a bird, a mouse, a white-and-brown puppy, and finally Mae, the foreman's wife, who had silky hair. So the posse went out to hunt him down, and George knew he had to find Lennie first to tell him again about the time they'd have their own little place—and to hold a gun to the back of his happily nodding head.

In summary this has a cruel, bizarre, ridiculous sound. But it doesn't seem that way on the screen. Tragedy dignifies people, even such little people as Lennie, George, Candy and Mae. Mr. Steinbeck and his adapters have seen the end all too clearly, the end

190

of George's dream and Lennie's life.
With sound dramatic instinct they
have not sought to hasten the inevitable, or stave it off. Doom takes
its course and bides its moment;
there is hysteria in waiting for the
crisis to come. And during the
waiting there is the rewarding opportunity to meet some of Steinbeck's interesting people, to listen
to them talk, to be amused or moved
by the things they say and do. For
here again, as in "Grapes of
Wrath," we have the feeling of seeing another third, or thirtieth, of
the nation, not merely a troupe of
play-actors living in a world of
make-believe.

Nc small share of that credit belongs to the men and the one young
woman Hal Roach has recruited for
his production. Miss Field has added stature to the role of the foreman's wife by relieving her of the
play's box-office-conscious order
that she behave like a hoyden.
Mae, in the film, is entitled to some
respect—and never more so than in
the splendid scene she has with
Lennie when they share a cross-
purposed soliloquy. Bob Steele's
Curly, Leigh Whipper's Crooks (the
only carry-over from the play),
Roman Bohnen's Candy, Charles
Bickford's Slim and the others, have
been scarcely less valuable in their
several ways. We noted but one
flaw in Mr. Milestone's direction:
his refusal to hush the off-screen
musicians when Candy's old dog
was being taken outside to be shot.
A metronome, anything, would
have been better than modified
"Hearts and Flowers." And that's
the only fault we can find with Mr.
Steinbeck's second Hollywood-to-
New York contribution.

F 17, 1940

REBECCA

By FRANK S. NUGENT

Before getting into a review of
"Rebecca," we must say a word
about the old empire spirit. Hitch
has it—Alfred Hitchcock that is, the
English master of movie melodramas, rounder than John Bull,
twice as fond of beef, just now
(with "Rebecca") accounting for
his first six months on movie-
colonial work in Hollywood. The
question being batted around by the

cineastes (hybrid for cinema-es-
thetes) was whether his peculiarly
British, yet peculiarly personal,
style could survive Hollywood, the
David O. Selznick of "Gone with
the Wind," the tropic palms, the
minimum requirements of the
Screen Writers Guild and the fact
that a good steak is hard to come
by in Hollywood.

REBECCA, adapted by Philip MacDonald
and Michael Hogan from the novel by
Daphne Du Maurier; screen play by
Robert E. Sherwood and Joan Harrison;
directed by Alfred Hitchcock for Selznick-
International; released by United Artists.
At the Radio City Music Hall.
Maxim de Winter..........Laurence Olivier
Mrs. de Winter.............Joan Fontaine
Jack Flavell..................George Sanders
Mrs. Danvers..............Judith Anderson
Giles ....Nigel Bruce
Frank Crawley.............Reginald Denny
Colonel Julyan.............C. Aubrey Smith
Beatrice....................Gladys Cooper
Mrs. Van Hopper..........Florence Bates
The coroner................Melville Cooper
Dr. Baker..................Leo G. Carroll
Ben ....Leonard Carey
Tabb ....Lumsden Hare
Frith ....Edward Fielding
Robert ....Philip Winter
Chalcroft ....Forrester Harvey

But depend on the native British-
er's empire spirit, the policy of doing in Rome not what the Romans
do, but what the Romans jolly well
ought to be civilized into doing.
Hitch in Hollywood, on the basis of
the Selznick "Rebecca" at the
Music Hall, is pretty much the
Hitch of London's "Lady Vanishes"
and "The Thirty-nine Steps," except that his famous and widely-
publicized "touch" seems to have
developed into a firm, enveloping
grasp of Daphne du Maurier's popular novel. His directorial style is
less individualized, but it is as facile
and penetrating as ever; he hews
more to the original story line than
to the lines of a Hitch original; he
is a bit more respectful of his cast,
though not to the degree of close-up
worship exacted by Charles Laughton in "Jamaica Inn." What seems
to have happened, in brief, is that
Mr. Hitchcock, the famous soloist,
suddenly has recognized that, in
this engagement, he is working
with an all-star troupe. He makes
no concession to it and, fortunately, vice versa.

So "Rebecca"—to come to it finally—is an altogether brilliant film,
haunting, suspenseful, handsome
and handsomely played. Miss du
Maurier's tale of the second mis-

From The New York Times Film Reviews

tress of Manderley, a simple and modest and self-effacing girl who seemed to have no chance against every one's—even her husband's—memories of the first, tragically deceased Mrs. de Winter, was one that demanded a film treatment evocative of a menacing mood, fraught with all manner of hidden meaning, gaited to the pace of an executioner approaching the fatal block. That, as you need not be told, is Hitchcock's meat and brandy. In "Rebecca" his cameras murmur "Beware!" when a black spaniel raises his head and lowers it between his paws again; a smashed China cupid takes on all the dark significance of a blood-stained dagger; a closed door taunts, mocks and terrifies; a monogrammed address book becomes as accusative as a district attorney.

Miss du Maurier's novel was an "I" book, its story told by the second, hapless Mrs. de Winter. Through Mr. Hitchcock's method, the film is first-personal too, so that its frail young heroine's diffident blunders, her fears, her tears are silly only at first, and then are silly no longer, but torture us too. Rebecca's ghost and the bluebeard room in Manderley become very real horrors as Mr. Hitchcock and his players unfold their macabre tale, and the English countryside is demon-ridden for all the brightness of the sun through its trees and the Gothic serenity of its manor house.

But here we have been giving Mr. Hitchcock and Miss du Maurier all the credit when so much of it belongs to Robert Sherwood, Philip MacDonald, Michael Hogan and Joan Harrison who adapted the novel so skillfully, and to the players who have recreated it so beautifully. Laurence Olivier's brooding Max de Winter is a performance that almost needs not to be commented upon, for Mr. Olivier last year played Heathcliffe who also was a study in dark melancholy, broken fitfully by gleams of sunny laughter. Maxim is the Heathcliffe kind of man and Mr. Olivier seems that too. The real surprise, and the greatest delight of them all, is Joan Fontaine's second Mrs. de Winter, who deserves her own paragraph, so here it is:

"Rebecca" stands or falls on the ability of the book's "I" to escape caricature. She was humiliatingly, embarrassingly, mortifyingly shy, a bit on the dowdy side, socially unaccomplished, a little dull; sweet, of course, and very much in love with—and in awe of—the lord of the manor who took her for his second lady. Miss du Maurier never really convinced me any one could behave quite as the second Mrs. de Winter behaved and still be sweet, modest, attractive and alive. But Miss Fontaine does it—and does it not simply with her eyes, her mouth, her hands and her words, but with her spine. Possibly it's unethical to criticize performance anatomically. Still we insist Miss Fontaine has the most expressive spine—and shoulders!—we've bothered to notice this season.

The others, without reference to their spines—except that of Judith Anderson's housekeeper, Mrs. Danvers, which is most menacingly rigid—are splendidly in character: George Sanders as the blackguard, Nigel Bruce and Gladys Cooper as the blunt relatives, Reginald Denny as the dutiful estate manager, Edward Fielding as the butler and—of course—Florence Bates as a magnificent specimen of the ill-bred, moneyed, resort-infesting, servant-abusing dowager. Hitch was fortunate to find himself in such good company but we feel they were doubly so in finding themselves in his.

Mr 29, 1940

PRIDE AND PREJUDICE, from a screen play by Aldous Huxley and Jane Murfin; based on the dramatization by Jane Austin's novel by Helen Jerome; directed by Robert Z. Leonard; produced by Hunt Stromberg for Metro-Goldwyn-Mayer. At the Music Hall.

Elizabeth Bennet	Greer Garson
Dr. Darcy	Laurence Olivier
Mrs. Bennet	Mary Boland
Lady Catherine de Bourgh	Edna May Oliver
Jane Bennet	Maureen O'Sullivan
Lydia Bennet	Ann Rutherford
Miss Bingley	Frieda Inescort
Mr. Bennet	Edmund Gwenn
Charlotte Lucas	Karen Morley
Kitty Bennet	Heather Angel
Mary Bennet	Marsha Hunt
Mr. Bingley	Bruce Lester
Mr. Wickham	Edward Ashley
Mr. Collins	Melville Cooper
Mr. Denny	Marten Lamont
Sir William Lucas	E. E. Clive
Mrs. Phillips	May Beatty
Lady Lucas	Marjorie Wood

By BOSLEY CROWTHER

If your fancy would be for a picture of a charming and mannered little English world which has long since been tucked away in ancient haircloth trunks—a quaint but lively world in which young laides were mainly concerned with dances and ribboned bonnets and the light in a guardsman's eye, and matrons had the vapors and worried only about marrying off their eligible daughters—then the picture for you is "Pride and Prejudice," which came yesterday to the Music Hall. For this, by your leave, we proclaim the most deliciously pert comedy of old manners, the most crisp and crackling satire in costume that we in this corner can remember ever having seen on the screen.

Jane Austen, who wrote the story away back at the turn of the nineteenth century, was an independent miss with a quick and affectionate eye for the nice little foibles and foibles of her frivolous age. Tolerantly, she comprehended the harmless absurdities of her middle-class provincial society, the trembling and dithering that wen on in a household full of girls when a likely bachelor hove into the vicinity. And she had an incomparable wit, and a facility with the pen to put down all she saw and felt in one of the most delightful of English novels.

And with an instinct such as Hollywood can seldom boast, Hunt Stromberg and his associates have managed to turn out a film which catches the spirit and humor of Miss Austen's novel down to the last impudent flounce of a petticoat, the last contented sigh of a conquering coquette. With no more of a plot than Miss Austen herself provided, they have told the simple but continuously captivating story of the five Bennet sisters in quest of husbands, of their frankly scheming mother, their wisely unmettlesome father, of Darcy and Bingley and the treacherous Wickham. The whole thing has been accomplished through a steady flow of superlative wit—most of it out of the novel and some of it supplied by Aldous Huxley and Jane Murfin—which puts a snapper on almost every scene; and also through a consistently artful inventiveness of detail and a keen appreciation of the subtleties of Miss Austen's characters.

It isn't often that a cast of such

uniform perfection is assembled. Greer Garson is Elizabeth—"dear, beautiful Lizzie"—stepped right out of the book, or rather out of one's fondest imagination: poised, graceful, self-contained, witty, spasmodically stubbron and as lovely as a woman can be. Laurence Oliver is Darcy, that's all there is to it—the arrogant, sardonic Darcy whose pride went before and as felicitous fall. Mary Boland is a completely overpowering Mrs. Bennet, a silly but determined mother hen to a brood of exquisitely fluffy chicks, which includes Maureen O'Sullivan, Ann Rutherford and Heather Angel. And Edmund Gwenn, Edna Mae Oliver, Friede Inescort and Bruce Lester do handsomely in their respective roles. Only Melville Cooper as Mr. Collins and Marsha Hunt as Mary Bennet permit their characterizations to degenerate into burlesque. Robert Z. Leonard's direction is the touchstone.

Pictures played in costume often have an artificial air. But for pure charm and romantic diversion, for bubbling and wholesome life, we most heartily recommend this exquisite comedy about the elegant young gentleman who was proud and the beautiful young lady who was prejudiced. Both are as real as any two young people you know today.

Ag 9, 1940

TIME IN THE SUN, based on the unfinished film, "Que Viva Mexico," directed by Sergei M. Eisenstein; photographed by E. Tisse; material edited by Marie Seton and Paul Burnford; produced by Miss Seton. At the Fifth Avenue Playhouse.

By BOSLEY CROWTHER

One of the most celebrated controversies in the annals of Hollywood was that raging some seven or eight years ago over a picture which was never released. In 1931 Sergei M. Eisenstein, the famous Russian director, had gone to Mexico to film what he presumably intended as an epic study of the Mexican people, the title of which was to have been "Que Viva Mexico." But for reasons variously disputed, Eisenstein never cut and edited the vast and assorted footage which he gathered; and, in

1933, when Upton Sinclair present- ed a picture culled from this cellu- loid mass under the title of "Thun- der Over Mexico," there were per- sons around and about who hotly held it didn't follow at all the in- tentions of Eisenstein.

Well, a lot of water has gone un- der the bridge since then, so a more dispassionate view is there- fore likely to be taken of Marie Seton's latest reworking of the Eis- enstein material. And furthermore, Miss Seton, who is a British jour- nalist, claims that the director him- self outlined the rough scenario that she followed in editing this second version, called "Time in the Sun," which opened at the Fifth Avenue Playhouse yesterday. So the boldness of her endeavor will probably cause neither riots nor bloodshed.

As a matter of fact, from this distance, the earlier controversy seems slightly foolish, and the film which Miss Seton has produced from the couple of hundred thou- sand feet which Eisenstein shot is probably as good a picture as could be distilled into a reasonable length. Basically, it is documentary in nature—a magnificently photo- graphed account of Mexican native life which attempts to get beneath mere externals to spiritual forces. For, whereas "Thunder Over Mex- ico" was concerned mainly with the question of peonage, "Time in the Sun" visualizes the inherence of a free, pagan spirit which has survived in the Mexican native, de- spite Spanish civilization and slav- ery. From the Mayan ruins in Yucatan, it traces the evidence of this spirit through the nature and customs of the people which have continued for centuries, and con- cludes with a spectacular display of the Mexican's attitude toward death.

Many technical faults are obvious in "Time in the Sun": it does not flow smoothly, its construction seems contrived and the main idea is conveyed more in narration than in picture. But the photography of E. Tisse is so stunning and of such dramatic strength that each indi- vidual shot offers an exciting expe- rience. This, we feel, is the chief distinction of the film—this, and the fact that it should make an

end to the "Que Viva Mexico" con- troversy.

O 1, 1940

THE LONG VOYAGE HOME, screen play by Dudley Nichols, based on four one-act plays of the sea by Eugene O'Neill; pro- duced and directed by John Ford; pre- sented by Walter Wanger and released by United Artists. At The Rivoli.

Ole Olson	John Wayne
Driscoll	Thomas Mitchell
Smitty	Ian Hunter
Cocky	Barry Fitzgerald
Captain	Wilfrid Lawson
Freda	Mildred Natwick
Axel	John Qualen
Yank	Ward Bond
Donkey Man	Arthur Shields
Davis	Joseph Sawyer
Limehouse Crimp	J. M. Kerrigan
Tropical Woman	Rafaela Ottiano
Bumboat Girl	Carmen Morales
Bumboat Girl	Carmen D'Antonio
Scotty	David Hughes
Joe	Billy Bevan
First Mate	Cyril McLaglen
Second Mate	Douglas Walton
Frank	Constantine Romanoff
Mr. Clifton	Lionel Pape

By BOSLEY CROWTHER

Out of Eugene O'Neill's four short plays of the sea, and under the haunting title of one, "The Long Voyage Home," John Ford has truly fashioned a modern Odys- sey—a stark and tough-fibered mo- tion picture which tells with lean economy the never-ending story of man's wanderings over the waters of the world in search of peace for his soul. It is not a tranquilizing film, this one which Walter Wan- ger presented at the Rivoli Theatre last night; it is harsh and relent- less and only briefly compassion- ate in its revelation of man's pa- thetic shortcomings. But it is one of the most honest pictures ever placed upon the screen; it gives a penetrating glimpse into the hearts of little men and, because it shows that out of human weakness there proceeds some nobility, it is far more gratifying than the fanciest hero-worshiping fare.

Mr. Ford has ever been noted for his muscular realism on the screen, for the rich and authentic flavor with which he imbues his films. And in "The Long Voyage Home" he has had an exceptional oppor- tunity to exercise not only his tal- ents but also his avowed affections. For the story is that of the tough crew of the British tramp freighter Glencairn on a present-day voyage from the West Indies, via an Ameri-

194

can port, to London in a rusty old tub loaded deep with highly explosive ammunition. And the loose and unresolved plot concerns the characters and reactions of the men in the face of lurking danger and their various bewildered impulses. Given a theme of this sort, Mr. Ford is a man inspired.

Although the O'Neill plays were written separately and with only the same characters and locale to give them unity, Mr. Ford and his scenarist, Dudley Nichols, have pulled them together handsomely. From "The Moon of the Caribbees" they have taken their departure—the departure of the S. S. Glencairn and its lusty, rum-soaking crew—and proceeded on through the dramatic incidents contained in "Bound East for Cardiff," "In the Zone" and, eventually, the poignant episode of frustration presented in "The Long Voyage Home." If the film does lack a conventional dramatic pattern, it is mainly because of this episodic construction. And this lack may be disturbing to some.

But the very essence of the theme lies exactly in its inconclusiveness, in deliberate fumbling onward toward a goal which is never reached, toward a peace which is never attained. Yank, the iron-muscled pal of the Irishman, Driscoll, dies at sea, but even in death he dreams of the land. Smitty, the outcast aristocrat, goes to his doom with a defiant gesture at the world which has overpowered him. Driscoll is lost to another ship, and the remaining members of the Glencairn's crew—with the exception of Olson, who does go home—creep back to sea after a spree in London. In the end, they are Mother Carey's chickens, and the only home they can ever know is the restless deep.

And this is the endless story which Mr. Ford has told with magnificent sharpness. His ship is really made of iron and his actors are really tough. Thomas Mitchell as the roaring, truculent Driscoll; Barry Fitzgerald as the viperish steward, Cocky; John Wayne as the gentle, powerful Olson; Ian Hunter as Smitty, the heartsick, and Wilfred Lawson, Ward Bond, all the rest are truly excellent. Suffice it to say that women only appear briefly in this odyssey, and then exclusively as agents of evil. For "The Long Voyage Home" is a story of men, of eternal suffering in a perilous trade, of life and tragic death in the dirty, heroic little cargo boats that sail the wet seas 'round.

O 9, 1940

THE GREAT DICTATOR, based on an original story written, directed and produced by Charles Chaplin and released through United Artists; musical direction by Meredith Willson. At the Astor and Capitol Theatres.
PEOPLE OF THE PALACE
Adenoid Hynkel, Dictator of Tomania,
Charles Chaplin
Benzini Napaloni, Dictator of Bacteria,
Jack Oakie
Schultz...................Reginald Gardiner
Garbitsch....................Henry Daniell
Herring.........................Billy Gilbert
Mme. Napaloni.................Grace Hayle
Bacterian Ambassador.....Carter de Haven
PEOPLE OF THE GHETTO
A Jewish Barber...........Charles Chaplin
Hannah...................Paulette Goddard
Mr. Jaeckel.............Maurice Moscovich
Mrs. Jaeckel....................Emma Dunn
Mr. Mann.................Bernard Gorcey
Mr. Agar......................Paul Weigel
Also Chester Conklin, Esther Michelson, Hank Mann, Florence Wright, Eddie Gribbon, Robert O. Davis, Eddie Dunn, Nita Pike and Peter Lynn.

By BOSLEY CROWTHER

Now that the waiting is over and the shivers of suspense at an end, let the trumpets be sounded and the banners flung against the sky. For the little tramp, Charlie Chaplin, finally emerged last night from behind the close-guarded curtains which have concealed his activities these past two years and presented himself in triumphal splendor as "The Great Dictator"—or you know who.

No event in the history of the screen has ever been anticipated with more hopeful excitement than the première of this film, which occurred simultaneously at the Astor and Capitol Theatres; no picture ever made has promised more momentous consequences. The prospect of little "Charlot," the most universally loved character in all the world, directing his superlative talent for ridicule against the most dangerously evil man alive has loomed as a titanic jest, a transcendent paradox. And the happy report this morning is that it comes off magnificently. "The Great Dictator" may not be the finest picture ever made—in fact, it possesses several disappointing shortcomings. But, despite them, it turns out to be a truly superb accomplishment by a truly great artist—and, from one point of view, perhaps the most significant film ever produced.

Let this be understood, however: it is no catch-penny buffoonery, no droll and gentle-humored social satire in the manner of Chaplin's earlier films. "The Great Dictator" is essentially a tragic picture—or tragi-comic in the classic sense—and it has strongly bitter overtones. For it is a lacerating fable of the unhappy lot of decent folk in a totalitarian land, of all the hateful oppression which has crushed the humanity out of men's souls. And, especially, it is a vithering revelation, through genuinely inspired mimicry, of the tragic weaknesses, the overblown conceit and even the blank insanity of a dictator. Hitler, of course.

The main story line is quite simple, though knotted with many complications. A little Jewish barber returns to his shop in the ghetto of an imaginary city (obviously Berlin) after a prolonged lapse of perception due to an injury in the World War. He does not know that the State is now under the sign of the double-cross, that storm troopers patrol the streets, that Jews are cruelly persecuted and that the all-powerful ruler of the land is one Hynkel, a megalomaniac, to whom he bears—as a foreword states—a "coincidental resemblance." Thus, the little barber suffers a bitter disillusionment when he naively attempts to resist; he is beaten and eventually forced to flee to a neighboring country. But there he is mistaken for Hynkel, who has simultaneously annexed this neighboring land. And pushed upon a platform to make a conqueror's speech, he delivers instead a passionate appeal for human kindness and reason and brotherly love.

Thus the story throws in pointed contrast the good man against the evil one—the genial, self-effacing but courageous little man of the street against the cold pretentious tyrant. Both are played by Chaplin, of course, in a highly comic vein, beneath which runs a note of eternal sadness. The little barber is our beloved Charlie of old—the fellow with the splay feet, baggy pants, trick mustache and battered bowler. And, as always, he is the pathetic butt of heartless circumstances, beaten, driven, but ever prepared to bounce back. In this role Chaplin performs two of the

most superb bits of pantomime he has ever done—one during a sequence in which he and four other characters eat puddings containing coins to determine which shall sacrifice his life to kill the dictator, and the other a bit in which he shaves a man to the rhythm of Brahms's Hungarian Rhapsody.

But it is as the dictator that Chaplin displays his true genius. Whatever fate it was that decreed Adolf Hitler should look like Charlie must have ordained this opportunity, for the caricature of the former is devastating. The feeble, affected hand-salute, the inclination for striking ludicrous attitudes, the fabulous fits of rage and violent facial contortions—all the vulnerable spots of Hitler's exterior are pierced by Chaplin's pantomimic shafts. He is at his best in a wild senseless burst of guttural oratory —a compound of German, Yiddish and Katzenjammer double-talk; and he reaches positively exalted heights in a plaintive dance which he does with a large balloon representing the globe, bouncing it into the air, pirouetting beneath it—and then bursting into tears when the balloon finally pops.

Another splendid sequence is that in which Hynkel and Napaloni, a neighboring dictator, meet and bargain. Napaloni, played by Jack Oakie, is a bluff, expansive creature —the anthesis of neurotic Hynkel —and the two actors contrive in this part of the film one of the most hilarious lampoons ever performed on the screen. Others in the cast are excellent—Paulette Goddard as a little laundry girl, Henry Daniell as a Minister of Propaganda, Billy Gilbert as a Minister of War—but Oakie ranges right alongside Chaplin. And that is tops.

On the debit side, the picture is overlong, it is inclined to be repetitious and the speech with which it ended—the appeal for reason and kindness—is completely out of joint with that which has gone before. In it Chaplin steps out of character and addresses his heart to the audience. The effect is bewildering, and what should be the climax becomes flat and seemingly maudlin. But the sincerity with which Chaplin voices his appeal and the expression of tragedy which is clear in his face are strangely overpowering. Suddenly one perceives in bald relief the things which make "The Great Dictator" great—the courage and faith and surpassing love for mankind which are in the heart of Charlie Chaplin.

O 16, 1940

FANTASIA, a feature-length musical cartoon produced by Walt Disney and interpreting Bach's "Toccata and Fugue in D Minor." Tchaikovsky's "The Nutcracker Suite," Dukas's "The Sorcerer's Apprentice," Stravinsky's "The Rite of Spring," Beethoven's "Sixth (Pastoral) Symphony," Ponchielli's "Dance of the Hours." Mussorgsky's "Night On Bald Mountain" and Schubert's "Ave Maria"; score conducted by Leopold Stokowski and recorded by the Philadelphia Symphony Orchestra; narrative introductions by Deems Taylor; recorded by the new RCA Fantasound System under the supervision of William E. Garity, C. O. Slyfield and J. N. A. Hawkins; story direction by Joe Grant and Dick Huemer; production supervision, Ben Sharpsteen; animation directors, Samuel Armstrong, James Algar, Bill Roberts, Paul Satterfield, Hamilton Luske, Jim Handley, Ford Beebe, T. Hee, Norm Ferguson, Wilfred Jackson; photographed in Multiplane Technicolor; distributed by Walt Disney, Inc. At the Broadway Theatre.

By BOSLEY CROWTHER

At the risk of being utterly obvious and just a bit stodgy, perhaps, let us begin by noting that motion-picture history was made at the Broadway Theatre last night with the spectacular world première of Walt Disney's long-awaited "Fantasia." Let us agree, as did almost every one present on the occasion, that the sly and whimsical papa of Mickey Mouse, Snow White, Pinocchio and a host of other cartoon darlings has this time come forth with something which really dumps conventional formulas overboard and boldly reveals the scope of films for imaginative excursion. Let us temperately admit that "Fantasia" is simply terrific—as terrific as anything that has ever happened on a screen. And then let's get on from there.

For the vital report this morning is that Mr. Disney and his troop of little men, together with Leopold Stokowski and the Philadelphia Orchestra and a corps of sound engineers, have fashioned with music and colors and animated figures on a screen a creation so thoroughly delightful and exciting in its novelty that one's senses are captivated by it, one's imagination is deliciously inspired. In the same fresh, light-hearted spirit which has marked all their previous cartoons Mr. Disney and the boys have gone aromping in somewhat more esoteric fields; they have taken eight symphonic numbers which are generally reserved for the concert halls, let Mr. Stokowski's band record them on multiple sound tracks, and have then given them visual accompaniments of vast and spellbinding range. In brief, they have merged high-toned music with Disney's fantastic imagery.

What the music experts and the art critics will think of it we don't know. Olin Downes is making the official observation for his department in an adjoining column. Probably there will be much controversy, and maybe some long hair will be pulled. Artistic innovations never breed content. But for this corner's money—and, we reckon, for the money of any one who takes it in the blithe and wondrous spirit in which it is offered—"Fantasia" is enchanting entertainment. This is one time, we warrant, you won't want to listen to music with your eyes shut.

For, as mentioned, you need not expect the customary collaboration of film and music. From the beginning—from before the beginning, in fact, when vague shadows of musicians appear on the screen, when the sound of instruments being tuned is heard and when finally the theatre lights go down and Deems Taylor steps up on the orchestra platform to introduce the show—it is obvious that this is a visual concert, with Mr. Taylor participating as commentator. It is, he explains, a representation of "designs and pictures and stories" which the selected music has inspired in the minds of a group of artists. Then Mr. Stokowski — or rather his shadow—dramatically ascends the podium, and the concert begins.

The first number is Bach's Toccata and Fugue, illustrated abstractly on the screen with brilliant colors flowing and merging, lacy figures cometing through space, a sky-writing cipher tracing patterns and sprays of falling stars. It is intended, obviously, to create the necessary mood of reverie, of immaterial detachment necessary to the complete comprehension and enjoyment of the entire program.

From The New York Times Film Reviews

197

At its conclusion, Mr. Taylor returns to explain the second selection — Tchaikovsky's "Nutcracker Suite"—and so the picture goes.

Space limitations prevent a detailed consideration of each number. But the high points cannot be overlooked. There is, for instance, the fragile and shimmering beauty of tiny fairies placing dewdrops on cobwebs in the first passage of the "Nutcracker Suite" and the lovable humors of the Chinese mushrooms dancing in the same selection; there is the familiar hectic comedy of Mickey Mouse in Dukas's "The Sorcerer's Apprentice," the titanic upheavals of the earth and the roaring battles of prehistoric animals in Stravinsky's "Rite of Spring," the winsome charm of baby fauns and sleek little centaurettes gamboling on pink fields of asphodel in Beethoven's "Pastoral Symphony" and the superb satire on ballet, with ostrich, hippopotamus and elephant performers, in Ponchielli's "Dance of the Hours." The final selections are Mussorgsky's "Night on Bald Mountain," visualized with a weird and terrifying assortment of skeletons, ghouls and imps swirling around the monstrous devil of the mountain, and then a solemn, liturgical illustration of Schubert's "Ave Maria."

Naturally, there are things about this film which one might readily criticize. The elaborate sound-projection system, of which there has been much talk, seems to possess many remarkable advantages, not least of which is its ability to "place" sounds. But it also amplifies them too much in certain passages—and that is hard on the ears. Also the length of the picture—more than two hours—tends to weary the senses, to dull one's receptiveness. Sometimes the color is too "pretty," especially in the "Pastoral," and frequently the dramatic action on the screen becomes so absorbing that the music, the primary music, takes an incidental place.

Both those are esthetic details which the majority will casually ignore. Mr. Disney said himself the other night that there are many problems he has yet to lick, that "Fantasia" is a frank experiment. Perhaps so, but it is also the most original and provocative film in some time. If you don't mind having your imagination stimulated by the stuff of Mr. Disney's fanciful

dreams, go to see it. It's a transcendent blessing these days.

N 14, 1940

PEPE LE MOKO; screen play by Henri Jeanson; adapted from the novel by D'Ashelbe; directed by Julien Duvivier; a French film with English dialogue titles, produced by Paris Film and released through Arthur Mayer and Joseph Burstyn; music by Vincent Scotto and Mohammed Yguerbuchen. At the World Theatre.

Pepe le Moko	Jean Gabin
Gaby	Mireille Balin
Carlos	Gabriel Gabrio
Slimane	Lucas Gridoux
L'Arbi	Dalio
Grandpere	Saturnin Fabre
Regis	Charpin
Ines	Line Noro
Pierrot	Gilbert Gil
Inspector	Bergeron
Frehel	Tania

By BOSLEY CROWTHER

Patience—that is, the patience of persons who enjoy fine French films—is being rewarded at the World Theatre, where Julien Duvivier's long-delayed "Pepe le Moko" opened last evening. For here, after quite a career, is the much-mentioned picture which was made in France and Algeria some five years ago but which had been withheld until now from release in this country by Walter Wanger, who bought the American rights and the story as the basis for his memorable "Algiers" of three years back. And, for all the delay—or perhaps because of it—"Pepe le Moko" turns out to be an item well worth the waiting, the most distinguished "new" French film in months and months.

Comparison with Mr. Wanger's "Algiers" is, of course, inescapable, since the two pictures tell substantially the same story in pretty much the same way. But, in one essential respect, the original has an incomparable advantage over the Hollywood-made imitation: it is a raw-edged, realistic and utterly frank exposition of a basically evil story, while Mr. Wanger's version was a romantic and necessarily cautious retelling of the same. The fact that "Pepe le Moko" has skinned past the New York censors but has failed to get a Hays office seal by a long shot—or rather by several close-ups and large chunks of dialogue—is sufficient comment upon the reasons why.

Don't get the idea, however, that "Pepe le Moko" is a risqué film. Rather it is the plain-spoken and honestly factual account of a Parisian crook's exile in the vicious and sordid Casbah of Algiers, that notorious area of corruption and native depravity from which he is eventually drawn to his doom by love for a woman. All the filthiness and vice of the Casbah are impressively shown in the film; there is no question at all about the ruthless wickedness of Pepe, and the woman who finally lures him into the open is obviously the mistress of another man.

But the very frankness of the picture is the secret of its power and distinction, for the quality of the melodrama is immeasurably enhanced thereby and the pathos of the ironic ending is given more subtle point. Likewise the manner in which M. Duvivier directed it for sharp and unadorned reality imbues it with a firmness to be found only in films which call spades by their names.

Consequently, Jean Gabin's tough, unsentimental performance of the title role is much more credible and revealing than Charles Boyer's sad-eyed mooning as Pepe in "Algiers"; Mireille Balin is indeed more authoritative as a practical femme fatale than was Hedy Lamarr, and Line Noro certainly looks much more the part of a cast-off Algerian mistress than did Sigrid Gurie. In the supporting roles, too, Lucas Gridoux combines cunning, lack of scruple and a slick face to perfection as a native police inspector; Charpin makes a properly deceptive informer, and Gabriel Gabrio, Saturnin Fabre and Dalio breathe life into other characters. Well-written and not too many English subtitles assist those patrons unfamiliar with the language.

Without criticizing "Algiers," which was an exciting film in its own right, it can be fairly said that "Pepe le Moko" tells the same story more trenchantly and with decidedly more true flavor. For, after all, it was made in a France which wasn't too squeamish about facts—the sort of facts, anyhow, which it contains.

Mr 4, 1941

CITIZEN KANE; original screen play by Orson Welles and Herman J. Mankiewicz; produced and directed by Orson Welles; photography by Gregg Toland; music composed and conducted by Bernard Herrmann; released through RKO-Radio. At the Palace.

Charles Foster Kane	Orson Welles
Kane, aged 8	Buddy Swan
Kane 3d	Sonny Bupp
Kane's Father	Harry Shannon
Jedediah Leland	Joseph Cotten
Susan Alexander	Dorothy Comingore
Mr. Bernstein	Everett Sloane
James W. Gettys	Ray Collins
Walter Parks Thatcher	George Coulouris
Kane's Mother	Agnes Moorehead
Raymond	Paul Stewart
Emily Norton	Ruth Warrick
Herbert Carter	Erskine Sanford
Thompson	William Alland
Miss Anderson	Georgia Backus
Mr. Rawlston	Philip Van Zandt
Headwaiter	Gus Schilling
Signor Matiste	Fortunio Bonanova

By BOSLEY CROWTHER

Within the withering spotlight as no other film has ever been before, Orson Welles's "Citizen Kane" had its world première at the Palace last evening. And now that the wraps are off, the mystery has been exposed and Mr. Welles and the RKO directors have taken the much-debated leap, it can be safely stated that suppression of this film would have been a crime. For, in spite of some disconcerting lapses and strange ambiguities in the creation of the principal character, "Citizen Kane" is far and away the most surprising and cinematically exciting motion picture to be seen here in many a moon. As a matter of fact, it comes close to being the most sensational film ever made in Hollywood.

Count on Mr. Welles; he doesn't do things by halves. Being a mercurial fellow, with a frightening theatrical flair, he moved right into the movies, grabbed the medium by the ears and began to toss it around with the dexterity of a seasoned veteran. Fact is, he handled it with more verve and inspired ingenuity than any of the elder craftsmen have exhibited in years. With the able assistance of Gregg Toland, whose services should not be overlooked, he found in the camera the perfect instrument to encompass his dramatic energies and absorb his prolific ideas. Upon the screen he discovered an area large enough for his expansive whims to have free play. And the consequence is that he has made a picture of tremendous and overpowering scope, not in physical extent so much as in its rapid and graphic rotation of thoughts. Mr. Welles has put upon the screen a motion picture that really moves.

As for the story which he tells—and which has provoked such an uncommon fuss—this corner frankly holds considerable reservation. Naturally we wouldn't know how closely—if at all—it parallels the life of an eminent publisher, as has been somewhat cryptically alleged. But that is beside the point in a rigidly critical appraisal. The blamable circumstance is that it fails to provide a clear picture of the character and motives behind the man about whom the whole thing revolves.

As the picture opens, Charles Kane lies dying in the fabulous castle he has built—the castle called Xanadu, in which he has surrounded himself with vast treasures. And as death closes his eyes his heavy lips murmur one word, "Rosebud." Suddenly the death scene is broken; the screen becomes alive with a staccato March-of-Time-like news feature recounting the career of the dead man—how, as a poor boy, he came into great wealth, how he became a newspaper publisher as a young man, how he aspired to political office, was defeated because of a personal scandal, devoted himself to material acquisition and finally died.

But the editor of the news feature is not satisfied; he wants to know the secret of Kane's strange nature and especially what he meant by "Rosebud." So a reporter is dispatched to find out, and the remainder of the picture is devoted to an absorbing visualization of Kane's phenomenal career as told by his boyhood guardian, two of his closest newspaper associates and his mistress. Each is agreed on one thing—that Kane was a titanic egomaniac. It is also clearly revealed that the man was in some way consumed by his own terrifying selfishness. But just exactly what it is that eats upon him, why it is there and, for that matter, whether Kane is really a villain, a social parasite, is never clearly revealed. And the final, poignant identification of "Rosebud" sheds little more than a vague, sentimental light upon his character. At the end Kubla Kane is still an enigma—a very confusing one.

But check that off to the absorption of Mr. Welles in more visible details. Like the novelist, Thomas Wolfe, his abundance of imagery is

so great that it sometimes gets in the way of his logic. And the less critical will probably be content with an undefined Kane, anyhow. After all, nobody understood him. Why should Mr. Welles? Isn't it enough that he presents a theatrical character with consummate theatricality?

We would, indeed, like to say as many nice things as possible about everything else in this film—about the excellent direction of Mr. Welles, about the sure and penetrating performances of literally every member of the cast and about the stunning manner in which the music of Bernard Herrmann has been used. Space, unfortunately, is short. All we can say, in conclusion, is that you shouldn't miss this film. It is cynical, ironic, sometimes oppressive and as realistic as a slap. But it has more vitality than fifteen other films we could name. And, although it may not give a thoroughly clear answer, at least it brings to mind one deeply moral thought: For what shall it profit a man if he shall gain the whole world and lose his own soul? See "Citizen Kane" for further details.

My 2, 1941

THE STARS LOOK DOWN, screen play by J. B. Williams; adapted by Dr. A. J. Cronin from his novel of the same name; directed by Carol Reed; produced in England by I. Goldsmith and released through Metro-Goldwyn-Mayer. At Loew's Criterion.

David Fenwick	Michael Redgrave
Jennie Sunley	Margaret Lockwood
Joe Gowlan	Emlyn Williams
Martha Fenwick	Nancy Price
Mr. Barras	Allan Jeayes
Mrs. Laura Millington	Linden Travers
Mr. Millington	Cecil Parker
Mr. Nugent, M. P.	Milton Rosmer
Robert Fenwick	Edward Rigby
Slogger Gowlan	George Carney
Religious Reformer	Ivor Barnard
Mrs. Sunley	Olga Lindo
Hughey Fenwick	Desmond Tester

When there are reasons for anger, most films tread softly. Usually the producers count ten before speaking their minds. But now and again there comes along a film that seems to have been struck off at white heat, that surges with indignation, that says what it has to say with complete and undeviating honesty. "The Stars Look Down," the English-made film which MGM has hesitantly brought into the Criterion after holding it for many a long month, is such a work.

As a story of catastrophe in a small Welsh mining town it is so stinging in its attack on those who made the disaster inevitable that one wonders how it came to be made at all. Fortunately it has more than indignation. Directed with brilliant restraint by Carol Reed, faithfully performed in even the smallest role, it has caught the slow anguish of its coal-blackened people in a splendid and overwhelming film.

For around Dr. Cronin's novel of men who go down into the pits and sometimes never return, Director Reed has produced a study of English miners that has the breath of life in it, that has the hard actuality and often the sweep of tragedy. The men who work the seams of the Neptune No. 17 are a begrimed and tight-lipped crew. Their lives on the earth above are spent in the sleazy, dim hovels that stretch in an endless pattern of monotony across the town. The risks of their occupation they accept as readily as daily bread. And it is a mark of Mr. Reed's truthfulness as a director that they emerge as heroic without knowing it. With the possible exception of one moment when the agonized suspense of a handful of entombed miners is shattered by the ravings of a religious fanatic, Mr. Reed has never allowed the film to lapse into the exaggerated heroics of melodrama; its compassion runs too deep.

Perhaps Mr. Reed has sacrificed a little in the unity of the film by deviating too long into the domestic contretemps of the miners' younger spokesman, who jeopardizes his own career by marrying a little trollop who never loved him at all. In itself harshly revealing, the great emotional impact comes more from the wider story of the miners' strike against the dangers of the pit, the slow corrosion of their resolve through months of hunger, their betrayal alike by mine owner and corrupt union leaders, and finally their return to the pit to meet death as they had feared.

In the shots of idle men passing a cigarette from mouth to mouth, of the inchoate angers suddenly brought into focus by a stone through a butcher's window, in the grim panic of men caught in the underground labyrinths by a rush of flood water, Mr. Reed has recorded their struggle and their tragedy with sensitive camera shorthand.

But even these sequences are surpassed by the account of the vigil at the mine's mouth. In the silent relays of weary rescue workers, in the click-clack of pulmotors, and above all in the drawn white faces of the women waiting hour after uncertain hour, Mr. Reed has created one of the magnificent passages of screen realism. For he has caught here more than the surface grimness, he has touched life at its quick. Because of that his film has more of heartfilling beauty than most of the flat fictions that pass across our screens.

To single out the performers is almost an impertinence, and yet one must mention the bitter portrait of Michael Redgrave as the aspiring young spokesman; the pitiless accuracy of Margaret Lockwood as the cheap little busybody; Edward Rigby as the patient, wife-ridden father, and Nancy Price's grimly impassive mother, who can say after all hope of rescue is gone, "A disaster's a disaster." Emlyn Williams as a scheming young knave and Milton Rosmer as a friendly Member of Parliament are both excellent. Beyond them stand the people of Sleescale for whom the director has let the camera speak with candor and compassion. In "The Stars Look Down" Mr. Reed has made a film to be remembered in this or any other season.   T. S.

JI 24, 1941

THE MALTESE FALCON; based on the novel by Dashiell Hammett. Screen play by John Huston; directed by Mr. Huston; produced by Hal B. Wallis for Warner Bros. Pictures, Inc. At the Strand.

Samuel Spade ....Humphrey Bogart
Brigid O'Shaughnessy ....Mary Astor
Iva Archer ....Gladys George
Joel Cairo ....Peter Lorre
Detective Lieutenant ......Barton MacLane
Effie Perine ....Lee Patrick
Kasper Gutman ....Sidney Greenstreet
Detective Polhaus ....Ward Bond
Miles Archer................Jerome Cowan
Wilmer Cook ....Elisha Cook Jr.
Luke ....James Burke
Frank Richman ....Murray Alper
Bryan ....John Hamilton

By BOSLEY CROWTHER

The Warners have been strangely bashful about their new mystery film, "The Maltese Falcon," and about the young man, John Huston, whose first directorial job it is. Maybe they thought it best to bring both along under wraps, seeing as how the picture is a remake of an old Dashiell Hammett yarn done ten years ago, and Mr. Huston is a fledgling whose previous efforts have been devoted to writing scripts. And maybe—which is somehow more likely—they wanted to give every one a nice surprise. For "The Maltese Falcon," which swooped down onto the screen of the Strand yesterday, only turns out to be the best mystery thriller of the year, and young Mr. Huston gives promise of becoming one of the smartest directors in the field.

For some reason, Hollywood has neglected the sophisticated crime film of late, and England, for reasons which are obvious, hasn't been sending her quota in recent months. In fact, we had almost forgotten how devilishly delightful such films can be when done with taste and understanding and a feeling for the fine line of suspense. But now, with "The Maltese Falcon," the Warners and Mr. Huston give us again something of the old thrill we got from Alfred Hitchcock's brilliant melodramas or from "The Thin Man" before he died of hunger.

This is not to imply, however, that Mr. Huston has imitated any one. He has worked out his own style, which is brisk and supremely hardboiled. We didn't see the first "Falcon," which had Ricardo Cortez and Bebe Daniels in its cast. But we'll wager it wasn't half as tough nor half as flavored with idioms as is this present version, in which Humphrey Bogart hits his peak. For the trick which Mr. Huston has pulled is a combination of American ruggedness with the suavity of the English crime school—a blend of mind and muscle—plus a slight touch of pathos.

Perhaps you know the story (it was one of Mr. Hammett's best): of a private detective in San Francisco who becomes involved through a beautiful but evasive dame in a complicated plot to gain possession of a fabulous jeweled statuette. As Mr. Huston has adapted it, the mystery is as thick as a wall and the facts are completely obscure as the picture gets under way. But slowly the bits fall together, the complications draw out and a monstrous but logical intrigue of international proportions is revealed.

Much of the quality of the picture lies in its excellent revelation of character. Mr. Bogart is a shrewd, tough detective with a mind that cuts like a blade, a temperament that sometimes betrays him, and a code of morals which is coolly cynical. Mary Astor is well nigh perfect as the beautiful woman whose cupidity is forever to be suspect. Sidney Greenstreet, from the Theatre Guild's roster, is magnificent as a cultivated English crook, and Peter Lorre, Elisha Cook Jr., Lee Patrick, Barton MacLane all contribute stunning characters. (Also, if you look closely, you'll see Walter Huston, John's father, in a bit part.)

Don't miss "The Maltese Falcon" if your taste is for mystery fare. It's the slickest exercise in cerebration that has hit the screen in many months, and it is also one of the most compelling nervous-laughter provokers yet.

O 4, 1941

TARGET FOR TONIGHT; a British documentary feature picture filmed by the Crown Film Unit of the British Ministry of Information; script and direction by Harry Watt. At the Globe.

By BOSLEY CROWTHER

Some fine reportorial films have come from England since this war began—films such as "London Can Take It" and "Christmas Under Fire"—which have conveyed in graphic details a sense of the courage and strength of the British under fire. But no film that they have sent over—and, in fact, no film about this war yet made—has surpassed, or can even equal, the extraordinary British document, "Target for Tonight," which arrived in this country only last week and which went on view at the Globe yesterday.

Here is one picture you may be certain no Hollywood production can ever touch, though many may try in the future, at great and elaborate expense. For this one was taken directly in the midst of this war's activity. It was made by the Crown Film Unit, under the direction of Harry Watt, with men of the R. A. F., from Air Marshal Sir Richard Peirse down, to the lowest mechanic, as its only actors. And it has been made with such fine and intelligent restraint, fashioned so simply and directly and photographed with such artistry that it constitutes both a brilliant motion picture and a splendid tribute to a wonderful bunch of men.

"Target For Tonight" is the authentic story of a bombing raid on Germany—a simple, factual account of how such a raid is planned and how it is executed, from the moment when a reconnoissance plane drops a picture of the target until the following fog-shrouded dawn when the last of the bombers —"F for Freddie"—comes roaring home to its base. It shows the manner in which the Bomber Command lays out its operations, how instructions are transmitted to the squadrons which are to participate, how the plan of attack is "briefed" by the men of one particular squadron and then how the crew of one powerful Wellington conducts its appointed task.

This is but the structure of the picture. The true, thrilling quality of it lies in the remarkable human detail which Mr. Watt has worked into it—the quiet, efficient way in which each man goes about his job; the interjection of humor which even the grimmest task and danger cannot suppress, and finally the tremendous suspense of the routine bombing attack when we ride with the crew of "F for Freddie" and get the feeling of being one of them. Mr. Watt has a fine eye for color, and his camera is used with eloquence. There is not a waste shot in this picture; not one that fails to carry a sharp effect.

Of them all, we will mention only one as a token of his sure dramatic sense: The lads of the bomber squadron have donned their flying togs in a small room and then have gone trooping out to board their planes, like prep school boys to play a game. The hubbub and confusion suddenly cease; the room is empty and still. But Mr. Watt holds his camera upon it—on scattered chairs and open locker doors. In that brief moment you feel the lurking fate which these young men have gone to face and a sense of their great but casual courage rushes over you.

"Target For Tonight" is a picture which quickens the pulse and cheers the heart.

O 18, 1941

'The Magnificent Ambersons,' Welles's Film From Novel by Tarkington, Opens at Capitol

THE MAGNIFICENT AMBERSONS, screen play by Orson Welles; based on the novel by Booth Tarkington; produced and directed by Mr. Welles for RKO Radio Pictures.

Eugene Morgan.............Joseph Cotten
Isabel Amberson..........Dolores Costello
Lucy Morgan..................Anne Baxter
George Amberson Minafer.......Tim Holt
Fanny Minafer..........Agnes Moorehead
Jack Amberson................Ray Collins
Major Amberson..........Richard Bennett
Wilbur Minafer..........Donald Dillaway
Bronson..................Erskine Sanford

With only two pictures to his credit, last year's extraordinary "Citizen Kane" and now Booth' Tarkington's "The Magnificent Ambersons," Orson Welles has demonstrated beyond doubt that the screen is his medium. He has an eloquent, if at times grandiose, flair for the dramatic which only the camera can fully capture and he has a truly wondrous knack for making his actors, even the passing bit player, behave like genuine human beings. And yet, with all his remarkable talent, Mr. Welles still apparently refuses to make concessions to popular appeal. The Capitol's new film, however magnificently executed, is a relentlessly somber drama on a barren theme.

In a world brimful of momentous drama beggaring serious screen treatment, it does seem that Mr. Welles is imposing when he asks moviegoers to become emotionally disturbed over the decline of such minor league American aristocracy as the Ambersons represented in the late Eighteen Seventies. While one may question Welles' choice of theme, as well as his conception of the Tarkington novel, it must be admitted that he has accomplished with marked success what he set out to do. For "The Magnificent Ambersons" is a dignified, resourceful character study of a family group, which incidentally reflects the passing of an era.

This time Welles does not participate as actor, but he does lend his impressive voice as an off-screen narrator, setting the scene and introducing the characters in much the same manner as he used to do on the radio. As the film opens, town gossipers are busily passing around word that beauteous Isabel Amberson is giving up fun-loving Eugene Morgan, because he imbibed too much and crashed through a bass fiddle, to marry the stuffy but more socially acceptable Wilbur Minafer.

Their marriage produces one son, George Amberson Minafer, a devilish, spoiled brat for all his beautiful golden curls, who imbues the elder townspeople with one burning desire—to witness the day that George gets his "come-up-ance." With the collapse of his grandfather's fortune George gets his "come-upance" with a vengeance in young manhood. But before fate delivers its humbling blows, the vain, arrogant youth cruelly wrecks the tender bitter-sweet romance that has been renewed between his now widowed mother and her old suitor, himself a widower and father of the girl whom George loves.

Tim Holt draws out all of the meanness in George's character, which is precisely what the part demands. As the mother, Dolores Costello proves that she is too beautiful and capable an actress to remain inactive for such long periods. Agnes Moorehead, playing the role of a romantically frustrated aunt, is splendid. Other fine performances are contributed by Ray Collins, Anne Baxter and the veteran Richard Bennett as the grandfather. Joseph Cotten, who has shown fine promise, gives an adequate though not distinguished performance as Eugene Morgan, a role which is not too well written.

All in all, "The Magnificent Ambersons" is an exceptionally well-made film, dealing with a subject scarcely worth the attention which has been lavished upon it.

T. M. P.

Ag 14, 1942

'In Which We Serve,' Depicting Cruel Realities of This War, Is Presented at Capitol. Noel Coward Heads Cast.

IN WHICH WE SERVE, written, scored and produced by Noel Coward; directed by Mr. Coward and David Lean; presented by Two Cities Productions and released through United Artists. At the Capitol.
Captain Kinross..............Noel Coward
Chief Petty Officer Walter Hardy,
  Bernard Miles
Ordinary Seaman Shorty Blake...John Mills
Alix (Mrs. Kinross)...........Celia Johnson
Freda Lewis..................Kay Walsh
Mrs. Hardy..................Joyce Carey
Number One............Derek Elphinstone
"Guns" ....Robert Sansom
"Torps" ....Philip Friend
"Flags" ....Michael Wilding
Pilot ....Hubert Gregg
Engineer Commander.....Ballard Berkeley
Doctor ....James Donald
Sub. Lieut. R. N. V. R.....Kenneth Carton
Colonel Lumsden........Walter Fitzgerald
Captain Jasper Fry...........Gerald Case
Lavinia ....Ann Stephens
Bobby ....Daniel Massey
Mrs. Lemmon...............Dora Gregory
Mrs. Blake..............Kathleen Harrison
Mr. Blake..................George Carney
Young Sailor........Richard Attenborough

By BOSLEY CROWTHER

One of the most eloquent motion pictures of these or any other times had its American première at the Capitol Theatre last night. It is Noel Coward's much-heralded British Navy film, "In Which We Serve," made within the last year in England under Mr. Coward's almost complete guidance and played by as fine a cast of actors as ever stepped up to a camera. There have been other pictures which have vividly and movingly conveyed in terms of human emotion the cruel realities of this present war. None has yet done it so sharply and so truly as "In Which We Serve."

"This is the story of a ship," says the voice of Mr. Coward to introduce the opening sequence of the picture—scenes of building a destroyer on the ways. But it is more than the story of one vessel which he is telling here; more than the log-book record of a British destroyer which was hastily commissioned for service in the Summer of 1939, fought through the howling watches around Britain's embattled isles and was finally knocked out by Nazi bombers off Crete in May of 1941. It is the human and vibrant story of the men who fought in her, of their stout devotion to their vessel and to the service in which they were pledged. And, above all, it is the story of man's heroic soul and the selfless, indomitable spirit by which a whole nation endures.

For the great thing which Mr. Coward has accomplished in this film is a full and complete expression of national fortitude. Yes, the men of H. M. S. Torrin, from her commander down to the lowest tar, are filled with deep pride in their vessel and a personal attachment to her. When the wife of the Torrin's commander wistfully explains that there is in the life of every navy woman "one undefeated rival —her husband's ship," she frankly acknowledges a relation to which she is dutifully resigned. And when Chief Petty Officer Hardy lifts his glass in a Christmas toast and solemnly says, "I love her—I love her with every fiber of my being; ladies and gentlemen—H. M. S. Torrin," it is a pledge of his very soul.

And that is the thing; this devotion of men to their ship and to their mates is a subtle symbolization of everything that they are. The ship represents themselves, their families. It is their nation. It is their world. The ship is the heart and sinew of all who sail in her. It is this profound realization which Mr. Coward has conveyed by graphically merging the lives of the

Torrin's company, ashore and afloat, in one resolve.

"In Which We Serve" is not a plot-film. Like Mr. Coward's previous "Cavalcade," it is rather a dramatic narrative, a pageant of tense experience. In the main, it is just the recollections of a handful of the Torrin's men as they cling to a tiny life-raft off Crete after their ship has been sunk. It is the poignant reflections of her commander upon the glories of his ship—of the night that they fought her desperately against the enemy in a North Atlantic storm and brought her home badly damaged, with thirty of their shipmates dead; of his talks with the crew, of Christmas services in the fo'c'sle and singing "Good King Wenceslaus," of the time that they helped bring the Army back from Dunkerque—and of the simple pleasures of his home.

It is the memories of C. P. O. Hardy and Ordinary Seaman Shorty Blake, typically overlapping, of their families and Plymouth homes—of Hardy's wife and her mother, and of the way Shorty met Hardy's niece on a train coming down from London and winningly married her. And it tells, in a correlated narrative, how the bombers came over Plymouth one fearful night and left poor Hardy a widower and Shorty a father by the grace of God..

It tells all of these things and others connected with the life of the ship in a manner as vivid and stirring as though it were actuality. It catches the "feel" of a destroyer with vibrant intensity—the sweep of her hull through the water, the pounding of pom-pom guns, the coordination in battle and the cool, efficient order on her bridge. And it visions civilian life in England as it really is—people doing their business with humor and hardihood. For Mr. Coward has written and he and David Lean directed this film out of knowledge and deep compassion.

for the people and the subject of which they treat.

And the actors have played it with the verity of close and keen observers of life. Mr. Coward himself is somewhat cryptic and attitudinized in the role of the ship's commander; for all his depth of sincerity, he still plays Mr. Coward. But Bernard Miles and John Mills are incomparable as a couple of Royal Navy men—Miles spare and gentle as Hardy and Mills bright and bustling as Blake. Celia Johnson, Kay Walsh and Joyce Carey play the wives of the three men as such should be—plain in appearance, unpretentious, but as real and dependable as home. And a large cast of truly excellent actors puts life and reality into other roles.

We may yet see a picture more rational about the large implications of this war. But this observer does not expect ever to see anything more moving on the screen than the looks of the oil-smeared sailors in this film as they watch their loved ship sink, or the way in which those tired Dunkerque survivors of the Coldstream Guards march off that Dover dock. Nor are we likely to hear ever anything which cuts more closely to the heart than Commander Kinross's valedictory to his sailors and to his ship: "Now she lies in 1,500 fathoms and with her most of our shipmates. We have lost her, but they are still with her. Now they lie in very good company."

Yes, this is truly a picture in which the British may take a wholesome pride and we may regard as an excellent expression of British strength. For it tells in this war's hard idiom what Kipling told in the last:

How in all time of our distress,
 And our deliverance too,
The game is more than the player
  of the game
 And the ship is more than the
  crew.

D 24, 1942

'Shadow of a Doubt' a Thriller, With Teresa Wright, Joseph Cotten, at Rivoli

SHADOW OF A DOUBT, screen play by
Thornton Wilder, Sally Benson and Alma
Reville; from an original story by Gordon
McDonell; directed by Alfred Hitchcock;
produced by Jack H. Skirball and released
by Universal. At the Rivoli.

Young Charlie	Teresa Wright
Uncle Charlie	Joseph Cotten
Jack Graham	Macdonald Carey
Emma Newton	Patricia Collinge
Joseph Newton	Henry Travers
Herbie Hawkins	Hume Cronyn
Fred Saunders	Wallace Ford
Ann Newton	Edna May Wonacott
Roger Newton	Charles Bates
Station master	Irving Bacon
Pullman porter	Clarence Muse
Louise	Janet Shaw
Catherine	Estelle Jewell

By BOSLEY CROWTHER

You've got to hand it to Alfred Hitchcock: when he sows the fearful seeds of mistrust in one of his motion pictures he can raise more goose pimples to the square inch of a customer's flesh than any other director of thrillers in Hollywood. He did it quite nicely in "Rebecca" and again in "Suspicion" about a year ago. And now he is bringing in another bumper crop of blue-ribbon shivers and chills in Jack Skirball's diverse production of "Shadow of a Doubt," which came to the Rivoli last night.

Yes, the way Mr. Hitchcock folds suggestions very casually into the furrows of his film, the way he can make a torn newspaper or the sharpened inflection of a person's voice send ticklish roots down to the subsoil of a customer's anxiety, is a wondrous, invariable accomplishment. And the mental anguish he can thereby create, apparently in the minds of his characters but actually in the psyche of you, is of championship proportions and—being hokum, anyhow—a sheer delight.

But when Mr. Hitchcock and/or his writers start weaving allegories in his films or, worse still, neglect to spring surprises after the ground has apparently been prepared, the consequence is something less than cheering. And that is the principal fault — or rather, the sole disappointment — in "Shadow of a Doubt." For this one suggests tremendous promise when a sinister character—a gentleman called Uncle Charlie—goes to visit with relatives, a typical American family, in a quiet California town. The atmosphere is charged with electricity when the daughter of the family, Uncle Charlie's namesake, begins to grow strangely suspicious of this moody, cryptic guest in the house. And the story seems loaded for fireworks and a beautiful explosion of surprise when the scared girl discovers that Uncle Charlie is really a murderer of rich, fat widows, wanted back East.

But from that point on the story takes a decidedly anticlimactic dip and becomes just a competent exercise in keeping a tightrope taut. It also becomes a bit too specious in making a moralistic show of the warmth of an American community toward an unsuspected rascal in its midst. We won't violate tradition to tell you how the story ends, but we will say that the moral is either anti-social or, at best, obscure. When Uncle Charlie's niece concludes cynically that the world is a horrible place and the young detective with whom she has romanced answers, "Some times it needs a lot of watching; seems to go crazy, every now and then, like Uncle Charlie," the bathos is enough to knock you down.

However, there is sufficient sheer excitement and refreshing atmosphere in the film to compensate in large measure for its few disappointing faults. Thornton Wilder, Sally Benson and Alma Reville have drawn a graphic and affectionate outline of a small-town American family which an excellent cast has brought to life and Mr. Hitchcock has manifest completely in his naturalistic style. Teresa Wright is aglow with maiden spirit and subsequent emotional distress as the namesake of Uncle Charlie, and Patricia Collinge gives amazing flexibility and depth to the role of the patient, hard-working, sentimental mother of the house. Henry Travers is amusing as the father, Edna May Wonacott is fearfully precocious as "the brat" and Hume Cronyn makes a modest comic masterpiece out of the character of a literal-minded friend.

As the progressively less charming Uncle Charlie, Joseph Cotten plays with smooth, insinuating ease while injecting a harsh and bitter quality which nicely becomes villainy. He has obviously kept an eye on Orson Welles. And MacDonald Carey and Wallace Ford make an adequate pair of modern sleuths.

The flavor and "feel" of a small town has been beautifully impressed in this film by the simple expedient of shooting most of it in Santa Rosa, Calif., which leads to the obvious observation that the story should be as reliable as the sets.

Ja 13, 1943

THE SCREEN

'Air Force,' South Sea Thriller, Arrives at the Hollywood

AIR FORCE; original screen play by Dudley Nichols; directed by Howard Hawks; produced by Hal B. Wallis for Warner Brothers. At the Hollywood.

Pilot (Capt. Quincannon)......John Ridgely
Co-Pilot (Lieut. Williams)......Gig Young
Bombardier (Lieut. McMartin),
                              Arthur Kennedy
Navigator (Lieut. Hauser)...Charles Drake
Crew Chief (Sgt. White)......Harry Carey
Asst. Crew Chief (Corp. Weinberger),
                              George Tobias
Radio Operator (Corp. Peterson),
                              Ward Wood
Asst. Radio Operator (Pvt. Chester),
                              Ray Montgomery
Aerial Gunner (Sgt. Winocki).John Garfield
Pursuit Pilot (Lieut. Rader)..James Brown
Major Mallory.............Stanley Ridges
Colonel ....Willard Robertson
Commanding Officer.........Moroni Olsen
Sgt. J. J. Callahan.....Edward S. Brophy
Major W. G. Roberts.......Richard Lane
Lieut. P. T. Moran.............Bill Crago
Susan McMartin............Faye Emerson
Major Daniels...........Addison Richards
Major A. M. Bagley.......James Flavin
Mary Quincannon.............Ann Doran
Mrs. Chester............Dorothy Peterson

By BOSLEY CROWTHER

On the natural assumption that Army fliers can do almost anything that requires grit, determination, high competence and just plain Yankee luck, the Warner Brothers have turned out a film about an Army bomber crew which matches in sheer incredibility some of the certified yarns that pop up every week. "Air Force" is its title. It came to the Hollywood yesterday. And although it draws about the longest and most pliant bow that has ever been drawn in the line of fanciful war films and goes completely overboard in the last reel, it is still a continuously fascinating, frequently thrilling and occasionally exalting show which leaves you limp and triumphant at the end of its two-hour ordeal.

For what the Warners have put together—with the help of Dudley Nichols, who wrote the script, and Howard Hawks, who directed a uniformly excellent cast—is a high-flying epic compounded from most, if not all, the ringing tales of the Air Forces' heroism in the far Pacific during the first months of this war. Inspired by the brilliant record which our Army fliers hung up, the boys gave way completely to their boundless enthusiasm and awe and ripped out a picture which tingles with the passion of spirits aglow.

The story recounts almost in toto the adventures of an Army bomber's crew and the ship itself, a Flying Fortress, labeled the Mary Ann. There are Captain Quincannon, a youthful veteran of the

208

Texas training fields, and Sergeant Rob White, the gray-haired crew chief who has a pilot-son in the Philippines. There are Corporal Weinberg from Brooklyn and Radioman Peterson from the Northwest and Sergeant Winocki, a cynic, and the four other men of the crew.

With a squadron of eight other bombers, the Mary Ann takes off from a field near San Francisco on Dec. 6—you know when. En route, on the "date which will live in infamy," the crew gets the startling report that the Japs are attacking Pearl Harbor and their destination, Hickam Field. (This is historically founded; a flight of Fortresses was coming in, you may recall.) So the crew set their ship down on Maui, where they are attacked by fifth columnists, get away and fly on to Hickam, only to find black destruction there and immediate orders to take off for danger points farther west.

And so the story follows Mary Ann and her sleepless crew—along with a bold pursuit pilot who is picked up at Hickam Field—on through storm and darkness to Wake Island, where they fall heir to a dog, and thence to Clark Field in the Philippines, for some breathless encounters with the Japs. And finally, flying on towards Australia, after the Philippines are lost, the Mary Ann's crew spots a Nip fleet—a huge flotilla—heading south and pitches in for a climactic action which is presumably that of the Coral Sea. Apparently Mr. Hawks and Mr. Nichols herewith let themselves go, and a noisier or more destructive battle (with models) you've never seen. For this one the Warners blew up practically everything but their studio.

Along the way, there is a succession of human dramas and comedies involving the crew, most of them of a nature peculiar to masculine films. The co-pilot loves the bombardier's sister. Winocki, the cynic, becomes a lion when fighting begins. Weinberg is a disarming jester. And the pursuit and

bomber pilots genially feud, of course. These little facets of the picture are generally obvious and routine.

But Mr. Hawks very wisely recruited a cast with no outstanding star, thus assuring himself the privilege of giving every one a chance. And his actors have responded handsomely. John Ridgely is refreshingly direct as the bomber's intrepid captain and sufficiently unfamiliar to seem real. Harry Carey gives a beautiful performance as the quiet and efficient crew chief, and John Garfield's tough creation of Winocki is superior despite its brevity. George Tobias is delightfully droll as Weinberg, James Brown is natural as a young pilot, and others in a rather large cast fulfill their roles with eminent success.

As usual, Mr. Hawks has directed the action for tremendous impact. When his actors move around, you believe it; when his bombs crash, you rock in your seat. The air fights, most of which are seen down gun barrels, are thrilling and highly accomplished special effects. And Mr. Hawks has assembled some striking and moving photography in this film. Maybe the story is high-flown, maybe it overdraws a recorded fact a bit. We'd hate to think it couldn't happen—or didn't—because it certainly leaves you feeling awfully good.

F 4, 1943

'The Ox-Bow Incident,' Drama of Mob Violence, With Dana Andrews and Henry Fonda in Leads, Opens at the Rivoli

By BOSLEY CROWTHER

An ugly study in mob violence, unrelieved by any human grace save the futile reproach of a minority and some mild post-lynching remorse, is contained in "The Ox-Bow Incident," which was delivered to the Rivoli on Saturday by Twentieth Century-Fox in as brazen a gesture as any studio has ever indulged. For it is hard to imagine a picture with less promise commercially. In a little over an hour, it exhibits most of the baser shortcomings of men—cruelty, blood-lust, ruffianism, pusillanimity and sordid pride. It shows a tragic violation of justice with little backlash to sweeten the bitter draught. And it puts a popular actor, Henry Fonda, in a very dubious light. But it also points a moral, bluntly and unremittingly, to show the horror of mob rule. And it has the virtue of uncompromising truth.

THE OX-BOW INCIDENT: produced and written for the screen by Lamar Trotti; from the novel by Walter Van Tilburg Clark; directed by William A. Wellman for Twentieth Century-Fox. At the Rivoli.

Gil Carter	Henry Fonda
Martin	Dana Andrews
Rose Mapen	Mary Beth Hughes
Mexican	Anthony Quinn
Gerald	William Eythe
Art Croft	Henry Morgan
Ma Grier	Jane Darwell
Judge Daniel Tyler	Matt Briggs
Arthur Davies	Harry Davenport
Major Tetley	Frank Conroy
Farnley	Marc Lawrence
Monty Smith	Paul Hurst
Darby	Victor Kilian
Pancho	Chris-Pin Martin
Kinkaid	Frank Orth
Joyce	Ted North
Mapes	Dick Rich
Old Man	Francis Ford
Gabe Hart	Rondo Hatton
Sparks	Leigh Whipper

The story is really no more than a single episode—an incident, as the title says—which is supposed to have occurred in Nevada back in 1885. But it might have happened at any place, for that matter, and at almost any time. A rancher is reportedly killed by cattle-rustlers and a mob gathers to seek revenge. Rancour, lust and curiosity fan a reckless fire. A deputy sheriff swears a posse; a demagogue takes command. And the self-assumed guardians of justice go tearing off into the hills to do their will. In the dark of night, they capture three men who are driving a herd. On the basis of circumstantial evidence, they assume these three are their prey. And, in a lather of hot brutality which takes no heed of the signs of innocence—nor of the valiant but do-nothing protests of a handful of clear-thinking men—the mob pulls a triplet lynching. When it is over, they learn that the "murdered" man still lives.

William Wellman has directed the picture with a realism that is as sharp and cold as a knife from a script by Lamar Trotti which is beautifully brief with situations and words. And an all-round excellent cast has played the film brilliantly. The manner in which Mr. Wellman has studied his characters is a lesson in close-up art. And the terror which he has packed into that night "trial," with the ruthless lynchers glowering around a mountain fire while the doomed men face their fate in pitiful misery, is drama at its cruel and cynical best.

A heart-wringing performance by Dana Andrews as the stunned and helpless leader of the doomed trio does much to make the picture a profoundly distressing tragedy, while Frank Conroy's performance of the demagogue (all rigged out in a Confederate officer's uniform) imparts to it a perceptive significance which is good to keep in mind. Mr. Fonda is cryptic and bitter as one of the stancher hold-outs for justice, while Harry Davenport and Leigh Whipper are more affecting emotionally as champions of the right. Mary Beth Hughes has been pulled in for one brief, ironic scene with Mr. Fonda which gives a justification for his mood. And the rest of the cast can take bows for small but impressive roles.

"The Ox-Bow Incident" is not a picture which will brighten or cheer your day. But it is one which, for sheer, stark drama, is currently hard to beat.

My 10, 1943

'For Whom the Bell Tolls,' a Drama From the Hemingway Novel, With Gary Cooper, Ingrid Bergman, at the Rivoli

FOR WHOM THE BELL TOLLS, screen play by Dudley Nichols; from the novel by Ernest Hemingway; produced and directed by Sam Wood; executive producer, B G DeSylva; production designed by William Cameron Menzies; presented by Paramount. At the Rivoli.

Robert Jordan	Gary Cooper
Maria	Ingrid Bergman
Pablo	Akim Tamiroff
Pilar	Katina Paxinou
Anselmo	Vladimir Sokolof
Augustin	Arturo de Cordova
Rafael	Mikhail Rasumny
Fernando	Fortunio Bonanova
El Sordo	Joseph Calleia
Andres	Eric Feldary
Primitivo	Victor Varconi
Joaquim	Lilo Yarson
General Golz	Leo Bulgakov
Captain Gomez	Frank Puglia
Andre Massa	George Coulouris
Colonel Miranda	Pedro de Cordoba
Kharkov	Konstantin Shayne
Paco	Alexander Granach
Gustavo	Adia Kuznetzoff
Ignacio	Leonid Snegoff
Captain Mora	Martin Garralaga
Staff Officer	Michael Visaroff
Colonel Duval	Jack Mylong
Kashkin	Feodor Chaliapin
Lieut. Berrendo	Duncan Renaldo
Sniper	Jean del Val

By BOSLEY CROWTHER

With such fidelity to the original that practically nothing was left out except all of the unmentionable language and the more intimate romantic scenes, Ernest Hemingway's wonderful novel of the Spanish civil war. "For Whom the Bell Tolls," has been brought to the screen in all its richness of color and character. By and large, it is the best film that has come along this year, and its opening last night at the Rivoli was a truly deserving "event." For, in spite of its almost interminable and physically exhausting length— it takes two hours and fifty minutes to cover less than four days in a group of people's lives—and in spite of some basic detruncations of the novel's two leading characters, it vibrates throughout with vitality and is topped off with a climax that's a whiz.

As often is the case with pictures which are based upon popular works, a thorough comprehension of this one may depend on whether one has read the book. For the fundamental emphasis of the novel upon the rapturous and tragic love of Robert Jordan, the American dynamiter, and Maria, the orphaned Spanish girl, has been vitiated in large measure by the obvious blanks compelled by the Hays code. And as a consequence, the cosmic symbolism of their regenerative love, set against a background of violence and the impending prospect of death, will barely be comprehensible only to those who have read the book. To others the love of Robert and Maria will be little more than good boy-meets-girl.

But so much that was fine in the novel and so much that was humanly true have been faithfully reproduced in the picture that the other is not too greatly missed. Now the emphasis is primarily upon the conflict within the band of Loyalist Spanish guerrillas to whom Robert Jordan goes for aid in his perilous mission to blow up an enemy bridge. And the study of character among those Spaniards, the definition of the braves and the cowards, is the matter of absorbing interest for at least two-thirds of the film.

The rest is the tingling action-business of the calculated blowing of the bridge, which is as tense and vivid melodrama as anyone could normally stand. And this is preceded by a thrilling representation of the fight of El Sordo's little band against the troop of Nationalist cavalry which comes into the mountains to ferret them out. Incidentally, the political sympathies of the characters are perfectly clear. The protagonists are plainly anti-fascists, and this fact is, at one point, well expressed. However, the political confusion and ramifications of the civil war are as vague and strangely amorphous as they were in Mr. Hemingway's book.

From The New York Times Film Reviews

211

In their fidelity to the novel, Dudley Nichols, who wrote the screen play, and Sam Wood, who directed for Paramount, were over-zealous, if anything, and lingered too long over matters which might have been profitably compressed. Mr. Nichols, in his script, caught the flavor and the spirit of the novel handsomely, and Mr. Wood gained an intimacy with the characters through constant close-ups which is well-nigh unique. The quality of their work is flawless. There is only too much of it.

However, the superb characterizations are the outstanding merit of the film. Gary Cooper as Robert Jordan and Ingrid Bergman as Maria are fine, though limited in their opportunities. Miss Bergman is perhaps a shade too gay. But Katina Paxinou as Pilar, the rugged Spanish woman who is the tower of strength, is a marvel of tenderness and violence, the Spanish peasant character in fluid mass. And Akim Tamiroff as Pablo is a masterpiece of dark and devious moods, as fine an expression of animal treachery and human pride as has ever been put on the screen.

Likewise, Vladimir Sokoloff as Anselmo, the aged man of iron; Joseph Calleia as El Sordo, the invincible; Mikhail Rasumny as Rafael, the gypsy clown; Fortunio Bonanova as Fernando, the realist, and many more perform excellently. The film is well worth seeing for its assorted characters alone.

And also it is produced as magnificently as any film has ever been. Photographed very largely in the High Sierras in technicolor that is breath-takingly fine, it has the hard texture of granite, the rough and vivid colors of all outdoors. And some of the close shots of the characters have the brilliance of Goya paintings. By and large, it is a picture which offers many rewards. It's a shame, to put it bluntly, that in it art is so long and life so short.

Jl 15, 1943

HEAVEN CAN WAIT, screen play by Samson Raphaelson; based on the play "Birthday" by Lazlo Bus-Fekete; produced and directed by Ernst Lubitsch for Twentieth Century-Fox. At the Roxy.

Martha	Gene Tierney
Henry Van Cleve	Don Ameche
Hugo Van Cleve	Charles Coburn
Mrs. Strabel	Marjorie Main
His Excellency	Laird Cregar
Bertha Van Cleve	Spring Byington
Albert Van Cleve	Allyn Joslyn
E. F. Strabel	Eugene Pallette
Mademoiselle	Signe Hasso
Randolph Van Cleve	Louis Calhern
Peggy Nash	Helene Reynolds
James	Aubrey Mather
Jack Van Cleve	Michael Ames
Jasper	Clarence Muse
Henry Van Cleve (age 15)	Dickie Moore
Albert Van Cleve (age 15)	Dickie Jones

By BOSLEY CROWTHER

It is an amusing anomaly that Twentieth Century-Fox displays a particular fondness for the nineteenth century and wolves. Never is the studio quite so profligate as when it has a film in which the background is fin-de-siècle and the hero is a lady-killing blade. The settings then ooze a horse-hair flavor and Technicolor rainbows the screen. And the hero has a patent-leather polish that would have dazzled Delmonico's.

No wonder, then, that the studio has been chortling with so much advance glee over its latest package of entertainment, "Heaven Can Wait," which came to the Roxy yesterday. For here is a shined and scented chromo which Ernst Lubitsch has produced for it with all the ornamental excess of the period so dear to the heart of the studio. Here is a nostalgic nosegay in which the hero is quite a wolf, indeed. And here is a comedy of manners, edged with satire, in the slickest Lubitsch style. The Twentieth Century-Fox has got a picture about fin-de-siècle conduct which rings a bell.

For this time Mr. Lubitsch (and his playwright, Sam Raphaelson) is not concerned with the present, as he was so embarrassingly in "To Be or Not To Be," but is poking very sly and sentimental fun at Eighteen Nineties naughtiness.

He—and Mr. Raphaelson, who based the script on a Lazlo Bus-Fekete play—are laughing with gentle affection at the pruderies of yesterday. Their picture has utterly no significance. Indeed, it has very little point, except to afford entertainment. And that it does quite well.

It begins with an elderly gentleman, obviously departed from this life, applying for permanent admission at the place to which so many have said he would go. Modestly he confesses that he wouldn't even apply up above. But His Excellency, who passes on the sinners, is a little bit doubtful of this case, so he sternly demands credentials, and the gentleman gives them—for nigh two hours—while Heaven waits.

He tells—or rather, does the picture—of his earliest experiences with girls, when he discovered, to his lasting confusion, that, to win them, you must have plenty of coin. And then he recounts his young manhood as the scion of wealthy New York aristocrats and of his frivolous ways with the ladies, which shocked h s parents and pleased his stiff granddad, concluding that phase by eloping with the fiancée of his strait-laced cousin.

The second—and less amusing—half of the picture continues the married life of this wayward gent, his silly estrangement from his darling and their reunion, with grandpa to egg them on. And it fritters out in old-age sentiment which is punctured by one sharp Lubitsch "touch." Mr. Lubitsch fortunately manages to top it off with an innocent, genial leer.

The character of the rakish hero is never clearly defined, nor is that of the girl who marries him. He remains an ambiguous changeling, and so does she. That may be one reason why Don Ameche and Gene Tierney are flat in the roles. Or rather, they lack the flexibility which such mannered comedy demands.

But so many other characters are so amusingly written and played that the lack is not overpowering. Charles Coburn as grandpa is great—a curmudgeon full of venom and gleeful naughtiness. Marjorie Main and Eugene Pallette play a pair of Kansas in-laws screamingly, and through them Mr. Lubitsch and Mr. Raphaelson satirize wealth in a lusty vein. Mention should be made of Allyn Joslyn's goody-goody prig and of Louis Calhern's Father and of several in lesser roles.

But those you will personally discover, for the film is certainly one you'll want to see. It loses tempo occasionally. It drags a bit toward the end. But—Heaven's above!

Ag 12, 1943

THE SCREEN
By MORDAUNT HALL

'Lady in the Dark,' With Ginger Rogers, Opens at Paramount

LADY IN THE DARK, screen play by Frances Goodrich and Albert Hackett; based on the play by Moss Hart with music by Kurt Weill and lyrics by Ira Gershwin; directed by Mitchell Leisen; produced by Dick Blumenthal; executive producer B. G. De Sylva; settings and costumes designed by Raoul Pene du Bois; presented by Paramount; song, "Suddenly It's Spring," by Johnny Burke and James Van Heusen. At the Paramount.

Liza Elliott	Ginger Rogers
Charley Johnson	Ray Milland
Randy Curtis	Jon Hall
Kendall Nesbitt	Warner Baxter
Dr. Brooks	Barry Sullivan
Russell Paxton	Mischa Auer
Maggy Grant	Mary Philips
Allison DuBois	Phyllis Brooks
Dr. Carlton	Edward Fielding
Adams	Don Loper
Miss Parker	Mary Parker
Miss Foster	Catherine Craig
Martha	Marietta Canty
Miss Edwards	Virginia Farmer
Miss Bowers	Fay Helm
Barbara, aged 17	Gail Russell
Liza's Mother	Kay Linaker
Liza's Father	Harvey Stephens
Ben	Rand Brooks

By BOSLEY CROWTHER

The slightly terrific spectacle of a couple of million dollars all laid out in eye-bedazzling costumes, dress creations and brilliant decor is something to which moviegoers have become more or less inured. But never, in this writer's memory, has the screen mounted such a display of overpowering splash and glitter as it does with Paramount's "Lady in the Dark." Imagine the gaudiest creations of all the fancy dressmakers in the trade; imagine the most resplendent spectacles of the Music Hall rolled into one; imagine a lacquered Ginger Rogers strolling sleekly through this compound mise en scène—and you have a moderate impression of this new film at the Paramount. For the studio, to use a common idiom, has completely shot the works and turned out a Technicolored marchpast which puts such previous screen parades to shame.

Not only are the picturesque dream scenes of Moss Hart's original musical play done up in such fantastic elegance as would make a child-romancer's whims seem pale. Raoul Pene du Bois designed them in a million-dollar trance, there is no doubt, and splashed them with a range of vivid colors that suggest he made a raid on stellar space. But the purely material demonstrations — for the most part, set in a fashion-magazine shop—are out of this world in gloss and richness. They are the ultimate in decorative chi-chi.

Small wonder, then, that the story which Mr. Hart's play originally told of a lady with an active psychosis becomes somewhat offset in this film. Small wonder that the human problem takes on a specious coloration, too. The psychoanalysis of Liza Elliott, editor of a slick magazine, who is strangely and violently irascible because of an unhappy past, was slightly ridiculous in the stage play. But it seems even more so in the film because of the lady's unreality in a completely artificial world. The relation of Liza Elliott to true personality is hard to find. Her psychological emancipation takes place in a rare vacuum.

Also the authors of the screen play have chopped the original in such a way that much that was wistful and tender in it has been curiously left out. And its musical passages have been shortened, so that its nature is basically changed. For instance, the lovely little theme song, "My Boat," which Kurt Weill composed, is hummed only briefly by Miss Rogers; it is never completely sung. And the childhood flashbacks have a hurried and undistinguished tone.

Except for her gay and raffish singing of "The Saga of Jenny" (slightly cut) and her burst of enthusiasm at the finish, Miss Rogers moves through it all in a variety of stunning costumes but in a plain brown study most of the time. Her mood is peculiarly depressing. Physically, however, she's all right. Ray Milland, on the other hand, is spirited and decidedly pleasant to know as her editorial associate whom she finally discovers is The Man. And Jon Hall, Warner Baxter and Mary Philips are agreeably placed in other roles. Mischa Auer screeches comically and broadly as the photographer (which Danny Kaye played on the stage). He does not, as a matter of record, sing the famous "Tchaikovsky" patter song.

Mitchell Leisen, the director, used his actors for display more than emotion, that is plain. And display in capital letters is the consequence. "Lady in the Dark" puts an I on a pedestal—and keeps it there.

F 23, 1944

'Gaslight,' Adapted From Play
'Angel Street,' at Capitol—

GASLIGHT, screen play by John Van Druten, Walter Reisch and John L. Balderston; based on the play by Patrick Hamilton; directed by George Cukor; produced by Arthur Hornblow Jr. for Metro-Goldwyn-Mayer. At the Capitol.
Gregory Anton ....Charles Boyer

By BOSLEY CROWTHER

That dark and shivering study of Victorian villainy which has been shaking the boards of Broadway for more than two years under the title of "Angel Street" is now doing similar violence to the Capitol Theatre's screen, where it arrived yesterday under the no more illuminating title of "Gaslight." But don't let that mellow come-on fool you, all ye who enter here. Prepare yourselves rather for a lengthy and restless stretch on tenterhooks. For Metro has given a pungent production to the Patrick Hamilton play. It has used Ingrid Bergman and Charles Boyer in the dominant roles of the distraught wife and her wicked spouse. And it has pulled such a ticklish assortment of melodramatic camera tricks that the audience was giggling with anxiety at a performance yesterday.

Maybe we shouldn't tell you what it is all about, even though that knowledge is rather general with theatre-goers by now. But we can, at least, slip the information that the study is wholly concerned with the obvious endeavors of a husband to drive his wife slowly mad. And with Mr. Boyer doing the driving in his best dead-pan hypnotic style, while the flames flicker strangely in the gas-jets and the mood music bongs with heavy threats, it is no wonder that Miss Bergman goes to pieces in a most distressing way. Both of these popular performers play their roles right to the hilt.

Nice little personality vignettes are interestingly contributed, too, by Joseph Cotten as a stubborn detective, Dame May Whitty and Angela Lansbury as a maid. But it must be stated frankly that the film doesn't match the play, mainly because of circumstances of an ambiguous physical sort. The play, by its rigid confinement within the limitations of one room, prevades the spectator with the horror and frustration of a claustrophobic mood. One is dragged imperceptibly right up there into that room and made to experience the same emotions as the bewildered and fear-driven wife. But the very flexibility of the camera, the constant cutting away from that one scene, induces the audience to take a comfortably objective point of view. Much of the fearful immediacy of the play is sadly lost in the film.

My 5, 1944

'Double Indemnity,' a Tough Melodrama, With Stanwyck and MacMurray as Killers, Opens at the Paramount

DOUBLE INDEMNITY, screen play by Billy Wilder and Raymond Chandler; from the novel by James M. Cain; directed by Billy Wilder for Paramount. At the Paramount.

By BOSLEY CROWTHER

The cooling-system in the Paramount Theatre was supplemented yesterday by a screen attraction designed plainly to freeze the marrow in an audience's bones. "Double Indemnity" is its title, and the extent of its refrigerating effect depends upon one's personal repercussion to a long dose of calculated suspense. For the sole question in this picture is whether Barbara Stanwyck and Fred MacMurray can kill a man with such cool and artistic deception that no one will place the blame on them and then maintain their composure under Edward G. Robinson's studiously searching eye.

Such folks as delight in murder stories for their academic elegance alone should find this one steadily diverting, despite its monotonous pace and length. Indeed, the fans of James M. Cain's tough fiction might gloat over it with gleaming joy. For Billy Wilder has filmed the Cain story of the brassy couple who attempt a "perfect crime," in order to collect some insurance, with a realism reminiscent of the bite of past French films He has detailed the stalking of their victim with the frigid thoroughness of a coroner's report, and he has pictured their psychological crack-up as a sadist would pluck out a spider's legs. No objection to the temper of this picture; it is as hard and inflexible as steel.

But the very toughness of the picture is also the weakness of its core, and the academic nature of its plotting limits its general appeal. The principal characters—an insurance salesman and a wicked woman, which Mr. MacMurray and Miss Stanwyck play—lack the attractiveness to render their fate of emotional consequences. And the fact that the story is told in flashback disposes its uncertainty. Miss Stanwyck gives ,a good surface performance of a destructively lurid female, but Mr. MacMurray is a bit too ingenuous as the gent who falls precipitately under her spell. And the ease of his fall is also questionable. One look at the lady's ankles and he's cooked.

The performance of Mr. Robinson, however, as a smart adjuster of insurance claims is a fine bit of characterization within its allotment of space. With a bitter brand of humor and irritability, he creates a formidable guy. As a matter of fact, Mr. Robinson is the only one you care two hoots for in the film. The rest are just neatly carved pieces in a variably intriguing crime game.

S 7, 1944

'Winged Victory,' Stunning Film Version of Air Force Show, Opens at the Roxy

WINGED VICTORY, stage and screen play by Moss Hart; directed by George Cukor; produced by Darryl F. Zanuck for Twentieth Century-Fox. At the Roxy.
Frankie Davis..............Pvt. Lon McCallister

Helen............................	Jeanne Crain
Irving Miller..............	Sgt. Edmond O'Brien
Jane Preston....................	Jane Ball
Alan Ross....................	Sgt. Mark Daniels
Dorothy Ross.............	Jo-Carroll Dennison
Danny (Pinky) Scariano.....	..Cpl. Don Taylor
Ruth Miller...............	Judy Holliday
Doctor.........................	Cpl. Lee J. Cobb
O'Brian.................	T/Sgt. Peter Lind Hayes
Major Halper.................	Cpl. Alan Baxter
Mrs. Ross....................	Geraldine Wall
Whitey	Cpl. Red Buttons
Bobby Grills.................	Cpl. Barry Nelson
Dave Anderson..............	Sgt. Rune Hultman
Captain McIntyre............	Cpl. Garry Merrill
Lieut. Thompson............	Sgt. George Reeves
Barker......................	Pfc. George Petrie
Milhauser....................	Pfc. Alfred Ryder
Adams......................	Cpl. Karl Malden
Gleason......................	Pfc. Martin Ritt
Cadet Peter Clark...........	Cpl. Harry Lewis
Flight Surgeon............	Corp. Henry Rowland
Carmen Miranda........	S/Sgt. Sascha Brastoff
Master of Ceremonies.......	Cpl. Archie Robbins
Andrews Sisters..............	Cpl. Jack Slate / Cpl. Red Buttons / Pfc. Henry Slate

By BOSLEY CROWTHER

The Army Air Force show, "Winged Victory," which was a big and deserving hit upon the stage, has now been transposed into the medium which was most appropriate to it all the time—the large-scale and swiftly fluid medium of the motion-picture screen. And, as it looked yesterday at the Roxy, where it opened amid a rout of brass and pomp, it gives every promise of being one of the most successful films about this war.

Successful, that is, in its disturbance of the public's interest and pulse and also in its encroachments upon the public's pocketbook. For Darryl F. Zanuck, who produced it as a film for Twentieth Century-Fox, has put into it all the spectacle that the original so narrowly implied. He and the Air Force's big-wigs—who, after all, are the "angels," as it were—have given it a stunning production, with real planes and training fields and men. They have photographed invivid actuality all the outdoor scenes that were limited on the stage and they have pictured, from the earth-bound looker's viewpoint, all the wonder that the "wide blue yonder" holds.

Furthermore, George Cukor, the director, has kept all the poignancy and zeal that was tightly compacted in the episodes of Moss Hart's original play. Only now the continuity flows easily and fast in a natural scenic pattern that carries great conviction on the screen. And the story of a group of fledgling airmen, from the day they are called into the Force until just one survivor of the trio takes off on a mission against the Nips, has the sweep and mounting tension of true visual narrative.

All profits from this picture will go to Army charities, which is all the more reason to be happy over the prospect of its popularity and success.

To be sure, Mr. Hart's play had something of an effervescent quality which may have been slightly more theatrical than literal, and this is also in the film. It is hard to believe that most new cadets are as volatile as some of the youngsters imaged here. And the story, both originally and in the picture, leans quite obviously on its sentimental props. But there is no question that Mr. Hart captured much of the gallantry and patros of youth rushing toward dangerous adventures wits surface enthusiasm and inner dread. There is no question that he sensed clearly the irony of young folks on the threshold of life having to live with the peril of death and killing. And all of this is staged well in the film, too.

Many of the Air Force soldiers who were in the stage play are likewise on the screen, and they perform their roles with the rare competence that was so marked in the original. Sgt. Edmond O'Brien as the chap from Brooklyn and Corp. Don Taylor as the voluble lad who "washes out" are distinguished, perhaps because they plainly have the most appealing things to do. But Pvt. Lon McCallister is effective as the youngster who gets killed on a training flight and Sgt. Mark Daniels is strikingly natural as the steadiest man in the group. Dozens of other fellows are splendid in minor roles, and the females enlisted for the picture are all most refreshing and good.

D 21, 1944

THE SOUTHERNER; screen play by Jean Renoir; adapted by Hugo Butler; based on the novel "Hold Autumn In Your Hand," by George Sessions Perry; directed by Mr. Renoir; produced by David L. Loew and Robert Hakim; a Producing Artists picture released through United Artists.

Sam Tucker	Zachary Scott
Nona Tucker	Betty Field
Granny	Beulah Bondi
Daisy	Jean Vanderwilt
Jot	Jay Gilpin
Devers	J. Carrol Naish
Finlay	Norman Lloyd
Tim	Charles Kemper
Ma	Blanche Yurka
Bartender	Nestor Paiva
Becky	Noreen Roth
Lizzie	Estelle Taylor
Doctor	Jack Norworth
Party Girl	Dorothy Grange

The poor, white sharecropper probably as unfashionable a subject for screen treatment as could be contemplated, has been given forthright, sympathetic and seemingly honest expression in "The Southerner." For the drama, which came to the Globe on Saturday, has invested its persevering farm family not only with the blights of poverty, pellagra and crop-destroying storm but also with dignity, humility, indigenous humor and a vestige of hope. Essentially the story of one man's overpowering love of the good earth in the face of bitter adversity and despite the prospects of a different, easier way of life, "The Southerner" is a worthy addition to the year's roster of fine films.

It does not matter greatly whether Jean Renoir, who wrote the screen play as well as directed this basically grim pastoral, adhered to the letter or the spirit of "Hold Autumn in Your Hand," the George Sessions Perry novel on which the picture was based. What does matter is that he has understandingly shown, through a series of leisurely paced but artistically integrated vignettes, the pathos and humor of a year's struggle in the life of Sam Tucker and his tenant-farming clan. There is genuine drama in the resolute endeavors of the migrant Tuckers to make their newly leased ramshackle house and brush-strewn fallow acres livable and productive. There is an absence of cliché and a wealth of humanity in little Jot Tucker's "spring sickness" for want of milk and fresh vegetables; or in the shooting of the possum which staves off starvation.

There is, too, the genuine humor of a riotous country wedding and a barroom brawl. There is Sam's vicious knife and fist fight with his sour, antagonistic neighbor, and there is the final heart-rending moment when the cotton, ready for harvest, is devastated by rain and flood. In all, Jean Renoir has subtly combined his camera with sparse dialogue in the native idiom to tell his story simply and beautifully and without resorting to opinion or prejudice. But it would be an injustice not to credit equally some of the cast. Zachary Scott is excellent and outstanding as the young, determined head of the despair-tagged group. His portrayal is at once restrained and powerful. And Betty Field, as his tireless wife; J. Carrol Naish, as the embittered neighbor; Charles Kemper, as the friend of the family; Beulah Bondi, as the acidulous grandmother of the brood, and Norman Lloyd, as a vindictive farm hand, all contribute vigorous characterizations.

"The Southerner" may not be an "entertainment" in the rigid Hollywood sense and it may have some flaws, but it is, nevertheless, a rich, unusual and sensitive delineation of a segment of the American scene well worth filming and seeing.   A. W.

Ag 27, 1945

'Spellbound,' a Psychological Hit Starring Ingrid Bergman and Gregory Peck, Opens at Astor — Hitchcock Director

SPELLBOUND; screen play by Ben Hecht; based on the novel, "The House of Dr. Edwardes," by Francis Beeding; directed by Alfred Hitchcock; produced by David O. Selznick and released by United Artists. At the Astor.

Dr. Constance Peterson........Ingrid Bergman
J. B. ....Gregory Peck
Matron ....Jean Acker
Harry ....Donald Curtis
Miss Carmichael ....Rhonda Fleming
Dr. Fleurot ....John Emery
Dr. Murchison ....Leo G. Carroll
Garmes ... .Norman Lloyd
Dr. Alex Brulov ....Michael Chekhov
Dr. Graff ... .Steven Geray
Dr. Hanish ....Paul Harvey
Dr. Gall ....Erskine Sanford
Sheriff ....Victor Kilian
Stranger ....Wallace Ford
House Detective ....Bill Goodwin
Bellboy ....Dave Willock
Norma ....Janet Scott
Sgt. Gillespie ....Regis Toomey
Police Captain ....Addison Richards
Lieut. Cooley ....Art Baker

By BOSLEY CROWTHER

This writer has had little traffic with practitioners of psychiatry or with the twilight abstractions of their science, so we are not in a position to say whether Ingrid Bergman, who plays one in her latest film, "Spellbound," is typical of such professionals or whether the methods she employs would yield results. But this we can say with due authority: if all psychiatrists are as charming as she— and if their attentions to all their patients are as fruitful as hers are to Gregory Peck, who plays a victim of amnesia in this fine film which came to the Astor yesterday —then psychiatry deserves such popularity as this picture most certainly will enjoy.

For Miss Bergman and her brand of treatment, so beautifully demonstrated here, is a guaranteed cure for what ails you, just as much as it is for Mr. Peck. It consists of her winning personality, softly but insistently suffused through a story of deep emotional content; of her ardent sincerity, her lustrous looks and her easy ability to toss off glibly a line of talk upon which most girls would choke.

In other words, lovely Miss Bergman is both the doctor and prescription in this film. She is the single stimulation of dramatic logic and audience belief. For the fact is the story of "Spellbound" is a rather obvious and often-told tale. And it depends, despite its truly expert telling, upon the illusion of the lady in the leading role.

It is the story of a female psychiatrist who falls suddenly and desperately in love with a man upon whom the dark suspicion of murder is relentlessly cast. All of the circumstantial evidence indicates that he has taken the dead man's place and is trying to assume his position—that is, until he prudently flees. But the lady, with full and touching confidence in the intuitive rightness of her love, is convinced that her adored one is most truly a victim of amnesia. And so she follows him to his place in hiding, begins the bold attempt to unlock his mind and, always two jumps ahead of detectives, finally delves the gnawing secret of his past.

This story, we say, has relation to all the faith-healing films ever made, but the manner and quality of its telling is extraordinarily fine. The script, which was based on the novel of Francis Beeding "The House of Dr. Edwardes," was prepared by Ben Hecht and the director was Alfred Hitchcock, the old master of dramatic suspense. So the firm texture of the narration, the flow of continuity and dialogue, the shock of the unexpected, the scope of image—all are happily here.

But, in this particular instance, Mr. Hecht and Mr. Hitchcock have done more. They have fashioned a moving love story with the elements of melodramatic use. More than a literal "chase" takes place here—more than a run from the police. A "chase" of even more suspenseful moment is made through the mind of a man. And in this strange and indeterminate area the pursuer—and, partially, the pursued—is the girl with whom the victim is mutually in love. Mr. Hitchcock has used some startling images to symbolize the content of dreams—images designed by Salvador Dali. But his real success is in creating the illusion of love.

Miss Bergman, as we say, is his chief asset in accomplishing the sincerity of this film, but Mr. Peck is also a large contributor. His performance, restrained and refined, is precisely the proper counter to Miss Bergman's exquisite role. Michael Chekhov is likewise responsible for some of the excellent humor in this film, playing an elderly psychiatrist and an accomplice in Miss Bergman's mental "chase." Leo G. Carroll, Wallace Ford and John Emery contribute excellent smaller roles.

Not to be speechless about it, David O. Selznick has a rare film in "Spellbound."

N 2, 1945

THE LOST WEEKEND, screen play by Charles Brackett and Billy Wilder; from the novel by Charles R. Jackson; directed by Mr. Wilder; produced by Mr. Brackett for Paramount. At the Rivoli.

Don Birnam .... Ray Milland
Helen St. James .... Jane Wyman
Wick Birnam .... Philip Terry
Nat .... Howard da Silva
Gloria .... Doris Dowling
Bim .... Frank Faylen
Mrs. Beveridge .... Mary Young
Mrs. Foley .... Anita Bolster
Mrs. St. James .... Lilian Fontaine
Mr. St. James .... Lewis L. Russell
Hat-check Man .... Frank Orth

By BOSLEY CROWTHER

The stark and terrifying study of a dipsomaniac which Charles R. Jackson wrote so vividly and truly in his novel, "The Lost Weekend," has been brought to the screen with great fidelity in every respect but one: the reason for the "dipso's" gnawing mania is not fully and convincingly explained. In the novel, the basic frustration which drove the pitiable "hero" to drink was an unconscious indecision in his own masculine libido. In the film, which bears the same title and which came to the Rivoli on Saturday, the only cause given for his "illness" is the fact that he has writer's cramp. That is, he can't make himself accomplish a burning ambition to write.

However, this single shortcoming is a minor detraction, at worst, from a shatteringly realistic and morbidly fascinating film. For Paramount's ace brace of craftsmen, Billy Wilder and Charles Brackett, have done such a job with their pens and their cameras as puts all recent "horror" films to shame. They have also achieved in the process an illustration of a drunkard's misery that ranks with the best and most disturbing character studies ever put on the screen. "The Lost Weekend" is truly a chef d'oeuvre of motion-picture art.

In imaging the gruesome details of five days in the life of a chronic 'lush'—five days during which this poor unfortunate is on one of his periodic "bats"—the Messrs. Brackett and Wilder have been as graphic and candid in their report as was Mr. Jackson in his novel—and that was almost too candid to bear. They have picked up their man at that moment when he is thirsting desperately for another go at his bottle, have indexed the dogged stratagems by which he evades his watchful brother and his sweetheart in getting at some booze, and then they have followed his debauch through a series of episodes which scarcely have a parallel as reflections of mortifying shame. These include his unblushing importunities of a bartender, begging for drinks; a horribly humiliating encounter when he is caught stealing money from a woman's purse, a racking walk along New York's Third Avenue, trying to pawn a typewriter for some cash, and a a staggeringly ugly experience in the Bellevue alcoholic ward. A bout of delirium tremens is also made blood-chillingly real—in a sharp, photographic comprehension, not with the usual phantasmagoric tricks.

Most impressive throughout the picture is the honesty with which it has been made. It seems a case-history documentation in its narrative and photographic styles. Mr. Wilder, who helped write and directed it, brought his camera and leading player to New York for those scenes which convey the grim relation of the individual to the vast, unknowing mass. And he kept a sharp tone of actuality in all of his studio work. The film's most commendable distinction is that it is a straight objective report, unvarnished with editorial comment or temperance morality.

And yet the ill of alcoholism and the pathos of its sufferers are most forcefully exposed and deeply pitied, thanks also to the playing of Ray Milland. Mr. Milland, in a splendid performance, catches all the ugly nature of a "drunk," yet reveals the inner torment and degradation of a respectable man who knows his weakness and his shame. Jane Wyman assumes with quiet authority the difficult role of the loyal girl who loves and assists the central character—and finally helps regenerate him. (This climactic touch is somewhat off key—like the "cute" way in which the two meet—but it has the advantage of relieving an intolerable emotional strain.)   Howard   da

Silva is tough and ironic as a disapproving bartender. Frank Faylen is glib as a sadistic male nurse and Philip Terry plays the brother meekly and well.

We would not recommend this picture for a gay evening on the town. But it is certainly an overwhelming drama which every adult movie-goer should see.

D 3, 1945

WALK IN THE SUN, screen play by Robert Rossen, from the novel by Harry Brown; directed by Lewis Milestone; ballad by Millard Lampell and Earl Robinson; produced by Mr. Milestone and distributed by Twentieth Century-Fox. At the Victoria.

Sergeant Tyne	Dana Andrews
Rivera	Richard Conte
McWilliams	Sterling Holloway
Friedman	George Tyne
Windy	John Ireland
Porter	Herbert Rudley
Tranella	Richard Benedict
Archimbeau	Norman Lloyd
Sergeant Ward	Lloyd Bridges
Carraway	Huntz Hall
Hoskins	James Cardwell
Rankin	Chris Drake
Tinker	George Offerman Jr.
Trasker	Danny Desmond
Cousins	Victor Cutler
Judson	Steve Brodie
Johnson	Al Hammer
Sergeant Halverson	Matt Willis
Lieutenant Rand	Robert Lowell
Giorgio	Anthony Dante

By BOSLEY CROWTHER

Your response to Lewis Milestone's brave film version of Harry Brown's classic war story, "A Walk in the Sun," will likely depend, proportionally speaking, on whether you have read the book. And if you haven't had the rare experience of absorbing the original, then you will surely find this film at the Victoria a swiftly overpowering piece of work. For Mr. Milestone, producing and directing, has followed Mr. Brown's intense report of a small beachhead maneuver near Salerno in a literal reproduction of episodes.

He has picked up the platoon of American infantry, which is the collective protagonist of the tale, at precisely the point that Mr. Brown did—as its landing barge drives toward the beach. He has faithfully recorded with his camera the calamity which befell the lieutenant, the confusion of the sergeants and their dilemma as they go ashore. And then, in a sequence of vignettes which include the subsequent actions and talk of twenty of the men, he has followed the platoon as it probes inland toward a farmhouse—its perilous "walk in the sun."

"The book was my script," said Mr. Milestone to someone, the other day, and that is substantially evident. For virtually every detail, with a few technical alterations, has been photographed sequentially from the book. As a consequence and in a manner which achieves the fullest from the photograph, he has captured in illustration the complex tensions of that desperate, ravaging "walk." He has given a completely graphic picture of the natures and responses of the various men, their humors and whims and nerve reflexes as they move in isolation toward the unknown.

In this, Mr. Milestone has been aided by a generally superlative cast—a score of speaking actors who play infantry men credibly. Most impressive is Dana Andrews, who makes of Corporal (here Sergeant) Tyne an intelligent acute and sensitive leader of the pathetically confused but stubborn group. Richard Conte is robutly endearing as a cheeky machine-gunner, and Sterling Holloway, George Tyne and Lloyd Bridges are variously appealing in other roles. A bit of theatrical ostentation is in Herbert Rudley's Sergeant Porter (he's the one who cracks up) and Norman Lloyd is plainly acting as the cold and cryptic Archimbeau. However, the performance in toto is consistent with the film's authentic tone.

But readers of the book are almost certain to find the picture falls considerably short of the cumulative force of the original—and that is, perhaps, inevitable. It is patent that the camera's observation cannot lay bare the insides of the men as did Mr. Brown's lean, unvarnished and thoroughly comprehending prose. The terrible uncertainty of the soldiers, the oppressive sense of lurking peril and doom, all the inner stress suggested in the writing is but surfacely envisioned on the screen. And the transcendent bomb-burst of emotion which forms the climax of the book is not achieved.

Mr. Milestone has hopefully endeavored to lift the audience to a high, reflective plane from time to time by handing the soundtrack to a singer of heroic ballad-verse. The music and words are disturbing but the device does not come off too well, mainly because it encroaches upon the illusion of the literal scene. Mr. Milestone should not have attempted to mix real and expressionistic styles. His picture is most effective when it dramatically documents.

However, don't let these side discourses deter you from seeing the film. "A Walk in the Sun" is unquestionably one of the fine, sincere pictures about the war.

Ja 12, 1946

OPEN CITY (CITTA APERTA). screen play by Sergio Amidel and F. Fellini: directed by Roberto Rosselini: English titles by Pietro di Donato and Herman G. Weinberg: produced in Italy by Excelsa and released in United States by Mayer-Burstyn, Inc. At the World.
Manfredi.....................Marcello Pagliero
Don Pietro.........................Aldo Fabrizi
Pina.............................Anna Magnani
Marcello....................Vito Annicchiarico
Marina Mari......................Maria Michi
Capt. Bergmann....................Harry Feist
Francesco............Francesco Grandjacquet
Ingrid........................Giovanna Galletti
Lauretta..........................Carla Revere
The Sexton.......................Nando Bruno
Police Warden.......................Passarelli
Chief of Police......................C. Sindici
Hartman..........................Van Hulzen
Austrian Deserter..................A. Tolnay

By BOSLEY CROWTHER

It may seem peculiarly ironic that the first film yet seen hereabouts to dramatize the nature and the spirit of underground resistance in German-held Europe in a superior way—with candid, overpowering realism and with a passionate sense of human fortitude—should be a film made in Italy. Yet such is the extraordinary case: "Open City" ("Citta Aperta"), which arrived at the World last night, is unquestionably one of the strongest dramatic films yet made about the recent war. And the fact that it was hurriedly put together

From The New York Times Film Reviews

by a group of artists soon after the liberation of Rome is significant of its fervor and doubtless integrity.

For such a picture as "Open City" would not likely be made under normal and established conditions. In the first place, it has the wind-blown look of a film shot from actualities, with the camera providentially on the scene. All of its exterior action is in the streets and open places of Rome; the interior scenes are played quite obviously in actual buildings or modest sets. The stringent necessity for economy compelled the producers to make a film that has all the appearance and flavor of a straight documentary.

And the feeling that pulses through it gives evidence that it was inspired by artists whose own emotions had been deeply and recently stirred. Anger, grim and determined, against the Germans and collaborationists throbs in every sequence and every shot in which the evil ones are shown. Yet the anger is not shrill or hysterical; it is the clarified anger of those who have known and dreaded the cruelty and depravity of men who are their foes. It is anger long since drained of astonishment or outrage.

More than anger, however, the feeling that flows most strongly through the film is one of supreme admiration for the people who fight for freedom's cause. It is a quiet exaltation, conveyed mainly through attitudes and simple words, illuminating the spirit of devotion and sacrifice. The heroes in "Open City" are not conscious of being such. Nor are the artists who conceived them. They are simple people doing what they think is right.

The story of the film is literal. It might have been taken from the notes of any true observer in occupied Europe—and, indeed, is said to have been based on actual facts. It is the story of an underground agent who is cornered by the Germans in a certain quarter of Rome and who barely escapes them until he is informed upon by his own girl friend. In the course of his flight he necessarily involves his resistance friends: a printer of an underground newspaper, his wife-to-be and her small son, and a neighborhood priest who uses his religious office to aid freedom's cause. The woman is killed during a raid on an apartment, the captured resistance leader is tortured to death and the priest is shot when he refuses to assist the Germans with any information.

All these details are presented in a most frank and uncompromising way which is likely to prove somewhat shocking to sheltered American audiences.

Yet the total effect of the picture is a sense of real experience, achieved as much by the performance as by the writing and direction. The outstanding performance is that of Aldo Fabrizi as the priest, who embraces with dignity and humanity a most demanding part.

Marcello Pagliero is excellent, too, as the resistance leader, and Anna Magnani brings humility and sincerity to the role of the woman who is killed. The remaining cast is unqualifiedly fine, with the exception of Harry Feist in the role of the German commander. His elegant arrogance is a bit too vicious—but that may be easily understood.

F 26, 1946

HENRY V, based on the play by William Shakespeare, edited by Laurence Olivier and Reginald Beck; directed and produced by Mr. Olivier; scenery and costumes by Paul Sheriff and Roger Furse; music by William Walton. A Two Cities Film, released by United Artists. At the City Center.

King Henry V................Laurence Olivier
Ancient Pistol..................Robert Newton
Chorus........................Leslie Banks
Princess Katharine............Renee Asherson
Fluellen.......................Esmond Knight
The Constable of France..........Leo Genn
Archbishop of Canterbury........Felix Aylmer
Mountjoy, the French Herald....Ralph Truman
King Charles VI. of France..Harcourt Williams
Alice, Lady-in-Waiting..........Ivy St. Helier
Duke of Berl..................Ernest Thesiger
The Dauphin.....................Max Adrian
Duke of Orleans................Frances Lister
Duke of Burgundy............Valentine Dyall
Duke of Bourbon............Russell Thorndike
Captain Gower.................Michael Shepley
Sir Thomas Erpingham........Morland Graham
Earl of Westmoreland............Gerald Case
Queen Isabel of France........Janet Burnell
Duke of Exeter................Nicholas Hannen
Bishop of Ely.............Robert Helpmann
Mistress Quickly.................Freda Jackson
Williams.....................Jimmy Hanley
Captain Jamie..................John Laurie
Captain MacMorris.............Niall MacGinnis
Sir John Falstaff...............George Robey

Lieutenant Bardolph..............Roy Emerton
Earl of Salisbury..... ....Griffith Jones
Bates ....Arthur Hambling
Corporal Nym................Frederick Cooper
Duke of Gloucester.............Michael Warre

By BOSLEY CROWTHER

Out of Will Shakespeare's rather turgid "Chronicle Historie of King Henry the Fifth"—more concisely and conveniently titled for this occasion simply "Henry V"—a fine group of British film craftsmen and actors, headed by Laurence Olivier, have concocted a stunningly brilliant and intriguing screen spectacle, rich in theatrical invention, in heroic imagery and also gracefully regardful of the conventions of the Elizabethan stage. They have further achieved the full eloquence of Shakespeare's tribute to a conquering English king in this Theatre Guild-sponsored motion picture, which opened at the City Center last night.

The reason for choosing this chronicle out of all the bard's better-known plays for production in Britain during wartime has not been mentioned by Mr. Olivier. But the enticement is fairly apparent: there was provided in "Henry V" a most tempting and timely opportunity for expansive cinematic display. The mounting and execution of the battle of Agincourt, which is the play's and the film's central drama, offered a spectacle too gorgeous to resist. And the theme of traditional English triumph on the Continent was appropriate to the day.

Certainly the story in this chronicle could not have lured Mr. Olivier too much, nor could the chance to explore a complex character have been the bait to draw him on. For the reasons for Henry's expedition against France, as laid down in the play, are neither flattering to him nor to his churchly counselors. The Bishops conspire to urge Henry to carry his claims against France in order to distract the Commons from confiscating their lands; and Henry apparently falls for it, out of sheer royal vanity and greed. His invasion of France is quite clearly a war of aggrandizement, and his nature appears slightly naive when he argues the justice of his cause.

But that, of course, is Shakespeare; and Mr. Olivier and his editor, Reginald Beck, have not attempted to change it. They have simply cut large chunks out of the play, especially the plot of the traitors, to get at the action and the meat. Thus reduced of excessive conversations (though it might have been trimmed even more), they have mounted the play with faithful service to the spirit and the word. That service is as truly magnificent as any ever given to a Shakespearian script, both in visual conception and in the acting of an excellent cast.

The film begins as a picturization of a performance at the Globe Theatre, with the arrival of the Elizabethan audience and preparation backstage. For students of Shakespearian stagecraft, this introduction is fascinating. And the early scenes are played within the confines and on the stages of the picturesque "wooden O." Then, as the Chorus advises to "eke out our performance with your mind," the character of the visualization lapses into naturalistic style, but with the scenes still played in the foreground against painted backdrops, as though seen through an invisible proscenium arch. This technique permits the embroidery of the motion-picture screen with images that have the texture of rich and silken animated tapestries.

It is only when the action develops to the night before Agincourt, in the quiet and vigilant camp of the English, that a realistic style is employed, and here Mr. Olivier has directed for action on a broad, spectacular scale. The night scenes in the camp are tense and thoughtful, as Henry, incognito, moves about, musing on war with his nervous soldiers. And then the violence explodes as the ringing, racing battle of Agincourt is fought in all its medieval pomp. The tumult of the armorers' preparations, the stretch of bowmen and the clash of steel-casqued knights is vividly recreated. Not since "The Birth of a Nation" do we recall a more thrilling and eerie charge of horsemen than the charge of the knights in "Henry V."

This emphasis upon the spectacular has not absorbed Mr. Olivier to the point of neglecting the subtleties and eloquence of Shakespeare's verse and prose. And Mr. Olivier's own performance of Henry sets a standard for excellence. His majestic and heroic bearing, his full and vibrant use of his voice, create a kingly figure around which the other characters rightly spin. And Leslie Banks, in the role of the Chorus, is his match in eloquence. Due and sufficient credit cannot be given the entire excellent cast, but mention must be made of Harcourt Williams' splendid portrait of the senile King of France, Max Adrian's pompous mincing as the Dauphin and Robert Newton's posturing as the clown Pistol. Renee Asherson is also very lovely and gracefully piquant in two scenes as the Princess Katharine, whose conversations are almost wholly in French.

Mr. Olivier has leaned perhaps too heavily toward the comic characters in the play—at least, for American audiences, which will find the dialects a little hard to get. The scenes with the Welsh and Irish captains are too parochial for our taste. And certainly the writing-in completely of the Falstaff deathbed scene, with the echoing voice of Harry carrying over from "Henry IV, Part Two," is obviously non-essential and just a bit grotesque.

However, in all other matters— in the use of music, in the brilliance of costumes (which appear most remarkably exciting in the Technicolor employed), in toning the whole film to the senses—Mr. Olivier has done a tasteful job. Thanks to him and to all those who helped him, we have a glowing "touch of Harry in the night."

Je 18, 1946

NOTORIOUS; screen play by Ben Hecht; directed and produced by Alfred Hitchcock for RKO-Radio Pictures. At the Radio City Music Hall.
Devlin ....Cary Grant
Alicia Huberman...............Ingrid Bergman
Alexander Sebastian..............Claude Rains
Paul Prescott...................Louis Calhern
Mme. Sebastian...........Madame Konstantin
"Dr. Anderson".............Reinhold Schunzel
Walter Beardsley.................Moroni Olsen
Eric Mathis......................Ivan Triesault
Joseph.............................Alex Minotis
Mr. Hopkins......................Wally Brown
Commodore..................Sir Charles Mendl

By BOSLEY CROWTHER

It is obvious that Alfred Hitchcock, Ben Hecht and Ingrid Bergman form a team of motion-picture makers that should be publicly and heavily endowed. For they were the ones most responsible for "Spellbound," as director, writer and star, and now they have teamed together on another taut, superior film. It goes by the name of "Notorious" and it opened yesterday at the Music Hall. With Cary Grant as an additional asset, it is one of the most absorbing pictures of the year.

For Mr. Hecht has written and Mr. Hitchcock has directed in brilliant style a romantic melodrama which is just about as thrilling as they come—velvet smooth in dramatic action, sharp and sure in its characters and heavily charged with the intensity of warm emotional appeal. As a matter of fact, the distinction of "Notorious" as a film is the remarkable blend of love story with expert "thriller" that it represents.

Actually, the "thriller" elements are familiar and commonplace, except in so far as Mr. Hitchcock has galvanized them into life. They comprise the routine ingredients of a South American Nazi-exile gang, an American girl set to spy upon it and a behind-the-scenes American intelligence man. And the crux of the melodramatic action is the peril of the girl when the nature of her assignment is discovered by one of the Nazis whom she has wed.

But the rare quality of the picture is in the uncommon character of the girl and in the drama of her relations with the American intelligence man. For here Mr. Hecht and Mr. Hitchcock have done a forthright and daring thing: they have made the girl, played by Miss Bergman, a lady of notably loose morals. She is the logically cynical daughter of a convicted American traitor when she is

224

pressed into this job of high-echelon spying by the confident espionage man. The complication is that she and the latter fall passionately and genuinely in love before the demands of her assignment upon her seductive charms are revealed. And thus the unpleasant suspicions and the lacerated feelings of the two as they deal with this dangerous major problem form the emotional drama of the film.

Obviously, that situation might seem slightly old-fashioned, too. But Mr. Hecht and Mr. Hitchcock have here treated it with sophistication and irony. There is nothing unreal or puritanical in their exposure of a frank, grown-up amour. And Miss Bergman and Mr. Grant have played it with surprising and disturbing clarity. We do not recall a more conspicuous—yet emotionally delicate—love scene on the screen than one stretch of billing and cooing that the principals play in this film. Yet, withal, there is rich and real emotion expressed by Miss Bergman in her role, and the integrity of her nature as she portrays it is the prop that holds the show.

Mr. Grant, who is exceptionally solid, is matched for acting honors in the cast by Claude Rains as the Nazi big-wig, to whom Miss Bergman becomes attached. Mr. Rains' shrewd and tense performance of this invidious character is responsible for much of the anguish that the situation creates. Reinhold Schunzel and Ivan Triesault are good, too, as Nazi worms, and a splendid touch of chilling arrogance as a German mother is added by Madame Konstantin. Louis Calhern and Moroni Olsen are fine in minor American roles.

Check up another smash hit for a fine and experienced team.

On the stage at the Music Hall is a revue spectacle entitled "Colorama," featuring Estelle Sloan, Joyce Renee, Bob Williams, Rabana Hasburgh and Charles Laskey, the Corps de Ballet, Glee Club and Rockettes.

Ag 16, 1946

BRIEF ENCOUNTER, screen play by Noel Coward, based on his one-act play, "Still Life"; directed by David Lean; produced by Mr. Coward in England and released in this country by Prestige Pictures, Inc. At the Little Carnegie Theatre.
Laura Jesson...............Celia Johnson
Dr. Alec Harvey............Trevor Howard
Fred Jesson................Cyril Raymond
Barmaid....................Joyce Carey
Station Guard..............Stanley Holloway
Stephan Lynn...............Valentine Dyall
Dolly Messiter.............Everley Gregg
Beryl......................Margaret Barton
Stanley....................Dennis Harkin

By BOSLEY CROWTHER

An uncommonly good little picture—and one which is frankly designed to appeal to that group of film-goers who are provoked by the "usual movie tripe"—is the British-made "Brief Encounter," which opened on Saturday at the Little Carnegie Theatre as the first of so-called Prestige imports.

Being no more than an expansion of one of Noel Coward's one-act plays—the conversational "Still Life," from his "Tonight at 8:30" group—it is plainly an intimate drama, limited in every respect to the brief and extremely poignant romance of a married woman and a married man. And virtually all of the action takes place in a railway waiting-room and in the small English town adjacent thereto, where the couple make their fleeting rendezvous.

That's all there is to the story—a quite ordinary middle-class wife, contentedly married and the mother of two children, meets a similarly settled doctor one day while on a weekly shopping visit to a town near that in which she lives. The casual and innocent acquaintance, renewed on successive weeks, suddenly ripens into a deep affection by which both are shaken and shocked. For a brief spell they spin in the bewilderment of conventions and their own emotional ties. Then they part, the doctor to go away and the wife to return to her home.

There are obvious flaws in the story. The desperate affection of the two develops a great deal more rapidly than the circumstances would seem to justify. And the cheerful obtuseness of the lady's husband is more accommodating than one would expect. But the whole thing has been presented in such a delicate and affecting way —and with such complete naturalness in characterization and fidelity to middle-class detail—that those slight discrepancies in logic may be easily allowed.

Under David Lean's fluid direction, Celia Johnson, who was memorable as the commander's wife in Mr. Coward's fine "In Which We Serve," gives a consuming performance as the emotionally shaken lady in the case. Unprettified by make-up and quite plainly and consistently dressed, she is naturally and honestly disturbing with her wistful voice and large, sad saucer-eyes. And Trevor Howard, who has none of the aspects of a cut-out movie star, makes a thoroughly credible partner in this small and pathetic romance. Excellent, too, as characters in a flat, middle-class milieu are Joyce Carey, Cyril Raymond, Everley Gregg and Stanley Holloway.

Ag 26, 1946

MY DARLING CLEMENTINE, screen play by Samuel G. Engel and Winston Miller; based on a story by Sam Hellman; from a book by Stuart N. Lake; directed by John Ford, produced by Mr. Engel for Twentieth Century-Fox. At the Rivoli.

Wyatt Earp	Henry Fonda
Chihuahua	Linda Darnell
Doc Holliday	Victor Mature
Old Man Clanton	Walter Brennan
Virgil Earp	Tim Holt
Clementine	Cathy Downs
Morgan Earp	Ward Bond
Thorndyke	Alan Mowbray
Billy Clanton	John Ireland
Mayer	Roy Roberts
Kate Nelson	Jane Darwell
Ike Clanton	Grant Withers
Bartender	J. Farrell MacDonald
John Simpson	Russell Simpson
James Earp	Don Garner
Town Drunk	Francis Ford
Barber	Ben Hall
Hotel Clerk	Arthur Walsh

By BOSLEY CROWTHER

Let's be specific about this: The eminent director, John Ford, is a man who has a way with a Western like nobody in the picture trade. Seven years ago his classic "Stagecoach" snuggled very close to fine are in this genre. And now, by George, he's almost matched it with "My Darling Clementine."

Not quite, it is true—for this picture, which came to the Rivoli yesterday, is a little too burdened with conventions of Western fic-

tion to place it on a par. Too obvious a definition of heroes and villains is observed, and the standardized aspect of romance is too neatly and respectably entwined. But a dynamic composition of Western legend and scenery is still achieved. And the rich flavor of frontiering wafts in overpowering redolence from the screen.

In this particular instance, Mr. Ford and Twentieth Century-Fox are telling an oft-repeated story from the treasury of Western lore. It's the story of that famous frontier marshal who "cleaned up" Tombstone, Ariz. — Wyatt Earp. And if that doesn't place him precisely in the history catalogue, rest assured that he's been model for film heroes ever since the days of William S. Hart. And since legend is being respected, as well as the conventions of the screen, it is the story of Wyatt's dauntless conquest of a gang of rustlers and a maiden's heart.

But even with standard Western fiction—and that's what the script has enjoined—Mr. Ford can evoke fine sensations and curiously-captivating moods. From the moment that Wyatt and his brothers are discovered on the wide and dusty range, trailing a herd of cattle to a far-off promised land, a tone of pictorial authority is struck—and it is held. Every scene, every shot is the product of a keen and sensitive eye—and eye which has deep comprehension of the beauty of rugged people and a rugged world.

As the set for this film, a fine facsimile of frontier Tombstone was patiently built in the desert of Monument Valley, and it was there that Mr. Ford shot most of the picture. And he is a man who knows that Westerns belong, in the main, out of doors. When he catches a horseman or a stagecoach thumping across the scrubby wastes, the magnificences of nature—the sky and desert—dwarf the energies of man. Yet his scenes of intensity and violence are played very much to the fore, with the rawness and meanness of the frontier to set his vital human beings in relief.

And the humans whom Mr. Ford imagines are not the ordinary stereotypes of films, no matter how hackneyed and conventional the things they are supposed to do. Henry Fonda, for instance, plays a Wyatt Earp such as we've never seen before—a leathery, laconic young cowpoke who truly suggests a moral aim. Through his quiet yet persuasive self-confidence—his delicious intonation of short words—he shows us an elemental character who is as real as the dirt on which he walks.

And Walter Brennan is completely characteristic as the scabby old desert rattlesnake whose villainous murder of Wyatt's brother sets off the dramatic fireworks. Even the mawkish fabrication of a young doctor gone to seed and turned bad-man (who later turns a good man) is soundly played by Victor Mature—not to mention the several rawhide buckos who twirl guns and hide behind beards, which are played by such competent actors as Tim Holt, Don Garner and Ward Bond. Mr. Ford is less knowing with the females. Linda Darnell makes a pin-up of a trull, and Cathy Downs is simply ornamental as a good little girl from back East.

However, the gentlemen are perfect. Their humors are earthy. Their activities are taut. The mortality rate is simply terrific. And the picture goes off with several bangs.

D 4, 1946

LES ENFANTS DU PARADIS (Children of Paradise); scenario and dialogue by Jacques Prevert; music by Joseph Kosma, Maurice Thiertz and Georges Mouque; directed by Marcel Carne; produced by Pathe Studios in France and released here by Tricolore Films. At the Ambassador.
Baptiste Deburau........Jean-Louis Barrault
Frederick Lemaitre............Pierre Brasseur
Garance ....Arletty
Lacenaire.....................Marcel Herrand
Jericho.........................Pierre Renoir
Avril..........................Fabien Loris
Anselme Deburau............Etienne Decroux
Nathalie.......................Maria Cassares
Madame Hermine..............Jeanne Marken
The Blind.....................Gaston Modot
Count de Montray..............Louis Salou
Director.......................Pierre Palau
Scarpia Barigni...............Albert Remy
Inspector of Police............Paul Frankeur

By BOSLEY CROWTHER

The strong philosophical disposition of the French film director, Marcel Carne, to scan through the medium of cinema the irony and pathos of life—a disposition most memorably demonstrated in his great pre-war film, "Quai des Brumes"—has apparently not been altered by the tragic experience of the last few years, as witness his most ambitious picture, "Les Enfants du Paradis." For, in this long and fervid French picture, which was more or less clandestinely made during the Nazi occupation under circumstances of the most exacting sort—and which had its American première at the Ambassador Theatre yesterday—M. Carne is Platonically observing the melancholy masquerade of life, the riddle of truth and illusion, the chimeras of la comedie humaine.

And if that sounds like a mouthful, you may rest emphatically assured that M. Carne has bitten off a portion no less difficult to chew. For his story concerns the crisscrossed passions of a group of Parisian theatre folks—clowns, charlatans and tragedians—in the mid-nineteenth century. It is a story of the fatal attraction of four different men to one girl, a creature of profound and rak impulses, in the glittering milieu of the demimonde. And to render it even more Platonic, he has framed this human drama within the gilded proscenium of the theatre, as though it were but a pageant on the stage—a pageant to hypnotize and tickle the shrilling galleries, the "children of the Gods'."

Obviously such an Olympian—or classical—structure for a film presumes a proportionate disposition to philosophize from the audience. And it assumes a responsibility of dramatic clarity. Unfortunately, the pattern of the action does not support the demand. There is a great deal of vague and turgid wandering in "Les Enfants du Paradis," and its network of love and hate and jealousy is exceptionally tough to cut through. Its concepts are elegant and subtle, its connections are generally remote and its sade, fatalistic conclusion is a capstone of futility.

It is said that the film was considerably cut down into its present two-hour and twenty-four-minute length, which may account for the lesions in the pattern and for the disjunction of the colorful musical score. That would not account, however, for the long-windedness of Jacques Prevert's script, sketchily transcribed in English titles, and for the generally archaic treatment of Passion and Destiny.

Withal, M. Carne has created a frequently captivating film which has moments of great beauty in it and some performances of exquisite note. Jean-Louis Barrault's impersonation of the famous French mime, Baptiste Deburau, is magically moody and expressive, especially in his scenes of pantomime, although it is hard to perceive the fascination which he is alleged to have for the lady in the case. And as the latter, the beauteous Areltty intriguingly suggests deep mysteries in the nature of a

richly feminine creature—but it is difficult to gather what they are. Pierre Brasseur is delightfully extravagant as a selfish, conceited "ham," Marcel Herrand is trenchant as a cut-throat and Louis Salou is brittle as a swell.

On the basis alone of performance and of its bold, picturesque mise en scene, "Les Enfants du Paradis" is worth your custom. What you get otherwise is to boot.

F 20, 1947

IVAN THE TERRIBLE (Part I), screen play and direction by Sergei M. Eisenstein; music by Sergei Prokofieff; sets and costumes by Isaac Shpinel; English titles by Charles Clement; produced by the Central Cinema Studio, Alma-Ata, U.S.S.R.; released in this country by Artkino. At the Stanley.
Ivan IV.......... ...Nikolai Cherkassov
Anastasia ....Ludmila Tsellkovskaya
The Boyarina Staritzkaya..Seraphima Birman
Vladimir Andreyevich.......Piotr Kadochnikov
Prince Andrei Kurbsky...............Nazvanov
Prince Fyodor Kolychov....Alexander Abrikosov
Nikola ....Vsevolod Pudovkin
Malyuta Skuratov..............Mikhail Zharov
Alexei Basmanov................Alexei Buchma
Fyodor ....Mikhail Kuznetzov

By BOSLEY CROWTHER

Everyone wise to cinema as a truly dynamic art, capable of charging the senses with galvanic sounds and images, will want to see Sergei M. Eisenstein's new and much-heralded Russian film, the first part of "Ivan the Terrible," which came to the Stanley on Saturday. And the desire to see it will be not only because it is the first film from Eisenstein, one of the really great artists in the medium, in nearly eight years; nor because of the recently reported difficulties of this irrepressible man with the guardians of Soviet culture over the second part of the "Ivan" trilogy, nor because they are passionately interested in a sixteenth-century Russian czar.

They will want to see it—or, rather, they should want to see it, very much—because it is, in its pure display of cinema, one of the most imposing films ever made. Mark you well, now—we are not saying that it is a great dramatic work nor a gem of historical narration nor of social philosophy. It is, in the recognized tradition of previous Eisenstein films, almost completely lacking in conventional narrative style, and the simplest liaisons of continuity, as we expect them in story-telling, are eschewed.

In staging a panorama of the reign of Ivan IV, from the time of his coronation to his first renunciation of the crown, Eisenstein has patterned his picture in a series of theatrical tableaux, vast and elaborate representations of episodes in the ruler's career. And, without making visible endeavor to show character in any more than the broadest strokes, he has put on the screen a human conflict of the sternest and most elemental sort. On the one hand is Ivan the Terrible, a tall and ferocious man, determined to unify Russia and expand its borders to the limits of his grasp. And on the other hand are the rich and greedy boyars, suspicious of Ivan and jealous of their power. In between are a few court intriguers and rather tentative intruders from the masses below.

And what there is of personal drama, Eisenstein has expansively worked out in ominous scenes of stylized acting and searching looks at expressions of face. There is the friend and most trusted associate of Ivan who secretly covets the throne and seeks to seduce the czarina when Ivan is believed to have died. And there is the dark and malicious boyarina who wants the throne for her imbecile son and

228

who presumably intrigues with other boyars to wrench it from Ivan's grasp.

But all of these aspects of drama —and even the assault by Ivan on the city of Kazan—are presented in a style of pageant acting, quite similar to pantomime. And they are accompanied—or orchestrated —to a magnificent score by Prokofieff. As a matter of fact, the musical scoring and the employment of tonal qualities are quite as important in this picture as the eloquent images cast upon the screen—images brilliantly created by sumptuous decor and splendid camera work.

The result is a film of awesome and monumental impressiveness, in which the senses are saturated in medieval majesty. The opening sequence, for instance, in which the coronation of Ivan is displayed, with the pomp of ceremonials and the glorious hymning of a cathedral choir, while the bells of Moscow ring in a silver paean outside, is one of the grandest sequences that we have ever seen. And some of Eisenstein's compositions with individuals and crowds are past all compare.

His performers, too, are fascinating. Nikolai Cherkassov as Ivan is superb, a monolith of a person, eloquent in bearing and speech. And Nazvanov is a creature of pale treachery as his most trusted friend, while Ludmila Tselikovskaya is a doll with odd expressions as his first wife.

To be sure, this conception of Ivan as a fierce and tempestuous man, bent on bringing all Russia into one nationality and achieving this aim, apparently, at the expense of anyone who stands in his way, is conspicuously totalitarian. And Ivan might just as well be one of Hitler's Teutonic heroes as a man venerated by the Soviet state. But, for all its suggestive ideology, the film is a work of art and not to be missed by those people who want to see the screen eloquently employed.

Mr 10, 1947

MONSIEUR VERDOUX, screen play by Charles Chaplin; directed and produced by Mr. Chaplin for United Artists release. At the Broadway.

Henri Verdoux alias Varnay alias Floray	Charles Chaplin
Mona, his wife	Mady Correll
Peter, his son	Allison Roddan
Maurice Bottello	Robert Lewis
Mme. Bottello	Audrey Betz

The Ladies:

Annabella Bonheur	Martha Raye
Marie Grosnay	Isobel Elsom
Lydia Floray	Margaret Hoffman
Annette	Ada-May
Yvonne	Helene Heigh
Maid	Marjorie Bennett
The Girl	Marilyn Nash

The Couvais Family:

Pierre	Irving Bacon
Jean	Edwin Mills
Carlotta	Virginia Brissac
Lena	Almira Sessions
Phoebe	Eula Morgan

The Law:

Prefect of Police	Bernard J. Nedell
Detective Morrow	Charles Evans

By BOSLEY CROWTHER

Let it be said for Charles Chaplin that, although his films are now few and far between, he really tries to deliver a hay-maker when he brings one up from the studio floor. Not one for sparring and flicking on the screen in these troubled times, Mr. Chaplin, the incomparable comedian, believes in using his talent for socking hard— socking, that is, at the evil and injustice that he sees in the world and aiming directly at the midriff of general complacency.

Thus it is that his latest picture, the much-guarded "Monsieur Verdoux," which was finally revealed to all and sundry at the Broadway Theatre last night, is no light and gentle slapstick comedy in the manner of Mr. Chaplin's earlier films. Neither is t freighted with the poignancy of his later satires upon modern life. Although it is labeled a "comedy of murders" and is screamingly funny in spots— funny as only the old Chaplin is able to make a comic scene—it is basically serious and bitter at the ironies of life. And those who go expecting to laugh at it may find themselves remaining to weep.

For Mr. Chaplin is treating on the subject of mass murder in a philosophic vein and upon the desperate dilemmas of making a living in this difficult world. His hero, if that is what you'd call him, is an apparently innocent ex-bank clerk who has a sick wife and a grand youngster whom he apparently loves very much. But to earn a livelihood for them in the pre-war France, where his scene is supposedly set, he finds that he must pursue a calling of a rare if not entirely original sort. And so he has gone into "the business of liquidating persons of the opposite sex"—which is to say that he marries foolish ladies of abundent means and then polishes them off.

In short, Mr. Chaplin plays a Bluebeard who murders his multiple "wives" with neat finesse, if not always with complete accommodation of the unfortunate victims themselves. In this way he does quite nicely by his little family, which never dreams of his career, until—well, of course, the inevitable is that Verdoux, the killer, is ironically caught.

Obviously, such a character is a monster by all our sane and ethical lights, and his ultimate conviction and destruction is only right and just. But as Mr. Chaplin plays him, he is both a satan and a faun —a devil in elegant clothing and a charming innocent with the manners of a dude. For each of his well-selected victims he plays a different role. For one he is a dapper sea captain, for another a pompous engineer. And for all he is a man of the greatest gentility and fastidiousness.

In this way, Mr. Chaplin is able to put variety into the quality of his clowning and oddity into his career. Most amusingg of his murderous enterprises is that directed against Martha Raye, a lady of uncouth and raucous manner, whom he finds impossible to destroy. Two sequences, one in which the subtle killer tries to poison the indestructible dame and the other in which he endeavors to drown her, a la "An American Tragedy" —are as comically inventive and hilarious as any Mr. Chaplin has ever played.

But, much more than grim, sardonic clowning, Mr. Chaplin is able to get across in this story a bitter philosophy on the ruthlessness of life. And that is that the "business of murder," when practiced on a moderately small scale, such as Verdoux practices it in this story, is a crime against society. But when practiced on a large scale, as in wars, it is acceptable.

Unfortunately, Mr. Chaplin has not managed his film with great success. It is slow—tediously slow —in many stretches and thus monotonous. The bursts of comic invention fit uncomfortably into the grim fabric and the clarity of the philosophy does not begin to emerge till near the end. By that time — almost two hours — Mr. Chaplin has repeated much and has possibly left his audience in an almost exhausted state.

However, it must be said for him that his performance is remarkably adroit and that those who assist him, especially Miss Raye, are completely up to snuff. Miss Raye's bumptious character is a mammoth of loud vulgarity and Isobel Elsom, Marilyn Nash and Robert Lewis are amusing in smaller roles.

There is no doubt that a lot of controversy will be created by "Monsieur Verdoux," but it is plain that Mr. Chaplin is still in the game—and hitting hard.

Ap 12, 1947

ODD MAN OUT, screen play by F. L. Green and Robert C. Sherriff, based on a novel by F. L. Green; directed and produced by Carol Reed for J. Arthur Rank in England and released here by Universal-International. At Loew's Criterion.

Johnny O'Queen	James Mason
Kathleen	Kathleen Ryan
Lukey	Robert Newton
Dennis	Robert Beatty
Pat	Cyril Cusack
Murphy	Roy Irving
Nolan	Dan O'Herlihy
Grannie	Kitty Kirwin
Teresa	Maureen Delany
Constable	Dennis O'Dea
Rosie	Fay Compton
Maudie	Beryl Measor
Tom	Arthur Hambling
Fenice	William Hartnell
Shell	F. J. McCormick
Tober	Elwin Brook-Jones
Father Tom	W. C. Fay
Gin Jimmy	Joseph Tomelty

By BOSLEY CROWTHER

The creative combination of James Mason, popular British star, and Carol Reed, the brilliant director of such films as "Night Train" and "The Stars Look Down," is sure to attract wide attention to the new British picture, "Odd Man

Out," which had its American première at Loew's Criterion yesterday. And the further fact that it
is fashioned from a novel by F. L.
Green which is current catnip for
thriller readers will not hurt the
film's draw one bit—all of which
is peculiarly propitious, for "Odd
Man Out" is a picture to see, to
absorb in the darkness of the theatre and then go home and talk
about.

Especially is it rewarding in its
first two-thirds or so, when the
galvanic talents of its director are
most excitingly demonstrated on
the screen. For in this part of the
picture, the story and Mr. Reed
are concerned almost exclusively
with a matter that gives his camera its most auspicious range. This
is the desperate endeavor of a
wounded man to escape the police
in the night-shrouded alleys of an
Irish city after committing a murder for a political cause.

Being a graduate master of the
cinematic "chase," Mr. Reed has
constructed this grim coursing like
nothing he has ever done before.
From the moment he joins with
his protagonist in the upstairs
room of a Belfast slum, plotting a
factory robbery in order to raise
funds for a rebel "cause," he had
colored and paced this terrible
manhunt with the precision of a
thundering symphony. The taut
stick-up of the bookkeepers, the
uncalculated shooting of one, the
critical wounding of the chieftain,
his fall from the get-away car and
then his first panicky flight to
cover in an air-raid shelter are
swiftly and throat-catchingly
achieved. Follows, then, the fugato
passages as the partisans of the
missing chief attempt to make
perilous contact with him and he
stumbles forth from his hiding
place under cover of night.

All of this part of the picture—
the horrible groping in the murk
and the rain, the harrowing contacts with terrified people, the desperation of brushes with the police
—is terrifically tense and dramatic
on a purely visual-emotional plane,
and Mr. Reed can be glowingly
commended for his artistry in
movement and mood. This part of

his picture bears most favorable
comparison with that classic film,
"The Informer," which John Ford
directed several years ago.

But the latter phases of the picture, while peculiarly challenging
to thought, lose the compactness
and impetus of this prime and precise portion. For here the focus
is expanded and the protagonist is
shelved for long spells while the
author and, perforce, the director
go searching for a philosophy of
life. In the backwaters of the city
and in the ways of a span of characters, they seek for some vague
illumination of the meanings of
charity and faith. Through a priest,
a mad portrait painter, a crafty
derelict and, especially, the girl
who loves and believes in the murderer, they endeavor to throw some
light. But Mr. Green and R. C.
Sherriff have fumbled this portion
of the script, and whatever it is
they are proving—if anything—is
anybody's guess.

Also, in switching attention from
the man-hunt to these cryptic characters, they have rudely relieved
the protagonist of the illustrative
role. As the fugitive, Mr. Mason
gives a terrifying picture of a
wounded man, disheveled, agonized
and nauseated, straining valiantly
and blindly to escape. But the
oblique dramatic construction, as
the picture draws toward the end,
neglects the responsibility of dramatizing the movements of his mind.
Clarification of the moral—or the
sympathy—is not achieved by him.

Nor is it achieved by the others,
no matter how finely they represent peculiar and picturesque people. Kathleen Ryan is beautiful as
the girl, cool, statuesque and stoical, but it is difficult to fathom her
thoughts. W. G. Fay, the great
Abbey Theatre veteran, is deeply
affecting as the priest and F. J.
McCormick apes his famous
"Joxer" Daly (of "Juno and the
Paycock") as the snivelling derelict. Allowance must be made for
specious writing in the performance which Robert Newton gives
as the wild-eyed and drunken
painter. But Dennis O'Dea is sobering as a constable and Robert
Beatty, Kitty Kerwin and many

others are as richly and roundly Irish as Patty's pig.

Granting its terminal confusions, "Odd Man Out" is still a most intriguing film. And, even if you can't perceive its wherefores, you should find it a real experience.

Ap 24, 1947

DUEL IN THE SUN, screen play by David O. Selznick, adapted by Oliver H. P. Garrett from a novel by Niven Busch; directed by King Vidor; produced by Mr. Selznick and released by Selznick Releasing Organization. At the Capitol and Loew's theatres.

Pearl Chavez	Jennifer Jones
Lewt McCanles	Gregory Peck
Jesse McCanles	Joseph Cotten
Senator McCanles	Lionel Barrymore
Mrs McCanles	Lillian Gish
Sam Pierce	Charles Bickford
Vashti	Butterfly McQueen
"The Sinkiller"	Walter Huston
Scott Chavez	Herbert Marshall
Mrs. Chavez	Tilly Losch
The Lover	Sidney Blackmer
Lem Smoot	Harry Carey
Sid	Scott McKay
Mr. Langford	Otto Kruger
Helen Langford	Joan Tetzel
Sheriff	Charles Dingle

By BOSLEY CROWTHER

There's a new sales technique in film business which has been rather cleverly evolved from scientific audience researching. It is this: If the public's "want to see" for a forthcoming picture samples higher than the reactions of test audiences, you sell your picture in a hurry before the curious have a chance to get wise. It follows, of course, the old pitch theory that you can fool all of the people some of the time provided your ballyhoo is super and you don't stick around too long.

That, we suspect, is one reason why David O. Selznick's "Duel in the Sun," as much ballyhooed a movie as we've had since "Gone With the Wind," was launched yesterday not only at the Capitol on Broadway but in thirty-eight (count 'em) houses of the Loew's circuit in and around New York. For, despite all his flashy exploitation, Mr. Selznick can't long hide the fact that his multimillion-dollar Western is a spectacularly disappointing job.

Those are harsh words for a movie upon which the producer of some memorably fine films has lavished some mighty production and close to a dozen stars. Those are also harsh words about a picture which promises very much and which, even for all its disappointments, has some flashes of brilliance in it. But the ultimate banality of the story and its juvenile slobbering over sex (or should we say "primitive passion," as says a ponderous foreword?) compels their use.

Reduced to its bare essentials and cleared of a clutter of clichés worn thin in a hundred previous Westerns, Mr. Selznick's two-hour-and-a-quarter tale is that of a sun-blistered romance involving a half-breed Indian girl and two dagger-eyed Texas brothers, one of them good and the other very bad. That, as a plot, might be sufficient for a sort of O'Neillian frontier tragedy —and, indeed, once or twice it looks faintly as though this might turn into a valid "Desire Under the Sun." Also, the locale of this fable —a baronial Texas ranch, ruled by a scalawag father wed to a faded flower of the Old South—and the incidental details of the raw life are sufficient to a drama of some point.

But Mr. Selznick, who wrote it from a novel by Niven Busch (and, we suspect, with occasional reference to Margaret Mitchell's famous tome), seems to have been more anxious to emphasize the clash of love and lust than to seek some illumination of a complex of arrogance and greed. As a consequence, most of the picture is devoted to the romantic quirks of a tawny-skinned Scarlett O'Hara who wants the noble brother with her heart but can't help loving the scoundrel with her notably feeble flesh.

Okay. On that elemental level, Mr. Selznick has turned quite a trick of lurid and lickerish illustration, by leave of the Production Code. He has got through some scenes of fancy wooing between Gregory Peck and Jennifer Jones, the bad boy and the half-breed doxy, and he has flashed a few broad suggestions. He—and his director, King Vidor—have also whipped up some eye-dazzling scenes of wide-open ranching and frontiering, all in color of the very best, of course. Indeed, some of the compositions, achieved with color and musical backgrounds, evoke sudden and singular sensations that are conspicuously superior to the whole. Oh, brother—if only the dramatics were up to the technical style!

But they're not. Nor are the performances, which are strangely uneven—all of them. The best and the most consistent is that of Mr. Peck, who makes of the renegade brother a credibly vicious and lawless character, and the next best is that of Walter Huston as a frontier evangelist. This is the role to which objection was voiced by elements on the West Coast and which was consequently trimmed by editing, as well as piously excused in an appended foreword. That seems to us unfortunate, for Mr. Huston's pungent thundering in this role is one of the bits of characterization which has real flavor and significance.

As the desert flower, cause of all the turmoil, Miss Jones gives occasional glints of the pathos of loneliness and heartbreak, but mostly she has to pretend to be the passion-torn child of nature in the loosest theatrical style. The final scene, in which she punctures Mr. Peck with several well-aimed rifle shots, is wounded herself and then crawls to him across the rocks to die with him in his arms, is one of those chunks of theatrics that ranks with Liza crossing the ice. Likewise, Lillian Gish and Lionel Barrymore are pretty porky as the Texas tycoons, and Joseph Cotten, Charles Bickford and many others are no better—nor worse—than the script allows.

However, we don't want to scare you. "Duel in the Sun" is still something to see—provided you understand clearly that it is the bankroll and not the emotions by which you will be shocked.

No stage show is being presented at the Capitol during the run of "Duel in the Sun."

My 8, 1947

GREAT EXPECTATIONS, screen play by David Lean and Ronald Neame, from the novel by Charles Dickens; directed by Mr. Lean; production designed by John Bryan, with musical score by Walter Goehr; produced by Mr. Neame for Cineguild, London; released by Universal-International. At the Radio City Music Hall.

Mr. Pip	John Mills
Pip (as a boy)	Anthony Wager
Estella	Valerie Hobson
Estella (as a girl)	Jean Simmons
Joe Gargery	Bernard Miles
Jaggers	Francis L. Sullivan
Magwitch	Finlay Currie
Herbert Pocket	Alec Guinness
Herbert (as a boy)	John Forrest
Miss Havisham	Martita Hunt
Wemmick	Ivor Bernard
Mrs. Joe	Freda Jackson
Bentley Drummil	Torin Thatcher
Biddy	Eileen Erskine
Uncle Pumblechook	Hay Petrie
Compeyson	George Hayes
Sergeant	Richard George
Sarah Pocket	Everley Gregg
Mr. Wopsle	John Burch
The Aged Parent	O. B. Clarence

By BOSLEY CROWTHER

If there is any lingering necessity of inspiring more Charles Dickens fans—not to mention more fans for British movies—the thing that should certainly do the job is the film made from "Great Expectations," which came to the Music Hall yesterday. For here, in a perfect motion picture, made in England (where it should have been made), the British have done for Dickens what they did for Shakespeare with "Henry V"; they have proved that his works have more life in them than almost anything now written for the screen.

Not that there haven't been previous delightful and inspiring Dickens films. "David Copperfield" was a winner a dozen years ago. And, from away back in antiquity, we recall a memorable, silent "Oliver Twist," while, more recently than either, came a sugar-cured "Christmas Carol." But, somehow, the fullness of Dickens, of his stories and characters—his humor and pathos and vitality and all his brilliant command of atmosphere—has never been so illustrated as it is in this wonderful film, which can safely be recommended as screen story-telling at its best.

That may sound slightly excessive to the fireplace-and-slippers Dickens fans, who seldom propose

"Great Expectations" as one of the novelist's most distinguished works. They might have asked for something stronger in the way of a narrative. But the every-day movie-goer—and even the casual reader of Dickens' books—will not recognize any weakness in either the structure or the characters of this film. For, despite necessary elisions and compressions of favorite scenes, the picture is so truly Dickens—so truly human and noble in its scope—that the quality of the author is revealed in every shot, in every line. Mid-nineteenth century England—and a thrilling story—are crowded on the screen.

Are you familiar with this story —the story of little Pip, the poor orphan boy who is accosted on the lone and shiverin' night by Magwitch, the granite-faced convict, escaped from the near-by hulks, whom Pip, in fear and compassion, befriends before the felon is caught and returned? Do you remember the contrivance by which Pip is later sent to "play" in the great, musty house of mad Miss Havisham; how he meets his love, Estella, there and is thus inspired with the ambition of becoming "a gentleman"? And do you recall how, years later, Pip is actually endowed with handsome means by a mysterious benefactor, how he goes to London and becomes a fancy blade and then suddenly runs into such adventures as only the nimble mind of Dickens could contrive?

Even if you do remember, it shouldn't lessen your enjoyment in the least from this glowing illumination of the warm and deliciously surprising tale. For the smooth team of Anthony Havelock-Allen, David Lean and Ronald Neame have caught it right down to the last shiver of a frightened youngster or the haughty flash in Estella's eye. A script that is swift and sure in movement, aromatic English settings and costumes and superlatively sentitive direction and acting are conjoined to make a rich and charming job. And a musical score of exceptional taste and understanding contributes too.

In the large cast of unsurpassed performers, John Mills, of course, stands out, since his is the paramount opportunity to play the grown-up Pip. He makes of this first-personal character such a full-bodied, gracious young man that Pip actually has more stature here than he has in the book. And little Anthony Wager, as the boy Pip, is so beautifully quiet and restrained, yet so subtly revealing of spirit, that he is certain to win every heart. Neither space nor words are sufficient to praise adequately the rest—the thundering Francis L. Sullivan as Jaggers, the shrewd solicitor; the sparrow-like Ivor Bernard as Wemmick, his Old Bailey clerk; the beautiful Valerie Hobson as the perverse Estella grown-up and the arrogant little Jean Simmons as this mettlesome creature as a girl; the tremendously comic Alec Guinness as Herbert Pocket, Pip's mad-hatter friend, or Finlay Currie as the beetling old Magwitch or Martita Hunt as mad Miss Havisham. Nor have we space or words to give more than a deeply grateful salute to Bernard Miles for making of Joe Gargery, the blacksmith, a vivid memory, nor to mention a half dozen others who are magically Dickensian in bits.

But we must say that all of them have managed to frame a Dickens portrait gallery to the life and to make real a tale of humble virtue elevated above snobbery and hate. It is such a tale as is enriching, for both young and old, in this day, and we offer as unforgettable some of its richest scenes. Like memorable moments from the novel, we will long cherish in our mind Pip's comical fight with the "pale young gentleman" that day at Miss Havisham's, or the desperate race to board the packet on the lower reaches of the Thames, with only the splash of water and the cry of gulls to break the tension of the scene. And always will we remember the sweetness in Joe's loving voice as he pours out his heart to his idol, "Dear old Pip, old chap!"

ZERO DE CONDUITE, a French film written and directed by Jean Vigo and distributed here by Cine Classics, Inc., in association with French Ideal Films, Inc.

Supt. Hugnet......................Jean Daste
Supt. Pete-Sec...............Robert Le Flon
Supt. Dec-de-Gaz....................Du Veron
Principal ....Delphin
Mother Haricot....................Mme. Emile
Professor ....Larive
Prefect..................L. de Gonzague-Frick
Fireman........................Raya Diligent

and

L'ATALANTE, a French film with a scenario by Jean Guinee and directed by Jean Vigo; distributed here by Cine Classics, Inc., in association with French Ideal Films, Inc.

Juliette.............................Dita Parlo
Jean.................................Jean Daste
"Father Jules"....................Michel Simon
The boy............................Lefevre
Traveling Salesman..........Gilles Margaritis

What the late Jean Vigo was attempting to illustrate back in 1933-34 when he made "Zero de Conduite" and "L'Atalante," the pair of Gallic importations which came to the Fifth Avenue Playhouse on Saturday, is nebulous and difficult to perceive today. Except for occasional moments of comedy, satire and tender romance, these intellectual exercises should prove of high interest only to avid students of the cinema.

The earlier of the two, "Zero de Conduite" (Zero for Conduct), a study of life in a French boarding school for boys, is a series of vignettes lampooning the faculty climaxed by a weird, dream-like rebellion of the entire student body. These amorphous scenes, strung together by a vague continuity may be art but they are also pretty chaotic.

"L'Atalante," Vigo's last film, hews closer to the standard concept of movie making. It is, in sum, the story of a pair of honeymooners aboard a barge slowly making its way on the Seine. Life aboard the barge, satirically named for the fleet Goddess, is tedious and dull for the young girl, who wants excitement.

She finds it when she deserts the boat to flirt with a stranger, a traveling salesman, and the aged barge hand seeks her out, and affects a reconciliation between the errant lady and her jealous bargemaster husband. Here too, the action is episodic and diffuse but Michel Simon, as the dour and cat-loving barge hand lends a bit of comic relief to the pallidly poetic proceedings.

Count "Zero de Conduite" and "L'Atalante" as examples of avant garde pictures which have now become passe.   A. W.

Je 23, 1947

GENTLEMAN'S AGREEMENT, based on the novel by Laura Z. Hobson; screen play by Moss Hart; directed by Elia Kazan; produced by Darryl F. Zanuck for Twentieth Century-Fox Pictures. At the Mayfair.

Phil Green.....................Gregory Peck
Kathy... ....Dorothy McGuire
Dave...........................John Garfield
Anne..........................Celeste Holm
Mrs. Green....................Anne Revere
Miss Wales ....June Havoc
John Minify....................Albert Dekker
Jane. . ...Jane Wyatt
Tommy.......................Dean Stockwell
Dr. Craigie....................Nicholas Joy
Professor Lieberman..............Sam Jaffe
Personnel Manager..........Harold Vermilyea
Bill Payson..... ....Ransom M. Sherman
Hotel Manager............. ....Roy Roberts
Mrs. Minify................Kathleen Lockhart
Bert McAnny....................Curt Conway
Bill . .. .John Newland
Weisman.....................Robert Warwick
Miss Miller.....................Louise Lorimer
Tingler ....Howard Negley
Apartment Superintendent.......Victor Kilian
Harry ....Frank Wilcox
Receptionist....................Marlyn Monk
Maitre D.........................Wilton Graff
Clerk.........................Morgan Farley

By BOSLEY CROWTHER

The shabby cruelties of anti-Semitism which were sharply and effectively revealed within the restricted observation of Laura Z. Hobson's "Gentleman's Agreement" have now been exposed with equal candor and even greater dramatic forcefulness in the motion-picture version of the novel which came to the Mayfair yesterday. In fact, every point about prejudice which Miss Hobson had to make in her book has been made with superior illustration and more graphic demonstration in the film, so that the sweep of her moral indignation is not only widened but intensified thereby.

Essentially, Miss Hobson's was a story of the emotional disturbance that occurs within a man who elects, for the sake of getting a magazine article, to tell people that he is a Jew and who experiences first-hand, as a consequence, the shock and pain of discriminations and social snubs. And it was the story of this same man's parallel romance with a supposedly unbigoted girl who, for all her intellectual convictions, can't quite shake the vicious prejudices of her particular group.

Shaped by Moss Hart into a

screen play of notable nimbleness and drive, the bewilderments of Miss Hobson's hero become absorbing and vital issues on the screen and the eventual outcome of his romance becomes a matter of serious concern. For such aspects of anti-Semitism as professional bias against Jews, discrimination by swanky hotels and even the calling of ugly names have been frankly and clearly demonstrated for the inhuman failings that they are and the peril of a normal and happy union being wrecked on the ragged edges of prejudice is affectingly raised.

Indeed, on the grounds of the original, every good and courageous thing has been done by Twentieth Century-Fox, the producer, to make "Gentleman's Agreement" a sizzling film. A fine cast, brilliant direction by Elia Kazan and intrepidity in citing such names as Bilbo, Rankin and Gerald L. K. Smith give it realism and authenticity. To millions of people throughout the country, it should bring an ugly and disturbing issue to light.

But the weaknesses of the original are also apparent in the film —the most obvious of which is the limited and specialized area observed. Although the hero of the story is apparently assigned to write a definitive article on anti-Semitism in the United States, it is evident that his explorations are narrowly confined to the upper-class social and professional level to which he is immediately exposed. And his discoveries are chiefly in the nature of petty bourgeois rebuffs, with no inquiry into the devious cultural mores from which they spring.

Likewise it is amazing that the writer who undertakes this probe should be so astonished to discover that anti-Semitism is cruel. Assuming that he is a journalist of some perception and scope, his imagination should have fathomed most of these sudden shocks long since. And although the role is crisply and agreeably played by Gregory Peck, it is, in a careful analysis, an extraordinarily naive role.

Also the role of his young lady,

which Dorothy McGuire affectingly plays, is written to link in a disquieting little touch of "snob appeal." Maybe the image of the actress in conjunction with the "station-wagon set" is a bit reminiscent of "Claudia" and her juvenile attitudes. But the suggestion of social aspiration—and accomplishment—confuses the issues very much.

It is likewise this reviewer's opinion that John Garfield's performance of a young Jew, lifelong friend of the hero, is a bit too mechanical and that a scene with Sam Jaffe as a Jewish scientist introduces a false note of low comedy. However, June Havoc, Albert Dekker, Celeste Holm and Anne Revere are variously brittle and competent as other characters, so we'll settle for a draw.

The film still has abundant meaning and should be fully and widely enjoyed.

N 12, 1947

BEAUTY AND THE BEAST, story, dialogue and direction by Jean Cocteau; from the fairy-tale by Mme. Leprince de eBaumont; produced by Andre Paulve, and released by Lopert Films, Inc. At the Bijou.
Avenant }
The Beast } ....Jean Marais
The Prince }
Beauty ....Josette Day
The Merchant ....Marcel Andre
Adelaide ....Mila Parely
Felicie ....Nane Germon
Ludovic ....Michel Auclair

By BOSLEY CROWTHER

The oft-tried but seldom-known accomplishment of telling a familiar fairy-tale with pure imagery and enchantment through the sensuous devices of the screen has been almost perfectly realized by the French poet-playwright, Jean Cocteau, in his beautifully measured French production of the old fable, "Beauty and the Beast." Except that it isn't in color, this film which came to the Bijou yesterday is an eminent model of cinema achievement in the realm of poetic fantasy.

This should be understood, however: the achievement is on a definitely adult plane and the beauties of Cocteau's conception will be most appreciated by sophisticated minds. It is not the sort of picture that will send the children into transports of delight, unless they are quite precocious youngsters of the new progressive school.

For Cocteau has taken the old story of the beautiful country girl who goes to live as a hostage for her impoverished father in the palace of a terrifying beast, there to be treated with such kindness that she falls in love with the unhappy brute, and has used it as a pattern for weaving a priceless fabric of subtle images. In the style of his "Blood of a Poet," though less abstract and recondite, it is a fabric of gorgeous visual metaphors, of undulating movements and rhythmic pace, of hypnotic sounds and music, of casually congealing ideas.

Freudian or metaphysician, you can take from it what you will. The concepts are so ingenious that they're probably apt to any rationale. From the long corridor of candelabra, held out from the walls by living arms, through which the wondering visitor enters the palace of the Beast, to the glittering temple of Diana, wherein the mystery of the Beast is revealed, the visual progression of the fable into a dream-world casts its unpredictable spell.

The dialogue, in French, is spare and simple, with the story largely told in pantomime, and the music of Georges Auric accompanies the dreamy, fitful moods. The settings are likewise expressive, many of the exteriors having been filmed for rare architectural vignettes at Raray, one of the most beautiful palaces and parks in all France. And the costumes, too, by Christian Berard and Escoffier, are exquisite affairs, glittering and imaginative, lacking only the glow of color, as we say.

As the Beast (and also as the Young Prince and as the churlish suitor of the heroine), Jean Marais has the grace of a dancer, the voice of a muffled baritone. Although his grossly feline make-up is reminiscent of some of the monsters of Hollywood (and could drive the little kiddies to hysterics), he wears it exceedingly well. And as Beauty, Josette Day is truly lovely, youthful and delicate, a convincingly innocent maiden and student to the mysteries of life. Mila Parely is despicably vain and greedy as one of Beauty's bad sisters and Marcel Andre is nicely theatrical as her doting, ineffectual papa.

Studied or not for philosophy, this is a sensuously fascinating film, a fanciful poem in movement given full articulation on the screen.

D 24, 1947

TREASURE OF SIERRA MADRE: Screen play by John Huston; based on the novel by B. Traven; directed by John Huston; produced by Henry Blanke for Warner Brothers Pictures, Inc. At the Strand.
Dobbs .... Humphrey Bogart
Howard .... Walter Huston
Curtin .... Tim Holt
Cody ... . Bruce Bennett
McCormick .... Barton MacLane
Gold Hat ... . Alfonso Bedoya
Presidente ....A. Soto Rangel
El Jefe .... Manuel Donde
Pablo .... Jose Torvay
Pancho .... Margarito Luna
Flashy Girl ....Jacqueline Dalay
Mexican Boy .... Bobby Blake

By BOSLEY CROWTHER

Greed, a despicable passion out of which other base ferments may spawn, is seldom treated in the movies with the frank and ironic contempt that is vividly manifested toward it in "Treasure of Sierra Madre." And certainly the big stars of the movies are rarely exposed in such cruel light as that which is thrown on Humphrey Bogart in this new picture at the Strand. But the fact that this steel-springed outdoor drama transgresses convention in both respects is a token of the originality and maturity that you can expect of it.

Also, the fact that John Huston, who wrote and directed it from a novel by B. Traven, has resolutely applied the same sort of ruthless realism that was evident in his documentaries of war is further assurance of the trenchant and fascinating nature of the job.

Taking a story of three vagrants on "the beach" in Mexico who pool their scratchy resources and go hunting for gold in the desolate hills, Mr. Huston has shaped a searching drama of the collision of civilization's vicious greeds with the instinct for self-preservation in an environment where all the barriers are down. And, by charting the moods of his prospectors after they have hit a vein of gold, he has done a superb illumination of basic characteristics in men. One might almost reckon that he has filmed an intentional comment here upon the irony of avarice in individuals and in nations today.

But don't let this note of intelligence distract your attention from the fact that Mr. Huston is putting it over in a most vivid and exciting action display. Even the least perceptive patron should find this a swell adventure film. For the details are fast and electric from the moment the three prospectors start into the Mexican mountains, infested with bandits and beasts, until two of them come down empty-handed and the third one, the mean one, comes down dead. There are vicious disputes among them, a suspenseful interlude when a fourth man tries to horn in and some running fights with the banditi that will make your hair stand on end. And since the outdoor action was filmed in Mexico with all the style of a documentary camera, it has integrity in appearance, too.

Most shocking to one-tracked moviegoers, however, will likely be the job that Mr. Bogart does as the prospector who succumbs to the gnawing of greed. Physically, morally and mentally, this character goes to pot before our eyes, dissolving from a fairly decent hobo under the corroding chemistry of gold into a hideous wreck of humanity possessed with only one passion—to save his "stuff." And the final appearance of him, before a couple of roving bandits knock him off in a manner of supreme cynicism, is one to which few actors would lend themselves. Mr. Bogart's compensation should be the knowledge that his performance in this film is perhaps the best and most substantial that he has ever done.

Equally, if not more, important

to the cohesion of the whole is the job done by Walter Huston, father of John, as a wise old sourdough. For he is the symbol of substance, of philosophy and fatalism, in the film, as well as an unrelenting image of personality and strength. And Mr. Huston plays this ancient with such humor and cosmic gusto that he richly suffuses the picture with human vitality and warmth. In the limited, somewhat negative role of the third prospector, Tim Holt is quietly appealing, while Bruce Bennett is intense as a prospecting lone wolf and Alfonso Bedoya is both colorful and revealing as an animalistic bandit chief.

To the honor of Mr. Huston's integrity, it should be finally remarked that women have small place in this picture, which is just one more reason why it is good.

On the stage at the Strand are Lionel Hampton and his orchestra, featuring Winni Brown, Roland Burton and Red and Curley.

Ja 24, 1948

THE NAKED CITY, screen play by Albert Maltz and Malvin Wald, from a story by Malvin Wald; directed by Jules Dassin; produced by Mark Hellinger for Hellinger Productions, and released by Universal-International Pictures. At the Capitol.

Lt. Dan Muldoon	Barry Fitzgerald
Frank Niles	Howard Duff
Ruth Morrison	Dorothy Hart
Jimmy Halloran	Don Taylor
Garzah	Ted De Corsia
Dr. Stoneman	House Jameson
Mrs. Halloran	Anne Sargent
Mrs. Batory	Adelaide Klein
Mr. Batory	Grover Burgess
Detective Perelli	Tom Pedi
Mrs. Hylton	Enid Markey
Captain Donahue	Frank Conroy

By BOSLEY CROWTHER

The late Mark Hellinger's personal romance with the City of New York was one of the most ecstatic love affairs of the modern day—at least, to his host of friends and readers who are skeptics regarding l'amour. Before he became a film producer and was still just a newspaper scribe, Mr. Hellinger went for Manhattan in a blissfully uninhibited way—for its sights and sounds and restless movements, its bizarre people and its equally bizarre smells. And he made quite a local reputation framing his fancies in flowery billets doux which stirred the hearts and the humors of readers of the tabloid press.

Now, in his final motion-picture, "The Naked City," which Mr. Hellinger produced and for which he spoke the commentary just before his untimely death, very much of the style and character of those missives has been achieved, for this picture, now at the Capitol, is a virtual Hellinger column on film. It is a rambling, romantic picture-story based on a composite New York episode, the detailed detection of a bath-tub murder by the local Homicide Squad. And it is also a fancifully selective observation of life in New York's streets, police stations, apartments, tenements, playgrounds, docks, bridges and flashy resorts.

Thanks to the actuality filming of much of its action in New York, a definite parochial fascination is liberally assured all the way and the seams in a none-too-good who-dunnit are rather cleverly concealed. And thanks to a final, cops-and-robbers "chase" through East Side Manhattan and on the Williamsburg Bridge, a generally talkative mystery story is whipped up to a roaring "Hitchcock" end.

But two of the memorable weaknesses of Mr. Hellinger's works are notable in this picture, even though the script was prepared by Albert Maltz and Malvin Wald and the direction was accomplished by Jules Dassin. The drama is largely superficial, being no more than a conventional "slice of life" — a routine and unrevealing episode in the everyday business of the cops. And the incidental details — the "humorous" and "poignant" vignettes—which have been scattered about in profusion seem studiously over-written and even contrived.

Furthermore, Mr. Dassin, in his direction, has not preserved them from staginess which, flagrant in several instances, rends the "actuality" disguise. This tendency towards "performance" is uncomfortably evident, too, in Barry Fitzgerald's pensive playing of the chief detective on the case. There has been a lot of rosy rumor about the "greatness" of his handling of this role, but to us it is just a combination of standard Fitzgerald and Sherlock Holmes. However, several others do pretty good jobs of playing "types," especially Howard Duff as a "con" man and Ted De Corsia as an athletic thug.

Also, the Hellinger interest in the seamier side of New York life, expressed in a flood of soundtrack rhetoric, seems a shade immature in graphic view. There are countless more fascinating facets to this city than the work of cops with crime and countless more striking characters in it than genial detectives and mumbling crooks.

However, within that range of interest, Mr. Hellinger has done a vivid job in this, his appropriate valedictory, which comes to you spontaneous and unrehearsed.

On the stage at the Capitol are Dean Martin and Jerry Lewis and Tex Beneke and his band.

Mr 5, 1948

PAISAN: scenario by Sergio Amidei, Klaus Mann, Alfred Hayes, Marcello Pagliero, Federico Fellini, Roberto Rossellini; directed and produced by Roberto Rossellini, and released here by Mayer-Burstyn, Inc. At the World.

Carmela	Carmela Sazio
Joe from Jersey	Robert Von Loon
American Soldiers	Benjamin Emanuel
	Raymond Campbell
	Harold Wagner
	Albert Hinze
	Merlin Berth
	Mats Carlson
	Leonard Penish
American MP	Dots M. Johnson
A Boy in Naples	Alfonsino
Francesca	Maria Michi
Fred	Gar Moore
Harriet, a Nurse	Harriet White
Renzo	Renzo Avanzo
Bill Martin, a Chaplain	Bill Tubbs
Dale, an O.S.S. Man	Dale Edmonds

By BOSLEY CROWTHER

Roberto Rossellini, the young Italian who first swam into our ken as the director of that fine Italian picture, "La Citta Aperta" ("Open City"), has now come forth with a film which, in many aspects, marks a milestone in the expressiveness of the screen. "Paisan" is the title and it opened at the World yesterday.

It is useless to attempt an explanation, in familiar and concrete terms, of its basic theme and nature, for it is not an ordinary film —neither in form nor dramatic construction nor in the things it has to say. In some ways, it is the antithesis of the classic "story film," and certainly it throws off glints of meaning which are strangely unfamiliar on the screen. Possibly for some persons who are accustomed to the routine sort of film, it will be completely bewildering and leave a sad sense of emptiness. But at least it cannot fail to rattle the windowpanes of your eyes. And for many it will crash into the consciousness and leave the emotions limp.

For, in a series of six dramatic incidents which supposedly occurred during the Allied war campaign in Italy—random incidents, with no connection, except by war —Mr. Rossellini constructs a terrifying picture of the disillusion, the irony, the horribleness of strife. More than that, he bluntly shows the tragic chasms which open between good people under circumstances of war and, without saying so, he makes evident the gant, sad thing that life is in a world of hate and killing.

The first incident involves an American patrol in Sicily. One soldier is shot; an Italian girl is blamed and killed—yet, a few minutes before, she has been listening, sensing and sympathizing without comprehending, while the soldier talked to her of his family back home. That is all.

The second incident is equally cryptic. An American Negro MP in Naples gets drunk, sings his sadness to a little street urchin, has his shoes stolen by the boy and tries to get them back next day, only to discover the horrible squalor in which the little fellow lives.

And so on through the picture. There is an episode involving a Roman street-walker and a heartsick "Joe"; one referring to the Partisans in Florence and an American nurse who hopes to meet an old lover there. Then there is a curious little incident in a Franciscan monastery in the Apennines and a final, cynical decimation of Italian partisans and American O.S.S. men in the marshy, bleak delta of the River Po.

As we say, there is no dramatic pattern in which all of these incidents are tied, yet the cumulative impact of them achieves an oddly disturbing effect. And the remarkable thing is that each incident is played for understatement straight through, with classic climaxes avoided and the anti-climax almost obviously applied. The consequence is a curious climate which accumulates as the film goes on— a climate such as that in the eye of a hurricane, windless and airless, in which all tragedy suddenly seems futile and flat. This is the ultimate expression which Mr. Rossellini has accomplished in his film.

The manner of its accomplishment is in his memorable "documentary" style, with this curious truncation of episodes. Through actuality photography, with an almost completely "pick-up" cast, including many Americans, he has developed a tremendous naturalness. And a musical theme of great pathos, running through the episodes, clinches the effect.

In Italian, "paisan" has the meaning of the common term "bud" in our tongue. Even the title is ironic. This is a film to be seen—and seen again.

Mr 30, 1948

DAY OF WRATH, screen play by Mogens Skot-Hansen, Poul Knudsen and Carl Dreyer, from the novel, "Anne Pedersdotter," by Wiers Jenssens; directed and produced in Denmark by Carl Dreyer. Released by George J. Schaefer Associates, Inc.
Anne .. .. Lisbeth Movin
Absalon .... Thirkild Roose
Meret, his mother .... Sigrid Neiiendam
Martin, his son .... Preben Lerdorff
The Bishop .... Albert Hoeberg
Herlofs Marte .... Anna Svierkier

By BOSLEY CROWTHER

The films of the veteran Danish producer and director, Carl Dreyer, have long been known for the perfection of their visual images, for their emphasis on facial expressions and for their austere— and often tedious—restraint. Best known, perhaps, of his pictures is "The Passion of Joan of Arc," which was a virtual facial study of the martyr and her oppressors, made in France some twenty years ago.

Now comes the latest of his pictures to reach this country, "Day of Wrath," a curious study of the power of evil, which opened at the Little Carnegie on Saturday. And again it manifests the stark integrity and the solid character of Dreyer's style—his absolute perfection of the image, his interest in faces and his heavy restraint.

Indeed, the visual richness of this picture and its brilliant instrumentation of the human face cause one to wish very strongly that the drama were more insistent than it is. But, unfortunately, in telling a story of love and hate in a Danish parish house back in the middle ages, Dreyer has kept his idea so obscure and the action so slow and monotonous that the general audience will find it a bore, especially those who do not speak Danish, regardless of the adequate subtitles.

To be sure, he does achieve a sense of darkness, of slow medieval wrath, in this tale of a solemn young woman who marries an elderly preacher, falls in love with his son and then is accused of being a witch by her mother-in-law and is condemned to burn after the preacher discovers the facts. And, true, when it finally emerges, the idea has intellectual force—it being that evil can wear the cloaks of sanctity and that some of the meanest witches in this life go unburned.

But in spite of the fine, tasteful production and the photogenic excellence of all the cast, the drama lacks any compulsion. "Day of Wrath" is handsome but dull (except for one early sequence when an aged witch is tossed into the fire).

Ap 26, 1948

THE LADY FROM SHANGHAI, screen play, based on a novel by Sherwood King, direction, and production by Orson Welles, for Columbia Pictures. At Loew's Criterion.
Elsa Bannister..................Rita Hayworth
Michael O'Hara.................Orson Welles
Arthur Bannister...............Everett Sloane
George Grisby..................Glenn Anders
Sidney Broome..................Ted de Corsia
Judge..........................Erskine Sanford
Goldie.........................Gus Schilling
District Attorney..............Carl Frank
Jake...........................Louis Merrill
Bessie.........................Evelyn Ellis
Cab Driver.....................Harry Shannon
Li.............................Wong Show Chong
Yacht Captain..................Sam Nelson

By BOSLEY CROWTHER

For a fellow who has as much talent with a camera as Orson Welles and whose powers of pictorial invention are as fluid and as forcible as his, this gentleman certainly has a strange way of marring his films with sloppiness which he seems to assume that his dazzling exhibitions of skill will camouflage.

Take "The Lady From Shanghai," for instance, which came to Loew's Criterion yesterday: it could have been a terrific piece of melodramatic romance. For the idea, at least, is a corker and the Wellesian ability to direct a good cast against fascinating backgrounds has never been better displayed. It's the story of a roving merchant seaman who falls in with some over-rich worldlings and who almost becomes the innocent victim of their murderous hates and jealousies. And for its sheer visual modeling of burning passions in faces, forms and attitudes, galvanized within picturesque surroundings, it might almost match "Citizen Kane."

The build-up, for instance, of the tensions among four people, in particular, aboard a yacht sailing from New York to San Francisco is tremendously captivating. In the group are the mesmerized sailor, his enchantress who is a sleek, seductive thing, her husband who is a famous criminal lawyer and his partner, a wild-eyed maniac. And in the subtle suggestion of corruption, of selfishness and violence in this group, intermingled with haunting wisps of pathos, Mr. Welles could not have done a better job.

And he couldn't have picked better actors—for three of the roles, anyhow. Everett Sloane is electrified with sharpness and malignance as the lawyer and husband, and Glenn Anders is exquisitely disturbing as the indefinite lunatic. Even Rita Hayworth, who is the Circe in the swinish company, is entirely adequate to the requirement of looking ravishing and acting vague.

But no sooner has Mr. Welles, director, deposited this supercharged group in literal San Francisco after a particularly vivid voyage up the Mexican Coast than Mr. Welles, the author, goes sloppy and leaves him in the lurch. For the protean gentleman's arrangement of triple-cross murder plot designed to entrap the sailor is a thoroughly confused and baffling thing. Tension is recklessly permitted to drain off in a sieve of tangled plot and in a lengthy court-room argument which has little save a few visual stunts. As producer of the picture, Mr. Welles might better have fired himself—as author, that is—and hired somebody to give Mr. Welles, director, a better script.

And he certainly could have done much better than use himself in the key role of the guileless merchant sailor who is taken in by a woman's winning charm. For no matter how much you dress him in rakish yachting caps and open shirts, Mr. Welles simply hasn't the capacity to cut a romantic swath. And when he adorns his characterization with a poetic air and an Irish brogue, which is painfully artificial, he makes himself—and the film—ridiculous.

Indeed, his performance in the picture—and his exhibitionistic cover-ups of the story's general untidiness—give ironic point to his first line: "When I start out to make a fool of myself, there's very little can stop me."

Je 10, 1948

LOUISIANA STORY: Story by Robert and Frances Flaherty; directed and produced by Mr. Flaherty for Robert Flaherty Productions. At the Sutton.
The Boy .. .. Joseph Boudreaux
His Father ....Lionel Le Blanc
His Mother ....Mrs. E. Bienvenu
The Driller ....Frank Hardy
His Boilerman ....C. T. Guedry

By BOSLEY CROWTHER

Heretofore, Robert Flaherty has shown a magnificent disregard for the implements of modern civilization in his few but classic documentary films. From Nanook of the North" through "Moana," "Man of Aran," "Elephant Boy" and even "The Land," his subjects have been individuals in more or less primitive states. The beauty and power of nature, the fluid grace and dauntless courage of man and the toil of his eternal struggle against the elements—these have been Flaherty's meat.

But now in his "Louisiana Story," which is his first film in more than six years, the "father of documentary" makes a gracious, formal nod toward the machine. It is not a submissive nod, mind you, and it should not be mistaken to mean that Flaherty is conciliated to the intrusion of the machine in nature's realm. Significantly, the intrusion—of an oil-drilling derrick, in this case—only briefly disturbs the serenity of a Louisiana bayou and of a small boy's life. But, at least, it is recognition that the machine can be a useful friend of man, no more rapacious, in some way, than primitive man or nature themselves.

The medium of this acknowledgment is a beautiful hour-and-a-quarter film, photographed with great patience in Louisiana and put on at the Sutton Theatre yesterday. Like all of Flaherty's pictures, it is a gem of the cinematographer's art and it ripples and flows with deep feeling for beauty and simplicity.

Leisurely it tells a story of a little "cajun" (Acadian) boy who lives in the swamps—the bayou country—of Louisiana and whose life is suddenly filled with wonder and dismay when a great floating derrick is brought in to sink an oil well beneath the muck of the swamps. Slowly the lad makes acquaintance with the drillers who operate the giant machine, instructs them in his brand of magic and beholds their miracles in turn. He has had an enriching experience with people from the outside world when eventually the well is spudded and the derrick is taken away.

Within this simple story framework, Flaherty — being his own writer as well as director—has devised a genial, romantic parable, a conspicuously idyllic union of the pulse and rhythm of primitive life with that of the machine. For, along with his rhapsodic sequences showing the swampland activities of the lonely boy—his silent, intent fishing expeditions with his pet raccoon and his more violent struggle with an alligator whom he suspects of eating his pet—are blended dynamic sequences showing the drilling for and discovery of oil.

Ironically, the most powerful and truly eloquent phases of this film are not those portraying the youngster, beautiful and tender though they be, but those demonstrating the great energy in the operations of a drilling crew. Bursting with grace and vitality is a sequence wherein the boy beholds the ballet-like rigging of a drill stem in a towering derrick on a sticky night. The swift movement of the machinery, the coordination of the "roughneck" crew, the metallic clang of the drill pipe and its writhing ripples as it is jerked from the "stack"—all are merged by Flaherty into a beautiful and exciting dance. And a roaring, explosive sequence in which a blowout of the well is shown caps his guarded admiration for the laconic crew.

Indeed, though his fuller attention is given to the little swamp boy, played with exquisite simplicity by an actual "cajun" lad named Joseph Boudreaux, the interest of Flaherty in the drillers as a type of "strong man" is evident. And the men who play these characters, drillers for the Humble Oil Company in fact, are worthy of this admiration, for they do put on a good show. This may be significant, since the picture was made with money supplied by Standard Oil, but we doubt it. The ring of sincerity is clear in Flaherty's film.

A fine musical score by Virgil Thomson, performed by the Philadelphia Orchestra under the baton of Eugene Ormandy, is a great asset to the sound track which Flaherty has most sensitively devised.

S 29, 1948

HAMLET, from the play by William Shakespeare; directed and produced by Laurence Olivier, under the management of Filippo Del Guidice, for Two Cities Films. At the Park Avenue.
Hamlet ....Laurence Olivier
The Queen.......................Eileen Herlie
The King.........................Basil Sydney
Ophelia ....Jean Simmons
Polonius ....Felix Aylmer
Horatio ....Norman Wooland
Laertes ....Terence Morgan
First Player ....Harcourt Williams
Player King.............Patrick Troughton
Player Queen................Tony Tarver
Osric ....Peter Cushing
Gravedigger ....Stanley Holloway
Priest ....Russell Thorndyke
Francisco ....John Laurie
Bernardo ....Esmond Knight
Marcellus ....Anthony Quayle
Sea Captain..................Niall MacGinnis

By BOSLEY CROWTHER

It may come as something of a rude shock to the theatre's traditionalists to discover that the tragedies of Shakespeare can be eloquently presented on the screen. So bound have these poetic dramas long been to the culture of our stage that the very thought of their transference may have staggered a few profound die-hards. But now the matter is settled; the filmed "Hamlet" of Laurence Olivier gives absolute proof that these classics are magnificiently suited to the screen.

Indeed, this fine British-made picture, which opened at the Park Avenue last night under the Theatre Guild's elegant aegis, is probably as vivid and as clear an exposition of the doleful Dane's dilemma as modern-day playgoers have seen. And just as Olivier's ingenious and spectacular "Henry V" set out new visual limits for Shakespear's historical plays, his "Hamlet" envisions new vistas in the great tragedies of the Bard.

It is not too brash or insensitive to say that these eloquent plays, in their uncounted stage presentations, have been more often heard than seen. The physical nature of the theatre, from the time of the Globe until now, has compelled that the audiences of Shakespeare listen more closely than they look. And, indeed, the physical distance of the audience from the stage has denied it the privilege of partaking in some of the most intimate moments of the plays.

But just as Olivier's great "Henry" took the play further away by taking it out into the open—and thereby revealed it visually—his "Hamlet" makes the play more evident by bringing it closer to you. The subtle reactions of the characters, the movements of their faces and forms, which can be so dramatically expressive and which are more or less remote on the stage, are here made emotionally incisive by their normal proximity. Coupled with beautiful acting and inspired interpretations all the way, this visual closeness to the drama offers insights that are brilliant and rare.

Further, a quietly-moving camera which wanders intently around the vast and gloomy palace of Elsinore, now on the misty battlements, now in the great council chamber, now in the bedroom of the Queen, always looking and listening, from this and from that vantage point, gives the exciting impression of a silent observer of great events, aware that big things are impending and anxious not to miss any of them.

Actually, a lot of material which is in the conventional "Hamlet" text is missing from the picture— a lot of lines and some minor characters, notably those two fickle windbags, Rosencrantz and Guildenstern. And it is natural that some fond Shakespearians are going to be distressed at the suddenly discovered omission of this or that memorable speech. But some highly judicious editing has not done damage to the fullness of the drama nor to any of its most familiar scenes. In fact, it has greatly speeded the unfolding of the plot and has given much greater clarity to its noted complexities.

Hamlet is nobody's glass-man, and the dark and troubled workings of his mind are difficult, even for Freudians. But the openness with which he is played by Mr. Olivier in this picture makes him reasonably comprehensible. His is no cold and sexless Hamlet. He is a solid and virile young man, plainly tormented by the anguish and the horror of a double shock. However, in this elucidation, it is more his wretched dismay at the treachery of his mother than at the death of his father that sparks his woe. And it is this disillusion in women that shapes his uncertain attitude toward the young and misguided Ophelia, a victim herself of a parent's deceit.

In the vibrant performance of Eileen Herlie as the Queen is this concept evidenced, too, for plainly she shows the strain and heartache of a ruptured attachment to her son. So genuine is her disturbance that the uncommon evidence she gives that she knows the final cup is poisoned before she drinks it makes for heightened poignancy. And the luminous performance of Jean Simmons as the truly fair Ophelia brings honest tears for a shattered romance which is usually a so-what affair.

No more than passing mention can be made at this point of the fine work done by Norman Wooland as Horatio and by Basil Sydney as the King, by Felix Aylmer as Polonius, Terence Morgan as Laertes and all the rest. Perfect articulation is only one thing for which they can be blessed. A word, too, of commendation for the intriguing musical score of William Walton and for the rich designing of Roger Furse must suffice. In the straight black-and-white photography which Mr. Olivier has wisely used—wisely, we say, because the study is largely in somber mood—the palace conceived for this "Hamlet" is a dark and haunted palace. It is the grim and majestic setting for an uncommonly galvanic film.

S 30, 1948

COMMAND DECISION, screen play by William R. Laidlaw and George Froeschel, based on the play by William Wister Haines; directed by Sam Wood; produced by Sidney Franklin for Metro-Goldwyn-Mayer. At Loew's State.
Brig. Gen. K. C. Dennis...........Clark Gable
Maj. Gen. Roland Kane........Walter Pidgeon
T/Sgt. Immanuel T. Evans......Van Johnson
Brig. Gen. Clifton Garnet......Brian Donlevy
Elmer Brockhurst ....Charles Bickford
Col. Edward Martin.............John Hodiak
Congressman Arthur Malcolm...Edward Arnold

Capt. George Washington Lee,
                              Marshall Thompson
Major George Rockton............Richard Quine
Lieut. Ansel Goldberg. ......Cameron Mitchell
Major Homer V. Prescott.....Clinton Sundberg
Major Desmond Lansing............Ray Collins
Col. Earnest Haley.........Warner Anderson
Major Belding Davis ....John McIntyre
Congressman Stone.............Moroni Olsen
James Carwood ....John Ridgely
Capt. Lucius Jenks...........Michael Steele
Congressman Watson ....Edward Earle
Lieut. Col. Virgil Jackson......Mack Williams
Major Garrett Davenport.......James Millican

By BOSLEY CROWTHER

This corner is not prepared to warrant that "Command Decision" at Loew's State is the best of all possibly conceivable films on World War II. It covers a limited area—this picture which Metro has made from the excellent play and novel of William Wister Haines. And it faithfully shuns the old temptation to pull in action outside its natural frame. But within its field of observation of the behavior of Air Forces personnel on the "brass" or command-decision level, it gives us a most impressive sense of real heroism in high places behind the actual battle scenes.

True, the Air Forces' generals may not often have been as emotionally concerned with the casualty losses of their operations as is the key general in this film. Maybe they rarely were confronted with the terrible necessity, as shown here, of sending their best friends on missions of suicidal nature to achieve essential aims. And maybe they weren't all as resolute and as magnificently full of fight when caught in political snafus as is Gen. "Casey" Dennis, hero of this tale.

Those are questions of verity which will probably come to the minds of only those persons who were closely associated with the Air Forces during the war. And although they are naturally pertinent to the historical accuracy of this film, they are not very likely to trouble the average person who plunks down his coin.

For Metro has made this drama of one Air Force general's private bout with short-sightedness. obstruction and Pentagon politics a first-rate, he-man character study with strong philosophical overtones. And it has seen that the whole thing is acted with exceptional competence.

Whereas one might have expected that the transfer of the play to the screen would permit a great deal of off-stage action and aerial warfare to be brought to the audience's view, it is significant that the scriptwriters and Director Sam Wood have avoided same. That seems a brilliant decision in dramatic analysis. For actually the vital drama of this story is within the physical range of General Dennis, an old-time flier now compelled to do his fighting on the ground. And it is his desperate battle with his superiors to continue a costly bombing campaign, with all it means to the war and to his emotions, that is our exclusive concern.

Withal, Mr. Wood has included some legitimate stuff which was not in the play, but which comes within the scan of General Dennis and the camera's flexible eye. A tremendously tense and affecting "talk-down" and crash of a plane on the general's base in England has been finely reproduced from one that occurred. A grim dawn take-off of heavy bombers, bound on a rought mission, is shown, with appreciation of the terror in one of those events—and also with the pregnant comment that "it is all in the kids' hands now." And a brief but vivid comprehension of turmoil and death in the sky is caught in reverberations of sounds in the mourning general's mind.

Indeed, it is the performance of Clark Gable in this scene of a soldier's momentary grieving that tests his competence in the leading role. For this is not only the least likely but it is the most sentimental moment in the film, and the fact that Mr. Gable takes it with dignity and restraint bespeaks his worth. Otherwise, he makes of General Dennis a smart, tough, straight-shooting man, disciplinary yet human and a "right guy" to have in command. He is not as crisp and dynamic as Paul Kelly was on the stage, but that is our incidental tribute to Mr. Kelly and no reflection on the star.

As Dennis' immediate superior—the buffer between him and the "top brass"—Walter Pidgeon is remarkably revealing, giving a brilliantly inclusive scan of a military wangler and conniver who feels that ends justify his means. It is through his credible performance that the ironies of professional militarism are exposed. And it might be added, incidentally, that this is a new characterization for him.

Edward Arnold, too,. is expressive in the thankless and devastating role of a small-minded Congressional investigator, and Charles Bickford comes through solidly as a skeptical newspaper correspondent (whose contribution, unfortunately, is not as clear as it was in the play). Less can be said for Brian Donlevy, who is artificial as a "Pentagon commando," or for Van Johnson's pretty-boyish clowning as the general's wised-up orderly. A sarge with Mr. Johnson's beaming arrogance would pretty soon be flying more missions. Others who do their jobs ably are Cameron Mitchell, John Hodiak and Ray Collins. Happily, Metro hasn't brought in a single female —not even in a dream.

That is the film's particular virtue. It is rugged. And it makes a point, as well as a most disturbing drama, about the background realities of war.

Ja 20, 1949

DEVIL IN THE FLESH, screen play by Jean Aurenche and Pierre Bost, from the novel by Raymond Radiguet; directed by Claude Autant Lara; produced by Paul Graetz and distributed by A. F. E. Corporation. At the Paris
Marthe Grangier............Micheline Presle
Francois Jaubert.............Gerard Philipe
M. Jaubert.........................Debucourt
Mme. Grangier...................Denise Grey
M. Marin................................Palau
Jacques Lacombe..............Jean Varas
Mme. Marin..................Jeanne Perez
Anselme......................Charles Vissieres
Mme. Jaudert............Germaine Ledoyen
Doctor..................Maurice Lagrenee
Reporter........................Andre Bervil
Headwaiter.............Richard Francoeur

By BOSLEY CROWTHER

An extraordinarily frank and understanding contemplation of a tragic love affair between a 17-year-old French schoolboy and the wife of a soldier during the first World War is beautifully and tenderly accomplished in a most formidable new French film. "Devil

in the Flesh," which was presented at the Paris Theatre last night.

Already celebrated by the controversies it has aroused on the Continent, where it was presented under the title "Le Diable au Corps," and also by some slight embarrassment in its admission to the United States, this film is plainly one for starting impassioned discussion, pro and con. And its merits will likely be debated on other than artistic grounds. For not only does it have forebearance for the youthful principals in an adulterous romance but it lays bare the merciless irony in certain conventional attitudes.

Based on a brilliant novel of Raymond Radiguet, who died at the age of 20 shortly after writing this frankly autobiographical tale, "Devil in the Flesh," explores the raptures and the torments of a sensitive boy and girl whose lives are confused and prostrated by the social abnormalities of war. And, in their deep emotional turmoil, it vainly seeks to find some basic rationalization of the weakness and inhumanity of man.

Told in the form of a flashback from Armistice Day, 1918, with the youth in the case gazing gravely into a mirror in a deserted room, the story unfolds the tragic romance of this lad with a 20-year-old girl whom he first meets while helping wounded soldiers into a hospital where she works. It tells of their first warm attraction, their excitement at finding youthful love and their confusion and despair at a separation, which leads to the girl's marrying a soldier fiancé.

And then the great torture of their romance is recounted as their meetings are resumed after the soldier's departure, when passion takes over their love and the bliss of their personal fulfillment is darkened by conscience and responsibility. Lost in the grip of natural impulse and the tearing grasp of their baffled loyalties, their happiness turns to bitter torment and their hopeless romance is brought to a shattering end.

Certainly, Radiguet's novel told this story with power and subtlety, and the film which has been made

246

from it lacks nothing of those major qualities. For the screen play by Jean Aurenche and Pierre Bost is a beautifully organized thing, with an orchestration of the visual that literally scores and iterates the melding themes. The romance is developed in cycles, with images designed to correspond and contrast in bringing out the shifting of impulse and decision between the two.

And Claude Autant Lara has directed a magnificently talented cast to achieve the maximum of poignance and clarity in this mordant tale. In Gerard Philipe, who plays the schoolboy, he had a most apt and eloquent actor, indeed, for Philipe is not only brilliant as a performer but has a hauntingly tragic face. And his consequent expositions of the moods and vagaries of the boy, his burning passions and frightening indecisions, are enhanced by his fine facial expressiveness.

In Micheline Presle, playing the woman, he had a beautiful and sensitive performer, too—a youthful, full-bodied little creature with remarkably tender mouth and eyes. And through Denise Grey, as the latter's mother, he got a rare picture of maternal anxiety, caution and discipline, matched by the moving indication of a father's solicitude which Debucourt gives.

Produced by Paul Graetz, this picture is perhaps the finest, most mature from post-war France, and its admission for exhibition by our assorted censors is a triumph to be hailed.

Also on the bill at the Paris is an interesting, beautiful short describing the life and creativity of the aged sculptor, Maillol.

My 10, 1949

GERMANY YEAR ZERO: Written, directed and produced by Roberto Rossellini; released here by Superfilm Distributing Corporation. At the Ambassador.
Edmund Koehler ....Edmund Meschke
Eva Koehler ....Ingetraude Hinze
Karl Koehler . ...Franz Cruger
Herr Koehler ....Ernst Pittschau
The Schoolmaster ....Erich Guhne

By BOSLEY CROWTHER

That shattering sense of futility which Roberto Rossellini evoked with the trenchant and unrelenting candor of his great Italian film, "Paisan," emerges again as the keynote of the picture that he has made about the grief and demoralization of people in post-war Berlin. But whereas a flood of compassion came forth from that other film, there is a strange emptiness of genuine feeling in this "Germany Year Zero," which opened at the Ambassador last night.

Possibly one reason for it is that Mr. Rossellini has made this film in a form and a style that are different from anything of his that we have seen. "Paisan" and "Open City," while plainly dissimilar in form, were films that turned sharply and deftly on withering dramatic twists. The terror and torture of those pictures came out of vivid, electric incidents—from things which happened to people for whose fate and anguish we could care.

But, even though human desolation — especially of children — is naturally deplored, and there is plenty of desolation in "Germany Year Zero," it is presented in an oddly passive way. What might be a terribly touching story of the ruin of a 12-year-old boy, surrounded by relatives and associates in a most miserably degraded state, becomes, in the cold accumulation by the camera of sordid details, little more than a literal (and depressing) presentation of an objective case.

The boy—an actual Berlin youngster whom Mr. Rossellini picked up, along with the rest of his performers when he made this film in Berlin two years ago—is certainly a tragic example of Europe's young innocents whose lives were torn and wasted by their fathers' unforgivable sins. And the hard and depraved circumstances in which he is forced to live are not only shocking to witness but they are a mockery to the decency of man.

Mr. Rossellini doesn't spare us—although it looks as though the censor often does. He shows us degradation and depravity at its most wretched and low. From scenes showing people in Berlin slicing meat off a dead horse in the streets to suggestions of vice among children, he puts post-war Berlin on the line. No irony of the desolation of Hitler's "empire" escapes his camera. The endless background of ruined buildings frames a foreground of scarred and ruined lives.

However, this manifest of details— this bill of particulars—is placed on the screen as though its showing was all the director aimed to do. Crowded dwellings, petty thievery, prostitution, black marketing, perversion and vice—these form the background of the youngster that seems Mr. Rossellini's main concern. Actually, his bit of a drama, wherein the boy poisons his ill father and then, overwhelmed by his anguish, commits suicide, is out of key. Following the realistic pattern the youngster more likely wouldn't care.

And here is a second possible reason for the picture's emotional emptiness: the barren and lethargic nature of most of the characters in it. The youngster, played by Edmund Meschke, is a sadly appealing lad, at times, especially in his final ordeal of wandering before jumping off a roof. But, in toto, he comes out a sallow and futile little thing. And Ingetraude Hinze, who plays his sister, seems a thoroughly contrived character. Ernest Pittschau, who plays the father, shows a weakling, hopeless and spent, while Franz Cruger makes the brother of the youngster a craven ex-Nazi clod.

It may be that "Germany Year Zero" is a social document beyond reproach. Certainly its pictorial brilliance and its social detail suggest it is. And certainly the characters in it—who all speak heavy German, by the way, with English subtitles for translation—are credible relics of the war's incalculable waste. But the sum effect of the presentation is a sense of bleak discomfort and despair, unrelieved by any purge of the emotions. That may be all we could expect.

S 20, 1949

ALL THE KING'S MEN, screen play by Robert Rossen, based on the Robert Penn Warren novel of the same name; directed and produced by Mr. Rossen for Columbia Pictures. At the Victoria.

Willie Stark	Broderick Crawford
Anne Stanton	Joanne Dru
Jack Burden	John Ireland
Tom Stark	John Derek
Sadie Burke	Mercedes McCambridge
Adam Stanton	Shepperd Strudwick
Tiny Duffy	Ralph Dumke
Lucy Stark	Anne Seymour
Mrs. Burden	Katharine Warren
Judge Stanton	Raymond Greenleaf
Sugar Boy	Walter Burke
Dolph Pillsbury	Will Wright
Floyd McEvoy	Grandon Rhodes
Pa Stark	H. C. Miller
Hale	Richard Hale
Commissioner	William Bruce
Sheriff	A. C. Tillman
Madison	Houseley Stevenson
Minister	Truett Myers
Football Coach	Phil Tully
Helene Hale	Helene Stanley

By BOSLEY CROWTHER

Out of Robert Penn Warren's prize novel, "All the King's Men," which was obviously based on the familiar rise and fall of the late Huey Long, Robert Rossen has written and directed, as well as personally produced, a rip-roaring film of the same title. It opened at the Victoria yesterday.

We have carefully used that descriptive as the tag for this new Columbia film because a quality of turbulence and vitality is the one that it most fully demonstrates. In telling a complicated story of a self-made and self-styled "redneck hick" who batters his way to political kingdom in an unspecified southern state, the picture bounces from raw-boned melodrama into dark psychological depths and thrashes around in those regions until it claws back to violences again. Consistency of dramatic structure—or of character revelation—is not in it. But it has a superb pictorialism which perpetually crackles and explodes.

And because of this rich pictorialism, which embraces a wide and fluid scene, it gathers a frightening comprehension of the potential of demagoguery in this land. From ugly illustrations of back-room spittoon politics to wild illuminations of howling political mobs, it catches the dim but dreadful aspect of ignorance and greed when played upon by theatrics, eloquence and bluff. It visions the vulgar spellbinders and political hypocrites for what they are and it looks on extreme provincialism with a candid and pessimistic eye.

In short, Mr. Rossen has assembled in this starkly unprettified film a piece of pictorial journalism that is remarkable for its brilliant parts. It clearly observes the beginnings of a Huey Long type of demagogue in an humble and honest lawyer fighting the "bosses" in a sleepy dirt-road town. It follows this disillusioned fellow as he gets the hang of politics and discovers the strange intoxication of his own unprincipled charm. And it wallows with him in egoism, corruption and dictatorial power until he is finally shot down by an assassin when his triumphs appear uncontrolled.

All of these things, Mr. Rossen, as director, has pictured stunningly. His final episode of personal violence and mob hysteria is superb for savagery. But in his parallel endeavors to transfer from Mr. Warren's book some real understanding of the character, he has met with much less success. In fact, the whole middle section of the film, which is deeply concerned with the brutal impact of the fellow upon his wife, son, mistress and friends, is a heavy confusion of dense dramatics that is saved from being downright dull only by the variety and vigor of pictorial detail.

And you may count as pictorial detail the performance which Broderick Crawford gives as the big, brawling, boisterous "hick" lawyer who makes himself a momentary "king." Mr. Crawford concentrates tremendous energy into every delineation he plays, whether it is the enthusiasm of a callow bumpkin or the virulence of a drunken demagogue. Although it is hard to know precisely why he gravitates and acts the way he does, he draws a compelling portrait, in two dimensions, of an egomaniac.

Less can be said for the other principal performers in the film—not because of their own shortcomings but because of the unresolved roles they play. Joanne Dru is a pretty, well-dressed cipher as the meaningless mistress of the man, and John Ireland is a loose-limbed, dead-panned puppet as a newspaper reporter who follows him around. Shepperd Strudwick fumbles vaguely with the passions of the doctor who assassinates the brute, and Mercedes McCambridge is picturesque but vagrant as a hard-boiled henchman in skirts. However, the various people who play cheap politicos, especially Will Wright and Ralph Dumke, are as genuine as pot-bellied stoves. As satellites to Mr. Crawford, in the raw, racy portions of the film, they help to bring color and excitement to this ironic "All the King's Men."

N 9, 1949

THE BICYCLE THIEF, story and screenplay by Cesare Zavattini, based on the novel of the same name by Luigi Bartolini; directed by Vittorio De Sica; produced in Rome by De Sica Production Company, and released here by Mayer-Burstyn. At the World.
Antonio .... Lamberto Maggiorani
Maria .... Lianella Carell
Bruno .... Enzo Staiola
The Medium .... Elena Altieri
The Thief .... Vittorio Antonucci
Baiocco .... Gino Saltamerenda

By BOSLEY CROWTHER

Again the Italians have sent us a brilliant and devastating film in Vittorio De Sica's rueful drama of modern city life, "The Bicycle Thief." Widely and fervently heralded by those who had seen it abroad (where it already has won several prizes at various film festivals), this heart-tearing picture of frustration, which came to the World yesterday, bids fair to fulfill all the forecasts of its absolute triumph over here.

For once more the talented De Sica, who gave us the shattering "Shoe Shine," that desperately tragic demonstration of juvenile corruption in post-war Rome, has laid hold upon and sharply imaged in simple and realistic terms a major—indeed, a fundamental and universal—dramatic theme. It is the isolation and loneliness of the little man in this complex social world that is ironically blessed with institutions to comfort and protect mankind.

Although he has again set his drama in the streets of Rome and has populated it densely with significant contemporary types, De Sica is concerned here with something which is not confined to

Rome nor solely originated by post-war disorder and distress. He is pondering the piteous paradoxes of poverty, no matter where, and the wretched compulsions of sheer self-interest in man's desperate struggle to survive. And while he has limited his vista to a vivid cross-section of Roman life, he actually is holding a mirror up to millions of civilized men.

His story is lean and literal, completely unburdened with "plot," and written by Cesare Zavattini with the camera exclusively in mind. Based on a novel by Luigi Bartolini, it is simply the story of a poor working man whose essential bicycle is stolen from him and who hunts feverishly to find it throughout one day. The man is a modest bill-poster; he must have a bicycle to hold his newly found job; he has a wife and small son dependent on him; the loss is an overwhelming blow. And so, for one long, dismal Sunday he and his youngster scour the teeming streets of Rome, seeking that vital bicycle which, we must tell you, they never find.

That is the picture's story—it is as stark and direct as that, and it comes to a close with a fade-out as inconclusive as a passing nod. But during the course of its telling in the brilliant director's trenchant style, it is as full and electric and compelling as any plot-laden drama you ever saw. Every incident, every detail of the frantic and futile hunt is a taut and exciting adventure, in which hope is balanced against despair. Every movement of every person in it, every expression on every face is a striking illumination of some implicit passion or mood.

Just to cite a few episodes and crises, there is the eloquent inrush of hope when the workman acquires his bicycle after his wife pawns the sheets from their beds; there is the horrible, sickening moment when he realizes that the bicycle is gone, seized and ridden away before his own eyes by a thief who escapes in the traffic swirl; there is the vain and pathetic expedition to hunt the parts of the bicycle in a second-hand mart and there is the bleak and ironic pursuit of a suspect into a church during a mass for the poor. There are also lighter touches, such as a flock of babbling German seminarians rudely crowding the father and boy out of a shelter into the rain and a dash after the thief into a bordello, with the little boy compelled to remain outside.

Indeed, the whole structure of this picture, with its conglomeration of experiences, all interlocked with personal anguish, follows a classic plan. It is a plan in which the comedy and tragedy of daily life are recognized. As a matter of fact, both the story and the structure of this film might have been used by Charlie Chaplin in the old days to make one of his great wistful films, for "The Bicycle Thief" is, in essence, a poignant and bitter irony—the irony of a little fellow buffeted by an indifferent world.

As directed by De Sica, however, the natural and the real are emphasized, with the film largely shot in actual settings and played by a non-professional cast. In the role of the anguished workman, Lamberto Maggiorani is superb, expressing the subtle mood transitions of the man with extraordinary power. And Enzo Staiola plays his small son with a firmness that fully reveals the rugged determination and yet the latent sensitivity of the lad. One of the most overpowering incidents in the film occurs when the father, in desperation, thoughtlessly slaps the anxious boy. Lianella Carell is also moving as the mother—a smaller role—and Vittorio Antonucci is hard and shabby as the thief. He is the only professional in the large cast.

One further word for the music which has been aptly written and used to raise the emotional potential—the plaintive theme that accompanies the father and son, the music of rolling bicycles and the "morning music," full of freshness and bells. De Sica has artfully wrapped it into a film that will tear your heart, but which should fill you with warmth and compassion.

250

People should see it—and they should care.

Excellent English subtitles translate the Italian dialogue.

D 13, 1949

BATTLE OF THE RAILS (BATAILLE DU RAIL), written by Colette Audry; produced and directed by Rene Clement with the cooperation of the Military Commission of the National Commission and the National Railroads of France; narration by Charles Boyer and released here by Mayer-Burstyn. At the Apollo.

Railroad Worker	Clarieux
Railroad Worker	Daurand
Chief Operations Room	Deagneaux
Camargue	Tony Laurent
Station Master	Leray
Locomotive Engineer	Redon
Seized Railroad Worker	Pauleon
Yard Worker	Rauzena
Railroad Worker	Lozach
Railroad Worker	Salina
Railroad Worker	Woll

By BOSLEY CROWTHER

It was four years ago that word first reached us of a powerful new picture made in France depicting in documentary manner the resistance of French railway workers during the war. "Bataille du Rail" was its title and, according to the glowing reports, it had been made by the French cinema cooperative with the assistance of the railway workers themselves. Here was the authentic picture of the slow-downs and sabotage by which the Nazis were hamstrung by the lowly "cheminots," the rumors said. Eager American exhibitors waited to show it—in vain. Seems that some sort of switch-throwers were on the track of the picture, too.

At long last, however, it has reached us. Under the translated title, "Battle of the Rails," it had its American première at the Apollo yesterday. And except that it isn't as timely as it might have been four years ago, when the excitement of the war was still upon us, it amply fulfills advance reports. For here, in this ninety-minute picture, is a sizzling dramatic account of realistic action and adventure in the fascinating realm of railway trains—of smuggling, spying, train-wrecking and correlated fighting by the bold Maquis.

Introduced and narrated by Charles Boyer, who gives a clear and restrained report on the critical nature of the railways for the American audience, the film begins with vivid details of the ways in which the railway workers used their unique opportunities to frustrate their country's enemies. Sharply and tautly it shows us, under René Clement's fine directorial hand, how the trainmen, with an appearance of great innocence, carried messages and men for the "underground," how they smuggled Jews across the country and caused impossible delays in the operation of vital trains. It also contains poignant episodes—no more than piercing glimpses, at times—of occasions when their devices did not always succeed. One shot of a frightened woman and her little girl being taken off a train or a sequence showing the execution of six hostage trainmen tell grim tales.

The better part of the film, however, is a rapid and suspenseful account of the efforts of the combined railway-worker and resistance fighters to stop a Nazi munitions train. And this part of the picture, full of rare actuality details, is a first-rate action thriller, aside from its conspicuous historical interest.

First, the key workers in the control room arrange to wreck an old freight across the right of way—a device which provides some wry humor, though only temporary success. Then they inspire a full-scale and relentless hold-up attack upon an armored train which precedes the munitions convoy—another device which is heroic but fails. Finally, they send some bold wreckers to dynamite the tracks directly in front of the train, and this device is successful—pictorially successful, too. To get this spectacular incident, the French producers actually ran a long train loaded with Nazi munitions over a high embankment. The consequent disaster is as fancy a one as you'd want to see. Unfortunately, it is succeeded by some anti-climactic episodes.

With plenty of trains, railway equipment and actual trainmen, Mr. Clement has achieved a picture of stunning realism as well as dramatic force. His "actors"—all carefully recruited for the familiar jobs they had to do—deserve a blanket commendation, with no one singled out for particular note. To him and to his scenarists go our respect and gratitude for keeping this film free of needless romance. It is one of the earliest—and still one of the top post-war French films.

D 27, 1949

CINEMA VS. TELEVISION

The fifties were a time of protracted crisis, characterized by desperate attempts to salvage the disintegrating American movie industry. Attendance figures were dropping alarmingly, largely due to the spread of television. For a short time, before the introduction of color television, movies in "gorgeous Technicolor" exerted a certain attraction. Another innovation Hollywood explored in this battle between the two media was size, the one feature the television screen could not match. The screen was horizontally extended by introducing several competing processes. Cinerama was introduced in 1952, Cinemascope in 1953, and many other designs followed in rapid succession. However, the wide screen required complex and costly technical adaptations; it was never standardized for universal distribution; and it created aesthetic problems in pictorial composition. These were not insurmountable obstacles. But in spite of favorable response to the wide screen image, the efforts to regain the lost ground were vain. Happy with the picture tube at home, and never much concerned with standards of taste and artistic quality, the public failed to return to the movie theatres, except for an occasional, intensively promoted giant production, emphasizing vast panoramic vistas and spectacular mass scenes. The standard feature production that had been the economic rock of the film industry, insuring its stability, and guaranteeing steady employment, declined inexorably. The traditional production system, with its strict division of labor, and with the studio boss or producer in absolute command, no longer worked. The only sound and constructive consequence of the crisis was the increase of so-called "independent" production which used the technical facilities and the promotional power of the big studios, but retained complete control of the production proper. This opened the door for young, new talent and more daring innovation.

Eventually, though, film and television producers arrived at mutually beneficial agreements. Television needed an endless supply of films to fill its programs, while the film industry owned an enormous stock of useless old films that now became unexpectedly a rich source of revenue—regardless of artistic qualities. The solution—which is still in effect today—may be merely an expedient, but it has proved to be a workable one. Moreover, many television features, especially serials like *Peyton Place* or *Gunsmoke*, are original productions. These are being shot in the well-equipped studios that had become deserted, providing steady employment for technicians and craftsmen as well as opportunities for new acting and directing talent. As television films are neither so long nor so elaborate nor remotely so expensive as feature film productions, the element of risk is considerably lower than the investment in a feature film that may fail at the box office. This arrangement was not in itself sufficient to save the film industry, but it assured the industry's survival during this difficult period.

Another factor affecting the domestic industry was the growing influx of foreign films. Although they did not attract the large masses on which the Hollywood empires were founded, they appealed nevertheless to a sizable segment of the more sophisticated population as well as to the spectacularly increasing contingent of the youthful "film generation" inside and outside the colleges. The proliferation of "art" theatres all over the country, as well as abroad, is evidence for this interest in non-Hollywood film fare. Since the end of World War Two, annual film festivals have exhibited the latest films from all over the world, affording an opportunity to get acquainted with the global production, with new techniques, trends, and personalities. Thus, for the first time, the films of Kurosawa, Mizoguchi, and Satyajit Ray, as well as provocative, highly accomplished productions from the Iron Curtain countries, could be seen and appreciated. Until then, it had been a fact almost unknown in this country that Hollywood had not exclusively dominated the world market. Japan and India, for example, had been steadily producing a considerably larger output of films than the United States. Although these films have not generally been of great merit, the oriental market was, and still is, saturated and satisfied with them. It was only in the fifties that the true stature of Buñuel, Bergman, and Dreyer was fully recognized; it was in the fifties that Fellini and Antonioni became established as major artists; it was in the late fifties that the "New Wave" burst upon the scene, a group of brilliant young French film makers, including Truffaut, Godard, Resnais, Chabrol and countless others. These events split the American film audience into two sections—summarily speaking, the "Art Theatre" and the Neighborhood Theatre patrons—that became even more sharply divided in the sixties.

THE THIRD MAN, story and screen play by
Graham Greene; music by Anton Karas; directed and produced by Carol Reed; a Selznick release, presented by David O. Selznick and Sir Alexander Korda. At the Victoria.
Holly Martins.... ....Joseph Cotten
Anna Schmidt ....Alida Valli
Harry Lime ....Orson Welles
Major Calloway ....Trevor Howard
Sergeant Paine ....Bernard Lee
Kurtz ... .Ernst Deutsch
Dr. Winkel ....Erich Ponto
Popesco ....Siegfried Breuer
Professor Crabbin ....Wilfrid Hyde-White
Harry's Porter ....Paul Hoerbiger
Anna's Housekeeper ....Hedwig Bleibtreu

By BOSLEY CROWTHER

The haunting music of a zither, the ring of Vienna's cobbled streets and a ghostly Graham Greene story, about a man-hunt in that seamy capital flow smoothly and beautifully together into one piece of top screen artifice in Carol Reed's most recent (and most touted) mystery-thriller-romance, "The Third Man." Trailing Continental glories and faint echoes of that zither's weird refrains, this extraordinarily fascinating picture began a run at the Victoria yesterday.

But we feel we are bound to inform you that our key word is "artifice" in that thoroughly enthusiastic introductory paragraph. For the simple fact is that "The Third Man," for all the awesome hoopla it has received, is essentially a first-rate contrivance in the way of melodrama—and that's all. It isn't a penetrating study of any European problem of the day (except that it skirts around black-markets and the sinister anomalies of "zones"). It doesn't present any "message." It hasn't a point of view. It is just a bang-up melodrama, designed to excite and entertain. In the light of the buzz about it, this is something we feel you should know. Once it is understood clearly, there is no need for further asides.

For into this strangely off-beat story of a young American visitor's attempts to get to the bottom of the mystery of a friend's dubious "death" in Vienna's streets, Mr. Reed has brilliantly packaged the whole bag of his cinematic tricks, his whole range of inventive genius for making the camera expound. His eminent gifts for compressing a wealth of suggestion in single shots, for building up agonized tension and popping surprises are fully exercised. His devilishly mischievous humor also runs lightly through the film, touching the darker depressions with little glints of the gay or macabre.

To be sure, Mr. Greene has contributed conspicuously to the job with a script that is cleverly constructed and pungently laced with dialogue. The smoothness and ease with which the edges of the mystery plot tongue and groove—with which the missing man's sweetheart joins the drama, the police build the case and such as that, while all the while little bits of color and character are worked in—make for complete fascination. Except for one far-fetched allowance for poor police-craft (a dead man is not properly identified) and a chase through the sewers for the climax (which is graphic but conventional) the script is tops.

So, too, are the performances of everyone in the cast—of Joseph Cotten as the American who blunders upon mystery and romance; of Valli, the cool Italian actress, who plays the refugee girl of the "dead" man; of Trevor Howard as a British police major, a beautifully crisp and seasoned gent; of Bernard Lee as his capable sergeant and of several grand continental "types." Even our old and perennially villainous friend, Orson Welles, does a right nice job of shaping a dark and treacherous shadow as the "third man."

However, with all due allowance, top credit must go to Mr. Reed for molding all possible elements into a thriller of superconsequence. And especially must he be credited with the brilliant and triumphant device of using the music of a zither as

256

the sole musical background in this film. This eerie and mesmerizing music, which is rhythmic and passionate and sad, becomes, indeed, the commentator—the genius loci —of the Viennese scene. Pulsing with hopefulness and longing with "menace" and poignance and love, it thoroughly completes the illusions of a swift and intriguing romance. **F 3, 1950**

THE RULES OF THE GAME, screen play by Jean Renoir and Koch, directed by Mr. Renoir, produced by Claude Renoir and released here by Cine-Classics, Inc.
Count Robert de La Chesnyest......Dalio
Christine ....Nora Gregor
Genevieve ....Mila Parely
Octave ....Jean Renoir
Jurieux ....Roland Tourain
Marceau ....Carette
Schumacher ....Gaston Modot
Lisette ....Paulette Dubost

Exactly what Jean Renoir had in mind when he wrote, performed in and directed "The Rules of the Game," Saturday's French import at the Fifth Avenue Playhouse, is anybody's guess. This is the same M. Renoir, if you please, who gave us those notable imports, "Grand Illusion" and "The Human Beast," not to mention "The Southerner," from Hollywood. The new arrival, however, is really one for the buzzards.

Here we have a baffling mixture of stale sophistication, coy symbolism and galloping slapstick that almost defies analysis. The distributors claim that the picture, made shortly before the war, was banned by the Occupation on grounds of immorality. Rest assured it wasn't immortality. And there's nothing particularly sizzling in this account of some addleheaded lounge lizards tangling up their amours on a week-end house party in the country.

One minute they're making sleek Noel Coward talk about art and free love, the next they're behaving like a Li'l Abner family reunion, chasing each other from pantry to boudoir to the din of wrecked furniture, yelling and random gunfire. One carefully picturesque sequence, a rabbit hunt, may or may not be fraught with Renoir meaning, but the grand

finale, in which everybody down to the cook joins in a hysterical conquest race, would shame the Keystone cops.

In the juicy role of a family friend, M. Renoir acts as though it were his last day on earth. The other principals, Dalio, Nora Gregor and Mila Parely, are right behind him. The picture ends abruptly with an unaccountable murder, whereupon one of the philanderers murmurs that the victim didn't learn the rules of the game. If the game is supposed to be life, love or hide-and-seek, which makes more sense, it's M. Renoir's own secret. At any rate, the master has dealt his admirers a pointless, thudding punch below the belt. **H. H. T.**

Ap 10, 1950

THE STORM WITHIN ("Les Parents Terribles"): a French film written and directed by Jean Cocteau, produced by Alexandre Mnouchkine and Francis Cosne and released by Discina International Films. At the Fifth Avenue Playhouse.
Michel ... .Jean Marais
Madeleine ....Josette Day
Yvonne ....Yvonne de Bray
Georges ....Marcel Andre
Aunt Leo ....Gabrielle Dorziat

As an artist who has been known to exercise a fertile imagination, Jean Cocteau is disappointingly unimaginative in "The Storm Within," his film adaptation of his play, "Les Parents Terribles," which arrived at the Fifth Avenue Playhouse on Saturday.

For M. Cocteau, who herein is inspecting the amours of a singularly unstable family, merely has come up with a series of tempestuous harangues, hysterical outbursts, nebulous soul-searchings and petty plots signifying nothing especially new about either sacred or profane love. And, despite a generally proficient cast, "The Storm Within" is, anomalously, a static drama, which talks a great deal about emotions while projecting little of same.

As the director of this study, M. Cocteau is equally unimaginative. He simply has photographed five characters in the two different apartments they occupy to tell the story of a 22-year-old youth, madly loved by his mother, a frantic dame who nearly ruins her son's newly-found romances. There are complications, of course. It turns out that the youth's girl friend also is his father's mistress, a fact unknown to the smitten young man. Eventually the fifth character, the spinster aunt and, obviously, the strongest of this flighty group, helps bring matters to a clear if somewhat tragic climax.

As the spoiled, fragile youth, Jean Marais is given to flamboyant tantrums, posturings and declamations to illustrate a complex-ridden nature, a performance that is tense but hardly subtle. As his mother, who commits suicide when she realizes she has lost her son, Yvonne de Bray is giving a wholly sensitive portrayal. And Gabrielle Dorziat, as the maiden aunt who aids in severing the attachment; Marcel Andre, as the philandering father, and Josette Day, as the young, blond cause of it all, contribute professional characterizations.

But despite their efforts and a profusion of literal English subtitles, which make the French dialogue eminently lucid, "The Storm Within" is only a tempest in a teapot.
                         A. W

                 Ap 24, 1950

THE ASPHALT JUNGLE screen play by Ben Maddow and John Huston, from a novel by W. R. Burnett; directed and produced by Mr. Huston for Metro-Goldwyn-Mayer. At the Capitol.

Dix Handley	Sterling Hayden
Alonzo D. Emmerich	Louis Calhern
Doll Conovan	Jean Hagen
Gus Ninissi	James Whitmore
Doc Erwin Riedenschnieder	Sam Jaffe
Police Commissioner Hardy	John McIntire
Cobby	Marc Lawrence
Lieut. Ditrich	Barry Kelley
Louis Ciavelli	Anthony Caruso
Maria Ciavelli	Teresa Celli
Angela Phinlay	Marilyn Monroe
Timmons	William Davis
May Emmerich	Dorothy Tree
Bob Brannom	Brad Dexter
Dr. Swanson	John Maxwell

By BOSLEY CROWTHER

Ever since W. R. Burnett's "Little Caesar" muscled into films with a quality of arrogance and toughness such as the screen had not previously known, this writer and this type of story—about criminals in the higher realms of crime—have been popular and often imitated, but "Little Caesar" has yet to be surpassed. However,

we've got to say one thing: a lot of pictures have come close—and one of them is "The Asphalt Jungle," also from a novel by Mr. Burnett.

This film, derived by Ben Maddow and John Huston from Mr. Burnett's book and directed by Mr. Huston in brilliantly naturalistic style, gives such an electrifying picture of the whole vicious circle of a crime—such an absorbing illustration of the various characters involved, their loyalties and duplicities, and of the minutiae of crime techniques—that one finds it hard to tag the item of repulsive exhibition in itself. Yet that is our inevitable judgment of this film, now on the Capitol's screen.

For the plain truth is that this picture—sobering though it may be in its ultimate demonstration that a life of crime does not pay—enjoins the hypnotized audience to hobnob with a bunch of crooks, participate with them in their plunderings and actually sympathize with their personal griefs. The vilest creature in the picture, indeed, is a double-crossing cop. And the rest of the police, while decent, are definitely antagonists.

Furthermore, unlike "Little Caesar," this picture does not expose any particular canker of society that has not often been displayed upon the screen. Its characters are ordinary criminals—a mastermind for a big jewel robbery, a safe-cracker, a hoodlum, a crooked lawyer and other types of the underworld—none of them novel or distinguished in the disturbance of society by crime. Mr. Burnett, Mr. Huston and this picture are merely concerned with the excitement of one case.

But, in that meager interest, we've got to hand it to the boys, particularly to Mr. Huston: they've done a terrific job! From the very first shot, in which the camera picks up a prowling thug, sliding along between buildings to avoid a police car in the gray and liquid dawn, there is ruthless authority in this picture, the hardness and clarity of steel, and remarkably subtle suggestion that conveys a whole involvement of distorted personality and inveterate crime. Mr. Huston's "The Maltese Fal-

258

con," which brought him to the fore as a sure and incisive director, had nothing in the way of toughness on this film.

Likewise, the story construction, both with pen and camera, is of a most intriguing nature. Slowly the elements merge—here a thwarted vagrant, there a conniving cop, here a greasy bookmaker and there an ex-convict with a plan. Smoothly and swiftly they're assembled until a masterful jewel robbery is afoot—a complex job of safecracking that will make you scream in suspense. And then comes the big double-dealing by the lawyer brought in to back the stunt, fireworks, flight into hideouts and the slow, inexorable hunt of the police. Mr. Huston has filmed a straight crime story about as cleverly and graphically as it could be filmed.

And that's the way his actors have played it. Louis Calhern as the big lawyer who tries to pull a doublecross and muffs it is exceptionally fluid and adroit and Sterling Hayden is sure-fire as a brazen hoodlum who just wants to go back home. Likewise Sam Jeffe does wonders as a coolheaded mastermind, James Whitmore is taut as a small "fixer" and John McIntire is crisp as a chief of police. But, then, everyone in this picture—which was produced, incidentally, by M. G. M.—gives an unimpeachable performance. If only it all weren't so corrupt!

Je 9, 1950

PANIC IN THE STREETS, based on a story by Edna and Edward Anhalt; adaptation by Daniel Fuchs; screenplay by Richard Murphy; directed by Elia Kazan and produced by Sol C. Siegel for Twentieth Century-Fox. At the Roxy.

Clinton Reed	Richard Widmark
Police Captain Warren	Paul Douglas
Nancy Reed	Barbara Bel Geddes
Blackie	Walter (Jack) Palance
Fitch	Zero Mostel
Neff	Dan Riss
John Mefaris	Alexis Minotis
Poldi	Guy Thomajan
Vince	Tommy Cook
Jordan	Edward Kennedy
Cook	H. T. Tsiang
Kochak	Lewis Charles
Dubin	Ray Muller
Tommy	Tommy Rettig
Jeanette	Lenka Peterson
Pat	Pat Walshe
Dr. Gafney	Paul Hostetler
Kleber	George Ehmig
Lee	John Schilleci
Ben	Waldo Pitkin
Sgt. Phelps	Leo Zinser
Dr. Mackey	Beverly C. Brown
Cortelyou	William A. Dean
Major Murray	H. Waller Fowler Jr.
Wynant	Rex Moad
Johnston	Irvine Vidacovich

Melodramas in which murderers and smugglers are the objects of intense manhunts are as much in evidence at Broadway movie houses just now as weeds are in suburban gardens. On Thursday "Edge of Doom" and "A Lady Without Passport" came to town and yesterday marked the arrival of "Panic in the Streets" and "Kiss Tomorrow Goodbye." As the saying goes, "Youse pays yur money and takes yur cherce."

The first choice this morning is "Panic in the Streets," a Twentieth Century-Fox contribution which Elia Kazan has directed with a keen sense of appreciation for violence and suspense. Now on the Roxy's screen, the film shapes up as a generally gripping entertainment, though there are some stretches when the story loses its tension.

A routine waterfront homicide suddenly becomes a source of frightening apprehension to city officials when a United States Public Health Service doctor discovers that the victim was infected with pneumonic plague. The problem of controlling a possible epidemic presents a seemingly insurmountable challenge to the police who have no idea about the dead man's identity much less that of the man or men who shot him. Although the audience knows who the killer is the search is conducted with such forceful pictorial imagery that this information does not detract from the excitement.

It is always dangerous to take the audience so much into confidence, but Mr. Kazan is a director who can manage to stay a step ahead of the crowd and in "Panic in the Streets" he keeps the action going at a pace which seldom permits interest to lag. The fact that the killer and his aides are ignorant of the murdered man's disease and may themselves be carriers of the deadly, virulent germ gives added impetus to the story.

Good acting helps out too, and

the people who carry the principal roles in "Panic in the Streets"— Richard Widmark as the doctor; Paul Douglas as the police captain who directs the manhunt with a cynical assurance of its futility with nothing definite to latch onto; Walter Palance as the killer and Zero Mostel as a cringing henchman—all give commendable performances. A newcomer to films, Mr. Palance is a tall, rugged man with deep-set, piercing eyes and a granite-like face that commands attention. Technically there can be no quarrel with Mr. Widmark's performance, but his mannerisms are not precisely those one would associate with a doctor.

Although it is excitingly presented, "Panic in the Streets" misses the mark as superior melodrama because it is not without obvious, sometimes annoying exaggeration that demands more indulgence than some spectators may be willing to contribute. However, there is an electric quality to the climax staged in a warehouse on the New Orleans waterfront that should compensate for minor annoyances which come to the surface spasmodically in "Panic in the Streets."

T.M.P.

Ag 5, 1950

SUNSET BOULEVARD, screen play by Charles Brackett, Billy Wilder and D. M. Marshman Jr.; directed by Mr. Wilder and produced by Mr. Brackett for Paramount Pictures. At the Music Hall.

Joe Gillis	William Holden
Norma Desmond	Gloria Swanson
Max Von Mayerling	Erich von Stroheim
Betty Schaefer	Nancy Olson
Sheldrake	Fred Clark
Morino	Lloyd Gough
Artie Green	Jack Webb
Undertaker	Franklyn Barnum
First Finance Man	Larry Blake
Second Finance Man	Charles Dayton
Themselves	Cecil B. DeMille Hedda Hopper Buster Keaton Anna Q. Nilsson H. B. Warner Ray Evans Jay Livingston

A segment of life in Hollywood is being spread across the screen of the Music Hall in "Sunset Boulevard." Using as the basis of their frank, caustic drama a scandalous situation involving a faded, aging silent screen star and a penniless, cynical young script writer, Charles Brackett and Billy Wilder (with an assist from D. M. Marshman Jr.)

have written a powerful story of the ambitions and frustrations that combine to make life in the cardboard city so fascinating to the outside world.

"Sunset Boulevard" is by no means a rounded story of Hollywood, past or present. But it is such a clever compound of truth and legend—and is so richly redolent of the past, yet so contemporaneous—that it seemingly speaks with great authority. "Sunset Boulevard" is that rare blend of pungent writing, expert acting, masterly direction and unobtrusively artistic photography which quickly casts a spell over an audience and holds it enthralled to a shattering climax.

Gloria Swanson was coaxed out of long retirement to portray the pathetic, forgotten film queen, Norma Desmond, and now it can be said that it is inconceivable that anyone else might have been considered for the role. As the wealthy, egotistical relic desperately yearning to hear again the plaudits of the crowd, Miss Swanson dominates the picture. Even in those few scenes when she is not on screen her presence is felt like the heavy scent of tuberoses which hangs over the gloomy, musty splendor of her memento-cluttered mansion in Beverly Hills.

Playing the part of Joe Gillis, the script writer, William Holden is doing the finest acting of his career. His range and control of emotions never falters and he engenders a full measure of compassion for a character who is somewhat less than admirable. Hounded by collectors from the auto-finance company, the struggling, disillusioned writer grabs an opportunity to make some money by helping Norma Desmond to fashion a screen play about Salome with which the hopeless egomaniac believes she will make a "return to the millions of people who have never forgiven me for deserting the screen."

Joe Gillis is indignant when Norma insists that he live in her house, but gradually his self respect is corroded by easy comforts and he does nothing strenuous to thwart her unsubtle romantic blandishments. Before an attachment to a girl of his own age jolts him out of this dark abyss and re-kindles his writing spark, Joe has become hopelessly entangled in the life of the psychopatic star who holds him down with lavish gifts and an attempted suicide.

With uncommon skill, Brackett and Wilder, who also produced and directed this splendid drama for Paramount Pictures, have kept an essentially tawdry romance from becoming distasteful and embar-rassing. Aside from the natural, knowing tone of the dialogue, the realism of the picture is heightened by scenes set inside the actual iron-grilled gates of the Para-mount Studio, where Norma Des-mond goes for an on-the-set visit with her old comrade, Cecil B. DeMille himself. And the fantastic, Babylonian atmosphere of an in-credible past is reflected sharply in the gaudy elegance of the de-caying mansion in which Norma Desmond lives.

The hope that propels young people to try their luck in Holly-wood is exemplified by Betty Schaefer, a studio reader with writing ambitions who is beauti-fully portrayed by Nancy Olson. Fred Clark makes a strong im-pression as a producer working for his second ulcer, and there is heartbreak in a simple card game scene where "the wax works," as Gillis cynically refers to Norma's friends, includes Buster Keaton, Anna Q. Nilsson and H. B. Warner.

Erich von Stroheim moves through "Sunset Boulevard" with a stiff, Prussian attitude that fits to a T his role as the devoted butler, who, in his day as a top director, discovered Norma as a young girl and became the first of her three husbands. But while all the acting is memorable, one always thinks first and mostly of Miss Swanson, of her manifestation of consuming pride, her forlorn despair and a truly magnificent impersonation of Charlie Chaplin.

"Sunset Boulevard" is a great motion picture, marred only slightly by the fact that the authors permit Joe Gillis to take us into the story of his life after his bullet-ridden body is lifted out of Norma Desmond's swimming pool. That is a device completely unworthy of Brackett and Wilder, but happily it does not interfere with the suc-cess of "Sunset Boulevard."

T.M.P.

Ag 11, 1950

ALL ABOUT EVE, screen play by Joseph L. Mankiewicz, adapted from a short story and radio play by Mary Orr; directed by Mr. Mankiewicz; produced by Darryl F. Zanuck for Twentieth Century-Fox. At the Roxy.

Margo	Bette Davis
Eve	Anne Baxter
Addison De Witt	George Sanders
Karen	Celeste Holm
Bill Simpson	Gary Merrill
Lloyd Richards	Hugh Marlowe
Birdie	Thelma Ritter
Miss Casswell	Marilyn Monroe
Max Fabian	Gregory Ratoff
Phoebe	Barbara Bates
Aged Actor	Walter Hampden
Girl	Randy Stuart
Leading Man	Craig Hill
Doorman	Leland Harris
Autograph Seeker	Barbara White
Stage Manager	Eddie Fisher
Pianist	Claude Stroud

By BOSLEY CROWTHER

The good old legitimate theatre, the temple of Thespis and Art, which has dished out a lot of high derision of Hollywood in its time, had better be able to take it as well as dish it out, because the worm has finally turned with a venom and Hollywood is dishing it back. In "All About Eve," a with-ering satire—witty, mature and worldly-wise — which Twentieth Century-Fox and Joseph Mankie-wicz delivered to the Roxy yester-day, the movies are letting Broad-way have it with claws out and no holds barred. If Thespis doesn't want to take a beating, he'd better yell for George Kaufman and Moss Hart.

As a matter of fact, Mr. Kauf-man and Mr. Hart might even find themselves outclassed by the daz-zling and devastating mockery that is brilliantly packed into this film. For obviously Mr. Mankiewicz, who wrote and directed it, had been sharpening his wits and his talents a long, long time for just this go. Obviously, he had been ob-serving the theatre and its charm-ing folks for years with something less than an idolator's rosy illusions and zeal. And now, with the excellent assistance of Bette Davis and a truly sterling cast, he is wading into the theatre's middle with all claws slashing and settling a lot of scores.

If anything, Mr. Mankiewicz has been even too full of fight—too full of cutlass-edged derision of Broadway's theatrical tribe. Apparently his dormant dander and his creative zest were so aroused that he let himself go on this picture and didn't know when to stop. For two hours and eighteen minutes have been taken by him to achieve the ripping apart of an illusion which might have been comfortably done in an hour and a half.

It is not that his characters aren't full blown, that his incidents aren't brilliantly conceived and that his dialogue, pithy and pungent, is not as clever as any you will hear. In picturing the inside story of an ambitious actress' rise from glamour-struck girl in a theatre alley to flinty-eyed winner of the Siddons Prize, Mr. Mankiewicz has gathered up a saga of theatrical ambition and conceit, pride and deception and hypocrisy, that just about drains the subject dry.

Indeed, he has put so many characters — so many vivid Broadway types—through the flattening and decimating wringer of his unmerciful wit that the punishment which he gives them becomes painful when so lengthily drawn. And that's the one trouble with this picture. It beats the horse after it is dead.

But that said, the rest is boundless tribute to Mr. Mankiewicz and his cast for ranging a gallery of people that dazzle, horrify and fascinate. Although the title character — the self-seeking, ruthless Eve, who would make a black-widow spider look like a lady bug —is the motivating figure in the story and is played by Anne Baxter with icy calm, the focal figure and most intriguing character is the actress whom Bette Davis plays. This lady, an aging ,acid creature with a cankerous ego and a stinging tongue, is the end-all of Broadway disenchantment, and

Miss Davis plays her to a fare-thee-well. Indeed, the superb illumination of the spirit and pathos of this dame which is a brilliant screen actress gives her merits an Academy award.

Of the men, George Sanders is walking wormwood, neatly wrapped in a mahogany veneer, as a vicious and powerful drama critic who has a licentious list towards pretty girls; Gary Merrill is warm and reassuring as a director with good sense and a heart, and Hugh Marlowe is brittle and boyish as a playwright with more glibness than brains. Celeste Holm is appealingly normal and naive as the latter's wife and Thelma Ritter is screamingly funny as a wised-up maid until she is summarily lopped off.

A fine Darryl Zanuck production, excellent music and an air of ultra-class complete this superior satire. The legitimate theatre had better look to its laurels

O 14, 1950

ORPHEUS, written and directed by Jean Cocteau; an Andre Paulve-Films du Palais Royal Production, released here by Discina International. At the Fifty-fifth Street Playhouse.
Orpheus.........................Jean Marais
Heurtebise.....................Francois Perier
The Princess..................Maria Casares
Eurydice..........................Maria Dea
The Man.....................Henri Cremieux
First Judge...............Jacques Varennes
The Inspector................./..Pierre Bertin
Aglaonice.............................Greco
The Writer.......................Roger Blin
Cegeste....................Edouard Dermithe

By BOSLEY CROWTHER

Perhaps the most tell-tale tip-off to the nature of the "Orpheus" of Jean Cocteau, a notably avant-garde French film which opened at the Fifty fifth Street Playhouse last night, is thoughtfully offered by the author in a signed statement in the program. "When I make a film," says M. Cocteau, "it is a slumber and I dream."

That is as fair a forewarning as any that we can provide to the curious conceits of fancy that you may expect in this film. For plainly the writer-director has let his imagination roam through a drama of images that resemble the vagrant phantasms of sleep. And while the famed legend of Orpheus

262

provides the framework of a plot and the pictorial character is concrete, the context is utterly abstract.

Indeed, at one point in this crisscross of phantoms and · images, which clearly defy interpretation along any logical line, the author permits one character to drop this significant remark: "You try too hard to understand and that is a mistake."

A mistake it is, beyond question—for, in telling a modern-dress tale of a young poet by the name of Orpheus who becomes strangely enamoured of Death and almost (but not quite) loses his pretty blond wife, Eurydice, M. Cocteau has so coagulated his picture with fantasies and stunts that a serious attempt to seek some meaning in all of them might drive one mad.

There is a chic and sophisticated lady who rides around in a Rolls-Royce car and ominously hangs over Orpheus. She seems quite simple. She is Death. Only she isn't all Death exactly. She is the Death of Orpheus. But she is also the personal Death of Cegeste, another poet. A little confused. There are also two mad motorcyclists who recklessly knock people down. They are quite clearly Death's agents. We can fathom them. But how about this fellow, Heurtebise, who drives the Rolls-Royce car? He is some sort of in-betweener. What is his place in Cocteau's realm?

And then there are all those mirrors through which people nonchalantly pass—that is, if they're properly departed or are wearing the magical rubber gloves. They are easy. As someone mentions, "Mirrors are the doors through which Death comes and goes." But what is the symbolism? And how about that stupid radio? Why does it drone monotonous numbers and speeches as though in code? You can say it again, M. Cocteau: "It is not necessary to understand; it is necessary to believe."

No doubt the true believers (whoever they are) will get much from this film, for it is produced with remarkable authority and photographed magnificently, thus enhancing the pictorial richness of its symbols and images. The music of Georges Auric is haunting, the direction is sharp and intense and the acting is generally impressive. In the title role, Jean Marais makes a finely agonized subject, Maria Dea is touching as his wife, François Perier is wistful as the chauffeur and Maria Casares makes a dark, hypnotic Death.

But for this corner's taste, the style of Cocteau, while valid, perhaps, does not embrace sufficient intellectual comprehension to justify so much film, and the visual here lacks the fascination of the same author's "Beauty and the Beast." Somnambulistic symbolism may be art for art's sake. Maybe not. This writer finds it slightly tiresome. It's more Morpheus than Orpheus by us.

N 30, 1950

'Marie du Port,' Marcel Carne Film With Jean Gabin as Star, at Paris Theatre

MARIE du PORT, adapted by Louis Chavance from the novel by George Simenon; directed and produced by Marcel Carne; released by Bellon-Foulke International Productions. At the Paris Theatre.
Chatelard ....Jean Gabin
Odile ....Blanchette Brunoy
Marie ....Nicole Courcel
Viau ....Carette
Marcel.......................Claude Romain
Cafe Proprietress..............Jeanne Marken

By BOSLEY CROWTHER

Marcel Carné, the French director who has ripped out such tormented films as "Daybreak," "Port of Shadows" and "Children of Paradise," is now represented at the Paris by an interestingly different film—less gloomy, less fatally conclusive—by the name of "Marie du Port." In this exploratory drama, based on a novel by Georges Simenon, M. Carné is leisurely discoursing on the humorous ironies of love. And while he persists in his old penchants for strange moods and seaport atmosphere, he is actually coming up with a fable that has the nature of an after-dinner joke.

We note the bewildering ambiguity with which the story is teasingly told because that is characteristic of the picture, as well as of M. Carné. From the way it begins with the funeral of an old fisherman at a salty Breton port and the dismal break-up of his poor family, you might well think it headed straight downhill. And, indeed, there are many times in it when it seems to insist on going that way.

But a tiny tip-off is given directly at the start when the dead fisherman's older daughter turns up at the funeral late. She has driven down from Cherbourg with her lover, who is an amiable restaurateur, and the reason they are late, to the townsfolks' horror, is because they have had a flat tire. That is the first indication of the sardonic nature of the film.

And the second one comes when the younger daughter and the sister's lover begin making eyes, almost directly after the funeral, in a well-populated fisherman's bar. They are not the kind of eyes, however, that forecast a surrender by closing time. They are the kind that indicate calculation, cool and cunning, on both parties' part. In short, they suggest the development of an odd and intriguing affair.

And that is precisely what happens. We won't bother you with details, but rest assured that M. Carné sees to it that they are not dull. Queer they may be and sometimes baffling, since M. Carné isn't sketching an amour of a commonplace, hit-and-run nature. It is complex, mature—and far from dull. Indeed, it is slyly fascinating, sparked by an occasional quick surprise. And it ends with a droll little comment that de Maupassant would have enjoyed.

The secret, of course, is character. M.Carné has a couple of good ones here and two very competent players to perform the substantial roles. The man is a sensible fellow, a tomcat but wise, nonetheless, and he is played with superb sophistication and dry humor by Jean Gabin. And tht girl is a smart, ambitious vixen, inexperienced and unsure but quick to learn, with a volatile physical attractiveness — all of which are contributed by Nicole Courcel. Blanchette Brunoy is interestingly casual as the older sister and mistress who is on the skids, Claude Romain makes a clumsy village Romeo and Carette is cute as his old man.

Henri Alekan's sensitive camera has done wonders with the streets and boats and sea against which the talented director has played his outdoor scenes.

Jl 24, 1951

A PLACE IN THE SUN, screen play by Michael Wilson and Harry Brown; based on the novel, "An American Tragedy," by Theodore Dreiser and Patrick Kearny play; produced and directed by George Stevens for Paramount. At the Capitol.

George Eastman	Montgomery Clift
ngela Vickers	Elizabeth Taylor
Alice Tripp	Shelley Winters
Hannah Eastman	Anne Revere
Marlowe	Raymond Burr
Charles Eastman	Herbert Heyes
Earl Eastman	Keefe Brasselle
Anthony Vickers	Shepperd Strudwick
Mrs. Vickers	Frieda Inescort
Dr. Wyeland	Ian Wolfe
Marcia Eastman	Lois Chartrand
Bellows (Defense Attorney)	Fred Clark
Jansan	Walter Sande
Boatkeeper	Douglas Spencer
Coroner	John Ridgley
Mrs. Louise Eastman	Kathryn Givney
Judge	Ted de Corsia
Kelly	Charles Dayton
Rev. Morrison	Paul Frees
Mr. Whiting	William R. Murphy

Although the term "remake" is, for some strange reason, shunned by the Coast's artisans as something vile, a stigma better left unheralded, Hollywood, Paramount and George Stevens, producer-director, in particular, can point with pride to "A Place in the Sun." For this second screen edition of Theodore Dreiser's monumental novel, "An American Tragedy," which was unveiled at the Capitol last night, is a work of beauty, tenderness, power and insight. And, though Mr. Stevens, his scenarists and cast have switched its time and setting to the present and avoided extreme concentration on the social crusading of the book, "A Place in the Sun" emerges as a credit to both the motion-picture craft and, we feel reasonably certain, the author's major intentions.

Out of Dreiser's often murky and turgid tale of the Twenties, now the present—the stream of words in "An American Tragedy,"

264

as has been noted many times previously, was not easy to navigate —scenarists Michael Wilson and Harry Brown have distilled the essence of tragedy and romance that is both moving and memorable. Retained, too, in this two-hour drama—representing the painstakingly edited end result of hundreds of thousands of feet of material shot—are characterizations which cleave to the Dreiser originals. And it is a tribute to deft dramatization that the young principals are projected as fully as the maelstrom of life in which they are trapped and with which they are unable to cope.

One may argue that Mr. Stevens has given only surface treatment to the society which appears to propel George Eastman to his tragic end and accentuated his love affairs and groping for a higher rung in the social ladder. That, it becomes apparent, is basically captious. George Eastman is obviously an intelligent youth whose background has not equipped him for anything better than menial endeavor. So it is not surprising that he grasps at the opportunity to work in his rich uncle's factory. And it is not surprising that the lonely, brooding young man, ignored by his rich relatives, will find an answer to his crying need for companionship in his drab, unlettered and equally lonely co-worker, Alice Tripp.

The forces pushing young Eastman to the final, horrible retribution are obvious and a tribute to the naturalism of Dreiser as the youth is suddenly exposed to the overwhelming opulence of his family and Angela Vickers to whose love and beauty he succumbs. Since his basic upbringing—a composite background of unbending Evangelism and slums from which he chose to escape—does not permit him to callously desert Alice—now frantic with the knowledge that she is bearing his child—he takes surreptitious steps to remedy his untenable position. This phase of his ordeal (and Alice's) is a wholly tasteful and compelling handling of a delicate situation. The questions of his morals and intrinsic cowardice here are placed squarely in the eyes of the viewer.

With similar integrity, the drama depicts Alice's drowning and the subsequent mounting terror and confusion of her lover, faced with the enormity of the tragedy and the reiteration of the insidious thought that while he did not commit murder he must have willed it. And, George Eastman, grappling with a transgression he cannot fully comprehend, is a pitiful, yet strangely brave individual as he explains his act and convictions in court. Despite his weaknesses he is a strong figure who admits in his death cell that "I wanted to save her but I just couldn't." He takes on stature as does his love for Angela whom he tells: "I know something now I didn't know before. I'm guilty of a lot of things—of most of what they say I am."

There may be some belief that Montgomery Clift, as the tortured George Eastman, is not nearly the designing and grasping youth conceived by Dreiser. But his portrayal, often terse and hesitating, is full, rich, restrained and, above all, generally credible and poignant. He is, in effect, a believable mama's boy gone wrong.

Equally poignant is Shelley Winters' characterization of the ill-fated Alice, Miss Winters, in our opinion, has never been seen to better advantage than as the colorless factory hand, beset by burgeoning anxieties but clinging to a love she hopes can be rekindled. Elizabeth Taylor's delineation of the rich and beauteous Angela also is the top effort of her career. It is a shaded, tender performance and one in which her passionate and genuine romance avoids the bathos common to young love as it sometimes comes to the screen.

And, under Mr. Stevens' expert direction, Raymond Burr, as the doggedly probing district attorney, and Anne Revere, as Clift's mother, a mission worker who feels that the blame for her son's crime is partly hers as well as most of the supporting players, contribute fitting bits to an impressive mosaic. Despite the fact that this version of Dreiser's tragedy may be criticized—academically, we think—

for its length or deviations from the author's pattern, "A Place in the Sun" is a distinguished work, a tribute, above all, to its producer-director and an effort now placed among the ranks of the finest films to have come from Hollywood in several years.—A. W.

Ag 29, 1951

'An American in Paris,' Arrival at Music Hall, Has Gene Kelly and Leslie Caron in Leads

AN AMERICAN IN PARIS, screen play and story by Alan Jay Lerner; directed by Vincente Minnelli; produced by Arthur Freed for Metro-Goldwyn-Mayer. At the Radio City Music Hall.
Jerry Mulligan.....................Gene Kelly
Lise Bourvier.......................Leslie Caron
Adam Cook..........................Oscar Levant
Henri Baurel.....................Georges Guetary
Milo Roberts...........................Nina Foch
Georges Mattieu..................Eugene Borden
Mathilde Mattieu............Martha Bamattre
Old Woman Dancer...............Mary Young

By BOSLEY CROWTHER

Count a bewitching French lassie by the name of Leslie Caron and a whoop-de-do ballet number, one of the finest ever put upon the screen, as the most commendable enchantments of the big, lavish musical film that Metro obligingly delivered to the Music Hall yesterday. "An American in Paris," which is the title of the picture, likewise the ballet, is spangled with pleasant little patches of amusement and George Gershwin tunes. It also is blessed with Gene Kelly, dancing and singing his way through a minor romantic complication in the usual gaudy Hollywood gay Paree. But it is the wondrously youthful Miss Caron and that grandly pictorial ballet that place the marks of distinction upon this lush technicolored escapade.

Alongside this crisp and elfin youngster who plays the Parisian girl with whom the ebullient American of Mr. Kelly falls in love, the other extravagant characters of the romance seem standard and stale, and even the story seems wrinkled in the light of her freshness and charm. Mr. Kelly

may skip about gaily, casting the favor of his smiles and the boon of the author's witticisms upon the whole of the Paris populace. Nina Foch may cut a svelte figure as a lady who wants to buy his love by buying his straight art-student paintings. And Oscar Levant may mutter wryly as a pal. But the picture takes on its glow of magic when Miss Caron is on the screen. When she isn't, it bumps along slowly as a patched-up, conventional musical show.

Why this should be is fairly obvious. Miss Caron is not a beauteous thing, in the sense of classic features, but she has a sweet face and a most delightful smile. Furthermore, she has winsomeness, expression and youthful dignity—and she can dance like a gossamer wood-sprite on the edge of a petal at dawn.

When she and Mr. Kelly first meet in a Paris cafe, the previous routine of "bon jours" and "voilas" and "mais ouis" is forgotten. Candor and charm invade the picture under Vincente Minnelli's helpful wand. And when they dance on a quai along the river, in hush of a Paris night, to "Our Love Is Here to Stay," the romance opens and unrepressed magic evolves. Then, in the final, bursting ballet, which is done to a brilliant score of Gershwin music orchestrated with his "American in Paris" suite, the little dancer and Mr. Kelly achieve a genuine emotional splurge. It is Mr. Kelly's ballet, but Miss Caron delivers the warmth and glow.

And a ballet it is, beyond question—a truly cinematic ballet—with dancers describing vivid patterns against changing colors, designs, costumes and scenes. The whole story of a poignant romance within a fanciful panorama of Paree is conceived and performed with taste and talent. It is the uncontested high point of the film.

Beside it such musical conniptions as Mr. Kelly and Mr. Levant giving out with "Tra-La-La," or Mr. Kelly doing a dance to "I Got Rhythm" with a bunch of kids, or

Mr. Levant performing all the key jobs in a large symphonic rendition of Concreto in F are purely coincidental. And Georges Guetary's careful oozing of Gallic charm in "I'll Build a Stairway to Paradise" and "'S Wonderful" could well be done without. As a matter of fact, some of these numbers leave the uncomfortable impression that they were contrived just to fill out empty spaces in Alan Jay Lerner's glib but very thin script.

However, all things are forgiven when Miss Caron is on the screen. When she is on with Mr. Kelly and they are dancing, it is superb.

O 5, 1951

THE RED BADGE OF COURAGE, screen play by John Huston, adapted by Albert Band from the novel by Stephen Crane; directed by Mr. Huston; produced by Gottfried Reinhardt. A John Huston Production, presented by Metro-Goldwyn-Mayer. At the Trans-Lux Fifty-second Street Theatre.

The Youth......................Audie Murphy
The Loud Soldier...............Bill Mauldin
The Tall Soldier................John Dierkes
The Tattered Man................Royal Dano
Bill Porter..................Arthur Hunnicutt
The General.......................Tim Durant
The Lieutenant................Douglas Dick
Thompson..............Robert Easton Burke

By BOSLEY CROWTHER

There are few, if any, old men now living who know from experience the exact look and "feel" of a battle in the War Between the States. Such knowledge, so common to so many until a few years ago, must now be derived from descriptions that are vivid in so many texts; from old photographs of battles, such as those that Matthew Brady made, and from the wells of imagination that have been fed by countless legends and tales.

Certainly a classic description, not only of a battle in full blast but of the tormenting fears and emotions of an untried youth in the ranks, is Stephen Crane's "The Red Badge of Courage," which says all that ever need be said about the terror of a man first entering battle, no matter which side he's on or in what war. Now, thanks to Metro and John Huston, "The Red Badge of Courage" has been transferred to the screen with almost literal fidelity. It opened here at the Trans-Lux Fifty-second Street yesterday.

Don't expect too much from it in the way of emotional punch—at least, not as much as is compacted in Mr. Crane's thin little book. For, of course, Mr. Crane was conveying the reactions of his hero to war in almost stream-of-consciousness descriptions, which is a technique that works best with words. When it is a matter of telling precisely how a young soldier feels at a time, for instance, when awaiting an enemy attack or when wandering behind the lines after lamming, it is easier to do so with words than with a camera going around with the soldier and frequently looking at his face.

This is a technical problem Mr. Huston has not been able to lick, even with his sensitive direction, in view of his sticking to the book. Audie Murphy, who plays the Young Soldier, does as well as anyone could expect as a virtual photographer's model whom the camera is mostly turned. And his stupefied facial expressions and erratic attitudes when grim experiences crowd upon him suggest what goes on in his mind. These, coupled with the visual evidence of all that surrounds him and all he sees, plus the help of an occasional narration that sketchily tells us what he feels, do all that can be expected to give us the inner sight of Mr. Crane's book.

But the major achievement of this picture is the whole scene, it re-creates of a battlefield near the Rappahannock (Chancellorsville) from the soldier's point of view—the ragged and nondescript infantry, the marches, the battlelines, the din, the dust, the cavalry charges, the enemy surging out of the clouds of smoke, and the pitiful, wretched lines of the wounded reaching and stumbling toward the rear. Mr. Huston, who made "San Pietro," one of the great documentaries of World War II, can conceive a Civil War battle, and he has done so magnificently in this film.

Furthermore, he has got the sense of soldiers in that long-ago day and war—their looks, their attitudes, their idioms—as suggested in the writings of the times. John Dierkes, as the Tall Soldier; Bill Maudlin as the loud, uneasy one, and Douglas Dick as the Lieutenant stand out in a small but excellent cast. All are the sort of soldiers that one's mind visions on those battlefields.

Also, Mr. Huston has captured and etched vividly most of the major encounters of the hero that Mr. Crane described—the heartbreaking death of the Tall Soldier, the stunning blow on the head—all but the shocking discovery of the rotting corpse in the woods. This is out of the picture as it is being shown here, probably out of deference for the squeamish.

But, in most respects, Mr. Huston has put "The Red Badge of Courage" on the screen, and that means a major achievement that should command admiration for years and years.

O 19, 1951

'Miracle in Milan,' an Italian Fable Directed by Vittorio De Sica, at the World

MIRACLE IN MILAN, screen play and story by Ceesare Zavattini, based on his novel, "Toto Il Buono"; directed by Vittoria De Sica; presented by Joseph Burstyn. At the World Theatre.
The Good Toto............Francesco Golisano
The Bad Rappi.................Paolo Stoppa
The Old Lolatta ....Emma Gramatica
The Rich Man ....Guglielmo Barnabo
The Little Edvidge............Brunella Bobo
Signora Altezzosa ....Anna Carene
The Statue ....Alba Arnova
The Unhappy Sweetheart.........Flora Cambi
The Sergeant ....Virgilio Riento
Alfredo ....Arturo Bragaglia
Gaetano ....Ermino Spalla
The Wrestler ....Riccardo Bertazzolo
The First Commander............Angelo Prioli
The Second Commander......Francesco Rissone

By BOSLEY CROWTHER

The rich vein of sly, compassionate humor that Charlie Chaplin and Rene Clair used to mine with unparalleled genius when they were turning out their best satiric films has been tapped by Vittorio De Sica in his "Miracle in Milan," the widely proclaimed Italian picture that arrived at the World yesterday. And although this uncommon vein of fancy is a way from De Sica's previous line, the great director has brought up from his digging a liberal return of purest gold.

Those who are mindful of De Sica as the maker of such realistic films as the tragically hopeless "Shoe Shine" and the heart-rending "Bicycle Thief" may be surprised to discover that he is not only in an antic mood but is openly toying with the fantastic in this "Miracle in Milan." Aspects of human degradation that have previously been for him the stuff of stark and shattering drama are here used as lush material for riotously comic demonstration of the outrageous ironies of life. And where he has previously discovered no balm for the miseries of man, he is here finding solace for his people in the working of miracles.

Obviously, this excursion, which is whimsically based upon a novel by Cesare Zavattini, entitled "Toto the Good," is meant as a frank and searching satire of modern society, put in the form of a fable that has the nature of a hard-boiled fairy tale. And, as such, it may represent De Sica, the realistic looker at life, gone to an extreme of mitigating his cynicism with ironic make-believe.

It is this reviewer's suspicion, however, that such is not the case —that "Miracle in Milan" is just De Sica enjoying a salty and complicated spoof—a spoof that has in it the poignance and the wormwood of life itself, indeed, but which is impishly bedded in the thesis that man lives in self-deluding dreams. This suspicion would seem to be supported by the fact that the yarn becomes involved beyond serious rationalization or symbolization before it reaches an end.

The beginning is nothing short of brilliant. In a typical Chaplinesque way, it opens with a little old lady finding a baby in her garden one day. With tender and guileless devotion, she teaches the growing child to be kind, to know the multiplication table and to make sport of any mishaps that occur. Then the old lady dies and the little boy, after going as the sole mourner to her grave, spends some time in an orphan asylum before sallying forth to face the world.

Bright and optimistic, he soon notes the dreariness of man, but nonetheless sets himself to spreading sunshine in a dismal hobo camp. He teaches the people to be cheerful, to improve their community life and to trust those who own the property on which the camp is built—that is, until they strike oil! Then the only salvation for the people and the shattered faith of the cheerful lad is a dove, from the old lady in heaven, permitting the lad to work miracles. With this magical portent, he has trouble satisfying his people, too, but finally all are transported (on broomsticks) to a place in the sky.

This bare outline of the fable reveals its fantastic quality, as well as the vagueness of its meaning that permits whatever deductions one desires. However, it does not begin to tell you of the tender and charming little glints of human nature and social ambiguities that run all the way through the film. And it is really these manifold inventions — some of them funny or revealing beyond words —that make for the glad surprises and refreshing stimulation of the film.

In the role of the cheerful Toto, a remarkably bright-eyed young man, Francesco Golisano, is infectiously appealing, without indulging any particular comic style. And the rest of the cast, made up largely of inexperienced "extras" and actual tramps, does a grand job of mimicking and mauling the social conceits of man.

Although it is questionable whether this picture has the simple, universal appeal of an old Chaplin film, for instance, or whether its meanings are as sharp as some may think, it is certainly a lively entertainment and should be a subject of discussion for months to come.

D 18, 1951

RASHO-MON, screen play by Akira Kurosawa and Shinobu Hashimoto; based on the novel "In the Forest" by Ryunosuke Akutagawa; directed by Akira Kurosawa; produced by Jingo Minoura. A Daiei Production released here by RKO Radio Pictures. At the Little Carnegie.

The Bandit ....Toshiro Mifune
The Woman.....................Machiko Kyo
The Man.......................Masayuki Mori
The Firewood Dealer.........Takashi Shimura
The Priest......................Minoru Chiaki
The Commoner................Kichijiro Ueda
The Medium...................Fumiko Homma
The Police.....................Daisuke Kato

By BOSLEY CROWTHER

A doubly rewarding experience for those who seek out unusual films in attractive and comfortable surroundings was made available yesterday upon the reopening of the rebuilt Little Carnegie with the Japanese film, "Rasho-Mon." For here the attraction and the theatre are appropriately and interestingly matched in a striking association of cinematic and architectural artistry, stimulating to the intelligence and the taste of the patron in both realms.

"Rasho-Mon," which created much excitement when it suddenly appeared upon the scene of the Venice Film Festival last autumn and carried off the grand prize, is, indeed, an artistic achievement of such distinct and exotic character that it is difficult to estimate it alongside conventional story films. On the surface, it isn't a picture of the sort that we're accustomed to at all, being simply a careful observation of a dramatic incident from four points of view, with an eye to discovering some meaning— some rationalization—in the seeming heartlessness of man.

At the start, three Japanese wanderers are sheltering themselves from the rain in the ruined gatehouse of a city. The time is many centuries ago. The country is desolate, the people disillusioned, and the three men are contemplating a brutal act that has occurred outside the city and is preying upon their minds.

It seems that a notorious bandit has waylaid a merchant and his wife. (The story is visualized in flashback, as later told by the bandit to a judge.) After tying up the merchant, the bandit rapes the wife and then—according to his story—kills the merchant in a fair duel with swords.

However, as the wife tells the story, she is so crushed by her husband's contempt after the shameful violence and after the bandit has fled that she begs her husband to kill her. When he refuses, she faints. Upon recovery, she discovers a dagger which she was holding in her hands is in his chest.

According to the dead husband's story, as told through a medium, his life is taken by his own hand, when the bandit and his faithless wife flee. And, finally, an humble wood-gatherer—one of the three men reflecting on the crime—reports that he witnessed the murder and that the bandit killed the husband at the wife's behest.

At the end, the three men are no nearer an understanding than they are at the start, but some hope for man's soul is discovered in the willingness of the wood-gatherer to adopt a foundling child, despite some previous evidence that he acted selfishly in reporting the case.

As we say, the dramatic incident is singular, devoid of conventional plot, and the action may appear repetitious because of the concentration of the yarn. And yet there emerges from this picture—from this scrap of a fable from the past—a curiously agitating tension and a haunting sense of the wild impulses that move men.

Much of the power of the picture—and it unquestionably has hypnotic power—derives from the brilliance with which the camera of Director Akira Kurosawa has been used. The photography is excellent and the flow of images is expressive beyond words. Likewise the use of music and of incidental sounds is superb, and the acting of all the performers is aptly provocative.

Machiko Kyo is lovely and vital as the questionable wife, conveying in her distractions a depth of mystery, and Toshiro Mifune plays the bandit with terrifying wildness and hot brutality. Masayuki Mori is icy as the husband and the remaining members of the cast handle their roles with the competence of people who know their jobs.

Whether this picture has pertinence to the present day—whether its dismal cynicism and its ultimate grasp at hope reflect a current disposition of people in Japan—is something we cannot tell you. But, without reservation, we can say that it is an artful and fascinating presentation of a slice of life on the screen. The Japanese dialogue is translated with English subtitles.

THE YOUNG AND THE DAMNED, screen play by Luis Bunuel and Luis Alcoriza; directed by Mr. Bunuel; produced by Oscar Dancigers. A Luis Bunuel Production presented by Arthur Mayer and Edward Kingsley. At the Trans-Lux Fifty-second Street Theatre.
The Mother .... Estela Inda
Pedro .... Alfonso Mejia
Jaibo .... Roberto Cobo
The Lost Boy................... Jesus Navarro
The Blind Man................... Miguel Inclan
The Young Girl................. Alma Fuentes
The Principal .... Francisco Jambrina

By BOSLEY CROWTHER

A brutal and unrelenting picture of poverty and juvenile crime in the slums of Mexico City is presented in "The Young and the Damned," a Mexican semi-documentary that was put on yesterday at the Trans-Lux Fifty-second Street. Although made with meticulous realism and unquestioned fidelity to facts, its qualifications as dramatic entertainment — or even social reportage—are dim.

For it is obvious that Luis Bunuel, who directed and helped write the script, had no focus or point of reference for the squalid, depressing tale he tells. He simply has assembled an assortment of poverty-stricken folk—paupers, delinquents, lost children and parents of degraded morals—and has mixed them altogether in a vicious and shocking melange of violence, melodrama, coincidence and irony.

To be sure, Mr. Bunuel does attract unstinted sympathy for a boy who appears the most pathetic victim of the state in which he lives. This lad is the son of a mother who has long since abandoned him, who resists his feeble bids for affection and who gives herself to his partner in crime. Bullied and dominated by the latter, the boy is led into murder and other crimes and finally is murdered by his partner, who appears some sort of irredeemable psychopath.

Mr. Bunuel also assaults us with visual details of poverty and crime that will stagger the most case-hardened and make the timids' hair stand on end. The vicious badgering of a blind beggar and the ruthless beating of a cripple by a gang of boys are only minor indiscretions. The frenzied flaying to death of chickens is the cue for the beating to death of humans by the bully. The suggestion of madness is plain.

But why there should be this wild coincidence of evil and violence is not explained, nor is any social solution even hinted, much less clarified. A foreword merely states that the correction of this problem of poverty and delinquency is left to the "progressive forces" (whatever they are) of our times.

In the role of the bully, Roberto Cobo is a slashing creature of harsh depravities, while Alfonso Mejia is boyish and touching as the lad who is lonely and doomed. Estela Inda is metallic as the mother, Miguel Inclan is repulsive as the blind man, and a youngster named Alma Fuentes is appealing as a girl of the slums.

This picture, under its original title of "Los Olvidados," previously was shown at the Cinema 48 without English subtitles. It is well provided with same in its present showing.

Mr 25, 1952

MISS JULIE, written and directed by Alf Sjoberg: based on the play by August Strindberg. A Sandrew Production released here by Trans-Global Pictures, Inc. At the World Theatre.
Miss Julie..........................Anita Bjork
Jean...................................Ulf Palme
Kristin.............................Marta Dorff
The Count................Anders Henrikson
Berta.............................Lissi Alandh
Viola...................................Inga Gill
The Fiance............Kurt-Olof Sundstrom
The Doctor.......................Ake Claesson
Miss Julie, as a child..........Inger Norberg
Jean, as a child................Jan Hagerman

By BOSLEY CROWTHER

August Strindberg's old play, "Miss Julie," which tells a grim, neurotic tale of the mad passion of a Swedish maiden for her father's handsome valet, may be considerably old-fashioned in its heavily labored social theme and also a trifle antiquated in its devious psychology. The wall between master and servant, which existed in 1888, at the time the play was written, seems ridiculously feudal today and shame over loving the butler seems a rather dull cause for suicide.

But, even so, Sweden's Alf Sjoberg, who wields a superb directorial hand, as well as puts together an excitingly cinematic script, has got from this Scandinavian drama a surprisingly fascinating film, which goes by the title of "Miss Julie" and opened at the World yesterday.

The best things about this Swedish picture are its strong imagistic qualities and a passionate, tormented performance of the principal role by Anita Bjork. Mr. Sjoberg has written a screen play that permits him to move with fluid ease from one time level to another, so that the ordinary flashback device becomes with him just a matter of panning from one to another scene. This makes for an interesting conjunction of immediate and previous events, all flowing suitably together for strong, impressive dramatic effects.

Also, the beautiful setting of a luxurious country estate, where all of the action takes place, with peasants laughing and making love on Midsummer Eve as a background for the violent drama that occurs, has been used by Mr. Sjoberg for handsome pictorial display and for appropriate demonstration of the anomalies of caste.

And Miss Bjorke's sensitive performance in the very difficult role of a girl torn by passion and convention is intriguing, for all its literary age. The lady is lovely and pliant, with a frail, blonde delicacy, and yet she manages to whip up some agonizing emotional storms. Alongside of her, Ulf Palme plays a vividly contrasting man as the low-born valet who is insensitive and who can never get over his sense of caste. Marta Dorff, as a comic kitchen servant, and Anders Henrikson, as the tormented count, complete a cast that is excellent down to the smallest bit role.

While the drama played out in this picture may seem turgid and obsolete, which it is beyond any question, the playing of it has hypnotic charm.

Ap 8, 1952

HIGH NOON

By BOSLEY CROWTHER

Every five years or so, somebody—somebody of talent and taste, with a full appreciation of legend and a strong trace of poetry in their soul—scoops up a handful of clichés from the vast lore of Western films and turns them into a thrilling and inspiring work of art in this genre. Such a rare and exciting achievement is Stanley Kramer's production, "High Noon," which was placed on exhibition at the Mayfair yesterday.

Which one of several individuals is most fully responsible for this job is a difficult matter to determine and nothing about which to quarrel. It could be Mr. Kramer, who got the picture made, and it be Scriptwriter Carl Foreman, who prepared the story for the screen. Certainly Director Fred Zinnemann had a great deal to do with it and possibly Gary Cooper, as the star, had a hand in the job. An accurate apportionment of credits is not a matter of critical concern.

HIGH NOON, screen play by Carl Foreman: directed by Fred Zinnemann; produced by Stanley Kramer. A Stanley Kramer Production released by United Artists. At the Mayfair.

Will Kane	Gary Cooper
Jonas Henderson	Thomas Mitchell
Harvey Pell	Lloyd Bridges
Helen Ramirez	Katy Jurado
Amy Kane	Grace Kelly
Percy Mettrick	Otto Kruger
Martin Howe	Lon Chaney
William Fuller	Henry Morgan
Frank Miller	Ian MacDonald
Mildred Fuller	Eve McVeagh
Cooper	Harry Shannon
Jack Colby	Lee Van Cleef
James Pierce	Bob Wilke
Ben Miller	Sheb Wooley
Sam	Tom London
Station Master	Ted Stanhope
Gillis	Larry Blake
Barber	William Phillips

What is important is that someone—or all of them together, we would say—has turned out a Western drama that is the best of its kind in several years. Familiar but far from conventional in the fabric of story and theme and marked by a sure illumination of human character, this tale of a brave and stubborn sheriff in a town full of do-nothings and cowards has the rhythm and roll of a ballad spun in pictorial terms. And, over all, it has a stunning comprehension of that thing we call courage in a man and the thorniness of being courageous in a world of bullies and poltroons.

Like most works of art, it is simple — simple in the structure of its plot and comparatively simple in the layout of its fundamental issues and morals. Plot-wise, it is the story of a sheriff in a small Western town, on the day of his scheduled retirement, faced with a terrible ordeal. At 10:30 in the morning, just a few minutes after he has been wed, he learns that a dreaded desperado is arriving in town on the noon train. The bad man has got a pardon from a rap on which the sheriff sent him up, and the sheriff knows that the killer is coming back to town to get him.

Here is the first important question: shall the sheriff slip away, as his new wife and several decent citizens reasonably urge him to do, or shall he face, here and now, the crisis which he knows he can never escape? And once he has answered this question, the second and greater problem is the maintenance of his resolution as noon approaches and he finds himself alone—one man, without a single sidekick, against a killer and three attendant thugs; one man who has the courage to take on a perilous, righteous job.

How Mr. Foreman has surrounded this simple and forceful tale with tremendous dramatic implications is a thing we can't glibly state in words. It is a matter of skill in movie-writing, but, more than that, it is the putting down, in terms of visually simplified images, a pattern of poetic ideas. And how Mr. Zinnemann has transmitted this pattern in pictorial terms is something which we can only urge you to go yourself to see.

One sample worth framing, however, is the brilliant assembly of shots that holds the tale in taut suspension just before the fatal hour of noon. The issues have been established, the townsfolk have fallen away and the sheriff, alone with his destiny, has sat down at his desk to wait. Over his shoulder, Mr. Zinnemann shows us a white sheet of paper on which is scrawled "last will and testament" by a slowly moving pen. Then he gives us a shot (oft repeated) of the pendulum of the clock, and then a shot looking off into the distance of the prairie down the empty railroad tracks. In quick succession, then, he shows us, the tense faces of men waiting in the church and in the local saloon, the still streets outside, the three thugs waiting at the station, the tracks again, the wife of the sheriff waiting and the face of the sheriff himself. Then, suddenly, away in the distance, there is the whistle of the train and, looking down the tracks again, he shows us a whisp of smoke from the approaching train. In a style of consummate realism, Mr. Zinnemann has done a splendid job.

And so has the cast, under his direction. Mr. Cooper is at the top of his form in a type of role that has trickled like water off his back for years. And Lloyd Bridges as a vengeful young deputy, Katy Jurado as a Mexican adventuress, Thomas Mitchell as a prudent townsman, Otto Kruger as a craven judge and Grace Kelly as the new wife of the sheriff are the best of many in key roles.

Meaningful in its implications, as well as loaded with interest and suspense, "High Noon" is a western to challenge "Stagecoach" for the all-time championship.

Jl 25, 1952

THE STRANGE ONES, screen play adapted by Jean Cocteau and Jean-Pierre Melville from the novel "Les Enfants Terribles," by M. Cocteau; directed and produced by M. Melville. Released here by Arthur Mayer and Edward Kingsley. At the Paris.

Elizabeth .... Nicole Stephane
Paul .... Edouard Dermithe
Agatha .... Renee Cosima
Gerard .... Jacques Bernard
Michael .... Melvyn Martin
Uncle .... Roger Gaillard
Maid .... Jean-Marie Revel
Mother .... Marie Cyliakus
Narrator ....Jean Cocteau

By BOSLEY CROWTHER

Whatever it is that Jean Cocteau and Director Jean-Pierre Melville are trying to say in their new French film, "The Strange Ones," this corner is unable to report.

According to the program thoughtfully passed along by the management of the Paris Theatre, where this picture is now on display, it is based on the celebrated novel, "Les Enfants Terribles," by M. Cocteau, and it is "a probing study of the private world of a brother and sister who share one room, with its secrets, treasures, memories and cluttered appurtenances that betray the total lack of emotional discipline and the disorderly lives of those who occupy it."

So long as the program says so, we imagine that's what it's about. We could make out a young man and a young woman, played by Edouard Dermithe and Nicolo Stephane, who are brother and sister in the fable and who certainly reside in a "cluttered" and "disorderly" room. We could also see very plainly—again as the program says—that "they are not the ordinary brother and sister; they are bizarre, eccentric, lovable, wicked and strange people—untouched and isolated by circumstances from the world."

But more than this we can't tell you—except that they steal watering cans, eat crabs in bed, walk through echoing chambers and eternally yap at each other like peevish dogs. They also have a couple of moody playmates in Renee Cosima and Jacques Bernard, who appear to be utterly bewildered by the tortured eccentricities of their friends.

Nor does M. Cocteau help matters any by breaking in on the sound track now and then to mutter mysterious phrases in poetic cadences—such things as "no sooner had Paul entered this deserted studio than he took possession of it like a cautious cat" and "all they could discover were shadows, phantoms of feeling." Rot!

In this corner's estimation, "The Strange Ones" is pretentious poppycock and the actors who have to swish through it look downright ridiculous in their roles. There may be some sympathetic patrons who will find Cocteau's fable meaningful and his images rich in symbolism, but to us the whole thing is a bore.

Jl 29, 1952

NOVEL TECHNIQUE IN FILMS UNVEILED

By BOSLEY CROWTHER

The new motion-picture projection system known as Cinerama was put on public display for the first time last night before an invited audience at the Broadway Theatre. And, with due account for the novelty of the system, it was evident that the distinguished gathering was as excited and thrilled by the spectacle presented as if it were seeing motion pictures for the first time.

The name is, of course, a combination of the words "cinema" and "panorama"—and that conveys most clearly the nature of the motion picture that was placed upon the screen. For Cinerama is a utilization of a giant wide-angle screen that sweeps in an arc of 146 degrees across the front of the theatre auditorium and is taller than the ordinary screen, and upon which is thrown from three projectors a tri-panel picture in color that actually has the appearance of one single panoramic display.

This huge semicircular picture screen is supplemented by a sound-projection system known as "stereophonic sound," which is arranged to throw the synchronized sounds of the picture to the audience from outlets around the theatre in such a way that the illusion of sound originating in sections of the screen—or from the sides or behind the audience—is achieved.

On the program last evening—and this is the program that will be offered to the public, beginning today—the most spectacular and thrilling presentations were those that combined magnificence of scenic spectacle with movement of an intensively actionful sort.

Introduced with a conventional screen appearance of Lowell Thomas, who is chairman of the board of the Cinerama company, recounting the development of man's graphic skills from the era of the cave paintings, the program, "This Is Cinerama," began with a ride on a roller-coaster, as viewed realistically from the front seat.

This was followed with a presentation of a ballet at the La Scala Theatre in Milan, a trip in a helicopter over Niagara Falls and a performance of Handel's "Messiah," sung by the robed choir of the Long Island Choral Society.

Thereafter came beautiful scenes of gondola boating on the canals of Venice, a parade by a Scottish Highlander band at Edinburgh Castle, a garden performance by the Vienna Boys Choir, a bull-fight crowd in a Madrid arena, a performance of the finale of Act II of "Aida," and a spectacular display of motor-boating and water-skiing at the Cypress Gardens in Florida. The program was concluded with airplane scenes of New York, Washington, Chicago, the Illinois farmlands, the Grand Tetons and other American locales.

Although no claim is made for the system actually projecting a three-dimensional image, the illusion of depth is variously achieved through the fact that the viewer's eye takes in a greater sweep of picture than is customary when viewing a standard theatre screen. The stimulation of what is called "peripheral vision"—the things that are seen out of the "corner of the eye"—accounts for the illusion of depth.

It was noticeable that last night's program was made up exclusively of purely scenic presentations—pictorial spectacles—without any attempt at story-telling in the customary cinematic sense. And the question arose immediately as to what might, indeed, be done with this new panoramic system in the way of developing a

274

dramatic story on the screen. All of the scenes were in long shots, with little or no use at all of "montage"—the cinematic means of expression and emphasis through cutting and juxtaposition of shots.

However, the quality of the color (by Technicolor) was generally excellent and the merging of the three images at the margins was only occasionally perceptible. The sound, while overwhelming in volume at times, was usually crisp and clear, and the presentation of voices was properly synchronized.

The process, invented by Fred Waller, has been under development for several years, and the present production on display at the Broadway was made by Merian C. Cooper and Robert L. Bendick.

Among those in the capacity audience which attended last evening were Governor Dewey, Fritz Kreisler, Rudolph Bing, James A. Farley, David Sarnoff, Robert R. Young, William S. Paley, Richard Rodgers and Louis B. Mayer.

O 1, 1952

LIMELIGHT, screen play by Charles Chaplin; directed and produced by Mr. Chaplin. Released by United Artists. At the Astor and Trans-Lux Sixtieth Street Theatres.
Calvero ....Charles Chaplin
Terry ....Claire Bloom
Neville ....Sydney Chaplin
Mr. Postant ....Nigel Bruce
Bodalink ....Norman Lloyd
Piano accompanist ....Buster Keaton
Mrs. Alsop ....Marjorie Bennett
                For the Ballet
Harlequin ....Andre Eglevsky
Columbine ....Melissa Hayden
The Clowns ......{Charles Chaplin Jr.
                {Wheeler Dryden

By BOSLEY CROWTHER

Out of his knowledge of the theatre and his sense of wistfulness of man in the ever-repeating cycle of youth taking over from age, Charlie Chaplin has drawn the inspiration and the poignantly sentimental theme of his most recent motion picture, which opened here yesterday. It is, of course, his "Limelight," into which the famed artist has poured a tremendous amount of mellow feeling and cinema artistry. Neither comedy nor tragedy altogether, it is a brilliant weaving of comic and tragic strands, eloquent, tearful and beguiling with supreme virtuosity. What Mr. Chaplin is telling in

this tensely awaited film, which is being presented at the Astor and the Trans-Lux Sixtieth Street, is simply a tale of a great comedian of the English music halls who has gone to seed, yet who passes on to a young ballet dancer his vast abundance of courage and hope. That is what he is telling as the author, producer and director of the film—and also as the composer of the music, of one ballet and the comedy routines. But as its principal performer, he is not only playing the role; he is feeling it in its essence and projecting it from the screen.

Herein lies the brilliance of "Limelight"—in the artistry of Mr. Chaplin in the use of his sensitive face and his supple, mobile person as a positive instrument for the capture of thoughts and moods. From the moment his eyes, confused by liquor, are first studied as they strangely gaze upon the young heroine who has been so foolish as to try to take her life, those eyes and that face of Mr. Chaplin become the core and the focus of the film. The drama takes place around them, like the concentric ripples in a pool.

For, with all the dramatic variety and pictorial beauty achieved by Mr. Chaplin in this picture—all the poignancy of the intimate scenes, the hilarity of the comic outbursts and the vitality and grace of the ballets—the essential expression of all the pathos of loneliness and age is in those eyes. It is in the beautiful close-ups of the old clown as he takes his make-up off in the dressing-room of a provincial theatre where he has just been a pitiful flop or, as he sits in the gloom observing the first fine triumph of his protege that all the dignity, anguish and surrender of an old trouper came through.

And this, in the final analysis, is the main thing that comes through in the film—an appreciation of the courage and the gallantry of an aging man. There is no social issue in "Limelight," no basic conflict to compare with those in some of Chaplin's earlier pictures, such as the "little man" against a mechanical world. The fate that confronts the aging comic is a natural inevitability. The satisfaction offered the beholder is that of seeing a gesture carried off well.

This limits the magnitude of the whole achievement. "Limelight" is not a great film. It is a genial and tender entertainment and a display of audacity and pride. There are those who will easily read into it a veiled biography of Mr. Chaplin himself, not to mention a pretty full expression of his personal philosophies. There may be some justification for this. One tangible weakness of the film is the garrulous discussion of human foibles and paradoxes that Mr. Chaplin permits himself.

But, within the two hours and fifteen minutes that the picture eventually runs, he also gives a full measure of inspired Chaplin comedy. By various devices, he gets into, first, one hilarious routine in which he plays a commanding flea-trainer, dressed up in a ring-master's duds, and then a rollicking music hall nonsense to "Oh, For the Life of a Sardine." Best of his numbers, however, is a slam-bang burlesque pantomime of a violin-piano concert, with Buster Keaton as the accompanist on the keys.

And certainly Mr. Chaplin's associates in this amiable enterprise contribute their comparable measure of artistry and charm to its success. Claire Bloom, the dark-haired English actress whom Mr. Chaplin chose to play his heroine, is beautifully sensitive and expressive of a youngster's complete idolatry. Nigel Bruce is robust as a theatrical producer, Norman Lloyd is crisp as a stage manager and Sydney Chaplin, the son of the maestro, plays a standard romantic lead well.

Beautiful dancing by Andre Eglevsky and Melissa Hayden in the ballets weaves a spell that is sustained by Mr. Chaplin's sweet, sad music.

"Limelight" is a very moving film.

O 24, 1952

BREAKING THROUGH THE SOUND BARRIER, story and screen play by Terence Rattigan; directed and produced by David Lean. Aerial Unit directed by Anthony Squire. A David Lean Production presented by London Films and released here by Lopert Films Corp. At the Victoria.

John Ridgefield	Ralph Richardson
Susan Garthwaite	Ann Todd
Tony Garthwaite	Nigel Patrick
Philip Peel	John Justin
Jess Peel	Dinah Sheridan
Will Sparks	Joseph Tomelty
Christopher Ridgefield	Denholm Elliott
Windy Williams	Jack Allen
Fletcher	Ralph Michael
A. T. A. Officer	Vincent Holman
Controllers	Douglas Muir, Leslie Phillips
Test Bed Operator	Robert Brooks Turner
Peter Makepeace	Anthony Snell
Baby John	Jolyon Jackley

By BOSLEY CROWTHER

A film of pictorial excitement and truly poetic eloquence about man's scientific imagination and his bold endeavors to move through the air at supersonic speed is cloaked behind what is surely the clumsiest title in years. It is "Breaking Through the Sound Barrier" and it arrived here at the Victoria last night. As documentary and pedantic as that lengthy and tedious title may sound, we urge you to overlook it and not let it stand in your way.

For this picture, which was directed and produced in England by David Lean from an uncommonly literate and sensitive original script by Terence Rattigan, is a wonderfully beautiful and thrilling comprehension of the power of jet airplanes and of the minds and emotions of the people who are involved with these miraculous machines. And it is played with consummate revelation of subtle and profound characters by a cast headed by Ralph Richardson, Nigel Patrick and Ann Todd.

Any capsule review of the story and the general nature of this superior film is likely to be inadequate to a conveyance of its moving qualities. For the story quite simply is that of a young woman who cannot understand the devotion of her father and her husband to experimentation with airplanes. So dark and disspiriting is her revulsion, especially after her husband has been killed in an attempt to fly a jet through the "sound barrier," that she prepares to leave her father's home. And it is only when she perceives his personal torment while "sweating out" the time of another attempt that she sees and understands the dedication to discovery that drives him on.

Just to outline this story is to give but a shadowy hint of the complex of issues and emotions that are involved in this human ordeal. And just to say that the picture is about the development of jets is to offer but meager suggestion of the mystery and magic of science that is revealed.

This cannot tell you, for instance, how impressively Mr. Richardson shows not only the passion and concentration of a rich and famous builder of planes but the almost fanatic absorption of a man in the challenge of space. It cannot convey the experience of torment and tension that is portrayed in a nervous and impassioned performance of this man's daughter by Miss Todd, nor the character of a blithe test pilot that Mr. Patrick so warmly clarifies. Neither can it make you begin to get the feel of speed and space and the elation of mechanical triumph that is in this film.

But to cite you as an appropriate sampling, the scene in which Miss Todd approaches the office of her father in his great airplane plant on the night after her husband has been killed and finds him dispassionately studying the tape-recordings of the dead man's radioed reports—this is an indication of the dramatic force and clarity of the film. Or to cite Mr. Patrick's breezy slanging about dangerous exploits may give some notion of his role.

And certainly to give you a description of the way in which Mr. Lean has suggested the drama of a jet flight from London to Cairo —by taking you aloft for a spell to look out upon the English Channel and France lying far below and then by watching trails of vapor above the Alps and the old ruins of Greece, to the sound of the distant roar of the jet engine— this should let you imagine the poetry.

In one allusive way and another, Mr. Lean has created visually a sense of the powerful impulses that are behind the mind of man and the machine. It may be a glimpse of Mr. Richardson listening-in to the inter-com between the technicians and the test-pilot in one of his latest planes. It may be a shot of a peaceful wheatfield when an unseen jet whooshes past, lashing the stalks of grain to fury even while the sudden roar fades away. Or it may be a bit of eerie music, composed by Malcolm Arnold, keying a quiet scene in which the unknown of the "sound barrier" is first discussed.

Incidentally, Mr. Lean and Mr. Rattigan have contrived a most effective way to explain in simple terms this air resistance to a plane flying at sonic speed.

All of these things about this picture, plus many, many more— including the excellent performances of such actors in subsidiary roles as John Justin as a brainier test pilot, Dinah Sheridan as his unimaginative wife, Denholm Elliot as a terrified student pilot and Joseph Tomelty as a veteran engineer merit the approving attention that we haven't the space to give. But this must be said about this picture: it soars far above its clumsy tag and it comes pretty close to being the most exalting of contemporary films.

N 7, 1952

FORBIDDEN GAMES, dialogue by Jean Aurenche and Pierre Bost; adaptation by M. Aurenche, M. Bost and Rene Clement from an original story by Francois Boyer; directed by Rene Clement; produced by Robert Dorfman. Released here by Times Film Corporation. At the Little Carnegie Theatre.
Paulette .... Brigitte Fossey
Michel .... Georges Poujouly
Father Dolle .... Lucien Hubert
Mother Dolle .... Suzanne Courtal
Georges Dolle .... Jacques Marin
Berthe Dolle .... Laurence Badie
Father Gouard .....,.......... Andre Wasley
Francis Gouard ....: Amedee
The Priest .. .. Louis Sainteve

By BOSLEY CROWTHER

It had been the vague hope of many that the French would eventually come through with a film which would boom such shattering comment upon the tragedy and irony of World War II as their memorable "Grand Illusion" did for World War I. That hope at last has been realized. Such a film came along yesterday to the Little Carnegie. It is Rene Clement's "Forbidden Games" ("Jeux Interdits").

A great deal of professional excitement was aroused in Europe by this film, and some of that bubbling excitement had been transmitted over here. For one thing, the film stirred howling protests last spring from visiting critics after a special screening at the Cannes Film Festival because it had not been selected as an official entry of France. For another, it almost got a fast brush at the subsequent Venice Festival, on the ground that it wasn't eligible because it already had been shown at Cannes—and then, when it was accepted, it won the Venice Grand Prize. And, finally, it has been lambasted (as was inevitable) by certain elements abroad as a vicious and unfair picture of the peasantry of France.

All of this rambling excitement may have sounded excessive over here, especially in the light of some confusions at previous European festivals. But now that the film has been exhibited and its qualities revealed on this side, it may be reported confidently that the excitement is not only understandable but entirely justified. For "Forbidden Games" is a brilliant and devastating drama of the tragic frailties of men, clear and uncorrupted by sentimentality or dogmatism in its candid view of life.

As "Grand Illusion" found its area for comment upon the irony of war outside the actual range of warfare—it was about war prisoners, you may recall—this film finds its area for comment upon the damage that has been done to humankind in the seemingly innocent realm of farmers and children in the undisturbed countryside. The towering symbol of the war's vast devastation is one little 5-year-old girl. And her immediate world, as we see it, is mostly that of a French peasant's farm.

But out of these plain and modest elements, M. Clement, who directed and helped to write the script with Jean Aurenche and Pierre Bost from an original screen story by François Boyer, has fused a powerful drama that cuts a wide swath through the fields of man's ripe hopes and symbolizes the frustration that many Europeans must feel about war.

For the little girl of this story is a pitiful orphan of the war—a child who has seen her two parents and her little dog killed on the road while they were fleeing from the oncoming Germans and has found sanctuary in a peasant home and in the wonderfully sympathetic companionship of a slightly older peasant boy. The only thing is that this youngster has a fondness for the symbols of death—a fondness in which her new companion encourages and comforts her by killing other animals and burying them, with ceremonials, beside the grave of her dog. And the irony is that the peasants have no way to help with this strange attitude because, as is demonstrated, they are burdened and confused by their own pitiably ignorant, hypocrital and inhuman fixed ideas about death.

We will not attempt a recital of the shattering details of this haunting film—of the swiftness of its dramatic passage from the most tender and heart-tearing scenes of attachment between the naïve children to scenes of earthy and ghoulish comedy in which the remarkably credible peasants demonstrate their pathetic crudity. Nor can we express sufficient admiration for the brilliant acting of it—for the 5-year-old girl, Brigitte Fossey, from whom M. Clement has got a performance that rips the heart out with its simplicity and sincerity; for a youngster named Georges Poujouly, who makes of the little boy not a creature of juvenile mischief but of spiritual magnificence; for Lucien Hubert as the boy's peasant father; Suzanne Courtal, as the latter's wife, and for all the remaining actors in this extraordinary film.

All to be said at the moment is that M. Clement has brought forth a film that has the irony of a "Grand Illusion," the authenticity of a "Harvest" and the fineness of French films at their best.

D 9, 1952

278

3 DIMENSION, a program of five short films produced in the stereoscopic process of Stereo-Techniques, Ltd.; Raymond Spottiswoode, technical director and presented by Sol Lesser. At the Globe.

By BOSLEY CROWTHER

Whatever prospects of improvement and added excitement in the projection of movies may reside in the new three-dimensional processes that are now being bally-hooed are only dimly and erratically suggested in the demonstration of stereoscopic films put on yesterday at the Globe Theatre, under Sol Lesser's sponsorship. For the total impression imparted by this forty-five-minute program of assorted shorts, produced by Stereo-Techniques, Ltd., of London and initially shown at the Festival of Britain two years ago, is one of indifferent achievement in the optical-illusion line and little or no departure in the way of novelty.

Outside of a few occasions when images seem to emerge from the standard-size screen and other occasions more or less uncertain, when there is an illusion of depth of image within the frame, the pictures presented in this program are no better pictorially—and are sometimes worse—than the average pictures' projected in the conventional and familiar "flat" way. The necessity of wearing polaroid glasses (provided by the theatre to all customers) in order to receive the optical effects is an incidental inconvenience that may also prove discomforting. This reviewer found the glasses not only oppressive but unpleasantly odorous—due, it appeared, to the plastic composition from which they are made.

Most effective of the five items, in both an optical and artistic way, is an animated abstract cartoon in color, entitled "Around Is Around," created by Norman McLaren and the National Film Board of Canada. In this little item, flying blobs of color and rhythmically oscillating whorls do appear at times to move out from the screen, bouncing about and gyrating over the heads of the customers down in front. How much of this tickling illusion is due to the stereoscopic process used and how much to the tricks of perspective that are obviously worked in the backgrounds is hard for a casual observer to determine on a first look. The effects, however, are surprising and amusing—when they do come off.

Also surprising and diverting is one little effect achieved when a supposedly humorous British professor seems to swing a ball suspended from a string out over the heads of the audience. This mildly phenomenal illusion evokes a few fearful gasps, especially when the string suddenly breaks and the ball appears to drop. Less effective in this professorial item are shots of animals in the London Zoo. Sea lions leaping at the camera, spraying water, are no more startling, to these eyes, than they would be if the picture were photographed "flat."

The use of the stereoscopic camera to get the illusion of depth is moderately well demonstrated in a pretty color film, illustrating a pleasantly placid and strictly scenic trip down the River Thames. But the use is imperfect and bewildering in a black-and-white ballet film, wherein the dancers are mostly flattened figures against the dismal background, but sometimes seem to leap as limbs or parts of bodies in or out around the sides of the screen's frame! It clearly appears that color is important to the three-dimensional effect and that it is perilously unrealistic to show human figures in any other than the whole.

Actually, the process demonstrated in this program at the Globe is, in optical principles, similar to the process shown before World War II in a series of Pete Smith shorts, released by Metro, called "Audioscopiks," and in a couple of films, produced by John A. Norling, shown at the New York World's Fair. With all due respect for innovations, this reviewer cannot see that any marked improvements in stereoscopic projection have been made in these latest films. Something more exciting will have to come forth to justify the noise being made about "3 D."

TRIORAMA: a program of four short films illustrating a stereoscopic process developed by the Bolex Company and known as Bolex Stereo. Editorial Supervision by Jean H. Lenauer.

———

The so-called "three-dimensional" tempest now buffeting the film industry is likely to continue, to judge by "Triorama," a stereoscopic process developed by the Bolex Company, which was publicly unveiled yesterday at the Rialto. For the program of four short subjects running about thirty-five minutes, which were photographed in Kodachrome and compiled under the aforementioned title to illustrate the Bolex Stereo photographic and projection systems, is largely imitative in its approach and only occasionally effective in achieving images in depth.

Perhaps, as was explained before the showing yesterday, the Bolex 16mm. process was fashioned primarily for amateur use. The sub-standard 16mm. films, viewed through polaroid glasses—as are the Globe Theatre's current Stereo Techniques offerings—and flashed on a narrow portion of the Rialto's screen, left much to be desired in the way of three-dimensional illusion or as an example of a new departure in the motion-picture field. And the need for glasses (provided by the management) does not appear to be an asset. This viewer found them uncomfortable on occasion and an impediment on other occasions in that they cut off some of the light needed for relaxed viewing.

Of the four subjects demonstrated, the last, termed "This Is Bolex Stereo" and filmed by Larry Crolius, Harold Reiff, Ewing Krainin and Prof. John F. Storr, came closest to imparting true optical depth. A travelogue, which skipped from Florida to Maine, Haiti, Nassau, Guatemala and Montego Bay, it made full use of panoramic shots, the natives and flora and fauna. Especially striking were some underwater scenes, filmed in the Bahamas, in which fish and multi-colored underwater rocks and vegetation seemed to approach viewers from the screen.

"Indian Summer," another travelogue filmed in the rugged fast-nesses of North Dakota by Ernest Wildi of the Paillard Bolex Company, used such visual tricks as arrows being shot at the camera and a pretty girl on a swing, but arrived at pictorially beautiful effects in capturing a genuinely stereoscopic sylvan scene from behind a waterfall. And a vista of a vast forest area, as momentarily seen from a precipitous ledge, had quality and depth.

However, "Sunday in Stereo," photographed by David Mage and Milton Fruchtman in such areas as the Playland Amusement Park in Rockaway, at a zoo and in other photogenic spots proved only occasionally that amateurs could invade professional precincts. A ride down a roller coaster, for example, just barely showed traces of three-dimensional illusion. And, in "American Life," also filmed by Ernest Wildi, a baseball or a beach ball tossed at a camera merely transmitted a mild shock effect an achievement paralleling that of the "Audioscopiks" shorts, released by Metro years ago, as well as the pictures produced by John A. Norling and shown at the World's Fair here.

Since "Triorama" is being offered as a demonstration of the results obtained by Bolex stereoscopic equipment—which has been marketed to amateurs for several months now—it would be unfair to appraise the pictures dramatically. But as examples of stereoscopic fare they are rarely more stimulating or imaginative than a two-dimensional or "flat" film. The management reportedly intends to enlarge the films to the conventional 35-mm. size any day now. But if the Rialto's present attraction is a yardstick, it is difficult to understand why.   A. W.

F 11, 1953

FROM HERE TO ETERNITY

Out of "From Here to Eternity," a novel whose anger and compassion stirred a post-war reading public as few such works have, Columbia and a company of sensitive hands have forged a film al-

280

most as towering and persuasive as its source. Although it naturally lacks the depth and fullness of the 430,000 words and 850 pages of the book, this dramatization of phases of the military life in a peacetime army, which was unveiled at the Capitol yesterday, captures the essential spirit of the James Jones study. And, as a job of editing, emending, re-arranging and purifying a volume bristling with brutality and obscenities, "From Here to Eternity" stands as a shining example of truly professional moviemaking.

FROM HERE TO ETERNITY, screen play by Daniel Taradash; based on the novel by James Jones; directed by Fred Zinnemann; produced by Buddy Adler for Columbia. At the Capitol.

Sgt. Milton Warden	Burt Lancaster
Robert E. Lee Prewitt	Montgomery Clift
Karen Holmes	Deborah Kerr
Angelo Maggio	Frank Sinatra
Alma (Lorene)	Donna Reed
Capt. Dana Holmes	Philip Ober
Sgt. Leva	Mickey Shaughnessy
Mazzioli	Harry Bellaver
Sgt. "Fatso" Judson	Ernest Borgnine
Sgt. Maylon Stark	George Reeves
Sgt. Ike Galovitch	John Dennis
Sgt. Pete Karelsen	Tim Ryan
Mrs. Kipfer	Barbara Morrison
Georgette	Kristine Miller
Annette	Jean Willes
Sal Anderson	Merle Travis
Treadwell	Arthur Keegan
Sgt. Baldy Thom	Claude Akins
Sgt. Turp Thornhill	Robert Karnes
Sgt. Henderson	Robert Wilke
Cpl. Champ Wilson	Douglas Henderson
Friday Clark	Don Dubbins
Cpl. Paluso	John Cason
Capt. Ross	John Bryant

As may be surmised, credit for this metamorphosis cannot be localized. The team of scenarist, director, producer and cast has managed to transfer convincingly the muscularity of the basically male society with which the book dealt; the poignance and futility of the love lives of the professional soldiers involved, as well as the indictment of commanding officers whose selfishness can break men devoted to soldiering. They are trapped in a world they made and one that defeats them. Above all, it is a portrait etched in truth and without the stigma of calculated viciousness.

Cleaves To Author's Thesis

Although the incisive script fashioned by Daniel Taradash sidesteps such matters as the shocking "Stockade" chapters of the book, it fundamentally cleaves to the author's thesis. Set in Schofield Barracks in Oahu, Hawaii, in the months preceding the attack on Pearl Harbor, it is the tragic story of the youthful Pvt. Robert E. Lee Prewitt, hard-headed Kentuckian whose convictions are strong enough to force him to forego his passionate devotion to both the bugle and prize fighting despite the knowledge that his superior officer, Capt. Dana Holmes, and his crew of athletes will give him "The Treatment."

It is the story, also, of First Sgt. Milton Warden, top kick of the company, a rough-hewn pillar of strength whose know-how guides and supports the pompous and philandering captain and the admiring contingent of G. I.'s in his command. It is the tale of sinewy Angelo Maggio, enlisted man from the sidewalks of New York whose brave revolt against the confinements of the Army system ends in tragedy. And it is the account of the ill-fated affair between Karen Holmes, the captain's wife, and Sergeant Warden, as well as the romance of Private Prewitt and Lorene, whose charms were purveyed in Mrs. Kipfer's New Congress Club.

Credit Fred Zinnemann with an expert directorial achievement in maintaining these various involvements on equal and lucid levels. While each yarn is pertinent and commands attention, the conflicts of its principals are fayed neatly into a compact whole. And the climactic strafing of Schofield Barracks is a fittingly explosive finish to the two hours of uncluttered drama culled from an immense and sometimes sprawling work of fiction.

Cast Plays Roles Well

Fortunately the cast members measure up to their assignments. In Burt Lancaster, the producer has got a top kick to the manner born, a man whose capabilities are obvious and whose code is hard and strange but never questionable. He is a "thirty-year man" respected by his superiors and the G. I.'s with whom he fights and plays. His view of officers leaves him only with hatred of the caste although he could easily achieve rank, which would solve his romantic problem. But he is honest enough to eschew it and lose the only love he has known.

Montgomery Clift adds another sensitive portrait to an already imposing gallery with his portrayal of Prewitt. Since he has blinded a man in the ring, no carefully planned scheme of harassment will get him in again. And, since he considers it a slight when he has been passed over as a bugler who once played taps at Arlington National Cemetery, he deems it his right to be "busted" from corporal to conform to his credo that "if a man don't go his own way, he's nothin'."

Although it is a deviation from the norm, Frank Sinatra is excellent in the non-singing role of Angelo Maggio, a characterization rich in comic vitality and genuine pathos. Deborah Kerr, heretofore the genteel lady in films, contributes a completely tender stint as the passionate Karen Holmes, defeated by a callous mate and a fruitless marriage, who clings to a doomed love.

While Donna Reed is not precisely the picture of a lady of the evening, her delineation of Lorene, wracked between a desire to be "proper" and her anomalous affair with Prewitt, is polished and professional. Although Philip Ober's weak captain is a comparatively slight and shallow role, the company of G. I.'s and the Schofield Barracks, where some of the film was shot, gave the drama and the authenticity required.

"From Here to Eternity" is being shown on a wide screen and with Stereophonic sound. It does not need these enhancements. It has scope, power and impact without them.   A. W.

Ag 6, 1953

THE WILD ONE

By BOSLEY CROWTHER

A little bit of the surface of contemporary American life is scratched in Stanley Kramer's "The Wild One," which came to the Palace yesterday, and underneath is opened an ugly, debauched and frightening view of a small but peculiarly significant and menacing element of modern youth. Although the reality of it goes soft and then collapses at the end, it is a tough and engrossing motion picture, weird and cruel, while it stays on the beam.

THE WILD ONE, screen play by John Paxton, based on a story by Frank Rooney; directed by Laslo Benedek; a Stanley Kramer Company production released by Columbia Pictures. At the Palace.
Johnny .... Marlon Brando
Kathie .... Mary Murphy
Harry Bleeker .... Robert Keith
Chino .... Lee Marvin
Sheriff Singer .... Jay C. Flippen
Mildred .... Peggy Maley
Charlie Thmas .... Hugh Sanders
Frank Bleeker .... Ray Teal
Bill Hannegan .... John Brown
Art Kleiner .... Will Wright
Ben .... Robert Osterloh
Wilson .... Robert Bice
Jimmy .... William Vedder
Britches .... Yvonne Doughty

The subject of its examination is a swarm of youthful motorcyclists who ride through the country in wolf-pack fashion and terrorize the people of one small town. Given to jive or be-bop lingo and the grotesque costumes and attitudes of the "crazy" cognoscenti, these "wild ones" resent discipline and show an aggressive contempt for common decency and the police. Reckless and vandalistic, they live for sensations, nothing more—save perhaps the supreme sensation of defying the normal world.

In bringing this gang into focus, Screenwriter John Paxton has contrived to give them some clarity through their leader, whom Marlon Brando plays. And in this taut and eerie hoodlum is fleetingly but forcibly revealed the consequence of youthful frustrations recompensed by association with a cult. Mr. Brando is vicious and relentless, so long as he is permitted to be; he barely exposes his battered ego from behind a ferocious front. In one line, muttered tersely and defiantly while he is being beaten by a vigilante mob, he reveals his whole pitiful ruination. "My old man hit harder than that," he snarls.

And in a second wolf-pack leader, whom Lee Marvin gruesomely portrays as a glandular "psycho" or dope-fiend or something fantastically mad, there is briefly injected into this picture a glimpse of utter monstrosity, loose and enjoying the privilege

282

of hectoring others in a fair society.

So long as the makers of this
pictur. permit it to stay in the
realm of graphic examination of
the behavior and depredations of
this mob, it is a powerful and
terrifying survey. And when they
wryly rush up the weak reserves
of a normal and baffled community in the form of one cowardly
cop and a snarling handful of
vigilantes they briefly project
their film onto the elevated level
of social drama with significance
and scope.

But, unfortunately, the picture
is not permitted to remain in these
realms. Mr. Paxton and Director
Laslo Benedek—or somebody—
have pulled it down. They begin
by bringing the gang leader, Mr.
Brando, into contact with a girl—
a good, clean, upright, small-town
beauty—who apparently fills him
with love. And before you know
it, this maiden and her father,
the cowardly cop, whom Robert
Keith plays in limpid fashion, are
pleading forgiveness for the
mugg. Although it is not clearly
stated that the obvious ties of
love are going to bind, the mugg
does ride off into the sunrise, a
presumably clean and fine young
man.

Mary Murphy, who plays the
maiden, is not to blame for the
patness of her role, any more
than Mr. Brando is responsible
for the fake repentant he must
turn out to be. All the others,
including Mr. Brando and Mr.
Marvin when they're on the beam,
give incisive and picturesque performances under the able direction of Mr. Benedek. It so happens that Mr. Marvin is permitted to disappear when the romance begins to blossom, and
that is unfortunate, too.

Withal, "The Wild One" is a
picture of extraordinary candor
and courage—a picture that tries
to grasp an idea, even though its
reach falls short. It is too bad
that some mutterings in the industry have seemed to deprecate
it, and it should turn up as the
passing feature on an eight-act
vaudeville bill.

D 31, 1953

BEAT THE DEVIL, screen play by John
Huston and Truman Capote, based on the
novel by James Helvick; directed by Mr.
Huston; a Santana-Romulus Production,
released through United Artists. At sixty-
eight metropolitan theatres.
Billy Dannreuther..........Humphrey Bogart
Gwendolen Chelm.............Jennifer Jones
Petersen ....Robert Morley
Maria Dannreuther.........Gina Lollobrigida
O'Hara ....Peter Lorre
Harry Chelm.............Edward Underdown
Major Ross.....................Ivor Barnard
Ravello ....Marco Tulli
C. I. D. Inspector.............Bernard Lee

A potential treat emerged as a
wet firecracker in some sixty-
eight neighborhood theatres yesterday where United Artists unveiled its singularly unorthodox
"Beat the Devil." From the marquee, or marquees, this Santana-
Romulus venture, made entirely
abroad, looks wonderful. Take
the cast, boasting Humphrey Bo-
bart, two luscious and talented
beauties like Jennifer Jones and
Gina Lollobrigida, and such supporting specialists as Robert Morley and Peter Lorre. Above all,
there is the distinguished directorial thumbprint of director John
Huston, who, with the estimable
Truman Capote, adapted the
script from a James Helvick
novel.

The result is a pointedly roguish and conversational spoof, generally missing the book's bite,
bounce and decidedly snug construction. Allowing for some
genuine, brazenly funny bits, the
format seems as brazenly piece-
meal. Mr. Helvick's lightweight
odyssey, like this transcription,
trailed a group of sophisticated
beachcombers in their race from
the Italian Riviera to Africa and
a vaguely confirmed uranium de-
posit, mixing a quartet of indo-
lently married couples and some
picaresque cutthroats.

Fun Wears Thin

However, off the printed page
and minus the glossy Hollywood
trimmings it needs, the fun wears
mighty thin. Even with the cast
braving a doomed freighter and
fantastically thrust into an Arabian uprising, the incidents remain on a naggingly arch and
lagging verbal keel. And the
business of wondering what will
happen next isn't too beguiling
when uneasily mirrored by about
half the cast. Add to this the

harsh, neo-realistic photography, which authentically stalks and X-rays the joke to death.

Mr. Bogart, as the kingpin, underplays with good-natured neutrality. The others seem, in turn, either nervous or plain determined, including a blonde Miss Jones as a rhapsodical liar; Miss Lollobrigida as the hero's spouse and Edward Underdown as a stuffy Briton.

The best moments belong to the sauntering cutthroats personified by Mr. Lorre, Ivor Barnard, Marco Tulli and the portly Mr. Morley, whose cherubic evil provides the spiciest interludes. And some of the dialogue is delicious, as when Miss Jones delivers a discourse on spiritual values to a stupefied Mr. Morley. The most hard-breathing scene, with an Arabic firing-squad practicing outside, has their captor leaning forward to ask Mr. Bogart, "Now tell me, do you really know Rita Hayworth?"

For all the studiedly suave professionalism, though, "Beat the Devil" ends up beating itself.

H. H. T.
Mr 13, 1954

[THE FUSION BOMB]

WASHINGTON, March 31—The world's most fearsome weapon, the fusion bomb, was shown in action for the first time here in public today before an audience of representatives of the press and other information media.

They saw a reproduction on color film of the phenomena that followed the explosion of the first full-scale hydrogen weapon on the Pacific proving grounds in the Marshall Islands in November, 1952.

The event marked the entry of mankind into the Hydrogen Age, taking the fateful step from the kiloton (thousands of tons) to the megaton (millions of tons) of explosive power in terms of TNT.

The film was released by the Atomic Energy Commission and the Department of Defense for public issuance by the Federal Civil Defense Administration. It was intended for general release at 6 P. M. April 7, and reviews of it were to be embargoed until then.

However, a descriptive review by a syndicated columnist appeared in newspapers a few hours after the showing. Because of this The Times is publishing its review now.

The test in November, 1952, was known as Operation Ivy and the device tested was known as Mike. At the time it was made the explosion was the greatest in history. Since then, however, it has been greatly exceeded by the test explosions on March 1 and 26.

The film opens with an introduction by President Eisenhower, who recites an excerpt from his historic address before the United Nations on Dec. 8, 1953, relating to the need of the peoples of the world to know the significant facts of today's atomic age.

Some of the dramatic facts about that first hydrogen explosion had already been made public by Representative W. Sterling Cole, Democrat of upstate New York and chairman of the Joint Congressional Committee on Atomic Energy, in an address in Chicago on Feb. 17.

The Mike shot, the Civil Defense Agency stated, was noteworthy in several respects:

¶It produced the greatest lateral destructive effects up to that time from a single explosive device: complete annihilation within a radius of three miles, severe to moderate damage out to seven miles, light damage as far as ten miles. In Washington, with the Capitol as Ground Zero (detona-

tion point), there would have
been complete annihilation west
to Arlington Cemetery, east to
the Anacosta River, north to the
Soldiers Home, and south to
Bolling Field.

¶It created the largest nuclear
explosive fireball produc d until
then—3½ miles in diameter at
its maximum, enough to engulf
about one-quarter of Manhattan
Island. With the Empire State
Building as Ground Zero, the
fireball would have extended from
Washington Square uptown to
Central Park.

¶It caused the particular test
island of the Eniwetok Atoll
named Elugelab, to disappear
leaving a crater roughly a mile
in diameter—into which fourteen
Pentagon Buildings could have
fitted easily. The crater sloped
down to 175 feet—equivalent to
a seventeen-story building.

¶Within two minutes after the
explosion the mushroom cloud
soared to 40,000 feet—the height
of thirty-two Empire State Buildings. Nearing its maximum ten
minutes later, the cloud-stem
pushed upward twenty-five miles,
deep into the stratosphere, while
the mushroom cap portion, ten
miles high, spread laterally for
100 miles.

As for the film itself, it was
generally criticized on the
grounds of poor photography,
conception and dramatization of
the tremendous scope and power
of the first full-scale hydrogen
explosion in history, a pictorial
record of the step from the
atomic into the hydrogen age.

At times music drowned out
the voice of the narrator. And
professional newsreel men criticized it for showing too much of
the narrator and too little of the
operation.

As one newsreel official put it:
"The film doesn't portray
what's happening. It shows a guy
telling you what is happening. It
is another case of false security
that keeps men who know the
business from participating."

The consensus among the
newsreel men was that the public will not get as much out of
their first hydrogen bomb film as
they did out of the atomic bomb
pictures, such as, for example,
were taken of the tests at Bikini
in the summer of 1946.

Val Peterson, Federal Civil Defense Administrator, in commenting on the effects of the hydrogen bomb on civil defense planning, said: "The same principles
of individual preparedness and
community organization for civil
defense which could cut our
casualties in half under A-bomb attack could also minimize our
losses if an H-bomb ever exploded over our cities."

Ap 1, 1954

DIARY OF A COUNTRY PRIEST, script
and dialogue by Robert Bresson from
the novel "Journal d'nu Cure de Cam-
pagne" by Georges Bernanos; directed
by M. Bresson; produced by Leon Carré
A Union Generale Cinematographique
Production released here by Brandon
Films. At the Fifth Avenue Cinema.

The Priest of Ambricourt....Claude Laydu
Louise ...., Nicole Maurey
The Priest of Torcy........Andre Guibert
The Count ....Jean Riveyre
The Countess................Mme. Arkell
Chantal .... Nicole Ladmiral
Seraphita .... Martine Lemaire
The Canon ....Gaston Severn
Dr. Delbende................... Balpetre
The Housekeeper ....Jean Etievant
Olivier .. .. Jean Danet

By BOSLEY CROWTHER

SOMETIMES it helps a little
to be able to understand the
motivations and maneuverings
of the characters in a film. A
few simple clues to their behavior do aid one to grasp
what's going on. But these
rather modest assistances are
not provided—to this reviewer,
at least—by the contents of
Robert Bresson's "Diary of a
Country Priest," the French
film that opened yesterday at
the refurbished Fifth Avenue
Cinema, formerly the Fifth
Avenue Playhouse, down near
Washington Square.

Despite the extraordinary
closeness one has to the hero
of this film—and Mr. Bresson
gets his camera so close that
you can study every bump on
the young priest's sad face,
every quiver and droop of his
sick body, every gesture of his

expressive hands, as he fumblingly tries to be a pastor to the people of a village parish in France—the scope of the personal relations and inner conflicts that agonize this man and hasten his death (of cancer) remains elusive and obscure.

What is the deep and dark misgiving that seems to be eating on him as he takes up his clerical duties in a curiously churlish little town? Why do the children torment him—especially one little girl, whose peculiarly sadistic taunting is never made reasonably clear? And what is this complicated business of a slyly adulterous Count, his neurotic wife and their strange daughter, who seems to have some complex towards the priest?

Don't ask us. We followed the picture as closely as we could, ears open and eyes darting diligently over the English subtitles for the dialogue. And still we could not catch the pattern of the poor young priest's misery nor penetrate the veil of mysticism that strangely enshrouds the whole film.

This may not be blamed on M. Bresson. The late George Bernanos, who wrote the original story, which is the basis for the film. was one of those French Catholic authors whose concern was the abstract regions of the soul. And it is into these difficult regions that M. Bresson obviously has attempted to have his camera delve.

His cinema technique is brilliant. Reflective of the work of Carl Dreyer, the old Danish master of the close-up and the hard, analytical camera style, it is a compound of searching realism and a tempo of movement that approaches poetry. Thanks to fine photography and authentic backgrounds, this is a pictorially beautiful film.

•

And the performances are gauntly impressive. Claude Laydu as the tortured young priest gives such a sense of general suffering that he is literally painful to watch. Madame Arkell as the embittered Countess is a credible sufferer, too. One long scene between these two characters, in which they talk out the tangles in their souls, is so mentally and physically agonizing that one feels exhausted when it's done. You may not know what has been accomplished, but you know you have been through an ordeal.

Others who play their parts fitly are Andrè Guibert as an old priest, Jean Riveyre as the Count, Nicole Maurey as his paramour and Nicole Ladmiral as the daughter of the Count.

Perhaps those more closely familiar with the states of grace discussed in this film will be more alert to its meanings. This reviewer was completely confused.

Also on the program is a delightful UPA cartoon that tells the moralistic story of "The Fifty-first Dragon," by the late Heywood Broun. A trenchant fable, done in sketches that has an amusingly satiric style, for all the economy in their drawing, it makes a point about catch-phrases and empty words.

Ap 6, 1954

THE EARRINGS OF MADAME DE: screen play by Marcel Achard and Max Ophuls; based on the novel by Louise de Vilmorin; directed by Max Ophuls; a Franco-London Production presented by Arlan Pictures, Inc. At the Little Carnegie.
Monsieur De (General)......Charles Boyer
Madame De ....Danielle Darrieux
Baron Donati ....Vittorio De Sica

THE French, who rarely are casual about l'amour, are being serious, tender and slightly ineffectual about a romantic triangle in "The Earrings of Madame De," a bittersweet confection that came from France to the Little Carnegie yesterday.

Like its turn-of-the-century décor and costuming, it is elegant and filled with decorative but basically unnecessary little

286

items, which give it gentility and a nostalgic mood, but nothing much more substantial. The principals of the Parisian haut monde involved in this affair of the heart—a lady, her general-husband and her lover, naturally — are well behaved, but unfortunately their problem seems more important to the producers than to a viewer.

Although the romantic trials in which the trio becomes enmeshed are fundamentally simple, the earrings on which this yarn hangs lead an uncommonly complex existence. First, the lady of the title sells them back to the jeweler from whom her husband bought them as a wedding present. She then tells her spouse a white lie about losing them. The jeweler, fearful of a scandal, reports the truth to the confused husband, who retrieves the trinkets and, in turn, gives them to his mistress. That luckless dame gambles them away and a noble, Italian diplomat snags them and, as may be guessed, turns up in Paris, is smitten by our heroine and donates the baubles to the lady as a token of his undying affection.

From here on in our Madame De and her paramour, whose love is real but unrequitted, spend considerable time together and apart but always pining desperately. When, by either a quirk of passion or devotion to her husband, the lady decides to wear the gems again, her mate, a strangely observant gent, learns of the deception and there is the inevitable duel. Madame De, a frail sort at best, succumbs to a heart attack on the field of honor.

Three fine performers such as Charles Boyer, Danielle Darrieux and Vittorio De Sica contribute polished characterizations in the principal roles, but fail to give insouciance and bite to this standard, gossamer romance. Mlle. Darrieux, who is fetching in the many pretty,

furbelowed costumes she wears, is a beautiful but ill-defined creature given to fits of vague illnesses. As her military husband, Charles Boyer is a handsome figure of a general who does, occasionally, inject Gallic nuance into gestures and speech. Sadly enough, Vittorio De Sica, as the lover who decides to step out of the picture, is afforded little opportunity to do more than be gallant. Although its charm is evident, the passion in this period piece is relegated, more often than not, to its French dialogue and English subtitles.   A. W.

Jl 20, 1954

SEVEN BRIDES FOR SEVEN BROTHERS: screen play by Albert Hackett, Frances Goodrich and Dorothy Kingsley; based on "The Sobbin' Women" by Stephen Vincent Benet; directed by Stanley Donen; produced by Jack Cummings for Metro-Goldwyn-Mayer; music by Gene de Paul and lyrics by Johnny Mercer. At the Radio City Music Hall.
The Pontipee Brothers:
Adam ....Howard Keel
Benjamin ....Jeff Richards
Caleb ....Matt Mattox
Daniel ....Marc Platt
Ephraim ....Jacques d'Amboise
Frank ....Tommy Hall
Gideon ....Russ Tamblyn
The Brides:
Milly ....Jane Powell
Dorcas ....Julie Newmeyer
Alice ....Nancy Kilgas
Sarah ....Betty Carr
Liza ....Virginia Gibson
Ruth ....Ruta Kilmonis
Martha ....Norma Doggett
and
Rev. Elcott ....Ian Wolfe
Mr. Bixby ....Russell Simpson
Mrs. Bixby ....Marjorie Wood
Dorcas' Father ....Dick Rich
Pete Perkins ....Howard Petrie

M-G-M, a movie manufactory that has not been represented by any outstanding musicals in recent months, has delivered a wholly engaging, bouncy, tuneful and panchromatic package labeled "Seven Brides for Seven Brothers" and deposited it at the Music Hall yesterday. A distant relation of "Oklahoma!" with such unrelated godfathers as Stephen Vincent Benét and Plutarch, this lively fable skilfully blends a warm and comic yarn about the rustic romances of a family of Oregonian pioneers with

strikingly imaginative chore-
ography and a melodic score
several notches above standard.
And, an amiable and talented
cast go to it with a will to
make these cheerful ingerdi-
ents infectious.

Perhaps it is not especially
important to divine precisely
what the author, or the scenarists who adopted his story,
"The Sobbin' Women," had in
mind. Suffice it to say that the
results add up to a gay tale
about seven strapping young
farmers whose unkempt persons and filthy cabin have
never benefited by the tender
distaff touch until, that is, the
oldest brings home a comely
bride.

That tiny but spirited lass
not only changes their manners
and habits but also in typically
feminine fashion, acts as Cupid's handmaiden by introducing them to Plutarch's legend
about the Sabine women (Mr.
Benet's "Sabbin' Women"). So,
hungering for companionship
and love, our rugged Romeos
raid the village according to
the Latin tradition and return
with six unwilling maidens,
who, as might be expected,
learn to like the arrangement
even if their parents do not.

Call this a somewhat thin
story line but it has been enhanced by the contributions of
Michael Kidd, whose dance
creations are in keeping with
the times (1850) and with the
seemingly unbounded energy of
the principals. He has provided them with a repertoire that
could be exhausting. But such
agile craftsmen as Jacques
d'Amboise, Marc Platt, Tommy
Rall, Russ Tamblyn, Matt Mattox and Jeff Richards give
them a dizzying whirl. And, it
might be noted specifically,
that the combination of ballet,
acrobatics and a knockdown
and drag-out fight he has con-
jured up to go with a barn-
raising scene should leave audiences panting and cheering.

The eight songs fashioned by
Gene de Paul and Johnny Mer-
ce rare fresh and lilting and

feyed neatly into the speedy
proceedings. Chances are that
"When You're In Love," a ballad delivered in fine, romantic
style by Howard Keel and Jane
Powell, will be hitting the juke
boxes soon. "Spring, Spring,
Spring," gaily warbled by both
the "brothers" and "sisters" of
the title, and 'Wonderful, Wonderful Day," to which Mr.
Keel's pretty bride, Miss Powell,
gives a smooth and tender rendition, are easy on the ears too.
And, "Sobbin' Women," a
rhythmic, bouncy ditty, is done
rousingly by Mr. Keel and his
"brothers."

Stanley Donen, a director
who is no stranger to M-G-M
musicals, has kept the pace of
this lark swift and in time with
the tunes. And, Mr. Keel, whose
baritone is as big and impressive as his frame; Miss Powell,
who sings and acts to the
pioneer manner born, as well
as their sturdy and energetic
kinfolk—and this must include
the nubile, dancing damsels
they abduct—are lovely to look
at and hear. Although the
powers at M-G-M are deviating
from the normal song-and-
dance extravaganza in "Seven
Brides for Seven Brothers," it
is a gamble that is paying rich
rewards.

Featured on the Music Hall's
stage are Nanci Crompton, the
ballet corps, the Rockettes, an
equestrian act featuring Roberto De Vasconscellos and Erika,
Larry Griswold, the Glee Club
and violinist Harry Cykman
and the Music Hall Symphony
Orchestra.

Jl 23, 1954

ON THE WATERFRONT

A SMALL but obviously dedicated group of realists
has forged artistry, anger and
some horrible truths into "On
the Waterfront," as violent and
indelible a film record of man's
inhumanity to man as has come
to light this year. And, while
this explosive indictment of the
vultures and the meek prey of

the docksides, which was unveiled at the Astor yesterday, occasionally is only surface dramatization and an oversimplification of the personalities and evils of our waterfront, it is, nevertheless, an uncommonly powerful, exciting and imaginative use of the screen by gifted professionals.

ON THE WATERFRONT: screen play by Budd Schulberg; based on an original story by Mr. Schulberg and suggested by the series of Pulitzer Prize-winning articles by Malcolm Johnson; directed by Elia Kazan; produced by Sam Spiegel; a Horizon picture presented by Columbia; at the Astor.

Terry Malloy	Marlon Brando
Edie Doyle	Eva Marie Saint
Father Barry	Karl Malden
Johnny Friendly	Lee J. Cobb
Charley Malloy	Rod Steiger
"Pop" Doyle	John Hamilton
"Kayo" Dugan	Pat Henning
Glover	Leif Erickson
Big Mac	James Westerfield
Truck	Tony Galento
Tillio	Tami Mauriello
Barney	Abe Simon
Mott	John Heldabrand
Moose	Rudy Bond
Luke	Don Blackman
Jimmy	Arthur Keegan
J. P.	Barry Macollum
Specs	Mike O'Dowd
Gillette	Marty Balsam
Slim	Fred Gwynne
Tommy	Thomas Handley
Mrs. Collins	Anne Hegira

Although journalism and television already have made the brutal feudalism of the wharves a part of current history, "On the Waterfront" adds a graphic dimension to these sordid pages. Credit for this achievement cannot be relegated to a specific few. Scenarist Budd Schulberg, who, since 1949, has lived with the story stemming from Malcolm Johnson's crusading newspaper articles; director Elia Kazan; the principals headed by Marlon Brando; producer Sam Spiegel; Columbia, which is presenting this independently made production; Leonard Bernstein, who herein is making his debut as a movie composer, and Boris Kaufman, the cinematographer, convincingly have illustrated the murder and mayhem of the waterfront's sleazy jungles.

•

They also have limned a bestial and venal boss longshoreman; the "shape-up" by which only his obedient, mulct, vassals can earn a day's pay; the hard and strange code that demands that these sullen men die rather than talk about these injustices and a crime commission that helps bring some light into their dark lives.

Perhaps these annals of crime are too labyrinthine to be fully and incisively captured by cameras. Suffice it to say, however, that while Mr. Kazan and Mr. Schulberg have not dug as deeply as they might, they have chosen a proper and highly effective cast and setting for their grim adventure. Moving cameras and crews to the crowded rookeries of Hoboken's quayside, where the film was shot in its entirety, they have told with amazing speed and force the story of Terry Malloy, ex-prize fighter and inarticulate tool of tough, ruthless and crooked labor leader, Johnny Friendly. The labor leader is an absolute unregenerated monarch of the docks who will blithely shake down his own men as well as ship owners; he will take cuts of pay envelopes and lend his impecunious union members money at usurious rates and he will have his pistol-toting goons dispatch anyone foolish enough to squeal to the crime commission attempting to investigate these practices.

•

It is the story also of one of these courageous few about to "sing" to the commission — a luckless longshoreman unwittingly set up for the kill by Terry Malloy, who is in his soft spot only because his older brother is the boss' slick, right-hand man. It is the tale of Terry's meeting with the dead man's agonized sister and a fearless, neighborhood priest, who, by love and reason, bring the vicious picture into focus for him. And, it is the account of the murder of Terry's brother; the rampaging younger man's defiant testimony before the commission and the climactic bloody battle that wrests the union from the boss' tenacious grasp.

Journalism may have made these ingredients familiar and certainly more inclusive and multi-dimension, but Mr. Kazan's direction, his outstanding cast and Mr. Schulberg's pithy and punchy dialogue give them distinction and terrific impact. Under the director's expert guidance, Marlon Brando's Terry Malloy is a shatteringly poignant portrait of an amoral, confused, illiterate citizen of the lower depths who is goaded into decency by love, hate and murder. His groping for words, use of the vernacular, care of his beloved pigeons, pugilist's walk and gestures and his discoveries of love and the immensity of the crimes surrounding him are highlights of a beautiful and moving portrayal.

In casting Eva Marie Saint —a newcomer to movies from TV and Broadway—Mr. Kazan has come up with a pretty and blond artisan who does not have to depend on these attributes. Her parochial school training is no bar to love with the proper stranger. Amid scenes of carnage, she gives tenderness and sensitivity to genuine romance. Karl Malden, whose importance in the scheme of this drama seems overemphasized, is, however, a tower of strength as the militant man of the cloth. Rod Steiger, another newcomer to films, is excellent as Brando's fearful brother. The pair have a final scene that is a harsh and touching revelation of their frailties.

Lee J. Cobb is muscularly effective as the labor boss. John Hamilton and Pat Henning are typical "longshoremen," gents who look at home in a hold, and Tony Galento, Tami Mauriello and Abe Simon —erstwhile heavyweight boxing contenders, who portray Cobb's chief goons—are citizens no one would want to meet in a dark alley. Despite its happy ending; its preachments and a somewhat slick approach to

some of the facets of dockside strife and tribulations, "On the Waterfront" is moviemaking of a rare and high order.   A. W.

Jl 29, 1954

THE ADVENTURES OF ROBINSON CRUSOE, adapted for the screen by Phillip Roll and Luis Bunuel from Daniel Defoe's novel; directed by Mr. Bunuel; produced by Oscar Dancigers and Henry Ehrlich. A Tepeyac Production released by United Artists. At the Trans-Lux Normandie
Robinson Crusoe...........Dan O'Herlihy
Friday ....James Fernandez
Captain Oberzo............Felipe De Alba
Bos'n ....Chel Lopez
Leaders of the Mutiny.....{Jose Chavez
                          {Emilio Garibay

By BOSLEY CROWTHER

NO plippancy is intended when we say that one of the most commendable things about "The Adventures of Robinson Crusoe," which arrived yesterday at the Normandie, is that Friday has not been transmuted into a beautiful native girl whom the famous castaway discovers and make a friend of on his lonely isle.

Such a strictly commercial alteration of the classic of Daniel Defoe might well have been pulled by some film-makers who might have attempted the tale, for there certainly is no other prospect of conventional romance in the book. And the story of one man's isolation for twenty-odd years would hardly seem the stuff of films.

Yet the fellows who made this picture — Oscar Dancigers, Henry Ehrlich and Luis Bunuel, three uncompromising independents who made the whole thing in color in Mexico—have gone right ahead and shot the story almost precisely as it unfolds in the book, with some natural omission of long descriptions and episodes that would only hold it up.

Indeed, they have hewed with such fidelity to the narrative line of Defoe that, for a good three-fifths of the picture, only one character appears on the screen. That character, of course, is Robinson Crusoe, the

English gentleman of the seventeenth century who is cast up on a deserted island off South America from 'a shipwreck that only he survives and for twenty-odd years makes himself cozy with no companions have a few animals.

And, what's more, Crusoe's lonely ordeal is recounted objectively, with no searching sweeps of introspection or psychological play. Except for two brief hallucinations, one when delirious and one when drunk, the hero goes blandly about the business of running a home way from home — building a stockade, fetching water, hewing wood, raising wheat and baking bread. The loneliness and longing of Crusoe are suggested largely in his narraive words.

This is not altogether tedious, since the color camera of Mr. Bunuel takes in a lot of lore of camping and a great deal of handsome scenery. The beauty of surf rolling strongly upon an endless, empty beach is slashed by a sense of the frustration of the captured and homesick man. And there is one scene in which the drunken exile runs into the surf carrying a torch that speaks his torment more clearly than any of the spoken words. But it does become heavily monotonous after a weary while, and it is quite a relief to have Friday show up on the isle.

The recount of the saving of the native from hungry cannibals, the making a loyal friend of him and the encounter with mutious sailors on the isle is good, run-of-mill adventure drama, eventful and exciting all the way. And the final departure of Crusoe hits a real note of poignancy.

The acting is simple in this picture. Dan O'Herlihy does a good straight job of playing the hermit hero, without getting inside the man. His only conspicuous condenscension to isolation is a trace of looniness, to be seen when the goat-skin-dressed old fellow wanders along the beach. And James Fernandez as Friday plays this primitve man with conventional broad gesticulation and humble attitude.

Ag 6, 1954

UGETSU, screen play by Matsutaro Kawaguchi and Yoshikata Yoda, from the stories of Akinari Ueda; directed by Kenji Mizoguchi; produced by Masaichi Nagata. A Daiei Film Production released by Harrison and Davidson. At the Plaza.
Lady Wakasa................Machiko Kyo
Genjuro ....Masayuki Mori
Miyagi ....Kinuyo Tanaka
Ohama ....Mitsuko Mito
Tobei ....Sakae Ozawa
The High Priest.........Sugisako Koyama
The Village Master.......Ryosuke Kagawa

By BOSLEY CROWTHER

MUCH more than the language that is spoken in "Ugetsu," the Japanese film that opened last night at the Plaza, will be hard for American audiences to comprehend—hard for even the most attentive patron to grasp as it goes along. For both the theme and the style of exposition in this Venice award-winning film have a strangely obscure, inferential, almost studiedly perplexing quality.

Indeed, it is this peculiar vagueness and use of symbolism and subterfuge that give to this Oriental fable what it has of a sort of eerie charm. They vex you at first with their confusions, but if you have patience, and hold on, intent upon finding out what's cooking, you'll get flavor from this weird, exotic stew.

•

For the mélange of strange adventures of two peasants and their wives in feudal Japan—back in the sixteenth century, when war lords were ravaging the land—is composed of all manner of pictured violence, demoniac shapes and sounds, hypnotic wailing of voices and some beautiful images. Terror is caught in monstrous faces and wildly contorted human forms; quietness and peace are indicated in gorgeous pictorial harmonies. Kenji Mizoguchi, who directed, has a fantastic flexibility in using his actors and his camera, as witness his range in this film.

Perhaps it will help if we tell you, here and now, that the point of it all—as nearly as we could finally make out—is that social ambition and greed are vices which the Japanese peasant would do very well to avoid. This is eventually illustrated, by the garbled misfortunes that befell the two somewhat reckless and disloyal husbands in the tale.

One of them, eager to be a soldier, an arrogant samurai, lets ambition lure him to such follies that he wholly neglects his poor wife and finally, in his moment of false triumph, discovers that she has been made a prostitute. The other, dreaming of riches, falls victim to a Japanese Lorelei, who seduces him away from his family and then turns out to be a ghost. This is a point of some confusion, since it isn't revealed until the end. Both fellows are stock fiction characters, and the lessons proved are banal.

It is this averageness of the stories that removes this legend-inspired film from a class with that previous artful and exciting Japanese picture "Rashomon." But the imagery and the acting are no less intriguing here, and the use of sound for weird disturbance is notably rarefied. Machiko Kyo and Masayuki Mori, who played the wife and husband in "Rashomon," are fine as the ghostly temptress and the man she vamps, to his chagrin. And Sakae Ozawa as the hot-headed fellow who wants to be a samurai has flamboyant airs.

We understand that "Ugetsu" means "pale and mysterious moon after the rain"—which is just about as revealing as a great deal else in this film.

S 8, 1954

A STAR IS BORN, screen play by Moss Hart, based on the Dorothy Parker, Alan Campbell, Robert Carson screen play; from a story by William A. Wellman and Robert Carson; music and lyrics by Harold Arlen, Ira Gershwin and Leonard Gershe; directed by George Cukor; produced by Sidney Luft for Warner Brothers. At the Paramount and Victoria.
Esther Blodgett..............Judy Garland
Norman Maine................James Mason
Libby ....Jack Carson
Oliver Niles..............Charles Bickford
Danny McGuire...............Tom Noonan
A Starlet.....................Lucy Marlow
Susan ....Amanda Blake
Graves ....Irving Bacon
Libby's Secretary...........Hazel Shermet
Glenn Williams.............James Brown
Miss Markham................Lotus Robb

By BOSLEY CROWTHER

THOSE who have blissful recollections of David O. Selznick's "A Star Is Born" as probably the most affecting movie ever made about Hollywood may get themselves set for a new experience that should put the former one in the shade when they see Warner Brothers' and George Cukor's remake of the seventeen-year-old film. And those who were no more than toddlers when that classic was starting floods of tears may warm themselves up for one of the grandest heartbreak dramas that has drenched the screen in years.

For the Warners and Mr. Cukor have really and truly gone to town in giving this hackneyed Hollywood story an abundance of fullness and form. They have laid it out in splendid color on the smartly used CinemaScope screen, and they have crowded it with stunning details of the makers and making of films. They have got Judy Garland and James Mason to play the important roles that were filled with such memorable consequence by Janet Gaynor and Fredric March in the original. And they have fattened it up with musical numbers that are among the finest things in the show.

●

And a show it is, first and foremost. Its virtually legendary account of the romance of an actress headed for stardom and an actor headed downhill would have very little force or freshness in this worldly wise day and age if it weren't played within the lush surroundings of significant performance and fancy show. So it is a build-up of this that gives grandeur and background to the poignance of this film, which was put on with fanfare last evening at the Paramount and Victoria Theatres.

The whole thing runs for three hours, and during this extraordinary time a remarkable range of entertainment is developed upon the screen. There is the sweet and touching love story that Moss Hart has smoothly modernized from the neat synthesis of Hollywood legends, which went into the original.

It is the story of a vocalist with a dance band who catches the bleary, wistful eye of a topnotch male star, now skidding on the downgrade, and gets his help toward motion - picture fame. It is the story of their marriage and their struggle to hold fast to the fragile thing of love as fame and failure divide them—and of the husband's sacrifice at the end. This is the core of the drama, and it is brilliantly visualized.

No one surpasses Mr. Cukor at handling this sort of thing, and he gets performances from Miss Garland and Mr. Mason that make the heart flutter and bleed. Such episodes as their meeting on the night of a benefit show, their talking about marrying on a soundstage under an eavesdropping microphone, their bitter-sweet reaching for each other in a million-dollar beach bungalow, their tormenting ordeal in a night court—these are wonderfully and genuinely played.

What matters that logic does not always underlie everything they do? What matters that we never really fathom Mr. Mason's flamboyant Norman Maine? Theirs is a credible enactment of a tragic little try at love in an environment that

packages the product. It is the strong tie that binds the whole show.

But there is more that is complementary to it. There is the muchness of music that runs from a fine, haunting torch-song at the outset, "The Man That Got Away," to a mammoth, extensive production number recounting the career of a singer. It is called "Born in a Trunk." Miss Garland is excellent in all things— but most winningly, perhaps, in the song, "Here's What I'm Here For," wherein she dances, sings and pantomimes the universal endeavors of the lady to capture the man. Harold Arlen, Ira Gershwin and Leonard Gershe are the authors of the songs.

•

And there is, through it all, a gentle tracing of clever satire of Hollywood, not as sharp as it was in the original, but sharp enough to be stimulating fun. Charles Bickford's calm and generous producer is a bit on the idealized side and Jack Carson's disagreeable press agent is not as vicious as he's supposed to be. But the sense of an artificial milieu wraps the whole thing, as in cellophane—all in colors that fill the eye with excitement.

It is something to see, this "Star Is Born."

———

Crowds of enthusiastic onlookers swirled around the Paramount and Victoria Theatres last night to attend and watch the gala activities surrounding the première of "A Star Is Born." Miss Garland made an appearance at the Victoria and and later arrived at the Paramount for the showing of the film.

The glare of flood lights and popping of flash-bulbs provided customary background for the event which was "covered" by television cameras, radio broadcasters, Armed Forces Overseas radio, press and newsreel photographers. The sidewalks in front of the two theatres were carpeted in the traditional red velvet and searchlights sent shafts of light high in the sky over Broadway.

The audiences at both theatres were made up, to a large extent, by notables from many fields. As they arrived, Martin Block, the master of ceremonies, and George Jessel greeted them.

O 12, 1954

GATE OF HELL, screen play and direction by Teinosuke Kinugasa, based on a play by Kan Kikuchi; produced by Masaichi Nagata. Presented by Harrison and Davidson. At the Guild Theatre.
Lady Kesa....................Machiko Kyo
Moritoh ....Kazuo Hasegawa
Wataru ....Isao Yamagata
Kiyomori ....Koreya Senda
Shigemori ....Yataro Kurokawa
Sawa ....Kikue Mohri
Rokuroh ...:................Kotaro Bando
Kogenta ....Jun Tazaki
Yachuta ....Tatsuya Ishiguro
Masanaka ....Kenjiro Uemura
Saburosuke ....Gen Shimizu

By BOSLEY CROWTHER

OUT of Japan has come another weird and exquisite film—this one in color of a richness and harmony that matches that of any film we've ever seen. It is a somber and beautiful presentation of a thirteenth century legendary tale, smoothly and awesomely unfolding behind the volcanic title, "Gate of Hell." Under the sponsorship of the Japan Society, it opened last night at the Guild.

It is hard to convey in simple language the moving qualities of this lovely film, which, among other things, was the winner of the grand prize at the Cannes film festival last spring. The secret, perhaps, of its rare excitement is the subtlety with which it blends a subterranean flood of hot emotions with the most magnificent flow of surface serenity. The tensions and agonies of violent passions are made to seethe behind a splendid silken screen of stern formality, dignity, self-discipline and sublime esthetic harmonies. The very essence of ancient Japanese culture is rendered a tangible stimulant in this film.

The story itself is quite simple—neither so complex nor abstruse as the stories of "Rashomon" and "Ugetsu," recent imports from post-war Japan. It is the story of a thirteenth century warrior — a handsome and proud samurai— who falls in love with a dainty Japanese lady whom he aids and saves during a palace revolt and later requests in marriage, only to learn that she already is wed. Burning with a mad desire for her, he besieges her in her happy married state and causes her such shame and sorrow that she commits suicide.

It is simple, and yet the strain and anguish that develop as the story moves on, out of the violence and turbulence of the initial insurrection into a consideration of the turbulence that occurs amid seemingly peaceful surroundings in a man's and a woman's hearts— are as gripping and full of silent terror as they might be in a more elaborate plot. The individual frustration that a social form imposes is the gist of its timeless tragedy.

How Teinosuke Kinugasa, who wrote the screen play and directed this film, has achieved such extrordinary emotional impact is a matter of true wizardry. His use of color (Eastman) as applied to the Japanese scene, with such economy in his composition and such texture and color subtleties in his materials, is on a level that renders it comparable to the best in Japanese art. And his use of music and physical movements has a weird eloquence and grace that are profound.

One could rhapsodize for a whole column on the beauty and excitement of individual scenes—a shot of a coral-colored temple ranked with white-kimoned priests by a blue sea; a sequence re-enacting a horse race, full of feudal pomp and panoply; a truly bewitching vision of a pale lady in a blossom-pink robe twanging the strings of a strange musical instrument in a quiet Japanese home.

And one could write reams of lush enthusiasm for the porcelain beauty and electrifying grace of Machiko Kyo, the lady of "Rashomon" and "Ugetsu," who is the heroine here. For it is she, with her great power of suggestion with a minimum of gesture and a maximum use of the tiny mouth and eyes, who conveys the sense of sadness and despair that suffuses this film.

Kazuo Hasegawa as the proud and insistent samurai is powerful, too, in his vigorous, vain formality, and Isao Yamagata is quietly compelling as the dignified husband of the harassed heroine.

There is much to be got from this picture—much to savor and deeply enjoy. English subtitles, which oddly glisten, carry the sense of the dialogue.

At last night's opening of "Gate of Hell" Jun Tsuchiya, Consul General of Japan, spoke of the impact of films from his country on the Western world.

"The successful entree of Japanese films in the world market," Mr. Tsuchiya said, "may well have not only cultural, but also, I venture to suggest, economic consequences for both our countries. . . . To me, it is entirely conceivable that the export of superior films will greatly help my country in its present unremitting struggle to become self-sufficient, to rely on trade, not aid."

The Consul General stated he expected the export of such films would stimulate tours and travel to Japan. "Both of these results," he said, "must promote the economic health of Japan and make for sounder trade relations between Japan and the U. S. A. . . . We will continue to strive side-by-side with the United States for human betterment and freedom in Asia."

D 14, 1954

STRATEGIC AIR COMMAND, screen play by Valentine Davies and Beirne Lay Jr., from a story by Mr .Lay; directed by Anthony Mann; produced by Samuel J. Briskin for Paramount Pictures. At the Paramount.
Col. Robert "Dutch" Holland
.................................James Stewart
Sally Holland ....June Allyson
Gen. Ennis C. Hawkes....Frank Lovejoy
Lieut. Col. Rocky Samford..Barry Sullivan
Ike Knowland.................Alex Nicol
General Espy ....Bruce Bennett
Doyle ....Jay C. Flippen
General Castle ....James Millican
Reverend Thorne.............James Bell
Mrs. Thorne ....Rosemary De Camp
Aircraft Commander ,.Richard Shannon
Captain Symington......John R. McKee
Sergeant Bible...........Henry Morgan

By BOSLEY CROWTHER

NEVER, in many years of looking at Air Force and aviation films, have we seen the familiar wide blue yonder so wide or so magnificently displayed as it is in the Vista-Vision process used to project "Strategic Air Command."

This latest Paramount service picture, which received a full-dress première under the sponsorship of the Air Force Association last night at the Paramount Theatre, is far and away the most elaborate and impressive pictoral show of the beauty and organized power of the United States air arm that has yet been put upon the screen.

Credit, first, the Air Force, which made available the equipment, personnel and installations that are shown to such advantage in this film. The picture, as indicated, honors the Strategic Air Command, which flies the long-range bombers that constitute the nation's retaliatory strength against attack. And its all-star performers—the great B-36 propeller planes, the new B-47 jet bombers and the nexus of bases and fields are truly the most photogenic and exciting things to be seen.

•

But, certainly, an equal measure of credit for the pictorial impressiveness of this show must go to the Vista-Vision process, which is here being revealed for the second time. The first use of Vista-Vision was in "White Christmas," several months ago, but that use was technically less finished and on a subject of less scope than is shown here.

Now the full advantage of the VistaVision wide film (explained in an adjoining column) in giving size, depth and clarity, as well as fidelity of color, to big and detailed outdoor scenes is richly and dramatically apparent. The great panoramic shots of air fields, crowded with colorful equipment, betoken the precision and clear focus of the large VistaVision lens. And the scenes in the air of cloud formations, of planes venting feathery vapor trails and of in-air refueling operations, all graphically shown, attest to the new dramatic potential of the sharp and well-proportioned image on a large scale.

VistaVision, in this particular showing, appears as grand as Cinerama, more felicitous and free than CinemaScope.

•

And what, one may ask, of the story that is told in this scenic display? That, too, deserves a share of credit for the total impact of this film. For it is an adroitly sentimental and personalized tale of the sort that creates a nice dramatic profile of warm emotions against the background of machines.

It is the story of a big-league baseball player called back into the Air Force at a time when he is at a critical point in his professional career; of his natural resistance to the summons, of the readjustments that must be made by him and his wife, and of their eventual good-natured satisfaction in responding to the call.

Script writers Valentine Davies and Beirne Lay Jr. have dressed it up with what —to avoid an expression of agricultural connotation — we'll call clichés. The ballplayer is a pal of generals; he runs into old World War II friends; he has a crack-up just

to show that he is human, and his wife has a baby just at that point! But it must be said for the writers that their story develops sentiment and it is studded with nice conversation, not to mention a few cheery gags.

Furthermore—and this is a blessing—the role of the hero is played by that old Air Force colonel, James Stewart, who knows his way around air fields and planes. He makes the "retread" a fellow you can follow and like, if not quite believe. And June Allyson is equally effective— and equally incredible—as his wife.

•

They're incredible, we say, because both of them are playing idealized roles—he the good-Joe-who-can-take-it and she the all-American wife. These characters have long been mastered by them. They know just how to hug, to gulp. Their reactions are as glib as advertisements. But they fall patly into this film.

So do the rest of the airmen, from Frank Lovejoy as the chief of the S. A. C., through Barry Sullivan, Alex Nicol and Bruce Bennett as lesser officers, right down to Henry Morgan as an old non-com.

But, above all, there are those airplanes, the roaring engines, the cluttered cockpits, the clouds and sky. These are the things that make your eyes bug and your heart leap with wonder and pride.

The invitational world première of "Strategic Air Command" was held under the auspices of the Air Force Association.

A large crowd thronged the Times Square area before the theatre, where searchlights heralded the occasion. The spectators watched the arrival of 3,500 guests, who included personalities in the armed services, politics, entertainment and business.

Among the military representatives were Gen. Thomas

D. White, Vice Chief of Staff, U. S. A. F.; Lieut. Gen. Emmett O'Donnell, Deputy Chief of Staff Personnel, U. S. A. F.; Maj. Gen. M. J. Asensio, Vice Commander, Continental Air Command, U. S. A. F.; and Vice Admirals L. T. Dubose and Arthur D. Struble, U. S. N.

Also present were Senator H. Alexander Smith of New Jersey, Grace Kelly, Danny Kaye, Barney Balaban, Spyros P. Skouras, Milton R. Rackmil, Adolf Zukor, Adam Gimbel and Alfred Gwynne Vanderbilt.

Interviews with James Stewart, co-star of the picture, and attending celebrities were telecast from the theatre lobby to a national audience on the Arthur Godfrey program. Mr. Godfrey served as moderator.

In a stage ceremony prior to the screening, Mr. Stewart accepted a citation of honor from Maj. Gen. C. R. Smith, representing the A. F. A., for "distinguished public service and outstanding artistic achievement" in connection with the film.

Ap 21, 1955

OKLAHOMA!, screen play by Sonya Levien and William Ludwig, from the musical comedy with music by Richard Rodgers and book and lyrics by Oscar Hammerstein 2d, based on a play by Lynn Riggs; directed by Fred Zinnemann; produced by Arthur Hornblow Jr., in the Todd-AO process; distributed by Magna Theatre Corporation. At the Rivoli.

Curly	Gordon MacRae
Laurey	Shirley Jones
Aunt Eller	Charlotte Greenwood
Will Parker	Gene Nelson
Ado Annie	Gloria Grahame
Ali Hakim	Eddie Albert
Jud Fry	Rod Steiger
Carnes	James Whitmore
Gertie	Barbara Lawrence
Skidmore	J. C. Flippen
Marshal	Roy Barcroft
Dream Curly	James Mitchell
Dream Laurey	Bambi Linn

The Dancers—Bambi Linn, Marc Platt, James Mitchell, Jennie Workman, Kelly Brown Lizanne Truex, Virginia Bosler, Evelyn Taylor, Jane Fischer.

By BOSLEY CROWTHER

AT long last, "Oklahoma!," the great Richard Rodgers-Oscar Hammerstein 2d musical show, which ran for more than five years on Broadway, has been brought to the motion picture screen in a production that magnifies and strengthens all the charm that it had upon the stage.

Photographed and projected in the new process known as Todd-AO, which reflects the images in color from a wide and deep Cinerama-like screen, the ever-popular operetta was presented before an invited audience at the Rivoli last night. It will be shown at two more invitation "premières" tonight and tomorrow night. Then it begins its two-a-day public showings on Thursday at the Rivoli.

•

Inevitably, the question which leaps to every mind is whether the essential magnificence and gusto of the original has been retained in the sometimes fatal operation of transfer to the screen. And then the question follows whether the mechanics of Todd-AO, which is being inaugurated with this picture, are appropriate to articulate this show.

To the first question, there is only one answer: under the direction of Fred Zinnemann —and, we might add, under the hawk-eyed observation of Messrs. Rodgers and Hammerstein — a full-bodied "Oklahoma!" has been brought forth in this film to match in vitality, eloquence and melody any musical this reviewer has ever seen.

With his wide-angle cameras catching backgrounds of genuine cornfields and open plains, red barns, yellow farmhouses and the blue sky full of fleecy clouds, Mr. Zinnemann has brought into the foreground all the warm, lively characters that swarm through this tale of the Oklahoma Territory and sing and dance its songs. By virtue of the sweeping motion picture, he has obtained a fresh, open-air atmosphere to embrace the same rollicking romance that tumbled upon the stage. And because he had the fine assistance of choreographer Agnes

De Mille, he has made the dances and ballet of the original into eloquent movements that flow beneath the sky.

•

In Gordon MacRae he has a Curly, the cowboy hero of the tale, who is wonderfully relaxed and unaffected (to this reviewer's delighted surprise). And in Shirley Jones, a strawberry-blonde newcomer, he has a Laurey, the girl Curly courts, so full of beauty, sweetness and spirit that a better Laurey cannot be dreamed. Both have excellent voices for the grand and familiar Rodgers' tunes. They are best, as one might hope and reckon, in the lyrical "People Will Say We're in Love."

Charlotte Greenwood's rangy Aunt Eller is an unmitigated joy. She has added a rare quality of real compassion to the robust rusticity of the role. And Gene Nelson's lanky Will Parker is a deliciously light-footed, dim-witted beau to the squeaky and occasionally pretentious Ado Annie of Gloria Grahame.

Rod Steiger's Jud Fry is less degenerate and little more human and pitiful than he is usually made, while Eddie Albert's Ali Hakim is the least impressive figure in the film. Both characters have been abbreviated, and a song of each has been dropped.

As for the "Out of My Dreams" ballet, with James Mitchell and Bambi Linn dancing the roles of Curly and Laurey, it is an exquisitely fluid and colorful thing, expansive and imagistic. The dancing boys and girls are as lithe as reeds. In colorful costumes and hairdos, they are pumpkin-seed-country come to town!

To the question of whether the dimensions and the mechanism of Todd-AO are appropriate to the material, one can only say that the generous expanse of screen is fetching, but the system has disconcerting flaws. The distortions of the

images are striking when the picture is viewed from the seats on the sides of the Rivoli's orchestra or the sides and rear of its balcony. Even from central locations, the concave shape of the screen causes it to appear to be arched upwards or downwards, according to whether one views it from the orchestra or the balcony.

While a fine sense of depth is imparted with some of the outdoor scenes—notably one looking down the rows of a cornfield and in a thrilling sequence of a horse-and-wagon runaway—the third-dimensional effect is not insistent. The color in the present film is variable. Some highly annoying scratches are conspicuous in many otherwise absorbing scenes.

However, the flaws in mechanism do not begin to outweigh a superlative screen entertainment, which is endowed with excellent sound and runs for two hours and twenty-five minutes, with a ten-minute pause for air.

———

"Oklahoma!" will have a special, invitational "première" showing tonight at the Rivoli for Gov. Raymond Gary of Oklahoma and other state officials, as well as guests from the civic, stage, screen, television and radio fields.

Governor Gary is scheduled to ride a white horse in the van of a cavalcade of surreys from the St. James Theatre on Forty-fourth Street, west of Broadway, to the Rivoli, at Broadway near Forty-ninth Street, where he will be welcomed by Richard Rodgers and Oscar Hammerstein 2d.

Governor Gary is slated to "annex" the Rivoli Theatre into "Oklahoma Territory" by stepping into transplanted Oklahoma soil in front of the theatre. He will also raise the Oklahoma flag atop the theatre building.

"Oklahoma!" which was screened for the press yesterday, will be shown again

Wednesday night before an invited audience under the sponsorship of the Vocational Advisory Service.

O 11, 1955

REBEL WITHOUT A CAUSE, screen play by Stewart Stern, from an adaptation by Irving Shulman and a story by Nicholas Ray; directed by Mr. Ray; produced by David Weisbart for Warner Brothers presentation. At the Astor.

Jim	James Dean
Judy	Natalie Wood
Jim's Father	Jim Backus
Jim's Mother	Ann Doran
Judy's Mother	Rochelle Hudson
Judy's Father	William Hopper
Plato	Sal Mineo
Buzz	Corey Allen
Goon	Dennis Hopper
Ray	Edward Platt
Mil	Steffi Sidney
Maid	Marietta Canty
Lecturer	Ian Wolfe
Crunch	Frank Mazzola

By BOSLEY CROWTHER

IT is a violent, brutal and disturbing picture of modern teen-agers that Warner Brothers presents in its new melodrama at the Astor, "Rebel Without a Cause." Young people neglected by their parents or given no understanding and moral support by fathers and mothers who are themselves unable to achieve balance and security in their homes are the bristling heroes and heroines of this excessively graphic exercise. Like "Blackboard Jungle" before it, it is a picture to make the hair stand on end.

The foremost of these youthful characters, played by the late James Dean, Natalie Wood and Sal Mineo, are several social cuts above the vocational high school hoodlums in that previous film. They are children of well-to-do parents, living in comfortable homes and attending a well-appointed high school in the vicinity of Los Angeles. But they are none the less mordant in their manners and handy with switch-blade knives. They are, in the final demonstration, lonely creatures in their own strange, cultist world.

Screenwriter Stewart Stern's proposal that these youngsters would be the way they are for the skimpy reasons he shows us may be a little hard to believe. Mr. Dean, he says, is a mixed-up rebel because his father lacks decisiveness and strength. "If he only had the guts to knock Mom cold once!" Mr. Dean mumbles longingly. And Miss Wood is wild and sadistic, prone to run with surly juveniles because her worrisome father stopped kissing her when she was 16.

As for Mr. Mineo, he is a thoroughly lost and hero-searching lad because his parents have left him completely in the care of a maid.

But convincing or not in motivations, this tale of tempestuous kids and their weird ways of conducting their social relations is tense with explosive incidents. There is a horrifying duel with switch-blade cutlery between the reluctant Mr. Dean and another lad (Corey Allen) on a terrace outside a planetarium, where the youngsters have just received a lecture on the tininess of man. There is a shocking presentation of a "chicky run" in stolen automobiles (the first boy to jump from two autos racing toward the brink of a cliff is a "chicken" or coward). And there's a brutal scene in which three hoodlums, villainous schoolboys in black-leather jackets and cowboy boots, beat up the terrified Mr. Mineo in an empty swimming pool.

To set against such hideous details is a wistful and truly poignant stretch where in Mr. Dean and Miss Wood as lonely exiles from their own homes try to pretend they are happy grown-ups in an old mansion. There are some excruciating flashes of accuracy and truth in this film.

However, we do wish the young actors, including Mr. Dean, had not been so intent on imitating Marlon Brando in varying degrees. The tendency, possibly typical of the behavior of certain youths, may therefore be a subtle commentary but it grows monotonous. And we'd be more convinced by Jim Backus and Ann Doran as parents of Mr. Dean if they weren't so obviously silly and ineffectual in treating with the boy.

There is, too, a pictorial slickness about the whole thing in color and Cinema-Scope that battles at times with the realism in the direction of Nicholas Ray.

O 27, 1955

UMBERTO D., screen play by Cesare Zavattini and Vittorio De Sica, from a story by Signor Zavattini; directed by Signor De Sica; a Rizzoli-De Sica-Amito Production, released by Harrison and Davidson. At the Guild.
Umberto D................Carlo Battisti
Maria..................Maria Pia Casilio
Landlady ....Lina Gennari

By BOSLEY CROWTHER

VITTORIO DE SICA'S genius as a director of realistic films has already been evidenced in this country by his "Shoe Shine" and "The Bicycle Thief." But nothing of his that has yet been seen here has had quite the pure simplicity and almost unbearable candor and compassion of his current "Umberto D."

This truly extraordinary picture, which is nothing more than a searching study of a lonely old man fighting a losing battle for existence on the piteous pension of a civil servant in Rome, is just now being offered in this country—it opened yesterday at the Guild —even though it has been finished for more than four years and has been shown considerably abroad.

●

The reason for this delay is to be suspected, once one has seen the film. It is an utterly heartbreaking picture, almost from the word go. The plight and destiny of the aging hero, who has only a mongrel dog and the casual friendship of a rooming-house slavey to comfort his loneliness, are plainly without prospect or hope. The only thing that could save the old gentleman is a happy contrivance of some sort. And this you may be sure that Signor de Sica, with his uncompromising integrity, will not invent.

The merchants obviously were anxious about the market for such a film.

But, hopeful or not, in comparison to the usual run of movie make-believe, this eloquent scan of a man's emotions under the most trying circumstances is a great and memorable achievement on the screen. It is an honest, noble study of human character with which few film exercises can compare.

●

The story, if such you can call it, that Signor de Sica and Cesare Zavattini tell is simply one of the old man's endeavors to sustain himself and his dog. The old man is about to be thrown out of his lodging by a proprietress who has no concern for him or his financial problem. He pitiably tries to sell his things to hang onto the room he has called home for the last twenty years. He goes to a charity hospital to try to save money. He loses his dog. He recovers the animal from the pound, but then is forced out of his room.

Weary, despondent and defeated, the gentle and dignified old man comes to the tragic extremity of attempting suicide, with his dog—which he has vainly attempted to give a good home — wrapped in his arms. But even that fails. The dog diverts him. At the plainly Charles Chaplinesque close, the old man is wistfully frolicking with his pet down an alley of autumnal trees.

But more than this simple continuity, the beautiful picture contains a comprehension of human feelings and fatalism that pierce the heart and mind. In Carlo Battisti, a college professor who never had acted before, Signor de Sica has a perfect reflector of the character of his lonely old man. Never have we seen shame and torment so clearly revealed on a man's face as when this old gentleman endeavors, unsuccessfully, to beg—or such absolute desolation as when he makes his decision to die. Signor de Sica has used him like a wonderfully mellow violin.

●

And the relations of the brave old fellow—who is not always cheerless, by the way—with the slavey, played gently by Maria Pia Casilio, give keen comment on the ages of man. For the young girl, too, has her troubles. She is pregnant and unwed. Her unwitting sense of the future as she comforts her old friend is deeply sad. Lina Gennari's landlady is an excellently etched character among the several minor persons that represent the flow of life in this film.

Also on the bill is a short film that recounts the life of the painter Goya in his works. It makes an appropriate supplement to Signor de Sica's philosophical perusal of old age.

N 8, 1955

THIS STRANGE PASSION, written and directed by Luis Bunuel; from the story "El," by Mercedes Pinto; adapted by Luis Alcoriza; produced by Oscar Dancigers for Tepeyac Productions, Mexico; an Omnifilms release presented by Noel Meadow. At the Fifty-second Street Trans-Lux.

Francisco .... Arturo De Cordova
Gloria .... Delia Garces
Raul .... Luis Beristain
Padre Velasco .. Carlos Martinez Baena
Pablo .... Manuel Donde
Beltran .... Fernando Casanova
Mother .... Aurora Walker
Ricardo .... Rafael Banquells

By A. H. WEILER

LUIS BUNUEL, the transplanted Spanish avante garde director whose Mexican features include such varied, impressive fare as "Robinson Crusoe" and "The Young and the Damned," has come a-cropper with "This Strange Passion," which was unveiled Saturday at the Fifty-second Street Trans-Lux. The warped jealousies of a husband and the desperate torment exhibited by his young wife in this import constitute merely an elementary and uninspired study of abnormal psychology. As drama, it is labored and often vague proof that soap opera can transcend national boundaries.

●

Perhaps Señor Bunuel, who adapted as well as directed, was attempting to indicate too many delicate nuances of his hero's psychoses. He is shown first as a middle-aged wealthy landowner, obsessed with the idea of regaining estates formerly held by his ancestors. And he is a devout churchgoer strangely captivated by some of the rituals of his religion when he falls in love with a beauteous parishioner engaged to one of his best friends. He succeeds in winning the lady but almost immediately is beset by some of the more frightening symptoms of paranoia and schizophrenia.

Our hero is a gent who is convinced his bride is being followed by an acquaintance she meets on their honeymoon. Later, he is certain she is paying too much attention to the lawyer he has hired to reacquire his lands. And, Señor Bunuel manages here to inject a suspicion of suspense as our now brutal hero, who has taken to beating his spouse on occasion, plans to murder her. Suffice it to say that the terrified heroine seeks solace and protection from her former sweetheart. The berserk husband, whose passions alternate from hate to love, finds the peace he seeks in a cloister.

As has been noted, Señor Bunuel's thesis is not especially profound. Call it somewhat cluttered. But with the aid of cinematographer Gabriel Figueroa, he has captured some photogenic scenes in

Mexican churches and their bell towers and in the brooding, baroque Mexico City mansion in which some of the action takes place.

•

He has also extracted professional performances from his principals. As the distracted husband, Arturo De Cordova gives a sensitive yet restrained portrayal of a man torn by love and mental illness. And Delia Garces is pretty and quietly effective as the object of his curious hate and affection. However, an abundance of English subtitles serves only to make the dialogue clear. "This Strange Passion" remains murky and turgid. It is rarely moving.

D 5, 1955

THE MAN WITH THE GOLDEN ARM, screen play by Walter Newman and Lewis Meltzer, from the Nelson Algren novel; produced and directed by Otto Preminger for United Artists release. At the Victoria.

Frankie	Frank Sinatra
Zosh	Eleanor Parker
Molly	Kim Novak
Sparrow	Arnold Stang
Louie	Darren McGavin
Schwiefka	Robert Strauss
Drunky	John Conte
Vi	Doro Merande
Markette	George E. Stone
Williams	George Mathews
Dominowski	Leonid Kinskey
Bednar	Emile Meyer

By BOSLEY CROWTHER

WHY there should be any question about showing "The Man With the Golden Arm," the new film about drug addiction that has been denied a screen Production Code seal, is—as the King of Siam said—a puzzlement. (It opened at the Victoria last night, despite that parochial disapproval, since it has been passed by the New York censor board.)

To the eyes of this watchful reviewer, this cleaned-up version of the Nelson Algren tale, which Otto Preminger has produced and directed and which has Frank Sinatra as its star, is nothing more than a long, torturous picture of one man's battle to beat a craving for dope. And there is nothing more bold or shocking in it

than a few shots of this guy writhing on the floor.

•

To be sure, there is one pregnant sequence in which the character, tormented to the point where he can no longer fight off his craving (from which he had thought himself "cured"), pops around to the place of a "pusher" and pops down $5 for a "fix." (A "fix" in the lingo of the "junkies" — or addicts — is a shot of dope.) The "pusher" gets out a pinch of powder, a hypodermic needle, a spoon and some other uncertain paraphernalia, preparatory to administering the drug. The next thing you see is him arranging to punch the needle in the character's arm. Then you see just the eyes of Mr. Sinatra as the drug presumably enters him.

We understand some footage that was in this sequence has been cut—footage that showed the mixing of the powder in water and the heating of it in the spoon. This was cut, we understand, to avoid trouble over instructing in the methods of taking dope. But either way, what you see or what you don't see is not likely to create anything—outside of the hardened addicts—but a revulsion toward the habit of drugs.

In short, for all the delicacy of the subject and for all the pathological shivers in a couple of scenes, there is nothing very surprising or exciting about "The Man With the Golden Arm." It is a pretty plain and unimaginative look-see at a lower-depths character with a perilous weakness for narcotics that he miraculously overcomes in the end. "The Lost Weekend" was much more arresting and shocking in its study of a drunkard.

Mr. Sinatra gives a plausible performance as the "junkie" who drifts back to the stuff when the pressures get too heavy for him after his return

302

to his old haunts from taking "the cure." His old haunts consist of the cheap spots in a big town—Chicago, perhaps —where he is a professional dealer for a floating poker game. One smoky session in a backroom with the card sharps is more exciting than all the stuff about dope.

But the other's in the cast are less effective. Eleanor Parker as an uncertain dame who manages to hang onto the hero by feigning a crippling illness is the least. She looks and talks like a well-bred, well-kept lady—living in a slum. Mr. Preminger weakened his film immensely by not having her a realistic drab.

Kim Novak makes a strangely pallid figure as the nightclub girl who finally helps the hero toss "the monkey off his back" merely by locking him in her room for a couple of days, and Darren McGavin is a stock oily villain as the peddler of the dope. Arnold Stang as a feeble-minded lackey, Robert Strauss as a cheap gambling tout and John Conte as a suitor to Miss Novak are standard types from gangster films.

D 16, 1955

THE NAKED NIGHT, screen play and direction by Ingmar Bergman; produced by Sandrew Productions and distributed by Times Film Corporation. At the Little Carnegie.
Anne ....Harriet Andersson
Albert ....Ake Groenberg
Frans ....Hasse Ekman
Frost ....Anders Ek
Alma ....Annika Tretow
Agda ....Kiki

By BOSLEY CROWTHER

THE shade of old Emil Jannings seems to stalk through "The Naked Night," a Swedish film written and directed by Ingmar Bergman, which came to the Little Carnegie yesterday. For this tale of a small circus owner tormented with lust and jealousy over a youthful bareback rider who is unfaithful to him with another man bears an almost morbid resemblance to

Jannings' old silent film, "Variety."

Mr. Bergman has slavishly copied the styles of the early Swedish and German films that had to do with passion and frustration in putting together this account, even to the point of working in a flashback sequence that is done in the silent technique. He dotes on close-ups of ugly, sweaty faces; shots of puddles spattered with rain; angle views of disheveled women, and silhouettes against the twilit sky.

He also dotes on exposing emotions in long and elaborate scenes of people clutching at themselves, panting hotly or going out into the barn and patting a horse. He has, too, a running symbolism: the circus owner—a big, puffy man—is juxtaposed to a caged bear, which he shoots at the climax, when he hasn't got the nerve to kill himself.

As you can see (if you've been around a long time), the shade of Mr. Jannings hovers nigh.

This kind of picture making has a certain poetic quality that is effective in some atmospheric stretches, such as the setting up of the pitiful little circus in the rain or the snooping of the wistful bareback rider in the wings of a theatre stage. (She goes there to rendezvous with a ham actor who seduces her with jewelry and then taunts her fat boy-friend—that being the general tenor of the story and the kind of picture this is.)

But the total effect of so much lushness and moody symbolism to tell a tale that is utterly maudlin and oldfashioned is at first oppressive, then provocative of laughs. An audience yesterday was mildly hooting at some of the more elaborate bits.

Ake Groenberg as the circus owner had them laughing at

him toward the end, when he was wallowing and heaving in torment after being humiliated by the seducer of his girl. And Anders Ek also drew a few chuckles as an aged clown who had been through something of the same sort with his woman and had jumped his trolley, as a consequence.

There was no laughing at Harriet Andersson, who plays the circus girl. She has a figure that attracts attention of an entirely different sort. You are permitted to see a good bit of it, especially when she goes to be seduced, but not as much, we suspect, as Mr. Bergman intended. It appears that some scenes have been cut. Miss Andersson also acts rather nicely the naive and clumsy girl.

This picture has English subtitles, some of them surprisingly blunt. But it could really do just as well without them. Everything is fully played in pantomime.

Ap 10, 1956

FORBIDDEN PLANET, screen play by Cyril Hume, based on a story by Irving Block and Allen Adler; directed by Fred McLeod Wilcox and produced by Nicholas Nayfack for Metro-Goldwyn-Mayer. At the Globe.
Dr. Morbius ....Walter Pidgeon
Altaira Morbius ....Anne Francis
Commander Adams ....Leslie Nielsen
Lieut. "Doc" Ostrow.....Warren Stevens
Lieut. Farman ....Jack Kelly
Chief Quinn ....Richard Anderson
Cook ....Earl Holliman
Bosun ....George Wallace
Grey ....Bob Dix
Youngerford ....Jimmy Thompson
Strong ....James Drury
Randall ....Harry Harvey Jr.
Lindstrom ....Roger McGee
Moran ....Peter Miller
Nichols ....Morgan Jones
Silvers ....Richard Grant

By BOSLEY CROWTHER

FASTEN your seat belts, fellows. Get those space helmets clamped to your heads and hang on tight, because we're taking off this morning on a wonderful trip to outer space. We are guiding you to "Forbidden Planet," which is appropriately at the Globe. And we suggest you extend an invitation to Mom and Dad to go along.

For this fanciful interstellar planet, which has been dreamed up at Metro - Goldwyn - Mayer and put on the screen in Eastman color and properly spacious CinemaScope, is the gaudiest layout of gadgets this side of a Florida hotel. It offers some of the most amusing creatures conceived since the Keystone cops.

Best of the lot is Robby, a phenomenal mechanical man who can do more things in his small body than a roomful of business machines. He can make dresses, brew bourbon whisky, perform feats of Herculean strength and speak 187 languages, which emerged through a neon-lighted grille. What's more, he has the cultivated manner of a gentleman's gentleman. He is the prettiest piece of mechanism on Planet Altaire .

You will note we said "piece of mechanism." The prettiest thing there, by far, is Anne Francis — also known as Altaira — the daughter of Dr. Morbius. He is the lone American scientist who has survived from a previous trip that was made to this distant planet twenty years before. And it is he and his beautiful daughter—who, we might add, has never been kissed—that intrigue and confound the handsome space-men that descend in their flying saucer to see what's what.

Take it from us, they see plenty—and so, we promise, will you, if you'll take our advice and fetch the family, from 8 to 80, to the Globe. You'll see the dry and ragged face of a worn-out planet, looking for all the (modern) world like some of those handsome illustrations in the slick-paper picture magazines. You'll see the vast subterranean powerhouses built by the superhuman Krells who inhabited this far-off planet 2,000 centuries before earth-man was born. And you'll see — or, rather, you won't see — the fearful monster created by the Id, which (according to Dr. Morbius) is the evil impulse of the subconscious mind.

You won't see him because he is invisible, but when he gets caught in the electronic grid that the fellows put around their flying saucer and he glows a fiery red, you'll get a vague idea of his giant proportions. And, brother, will you hear him roar!

Don't ask us who deserves top credit for the creation of this film—whether it be Irving Block and Allen Adler, who wrote the story, or director Fred McLeod Wilcox or screen-playwright Cyril Hume. The people who built the vast arrangements of queer machinery and multicolored lights that constitute the flying saucer and the fabulous ranchhouse of Dr. Morbius did their share.

So did Louis and Bebe Barron, who developed the "tonalities"—the accompaniment of interstellar gulps and burbles—that take the place of a musical score. And so did Walter Pidgeon as Dr. Morbius, the counterpart of the old "mad scientists," and Leslie Nielsen as the captain of the spaceship and Miss Francis and all the crew.

Also, a mention is merited by whoever is inside Robby, the Rover Boyish robot, and whoever speaks his courteous words.

Certainly, every one of them had a barrel of fun with this film. And, if you've got an ounce of taste for crazy humor, you'll have a barrel of fun, too.

My 4, 1956

LA STRADA, story and screen play by Federico Fellini and Tullio Pinelli; dialogue by Signor Pinelli; directed by Signor Fellini; produced by Dino De Laurentiis and Carlo Ponti and released by Trans-Lux Films. At the Fifty-second Street Trans-Lux.
Zampano ....Anthony Quinn
Gelsomina ....Giulietta Masina
Matto (The Fool)......Richard Basehart
Colombaini ....Aldo Silvani
and
Marcella Rovere and Livia Venturini

By A. H. WEILER

ALTHOUGH Federico Fellini's talents as a director have not been displayed to advantage heretofore in these parts, his "La Strada" ("The Road"), which arrived at the Fifty-second Street Trans-Lux yesterday, is a tribute both to him and the Italian neo-realistic school of film-making.

His story of an itinerant strong man and the simple-minded girl who is his foil and helpmeet is a modern picaresque parable. Like life itself, it is seemingly aimless, disjointed on occasion and full of truth and poetry. Like the principals, it wanders along a sad and sometimes comic path while accentuating man's loneliness and need for love.

We have no idea why "La Strada," which won a prize at the 1954 Venice Film Festival, has not been exposed to American audiences until now. Perhaps it is because Signor Fellini's theme offers neither a happy ending so dear to the hearts of escapists nor a clear-cut and shiningly hopeful plot. Suffice it to say that his study of his principals is honest and unadorned, strikingly realistic and yet genuinely tender and compassionate. "La Strada" is a road well worth traveling.

The story, let it be said at the outset, is, like its protagonists, simplicity itself. A boorish and brutish strong man literally buys a happy but mentally incompetent lass from her impoverished mother to serve as his clown, cook and concubine. She is replacing her sister, who has died. He teaches her some simple routines as they bowl along in his motorcycle-trailer—clowning and simple tunes on a cornet—to serve as a come-on to his pitifully corny act of breaking chains across his chest.

Although her timorousness fades into happiness as they play villages, fairs and country weddings, her idyllic existence is broken when they join a small circus on the outskirts of Rome. Here a clown and high-wire artist goad her man, who is finally jailed for threatening the buffoon with a knife.

The clown, who has invited her to join him on the road, realizes that she is peculiarly dedicated to her hard master and advises her to wait for the bestial strong man.

"Everyone serves some purpose," he tells her, "and perhaps you must serve him."

Later, the pair meet the clown and the strong man beats and unwittingly kills him. Since the girl's constant whimpering serves as the strong man's conscience, he deserts his ill-fated companion. At the drama's climax, when he accidentally learns of her death, he breaks down in sudden and helpless realization of his solitude.

Despite this doleful outline, Signor Fellini has not handled his story in merely tragic or heavily dramatic fashion. In Giulietta Masina (Mrs. Fellini in private life) he has an extremely versatile performer who mirrors the simple passions and anxieties of the child-like girl with rare and acute perception. She is expert at pantomime, funny as the low-headed, doe-eyed and trusting foil and sentient enough to portray in wordless tension her fear of the man she basically loves.

•

Anthony Quinn is excellent as the growling, monosyllabic and apparently ruthless strong man, whose tastes are primitive and immediate. But his characterization is sensitively developed so that his innate loneliness shows through the chinks of his rough exterior. As the cheerful and prescient clown, Richard Basehart, like the haunting background score by Nino Rota, provides a humorous but pointed counterpoint to the towering and basically serious delineations of the two principals.

Signor Fellini has used his small cast, and, equally important, his camera, with the unmistakable touch of an artist. His vignettes fill his movie with beauty, sadness, humor and understanding.

Although there are English subtitles and the voices of the Messrs. Quinn and Basehart have been dubbed into Italian, "La Strada" needs no fuller explanations. It speaks forcefully, poetically and often movingly in a universal language.

Jl 17, 1956

VITELLONI, screen play by Federico Fellini and Ennio Flaiano; derived from a story by Signor Fellini, Flaiano and Tullio Pinelli; directed by Signor Fellini; a Peg Film-Cite Film production released by API-Janus. At the Fifty-fifth Street Playhouse.
Moraldo ....Franco Interlenghi
Fausto ....Franco Fabrizi
Alberto ....Alberto Sordi
Leopoldo ....Leopoldo Trieste
Riccardo ....Riccardo Fellini
Sandra ....Leonora Ruffo
Giulia ....Lida Baarowa
Woman in the cinema..Arlette Sauvage
Actress ....Maja Nipora
Father of Fausto ....Jean Brochard
Sister of Alberto ....Claude Farere
Michele ....Carlo Romano

By BOSLEY CROWTHER

A presumably irritating problem in post-war Italy —that of the lazy, parasitic sons of good middle-class families—is explored by Federico Fellini with a sense of its tragi-comic character in the Italian film, "Vitelloni," which came to the Fifty-fifth Street Playhouse yesterday. If director Fellini makes it seem a little more urgent than it is, you may charge that off to his volatile disposition and a desire to make a stinging film.

•

For he does certainly take a vigorous whiplash to the breed of over-grown and over-sexed young men who hang around their local poolrooms and shun work as though it were a foul disease. He ridicules them with all the candor of his sharp neo-realist style, revealing their self-admiration to be sadly immature and absurd. And, without going into reasons for the slack state of these young men, he indicates that they are piteous and merit some sympathy, too.

His hero in this sardonic picture, which actually was made before his tender and compassionate "La Strada," now running in its fourth month at the Fifty-second Street Trans-Lux, is a vain and smirking Narcissus who, at the start, is forced to wed the sister of one of his companions. He has casually got her in a family way.

But marriage does not bring him to a sense of responsibility. He continues to chase after women and act like an adolescent boy. So do his friends. They are children—big, hulking babies and cowards. They don't even have the nerve or the desperation to indulge in crime.

Signor Fellini runs a fine line between gravity and burlesque in exposing the sleazy involvements and the grotesque behavior of these young men. At one moment, he is soberly musing with the brother of the girl who has to wed; at the next, he is showing him carousing with his irresponsible friends. From a comical scene of all the fellows listening to an old actor spout, he leaps to a shuddering revelation of the insidiousness of the old man. Signor Fellini loves to mirror the rapid shiftings in the human comedy.

The weakness of this picture is that it reaches a weak conventional end. The bawdy hero forsakes his infidelities when his wife runs away from him, and the philosophical brother pulls himself together and leaves town to find a job. It seems as though Signor Fellini simply got tired and called it off.

●

But when the drama is spinning, it is lively and interesting, and everybody in it does a commendable job. Franco Fabrizi is excellent as the plump, pretty, self-indulgent lad who has to marry, and Franco Interlenghi is quiet and and seemingly sensitive as his friend. Alberto Sordi, Leopoldo Trieste and Ricca de Fellini are eccentric as some of the boys, and Leonora Ruffo is pretty and appropriately banal as the girl.

As usual, Signor Fellini uses music to comic and poignant effect. The dialogue that he and Ennio Flaiano have written is obviously more lively than the English subtitles that translate it.

O 24, 1956

THE TEN COMMANDMENTS, screen play by Aeneas MacKenzie, Jesse L. Lasky Jr., Jack Gariss and Frederic M. Frank; directed and produced by Cecil B. De Mille for Paramount Pictures. At the Criterion.

Moses	Charlton Heston
Nefretiri	Anne Baxter
Rameses	Yul Brynner
Sephora	Yvonne DeCarlo
Sethi	Sir Cedric Hardwicke
Lilia	Debra Paget
Dathan	Edward G. Robinson
Joshua	John Derek
Bithiah	Nina Foch
Memnet	Judith Anderson
Aaron	John Carradine
Baka	Vincent Price
Yochabel	Martha Scott
Miriam	Olive Deering
Jannes	Douglass Dumbrille
Pentaur	Henry Wilcoxon
Amminadab	H. B. Warner
Jethro	Eduard Franz
Abiram	Frank DeKova
Mered	Donald Curtis
Hur Ben Caleb	Lawrence Dobkin
Elisheba	Julia Faye

By BOSLEY CROWTHER

AGAINST the raw news of modern conflict between Egypt and Israel—a conflict that has its preamble in the Book of Exodus—Cecil B. De Mille's "The Ten Commandments" was given its world première last night at the Criterion Theatre, and the coincidence was profound. For Mr. De Mille's latest rendering of Biblical literature in the spectacular framing and colloquial idiom of the screen tells an arresting story of Moses, the ancient Israelite who was a slave with his people in Egypt and who struggled to set them free.

As Mr. De Mille presents it in this three-hour-and-thirty-nine-minute film, which is by far the largest and most expensive that he has ever made, it is a moving story of the spirit of freedom rising in a man, under the divine inspiration of his Maker. And, as such, it strikes a ringing note today.

But aside from the timely arrival and contemporary context of this film, it is also a rather handsome romance in Mr. De Mille's best massive style. To the fundamental story of Moses, as told in the Old Testament and reflected in other ancient writings consulted by Mr. De Mille, he and his corps of screen playwrights have added some frank apocrypha which, while they may not be traceable in history (or even in legend), make for a robust tale.

In this imaginative recount, Moses is raised as a prince in the palace of Egypt's Pharaoh, after being found, as the Bible tells, by the Pharaoh's daughter in the bullrushes, where he was hidden by his mother, a Hebrew slave. And as a presumed Egyptian, he is a candidate for the Pharaoh's throne and a rival for the love of a luscious princess with the Pharaoh's own son, Rameses.

As one might well imagine, the plot-minded Mr. De Mille does not pass lightly or briefly over this phase of his tale. Moses, as played by Charlton Heston, is a handsome and haughty young prince who warrants considerable attention as a heroic man of the ancient world. And Anne Baxter as the sensual princess and Yule Brynner as the rival, Rameses, are unquestionably apt and complementary to a lusty and melodramatic romance.

•

But the story is brought back to contact with the Bible and with its inspirational trend when Moses discovers,

acknowledges and is exiled from Egypt because of his Hebraic birth. Then Mr. De Mille, who, incidentally, acts as narrator for his film in many of its more exalted stretches, takes him into the wilderness and establishes his contact with his Maker, which leads to the Exodus and the Covenant on Mount Sinai.

In the latter phases of the drama, wherein the impulse to set his people free from the bondage of Egypt flames in Moses, the spiritual and supernatural surge comes somewhat bluntly in the picture, and the performance of such awesome miracles as the crossing of the Red Sea and the burning of the Ten Commandments into the tablets of stone may strike the less devout viewer as a bit mechanical and abrupt.

Also, and with all due regard for the technical difficulties besetting Mr. De Mille, we must say his special effects department was not up to sets or costumes. The parting of the Red Sea is an obvious piece of camera trickery in which two churning walls of water frame a course as smooth and dry as a race track. And the striking off of the Ten Commandments by successive thunderbolts, while a deep voice intones their contents, is disconcertingly mechanical.

•

However, in its other technical aspects—in its remarkable settings and décor, including an overwhelming facade of the Egyptian city from which the Exodus begins, and in the glowing Technicolor in which the picture is filmed—Mr. De Mille has worked photographic wonders. And his large cast of characters is very good, from Sir Cedric Hardwicke as a droll and urbane Pharaoh to Edward G. Robinson as a treacherous overlord. Yvonne DeCarlo as the Midianite shepherdess to whom Moses is wed is notably good in a severe role, as is John Derek as a reckless Joshua.

This is unquestionably a picture to which one must bring something more than a mere wish for entertainment in order to get a full effect from it. But for those to whom its fundamentalism will be entirely credible, it should be altogether thrilling and perhaps even spiritually profound.

N 9, 1956

THE MAGNIFICENT SEVEN, written by Akira Kurosawa, Shinodou Hashimoto and Hideo Oguni; directed by Mr. Kurosawa and produced by Sojiro Motoko for Toho Studios of Japan. a Columbia presentation; at the Guild.

Samurai

Kambei	Takashi Shimura
Gorobei	Yoshio Inaba
Katsushiro	Isao Kimura
Kyuzo	Seiji Miyaguchi
Heihachi	Minoru Chiaki
Shichiroji	Daisuke Kato
Kikuchiyo	Toshiro Mifune

Villagers

Rikichi	Yoshio Tsuchiya
Shino	Keiko Tsushima
Manzo	Kamatari Fujiwara
Yohei	Bokuzen Hidari
Gisaku	Kunihori Kodo

By BOSLEY CROWTHER

THE Japanese film director Akira Kurosawa, who gave us that eerily exotic and fascinating picture "Rasho-Mon," is now, after five years, represented by another extraordinary film, which matches his first for cinema brilliance, but in another and contrasting genre. It is called "The Magnificent Seven," though it was known in Japan and abroad as "Seven Samurai," and it was put on public exhibition yesterday at the Guild.

To give you a quick, capsule notion of the nature of this unusual film, let us say it bears cultural comparison with our own popular western "High Noon." That is to say, it is a solid, naturalistic, he-man outdoor action film, wherein the qualities of human strength and weakness are discovered in a crisis taut with peril. And although the oc-currence of this crisis is set in the sixteenth century in a village in Japan, it could be transposed without surrendering a basic element to the nineteenth century and a town on our own frontier.

•

The drama, to put it briefly—which is not what Mr. Kurosawa does, since his film runs for two hours and thirty-eight minutes, after some considerable trimming, we understand—is concerned with the defense of a farming village against a horde of bandits by seven samurai (independent professional soldiers), who are hired by the poor farmers to do the job.

That is the sum and substance of it: seven warriors are persuaded to come in and guard the village against the fearful bandits who have warned they will return when the crops are ripe. Seven sword-swinging, bow-and-arrow footmen of varied courage and personality are on hand to oppose the forty mounted bandits when they come charging down from the hills.

But on that simple framework and familiar story line, director Kurosawa has plastered a wealth of rich detail, which brilliantly illuminates his characters and the kind of action in which they are involved. He has loaded his film with unusual and exciting physical incidents and made the whole thing graphic in a hard, realistic western style.

There are things about the picture to question and criticize. It is much too long for comfort or for the story it has to tell. The director is annoyingly repetitious. He shows so many shots of horses' feet tromping in the mud in the course of battle that you wonder if those horses have heads. And his use of modern music, which is as pointed as the ballad in "High Noon," leads you to wonder whether this picture is any more authentic to its period of culture than is the average American western film.

However, it sparkles with touches that would do honor to Fred Zinnemann or John Ford, particularly in close-ups of faces and in sudden changes of mood within scenes. There is one switch, for instance, from a couple making luxurious love in the woods to a blood-chilling indication that the bandits have returned.

●

And Mr. Kurosawa's actors are, in their métier, superb, beginning with Takashi Shimura as the cool, collected leader of the samurai and continuing through the one conspicuous female, Keiko Tsushima, as the frightened but ardent village girl. Outstanding for his rare command of humor, however, is Toshiro Mifune, who played the bandit in "Rasho-Man." Here he is brilliant as a crazy but courageous Samurai.

Again, as in his previous triumph, the director has got photography that is perfectly calculated and effected to evoke appropriate moods, from harshly realistic to poetic. It is in black-and-white. And the English subtitles for the Japanese dialogue are brief and to the point.

N 20, 1956

———

THE SUN ALSO RISES, screen play by Peter Viertel, based on the Ernest Hemingway novel; directed by Henry King; produced by Darryl F. Zanuck for Twentieth Century-Fox. At the Roxy.
Jake Barnes ....Tyrone Power
Lady Brett Ashley........Ava Gardner
Robert Cohn................Mel Ferrer
Mike Campbell..............Errol Flynn
Bill Gorton..............:...Eddie Albert
Romero ....Robert J. Evans
Montoya ....Carlos Muzquiz
Georgette ....Juliette Greco
Count Mippipopolous....Gregory Ratoff
Doctor ....Henry Daniell

———

IN all probability, many bristling book-readers are going to march into the Roxy for the screen version of Ernest Hemingway's "The Sun Also Rises" with a unanimous, grim conviction: it had better be good. It is.

Bravely tackling one of the most hallowed of all American novels, as his second independent project under the Twentieth Century-Fox banner, Darryl F. Zanuck has assembled a glitteringly spacious and beautiful background canvas, on location in France, Spain and Mexico.

This visual magnificence, in CinemaScope and color, frames a picturesque cast, headed by Tyrone Power, Ava Gardner and Mel Ferrer, that looks hand-picked down to the last bit "extra." Director Henry King has staged a personalized, handsome big "show," from Peter Viertel's admirably faithful script, which slices a few corners and minor characters from the source.

While the result is emotionally intriguing, rather than powerful, it remains, nevertheless, Hemingway all the way.

Outwardly, the author's revered "lost" American expatriates of the post-war mid-Twenties have changed little in some thirty years. Jake—good old Jake Barnes, played by Mr. Power—is the same cynical Paris Herald writer, the platonic soul-mate of the disillusioned Brett Ashley, portrayed by Miss Gardner, who is trailed, in turn, by their hanger-on crony, Robert Cohn, played by Mr. Ferrer.

Their aimless Parisian prowlings in a superbly atmospheric assortment of vintage bars, hotels and thoroughfares immediately convey Mr. Hemingway's unyielding tone of futility. These rather stilted early scenes, unfortunately, are full of endless, if incomparable, talk.

What amounts to an adult, lifelike charade suddenly bursts forth with a clanging, hypnotically stunning close-up of a Spanish bullfighting town in full traditional fiesta blast. Here, in Pamplona (adroitly juxtaposed with additional Mexican footage), the crossed tensions of the trio begin to attain real urgency.

The derelicts, by now linked up with Bill Gorton (Eddie Albert) and Mike Campbell, Brett's "fiancé," (Errol Flynn), are so smoothly piloted through the fascinating little town by Mr. King that their child-like abandon, their snapping nerves and Brett's climactic dalliance with a young toreador all come across with keen-edged credibility.

•

We doubt, indeed, if Mr. Hemingway's pen, or anybody's, could improve some occasional camera magic: the huge arena itself: Jake's poster-lined stalk through the streets; Brett's first, fleeting glimpse of her young quarry, Romero (perfectly personified by Robert J. Evans—let's forget his Irving Thalberg in "Man of a Thousand Faces).

The picture needs, and lacks, just one great performance, although Mr. Power is certainly a professionally convincing hero. Mr. Ferrer is fine, considering the slight sketchiness of his motivations. A grinning, portly Mr. Flynn and the jovial Mr. Albert fit their roles like gloves.

As for Brett, that tarnished beauty loved for years by so many male readers (including this one), Miss Gardner, with an occasional look of real, fleeting anguish, excellently pegs her predatory aspects. She simply doesn't, or can't, convey the lady's innate, poignant air of breeding, for all Brett's promiscuity. Sorry, Miss Gardner.

Again, thirty years is a long time between mediums. In an age of galvanized tourism, short on introspection, this picture deals with some none-too-youthful barflys who might be called merely idle, rather than (as they insist) "lost." But if Mr. Heming-

way's book seems somewhat of a curio on the screen, blame it on the respect, intelligence and technical splendor that roving Hollywood has accorded a classic.

H. H. T.

Ag 24, 1957

A MAN ESCAPED, written and directed by Robert Bresson; adapted from the true story by Andre Devigny; produced by Jean Thuillier and Alain Poire; released here by Continental Distributing, Inc. At the Baronet.
Lieutenant Fontaine..Francois Leterrier
Jost ....Charles Leclainche
Blanchet ....Maurice Beerblock
The Pastor of Leiris....Roland Monod
Orsini ....Jacques Ertaud
Hebrard ....Jean-Paul Delhumeau
Terry ....Roger Treherne
Prisoner 110.....Jean-Philippe Delamare
Prison Guard........Jacques Oerlemans
Security Officer
          Klaus Detlef Grevenhorst
Prisoner's Escort.....Leonhard Schmidt

By BOSLEY CROWTHER

THE French film director, Robert Bresson, is an extraordinary artist in his realm. He makes his pictures with patience, simplicity and the uncompromising devotion of a saint. This was clearly demonstrated in his mystical and austere "Diary of a Country Priest." It is evident again in his "A Man Escaped," known in France as "Un Condamné à mort s'est échappé," which came to the Baronet yesterday.

Here concentrating his attention upon the quiet resolve of a French Underground prisoner to escape from a Nazi jail during the wartime Occupation, M. Bresson spends an hour and one-half detailing the prisoner's painful preparations and then his perilous execution of the break.

It is a raw, lean, mechanical operation, beginning with the man's unblinking realization that he must get himself out of that prison or certainly be put to death, and continuing with his patient calculation and accumulation of the means to get away.

He steals a spoon, makes a tool of it, opens a secret portal out of his cell and then scouts among the other prisoners to learn the best avenues of escape. From an unsuccessful escapee, he hears that there is a moat over which he must pass before gaining freedom. For this, he must make himself a rope.

So, with a searching eye to detail, M. Bresson documents the enterprise, looking often at the face of the prisoner to comprehend his deliberate, desperate moods. And so, through a train of tense experience, we are brought to know the fervor of the man—the fervor of a condemned man for freedom—and the grim, suspenseful trial of his escape.

The picture is based upon an actual account of a prisoner's break from Fort Montluc in Lyons, where, we are told, much of this film was made. The claim is credibly supported by the severity of the scene. And the appearance and behavior of the prisoners are easy to believe.

François Leterrier as the principal character is impressively gaunt and engrossed, giving a sure, integrated performance that makes it hard to accept the report that he is an amateur. If so, an exceptional credit must be given the direction of M. Bresson. Charles Leclainche as a second prisoner who is threaded into the escape also plays with remarkable realism.

This is not the sort of picture that one should view without knowing what it is. The strain is hard and the reward is limited. But it is a fine reflection of a cruel experience.

Ag 27, 1957

THE THREE FACES OF EVE, written, produced and directed by Nunnally Johnson; based on the book by Drs. Corbett H. Thigpen and Hervey M. Cleckley; presented by Twentieth Century-Fox. At the Victoria.
Eve ....Joanne Woodward
Ralph White ....David Wayne
Dr. Luther ....Lee J. Cobb
Dr. Day ....Edwin Jerome
Secretary ....Alena Murray
Mrs. Black ....Nancy Kulp
Mr. Black ....Douglas Spencer
Bonnie ....Terry Ann Ross
Earl ....Ken Scott
Eve—Age 8 ....Mimi Gibson

By BOSLEY CROWTHER

A YOUNG Georgia woman with a personality that is prone to a severe three-way stretch is the subject of Nunnally Johnson's new drama—or melodrama—"The Three Faces of Eve," which came with a faint jangle of sweet bells into the Victoria yesterday.

When we first come upon this heroine she is a wan and emotionally troubled dame, nervously accompanied by her husband, seeking the aid of a psychiatrist. It seems that she has terrible headaches and strange lapses of memory. The psychiatrist offers some pat suggestions and sends her home to her husband and child.

However, she comes back some time later. Now a second personality has begun to emerge. This one is a loose, lurid creature with a brash go-to-hell attitude. She doesn't care beans for her husband, denies that she's the mother of her child and generally raises mischief when she takes over and goes out on the town.

Naturally, the woman is bewildered when she slips back into her pallid state. The doctor is fascinated. And the dumb husband thinks it's all a fake. He watches a couple of these cycles of changing personality, then washes his hands of the whole business and gets himself a divorce.

Left alone with her psychiatrist, the woman degenerates

312

until she is switching back and forth from one to the other personality almost as fast as she can close and open her eyes. The doctor seems to find it so intriguing that he prompts her to change, like a magician doing a trick.

"Let's have Eve Black," he will tell her. "Now, let's go back to Mrs. White." She does.

And then something curious happens. Mrs. White tries to commit suicide, but Eve Black takes possession of the situation and saves herself — or both of herselves — just in time. Whereupon, as she tells the doctor of it, a third personality begins to emerge. This one is sweet, serene, intelligent and conspicuously self-possessed.

Well, this occurrence flips the doctor. Now he has THREE changes that he can ring, and he spins the poor woman around the circuit as though her three personalities were playing tag. Finally, he hits upon something. Seems that when she was a little girl, her mother made her kiss her dead grandmother and that did something awful to her nerves. What it was is not explained to the audience, but once the doctor and the woman have it tagged, they are able to "kill" the other personalities and let the sweet, serene one live.

The last we see of the woman and her recovered daughter they are going off with a fine young fellow name of Earl.

●

This story, which Alistair Cooke sincerely tells us at the beginning is absolutely true—and is, indeed, based upon a clinical study written up by two Georgia psychiatrists. It is written, produced and directed by Mr. Johnson with a clean documentary clarity, and played with superlative flex-

ibility and emotional power by Joanne Woodward in the main role.

Miss Woodward, a comparative newcomer, stretches three ways convincingly. David Wayne is pretty good as her crude husband and Lee J. Cobb plays the psychiatrist well.

But when you come right down to it, this is simply a melodramatic exercise—an exhibition of psychiatric hocus-pocus, without any indication of how or why. It makes for a fairly fetching mystery, although it is too verbose and too long. But like the similar film, "Lizzie," before it, it leaves one feeling gypped and gulled at the end.

S 27, 1957

ORDET, written and directed by Carl Dreyer, based on a play by Kaj Munk; produced by Palladium Film, Copenhagen; released here by Kingsley International Pictures. At the Fifth Avenue Playhouse.
Morten Borgen.........Henrik Malberg
Mikkel..........Emil Hass Christensen
Johannes..........Preben Lerdorff Rye
Inger.................Birgitte Federspiel
Peter, the tailor.......Ejner Federspiel
Anders................Cay Kristiansen
Kirstine...............Sylvia Eckhausen
Anne....................Gerda Nielsen
Doctor....................Henry Skjaer
Clergyman....................Ove Rud
Maren..........Ann Elisabeth Hansen

TWO unyielding forces permeate Carl Dreyer's "Ordet" — the revered old Danish film-maker himself, and his beloved, omnipotent God of Elijah. And since each demands the same thing total submission — every paying customer at the Fifth Avenue Playhouse must eventually gauge "Ordet" for himself. For in his latest screen drama the painstaking scenarist-director has remolded, as only he could, or would, a "miracle" play, originally penned by the late Rev. Kaj Munk in 1932.

This Kingsley International release, which opened Saturday, is an experience, not a show, and certainly no entertainment—a visual sermon of scalding, spiritual intensity. It uncoils, when it moves at all, like a majestic snail. Dreyer novices are warned.

•

The time, apparently, is some twenty-five years ago. At the fade-in, a family of marshland farmers worriedly trails an idiot son, who calls himself Christ. It closes, like the thickest of Bibles, as the demented theological student approaches the open coffin of his sister-in-law and, at the simple urging of her child, calls her back to life. These simple-living people are stern practicing Christians, frankly puzzled by varying doubts and at ideological odds with an even sterner clan down the road.

Mr. Dreyer's primary concern is the first patriarch, magnificently played by Henrik Malberg. The old realist simply can't accept the idea of modern miracles, not with one vigorously indifferent son, Emil Hass Christensen, and the other, his "cross," a scriptural-tongued lunatic. In this role, as the catalyst who miraculously solidifies the family, Preben Lerdorff Rye (from "Day of Wrath") glides in and out eerily, moaning in concert with a relentless wind howling outdoors.

Confronted with such a plot, most film producers would take to the hills. Mr. Dreyer, instead, reportedly took a quarter-century for thought, and it shows.

Framing a superlative cast in the simplest of settings, he has evoked a rigid but powerful blend of speeches and faces—the Dreyer trademark. Photographically, the canvas suggests a stained-glass window, with graying daylight, more often lamp glow, washing over a few cottage interiors. Very rarely, a wagon lumbers across the grassy horizon outside.

•

Both emotionally and intellectually the picture is hypnotic, and some portions will nail the spectator to his seat.

One sequence of a sheeted woman, Birgitte Federspiel, dying in childbirth, as upstairs her unhinged brother and little daughter equably discuss the hereafter, is even more harrowing than the witch-burning in "Day of Wrath." In perhaps the most indicative scene of all — Mr. Rye's spiritual babbling about a car's sweeping headlights— the car remains out of sight.

Both the dedicated old man who created it and this extraordinary film are best appraised in two lines of the competently subtitled dialogue. "It takes him a little too long to make the Amen," notes Mr. Malberg (of the village pastor). Then, "I prayed with all my heart; you see the result."   H. H. T.

D 16, 1957

THE BRIDGE ON THE RIVER KWAI, screenplay by Pierre Boulle; based on his novel; directed by David Lean; produced by Sam Spiegel for Horizon Pictures; presented by Columbia. At the Palace. Running time: 161 minutes.

Shears	William Holden
Colonel Nicholson	Alec Guinness
Major Warden	Jack Hawkins
Colonel Saito	Sessue Hayakawa
Major Clipton	James Donald
Lieutenant Joyce	Geoffrey Horne
Colonel Green	Andre Morell
Captain Reeves	Peter Williams
Major Hughes	John Boxer
Grogan	Percy Herbert
Baker	Harold Goodwin
Nurse	Ann Sears
Captain Kanematsu	Henry Okawa
Lieutenant Miura	K. Katsumoto
Yai	M. R. B. Chakrabandhu
Siamese Girls	Vilaiwan Seebooreaung, Ngamta Suphaphongs, Javanart Punynchoti, Kannikar Bowklee.

By BOSLEY CROWTHER

THERE are actually two motion picture dramas— two strong, suspenseful issues—embraced in Sam Spiegel's exceptional film production, "The Bridge on the River Kwai."

The first is a powerful personal drama of a conflict of wills between two military men, one the Japanese commander of a prisoner-of-war camp in the Burmese jungle and the other a British colonel brought there with a handful of his men. The second drama is a tingling action thriller that follows smoothly upon the resolution of the first. The crux of it is a bold maneuver to blow up a jungle railway bridge.

This mounting of drama upon drama in Mr. Spiegel's magnificent color film, which opened last night at the Palace for an extended two-a-day run, makes it more than a towering entertainment of rich variety and revelation of the ways of men. It makes it one of the niftiest bargains to be had on the screen this holiday.

•

Since both of the issues in this picture—the conflict of wills between two men and the subsequent contest to accomplish the destruction of the prisoner-built bridge—are loaded with mortal tension that holds the viewer in sweating suspense, it seems a shame that we have to give an inkling of the outcome of either one. But so much of the theme of the whole picture is conveyed in the resolution of the first that we have to tip you off to that one: the British colonel wins.

That is to say, he outfaces and outwits the camp commandant in compelling the latter's surrender on a military technicality. He refuses to permit himself or his officers to do manual labor on the building of the strategic bridge, as is brutally and illegally demanded by the snarling commandant. And for the first hour or so of the picture, he undergoes torture of a terrible, withering sort, until he catches his adversary in an ironic weakness and compels him to respect the military code.

He wins, but he wins at the expense of a shocking, significant compromise. He agrees to apply himself and officers as supervising engineers. He accepts the narrow technical victory with satisfaction and even pride, without regard for—or even apparent awareness of—the aid he will thus give the enemy. The building of the bridge for the one-track railway becomes the sole aim of this man with the one-track mind.

Here is the heart of this fine picture, here is its stark and potent theme: discipline and conformity are the obsession of the professional militarist. And upon this rising realization hinges all the subsequent drama and suspense as a small commando team inches into the jungle to destroy the colonel's precious bridge. Does the colonel actually stop his own countrymen? This one we will not reveal!

Brilliant is the word, and no other, to describe the quality of skills that have gone into the making of this picture, from the writing of the script out of a novel by the Frenchman Pierre Boulle, to direction, performance, photographing, editing and application of a musical score.

David Lean has directed it so smartly and so sensitively for image and effect that its two hours and forty-one minutes seem no more than a swift, absorbing hour. In addition to splendid performance, he has it brilliantly filled with atmosphere—the atmosphere of war's backwash and the jungle—touched startlingly with humor, heart and shock.

In the line of performance, Alec Guinness does a memorable—indeed, a classic—job in making the ramrod British colonel a profoundly ambiguous type. With a rigid, serene disposition, he displays the courage and tenacity of a lion, as well as the denseness and pomposity of a dangerously stupid, inbred snob. He shows, beneath the surface of a hero, the aspects of an inhuman fool. He gives one of the most devastating portraits of a militarist that we have ever seen.

•

As his Japanese opposite number, old Sessue Hayakawa is superb—brutal, stubborn, sluggish an equally grotesque fool. Jack Hawkins is droll and determined as the British major who leads the commando raid and William Holden is delightfully gallant as an American sailor mixed up in this strange affair. James Donald, Geoffrey Horne and Peter Williams are splendid as British army chaps, and a bunch of little Oriental females add spice as native porters on the raid.

A real bridge and natural settings in Ceylon have been exquisitely photographed by Jack Hildyard's color cameras.

Here is a film we guarantee you'll not forget.

D 19, 1957

PATHS OF GLORY: screenplay by stanley Kubrick, Calder Willingham and Jim Thompson; based on the novel by Humphrey Cobb; directed by Mr. Kubrick; produced by James B. Harris; presented by Bryna Productions and released through United Artists. At the Victoria. Running time: eighty-six minutes.

Colonel Dax..............Kirk Douglas
Corporal Paris...........Ralph Meeker
General Broulard.....Adolphe Menjou
General Mireau.......George Macready
Lieutenant Roget.........Wayne Morris
Major Saint-Auban....Richard Anderson
Private Arnaud.........Joseph Turkel
Private Ferol...........Timothy Carey
Colonel Judge............Peter Capell
German Girl.........Susanne Christian
Sergeant Boulanger ....Bert Freed
Priest ....Emile Meyer
Private Lejeune............Kem Dibbs
Private Meyer............Jerry Hausner
Shell-Shocked Soldier. .. .Frederic Bell
Captain Nichols.........Harold Benedict
Captain Rousseau..........John Stein

By BOSLEY CROWTHER

CREDIT Kirk Douglas with having the courage to produce and appear in the screen dramatization of a novel that has been a hot potato in Hollywood for twenty-two years. That is Humphrey Cobb's "Paths of Glory," a

shocking story of a shameful incident in World War I—the court-martial and execution of three innocent French soldiers on charges of cowardice, only to salve a general's vanity.

Obviously, this is a story—based on an actual occurrence, by the way—that reflects not alone on France's honor but also on the whole concept of military authority. Yet Mr. Douglas has made a movie of it—an unembroidered, documentary-like account—with himself playing the role of an outraged colonel who tries vainly to intercede. It opened at the Victoria yesterday.

To a certain extent, this forthright picture has the impact of hard reality, mainly because its frank avowal of agonizing, uncompensated injustice is pursued to the bitter, tragic end. The inevitability of a fatal foul-up is presented right at the start, when an ambitious general agrees to throw one of his regiments into an attack that he knows has little chance to succeed. And it looms with ever mounting horror as he orders an example to be made of three men picked at random from the thwarted attackers and dogs them unmercifully to their doom.

All this is shown with shattering candor in this film, which was shot in Germany and was directed by Stanley Kubrick, who also helped to write the screenplay with Jim Thompson and Calder Willingham. The close, hard eye of Mr. Kubrick's sullen camera bores directly into the minds of scheming men and into the hearts of patient, frightened soldiers who have to accept orders to die.

Mr. Kubrick has made it look terrific. The execution scene is one of the most craftily directed and emotionally lacerating that we have ever seen.

316

But there are two troubling flaws in this picture, one in the realm of technique and the other in the realm of significance, which determine its larger, lasting worth.

We feel that Mr. Kubrick — and Mr. Douglas — have made a damaging mistake in playing it in colloquial English, with American accents and attitudes, while studiously making it look as much as possible like a document of the French Army in World War I. The illusion of reality is blown completely whenever anybody talks.

•

Mr. Douglas exudes tremendous passion as the colonel who tries to stave off a sacrifice, but he speaks with the same kind of English that he used in "Gunfight at the O. K. Corral." Adolphe Menjou is a bit more clipped and Gallic as a staff general who plays sly politics, but George Macready acts and speaks the vengeful general as if he were a slimy Harvard man. Ralph Meeker, Joseph Turkel and Timothy Carey play the doomed poilus (remember that fine word?) with the swagger, slouches and speech slurs of assorted G. I.'s in World War II. Emile Meyer is perhaps least effective (when he speaks) in the role of a French priest.

As for the picture's significance, it comes to an inconclusive point. Its demonstration of injustice is like an exhibit in a bottle in a medical museum. It is grotesque, appalling, nauseating—but so framed and isolated that, when you come away, you are left with the feeling that you have been witness to nothing more than a horribly freakish incident.

Also, merely as a footnote —what a picture to open on Christmas Day!

D 26, 1957

THE NAKED AND THE DEAD; screen play by Denis and Terry Sanders; based on the novel by Norman Mailer; directed by Raoul Walsh; produced by Paul Gregory; an R. K. O. Telaradio Pictures Production released by Warner Brothers. At the Capitol Theatre, Broadway and Fifty-first Street. Running time: 131 minutes.

Sergeant Croft .... Aldo Ray
Lieutenant Hearn ..... Cliff Robertson
General Cummings ... Raymond Massey
Brown .... William Campbell
Gallagher .... Richard Jaeckel
Ridges .... James Best
Roth .... Joey Bishop
Goldstein .... Jerry Paris
Red .... Robert Gist
Wilson .... L. Q. Jones
Lieutenant Colonel Dalleson
                            Casey Adams
Mantelli .... John Berardino
Conn .... Edward McNally
Minetta .... Greg Roman
Martinez .... Henry Amargo
Lily .... Lili St. Cyr
Mildred .... Barbara Nichols

_____

By A. H. WEILER

THE praiseworthy effort to produce a giant of a film from Norman Mailer's towering World War II novel, "The Naked and the Dead," has resulted in a professionally turned but derivative action drama no more memorable than similar sagas of strife that have preceded it. Director Raoul Walsh has filled the screen with striking vistas in beautiful color and with the chilling sound and fury of conflict, but the hearts, minds and motives of men exposed to sudden and often useless death, which gave the book its awesome power, serve merely as sketchy background to battle in this uneven picturization that was unveiled at the Capitol yesterday.

Attempts have been made to transcribe "The Naked and the Dead" into cinema terms ever since its publication more than decade ago. But its 721 pages, its large canvas of people and places and the obviously censorable obscenity of its G. I.'s proved stumbling blocks for adapters and official guardians of morality in films.

Credit the director, producer Paul Gregory and especially the writing team of Denis and Terry Sanders with laundering the billingsgate of the original and in extracting the derring-do of the author's impassioned work. But in so doing they have simply come up with a surface recounting of a platoon doomed to decimation in securing a small island in the Pacific in 1943. They have quickly limned a general who is a black-and-white militarist, nothing more, and of officers who only appear as quickly passing figures in a kaleidoscope of briefings and small talk.

The hates, passions, brutalities and backgrounds of the men are stated and restated but one is generally left with the impression of actors speaking lines. Although the authors' over-all view was sometimes clouded, his men, who rarely understood why they fought, were honest, realistic, vibrantly alive citizens.

Here we see the platoon in brief personal outline. They are lonely in a terrible world they never made. They are afraid, they hate the jungle, their rugged assignment, themselves and each other. They recall in flashback sweethearts and wives and lusts. Some are lucky and survive and others do not. It's nearly always as simple as that.

The adaptation, which does not always adhere to the book, concentrates on typing each man. One is the ill-fated Sergeant Croft, who it is explained, is driven by an overweening urge to command because of the memory of an unfaithful wife. From his actions, however one is led to think that he just likes killing. As portrayed by Aldo Ray in rough-hewn, laconic style, he is the standard, hard platoon leader seen in more than one movie. The other members of the detail are competent, but also appear to have been chosen solely to represent the types that comprised our citizen army.

There are, to name a few, Joey Bishop, as the wry, comic Jew; L. Q. Jones, as the hillbilly cut-up who is the darling of a strip-teaser and the

platoon for whom he brews "jungle juice"; there is the hard-bitten, cynical loner played in dour fashion by Robert Gist; Henry Amargo, as the Indian scout; James Best, as the Southern religious boy, and Richard Jaeckel, as the youngster saddened by the loss of his wife and yearning for their child he never has seen. Their women, namely Lili St. Cyr, as the stripper; Barbara Nichols, as Mr. Ray's voluptuous, two-timing wife, and a covey of cuties recalled by the platoon's lieutenant only pass briefly in review.

Cliff Robertson contributes a few solid scenes as the former playboy, who is the compassionate "ninety-day wonder" leader of the group. The context of the script is well-handled also by Raymond Massey, as the general, who is convinced he has to make his men hate him to gain their respect. But the talks between the two men often seem to be sober discussions rather than the baring of souls.

Although the Sanders' dialogue is plentiful but short of nuances, the platoon's stealthy trek, its skirmishes with Japanese patrols and the massive, climactic assault have been directed with terrifying realism. A viewer cannot help but recall scenes of the burning of enemy troops as the lush grass is ignited by the hidden G. I.'s; the death throes of a private bitten by a snake; the tension of the men as they try to scale a sheer cliff, the sounds and look of the jungle, which have been beautifully captured in this color film.

Director Walsh and his associates have carefully drawn an impressively stark face of war from "The Naked and the Dead" but only seldom do they deeply dissect the people involved in it.

Ag 7, 1958

PATHER PANCHALI, screen play by Satyajit Roy; based on the novel by B. Bandopadhaya; directed by Mr. Roy; presented by Edward Harrison. At the Fifth Avenue Cinema, Fifth Avenue, south of Twelfth Street. Running time: 112 minutes.

The father	Kanu Banerji
The mother	Karuna Banerji
Apu	Subir Banerji
Durga, as a child	Runki Banerji
Durga, as a young girl	Uma Das Gupta
Old aunt	Chunibala Devi
Mrs. Mookerji	Reva Devi
Ranu Mookerji, her daughter,	Rama Gangopadhaya
Schoolmaster	Tulshi Chakraborty
Doctor	Harimoran Nag

By BOSLEY CROWTHER

THE Indian film, "Pather Panchali" ("Song of the Road"), which opened at the Fifth Avenue Cinema yesterday, is one of those rare exotic items, remote in idiom from the usual Hollywood film, that should offer some subtle compensations to anyone who has the patience to sit through its almost two hours.

Chief among the delicate revelations that emerge from its loosely formed account of the pathetic little joys and sorrows of a poor Indian family in Bengal is the touching indication that poverty does not always nullify love and that even the most afflicted people can find some modest pleasures in their worlds.

This theme, which is not as insistent or sentimental as it may sound, barely begins to be evident after the picture has run at least an hour. And, in that time, the most the camera shows us in a rambling and random tour of an Indian village is a baffling mosaic of candid and crude domestic scenes.

There are shots of a creaky old woman, a harassed mother, her lively little girl and a cheerful husband and father who plainly cannot provide for his small brood. There are scenes, as familiar as next-door neighbors, of the mother trying to get the child to eat, washing clothes, quarreling with the husband or pushing the child toward school.

Satyajit Roy, Indian artist, who wrote the screen play and directed this film, provides ample indication that this is his first professional motion picture job. Any picture as loose in structure or as listless in tempo as this one is would barely pass as a "rough cut" with the editors in Hollywood.

But, oddly enough, as it continues—as the bits in the mosaic increase and a couple of basically human and dramatic incidents are dropped in, such as the pitiful death of the old woman and the sickness and death of the little girl—the poignant theme emerges and the whole thing takes a slim poetic form. By the time it comes to its sad end, it has the substance of a tender threnody.

Much of the effect is accomplished by some stunningly composed domestic scenes, well performed—or pictured—by an excellent Indian cast, and exquisitely photographed by Subrata Mitra in tastefully filtered blacks and whites. And a finely conceived and sympathetic original musical score, composed by Ravi Shankar, in which native instruments are employed, sets the whole sad story in the frame of a melancholy mood.

Karuna Banerji is touching as the mother who is most distressed by poverty and Uma Das Gupta is lovely and sensitive as the girl. Chunibala Devi is fantastically realistic and effective as the aging crone and Subir Banerji is wistful and beguiling as the small son of the family.

As we say, it is quite exotic. The dialogue often sounds like a Gramophone record going at high speed. English subtitles barely make some sense. But there are lovely little threads in the strange fabric. It's a film that takes patience to be enjoyed.

S 23, 1958

THE SEVENTH SEAL, written and directed by Ingmar Bergman; produced by AB Svensk Filmindustri; distributed by Janus Films. At the Paris, 4 West Fifty-eighth Street. Running time: 105 minutes.

Knight	Max von Sydow
Squire	Gunnar Bjornstrand
Death	Bengt Ekerot
Jof	Nils Poppe
Mia	Bibi Andersson
Lisa	Inga Gill
Witch	Maud Hansson
The Knight's spouse	Inga Landgre
Girl	Gunnel Lindblom
Raval	Bertil Anderberg
Monk	Anders Ek
Smith	Ake Fridell
Church painter	Gunnar Olsson
Skat	Erik Strandmark

By BOSLEY CROWTHER

SWEDISH director Ingmar Bergman, whose "Smiles of a Summer Night" proved him an unsuspected master of satiric comedy, surprises again in yet another even more neglected vein with his new self-written and self-directed allegorical film, "The Seventh Seal."

This initially mysitfying drama, known in Swedish as "Det Sjunde Inseglet," opened yesterday at the Paris, and slowly turns out to be a piercing and powerful contemplation of the passage of man upon this earth. Essentially intellectual, yet emotionally stimulating, too, it is as tough —and rewarding—a screen challenge as the moviegoer has had to face this year.

•

The specified time of its action is the fourteenth century and the locale is apparently Sweden—or it could be any other medieval European country—in the fearful throes of the plague. A knight, just returned from the Crusades, meets black-robed Death on the beach and makes a bargain for time to do a good deed while the two of them play a sort of running game of chess.

While the game is in progress, the knight and his squire go forth to find the land full of trembling people who darkly await the Judgment Day. Some are led to self-pity and torturing themselves by their priests, who also have provided a symbol of wickedness in an innocent girl condemned as a "witch." Others are given to snatching a little fun while they may; and, recalling Mr. Bergman's last picture, you should guess what sort of fun that it.

But en route, the knight, who significantly was disillusioned by the Crusaders and is still seeking God, comes across a little family of traveling actors who are as fresh and wholesome as the morning dew. Except that the young father of the little family has a way of seeing visions from time to time (to his pretty wife's tolerant amusement), the happy couple are as normal as their chubby child. And it is this little family that the sad knight, still uncertain, arranges to save when he and a gathering of weary wanderers, including his defiant square, must submit to Death at the end of the game.

If this sounds a somewhat deep-dish drama, laden with obscurities and costumes, it is because the graphic style of Mr. Bergman does not glow in a summary. It is a provocative picture, filled with intimations, that it true— some what you want to make of them and some as clear as the back of your hand.

For instance, it could be that Mr. Bergman means the plague ot represent all mortal fears of threats beyond likely containment that hang over modern man. Certainly, there can be little question what he means when he shows the piteous herds of anguished and self-tormenting people driven by soldiers and priests.

•

But the profundities of the ideas are lightened and made flexible by glowing pictorial presentation of action that is interesting and strong. Mr. Bergman uses his camera and actors for sharp, realistic effects. Black-robed Death is as frank and insistent as a terrified girl being hustled to the stake. A beach and a cloudy sky are as literal and dramatic as a lusty woman's coquerties. Mr. Bergman hits you with it, right between the eyes.

And his actors are excellent, from Max von Sydòw as the gaunt and towering knight, through Gunnar Bjornstrand as his squire and Bengt Ekerot as Death to Maud Hansson as the piteous "witch." Nils Poppe as the strolling player and Bibi Andersson as his wife are warming and cheerful companions in an uncommon and fascinating film.

O 14, 1958

HE WHO MUST DIE: screen play by Ben Barzman and Jules Dassin; from the novel, "The Greek Passion," by Nikos Kazantzakis; dialogue by Andre Obey; directed by Jules Dassin; presented by Henri Berard; released by Kassler Films. Inc. At the Beekman Theatre, Second Avenue and Sixty-fifth Street. Running time: 122 minutes.

Pope Fotis	Jean Servais
Lukas	Carl Mohner
Agha	Gregoire Aslan
Patriarcheas	Gert Froebe
Hadji Nikolis	Teddy Bilis
Yannakos	Rene Lefevre
Kostandis	Lucien Raimbourg
Katerina	Melina Mercouri
Pannayotaros	Roger Hanin
Manollos	Pierre Vaneck
Ladas	Dimos Starenios
Mariori	Nicole Berger
Michelis	Maurice Ronet
Pope Grigoris	Fernand Ledoux

By BOSLEY CROWTHER

OUT of Nikos Kazantzakis' powerful novel, "The Greek Passion," American film director Jules Dassin has made an equally powerful and frightening French film. It is called "He Who Must Die" ("Celui Qui Doit Mourir"), and it opened at the Beekman Theatre yesterday.

The scene of this stark and staggering drama is a poor town on the island of Crete at a time during the Turkish occupation at the end of World War I. This town, which has a truce with its Turkish governor, is preparing to stage its annual Passion Play and has chosen the local citizens to play tht chief roles, when a horde of starving dispossessed people from a distant town wanders into its streets.

The natural inclination of the townsfolk is to shelter these poor people and give them food, but their priest and the head of the town council strongly oppose this charity. They fear the wanderers will disturb the truce with the Turkish governor and, more important, prove an economic strain. So they succeed in arousing the townsfolk to drive the wanderers out.

However, a few of the people who have been chosen to take the leads in the Passion Play, are to imbued with the spirit of their Christian forebears that they want to help the sufferers who have camped on a near-by hill. Especially the young man who will play the Christus wants to live up to the Golden Rule. But the bosses of the town are inflexible and in a final devastating scene the young man is murdered by the town leaders (he is actually stabbed by the man who would play Judas) within the walls of the church.

This is the gist of the drama, which plainly has as its theme the horrible irony in the pretense of Christian virtue that some worldly people make. If Christ returned to Earth today, these selfish people would still crucify Him for His social teachings, this drama says.

On that theme, magnified by the Greek author, Mr. Dassin has constructed a film that is as brutally realistic as the bare, dried-out Cretan town and the stony hills in which it was photographed. It abounds in a daring sort of candor and relentless driving toward its points of allegorical contact in a succession of searching and searing episodes.

For instance, the affinity of the Christus toward the widow who plays Mary Magdalene is developed in a sensitive, poignant and irreproachably honest way. It is human and emotionally complicated, yet deeply respectful and in good taste. Mr. Dassin with an excellent cast of actors and large groups of Cretan townsfolk and peasants to play his crowds, has made his picture so truly and sympathetically that it could be a documentary of an occurrence in life.

Every one of his professional players does a superlative job, with Pierre Vaneck perhaps most affecting as the young man who would play the Christus. Jean Servais, who may be remembered as the senior member of the safe-cracking gang in Mr. Dassin's previous triumph, "Rififi," is fine as the patriarch who leads the wanderers, and Fernand Ledoux is equally sturdy in a tyrannical way as the town priest. Gregoire Aslan as the urkish Governor, Gert Froebe as the head of the council and Melina Mercouri as the widow distinguish themselves.

The film has good English subtitles and is in sharp black-and-white photography.

D 29, 1958

ROOM AT THE TOP; screen play by Neil Paterson; from the novel by John Braine; directed by Jack Clayton; produced by John and James Woolf; a Romulus Production released by Continental Distributing, Inc. At the Fine Arts, Fifty-eighth Street, west of Lexington Avenue. Running time: 115 minutes.

Joe Lampton .... Laurence Harvey
Alice Aisgill .... Simone Signoret
Susan Brown .... Heather Sears
Mr. Brown .... Sir Donald Wolfit
Mrs. Brown .... Ambrosine Philpotts
Charles Soames ..... Donald Houston
Mr. Hoylake .... Raymond Huntley
Jack Wales .... John Westbrook
George Aisgill ...... Allan Cuthbertson
June Samson .... Mary Peach
Elspeth .... Hermione Baddeley
Miss Gilchrist .... Avril Elgar
Aunt .... Beatrice Varley
Darnley .... Stephen Jack
Mayor .... John Welsh
Mayoress .... Everley Gregg
Mavis .... April Olrich

By A. H. WEILER

THE cynical, disenchanted and footloose post-war youths of England, who justifiably have been termed "angry," never have been put into sharper focus than in "Room at the Top." The British-made import, which was unveiled at the Fine Arts Theatre yesterday, glaringly spotlights them in a disk of illumination that reveals genuine drama and passion, truth as well as corruption. Although it takes place 3,000 miles away, it is as close to home as a shattered dream, a broken love affair or a man seeking to make life more rewarding in an uneasy world.

Unlike John Osborne, who, in "Look Back in Anger," merely shouted the sensitive younger Britishers' fiery protests against class distinctions and other contemporary English inequities, John Braine, out of whose brilliant first novel this careful dissection was made, is more adult and scientifically observant about a grievous malaise, Mr. Braine, Neil Paterson, the scenarist, and Jack Clayton, who did a superb job in directing an excitingly effective cast, are angry, too. But they see the picture whole. They are basically moral people who know that, come what may, a price must be paid for revolt sometimes.

As has been noted, Mr Braine is concerned with a type of schemer, whose accent may be exotic but one who is becoming more and more symbolic of the restless young men of the world. In this case, he is Joe Lampton, born to poverty in a North Country manufacturing town but determined to catapult himself out of a world he never made or wanted. As a civil servant in another city, he meets the nubile and naïve daughter of the richest tycoon who represents the prize and escape he has been waiting for. But this is a consummation not easily achieved. And, when thrown into the orbit of a married woman, ill-used, worldly wise, anxiously groping for real affection, it is fairly obvious that he will succumb first to lust and then to genuine love.

That this dual affair is doomed to tragedy is inevitable. But the artisans who fashioned this shaky triangle are neither crude nor insensitive. Joe is a calculating, shrewd and realistic campaigner, yearning for wealth and the opportunity to rid himself of low-caste stigma through marriage with the heiress to a great fortune. He is, however, also pictured as a man in whom all conscience has not been killed. He is a hero without medals and one mourning defeat when he should be enjoying victory.

The director and scenarist also have shown us a multidimensional figure in the married woman he is forced to reject, a deed that indelibly underlines the sadness, desperation and tragedy that surrounds these truly ill-fated lovers. And they have done equally well by the rich, sheltered young girl he marries at long last, an untutored youngster wholly engulfed by the sweetness, wonder and uneasiness of first love and sex.

•

A prudish observer perhaps might be shocked by some of the drama's explicit dialogue and situations, but these, too, are adult and in context. One also might be thrown by the thick, Yorkshire-like accents of the cast, which strike foreign and harsh on American ears. A viewer might take exception to the slowness of pace as this somber play is first exposed.

But these are minor faults that are heavily outweighed by the superb performances of Simone Signoret, as the married woman clutching at her last chance at happiness, and Laurence Harvey, the seemingly selfish schemer, who discovers that he cannot destroy all of his decency. Heather Sears is gentle, fresh and properly naïve as the heiress he is forced to marry; and Sir Donald Wolfit, as her outspoken, self-made millionaire father; Donald Houston, as Mr. Harvey's room-mate and confidant, and Hermione Baddeley, as Miss Signoret's trusted friend, are among those supporting players who add distinctive bits to an engrossing picture.

Jack Clayton's vigorous and discerning direction has involved them in more than just a routine romantic drama. "Room at the Top" may be basically cheerless and somber, but it has a strikingly effective view.

Mr 31, 1959

APARAJITO, screen play by Satyajit Ray; adapted from the novel by Bibhutibhushan Bandopadyaya; directed by Mr. Ray; presented by Edward Harrison. At the Fifth Avenue Cinema at Twelfth Street. Running time: 108 minutes.
Apu (as boy)..........Pinaki Sen Gupta
Apu (as adolescent).....Smaran Ghosal
Sarbojaya................Karuna Banerji
Harihar..................Kanu Banerji
The Old Uncle.......Ramani Sen Gupta
Nanda Babu...............Charu Ghosh
Headmaster ... .Subodh Ganguly
Press Proprietor.......Kali Charan Ray
Landlord's Wife............Santi Gupta
Pandey ....K. S. Pandey
Nirupama...................Sudipta Ray
Anil.......................Ajay Mitra

By BOSLEY CROWTHER

FURTHER adventures of the family that was so leisurely and tenderly introduced in the Indian film, "Pather Panchali," the tenant at the Fifth Avenue Cinema for the last six months, are presented in "Aparajito," which opened at that theatre yesterday. It is a sequel that carries on with the same principal players and was likewise produced and directed by Satyajit Ray.

And, as with "Pather Panchali," the format and content of this film are remote from and very much in contrast to what we generally get from Hollywood. Like its exotic predecessor, it is a compound of documentary views of life in pre-liberation India, with some personal experiences and moods of its few principal characters conveyed at a pace that would try the patience of Job.

Still, it is done with such rare feeling and skill at pictorial imagery, and with such sympathetic understanding of Indian character on the part of Mr. Ray, that it develops a sort of hypnotism for the serene and tolerant viewer who is willing to sit still for an hour and forty-eight minutes and let some stunning black-and-white pictures pass before his eyes.

Actually, there is very little story or drama, in the usual sense, this being more in the nature of a chronicle of a woman's affection for her husband and her son. This is the woman who, in "Pather Panchali," saw her little family disintegrate through her husband's going off to a distant city from their poor village and the death of her entrancing little daughter.

Now, the mother, husband and son are together in the holy city of Benares, when this picture begins, and once more the family goes through a cycle of life, death and life going on. This persistence of life in the midst of difficulties probably accounts for the title, which, we are told, means "The Unvanquished" in our language. And persistence is in the tempo of the film.

Slowly, in episodic sequence, we see the husband take ill and die, the mother and small son leave Benares and go to a distant village to live, the son start his education in a local school and win a scholarship to a college in Calcutta, whither he goes.

Now the son is an older fellow, not the lively youngster played by Subir Banerji in the early picture and by Pinaki Sen Gupta in the early part of this one. He is a tall, skinny, solemn adolescent, portrayed convincingly by Smaran Ghosal, and he acts in the undemonstrative manner that is no doubt authentic to his class.

It is while he is away at college that the mother, lonesome for him, becomes ill and, in a series of scenes, conveys the essence of her deep but stoical love. Beautifully portrayed again by Karuna Banerji, the mother eventually dies and the son returns to college rather than remain in the village as a priest.

Despite the meagerness of action, there are clear undertones in this film. Social customs and religious superstitions are subtly exposed and criticized. The fatal illness of the ineffectual father, again played touchingly by Kanu Banerji, is suggested as the consequence of bathing in the Ganges with the swarms of pilgrims who visit the Benares shrines. The old suspicion of education is interestingly implied, as is a comment on its English character in the pre-liberation schools.

And Mr. Ray's remarkable camera catches beauty in so many things, from the softness of a mother's sad expression to the silhouette of a distant train, that innuendos take up the slack of drama. Hindu music and expressive natural sounds complete the stimulation of the senses in this strange, sad, evocative film.

There are English subtitles.

Also on the bill at the theatre is a thoroughly delightful little color cartoon, titled "Moonbird," which sketches the experience of two youngsters who sneak out at night to try to catch a bird. It was designed and directed by John Hubley, and his two children provide the voices of the tots, who are just about the cutest animations in the modern style that we have ever seen.

Ap 29, 1959

WILD STRAWBERRIES: screen play by Ingmar Bergman; directed by Mr. Bergman; produced by Allan Ekelund; presented by Svensk Filmindustri and released by Janus Films. At the Beekman Theatre, Second Avenue and Sixty-fifth Street. Running time: ninety minutes.

Prof. Isak Borg,
                Victor Seastrom (Sjostrom)
Sara ....Bibi Anderson
Marianne ....Ingrid Thulin
Evald ....Gunnar Bjornstrand
Agda ....Jullan Kindahl
Anders ....Folke Sundquist
Viktor ....Bjorn Bjelvenstam
Isak's Mother........Naima Wifstrand
Mrs. Alman...........Gunnel Brostrom
Isak's Wife............Gertrude Fridh
Her Lover...................Ake Fridell
Aunt ....Sif Ruud
Alman ....Gunnar Sjoberg
Akerman ....Max Von Sydow
Uncle Aron ......Y....ngve Nordwall
Sigfrid ....Per Sjostrand
Sigbritt ....Gio Petre
Charlotta ....Gunnel Lindblom
Angelica ....Maud Hansson
Mrs. Akerman.......Anne-Mari Wiman
Anna ....Eva Noree
The Twins..............｛Lena Bergman
                    ｛Monica Ehrling
Hagbart ....Per Skogsberg
Benjamin ....Goran Lundquist
Promoter ....Prof. Helge Wulff

By BOSLEY CROWTHER

IF any of you thought you had trouble understanding what Ingmar Bergman was trying to convey in his beautifully poetic and allegorical Swedish film, "The Seventh Seal," wait until you see his "Wild Strawberries" ("Smultron-Stallet"), which came to the Beekman yesterday. This one is so thoroughly mystifying that we wonder whether Mr. Bergman himself knew what he was trying to say.

As nearly as we can make out—and, frankly, we found "The Seventh Seal" a tough but comparatively lucid and extraordinarily stimulating film—the purpose of Mr. Bergman in this virtually surrealist exercise is to get at a comprehension of the feelings and the psychology of an aging man.

His hero is a 78-year-old doctor—whether a physician or a scientist is not made clear—who is going from his place of retirement to the university at Lund to be honored on an anniversary. Before he starts out, he has a shocking and plainly depressing dream in which he sees his own mournerless funeral and his own corpse trying to pull him into the grave. This rather ill prepares him for an admission made a few hours later by his daughter-in-law, who accompanies him on the journey, that she and her husband consider him a cold and egotistical old man.

Therefore, the journey becomes a series of actual and dream experiences, of encounters with mortal beings and with ghosts and fantasies, in which the old man runs a recapitulation of many events and phases of his life, and apparently comes to the conclusion that he has been admired but not loved. The consensus of those who have known him, including his still-living mother and his dead and faithless wife, seems to be that he has been standoffish and emotionally cold.

This is as close as we can make it in the way of a general résumé, but this doesn't give an explanation of several details that we still don't dig. And it also doesn't carry much conviction in the light of the sweet and charming character of the old man portrayed by Victor Seastrom (Sjostrom), one of the great actors and directors of Swedish films.

Mr. Seastrom, whom we older moviegoers remember from the silent films as the visiting director of such fine American pictures as Lon Chaney's "He Who Gets Slapped" and Lillian Gish's "The Scarlet Letter" and "The Wind," is wonderfully warm and expressive as the old gentleman who finds the wild strawberry patch where his first love fatefully forsook him and then goes off from there. He is so real and sensitive and poignant, so winning of sympathy in every way, that Mr. Bergman's apparent explanation doesn't make sense.

This is not to say, however, that the film doesn't have its brilliant scenes and its beautifully touching moments, its tatters of sheer nostalgia. These, with Mr. Seastrom, are most rewarding. So are the straight performances of Ingrid Thulin as the daughter-in-law and Bibi Anderson as a modern girl who is a duplicate of an old love. Mr. Bergman, being a poet with the camera, gets some grand, open, sensitive images, but he has not conveyed full clarity in this film. And the Engish subtitles are not much help.

Also on the program is a pretty and interesting color short, "Swedish Peasant Painting," which represents the work of primitive painters who have used the gourd as a motif.

Je 23, 1959

NORTH BY NORTHWEST; written by Ernest Lehman; produced and directed by Alfred Hitchcock and released by Metro-Goldwyn-Mayer. At the Radio City Music Hall. Running time: 136 minutes.
Roger Thornhill..............Cary Grant
Eve Kendall.............Eva Marie Saint
Phillip Vandamm ....James Mason
Clara Thornhill ....Jessie Royce Landis
Professor..................Leo G. Carroll
Lester Townsend...........Philip Ober
Handsome Woman..Josephine Hutchinson
Leonard ....Martin Landau
Valerian ....Adam Williams
Licht ....Robert Ellenstein
Victor Larrabee...........Edward Platt
Auctioneer ....Les Tremayne
Dr. Cross ....Philip Coolidge
Captain Junket...........Edward Binns

By A. H. WEILER

SINCE he is a peripatetic operative who loves to beat about the bush while beating about the countryside, director Alfred Hitchcock and a covey of willing and able traveling companions have made "North by Northwest," which was unveiled at the Music Hall yesterday, a suspenseful and delightful Cook's Tour of some of the more photogenic spots in these United States.

Although they are involved in lightning-fast romance and some loose intrigue, it is all done in brisk, genuinely witty and sophisticated style. With Mr. Hitchcock at the helm, moving "North by Northwest" is a colorful and exciting route for spies, counterspies and lovers.

The director and Ernest Lehman, his scenarist, are not, to put a fine point on it, really serious about their mystery. With a tongue-in-cheek attitude and a breezy sense of humor, they are off in high gear right at the beginning as they spin the somewhat improbable yarn of a successful, handsome Madison Avenue executive, who is mistaken for a Federal intelligence man by foreign agents and forcibly pushed into a succession of macabre situations that shock, amaze, perplex and anger our once-debonair hero.

Mr. Hitchcock, who, as has been noted, knows that travel is both fun and broadening, quickly shifts his cast from such locales as the Oak Room of the Plaza Hotel and the modernistic interiors of the United Nations Headquarters, to the fancy confines of the Twentieth Century Limited, to the posh Amassador East Hotel in Chicago, to a vast, flat Midwest cornfield and finally to the giant faces of the Presidents sculptured on Mount Rushmore high above Rapid City, S. D.

The complications are introduced with about the same rapidity as the ever-changing scenery. Our beleaguered hero, it appears, is being harried by the villains who want to dispatch him because he seems to be on to their skulduggery. It is, of course, merely a case of mistaken identity, an illusion the Federal boys are desperate to maintain.

In any event, Mr. Hitchcock, et al, take time out

326

now, and again to stop strew-
ing red herrings and inject a
funny scene here and there,
such as one involving our
drunken hero in a local hoose-
gow, or to point up the quickly
burgeoning romance between
him and the blonde Mata Hari
who apparently is aiding him.
dastards chasing him. Their
interlude, to the sounds of
slick, romantic dialogue, in a
train drawing room, for example, is guaranteed to send
viewers' temperatures soaring. The lines and the expert
manipulation of the principals
are tributes to the outstanding
talents of Messrs. Lehman
and Hitchcock.

Cary Grant, a veteran
member of the Hitchcock
acting varsity, was never
more at home than in this
role of the advertising-man-
on-the-lam. He handles the
grimaces, the surprised look,
the quick smile, the aforementioned spooning and all
the derring-do with professional aplomb and grace, In
casting Eva Marie Saint as
his romantic vis-à-vis, Mr.
Hitchcock has plumbed some
talents not shown by the
actress heretofore. Although
she is seemingly a hard, designing type, she also emerges
both the sweet heroine and a
glamorous charmer.

Jessie Royce Landis con-
tributes a few genuinely humorous scenes as Mr. Grant's
slightly addle-pated mother.
James Mason is properly
sinister as the leader of the
spy ring, as are Martin Landau, Adam Williams, Robert
Ellenstein and Josephine
Hutchinson, as members of
his malevolent troupe. And
Leo G. Carroll is satisfyingly
bland and calm as the studious
intelligence chief.

Perhaps they and Messrs.
Hitchcock and Lehman are
kidding, after all. Their climax is a bit overdrawn and
there are a few vague spots
along the way. But they do
lead us on the year's most
scenic, intriguing and mer-
riest chase.

Ag 7, 1959, 28:1

THE MAGICIAN: written and directed
by Ingmar Bergman; produced by
Carl-Henry Cagarp; presented by
Svensk Filmindustri and released here
by Janus Films, Inc. At the Fifth
Avenue Cinema. Running time: 102
minutes.
Vogler .... Max von Sydow
Manda Aman .... Ingrid Thulin
Vergerus .... Gunnar Bjornstrand
Grandmother .... Naima Wifstrand
Spegel .... Bengt Ekerot
Sara .... Bibi Andersson
Ottilia .... Gertrud Fridh
Simson .... Lars Ekborg
Starbeck .... Toivo Pawlo
Egerman .... Erland Josephson
Tubal .... Ake Fridell
Sofia .... Sif Ruud
Antonsson................. Oscar Ljung
Henrietta................. Ulla Sjoblom
Rustan .... Axel Duberg
Sanna .... Birgitta Pettersson

By BOSLEY CROWTHER

DON'T knock the spell of illusion That's what Swe-
den's Ingmar Bergman says
in the latest of his highly
esoteric and technically exquisite films, "The Magician"
("Ansiktet"). It opened at
the Fifth Avenue Cinema
yesterday.

More than in either of his
pictures exhibited hereabouts
recently ("The Seventh Seal"
and "Wild Strawberries"),
Mr. Bergman is offering in
this a mystical contemplation
that could well have wide popular appeal. For he is dealing with magic, spiritual man-
ifestations, spells and "animal
magnetism," which are more
exciting when they're not
fully understood.

And it's a safe bet that
very few viewers are going
to understand everything that
Mr. Bergman here levitates
and puts forth in his bewitch-
ingly imagistic style. That
drunken and dying actor who
is found in a haunted woods
by a vagrant troupe of medicine-show performers—what
does he symbolize? What is
the esoteric meaning of his
seeming to die and then come
back to life? And who is that
weird old woman who tags
along with the troupe?

These are a few of the mysteries that rise from the shadows and the glooms of this
eerie and Rabelaisian study
of the susceptibility of the
human mind to the powerful
sway of illusion and of the
ephemeral nature of Truth.

But never mind about those

details that may be vaporous and vague. The important thing is that this picture is full of extraordinary thrills that flow and collide on several levels of emotion and intellect. And it swarms with sufficient melodrama of the blood-chilling, flesh-creeping sort to tingle the hide of the least brainy addict of outright monster films.

Is it something supremely contemplative of the marginal regions between reality and unreality that you would care to cogitate? Then watch the subtle inquisition of the pitifully tawdry little troupe when, in its travels through the country in the mid-nineteenth century, it is strangely incarcerated in a quizzical merchant's home. Is it eroticism you are after? Then study what occurs to the neurotic wife of the merchant when she watches the hypnotist. Or are you for Rabelaisian humor? Then get those servant girls when they drink the fake love-potions and start going after the lads.

As for the sheer melodrama, you'll look far to find a creepier scene than the one in which the skeptical surgeon is hounded by the "body" on which he has just performed an autopsy! The practical uses of suggestion are beautifully indicated here.

As in all his pictures, Mr. Bergman (who does everything) has achieved remarkable magic with his camera and with his cast. Max von Sydow as the magician is a haunting figure who floats between the realms of an agonized mystic and a vulgar charlatan. And he recalls the late Lon Chaney in his sad unmasking scene and in the one he plays with the surgeon, brilliantly performed by Gunnar Bjornstrand.

Ingrid Thulin as the wife of the magician, Erland Josephson as the merchant-dilletante, Ake Fridell as the medicine-show barker and Bibi Andersson as one of the servant girls stand out in a cast that is superior in absolutely every role.

Brilliant use of the sound-track—lengthy silences broken by weird guitar phrases, thumps and strikings of clocks—is a notable feaure. It is just too bad one has to read so many English subtitles to follow the Swedish dialogue.

Ag 28, 1959

THE 400 BLOWS (Les Quatre Cents Coups), screen play by Francois Truffaut and Marcel Moussy; directed and produced by M. Truffaut; produced by Les Films du Carosse and Sedif and presented by Zenith International Film Corporation. At the Fine Arts, Fifty-eighth Street west of Lexington Avenue. Running time: ninety-eight minutes.
Antoine Doinel ......Jean-Pierre Leaud
Rene ....Patrick Auffay
Mme. Doinel ....Claire Maurier
M. Doinel ....Albert Remy
The Teacher ....Guy Decomble

By BOSLEY CROWTHER

LET it be noted without contention that the crest of the flow of recent films from the "new wave" of young French directors hit these shores yesterday with the arrival at the Fine Arts Theatre of "The 400 Blows" ("Les Quatre Cents Coups") of François Truffaut.

Not since the 1952 arrival of René Clement's "Forbidden Games," with which this extraordinary little picture of M. Truffaut most interestingly compares, have we had from France a cinema that so brilliantly and strikingly reveals the explosion of a fresh creative talent in the directorial field.

Amazingly, this vigorous effort is the first feature film of M. Truffaut, who had previously been (of all things!) the movie critic for a French magazine. (A short film of his, "The Mischief Makers," was shown here at the Little Carnegie some months back.) But, for all his professional inexperience and his youthfulness (27 years), M. Truffaut has here turned out a picture that might be termed a small masterpiece.

The striking distinctions of it are the clarity and honesty with which it presents a moving story of the troubles of a 12-year-old boy. Where previous films on similar subjects have been fatted and fictionalized with all sorts of adult misconceptions and sentimentalities, this is a smashingly convincing demonstration on the level of the boy—cool, firm and realistic, without a false note or a trace of goo.

And yet, in its frank examination of the life of this tough Parisian kid as he moves through the lonely stages of disintegration at home and at school, it offers an overwhelming insight into the emotional confusion of the lad and a truly heartbreaking awareness of his unspoken agonies.

It is said that this film, which M. Truffaut has written, directed and produced, is autobiographical. That may well explain the feeling of intimate occurrence that is packed into all its candid scenes. From the introductory sequence, which takes the viewer in an automobile through middle-class quarters of Paris in the shadow of the Eiffel Tower, while a curiously rollicking yet plaintive musical score is played, one gets a profound impression of being personally involved—a hard-by observer, if not participant, in the small joys and sorrows of the boy.

Because of the stunningly literal and factual camera style of M. Truffaut, as well as his clear and sympathetic understanding of the matter he explores, one feels close enough to the parents to cry out to them their cruel mistakes or to shake an obtuse and dull schoolteacher into an awareness of the wrong he does bright boys.

Eagerness makes us want to tell you of countless charming things in this film, little bits of unpushed communication that spin a fine web of sympathy—little things that tell you volumes about the tough, courageous nature of the boy, his rugged, sometimes ruthless, self-possession and his poignant naïveté. They are subtle, often droll. Also we would like to note a lot about the pathos of the parents and the social incompetence of the kind of school that is here represented and is obviously hated and condemned by M. Truffaut.

But space prohibits expansion, other than to say that the compound is not only moving but also tremendously meaningful. When the lad finally says of his parents, "They didn't always tell the truth," there is spoken the most profound summation of the problem of the wayward child today.

Words cannot state simply how fine is Jean-Pierre Leaud in the role of the boy—how implacably deadpanned yet expressive, how apparently relaxed yet tense, how beautifully positive in his movement, like a pint-sized Jean Gabin. Out of this brand new youngster, M. Truffaut has elicited a performance that will live as a delightful, provoking and heartbreaking monument to a boy.

Playing beside him, Patrick Auffay is equally solid as a pal, companion in juvenile deceptions and truant escapades.

Not to be sneezed at, either, is the excellent performance that Claire Maurier gives as the shallow, deceitful mother, or the fine acting of Albert Remy, as the soft, confused and futile father, or the performance of Guy Decomble, as a stupid and uninspired schoolteacher.

The musical score of Jean Constantin is superb, and very good English subtitles translate the tough French dialogue.

Here is a picture that encourages an exciting refreshment of faith in films.

N 17, 1959

IVAN THE TERRIBLE, PART II.
written and directed by Sergei Eisenstein; produced by Central Cinema Studio, Alma Ata, U. S. S. R.; distributed by Janus Films and presented by Sovexportfilm and Artkino. At the Murray Hill Theatre, Thirty-fourth Street east of Lexington Avenue. Running Time: eighty-seven minutes.

Ivan IV	Nikolai Cherkassov
The Boyarina	Serafima Birman
Vladimir Andreyevich	Piotr Kadochnikov
Malyuta Skuratov	Mikhail Zharov
Philip	Andrei Abrikosov
Pimen	Alexander Mgebrov
Prince Andrei Kurbsky	Nikolai Nazvanov
Alexei Basamanov	Alexei Buchma
Fyodor	Mikhail Kuznetsov
Piotr Volynets	Vladimir Balashov
King Sigismund Augustus	Pavel Massalsky

By BOSLEY CROWTHER

WHOEVER it was in Soviet Russia that compelled withholding for twelve years the release of Part II of the late Sergei Eisenstein's "Ivan the Terrible" was every bit as good a movie critic as he was a stern Russian chauvinist. He might have ordered the film put away forever and have done a service to Eisenstein.

For this second part of what the great director originally intended to be an Ivan trilogy (which he was prevented from completing by a series of heart attacks and then death in 1948) is a murkily monolithic and monotonous series of scenes with little or no dramatic continuity and only fitful dynamic quality.

The first part of "Ivan the Terrible" proved a monumental sort of film, conveying the dark magnificence of Russian medievalism, when it was shown here twelve years ago. This second part, which went on last evening at the Murray Hill Theatre, is but a pale extension of that great tableau, appearing to have been made from pieces of it picked up from the cutting-room floor.

Evidently the spark of inspiration and vigorous concept along pictorial lines that fired Eisenstein when he was making his first study of the reign of Ivan IV had burned out when he got around to this look-in on the phase of the sixteenth-century czar's career that embraced his return to Moscow from foreign adventures and his suppression of intriguers in the land.

None of the fine panoramic sweep of medieval spectacle that was in the coronation sequence in the earlier film is anywhere matched in this. Nor is there anything here to compare with the sense of supreme ferocity and almost barbaric aggressiveness that ran through the earlier film.

All there really is in this picture is a series of slowly paced scenes, most of them done with facial close-ups, intended to represent Ivan's bitter dispatch of treacherous boyars (feudal aristocrats) and his ponderously planned trap to catch a plotter who would assassinate him. The political explanations are long and tedious, becoming much confused in the hurried flashing of English subtitles to convey the Russian dialogue. Who is chasing whom and who gets butchered are matters of some doubt and less dramatic concern.

Nikolai Cherkassov's performance—or, rather, his appearance—in the Ivan role is mainly a matter of his posing in grotesque get-ups and attitudes. The indication is that he is supposed to represent a lonely and angry man. He appears to be more of a mad one, with a peculiarly pointed head. The rumor that the reason this picture was suppressed for so long was because it made Ivan look maniacal may well be true and reasonable. In this film he

330

seems akin to Rasputin, the latter-day Mad Monk.

•

As the gullible boy who would kill him, Piotr Kadochnikov is stupid in looks and generally static in behavior, and as the intriguing mother of this lad, Serafima Birman resembles a Halloween witch. Andrei Abrikosov is a heavily cowled villain in the role of the treacherous religious leader of Moscow, and swarms of extras play boyars with beards.

The musical score of Sergei Prokofieff fails to put much more than sound behind the scenes.

The place for this last of Eisenstein's pictures is in a hospitable museum.

Also on the bill at the Murray Hill is "The World of Rubens," a twenty-minute film that tells the story of the great Flemish painter's life through reflection on his works.

N 25, 1959

THE FILM GENERATION

The last decade recorded in our reviews conveys, at a glance, a picture of enormous vitality and diversity. There are conventional films, experimental films, art films, musicals and documentaries; there is the work of the established masters side by side with the contributions of untried talent; tradition prevails next to rebellion, standard method next to advanced technology. It is obvious, then, that television has not eliminated the cinema so much as liberated it, that the foreign films have not supplanted the domestic production so much as stimulated, challenged, and alerted it. Never before has the American cinema been so aggressively provoked and threatened both on its home ground and abroad; never before had so many Hollywood-based productions been shot and processed in foreign countries, often with foreign actors and crews. While the motivation was purely economic, the incidental benefit was an increased awareness of cultural interdependency. Only Soviet Russia inflexibly maintained the principle of isolation, producing films of impeccable technical finish but of incongruously conservative character. In contrast, the satellite countries, Poland, Hungary, Czechoslovakia, Yugoslavia, exported films of vigor and originality with an entirely contemporaneous feeling.

The full significance of this worldwide activity cannot be conveyed in statistics, merely listing the sum total of productions per country, the costs and revenues, and the attendance figures. Although impressive, they would hardly reflect the ingenuity and creative energy animating the film makers; nor would they intimate the responsiveness and aesthetic sensibility of the new audiences. Statistically, television can boast of a vastly larger attendance than the cinema. But its very omnipresence and easy availability, any time from morning into the night, deprives it of the excitement of deliberate choice and the unique occasion. Requiring little effort or attention or concentration or any other form of cooperation, the television event remains on the surface of experience. Unlike television, still in an infant stage of development, the cinema has matured into the most powerful creative medium of our time. After only a few decades, there are telling instances of distinctive, sustained careers that have produced a lasting oeuvre over the years. To recall just a few masters of the older generation who are still productive: Renoir and Bresson in France; Buñuel in Mexico and France; Mizoguchi in Japan; Ford, Hawks and Hitchcock in the United States.

We might observe here that at one time dominant national characteristics were easily recognizable, accounting for cultural variants between different countries. But in the same measure in which cinema has become a global language, those distinctions have tended to vanish. Today, nationality is more definitely represented in personalities than in generalized attitudes; thus we can unequivocally say: a film as French as Renoir, as Japanese as Ozu, as Swedish as Bergman, as British as Lean, as Italian as Fellini, as American as John Ford. This is not an idle game but a key toward the comprehension of the specific quality of "foreignness" in imported films, a quality that is the more precious for becoming more and more absorbed into an international style, similar to what has happened in contemporary painting.

Today, a younger generation of film artists has come into prominence, assuring the cinema of growth and continuity. Considering the astonishing proliferation of young creative film makers, it seems as if there was an inexhaustible supply of fresh talent, not only in the United States but in many other Western countries as well. They adopted the cinema as uniquely appropriate for the urgency to express and communicate the concerns of their age group, and they manipulate it with perfect ease and competence. They are frequently the exponents of acute, emotionally charged issues: the polarity of the "generation gap;" the conflicts between the "establishment" and youth in revolt; racial, sociological, and ideological tensions; the repercussions of the Vietnam situation; campus unrest, police action, the drug scene; the abolishment of sexual taboos. These and many related problems are filling the screen with vital, often violent, reflections of our time, disturbing the wonted comfort of "entertainment" and "escape." There is unquestionably a more sharply defined differentiation than ever before between the traditional movies and the "new cinema" and, as a consequence, between the "cinema generation" and the more conservative movie audience. The conflicts of opinion and taste between these two widely separated spheres have actually contributed to the richness of the recent cinema scene. The sixties will probably be remembered by a phenomenon without precedent, best described as a new cinema awareness that pervades the public arts. At the close of the sixth decade, two powerful, active forces carry promise for the future: diversity and vitality.

"IKIRU" ("To Live"), scenario by Hideo Oguni and Shinobu Hashimoto; directed by Akira Kurosawa; produced by the Toho Company, and presented here by Brandon Films, Inc. At the Little Carnegie Theatre, Fifty-seventh Street east of Seventh Avenue. Running time: 140 minutes.

Kanji Watanabe ......Takashi Shimura
Toyo ....Miki Odagiri
Mitsuo ....Nobuo Kaneko
Kazue ....Kyoko Seki
Ohno ....Kamatari Fujiwara
Saito ....Minosuke Yamada
Kiichie Watanabe ....Makoto Kobori
Tatsu ....Kumeko Urabe
Hayoshi ....Yoshie Minami
Novelist ....Yunosuke Ito

By BOSLEY CROWTHER

FOR a varied and detailed illustration of middle-class life in contemporary Japan, with a good deal of caustic social comment and extra thick sentiment thrown in, Akira Kurosawa's "Ikiru" ("To Live"), which opened at the Little Carnegie yesterday, is the best of the series of Japanese films that Thomas J. Brandon has shown at that theatre in the last several weeks. It is also the most expressive in its cinematic style, and if it weren't so confused in its story-telling, it would be one of the major postwar films from Japan.

•

As it stands, it is a strangely fascinating and affecting film, up to a point—that being the point where it consigns its aged hero to the great beyond. Then the last third (or forty-five minutes) of it is an odd sort of jumbled epilogue in which the last charitable act of the deceased man is crudely reconstructed in a series of flashbacks that are intercut with the static action of a tedious funeral.

The essential drama of the picture is that of an aging widower, a petty government official who has done nothing but shuffle papers and pass the buck for thirty years. Then, on the shattering discovery that he has cancer and has only a few months to live, he fearfully and frantically endeavors to make up for all the life and gratification he has lost.

•

In company with a disenchanted novelist, he tours the fleshpots of Tokyo, seeking joy in girls and liquor. That doesn't do any good. Then he tries to arrange for a calm retirement with his much adored son and daughter-in-law. They misunderstand his dilemma and rebuff him, which breaks his heart. A poignant attempt to have a friendship with a cheerful young woman does not succeed. Finally, he turns to a project of civic improvement that has been held up by government red tape for years, and it is upon this that he is working when he dies.

•

If the drama were clearly completed in continuity, it would be a proper progression to a climax with character and force. For the pathos of loneliness and searching in a friendless and meretricious world is brought out with vivid illustration in the first two-thirds of this film. And the idea of misunderstanding and callous disregard for other men that is the charge brought against the government officials could be continued to a straight ironic end.

It's that long-drawn, funereal maundering by the dead man's family and dull associates, all of them drinking and talking and showing their pettiness, that is the

333

anti-climactic death of the film.

Even so, in this flat phase, Kurosawa often flashes that cinematic style of sharp reportage and introspection of his characters that distinguishes his film. He patiently studies his people, gives them plenty of time to move and surrounds them with rich and meaningful details in composing the comment of a scene. As a consequence, you see more human nature and more Japanese customs in this film—more emotion, personality and ways of living—than in most of the others that have gone before.

Particularly does Takashi Shimura give a deep and exhaustive notion of a man tormented by frustration and the dread of approaching death. Unquestionably, Shimura, who was the woodcutter in "Rashomon," measures up through his performance in this picture with the top film actors anywhere. Miki Odagiri as the girl he seeks as a companion, Nobuo Kaneko as his unfeeling son and Yunosuke Ito as the novelist are also remarkably good.

Although the English subtitles are somewhat pallid against the bottom margins of this black-and-white film, they are generally decipherable and sufficient to convey the thought of the Japanese dialogue.

Ja 30, 1960

THE CRANES ARE FLYING: produced and directed by Mikhail Kalatozov; screen play by Victor Rozov; a Mosfilm production distributed by Warner Brothers. Running time: ninety-four minutes. At the Fine Arts Theatre.
Veronica............Tatyana Samoilova
Boris.................Alexei Batalov
Fyodor Ivanovich.....Vasily Merkuryev
Mark................Alexander Shvorin
Irina...............Sophola Kharitonova
Volodya............Konstantin Nikitin
Stepan..............Valentine Zubkov
Grandmother..........Alla Bogdanova

By BOSLEY CROWTHER

SOME things that many people may be surprised to find in a Soviet film are the warp and weft of "The Cranes Are Flying," which came to the Fine Arts yesterday. These are a downright obsessive and overpowering revulsion to war and, in contrast, a beautifully tender, almost lyric, feeling for romantic love.

These two amazing expressions, so uncommon in Soviet films, which are more often given to extolling patriotic fervor and the lovable qualities of hydroelectric plants, are the particular thematic distinctions of this extraordinary prize-winning film, offered here under the cultural exchange agreement promoted by the Soviet Union and our Department of State.

Unusual, too, is the employment of a highly intimate, impressionistic style of cinematic narration to tell the story of a sensitive Moscow girl who weakens and is unfaithful to her sweetheart when he is at the front in World War II. Mikhail Kalatozov, the director, has harked back to a cinematic style that was popular in the days when Pudovkin and Dovzhenko were making heroic revolutionary films. It is a style used in silent pictures, full of angular shots and close-up views of running feet and anguished faces. But M. Kalatozov has brought it up to date to blend with sound and the overlapping idioms of modern screen reportage. It might be called neo-romanticism, applied to a tragic tale.

The story is that of two lovers who are parted by the war—he a stalwart and patriotic fellow who willingly volunteers and marches off, while she, a wholesome maiden, remains behind and tends her hospital job. But under the strain of wartime torments, the loss of her family and her home in an air raid and the loneliness of waiting and not hearing from her beau, she submits to the latter's pianist cousin, who has got out of going to war. And, in the turmoil of the moment, she lovelessly marries him.

The illogic of this marriage is the most glaring fault of the plot, since it represents a conspicuous old-fashioned romantic cliché. But the twist does provide the solid basis for the heroine's subsequent despair and the high moral of the fable, which is that one should stay faithful to one's love.

Other familiar little details may be noted in the film, possibly signifying deliberate propaganda aims. For instance, an aged grandmother bestows upon the departing soldier the sign of the cross. The piano used by the musician is a Steinway. And family affections are strongly pronounced. But most genuine and touching is the emphasis on the steadfast love and devotion of the heroine for her sweetheart—and his for her, as caught in quick scenes at the front.

Thanks to Mr. Kalatozov's direction and the excellent performance Tatyana Samoilova gives as the girl, one absorbs a tremendous feeling of sympathy from this film— a feeling that has no awareness of geographical or political bounds. She is simply a fine, fecund-looking young woman torn from her lover by war. And he, played by Alexei Batalov, is a pleasant and credible young man moved by romantic impulses and shattered by fates outside himself.

Vasily Merkuryev as the soldier's father, Alexander Shvorin as the pianist and Alla Bogdanova as the grandmother make solid characters, too.

Strong music and good English subtitles to translate the Russian dialogue complete a moving drama that carries a message of love.

Mr 22, 1960

I'M ALL RIGHT, JACK; screen play by Frank Harvey, John Boulting and Alan Hackney; directed by Mr. Boulting; produced by Roy Boulting and distributed by Lion International Films, Inc. At the Guild Theatre, 33 West Fiftieth Street. Running time: 104 minutes.
Fred Kite ....Peter Sellers
Stanley Windrush ......Ian Carmichael
Major Hitchcock ....Terry-Thomas
Sidney De Vere Cox.
............................Richard Attenborough
Bertram Tracepurcel ......Dennis Price
Aunt Dolly ....Margaret Rutherford
Mrs. Kite ....Irene Handl
Cynthia Kite ....Liz Fraser
Stanley Windrush Sr....Miles Malleson
Mr. Mohammed.......Marne Maitland
Waters ....John Le Mesurier
Magistrate ....Raymond Huntley
Knowles ....Victor Maddern
Dai ....Kenneth Griffith
Charlie ....Fred Griffiths
Perce Carter ....Donal Donnelly
Shop Stewards..........John Comer,
............Sam Kydd, Cardew Robinson.
TV-panel chairman.Malcolm Muggeridge

By BOSLEY CROWTHER

OF all the unlikely subjects for successful satirizing on the screen—organized labor and management in modern industry — the British Boulting brothers, John and Roy, have picked it for their film "I'm All Right, Jack." And, what do you know!— they have run it into the brightest, liveliest comedy seen this year.

Much like their "Private's Progress," which took a decidedly scandalous view of life in the British Army during World War II, this new satire at the Guild Theatre plays absolutely devastating hob with the obstructive tactics of trade unions—and with the intrigues of management, too.

•

As a matter of fact, most of the characters in this delightfully sharp and rowdy farce are the same as were in "Private's Progress," only grown a little longer in the tooth. There's Ian Carmichael, the private, still a naïve and dizzy gentleman, seeking a place to dispose his peacetime talents and finding it as a laborer in a missile-making plant.

There's Richard Attenborough, the Cockney schemer, now become a dapper man of affairs, and Dennis Price, the art-purloining major, now the head of the arms factory. These two arch and practiced connivers are joined in a clearly crooked plot, with Marne Maitland as a shifty-eyed Mohammedan, to mulct an unnamed Arab country on a big arms deal.

And whom do you think these fine industrialists have as the labor-relations manager in their plant? None other than bucktoothed Terry-Thomas, the snarling major in that other film. He's the frenzied but foxy fellow who is now stuck with the patience-fraying job of dealing with the bland, lint-picking workers and spying on their time-wasting toils.

However, someone new has been added—an outsider to complicate the lives of these memorable and mischievous war buddies and make their best-laid schemes gang agley. He is a stalwart and solemn-faced shop steward, a provokingly pompous, priggish type. And he is played so sensationally by Peter Sellers that the whole film is made to jump and throb.

Truly, it's hard to tell you what it is that Mr. Sellers does to make this figure of a union fanatic devastatingly significant and droll. Up to the point of his entrance, the comedy runs along in an innocent, charming fashion, poking fun at the British upper class and making a mockery of modern manufacturing and merchandising, somewhat in the manner of Charlie Chaplin's "Modern Times."

But when Mr. Sellers strides into the picture at the head of a shop committee, breathing fire and rattling off union specifications in an educated Cockney tone of voice, it is as if Mr. Chaplin's Great Dictator has come upon the scene. He is all efficiency, righteous indignation, monstrous arrogance and blank ineptitude. He is the most scathing thing that union labor has ever had represent it on the screen. He is also side-splittingly funny, as funny as a true stuffed shirt can be.

We're not going to try to tell you how it all comes out; how Mr. Carmichael, with the best intentions, upsets the labor apple cart and precipitates a strike that puts a spoke in the conniving management's scheme and how this arouses the nation and compels a television panel show, in which the honest Mr. Carmichael exposes labor and management alike.

All we'll say further is that John Boulting, Frank Harvey and Alan Hackney have written a script that is one of the liveliest in a long time, although loaded with cryptic British slang; that Mr. Boulting has directed it briskly; that Margaret Rutherford, Irene Handl, Liz Fraser and Victor Maddern play it finely, along with all those mentioned above—and that this is a picture that only members of the National Association of Manufacturers, the unions and a few million other Americans should be sure to see.

Ap 26, 1960

HIROSHIMA, MON AMOUR; story and screen play by Marguerite Duras; produced and directed by Alain Resnais; an Argos-Daiei-Pathe Overseas production released by Zenith International. At the Fine Arts Theatre. Fifty-eighth Street, west of Lexington Avenue. Running time: eighty-eight minutes.
She .... Emmanuelle Riva
He .... Eiji Okada
Mother .... Stella Dassas
Father .... Pierre Barbaud
German Lover......... Bernard Fresson

By A. H. WEILER

IF ALAIN RESNAIS, producer-director of "Hiroshima, Mon Amour," may be classified a member of the French "new wave," then he also must be listed as riding its crest. For his delicately wrought drama, which had its local première at the Fine Arts Theatre yesterday, is a complex yet compelling tour de force—as a patent plea for peace and the abolition of atomic warfare; as a poetic evocation of love lost and momentarily found, and as a curiously intricate but intriguing montage of thinking on several planes in Proustian style.

Although it presents, on occasion, a baffling repetition of words and ideas, much like vaguely recurring dreams, it, nevertheless, leaves the impression of a careful coalescence of art and craftsmanship.

With the assistance of Marguerite Duras, one of France's leading symbolic novelists ("The Sea Wall," "Moderato Cantabile"), as well as the Nipponese technicians involved in this Franco-Japanese co-production, M. Resnais is not merely concerned with the physical aspects of a short (two-day) affair between a Gallic actress, in Hiroshima to make a film, and a Japanese architect. He also explores the meanings of war, the woman's first love and the interchange of thoughts as they emerge during the brief but supercharged romantic interlude.

●

A viewer, it must be stated at the outset, needs patience in order to appreciate the slow but calculated evolvement of the various levels of the film's drama, despite its fine, literal English subtitles. Neither M. Resnais nor Mlle. Duras are direct in their approach.

For the first fifteen minutes, our lovers, in intimate embrace, seemingly are savoring the ecstacies of their moment. Simultaneously, however, they are discussing Hiroshima, the 200,000 dead, the remembrance (shown in harrowingly stark newsreel and documentary footage of that monumental holocaust) of that frightful period in

history. It is, in striking effect, an oblique but vivid reminder of the absolutes of love and death.

As his parable progresses, however, M. Resnais reveals through his principals, both of whom indicate that they are happily married, that our love-wracked heroine has been through a similar situation before. This elegiac affair is the sudden outgrowth of her previous liaison during World War II in her native Nevers, with a young German soldier, an act for which she was ostracized both by Nevers' citizens and her parents. Now, fourteen years later, she divulges in tortured snatches of remembrance that she is again suddenly, experiencing that initial, exquisite happiness.

It is here, when the pain of memory forces the actress to refer to her Japanese vis-a-vis as if he were the German of her "amour impossible," that Mlle. Duras' script becomes slightly bewildering. Also in the final quarter of the film, when the distracted lovers merely state and restate their devotion and indecision, the drama drops into unnecessary romantic vagueness and repetition.

●

Mlle. Duras' screen play is, of course, largely a woman's point of view, one in which the nuances of love, physical and ephemeral, are dissected to a fare-thee-well. Despite this overemphasis, Emmanuelle Riva, a French actress who is making her screen debut in "Hiroshima, Mon Amour," gives each word and phrase meaning and tenderness.

Since she and her partner, are, in effect, the only two important players in the picture, it is notable that Mlle. Riva, a pale, blonde, wan type whose large eyes mirror beautifully the variations in her emotions, gives her heavy assignment professional polish and expression. Eiji Okada, as her confused lover, is obviously cast in a less weighty role, but the dark-haired intense Mr. Okada, speaking French in strange, Oriental accents, nevertheless, lends dignity and understanding to the characterization.

●

There is no doubt now that M. Resnais has chosen his proper metier. As a director who set himself an extremely difficult task, he expertly sustains the fragile moods of his theme most of the way. He also illustrates a rare expertise in his ability to show flashbacks; to intercut scenes of France and Hiroshima (where the picture was filmed) of today and yesterday, and to draw the most from his principals and the factual footage he uses.

This offering represents the first feature film M. Resnais has done, although he has won a niche for himself with such documentaries as the Picasso "Guernica," and others, not yet shown here publicly, like 'Nuit et Brouillard" ("Night and Fog"), which deals with concentration camps. If "Hiroshima, Mon Amour" is any yardstick, M. Resnais seems to have assured himself a niche in the feature-film field, too.

My 17, 1960

THE THREEPENNY OPERA; screen play by Leo Lania, Ladislas Vajda and Bela Balazs; based on John Gay's "Beggar's Opera"; adapted from the play by Bertolt Brecht; music by Kurt Weill; directed by G. W. Pabst; released by Brandon Films. Running time: 113 minutes. At the Fifty-fifth Street Playhouse, east of Seventh Avenue.
Macheath (Mack the Knife)
.......Rudolph Forster
Polly Peachum ....Carola Neher
Jenny ....Lotte Lenya
The Street Singer ....Ernst Busch
Peachum ....Fritz Rasp
Mrs. Peachum..............Valeska Gert
Tiger Brown..........Reinhold Schunzel
The Pastor ....Hermann Thimig
Smith, the Jailer.......Vladimir Sokolov
Filch ....Herbert Grunnbaum
Mack's Gang ....Paul Kemp
Gustav Puettjer
Oscar Hoecker
Kraft Raschig

By A. H. WEILER

ALTHOUGH despots, wars and several theatrical pro-

ductions of the Bertolt Brecht-Kurt Weill "Threepenny Opera" have come and gone since the German-language film edition first was shown here in 1931, it must be noted that the deservedly indestructible musical play, which came to the Fifty-fifth Street Playhouse on Saturday, has not been hurt to any great extent by the passage of time or malevolent men.

According to the distributors, the original negative was destroyed by the Nazis and the present edition is the result of many years of search and reconstructive work to make it the first complete version ever screened here. As such, the nearly two-hour feature, which has good literal English subtitles, is a strange, quaint, artistic and wryly humorous period piece that may be a curio but still is a tribute to the artistry of the men who fashioned it and the professionals who performed in it.

There is little need to remind the New Yorkers who have been flocking to the off-Broadway revival for more than five years that "The Threepenny Opera" stems from John Gay's early eighteenth-century "Beggar's Opera" and, in this case, is set in a world of cutthroats, thieves, beggars and prostitutes of the Soho of mid-Victorian London. It is more important to indicate that the cynical saga of the dashing Mack the Knife; his uninhibited band of robbers; Peachum, the beggar king; Polly, his daughter, who loses her heart to Mack, and Jenny, the strumpet who loves him, is satire that may be missed.

Despite the fact that the film's foreword states that its "theme of ironic disenchantment and wry optimism was universal," a viewer must bring an intimate knowledge of the disenchantment that existed in Germany in the Nineteen Twenties to this "opera" to understand and appreciate the scenarists' and Brecht's oblique digs through the film's dialogue and lyrics.

There are not too many songs, oddly enough, although audiences, conditioned by the current long-run stage revival, may expect a great many more. The popular "Mack the Knife" ("Moritat") begins and ends the film as it is done in fine style by Ernst Busch. A youthful and sad Lotte Lenya (Weill's widow), who created the role of Jenny on the German stage in 1928, and repeated the role on stage here, is properly bitter and slightly lachrymose in "Pirate Jenny." The thieves pitch in with a chorus or two, and there are a couple of other numbers. A brassy, jazzy musical background, while not in keeping with the era, is, nevertheless, in tune with the kind of singing and singers involved.

Since this production came only some two years after the advent of sound, the unevenness of the sound track is not surprising. It is, considering the vagaries of reconstructing a pioneer job, a stint worth commendation. Director G. W Pabst, who with the aid of Andrei Andreiev's stylized settings, has turned out a flavorsome, albeit sometimes murky and jerky production that fades in and out with rapidly and, on occasion, surprising cuts. And, he has handled his crowds, such as those legions of beggars, who swarm in madly on a coronation parade, and his principals with a true feeling for visual effects

By today's standards, the performance of Rudolph Forster as Mack the Knife, is vigorous but odd. In gray bowler, mustache, loud suit, white gloves and white shoes, he is a dapper, proud gang chief, who seems a caricature but, nevertheless, emerges as a forceful gent. Carola Neher, as his brunette Polly, is handsome and winsome; Reinhold Schuenzel is properly scatterbrained and terrified as Mack's police chief buddy; Fritz Rasp is, again by present yardsticks, a larger than life conniver, as are the comics who serve as Mack's henchmen.

In "The Threepenny Opera," they not only restore a page of the talking film's colorful early history but prove that even the quaint and archaic can be entertaining.

Jl 11, 1960

THE WORLD OF APU (APUR SANSAR), screen play by Satyajit Ray, from the novel, "Aparajito," by Bibhutibhusan Bannerji; directed and produced by Mr. Ray. Released by Edward Harrison. At the Fifth Avenue Cinema, 66 Fifth Avenue. Running time: 103 minutes
Apu .... Soumitra Chatterjee
Aparna .... Sharmila Tagore
Kajol .... Alok Chakravarty
Pulu .... Swapan Mukherji

By BOSLEY CROWTHER

THE cycle of life in India that film-maker Satyajit Ray determined to make graphic and poetic in an uncommon film trilogy is finally brought full circle in "The World of Apu" ("Apur Sansar"), which opened yesterday at the Fifth Avenue Cinema. The fulfillment honors the screen.

For with this beautiful picture, which completes the story of the Hindu lad we first met as a boy in "Pather Panchali" and saw grow into a raw young man in the succeeding "Aparajito," an impressive capstone is put not only upon a touching human drama but also upon the development of a genuine artist's skill. Mr. Ray, whose grasp of the cinema medium was uncertain in "Pather Panchali," his first film, demonstrates in "The World of Apu" that he is master of a complex craft and style.

•

Here he is telling us what happens to Apu, the lad of his previous films, when he has completed his skimpy education and gone out into the cold and challenging world. It is helpful to know about Apu, his broken family and his boyhood trials from the previous films. But it isn't essential or even vital, for this is a complete and rounded drama in itself.

It is the drama of a young man, shy and lonely, who is drawn into marriage with a girl, whom he doesn't know, out of regard for friendship and for a Hindu custom that is patently absurd; of his quick realization of love for her and their blissful happiness together for one year, until she dies in childbirth and he is left desolate, the stricken father of an unwanted child.

Through all of this tender experience, Mr. Ray pursues the story and constructs the film with an attention to the finer spiritual values that is extraordinarily sensitive and rare. Being a man who won't be hurried—or, at least, will not allow the tempo of a placid, pensive people to be stepped up to suit the custom of the screen—he follows the life stream of his hero with elaborate serenity, observing his world with close attention and delicately molding the beauties along the way.

Life is an everlasting poem in the canon observed by Mr. Ray. It is a slow flow of sensuous experience, surrounded by esthetic qualities. A man comes home in disappointment after having failed to get a job; he pensively shuts the windows, lies on his bed and plays a flute. A bride adorned in all her finery dares nothing more than a soft smile and whatever delight shows in her large eyes to express her gratitude at being wed. A woman goes home to have a baby; a message comes that she is dead.

Mr. Ray conveys in simple symbols the inexorable swing of life and death.

But the climax and triumph of his picture is its final phase in which the hero, the husband of the dead wife, the father of the unwanted child, goes into a period of several years of wandering and seeking for peace, finally to return to pick up his youngster and start another cycle of Apu.

Mr. Ray's command of the telling image and of tempo is superior in this film, and he seems to have elicited from his actors as fine performances as he has ever had. In the role of Apu, Soumitra Chatterjee is timid, tender, sad, serene, superb. He is the perfect extension of Apu as a man. Sharmila Tagore is an idol—an animated idol—as his bride, and Swapan Mukherji is striking as his modern, educated, practical friend. An incredibly slight and sad-eyed youngster named Alok Chakravarty is heartbreaking as the child.

A lovely musical score by Ravi Shankar complements the imagery of Mr. Ray. English subtitles apparently give us the gist of the conglomerate dialogue.

O 5, 1960

THE VIRGIN SPRING ("Jungfrukallan"), screen play by Ulla Isaksson, based on a thirteenth-century Swedish legend; directed by Ingmar Bergman; produced for Svensk Filmindustri and distributed by Janus Films. At the Beekman Theatre. Second Avenue at Sixty-fifth Street. Running time: eighty-eight minutes.
Herr Tore..............Max von Sydow
Fru Mareta............Birgitta Valberg
Ingeri................Gunnel Lindblom
Karin..................Birgitta Pettersson
The Thin Man.............Avel Duberg
The Mute...................Tor Isedal
Beggar..................Allan Edwall
Boy......................Ove Porath
Bridge Keeper............Axel Slangus
Frida...................Gundrun Brost
Simon................... Oscar Ljung

By BOSLEY CROWTHER

INGMAR BERGMAN is full of surprises. In his more recent films—"The Seventh Seal," "Wild Strawberries" and "The Magician"—the Swedish director has shown a tendency to ever greater intellectual complexity of theme. But now, in his latest to be released here (and successor to the above), "The Virgin Spring," he has done a substantial about face and tackled a theme of supreme simplicity.

It is a straight equating of violence and revenge, of brutality and compassion or—to reduce it to simplest terms—of evil and good. The film, called "Jungfrukallan" in Sweden, opened at the Beekman last night. It might be termed a morality play, so direct and uncomplicated is it.

But for all its directness and simplicity—its barrenness of plot and perplexities—it is far from an easy picture to watch or entirely commend. For Mr. Bergman has stocked it with scenes of brutality that, for sheer unrestrained realism, may leave one sickened and stunned. As much as they may contribute to the forcefulness of the theme, they tend to disturb the senses out of proportion to the dramatic good they do. However much one may welcome an easier clarity in a Bergman theme, there is a point beyond which the sophistication of the artist may be reduced with peril.

•

The story Mr. Bergman is telling, from a screen play by Ulla Isaksson, based on a thirteenth-century legend and folk song, is that of violence done by two goatherds upon an innocent maiden, of the revenge her father takes and then of his Christian repentance for the un-Christian wrong he has done.

Set in the Middle Ages, against the background of what appears to be a feudal farm, which Mr. Bergman has rendered graphic with much the same texture of rough-hewn image he had in "The Seventh Seal," the conflict is simply and clearly what it probably was in that age—between the pagan urge to have vengeance and the Christian will to forgive.

When the maiden, sent by her father to deliver candles to the church at Easter time, has been stopped in the forest by the goatherds, raped and murdered by them, the initial violence is committed. It is a brutish and horrible offense, which Mr. Bergman has represented for all the hideousness and terror it contains.

The maiden, played by Birgitta Pettersson, is a fresh and lovely thing. The goatherds, played by Avel Duberg and Tor Isedal, are brutes. Their deception of the child is nauseating, as is frankly depicted by the reaction of a boy who is with them and watches the violence done. And when they ravish her, the act is imaged — well, almost too candidly. Although the scene has been cut from the way it was shown in Europe, it is still sickening on our screen.

The response of the father to this violence, when he learns of it, is of equal ugliness and terror. After he prepares himself. by lashing his body with birch branches while taking a Swedish steam bath, he corners the goatherds in an outhouse, cuts one's throat with a knife and chokes and forces the other backward into a fire. Then he takes the boy, for whom sympathy and compassion have been aroused—he is the second symbol of innocence in the picture—and kills him by hurling him bodily against the wall.

In all of this representation, Mr. Bergman has achieved a tremendous sense of mental heaviness, primeval passion and physical power. The father, played by Max von Sydow, the feudal knight of "The Seventh Seal," is a gaunt and stubborn figure, the image of fierce, fanatical zeal. The mother, played by Birgitta Valberg, is less rigid and obtuse, more inclined to be understanding but more drugged in pagan superstition, too. Other figures — a terror-haunted farmgirl, an

342

old bridge keeper, a farmhand and a cook—contribute glints of human frailness and feudal ferocity.

If one wishes, of course, it is possible to find urgent symbolism in this film. Each character may be a representation of some contemporary element in the world. But we rather feel Mr. Bergman has here given us nothing more than a literal, very harsh, very vivid and occasionally touching statement of a moral. When water springs from the earth beneath the dead child, after the father has repented his wrong, the simple — almost naïve — conception is resolved in a miracle.

This is a simplification we feel Mr. Bergman is above.

The dialogue is in Swedish with English subtitles.

N 15, 1960

BALLAD OF A SOLDIER, screen play by Valentin Yoshov and Grigori Chukhrai; directed by Mr. Chukhrai; a Mosfilm Production released by M. J. P. Enterprises and Kingsley International. At the Murray Hill Theatre, 160 East Thirty-fourth Street. Running time: eighty-nine minutes.
Alyosha ....Vladimir Ivashov
Shura ....Shanna Prokhorenko
Mother ....Antonina Maximova
General ....Nikolai Kruchkov
Crippled Soldier ....Evgeni Urbanski

By BOSLEY CROWTHER

ONCE more, as in "The Cranes Are Flying," one of the best Soviet films in years, the Russians are poignantly protesting the damage done to people's lives by the occurrence of war. In their new picture, "Ballad of a Soldier," which opened at the Murray Hill yesterday, they are stating the case about as simply and touchingly as it could be put. At the same time, they are continuing the humane concept, embraced in "Cranes" and other recent Soviet films, that anxiety for the individual in warfare transcends anxiety for the state.

The hero of this tragic "ballad" is an innocent, beardless soldier-boy who earns a ten-day leave to go home to visit his mother by performing a desperation act of bravery at the front. More important to him than a medal is a chance to see his parent and to repair the roof of their house. And so, with the blessing of a compassionate general and the cheers of his comrades, off he goes.

On the way he has many small adventures—small, that is, when exposed against the background of national crisis and massive hardship that is unobtrusively made evident throughout the film. He takes up with a legless soldier who is terrified at the thought of going home, and sticks with him and spurs him with encouragement until he has seen him safely deposited in the arms of a comforting wife.

He wastes a half day in a city on the route trying to find the wife of a comrade to whom he has promised to deliver some soap, and when he finds her he discovers that she is living with another man.

Most momentously, he encounters a homeless and wandering girl when she jumps into a freight car of a military train that he has been permitted to ride. And out of this clumsy, humorous meeting a tender, innocent, warm attachment grows and glows rapturously for a few hours before the two youngsters are separated forever in a railway switching yard.

Eventually, the soldier gets home, but he has only the briefest time to embrace his mother and let her feast her eyes upon him before he has to start back to the front.

Small adventures, yes. But in the context in which they have been arranged by Grigori Chukhrai, who directed and helped to write the script, they become the moving episodes, the stanzas, in a profound and cumulative lament for the disorder, the grief and the frustration of people borne down upon by war. They become the heart-rending dilemmas and the strength-testing challenges set one upon the other in a ballad that states the cruelties of a monstrous agony.

Yet Mr. Chukhrai has made his picture to flow in such a swift, poetic way that the tragedy of it is concealed by a gentle lyric quality. And it is not until the cruel and final import of the terminal episodes is brought home to us at the fadeout that we sense how vastly sad it is.

He has done such lovely things as use his camera to pace the tempo of his story with the train, to catch the poetry of a girl's hair blowing wildly in the wind, to note the irony of a child's soap bubbles floating down a stairwell as the hero descends from his dismal discovery in the apartment where he went to deliver the soap. It is with such lyric touches that the deathless beauty in the tragedy is traced.

And it is through two splendid performances by Vladimir Ivashov and Shanna Prokhorenko as the soldier and the girl that he brings out the deep human meanings of the experiences through which they go. The lad, ever bright and energetic, is the essence of always hopeful youth, apparently never aware of impending tragedy. The girl, sad-eyed and apprehensive, generous and yet reserved, is the eternal woman who must bear the lasting loneliness of war.

This theme of the woman's suffering is also beautifully conveyed by Antonina Maximova in the mother role. Her alertness, her breath-taxing racing from the fields to greet her boy, and her final statuesque standing alone in the empty road after he has gone (as the text states, forever) give great depth, strength and heart to this strong film.

Michael Siv has contributed an appropriately eloquent musical score. English subtitles distill the gist of the Russian dialogue.

D 27, 1960

THE RULES OF THE GAME; written and directed by Jean Renoir, based on the play, "Les Caprices de Marianne" by Alfred de Musset; produced by La Nouvelle Edition Francaise; released by Janus Films. At the Eighth Street Playhouse, at the Avenue of the Americas. Running time: 110 minutes.
Robert de La Chesnyest ....Dalio
Christine de La Chesnyest..Nora Gregor
Genevieve ....Mila Parely
Octave ....Jean Renoir
Andre Jurieux ....Roland Tourain
Marceau ....Carette
Schumacher ....Gaston Modot
Lisette ....Paulette Dubost
General ....Pierre Magnier

Renoir Classic

TWENTY-TWO years after "The Rules of the Game" was made, and twelve years after a mutilated print was exhibited here, the full version of Jean Renoir's study of the manners and mores of prewar France opened yesterday at the Eighth Street Playhouse and completely justified its European reputation.

This remarkable film was photographed in the Sologna valley, where a year later French armies were fighting their last battles against the Nazis. While the film was in production, Hitler's troops invaded Czechoslovakia. The film opened in Paris while the city was celebrating the 150th anniversary of the French Revolution.

All these factors are subtly evoked in M. Renoir's trenchant examination of the decaying social structure of France before its fall. His screen play, loosely based on a modernized play by Alfred de Musset, deals with a house party given by a wealthy French aristocrat and his Viennese wife. Among the guests are his possessive mistress, a family friend who worhips the wife from a distance and her lover, a heroic aviator.

Downstairs, where the servants watch and imitate their employers, a parallel triangle develops among a flirtatious maid, her jealous gamekeeper husband and an amorous poacher. The situation erupts into a wildly comic chase in the midst of a costume ball, when the masquerading lovers intermingle in the confusion and the marquis reluctantly discharges the distraught gamekeeper for taking pot shots at his guests.

In an abrupt change of mood, reality intrudes upon the artificial surface, leaving the dazed and frightened guests gathered around the body of the only inocent victimthe man who broke the rules of a society founded upon a superficial display of manners by revealing the sincerity of his emotions. As a final coda, the marquis apologizes for the "accident," while a bystander remarks that "he has class—and, belive me, the race is dying out."

Entirely a director's film, "The Rules of the Game' is unevenly acted, although Dalio as the marquis, Carette as the poacher and M. Renoir himself as the awkward family friend are fascinating to observe.

The technique is admirable throughout, with at least two sequences emerging as classics of their kind—a rabbit hunt, emphasizing the barbarity of the ritual, and a masquerade foreshadowing the finale, in which guests dressed as skeletons perform a grotesque dance of death.

Admirers of the director's work will not find the moving simplicity of his expression of a pacifist theme in "Grand Illusion" or the colorful décor of "The River,' but will discover instead a deeply personal statement of unusual richness and complexity. M. Renoir obviously set out to make a masterpiece, closely following the literary tradition of Beaumarchais—who also foreshadowed the fall of a decadent aristocracy on the eve of the French Revolution.

Janus Films is presenting the film in a complete, uncensored print equipped with intelligent English sub-titles, which help to clarify the directors conception. For discerning audiences, "The Rules of the Game" affords a memorable experience.

EUGENE ARCHER

Ja 19, 1961

BREATHLESS, screenplay by Jean-Luc Godard based on a story by Francois Truffaut; directed by M. Godard; produced by Georges De Beauregarde; presented by Films Around the World, Inc. At the Fine Arts Theatre, Fifty-eighth Street west of Lexington Avenue. Running time: eighty-nine minutes.
Patricia Franchini.........Jean Seberg
Michel Poiccard....Jean-Paul Belmondo
Liliane...................Liliane David
Inspector ....Daniel Boulanger
Parvulesco...........Jean-Paul Melville
Berrouti...........Henri-Jacques Huet
Used Car Dealer........Claude Mansart
Editor......................Van Doude
Informer............Jean-Luc Godard

By BOSLEY CROWTHER

AS sordid as is the French film, "Breathless" ("A Bout de Souffle"), which came to the Fine Arts yesterday—and sordid is really a mild word for its pile-up of gross indecencies—it is withal a fascinating communication of the savage ways and moods of some of the rootless young people of Europe (and America) today.

Made by Jean-Luc Godard, one of the newest and youngest of the "new wave" of experimental directors who seem to have taken over the cinema in France, it goes at its unattractive subject in an eccentric photographic style that sharply conveys the nervous tempo and the emotional erraticalness of the story it tells. And through the American actress, Jean Seberg, and a hypnotically ugly new young man by the name of Jean-Paul Belmondo, it projects two downright fearsome characters.

•

This should be enough, right now, to warn you that this is not a movie for the kids or for that easily shockable individual who used to be known as the old lady from Dubuque. It is emphatically, unrestrainedly vicious, completely devoid of moral tone, concerned mainly with eroticism and the restless drives of a cruel young punk to get along. Although it does not appear intended deliberately to shock, the very vigor of its reportorial candor compels that it must do so.

On the surface, it is a story of a couple of murky days in the lives of two erratic young lovers in Paris, their temporary home. He is a car thief and hoodlum, on the lam after having casually killed a policeman while trying to get away with a stolen car. She is an expatriate American newspaper street vender and does occasional stories for an American newspaper man friend.

But in the frenetic fashion in which M. Godard pictures these few days—the nerve-tattering contacts of the lovers, their ragged relations with the rest of the world—there is subtly conveyed a vastly complex comprehension of an element of youth that is vagrant, disjointed, animalistic and doesn't give a damn for anybody or anything, not even itself.

•

The key is in the character that M. Belmondo plays, an impudent, arrogant, sharp-witted and alarmingly amoral hood. He thinks nothing more of killing a policeman or dismissing the pregnant condition of his girl than he does of pilfering the purse of an occasional sweetheart or rabbit-punching and robbing a guy in a gentlemen's room.

For a brief spell—or, rather a long spell, for the amount of time it takes up in the film—as he casually and coyly induces his pensive girl friend to resume their love affair, it does look as if there may be a trace of poignant gentleness in him, some sincerity beneath the imitation of a swaggering American movie star. But there isn't. When his distracted girl finally turns him in and he is shot in the street, he can only muster a bit of bravado and label his girl with a filthy name.

The girl, too, is pretty much impervious to morality or sentiment, although she does indicate a sensitive nature that has been torn by disappointments and loneliness. As little Miss Seberg plays her, with her child's face and closely cropped hair, she is occasionally touching. But she is more often cold and shrewd, an efficiently self-defensive animal in a glittering, glib, irrational, heartless world.

•

All of this, and its sickening implications, M. Godard has got into this film, which progresses in a style of disconnected cutting that might be described as "pictorial cacaphony." A musical score of erratic tonal qualities emphasizes the eccentric moods. And in M. Belmondo we see an actor who is the most effective cigarette-mouther and thumb-to-lip rubber since time began.

Say this, in sum, for "Breathless": it is certainly no cliché, in any area or sense of the word. It is more a chunk of raw drama, graphically and artfully torn with appropriately ragged edges out of the tough underbelly of modern metropolitan life.

F 8, 1961

L'AVVENTURA, written and directed by Michelangelo Antonioni; produced by Cino del Duca; presented by Robert and Raymond Hakim; distributed by Janus Films, Inc. At the Beekman Theatre, Second Avenue and Sixty-fifth Street. Running time: 145 minutes.

Claudia ....Monica Vitti
Sandro ....Gabriele Ferzetti
Anna ....Lea Massari
Giulia ....Dominique Blanchar
Corrado ....James Addams
Anna's father ....Renzo Ricci
Patrizia ....Esmerelda Ruspoli
Raimondo ....Lelio Luttazi
Gloria Perkins.......Dorothy De Poliolo
Young Prince ....Giovanni Petrucci

By BOSLEY CROWTHER

WATCHING "L'Avventura" ("The Adventure"), which came to the Beekman yesterday, is like trying to follow a showing of a picture at which several reels have got lost.

Just when it seems to be beginning to make a dramatic point or to develop a line of continuity that will crystallize into some sense, it will jump into a random situation tnat appears as if it might be due perhaps three reels later and never explain what has been omitted.

At least, that's how it strikes us.

What Michelangelo Antonioni, who wrote and directed it, is trying to get across in this highly touted Italian mystery drama (which is what we take it to be) is a secret he seems to be determined to conceal from the audience. Indeed he stated frankly to a reporter from this paper last week that he expects the customers to search for their own meanings. "I want the audience to work," he said.

That would be all right, if the director would help us a bit along the way, if he would fill in a few of the big potholes in this two-hour-and-twenty-five minute film. But he doesn't. Like a breathless storyteller who has a long and detailed story to tell and is so eager to get on to the big doings that he forgets to mention several important things, Signor Antonioni deals only with what seems to interest him. He omits such little details as whatever happens to some key characters and why others turn up in certain places and do what they do.

For instance, it might be helpful if he would have the kindness to explain what gives on a curious, barren island, where his drama presumably begins. To this lava rock off the coast of Sicily he brings a peculiarly viperous group of jaded and selfish worldings in a conspicuously crowded little yacht. While they are wandering across its waste space, he has one of the party disappear—a sad young woman who has been having a bit of a dido with one of the handsome bachelors in the group.

What has happened to this poor young woman? Has she committed suicide? Has her lover stuffed her in a cozy crevice? Signor Antonioni never explains. He just keeps us there on that ugly island for what seems an interminable length of time while the party and police hunt for the body. Then he suddenly jumps the scene to Sicily, where the lover and another young woman in the party somehow meet on strangely disagreeable terms.

Has that prelude on the island been symbolic? Are the two, now isolated, meant to be the forlorn and exhausted relics of a social catastrophe? Maybe so, maybe not, but in a short time they are on anything but disagreeable terms. They are suddenly enthusiastic lovers, embracing frequently.

However, their affair does not run smoothly. They have doubts, anxieties, violent spats. One time they drive together into an empty city and look at the cold austere facade of a concrete church. ("These buildings are madness," the girl says.) They are lonely amid gay people. One night the man stays away with another girl. The woman finds them together the next morning. They have a dismal reunion in the cheerless dawn.

●

Perhaps Signor Antonioni is saying something valuable in this. We would very much hate to think he isn't, for he has put a lot of craft into his film. His photography is exquisite—sharp and immensely picturesque. Much of it is shot on location, in the cities and countryside of Sicily, and there is a great deal of beauty and excitement in the pure composition of movement against architectural forms.

Signor Antonioni also has great skill in conceiving and conveying provocative isolated images. A shot of the woman walking from her first assignation past a lineup of ogling, leering men, or one of her running distractedly down an endlessly long hall to seek aid, flash vivid concepts of feeling. And the actors are all provocative types and interesting performers of the odd things they have to do.

Gabriele Ferzetti as the lover has a taut, tireless energy, and Monica Vitti, as his second mistress, is weirdly coquettish and intense. Lea Massari, Dominique Blanchar and James Addams make odd sybarites—until they are dropped like hot potatoes. Several others fit into that class.

A wry musical score and sound track and English subtitles that seem inadequate contribute to the mystification of this picture, which won prizes in Europe. 'Tis strange.

Or maybe Signor Antonioni isn't out to prove anything— just to give us a weird adventure. Well, it gives us that.

Ap 5, 1961

LA DOLCE VITA, scenario by Federico Fellini, Tullio Pinelli, Ennio Flaiano and Brunello Rondi; directed by Signor Fellini; produced by Giuseppe Amato; presented here by Astor Films. At Henry Miller's Theatre, Forty-third Street east of Broadway. Running time: 175 minutes.

Marcello Rubino...Marcello Mastroianni
Photographer............Walter Santesso
Maddalena ....Anouk Aimee
The Prostitute.........Adriana Moneta
Marcello's mistress....Yvonne Furneaux
A Hollywood Star.........Anita Ekberg
The Producer.........Carlo Di Maggio
Robert.....................Lex Barker
Frankie Stout.................Alain Dijon
Steiner.....................Alain Cuny
Paola................Valeria Ciangottini
Mrs. Steiner...........Renee Longarini
Marcello's father.......Annibale Ninchi
The Clown....................Polidor
Fanny.................Magali Noel
Blonde Prostitute...........Nico Otzak
Prince Mascalchi
                Prince Vadim Wolkonsky
Don Eugenio Mascalchi
                Prince don Eugenio
                Ruspoli di Poggio Suasa
Nadia ....Nadia Gray
The Matinee Idol.......Jacques Sernas
Riccardo...............Riccardo Garrone

By BOSLEY CROWTHER

FEDERICO FELLINI'S "La Dolce Vita" ("The Sweet Life"), which has been a tremendous hit abroad since its initial presentation in Rome early last year, finally got to its American première at Henry Miller's Theatre last night and proved to deserve all the hurrahs and the impressive honors it has received.

For this sensational representation of certain aspects of life in contemporary Rome, as revealed in the clamorous experience of a free-wheeling newspaper man, is a brilliantly graphic estimation of a whole swath of society in sad decay and, eventually, a withering commentary upon the tragedy of the over-civilized.

The critic is faced with a dilemma in attempting to assess and convey all the weird observations and intimations that abound in this titanic film. For Signor Fellini is nothing if not fertile, fierce and urbane in calculating the social scene around him and packing it onto the screen.

He has an uncanny eye for finding the offbeat and grotesque incident, the gross and bizarre occurrence that exposes a glaring irony. He has, too, a splendid sense of balance and a deliciously sardonic wit that not only guided his cameras but also affected the writing of his script. As a consequence there are scores of piercing ideas that pop out in the picture's nigh three hours and leave one shocked, amused, revolted and possibly stunned and bewildered at the end.

Perhaps the best way to give the reader a hint as to the flavor of this work is to describe its amazing beginning. A helicopter is seen flying toward Rome with an uncertain object dangling beneath it by a rope. As the machine comes closer, we see the object is a statue of Jesus, arms outstretched as if in blessing, a sweet, sad expression on its face.

Casually, the whirring "chopper" flies past an ancient aqueduct, the modern machine and its strange burden looking incongruous against the ruin. On it goes past piles of buildings, the ugly post-war apartment houses on the fringe of Rome and over the heads of a bevy of voluptuous females sunbathing in Bikinis on a penthouse roof. Then alongside it comes a second helicopter bearing our young newspaper man and his persistent photographer recording the bizarre scene.

Here is the flavor of the picture and, in a fast glimpse, its theme. Dignity is transmuted into the sensational. Old values, old disciplines are discarded for the modern, the synthetic, the quick by a society that is past sophistication and is sated with pleasure and itself. All of its straining for sensations is exploited for the picture magazines and the scandal sheets that merchandise excitement and vicarious thrills for the mob.

This is Signor Fellini's comment, not put into words,

of course, but fully illuminated in his accumulation of startling episodes. It is clear in the crazy experience of his questing newspaper man (played brilliantly by Marcello Mastroianni) with a visiting Hollywood movie star (enacted by Anita Ekberg with surprising personality and punch.)

It comes through with devastating impact in an episode wherein two frightened kids are used to whip up a religious rally for the benefit of television. It is implicit in the contact of the hero with a strange and motley mob of jaded aristocrats and worldlings at an all-night party in a palace outside Rome.

It finally comes home to the hero (at least we think it does) when he sees his own pack of voracious photographers trying to make a sensation of the suicide of his most respected friend (Alain Cuny) for whom the "sweet life" becomes too grim. And it is evident in unmistakable symbols at a mammoth orgy the hero attends with a gang of depraved sensation seekers who face their loneliness and emptiness in the dawn.

. Possibly Signor Fellini has rambled a bit in his film. Possibly he has strained logic and exaggerated somewhat here and there. (He has a character say "The public demands exaggeration," which does support the theme.)

In sum, it is an awesome picture, licentious in content but moral and vastly sophisticated in its attitude and what it says. An excellent cast performs it. In addition to those named above, Yvonne Furneaux as the hero's mistress, Anouk Aimee as a nymphomaniac, Annibale Ninchi as the hero's father and Magali Noel as a night-club chorus girl make most vivid impressions in a stupendous cast.

An all-purpose musical melody, as persistent and haunting as the memorable "Third

Man" theme, is aptly played in the right places. The use of multilingual dialogue (the French and Italian translated with English subtitles) makes the yakkity-yak really sound like Rome. If the subtitles are insufficient, the picture itself speaks louder than any words.

Ap 20, 1961

ASHES AND DIAMONDS, screen play by Andrzej Wajda and Jerzy Andrzejewski, based on a novel by Mr. Andrzejewski; directed by Mr. Wajda and produced for Film Polski by Film Unit KADR. Released by Janus Films, Inc. At the Fifth Avenue Cinema, Fifth Avenue at Thirteenth Street. Running time: 105 minutes.

Maciek	Zbigniew Cybulski
Christine	Eva Krzyzewska
Andrzej	Adam Pawlikowski
Szczuka	Waclaw Zastrzezynski
Drewnowski	Bogumil Kobiela
Porter	Jan Ciecierski
Journalist	Stanislaw Milski
Kotowicz	Artur Mlodnicki
Mrs. Staniewicz	Halina Kwiatkowska
Waga	Ignacy Machowski

By BOSLEY CROWTHER

DETERIORATION in Poland as a consequence of World War II is a subject from which Andrzej Wajda, one of that country's best young film directors, has evidently found it hard to get away.

In his first feature film, "A Generation," not yet released in this country, he examined the dismal condition of juvenile gangs in Poland after the war. In his subsequent "Kanal," now showing at the New Yorker Theatre on upper Broadway, he reflected upon the painful happenings in the disastrous Warsaw uprising of 1944. Now, in his "Ashes and Diamonds," which opened at the Fifth Avenue Cinema yesterday, he is doing a melancholy recapitulation on the political and social chaos at the end of the war.

•

As in his previous pictures, M. Majda is putting forth here something more than a trenchant observation of a highly dramatic episode.

While his action is set within the area of a small Polish city in one full day—the day of Germany's surrender—and mainly revolves around the efforts of a young resistance fighter to spot and assassinate a new Polish Communist leader, his camera takes in a shattering sweep of the litter of a lost and ruined country at the symbolic dawn of a new day.

There are greedy politicians in his round-up, smug and sharp-eyed fellows who pretend that a hastily arranged victory banquet is a welcome to their new political chief but wind up in the gray light of the morning reeling drunkenly to the off-key Polonaise.

There is a tough and tense resistance leader who will never say surrender or die and who makes his getaway into the darkness when he thinks that he has his murder plot arranged. There is the mellow, serene, paternalistic incoming commissar who grieves when he learns that his own son is one of a band of captured and condemned resistance troops. And there is the young, idealistic assassin who hesitates at dealing out more death and spends the long night of the vulgar banquet paying court and making love to a clear-eyed girl.

•

With the literary help of Jerzy Andrzejewski, upon whose novel this drama is based, director Wajda has shaped the story in strong and striking visual images. His sharply etched black-and-white action has the pictorial snap and quality of some of the old Soviet pictures of Pudovkin and Eisenstein. Facial expressions are highlighted, bodily movements are swift and intense and the light that comes in from the outside in the shaky morning is as dense as luminous smoke.

Likewise, Wajda has created some vivid ideas through imagery—ideas that carry cynicism, melancholia, wistfulness and shock. There is a beautiful scene of the killers remembering dead comrades at a bar, marking each recollection with a glass of brandy set aflame. There is a scene of the lovers wandering restlessly among ruins, coming upon a large crucifix dislodged and swaying perilously head down. And there's the idea conveyed with the shot commissar dying in his assassin's arms, and finally that of the young hero twitching convulsively to his death on a rubbish heap.

The mood of despair in this picture is as heavy as that in "Kanal," but the film itself is much more searching and infinitely better performed. Zbigniew Cybulski as the hero is sensitive, attractive and alert—a lad with humor and compassion. One is strongly drawn to him. Eva Krzyzewska as the barmaid with whom he has one last lyrical love looks like Gina Lollobrigida and acts decently to boot. Others, whose names are equally difficult, make vigorous and valid characters. The musical score is excellent and the English subtitles will do.

My 30, 1961

THE HUSTLER, screen play by Robert Rossen and Sidney Carroll; based on a novel by Walter Tevis; directed and produced by Mr. Rossen for Twentieth Century-Fox. At the Paramount, Seventh Avenue and Forty-third Street, and the Seventy-second Street Playhouse, 346 East Seventy-second Street. Running time: 133 minutes.

Eddie Felson...............Paul Newman
Minnesota Fats...........Jackie Gleason
Sarah Packard..............Piper Laurie
Bert Gordon.............George C. Scott
Charlie Burns.........Myron McCormick
Findlay................Murray Hamilton
Big John...........Michael Constantine
Preacher.................Stefan Gierasch
Bartender.................Jake LaMotta
Cashier................Gordon B. Clarke
Scorekeeper.............Alexander Rose
Young Hustler.................Carl York

By BOSLEY CROWTHER

DAD always said stay out of poolrooms, and obviously he was right, to judge by what one sees in "The Hustler," which came to the Paramount and the Seventy-second Street Playhouse yesterday. For the characters one meets in the succession of sunless and smoky billiard halls (to use a more genteel term for them) that are tenanted in the course of this tough film are the sort to make your flesh creep and whatever blood you may have run cold.

Indeed, one character says in the beginning that a poolroom looks like a morgue and "those tables are the slabs they lay the stiffs on."

We're glad we took the good advice of Dad.

But this doesn't say the weird assembly of pool players, gamblers, hangers-on and hustlers—especially the hustlers—which they used to call "pool sharks" in our youth, are not fascinating and exciting to watch at a safe distance from the screen. They're high-strung, voracious and evil. They talk dirty, smoke, guzzle booze and befoul the dignity of human beings. At least, the hustlers' wicked betting managers do. They have a consuming greed for money that cancels out charity and love. They're full of energy and action.

That's the virtuous quality of this film.

Under Robert Rossen's strong direction, its ruthless and odorous account of one young hustler's eventual emancipation is positive and alive. It crackles with credible passions. It crackles briskly and brusquely to sharp points. It doesn't dawdle with romantic nonsense, except in one brief unfortunate stretch.

Along about midway, after its hero has been washed out in a herculean game and has sneaked away into a cheap New York apartment with a fortuitously picked-up girl, it does mush about a bit with chitchat anent the deep yearnings of the heart and the needful direction a man takes to get onto solid ground.

But even in this mushy area, Mr. Rossen and Sidney Carroll have provided their characters with dialogue that keeps them buoyant and alive. And soon they are potently projected into the world of the realists again—into a brutally cynical connivance and a gorge-raising sweep to an ironic end.

There may not be much depth to the hero, whom Paul Newman violently plays with a master's control of tart expressions and bitterly passionate attitudes. Nor may there be quite enough clarity in the complicated nature of the girl, whom Piper Laurie wrings into a pathetic and eventually exhausted little rag. But they're both appealing people, he in a truculent, helpless way and she in the manner of a courageous, confused and uncompromising child.

The real power is packed into the character of an evil gambler, whom George C. Scott plays as though the devil himself had donned dark glasses and taken up residence in a rancid billiard hall. Mr. Scott is magnificently malefic. When he lifts those glasses and squints, it is as though somebody had suddenly put a knife between your ribs.

Jackie Gleason is also excellent—more so than you first realize—as a cool, self-collected pool expert who has gone into bondage to the gambling man. His deceptively casual behavior in that titanic initial game conceals a pathetic robot that you only later perceive.

Myron McCormick is touchingly futile as a tin-horn manager and Murray Hamilton, too, is effective in the brief role of a wealthy billiards buff. Michael Constantine, Carl York and Jale LaMotta are colorful as poolroom types.

"The Hustler" is not a picture to take the children to see, but it is one a father might wisely recommend to a restless teen-age son.

An appropriately nervous jazz score keeps the eardrums sharp.

S 27, 1961

WEST SIDE STORY screen play by Ernest Lehman; directed by Robert Wise and Jerome Robbins; produced by Mr. Wise for Mirisch Pictures in association with Seven Arts Productions; released by United Artists. At the Rivoli Theatre, Seventh Avenue and Forty-ninth Street. Running time: 155 minutes.

Maria	Natalie Wood
Tony	Richard Beymer
Riff	Russ Tamblyn
Anita	Rita Moreno
Bernardo	George Chakiris
Ice	Tucker Smith
Action	Tony Mordente
A-rab	David Winters
Baby John	Eliot Feld
Snowboy	Bert Michaels
Anybodys	Sue Oakes
Graziella	Gina Trikonis
Velma	Carole D'Andrea
Chino	Jose De Vega
Pepe	Jay Norman
Indio	Gus Trikonis
Juano	Eddie Verso
Loco	Jaime Rogers
Rocco	Larry Roquemore
Consuelo	Yvonne Othon
Rosalia	Suzie Kaye
Francisca	Joanne Miya
Lieutenant Schrank	Simon Oakland
Officer Krupke	William Bramley
Doc	Ned Glass
Glad Hand	John Astin

By BOSLEY CROWTHER

WHAT they have done with "West Side Story" in knocking it down and moving it from stage to screen is to reconstruct its fine material into nothing short of a cinema masterpiece.

In every respect, the recreation of the Arthur Laurents-Leonard Bernstein musical in the dynamic forms of motion pictures is superbly and appropriately achieved. The drama of New York juvenile gang war, which cried to be released in the freer and less restricted medium of the mobile photograph, is now given range and natural aspect on the large Panavision color screen, and the music and dances that expand it are magnified as true sense-experiences.

The strong blend of drama,

dance and music folds into a rich artistic whole. It may be seen at the Rivoli Theatre, where it had its world première last night.

Perhaps the most striking aspect of it is the sweep and vitality of the dazzling Jerome Robbins dances that the kids of the seamy West Side do. Here is conveyed the wild emotion that burns in these youngsters' tough, lithe frames. Here are the muscle and the rhythm that bespeak a collective energy.

From the moment the camera swings grandly down out of the sky at the start of the film and discovers the Jets, a gang of tough kids, twitching restlessly in a playground park, bodies move gracefully and fiercely in frequent spontaneous bursts of dance, and even the movements of the characters in the drama have the ' grace of actors in a ballet.

This pulsing persistence of rhythm all the way through the film—in the obviously organized dances, such as the arrogant show-offs of the Jets, that swirl through playgrounds, alleys, school gymnasiums and parking lots, and in the less conspicuous stagings, such as that of the "rumble" (battle) of the two kids—gives an overbeat of eloquence to the graphic realism of this film and sweeps it along, with Mr. Bernstein's potent music, to the level of an operatic form.

Against, or within, this flow of rhythm is played the tender drama of two nice kids, a Puerto Rican girl and a Polish boy, who meet and fall in love, despite the hatred and rivalry of their respective ethnic groups, and are plunged to an end that is tragic, just like Romeo and Juliet.

Every moment of the drama has validity and integrity, got from skillful, tasteful handling of a universal theme. Ernest Lehman's crackling screen play, taken from Arthur Laurent's book, and Robert Wise's incisive direction are faithful and cinema-wise, and the performances are terrific except in one major role.

Richard Beymer's characterization of the boy who meets and loves the girl is a little thin and pretty-pretty, but Natalie Wood is full of luster and charm as the nubile Puerto Rican who is poignantly drawn to him. Rita Moreno is a spitfire as Miss Wood's faithful friend, and George Chakiris is proud and heroic as her sweetheart and leader of the rival gang.

Excellent as young toughs (and dancers) in a variety of characterizations are Russ Tamblyn, Tucker Smith, Tony Mordente, Jose De Vega, Jay Norman and many more, and outstanding girls are Gina Trikonis, Yvonne Othon, Suzie Kaye and Sue Oakes.

Although the singing voices are, for the most part, dubbed by unspecified vocal performers, the device is not noticeable and detracts not one whit from the beauty and eloquence of the songs.

In the end, of course, the moral of the tragedy comes through in the staggering sense of wastage of the energies of kids. It is screamed by the candy-store owner, played trenchantly by Ned Glass, when he flares, "You kids make this world lousy! When will you stop?"

It is a cry that should be heard by thoughtful people—sympathetic people—all over the land.

O 19, 1961

THE NIGHT (LA NOTTE)

By BOSLEY CROWTHER

AT least, Michelangelo Antonioni lets us know what he's about in his new film, "The Night" ("La Notte"), which came to the Little Carnegie yesterday.

He is coolly cataloguing

with his camera the wealth of telltale things that occur in the course of an afternoon and evening in the life of an Italian novelist's wife as she comes to the dismal conclusion that her husband no longer loves her, that she no longer loves him and she wishes she were dead.

Where Signor Antonioni was elusive, if not obscure, in tracing a dramatic line in "L'Avventura," his controversial film of last year, he is absolutely explicit in tracing the line in this.

THE NIGHT (LA NOTTE), screen play by Michelangelo Antonioni, Ernio Flaiano and Tonino Guerra; directed by Signor Antonioni and produced by Emanuele Cassuto. A Sofitedip-Nepi Film, released by Lopert Pictures Corp. At the Little Carnegie, 146 West Fifty-seventh Street. Running time: 120 minutes.
Lidia .... Jeanne Moreau
Giovanni .... Marcello Mastroianni
Valentina G. .... Monica Vitti
Tomasso .... Bernhard Wicki
Resy .... Rosy Mazzacurati
The Young Patient....... Maria Pia Luzi
Gerardini .... Vincenzo Corbella
Signora Gerardini.......... Gitt Magrini
Roberto .... Giorno Negro

He begins with the wife and her husband on their way to a hospital in Milan to visit a dear friend who is dying (this is told to them before they enter the room). And after this harrowing experience, during which everyone tries to be brave, they go on to a chic cocktail party to celebrate the publication of the husband's new book.

Here the wife, still oppressed by sadness, begins to feel lonely, out of place, and wanders off on an aimless excursion that ultimately takes her to a run-down park on the edge of Milan. It is a place she used to visit with her husband. She thinks of him and telephones him at home. Relieved to know where she is, he comes to fetch her. But she still can't make contact with him.

So it goes through the evening. The couple visit a dinner club and watch a smoothly erotic dance act. They are both detached and bored. Then they go on to a huge garden party at the elegant, modernistic home of a Milanese business magnate and spend the long, humid tedious night fumbling with other people and finding themselves ever more apart and alone.

The husband is soundly frustrated in his pursuit of a solemn, lonely girl, and the wife is violently shaken by the evident indifference of her spouse. Finally, they leave the dying party to go out onto a golf course at dawn and face the sober truth of their lost union and the feeble hope that they may still patch it up.

That is the line of the drama, and we state it in order to reveal the simplicity of the progression and the complexity of the tensions implied. For here, as in "L'Avventura," it is not the situation so much as it is the intimations of personal feelings, doubts and moods that are the substance of the film.

And these Signor Antonioni has implanted and developed with a skill that is excitingly fertile, subtle and awesomely intuitive. Upon a crisply graphic background of real buildings and places in Milan that would lead one to expect the exposition of a virtually objective document, he has superimposed and intruded a completely subjective account of the interior loneliness, boredom and emotional exhaustion of a woman and a man.

Too sensitive and subtle for apt description are his pictorial fashionings of a social atmosphere, a rarefied intellectual climate, a psychologically stultifying milieu—and his haunting evocations within them of individual symbolisms and displays of mental and emotional aberrations. Even boredom is made interesting by him.

There is, for instance, a sequence in which a sudden downpour turns a listless garden party into a riot of fool-

354

ish revelry, exposing the lack of stimulation before nature takes a flagellating hand. Or there's a shot of the crumpled wife leaning against a glass wall looking out into the rain that tells in a flash of all her ennui, desolation and despair.

●

As the wife, Jeanne Moreau does a fine job of generating the sodden spirit of vagrant moods and catching the glints of resignation and accusation in her eyes. Marcello Mastroianni, the "La Dolce Vita" lad, is foggy and obtuse as the husband, and Monica Vitti is peculiarly flat and lackluster as the young woman with whom the husband is unable to "communicate." Bernhard Wicki, the German film director, is impressive in the brief role of the dying man, and several Milanese citizens are colorful as garden-party types.

There is a lot of Italian conversation that is complicated and hard to get from the heavy English subtitles. This adds further to the difficulty of fathoming this film, which already demands a large measure of sophistication and sensitivity in its audience. Whether one finds it stimulating or a redundant bore will depend, we suspect, in large measure upon the subtle attunement of one's mood.

F 20, 1962

LAST YEAR AT MARIENBAD
By BOSLEY CROWTHER

BE prepared for an experience such as you've never had from watching a film when you sit down to look at Alain Resnais' "Last Year at Marienbad," a truly extraordinary French film, which opened at the Carnegie Hall Cinema last night.

It may grip you with a strange enchantment, it may twist your wits into a snarl, it may leave your mind and senses toddling vaguely in the regions in between. But this we can reasonably promise: when you stagger away from it, you will feel you have delighted in (or suffered) a unique and intense experience.

LAST YEAR AT MARIENBAD, screen play by Alain Robbe-Grillet; directed by Alain Resnais; a French-Italian co-production of Terra Films, Societe Nouvelle des Films Cormoran, Preceitel, Como-Films, Argos-Films Les Films Tamara, Cinetel, Silver-Films and Cineriz of Rome. Released by Astor Films. At the Carnegie Hall Cinema, Seventh Avenue and Fifty-seventh Street. Running time: ninety-three minutes.

The Woman.............Delphine Seyrig
The Stranger..........Giorgio Albertazzi
The Husband..............Sacha Pitoeff

and

Francoise Bertin	Wilhelm von Deek
Luce Garcia-Ville	Jean Lanier
Helena Kornel	Gerard Lorin
Francoise Spira	Davide Montemuri
Karin Toeche-Miltier	Gilles Queant
Pierre Barbaud	Gabriel Werner

And that, it appears, is precisely what M. Resnais means you to feel—the extreme and abnormal stimulation of a complete cinematic experience. For this is no usual movie drama that he is dishing up from a script of radical construction by Alain Robbe-Grillet. This is no lucid exposition of human behavior in terms of conventional dramatic situation, motivation and plot.

This is an eye-opening example of the use of the cinema device—the machinery of visual image-making, conjoined with musical sounds and the contrapuntal assistance of vocalized images and ideas—to excite the imagination as it might be excited by a lyrical poem or, better, by the tonal colorations and rhythms of a fine symphony.

To this observer's way of thinking (which we might as well recognize right now is going to be countered or challenged by others that may be just as good), it is not to be taken even as what it may seem to be—that is, a surrealistic picture of a romantic encounter between a man and a married woman, who meet at a European spa and drift into an affair that he cons her into believing began the previous year.

To our way of thinking and responding to the flow of sensuous stimuli, it is a web of complete imagination, a visualization of the thoughts, the mental associations, the wishes and fantasies that swirl through the mind of this fellow—the fellow conveying his dream to us—beneath the spell of an elegant palace that suggests all sorts of romantic things.

It suggests, as he walks us through it, looking at the decorated walls, the ballroom full of formal people, a stiff performance of Ibsen's "Rosmersholm," something of the cold, embalmed emotions that lived and died here in long-gone years. And as he picks up his married woman, his dream of love, and begins his pursuit, it suggests that time and emotions have no terminal points, that they whirl in fields of gravity surrounding material things and magnetize the sensitive people that come within these fields.

As a consequence of this concept, there is not time continuity in this film. The images change, jump, reverse, become fantastic, as the man continues his pursuit, pleading, reminiscing, always as in a desperate quest to escape the tension of loneliness, longing and desire. When he finally completes his persuasion and gets the woman to agree to go away with him, it is as though a stream of consciousness has ended its flow through a sea of memories.

The artfulness of this picture is in its brilliant photography, in black and white and (what is wondrous) on a radically wide screen; in its sumptuous setting and staging (most of it was shot in a palace and park near Munich); in its hypnotic rhythmical flow and in the radical use of actors almost as models within in the architectural frame.

Delphine Seyrig as the woman, Giorgio Albertazzi as the man (who also performs as narrator through the better part of the film) and Sacha Pitoëff as the husband walk through their roles eloquently, speak occasionally in slumberous intonations and use their eyes tellingly. Dozens of other handsome people, stylishly and impeccably dressed, surround them with a dazzling aura of the haut monde and haute couture.

Francis Seyrig's music, mostly for the organ, has a sad, lyrical quality, and the French narration is poetic. It is too bad that it cannot be spoken in English by a beautiful voice, so to free the eye from the English subtitles, which keep one glued to the bottom of the screen.

●

To be sure, this is not a picture in which a vital "message" is conveyed. It is a romantic excursion—or perhaps a serious sort of travesty on same. It is, in short, an experience, full of beauty and mood.

Take it thus and you should find it fascinating; try to make some sense of it—to discover some thread of proof or logic—and it is likely to drive you mad, like that clearly illogical match game that is played like a running gag through it.

Mr 8, 1962

THROUGH A GLASS DARKLY, written and directed by Ingmar Bergman; a Svensk Filmindustri presentation, distributed by Janus Films. At the Beekman Theatre, Sixty-fifth Street and Second Avenue. Running time: ninety-one minutes.
Karin ....Harriet Andersson
David ....Gunnar Bjornstrand
Martin ....Max von Sydow
Minus ....Lars Passgard

By BOSLEY CROWTHER

SWEDISH director Ingmar Bergman seems to be turning more and more into himself—or, at least, into a type of picture-making that economically packs a rather limited but powerful personal experience within a comparatively narrow frame. Such was his simple, impassioned and strongly moralistic "The Virgin Spring." And such is "Through a Glass Darkly," his latest import, which opened at the Beekman yesterday.

Here, in this tightly constructed and starkly realistic little film, which concentrates upon the experiences of our people on an isolated island in Sweden within a time span of twenty-four hours, Mr. Bergman is tensely exposing some aspects of shock and tragedy that evolve from the painful paroxysms of a young woman going mad.

That's it. That's all that happens. This young woman, who is the wife of one of the men, the daughter of another and the older sister of the third, is revealed as an incurable sufferer from schizophrenia. This is shortly after the picture begins with the return of the father from Switzerland for a little vacation with his family.

Each man reacts to this knowledge—or to this condition—in his own particular way. The father is silently shaken, yet moved with a curiosity of a seemingly callous nature because of his absorption as a novelist. The husband, himself a physician, is paralyzed with helplessness and grief. And the kid brother, unaware of the real disorder, is sexually stirred by his sister's restlessness.

As she goes through one phase of mental wandering and then into an episode with the lad, wherein she evidently (though not specifically) lures him into an incestuous act, the pathos and hopelessness of the situation assume fearful proportions. Then they burst in a horrifying display of violent madness and spiritual voiding that makes ones senses reel.

The conclusion is an exchange of conversation about God between father and son that, for all its solemn sound of deep simplicity, brings the curtain down with a hollow thud.

Like all—or most—of Mr. Bergman's pictures, this one may be dissected and scanned for profound implications and pregnant symbols of the loneliness and hunger of the human soul. Guidelines may be found in the frightened gropings and warped illusions of a dark, disordered mind to lead one to a harsher awareness of the tricks the mind can play upon man. Glints of the cruelty of obtuseness and the pathos of ignorance may be seen in the too-late solicitude of the father and the callowness of the brother toward this girl, this still sweet and virginal Ophelia, whose yearning for them has been stunted and befouled.

●

This and more may be drawn from the drama, if one has the inclination and the wits (and the psychological sensitivity) to feel around for it. Mr. Bergman has laid out the materials upon a narrow and forbidding plateau and has got some magnificent performers to give light and shadow to it.

Harriet Andersson is beautifully expressive of the haunting awareness, the agony of madness, that move the girl. In one scene, where she takes leave of her senses, she does a masterpiece of marbling her face. Through her, one sees the mysteries that move within the dark glass of the soul. They are barren and still mysterious, rootless and bewildering, but there they are.

Gunnar Bjornstrand is stolid as the father, a little pompous, a little gauche, but subtly communicative of a sense of guilt in a selfish man. Max von Sydow is gaunt and submissive as the husband who bids his love adieu, and young Lars Passgard is wild and baffled as the tormented boy.

●

They say that Mr. Bergman constructed his film in the form of a fugue, with Bach's Suite No. 2 in D Minor for Violoncello as its musical score. This sounds a bit pretentious. It has a simple, straight cinematic form, unifying a little tangle of experience within a modest frame. It may strike one as slight and disappointing alongside the intellectual magnitude of such as his film "The Seventh Seal." But it suggests a new mood of its author—introspective, troubled, cold. It seems to seek faith—and yet is without faith.

English subtitles are well provided for its Swedish dialogue.

Mr 14, 1962

VIRIDIANA, written and directed by Luis Bunuel; produced by Gustavo Alatriste and released by Kingsley International. At the Paris Theatre, 4 West Fifty-eighth Street. Running time: ninety minutes.
Jorge....................Francisco Rabal
Viridiana...................Silvia Pinal
Don Jaime................Fernando Rey
Ramona................Margarita Lozano
Lucia.....................Victoria Zinny
Rita.......................,....Teresa Rabal

By BOSLEY CROWTHER

LUIS BUNUEL is presenting a variation on an ancient theme in his new Spanish film, "Viridiana," which came to the Paris yesterday. The theme is that well-intended charity can often be badly misplaced by innocent, pious people. Therefore, beware of charity.

That is the obvious moral that forms in this grim and tumorous tale of a beautiful young religious novice who gets into an unholy mess when she gives up her holy calling to try to atone for a wrong she has done. But we strongly suspect that Señor Buñuel had more than this in mind when he made this intense and bitter picture, the first he's made in Spain in thirty years.

●

We sense all the way through this drama of the shocking education of this girl in the realities of passion and the grossness of most of mankind a stinging, unmerciful sarcasm directed at the piously insulated mind and a strong strain of guarded criticism of social conditions in Spain.

When his heroine, Viridiana, is violently and unhealthily repelled by the tendered affection of her uncle, who sees in her a perfect image of his long-dead wife, there is clearly implied recognition of the tangled libido of the girl and the pitiful confusion of 'the uncle in a bind of propriety, sentimentality and lust. That he hangs himself in remorse and anguish after the girl has fled reveals Señor Buñuel's recognition of the grotesqueness of the gentlemen's code.

And when the girl gives up her holy calling and returns to her dead uncle's farm with a rabble of derelicts and beggars to make amends for what she has done, there is stark evidence of his disgust at the pallid charitable gesture in the greed and meanness with which he has imbued these bums.

Señor Buñuel makes no bones about it. The most powerful stuff in his film are the macabre scenes of these people showing how vicious and contemptible they are. They snivel, cheat, steal, abuse one another, ostracize and brutalize one who has a foul disease and finally cut loose in a wild carouse that fairly wrecks the place. Played as a thundering obbligato to the milky generosity of the girl, these scenes carry the moralizing muscle and ironic punch of the film.

Following them, there is little more than drabness in

the evidence that the girl ends up playing cards and listening to rock 'n' roll music with her uncle's robust illegitimate son.

•

Whether Señor Buñuel means his picture as a reflection of all people or just the people of Spain is not clear nor, indeed, is it essential. It is an ugly, depressing view of life. And, to be frank about it, it is a little old-fashioned, too. His format is strangely literary; his symbols are obvious and blunt, such as the revulsion of the girl toward milking or the display of a penknife built into a crucifix. And there is something just a bit corny about having his bums doing their bacchanalian dance to the thunder of the "Hallelujah Chorus."

However, it is stringently directed and expertly played. Silvia Pinal is lovely and precisely as stiff and forbidding as she should be as the misguided novice. Fernando Ray makes the uncle a poignant dolt and Francisco Rabal is aggressive and realistic as the illegitimate son. Margarita Lozano does a good job as a cowed and inhibited maid and Teresa Rabal is lively as the latter's nosey child.

As usual in Señor Buñuel's pictures, the black-and-white photography is artful and true, and the English subtitles do politely by the sometimes coarse Spanish dialogue.

Mr 20, 1962

JULES AND JIM

By BOSLEY CROWTHER

FRANCOIS TRUFFAUT, the French director whose first film, "The 400 Blows," was a strong, sensitive study of a boy's rebellion (and a first powerful thrust of the French "new wave"), has come up with something quite different in his third film (his second to be shown here). He has come up with an arch and arty study of the perver-

sities of woman and the patience of man in this "Jules and Jim," which opened at the Guild yesterday.

At least, that is putting it as clearly as one can in a few well-chosen words—and almost as clearly as he does in a continual, complex, babbling flow of same. For not only is woman evasive and enigmatic in this film; M. Truffaut himself is quite as shifty and puzzling as its agile cinematist.

JULES AND JIM; screen play by Francois Truffaut and Jean Grualt, from a novel by Henri-Pierre Roche; produced and directed by M. Truffaut; a Janus Films release. At the Guild Theatre, Fiftieth Street and Avenue of the Americas. Running time: 105 minutes.
Catherine ....Jeanne Moreau
Jules ....Oskar Werner
Jim ....Henri Serre
Therese ....Marie Dubois
Gilberte ....Vanna Urbino
Sabine ....Sabine Haudepin
Albert ....Boris Bassiak
Birgitta ....Kate Noelle
Lucie ....Anny Nelsen
Helga ....Christiane Wagner

Taking his cue from a novel by Henri-Pierre Roché, who was in his seventies when he wrote it and therefore should have known whereof he wrote, Truffaut is endeavoring to express (and presumably let us know) what it's like when two happy fellows fall in love with one whimsical girl. To put it quickly and crisply, it is charming, exciting and sad.

He begins with a lively, spicy look-in on Paris around 1912 and upon the bachelor escapades of his two heroes, two young bohemians, Jules and Jim. They are cheerful, inseparable companions. Jules is German, Jim is French. They even find enjoyment in their casual exchanges of girls.

Then they meet a young woman who becomes more than a passing pal of theirs. She becomes, after certain gay frivolities, the focal point in their lives. And from here on, the text of the drama, as well as its character and tone, becomes reflective, philosophic, strangely resigned and sad.

For with the young woman's capricious marriage to Jules, there begins a long series of sexual and emotional adjustments among them that extend over a period of years. And it ends in a tragic occurence and a wistful resignation to life.

The fascination in M. Truffaut's telling of this curious relationship is not so much in the personal conflicts. They are deviously intellectualized —talked and talked over so deeply that they become academic and strangely sterile. It is in the involved and artful structure of the scenic elements and in the demonstrations of personalities.

●

Jeanne Moreau is as variable as a prism that gives off lights and glints as she puts into the role of the woman a bewitching evanescent quality. Oskar Werner gives a haunting presentation of the cerebral nature of Jules, and Henri Serre makes a vivid, melancholy and finally tragic figure of Jim. Little Sabine Haudepin is winning as the daughter of Jules, and Boris Bassiak is rather funny as a marginal lover.

Actually, the emotional content is largely carried in the musical score, which Georges Delerue has constructed as a dominant element in the film. It and the lengthy conversations and intrusions of a commentator's voice, which are translated in English subtitles that are tedious to read, impart to the film a perceptible aural character that is odd for a film of an artist as "cinematic" as M. Truffaut.

Ap 24, 1962

A TASTE OF HONEY

By A. H. WEILER

SHELAGH DELANEY'S "A Taste of Honey," which justifiably drew theatregoers like flies, to London and Broadway, is more memorable on film. The Brit-

ish-made drama, which was unveiled at the Paris Theatre yesterday, has been given specifically effective scope in the movie medium. Freed from the constricting confines of the stage, the shining honesty, the trials, the disenchantment of the drama's low-born Lancashire principals have become all the more striking and true. The dedicated producers have concocted a bitter "Honey" that is rare and travels well.

A TASTE OF HONEY; screen play by Shelagh Delaney and Tony Richardson; from the play by Miss Delaney; produced and directed by Mr. Richardson; a Woodfall Production presented here by Continental Distributing, Inc. At the Paris Theatre, 4 West Fifty-eighth Street. Running time: 100 minutes.
Jo .... Rita Tushingham
Helen .... Dora Bryan
Geoffrey .... Murray Melvin
Peter .... Robert Stephens
Jimmy .... Paul Danquah
Bert .... David Bolivar
Doris .... Maira Kaye
Shoe Shop Owner .... Herbert Smith
School Mistress .... Eunice Black
Nurse .... Rosalie Scase
Gladys .... Veronica Howard
Landlady .... Margo Cunningham

"A Taste of Honey" obviously is a labor of love. Tony Richardson, its producer-director, and Miss Delaney have been a team ever since it was staged here. Miss Delaney, it will be recalled, wrote the play when she was an astounding 19 years old, out of conviction and the perceptions of an artist. Mr. Richardson, no less an artist, treated the work with appreciation of a shining and unusual talent. The result is a fittingly unadorned, sometimes drab, vehicle freighted with meaning and compassion that is universal despite its seemingly restrictive locale.

●

They and their sensitive cast have cleaved to the original story and to Miss Delaney's wry style. "A Taste of Honey" was and is less of a formalized narrative than it is a restrained, circuitous manner of presenting moods and moments of living. As such, Miss Delaney's slice of life evolves whole and with impact. It bursts with vitality against the sleazy environs of a North Country city slum, its dirty flats, dank docksides and the kaleidoscopic sights and the raucous, tinny sounds of Blackpool's fun fairs.

Having evoked complementary drama from a variety of sites, Mr. Richardson collaborated with Miss Delaney to keep her original lines intact. Her wide-eyed but worldly wise teen-ager, who is constantly fighting loneliness and seeking affection she never gets from her man-chasing mother, meets an equally lonely Negro sailor and, after an idyllic interval, finds she is with child. After his tender departure for other ports, our heroine is a the more confused, frightened and unloved, especially when her brassy, roving mother marries a loud, free-spending type who plainly abhors the sight of the girl.

Since she is a resilent sort, she gives understanding and sanctuary to an effeminate youth from whom, for the first time, she receives tender care and tacit affection. But, as a realist, Miss Delaney finds life not only real and earnest but also hard. And, when childbirth is imminent, her mother, who has come to a parting of the ways with her spouse, returns to drive her delicate companion away. While she nominally takes up her maternal duties, a viewer is left with the idea that the daughter may yet be lonely and lovelorn.

As in the play, Miss Delaney is not compromising. One has the feeling that she chose abnormal characters to accent more forcefully society's indifference to its disenfranchised. They are neither angry nor lachrymose and they are, on occasion, a happy lot ready to laugh at themselves. Though they are involved in sordid circumstances, they manage to tug

at the heart without breaking it.

Call it fateful or a matter of professionalism, but Mr. Richardson has been fortunate in finding Rita Tushingham, a 19-year-old newcomer to films, to portray Jo, the daughter. A plain Jane, she uses her saucer-eyed visage subtly to convey the pains and joys of her predicament, and her North Country accents, which may confuse some, beautifully transmit her humor and her self-protective cynicism. Mr. Richardson had a hand in shaping her performance but she is, nevertheless, a wondrous discovery.

Murray Melvin, who is repeating the role of the homosexual he created in the British play, handles this difficult assignment in muted but effective fashion. Like Miss Tushingham he is flesh and blood and not a caricature. Dora Bryan, a veteran of stage and screen comedy, is equally real as the hard and footlose mother. Paul Danquah in his movie debut as the Negro sailor, is gentle and subtle in a small but demanding role and Robert Stephens is properly brash, vulgar and oafish as Miss Bryan's husband.

With the aid of Walter Lassally's expert camera work, which caught sooty, canal-lined Manchester exteriors, as well as grubby streets and happy, grubby, singing kids, Mr. Richardson and the company, who acted as though they lived there, have given a new dimension to an already sobering view of life among the lowly. In being transported out of the theatre, this "Honey" has been enriched.

My 1, 1962

SHOOT THE PIANO PLAYER

By BOSLEY CROWTHER

FRANCOIS TRUFFAUT, the French director who

showed in "The 400 Blows" that he had a rare talent for lacing pathos with slapstick comedy, pulled all the stops on that talent and let it run rampant when he made "Shoot the Piano Player," which arrived at the Fifth Avenue Cinema yesterday.

SHOOT THE PIANO PLAYER; screen play by Francois Truffaut; based on the novel "Down There" by David Goodis; directed by M. Truffaut; produced by Pierre Braunberger for Films de la Pleiade and presented by Astor Pictures, Inc. At the Fifth Avenue Cinema at Twelfth Street. Running time: ninety-two minutes.

Charlie Koller	Charles Aznavour
Lena	Marie du Bois
Theresa	Nicole Berger
Clarisse	Michele Mercier
Chico	Albert Remy
Richard	Jacques Aslanian
Fido	Richard Kanavan
Momo	Claude Mansard
Ernest	Daniel Boulanger
Plyne	Serge Davri
Lars Schmeel	Claude Heyman
Passerby	Alex Joffe

Nuttiness, pure and simple —nuttiness of the sort that has a surly kidnapper in a presumably serious scene swearing to something on the life of his mother, whereupon there's a cut to the mother dropping dead—surges and swirls through the tangle of solemn intimations in ·this film until one finds it hard to see or figure what M. Truffaut is about.

Evidently he is asking that the audience pay gentle heed to the significance of the old barroom legend, "Don't shoot the piano player; he is doing the best he can." For his hero is a small piano player in a noisome Parisian bar who turns out to be a poignant victim of fate and his own timidity.

●

This little ivory-tickler, played by Charles Aznavour with an almost Buster Keaton-like insistence on the eloquence of the dead pan, is more than a tired and pallid jangler of popular ragtime tunes. Oh, yes. He is a former concert pianist with a brilliant and glamorous past.

But for some unspecified reason he couldn't get along with his wife, who finally tells him she bought him his big chance with her virtue, and this dumps him into the bars.

Maybe, in this little fellow, M. Truffaut is trying to construct an arch example of a sentimental hero that he is subtly attempting to spoof. But if this is the case, why does he bear down on the little fellow's piety so hard and bring his serio-comic roughhouse to a mawkishly tearful end? Why does he scramble his satire with a madly melodramatic plot and have the little piano player kill a man in .defense of a girl?

It looks, from where we are sitting, ·as though M. Truffaut went haywire in this film, which he made as his second feature picture, following the great success of "The 400 Blows." It looks as though he had so many ideas for movie outpouring in his head, so many odd slants on comedy and drama and sheer clichés that he wanted to express, that he couldn't quite control his material, which he got form a novel by David Goodis called "Down There."

Else why would he switch so abruptly from desperately serious scenes and moods to bits of irrelevant nonsense or blatant caricature? Why would he let Nicole Berger play a lengthy, heart-breaking scene in which she boldly explains to her husband how she was unfaithful to him, them turn around a few minutes later and put two gangsters through a frolic of farce?

●

It is a teasing and frequently amusing (or moving) film that M. Truffaut has made, but it simply does not hang together. It does not find a sufficiently firm line, even one of calculated spoof or mischief, on which to hang and thus be saved.

M. Aznavour is touching as the hero, when he is supposed to be, but his character is much too shallow and vagrant for substantiality. Marie du Bois is appealing as a young barmaid who tries to help him out, and Mlle. Berger is excellent in her brief role as his flashback wife. Several other fellows overact in various roles. The English subtitles do bare justice to the lusty colloquial· French.

Jl 24, 1962

YOJIMBO, screenplay by Ryuzo Kiku-shima and Akira Kurosawa; directed and produced by Mr. Kurosawa for Toho Company, Ltd. Distributed by Seneca International, Ltd. At the Carnegie Hall Cinema, Seventh Avenue at 56th Street. Running time: 75 minutes.

Sanjuro	Toshiro Mifune
Gonji	Eijiro Tono
Seibei	Seizaburo Kawazu
Orin, his wife	Isuzu Yamada
Yoichiro	Hiroshi Tachikawa
Nosuke	Tatsuya Nakadai
Ushi-Tora	Kyu Sazanka
Ino	Daisuke Kato
Sukasa	Kamatari Fujiwara
Kuemon	Takashi Shimura
Hansuke	Ikio Sawamura

By BOSLEY CROWTHER

AKIRA KUROSAWA'S obvious taste for American Western films, manifested most clearly in his "Magnificent Seven" (known in Japan as "Seven Samurai"), is evident again in his "Yojimbo," which opened yesterday at the Carnegie Hall Cinema. Underneath its Japanese kimonos lurk the aspects of a "High Noon" or "Shane."

Consider simply its story. A jobless and vagrant samurai (a mercenary or sword fighter) comes into a 19th-century Japanese town where two lawless and vicious factions are battling for control. He goes to the local tavern, orders sake (counterpart for "red eye"), gets briefed on the local situation and offers his sword for hire. He will work as a bodyguard (yojimbo) for the side that makes the better bid.

This leads to considerable contention. Both sides are suspicious of him, yet neither wants the other to get him because he is so fast and powerful on the draw. There's a good deal of back-and-forth jockeying, in which the awesome samurai (who is really a peace-loving fellow) works the factions into a stand-off spot.

Then into town charges the brother of the leader of one of the gangs. He is a wicked and reckless young fellow, and he brandishes a Colt .45. This changes the situation. Swords would appear obsolete. The power of the old sword fighter would appear irrevocably doomed.

And it is—for a while. Caught off guard in the performance of a sentimental act, he is beaten up by the henchmen of the gunman and presumably rendered null and void. But he crawls into a hideout, slowly gets back his strength and finally sallies forth to challenge the gunman, sword (and heroism) versus gun. He meets him and faces off with him, right out in the middle of the windy, empty street. Needless to say, the old sword fighter—all canniness and heroism—wins.

As he leaves, with the warring factions scattered and himself in a mood of disgust, he remarks (according to the English subtitle), "Now it will be quiet in this town."

So help us, that is the melodrama that occurs in this Japanese film—and we leave you reckon how closely it reflects the historical and cultural features of Japan. It is, beyond any question, a straight transposition of Western film clichés, which in turn may be dubious reflections of the historical and cultural truth of our frontier. Still, they stem from our tradition, not that of the Japanese.

But despite the sometime

appearance of the whole thing as a forthright travesty, it does have stretches of excitement and cinematic power. Kurosawa is a master director. He can work up a melodramatic scene, such as that final street fight (as in "High Noon" or "Red River"), so that it gets you, kimonos and all. Or he can catch a close-up of his hero's battered face in a deep shadow, with one good eye lit by a beam of light that fires it with invincible savage defiance.

Also, Toshiro Mifune, who plays the leading role, is always an interesting actor, commanding and apt at imaging strain. He passes well in this picture for a Japanese Gary Cooper or John Wayne. Tatsuya Nakadai plays the fellow with the gun in broad, wild style, and Seizaburo Kawazu is knotty as the leader of one of the gangs.

However, as in most Westerns, the dramatic penetration is not deep, and the plot complications are many and hard to follow in Japanese. Kurosawa is here showing more virtuosity than strength. "Yojimbo" is a long way (in the wrong direction) from his brilliant "Rashomon."

O 16, 1962

LAWRENCE OF ARABIA. Original screen play by Robert Bolt; directed by David Lean. / Sam Spiegel Production for Columbia Pictures At the Criterion. Running time 220 minutes. Running time 220 minutes.

Lawrence	Peter O'Toole
Prince Feisal	Alex Guinness
Auda Abu Tayi	Anthony Quinn
General Allenby	Jack Hawkins
Turkish Bey	Jose Ferrer
Colonel Brighton	Anthony Quayle
Mr. Dryden	Claude Rains
Jackson Bentley	Arthur Kennedy
General Murray	Donald Wolfit
Sherif Ali	Omar Sharif
Gasim	I. S. Johar
Majid	Gamil Ratib
Farraj	Michael Ray

By BOSLEY CROWTHER

Special to The New York Times.

NEW YORK.

Like the desert itself, in which most of the action in "Lawrence of Arabia" takes place, this much - heralded film about the famous British soldier-adventurer, which opened last night at the Criterion, is vast, awe-inspiring, beautiful with ever-changing hues, exhausting and barren of humanity.

It is such a laboriously large conveyance of eye-filling outdoor spectacle—such as brilliant display of endless desert and camels and Arabs and sheiks and skirmishes with Turks and explosions and arguments with British military men—that the possibly human, moving T. E. Lawrence is lost in it. We know little more about this strange man when it is over than we did when it begins.

Sure, a lean, eager, diffident sort of fellow, played by blue-eyed Peter O'Toole, a handsome new British actor, goes methodically over the ground of Lawrence's major exploits as a guerrilla leader of Arab tribesmen during World War I. He earnestly enters the desert, organizes the tribes as a force against the Turks for the British, envisions Arab unity and then becomes oddly disillusioned as the politicians move in.

Why Lawrence had a disposition to join the Arab tribes, and what caused his streak sadism, is barely hinted in the film. The inner mystery of the man remains lodged behind the splendid burnoosed figure and the wistful blue eyes of Mr. O'Toole.

The fault seems to lie, first in the concept of telling the story of this self-tortured man against a background of action that has the characteristic of a mammoth Western film. The nature of Lawrence cannot be captured in grand Super-Panavision shots of sunrise on the desert or in scenes of him arguing with a shrewd old British general in a massive Moorish hall.

The fault is also in the

lengthy but surprisingly lusterless dialogue of Robert Bolt's over-written screenplay. Seldom has so little been said in so many words. There are some great things in the picture—which runs, incidentally, for 3 hours and 40 minutes, not counting intermission. There is some magnificent scenery, barbaric fights, a mirage in the desert that is superb (the one episode in the picture that conveys a sense of mystery). And there are some impressive presentations of historic characters.

Alex Guinness as the cagey Prince Feisal, Anthony Quinn as a fierce chief, Omar Sharif as a handsome Arab fighter and Jack Hawkins as General Allenby stand out in a large cast that is ordered into sturdy masculine ranks by David Lean.

But, sadly, this bold Sam Spiegel picture lacks the personal magnetism, the haunting strain of mysticism and poetry that we've been thinking all these years would be dominant when a film about Lawrence the mystic and the poet was made. It reduces a legendary figure to conventional movie-hero size amidst magnificent and exotic scenery but a conventional lot of action-film cliches.

It is, in the last analysis, just a huge, thundering camel-opera that tends to run down rather badly as it rolls on into its third hour and gets involved with sullen disillusion and political deceit.

D 17, 1962

ECLIPSE, Story and Screenplay by Michaelangelo Antonioni and Tinino Guerra, Directed by Victor Antanioni; Produced by Robert and Raymond Hakim, for Times Film Release. At the Little Carnegie, West 57th Street, and the Murray Hill, 34th Street at Third Avenue. Running time: 123 minutes.
Piero....................... Alain Delon
Vittoria.................... Monica Vitti
Ricardo................. Francisco Rabal
Vittoria's Mother.......... Lilla Brignone
Stockbroker................ Louis Seigner
Anita..................... Rassana Rory
Marta................... Mirella Ricciardi

By BOSLEY CROWTHER

Special to The New York Times.

NEW YORK.
Another of those capricious women of the sort that has preoccupied the Italian director Michelangelo Antonioni, in his previous films, "L'Avventura" and "The Night," is the fidgety focus of attention in his new Italian film, "Eclipse," which arrived yesterday at the Little Carnegie and the Murray Hill Theaters. And again the capricious creature is played by Monica Vitti, the gawky blonde who also played human enigmas in those previous Antonioni films.

But this time, thank heaven, the disturbance of the haggard heroine is not so dense as it was in those other pictures, nor is the cinematic quality so vague. Here she is simply a young woman who is sadly breaking off a love affair with a baffled man at the beginning, because, as slowly comes clear as the essential revelation of the drama, she is a timid, introverted, cautious girl.

●

She is fearful of complications, suspicious of the greed and lust of men, perhaps distrustful of her own emotions and a little bored with the frantic modern world. She finds relaxation and refreshment by walking among the pines of Rome at dawn, by playing at being an African native or flying high above the Euganean hills in a plane. Thus she is ultra-cautious, even cold, when she meets a young man who is thoroughly involved as a stockbroker on the floor of the Rome stock exchange. She resents and resists his mild advances, but, as she sees him more and more, she finds herself warming to him as he warms and relaxes toward her.

That's all there is to the drama—a prolonged detailed illustration of the moody surrender of the woman to a rare and elusive love. This takes, for its full illumination, a few minutes over two hours.

But Antonioni is so selective and sensitive with his use of camera, so deft in catching intonations of emotional flux and flow in the graphic relations of individuals to the vividly passing scene, that what might be slow and tedious as a cinematic style actually turns out quite fascinating in his skillful command of it.

●

For instance, what first seems a redundant contemplation of frenzy on the stock exchange during a big break in the market becomes pervasive and apt as it goes on, rising in noisiness and tempo. It is hypnotic, frightening, and serves to establish a pinnacle of animalistic madness from which to descend to softer, truer personal moods.

Alain Delon, the handsome actor who was in "Rocco and his Brothers" and "Purple Noon," complements Miss Vitti's sullen nature with a springy, sassy attitude that slides into a gentle disposition as he, too, is softened by love. Lilla Brignone is thoroughly lacking as the market-mad mother of the girl, and Louis Seigner is laconic as an old stock exchange man.

The virtual orchestration of graphic detail that Antonioni has managed here, the interesting blend of the human idea with pictorial chic, is affectingly complemented by an excellent musical score. Adequate English sub-titles take care of the Italian dialogue.

D 21, 1962

PICKPOCKET, screenplay by Robert Bresson. Directed by Mr. Bresson and produced by Agnes Delahaye. Released by Agnes Delahaye. At the New Yorker Theater, Broadway and 88th Street. Running time: 75 minutes.
Michel .... Martin La Salle
Jeanne .... Marika Green
Chief Detective ....Jean Pelegri
Mother .... Dolly Scal
Jacques .... Pierre Leymarie
First Accomplice .. .. Kassagi
Second Accomplice .... Pierre Etaix
Detective ....Cesar Gattegne

By BOSLEY CROWTHER

IN line with its chivalrous policy of occasionally programing foreign films that have gained distinction in their own countries but have failed to get distribution in the United States, the uptown New Yorker Theater is showing "Pickpocket." The 1959 French film was made by Robert Bresson, best known for his "Diary of a Country Priest."

Ten minutes with this slow and cryptic study of the movements of a young compulsive thief will give you a pretty good idea of why no distributor over here has wanted to try to push it.

It is clearly an esoteric effort. Coldly objective and remote, it observes in studious detail the goings and comings of this young man and his technique of lifting wallets and committing other personal-contact thefts. There are painfully shy and taut encounters with a young woman whom, it suddenly turns out, he loves.

It is a difficult film to follow—so inexpressive, detached and devoid of acknowledged emotion and dramatic emphasis. Its hero is played flatly by Martin La Salle. His ultimate arrival at the realization that he loves the girl (Marika Green), an equally colorless creature, comes as a mild surprise.

But the camera work is exquisite. Mr. Bresson has a sharply graphic style well worth the study of film fans. And the picture has a moral:

Keep your hand on your wallet. Those pickpockets work like worms in crowds.

My 22, 1963

HUD, screenplay by Irving Ravetch and Harriet Frank Jr., adapted from a novel by Larry McMurty. Directed by Martin Ritt and produced by Mr. Ritt and Mr. Ravetch. A Paramount Pictures release. At the Paramount Theater, Broadway and 43d Street, and the Coronet Theater, Third Avenue and 59th Street. Running time: 112 minutes.

Hud Bannon	Paul Newman
Homer Bannon	Melvyn Douglas
Alma	Patricia Neal
Lon Bannon	Brandon de Wilde
Hermy	John Ashley
Burris	Whit Bissell
Jesse	Crahan Denton
Jose	Val Avery
Thompson	Sheldon Allman
Larker	Pitt Herbert
George	Peter Brooks
Truman Peters	Curt Conway
Lily Peters	Yvette Vickers
Joe Scanlon	George Petrie

By BOSLEY CROWTHER

ANY film with a title as cryptic and ugly-sounding as "Hud" better have more to recommend it than its name. So, take it from me, "Hud," which came to the Paramount and the Coronet yesterday, does have more—so much more, in every aspect—that it shapes up now as this year's most powerful film.

This is a daring endorsement for a picture in which the principal character is a heel and the setting is the Texas cow country that we've seen a thousand times (or more) in films. But the heel in this instance is different. He's more than a stock Western brute, banging the bar for red-eye and sneaking out to steal cattle in the dark.

This heel, named Hud, is a rancher who is fully and foully diseased with all the germs of materialism that are infecting and sickening modern man. He is a nineteen-sixties specimen of the I'm-gonna-get-mine breed—the selfish, snarling smoothie who doesn't give a hoot for anyone else.

And the place where he lives is not just Texas. It is the whole of our country today. It is the soil in which grows a gimcrack culture that nurtures indulgence and greed.

●

Here is the essence of this picture, which Martin Ritt and Irving Ravetch have produced, and Mr. Ritt has directed in a powerfully realistic style. While it looks like a modern Western, and is an outdoor drama, indeed, "Hud" is as wide and profound a contemplation of the human condition as one of the New England plays of Eugene O'Neill.

As a matter of fact, the structure of it is close to the spare and simple lines of one of those great O'Neill dramas —say, "Desire Under the Elms." For the human elements are simply Hud, the focal character, with his aging father, a firm and high-principled cattleman, on one hand, and Hud's 17-year-old nephew, a still-growing and impressionable boy, on the other. The conflict is simply a matter of determining which older man will inspire the boy. Will it be the grandfather with his fine traditions or the uncle with his crudities and greed?

It would not be proper to tell which influence prevails. Nor is that answer essential to the clarification of this film. The striking, important thing about it is the clarity with which it unreels. The sureness and integrity of it are as crystal-clear as the plot is spare.

Mr. Ritt, working from an excellent screenplay that Mr. Ravetch and Harriet Frank Jr. wrote from a novel by Larry McMurty, has caught the whole raw-boned atmosphere of a land and environment lying between nature and cheap urbanity, between the vastness of yesterday's open country and the closeness' of the claptrap of tomorrow. And with a fine cast of performers, he has people who behave and talk so truly that it is hard to shake them out of your mind.

Paul Newman as Hud is tremendous—a potent, voracious man, restless with all his crude ambitions, arrogant with his contempt and churned up inside with all the meanness and misgivings of himself.

And Melvyn Douglas is magnificent as the aging cattleman who finds his own son an abomination and disgrace to his country and home. It is Mr. Douglas's performance in the great key scene of the film, a scene in which his entire herd of cattle is deliberately and dutifully destroyed at the order of government agents because it is infected with foot-and-mouth disease, that helps fill the screen with an emotion that I've seldom felt from any film. It brings the theme of infection and destruction into focus with dazzling clarity.

•

As the young fellow, Brandon de Wilde is eloquent of clean, modern youth—naïve, sensitive, stalwart, wanting so much to be grown-up. And Patricia Neal is brilliant as the lonely housekeeper for these men. She is a rangy, hard-bitten slattern with a heart and a dignity of her own.

There is also much else that is excellent: the camerawork of James Wong Howe, the poignant musical score of Elmer Bernstein, the insinuating use of natural sounds. They merge in an achievement that should be honored as a whole.

In spite of the title, "Hud' has it. That's all you have to know.

My 29, 1963

8½--screenplay by Federico Fellini, Tullio Pinelli, Ennio Flaiano and Brunello Rondi; directed by Mr. Fellini and produced by Angelo Rizzoli. A Joseph E. Levine Presentation for Embassy Pictures release. At the Festival Theater, Fifth Avenue and 57th Street and the Embassy, Seventh Avenue at 46th Street. Running time: 135 minutes.
Guido Anselmi......Marcello Mastroianni
Claudia ....Claudia Cardinale
The Dream Girl ......Claudia Cardinale
Luisa Anselmi ....Anouk Aimee
Carla ....Sandra Milo
Rosella ....Rosella Falk
Gloria Morin ....Barbara Steele
The Producer ....Guido Alberti
An Actress ....Madeleine Lebeau
The Writer ....Jean Rougeul
Fashionable Woman .....Caterina Boratto
Father ....Annibale Ninchi
Mother ....Giuditta Rissone
The Mind-Reader ....Jan Dallas
La Saraghina ....Edra Gale
Aging Dancer .....:.Jacqueline Bonbon
Producer's Girl Friend ...Annie Gorassini
The Cardinal ....Tito Masini
The Journalist ....Eugene Walter
Journalist's Wife ....Gilda Dahlberg
The Model ....Hedy Vessel
Airline Hostess ....Nadine Sanders
Grandmother ....Georgia Simmons
Negro Dancer ....Hazel Rogers
Guido as a Farm Boy .Riccardo Guglielmi
Guido as a Schoolboy ....Marco Gemini

By BOSLEY CROWTHER

IF you thought Federico Fellini's "La Dolce Vita," was a hard-to-fathom film, random and inconclusive, wait until you see "8½," his latest.

It opened yesterday at the handsome new Festival Theater, on 57th Street West of Fifth Avenue, and at the Embassy on Seventh Avenue and 46th Street.

Here is a piece of entertainment that will really make you sit up straight and think, a movie endowed with the challenge of a fascinating intellectual game. It has no more plot than a horse race, no more order than a pinball machine, and it bounces around on several levels of consciousness, dreams and memories as it details a man's rather casual psychoanalysis of himself. But it sets up a labyrinthine ego for the daring and thoughtful to explore, and it harbors some elegant treasures of wit and satire along the way.

Cannily, Mr. Fellini has chosen a character he knows as the subject of his introspection. He has chosen a director of films. A person familiar with his nature might even suspect it is Mr. Fellini himself. And he has planted this character in a milieu of luxury and toil he knows so well that you sense that every detail of the canvas must be wrenched from his own experience.

The picture begins with this fellow sitting trapped in his car in a traffic jam, immobilized among a crowd of zombies that might be dead souls crossing the River Styx. Suddenly suffocating, he struggles wildly to be released. And the next thing —he's floating upward, out of the traffic jam and above a beach, where he is magically hauled back earthward by a kite-string tied to his leg.

Thus does Mr. Fellini notify us right away that he has embarked on a fanciful excursion with a man who has barely escaped death. By the obvious implications of his pictorial imagery this would be the only release from the stagnation and deadness he feels himself to be in.

Now the fellow comes to in bed in a luxurious health-resort hotel, attended by truculent physicians, needled by a nurse (who asks if she may borrow his typewriter) and watched by a hawk-like little man who turns out to be a script writer waiting to go to work with him. Reality is re-established. We are among the living now.

But not for long. And, indeed, there is some question as to whether Mr. Fellini sees the old and antiquated people he parades at this health resort as actually living creatures. May not they, too, be dead and decayed, the relics and shells of a society that is struggling feebly and ironically to regain its health?

Anyhow, it is in this environment that the fellow, who is now identified as a famous movie director, tried to apply himself to preparing a new movie, while his mistress comes to stay nearby and swarms of idlers and job hunters persistently keep after him.

But, alas, he cannot get going. He is full of anxieties, doubts and disbelief in the value of movies. And, in this uncertain state, his mind takes to wandering off in memories and building fantasies.

He sees himself in his childhood. He visions painful experiences with priests. He goes from actual encounters with his mistress to recollections of his education in sex. The present, the past and wishful thinking are wryly and poignantly blurred. (Last year we were at Marienbad, remember? Well, we're at Montecatini or some such place this year!)

However, Mr. Fellini does give us sufficient clues to the nature and problems of his fellow to lead us to understand—that is, if we have the patience and the prescience. And what we discover (at least, I do) is an outrageous egotist, a man of supreme romantic notions with a charmingly casual conceit, who has been attended and spoiled by women ever since he was a tot.

One of the most delightful fabrications is a wild and robust fantasy in which the director sees himself as the master of a harem of all the women he has known (or desired) ordering them to do his bidding, slapping them with a whip, receiving their utter adulation in a state of complete harmony. And this is an adult variation of one of his cozy childhood memories.

Mr. Fellini has managed to compress so much drollery and wit, so much satire on social aberrations, so much sardonic comment on sex and, indeed, when you come right down to it, even a bit of a travesty of Freud, that it pains me to note that he hasn't thought his film through to a valid end.

He has his erratic hero, whom Marcello Mastroianni plays in a beautifully bored and baffled fashion, suddenly become aware that the trouble with him is that he has always taken but never given love. And when he grasps this, he is able to get all the people he knows to join hands and get ready to make a fine movie on the set of a rocket launching pad.

This is a romantic side-step — as romantic as the whole film, the title of which, incidentally, means simply Mr. Fellini's Opus 8½. (This is his seventh full-length film; he has also made three shorts.) And it leaves an uncomfortable feeling of letdown at the end.

But this is, in large part, compensated by much that is wonderful — by Mr. Fellini's tremendous pictorial poetry, his intimations of pathos and longing, his skill with the silly and grotesque; by some splendid and charming performing—Sandra Milo as the mistress (she's a doll!), Guido Alberti as a producer, Anouk Aimée as the director's jealous wife, Claudia Cardinale as a "dream girl" and many, many more. There is also another delicious Nino Rota musical score.

So if Mr. Fellini has not produced another masterpiece —another all-powerful exposure of Italy's ironic sweet life — he has made a stimulating contemplation of what might be called, with equal irony, a sweet guy.

The English subtitles are good ones, but they miss the total substance of the Italian dialogue.

Je 26, 1963

THE LEOPARD

By BOSLEY CROWTHER

THE film that Luchino Visconti and his star, Burt Lancaster, have made from Giuseppe di Lampedusa's fine novel "The Leopard" is a stunning visualization of a mood of melancholy and nostalgia at the passing of an age.

THE LEOPARD, screenplay by Suso Cecchi D'Amico, Pasquale Festa Campanile, Masssimo Francojsa, Enrico Medioli and Luchino Visconti; directed by Mr. Visconti; produced by Goffredo Lombardo for Titanus Productions and released by 20th Century-Fox. At the Plaza, 42 East 58th Street. Running time: 160 minutes.
Prince Don Fabrizio
  Salina (The Leopard) Burt Lancaster
Tancredi .... Alain Delon
Angelica Sedara ..... Claudia Cardinale
Princess Maria Stella ..... Rina Morelli
Don Calogero Sedara ..... Paolo Stoppa
Father Pironne .... Romolo Valli
Concetta .... Lucilla Morlacchi
Don Ciccio Tumeo ...... Serge Reggiani
Carolina .... Ida Galli
Caterina .... Ottavia Piccolo
Count Cavriaghi .... Mario Girotti
Cavalier Chevally .... Leslie French
Colonel Pallavicino .... Ivo Gerrani
Francesco Paolo ...... Pierro Clementi
Paolo .... Carlo Valenzano
Mlle. Dombreuil .... Annamaria Bottini

Sentiment and sadness whisper through it like the soft Mediterranean breeze tha flutters the curtains in the windows of the palace in the stark Sicilian hills, on the outskirts of Palermo, as the unhurried story begins. They waft through the slow and stately tableaux of incidents in the stilted, baroque life of a noble Sicilian family in the mid-19th century.

They even rustle in the laughter of young people who are the inheritors of the change that the Risorgimento of Garibaldi is allegedly bringing to the land. And they hang like a softly soaking vapor over the great, gaudy end-of-an-era ball that takes up the last 40 minutes of this 2 hour and 40 minute film.

For the one thing that Mr. Visconti has been able to do magnificently — and it's the only thing I imagine he figured he could possibly do with the shimmering, atmospheric material of Mr. di Lampedusa's book—is translate in terms of brilliant pictures, almost like paintings, the autumnal mood of change and decay that the onrush of social revolution brought to one family and to the spirits of one strong man.

Faithful to the contours of the novel, he hasn't attempted to intrude into this handsome color picture, which opened at the Plaza last night, any more sense of the melodrama of Garibaldi's conquest of Sicily than a few lurid shots of fiery Redshirts fighting Bourbons in the narrow Palermo streets. Neither have he and his scenarists told us any more about the nature of the Risorgimento than simply that it freed and elevated a middle class.

All that he gives us in this picture in the way of plot and dramatic clash are loose suggestion of the personal accommodations to the pressures of the revolution that the Prince and his family have mild confrontations of the Prince with members of the middle class. And since the supreme accommodation is to accept the marriage of a nephew with a girl of the bourgeoise who is both beautiful and wealthy, the hardship does not appear great.

But the quality of the presentation is not in a running display of plotted, emotional crises. It is in a slow, rhythmic, tempered account of the yielding of the Prince to changes that he realizes are inevitable, but perhaps not as gracious as he would have them, and that is why he is sad.

It is in the superb illustration of a special way of life, elaborate and luxurious, but confined by rigid restraints, surrounded by lush decoration but internally cramped and dour. And it is in the interesting suggestions of the nature of the Prince, the soi-disant Leopard of the title, played by Mr. Lancaster.

Got up in side-burns and tail coats, plug hats and canes, the American star gives a physically forceful presentation of the massive, imperious man whom the mood of melancholy descends most heavily at the ball. He is mighty in moments of anger, harsh in his sarcastic bursts and amazingly soft and sympathetic when the call is for tenderness.

But unfortunately Mr. Lancaster does have that blunt American voice that lacks the least suggestion of being Sicilian in the English-dialogue version shown here. And either the role lacks the humor—the gentle irony—of di Lampedusa's Prince or Mr. Lancaster does not get it, which is a most regrettable miss.

Alain Delon is also handsome and physically correct as the Prince's high-spirited nephew, but there isn't enough body in the role, not enough self-assertion, to make it truly meaningful. And the American voice that speaks for him is not appropriate.

As for Claudia Cardinale in the role of the bourgeoise girl this young man choses to marry, she is strangely, almost grotesquely made-up to look and act like a gypsy in the earlier scenes, and in the later she is rendered so stylish and compelled to act so subdued that a curiously uneven character and social significance come from her.

Paolo Stoppa as her father, the crude, pushy mayor of a Sicilian town, is unmistakably vulgar, however, and Romolo Valli as the Prince's personal priest and Serge Regianni as a small-town traditionalist have the proper air of minor snobs. Lucilla Morlacchi as the Prince's daughter, Rina Morelli as his wife and Mario Girotti as an aristocratic suitor blend perfectly with the atmosphere.

For the most part, Nino Rota's music provides a rich melodic surrounding for the pictorial magnificence, and a heretofore unknown Verdi waltz that is played at the

ball at the finish appropriately supplements this remarkably vivid, panoramic and
eventually morbid show.

I just wonder how much
Americans will know or care
about what's going on, how
much we will yield to a nostalgia very similar to that in
"Gone With the Wind."

Ag 13, 1963

MY LIFE TO LIVE, screenplay in 12
episodes, written and directed by Jean-
Luc Godard and produced by Pierre
Braunberger. A Union Films release
presented by Pathe Cinema Corporation. At the Paris Theater, 4 West
58th Street. Running time: 85 minutes.

Nana ....Anna Karina
Raoul ....Saddy Rebbot
Paul ....Andre Labartre
Yvette ....Giselle Schlumberger
The Cook...............Gerard Hoffman
Elizabeth ....Monique Messine
A Journalist.................Paul Favel
A Youth..................Dimitri Dineff
A Young Man..........Peter Kassowitz
Luigi ....E. Schlumberger
The Philosopher............Brice Parain

By BOSLEY CROWTHER

JEAN-LUC Godard, who
made "Breathless," that
sordid French film in which
he got across a curious, offbeat comprehension of the
degradation of a young Parisian punk, is at it again, only
more so, in his new film, "My
Life to Live" ("Vivre Sa
Vie"), which opened at the
Paris yesterday.

Where he was more or less
conventional in his narrative
approach in the former film
—that is to say, he followed
a fairly clear line in a strange
erratic style—he has chosen
to be completely offbeat in
the method and structure of
this tale of the far from happy experiences of a young
Parisian prostitute.

The simplest way to de-
scribe it is as a simulated
documentary film, recounting
in episodic sections the decline and fall of a pretty,
shallow girl.

Each section is introduced
with a title, such as "2 - The
record shop - 2,000 francs -
Nana lives her day" or "5 -
On the street - the first client

- the room." And the point of
view of the camera is objective and reportorial through
out. In a sense, this might be
regarded as a social worker's
case report.

•

Indeed, in one section, the
narrative purpose is pursued
in a question-and-answer
stunt, with the voice of the
girl on the soundtrack asking her procurer how to go
about her work and the voice
of the procurer telling her in
detail, very professionally,
while the pictures on the
screen are a montage of shots
of the girl doing as she is
told. Significantly, these
glimpses, while candid and
sordid as screen material, are
not erotic or lascivious. They
have an ugly, repulsive look.

Thus it is evident that Mr.
Godard did not intend this
film to be a glamorization of
the life of the prostitute. Evidently his intention is to
catch in a novel, forthright
way an external sense of the
aloneness, inadequacy and
pathos of the girl.

And he has oddly intruded
techniques and details that
seem aimed toward this end
—to involve the viewer with
the girl's emotions without
visually describing them.
Thus the opening scene of the
the picture finds the girl sitting
on a bar stool with her back
to the camera, talking to a
friend (who also has his back
to the camera), with whom
she is ending a love affair.

The scene, lasting several
minutes, is shot entirely that
way, with only an occasional
glimpse of the girl's face in
the mirror. This is strictly an
outsider's view of what is obviously a crucial personal experience.

Or to give an objective understanding of how the in-
cipient streetwalker feels
when she goes to see a movie,
which appears to be the
classic "Passion of Joan of
Arc," Mr. Godard simply
shows several minutes of this

tormenting intimate film, then he cuts to a close-up of his girl's face, with tears in her eyes, at the end. The intention of this juxtaposition is theoretically good.

●

Yet, somehow, it isn't very effective, and that's how it is through the film. The girl, played by Anna Karina (who is Mr. Godard's wife) with a delicate grace and luminescence that he thoroughly captures in a succession of close shots—shots in which the camera moves all around her head—never emerges as much more than an amiable, stupid, helpless thing preyed upon by a standard procurer, whom Saddy Rebbot plays standardly.

And the tedious devices of suggesting some spiritual hunger by having her listen to a young man read pages from Edgar Allan Poe or talk for several minutes, merely talk, to an old philosopher, do little but slow the picture from reaching a meledramatic end.

Mr. Godard is a bold experimenter, but it's time he picked himself a stronger theme.

The usual English subtitles do fairly well by the French dialogue.

S 24, 1963

KNIFE IN THE WATER, screenplay by Roman Polanski, Jerzy Skolimowski and Jakub Goldberg; directed by Mr. Polanski; produced by Kamera Unit of Film Polski; released by Kanawha Films, Ltd. At the Beekman Theater, Second Avenue and 65th Street. Running time: 95 minutes.

Andrzej .... Leon Niemczyk
Christine .... Jolanta Umecka
The Young Man..... Zygmunt Malanowicz

By BOSLEY CROWTHER

THE odd sort of personal hostility that smolders in many men who have trouble asserting their egos in this complex modern world is casually, cryptically and even comically dissected by the probing camera of Roman Polanski in his "Knife in the Water," which opened at the Beekman yesterday.

This strange little film from Poland, which was one of the more popular among the 21 multi-national features shown at the First New York Film Festival last month, is the first of that lot of offbeat pictures to be presented commercially here. And it eminently justifies the interest in its acid contents and in the techniques of its young director that it stirred.

●

Using his naturalistic camera as though it were an outsized microscope set up to observe the odd behavior of three people completely isolated for 24 hours aboard a weekend pleasure boat, Mr. Polanski evolves a cryptic drama that has wry humor, a thread of suspense, a dash of ugly and corruscating evil — and also a measure of tedium because of the purposeful monotony of its pace.

What he has done, as co-author as well as director, is merely place these people— an edgy, snarling husband, his cool and calmly critical wife and a surly and sassy young hitchhiker whom they have picked up en route to their boat — within the controlled confinement of a trim little sailing sloop and there has them work out their aggressions and their sly sexual rivalries.

From their first harsh exchange of hostilities as they almost collide on the road, the husband and his virtually shanghaied passenger casually taunt each other and contend to show their superior skills and prowess, while the smirking wife silently observes. The husband vaunts himself as a sailor and mocks the clumsiness of the youth; the latter shows off his agility with a murderous switchblade knife.

Comical and trifling at the outset, these rivalries between the two men appear to be no more consequential than the jostling of two hostile kids, daring one another to step over a line. And the casual goings and comings of the pretty young wife about the boat, innocently but very seductively patched in a two-piece bathing suit, appear no more pertinent to the wrangling than the picnic lunch she serves.

But Mr. Polanski is sneaky. In carefully guarded ways, he has the competition become more vicious, the distraction of the woman more intense, until suddenly he has a situation where hostilities flare into hate and the two men vie with each other in a series of water shenanigans that thinly veil their lethal inclinations and the hideous possibilities of death.

In this situation, he flashes the chemistry of sex—the natural bestowal by the woman of her token of sympathy upon the more pathetic of these rivals and then her ultimate display of contempt for both immature male creatures. It makes for a neat ironic twist.

As I say, the style is so casual and random at the start that the clambering of only three people about a sailboat tends to become monotonous. And unless one is quickly perceptive of the subtle drama Mr. Polanski is about, the use of attending their behavior may be disastrously missed.

But the performances are engaging. Leon Niemczyk is mephitic and intense as the nasty husband, Zygmunt Malanowicz is dry and droll as the young man and Jolanta Umecka is obligingly attractive and provokingly scornful as the wife. The décor is

entertaining, if you can overlook the facts that the sailing is laughably sloppy and that there are no other boats on the lake.

Once you realize that this is a devilish dissection of man in one of his more childish and ridiculous aspects, you should get some laughs and tingles out of it.

It is too bad about that Polish dialogue. The English subtitles are good.

O 29, 1963

MURIEL, screenplay by Jean Cayrol; directed by Alain Resnais and produced by Anatol Dauman. A co-production of Argos Films, Alpha Productions, Eclair, Les Films de la Pleiade (Paris) and Dear Films (Rome). Distributed by Lopert Pictures Corporation. At the Plaza Theater, 58th Street east of Madison Avenue. Running time: 115 minutes.

Helene	Delphine Seyrig
Alphonse	Jean-Pierre Kerien
Francoise	Nita Klein
Bernard	Jean-Baptiste Thierree
De Smoke	Claude Sainval
Claudie	Laurence Badie
Ernest	Jean Champion
The Goat Man	Jean Daste
Marie-Dominique	Martine Vatel

PERHAPS there are those who can follow the scattered clues in the devious mystery that Alain Resnais has thrown together in his new French film, "Muriel." But I am not one, and having tried twice—first at the New York Film Festival where "Muriel" was shown and at the Plaza, where it opened yesterday — I feel I can fairly advise you that this is a very bewildering, annoying film.

Oh, sure, I can sift a few vague notions from the jumble of disconnected scenes and crazily edited footage in this beautifully photographed color film from the director of "Last Year at Marienbad" and, before that, "Hiroshima, Mon Amour."

I can see that he's giving us another of those wistful reflections upon the moods of a lonely woman who is trying to sort her memories and her present desires for the resumption of a long past love. That's obvious enough at the beginning, when he has this woman, who lives in Boulogne-sur-Mer, visited by a solemn, gray-haired fellow who keeps talking about their old affair and trying to rekindle the woman's ardor, even though he has his young mistress with him.

I can see that the woman is also dangling on the edge of an affair with another man, and that her stepson, who is just back from military service in Algeria, is having romantic troubles, too. And I detect that the stepson and the visitor both know more than is explained about the death of a girl named Muriel back in Algeria.

But that's about as much as I can fathom or tell you is evident in the fantastic display of hodge-podge movements, random details, erratic images and utterly nonsequential cutting that Mr. Resnais has arranged. I can't tell you who is that weird girl the stepson drags in from time to time or why the soundtrack is occasionally shattered by a strange, keening siren-song. And I can't tell you what is intended by such things as the stepson's fixation on a horse or what the whole thing symbolizes, if it is meant to symbolize anything.

For it strikes me that Mr. Resnais has here carried intentional elusiveness so far, without any evident justification for it, that he has killed the effectiveness of his film. Sure, he was opaque and elusive in "Last Year at Marienbad," and he was psychologically esoteric and evasive in "Hiroshima, Mon Amour." But his style was expressing the nature of subliminal emotions in both those films, and it also achieved a distinctive poetic effect and harmony.

I get none of that in this picture. All I get is a stunning mise-en-scène, a nervous performance by Delphine Seyrig, who was also the woman in "Last Year at Marienbad," and some vivid but baffling performances by the other people in the cast. I get a feeling that Mr. Resnais is somehow pulling our legs, and I don't find it amusing. He's too good with the camera for that.

B. C.

O 31, 1963

DR. STRANGELOVE OR: HOW I LEARNED TO STOP WORRYING AND LOVE THE BOMB, screenplay by Stanley Kubrick, Terry Southern and Peter George, based on the book "Two Hours to Doom," by Mr. George; produced and directed by Mr. Kubrick. Presented by Columbia Pictures Corporation. At the Victoria Theater, Broadway and 46th Street, and the Baronet Theater, Third Avenue and 59th Street. Running time: 93 minutes.
Group Captain Lionel Mandrake, President Muffley, Dr. Stanrgelove .... Peter Sellers
Gen. Buck Turgidson .... George C. Scott
Gen. Jack D. Ripper ..... Sterling Hayden
Col. Bat Guana .... Keenan Wynn
Maj. T. J. King Kong .... Slim Pickens
Ambassador de Sadesky .... Peter Bull
Miss Scott .... Tracy Reed
Lieut. Lothar Zogg ...... James Earl Jones
Staines .... Jack Creley
Lieut. H. R. Dietrich .... Frank Berry
Lieut. W. D. Kivel .... Glenn Beck
Capt. G. A. (Ace) Owens) . Shane Rimmer
Lieut. B. Goldberg .... Paul Tamarin
General Faceman .... Gordon Tanner
Admiral Randolph .... Robert O'Neil
Frank .... Roy Stephens

By BOSLEY CROWTHER

STANLEY KUBRICK'S new film, called "Dr. Strangelove or: How I Learned to Stop Worrying and Love the Bomb," is beyond any question the most shattering sick joke I've ever come across. And I say that with full recollection of some of the grim ones I've heard from Mort Sahl, some of the cartoons I've seen by Charles Addams and some of the stuff I've read in Mad Magazine.

For this brazenly jesting speculation of what might happen within the Pentagon and within the most responsible council of the President of the United States if some maniac Air Force general should suddenly order a nuclear attack on the Soviet Union is at the same time one of the cleverest and most incisive satiric thrusts at the awkwardness and folly of the military that have ever been on the screen. It opened yesterday at the Victoria and the Baronet.

My reaction to it is quite divided, because there is so much about it that is grand, so much that is brilliant and amusing, and much that is grave and dangerous.

On the one hand, it cuts right to the soft pulp of the kind of military mind that is lost from all sense of reality in a maze of technical talk, and it shows up this type of mentality for the foolish and frightening thing it is.

In a top-level Air Force general, played by George C. Scott with a snarling and rasping volubility that makes your blood run cold, Mr. Kubrick presents us with a joker whose thinking is so involved with programs and cautions and suspicions that he is practically tied in knots.

It is he who is most completely baffled, bewildered and paralyzed when word comes through to Washington that a general in the Strategic Air Command has sent a wing of bombers off to drop bombs and that the planes cannot be recalled. It is he who has to answer to the President for this awesome "accident" when the President gathers his council in the War Room at the Pentagon. And it is he who looks the most unstable and dubious in the causes of peace when it begins to appear that the Russians have a retaliatory "doomsday device."

Some of the conversations in that War Room are hilarious, shooting bright shafts of satire through mounds of ineptitude. There is, best of all, a conversation between the President and an unseen Soviet Premier at the other end of a telephone line that is a titanic garble of nuttiness and platitudes.

Funny, too, in a mad way, is the behavior of the crew in one of the planes of the airborne alert force ordered to drop the bomb. The commander is a Texan who puts on a cowboy hat when he knows the mission is committed. Slim Pickens plays this role. He and Keenan Wynn as a foggy colonel are the funniest individuals in the film.

As I say, there are parts of this satire that are almost beyond compare.

On the other hand, I am troubled by the feeling, which runs all through the film, of discredit and even contempt for our whole defense establishment, up to and even including the hypothetical Commander in Chief.

It is all right to show the general who starts this wild foray as a Communist-hating madman, convinced that a "Red conspiracy" is fluoridating our water in order to pollute our precious body fluids. That is pointed satire, and Sterling Hayden plays the role with just a right blend of wackiness and meanness to give the character significance.

But when virtually everybody turns up stupid or insane —or, what is worse, psychopathic—I want to know what this picture proves. The President, played by Peter Sellers with a shiny bald head, is a dolt, whining and unavailing with the nation in a life-or-death spot. But worse yet, his technical expert, Dr. Strangelove, whom Mr. Sellers also plays, is a devious and noxious ex-German whose mechanical arm insists on making the Nazi salute.

And, oddly enough, the only character who seems to have much common sense is a British flying officer, whom Mr.

Sellers—yes, he again—plays.

The ultimate touch of goulish humor is when we see the bomb actually going off, dropped on some point in Russia, and a jazzy sound track comes in with a cheerful melodic rendition of "We'll Meet Again Some Sunny Day." Somehow, to me, it isn't funny. It is malefic and sick.

Ja 31, 1964

THE SILENCE, written, directed and produced by Ingmar Bergman. Presented by Svensk Filmindustri. A Janus Films release. At the Trans-Lux East Theater, Third Avenue at 58th Street, and the Rialto Theater, Broadway at 42nd Street. Running time: 95 minutes.

Ester .... Ingrid Thulin
Anna .... Gunnel Lindblom
Old Waiter.. .... Hakan Jahnberg
The Man .... Birger Malmsten
The Boy .... Jorgen Lindstrom.

By BOSLEY CROWTHER

THE grapplings of Ingmar Bergman with loneliness, lust and loss of faith, so weirdly displayed in his last two pictures, "Through a Glass Darkly" and "Winter Light," have plunged him at last into a tangle of brooding confusions and despairs in his latest film, which, he tells us, completes a trilogy begun with those previous films. It is titled appropriately "The Silence" and it opened yesterday at the Rialto (lately a house for strip-tease movies) and the Trans-Lux East.

What Mr. Bergman is trying to tell us is something each individual viewer must fathom and discover for himself. Or, indeed, one may reasonably question whether he is trying to give us anything save a grim philosophical observation of a tragic aspect of life.

For here, as in the previous pictures in his trilogy, he has fashioned his drama from the tensions of only a few people in a narrow frame. He has let his action develop in a casual, almost haphazard form. And he has brought it to a conclusion on a deliberately enigmatic note. What there is of commentary must be studiously inferred from dark psychological implications and heavy symbolic strokes.

Evidently the situation that Mr. Bergman presents is to be viewed as a singular speculation, a dramatic hypothesis. To a strange hotel in a strange city, he brings two women and one little boy, as though they were lonely wanderers and seekers in a stark, unfriendly world.

The women are obviously sisters and the tension between them seems to be over the latent predilection of the older to possess the younger one. She seems to want to clutch the younger in a sexual embrace that would include an emotional expression of their family associations and their youth. But the younger one, restless and resentful, resists her and takes revenge by finding a nameless lover and having a wild affair with him.

Meanwhile, the lonely youngster, the son of the younger woman, wanders in solemn desolation through the almost empty hotel. He has a briefly bright encounter with a theatrical troupe of dwarfs who entertain him with a bit of playful make-believe, until their leader comes along and calls it off. He hobnobs a bit with a nice old waiter who mutely attends his aunt, brings her bottles of brandy and helps her when she has a racking cough. And, finally, the sad little fellow watches secretly while his mother embraces her lover and goes with him into a room.

Whether this strange amalgam of various states of loneliness and lust articulates a message may be questionable, but it does, at least, resolve into a vaguely affecting experience that moves one like a vagrant symphony.

Mr. Bergman has ordered his images as though presenting a musical score, with separate themes projected and developed and with supplementary phrases struck.

His actors are all superbly tempered and paced in their strange, allusive roles. Ingrid Thulin is sterile and anguished as the older sister who struggles in vain, and Gunnel Lindblom is earthy and arrogant as the younger one. Jorgen Lindstrom is touchingly spiritual yet entirely natural as the boy, and Hakan Jahnberg plays the old waiter as though he were a shadowy ghost from a happier age.

It is notable, for instance, that he handles the poignant theme of the boy with an affecting use of close-ups that have deep emotional quality. Through the impersonal streets of the city, he suddenly rumbles an army tank, intruding a thought of menace in the alien community. Or down in the streets he shows his women an old junk wagon drawn by a nag, which calls up a contemplation of degeneration and death.

But, unfortunately, Mr. Bergman has not given us enough to draw on, to find the underlying meaning or emotional satisfaction in this film. They say when it was shown in Sweden, its several erotic scenes were so detailed and explicit that they literally shocked audiences. Perhaps these scenes are essential to a superheated mood required for the psychological context. But obviously these scenes have been cut or trimmed for this market. Here the whole thing is rather tame, mystifying and morbid. 'The Silence" is almost like death.

F 4, 1964

THE CRIME OF MONSIEUR LANGE, screenplay by Jacques Prevert from an original story by Jean Renoir and Jean Castanier; directed by Mr. Renoir; released by Brandon Films, Inc. At the Normandie Theater, 57th Street near Fifth Avenue. Running time: 90 minutes.

Monsieur Lange	Rene Lefever
Valentine	Florelle
Meunier	Henri Guisol
Bessard	Marcel Levesque
Mme. Bessard	Odette Talazac
Charles	aurice Baquet
Estelle	Nadia Sibirskaia
Batala	Jules Berry
Edith	Sylvia Battille

and

LES DAMES DU BOIS DE BOULOGNE (LADIES OF THE PARK), screenplay by Robert Bresson, adapted from a chapter of "Jacques le Fataliste," by Denis Diderot; dialogue by Jean Cocteau; directed by Mr. Bresson. Released by Brandon Films, Inc. At the Normandie, Theater. Running time: 84 minutes.

Jean	Paul Bernard
Helene	Maria Casares
Agnes	Elina Labourdette
Jacques	Jean Marchat
Agnes's Mother	Lucienne Bogaert

By BOSLEY CROWTHER

THE series of French film revivals that has been running at the Normandie for the last five weeks was topped off yesterday with the showing of two historically important films, each from a prominent director, that have never been shown theatrically in this country. They are "The Crime of Monsieur Lange," which Jean Renoir made in 1935, and 'Les Dames du Bois de Boulogne," which Robert Bresson made in 1944.

Neither will stand comparison with the technically more expert films of today; and, indeed, it is not difficult to fathom why they probably were not released here previously. For both manifest shortcomings that were no less critical at the time they were made, and time has only served to date them further, so that now they appear complete antiques.

●

But the student should find them interesting, especially the one of Renoir, which offers some fascinating glints of his developing thoughts and style.

It spins a loose and non-descript story, which ranges

378

uncertainly between romantic comedy and solemn melodrama, about a publishing enterprise in which an author of cheap French Western fiction is the pivotal element.

He is a naive and helpless little fellow, but he has the spunk to join the employes of his publishing company in a cooperative venture when the head of the company skips out with the company funds. And he has the audacity to shoot the latter when he returns and tries to take over again—an act that is justified in the telling by a build-up of sentiment for the little man.

Significantly, this picture was made at the time of the Popular Front in France, in the period immediately following the Depression, when the "little people" of the nation were feeling strong. And it follows somewhat in the rebellious spirit of the classic comedy - satires of René Clair. Indeed, the hero is played by René Lefevre, who was the hero in Clair's "Le Million."

In it is evident Renoir's fervor for the spirit and courage of the French workingman. Two years later, he made "Grand Illusion," which is his masterpiece.

Bresson's film was made in Paris during the Occupation, and is a very stiff, over-formalized account of an abandoned mistress's endeavor to get revenge upon her lover by ensnaring him in a marriage with a so-called "tramp."

It is slow, solemn, rigidly conventional and as stilted as a silent film, but it shows Bresson's early ability to catch sober and smoldering moods with his camera. Maria Casares is handsome and icy as the mistress scorned. Elina Labourdette is no more trampish than Ginger Rogers in "Top Hat."

This was Bresson's second picture. He was later to make

"The Diary of a Country Priest" and "A Man Escaped."

Both films have English subtitles.

Ap 4, 1964

A HARD DAY'S NIGHT, screenplay by Alun Owen; directed by Richard Lester and produced by Walter Shenson for United Artists. At the Astor, Broadway at 45th Street; the Trans-Lux East, Third Avenue at 58th Street, and other theaters in the metropolitan area. Running time: 87 minutes.

John ....John Lennon
Paul ....Paul McCartney
George ....George Harrison
Ringo ....Ringo Starr
Grandfather ....Wilfrid Brambell
Norm ....Norman Rossington
T V Director ....Victor Spinetti
Shake ....John Junkin
Millie ....Anna Quayle
Simon ....Kenneth Haigh
Man on Train ....Richard Vernon
Hotel Waiter ....Eddie Malin

By BOSLEY CROWTHER

THIS is going to surprise you—it may knock you right out of your chair—but the new film with those incredible chaps, the Beatles, is a whale of a comedy.

I wouldn't believe it either, if I hadn't seen it with my own astonished eyes, which have long since become accustomed to seeing disasters happen when newly fledged pop-singing sensations are hastily rushed to the screen. But this first fiction film of the Beatles, entitled "A Hard Day's Night," which exploded last night at the Astor, tne Trans-Lux East and other theaters hereabouts, has so much good humor going for it that it is awfully hard to resist.

●

In the first place, it's a wonderfully lively and altogether good-natured spoof of the juvenile madness called "Beatlemania," the current spreading craze of otherwise healthy young people for the four British lads with the shaggy hair.

The opening shots, behind the credits, are of three of the fellows running ahead of a mob of howling admirers chasing after them as they break away from a theater where they have played a singing engagement and race for a waiting train. And all the way through the picture, there are frenzied episodes of the Beatles' encounters with squealing fans and with reporters who ask silly questions, all in a facile, witty vein.

But more than this, it's a fine conglomeration of madcap clowning in the old Marx Brothers' style, and it is done with such a dazzling use of camera that it tickles the intellect and electrifies the nerves.

This is the major distinction of this commercially sure-fire film: It is much more sophisticated in theme and technique than its seemingly frivolous matter promises. With practically nothing substantial in the way of a story to tell — nothing more than a loosely strung fable of how the boys take under their wings the wacky old grandfather of one of them while preparing for a London television show—it discovers a nifty little satire in the paradox of the old man being more of a problem, more of "a troublemaker and a mixer," than the boys.

"'e's a nice old man isn't 'e?,'" notes one of the fellows when they first meet Granddad on a train. And another replies, with courteous unction, which parodies the standard comment about the Beatles themselves, "'e's very clean."

This line, which runs through the picture, may be too subtle for the happily squealing kids who will no doubt be its major audience, but the oldsters may profitably dig. And, of course, everybody will be able to enjoy the rollicking, madcap fun.

There's no use in trying to chart it. It comes in fast-flowing spurts of sight gags and throw-away dialogue that is flipped about recklessly. Alun Owen, who wrote the screenplay, may have dug it all out of his brain, but Richard Lester has directed at such a brisk clip that it seems to come spontaneously.

And just one musical sequence, for instance, when the boys tumble wildly out of doors and race eccentrically about a patterned playground to the tune of their song "Can't Buy Me Love," hits a surrealistic tempo that approaches audio-visual poetry.

Sure, the frequent and brazen "yah-yah-yahing" of the fellows when they break into song may be grating. To ears not tuned to it, it has moronic monotony. But it is always relieved by pictorial compositions that suggest travesties—or, at least, intelligent awareness of the absurdity of the Beatle craze.

Unless you know the fellows, it is hard to identify them, except for Ringo Starr, the big-nosed one, who does a saucy comic sequence on his own. But they're all good —surprisingly natural in the cinema-reality style that Mr. Lester expertly maintains. And Wilfrid Brambell as the old man is dandy, a delightfully comic Irishman. Many others are also funny.

It is good to know there are people in this world, up to and including the major parties, who don't take the Beatles seriously.

Ag 12, 1964

ANTONIONI MOVIE

DESERTO ROSSO

(RED DESERT)

By THOMAS QUINN CURTISS

Special to The New York Times

VENICE, Italy, Sept. 7— Michelangelo Antonioni's new

film, "Deserto Rosso" ("Red Desert"), shown at the Venice Festival, has the look of a winner.

Its imaginative use of color (the director's first experiment in this field of the motion picture), the compelling performance of Monica Vitti in the leading role, the intense personal style of the narration and the bold strokes with which mood and atmosphere are achieved have drawn praise from the various and opposing factions of the audience.

Mr. Antonioni again indulges in probing the motives of neurotic behavior, this time investigating the case of a Ravenna engineer's wife who is in a state of mental shock as a result of an automobile accident.

On the verge of manic depression, she is tortured by her oppressive surroundings. The factory dynamos, the radar towers, the noise, smoke, steam and tempo of modern industrialization take on an ominous aspect for her. She is never at peace, the prey of a thousand nameless terrors.

Her husband is somewhat indifferent to her suffering, and in despair she takes a friend of his, another engineer, as her lover. It is a brief and in no way soothing romance, and when he goes off on an assignment in South America, she seeks to readjust herself to her family life.

Her panic fears are the main business of the film, and Mr. Antonioni has pictured them vividly and to fine dramatic effect. He has employed color artfully, drawing the foggy winter-time harbor and the gaunt factory yards in subdued tones.

In contrast, he offers a brilliant, sun-flooded sequence of a tropical island, about which the woman tells her little boy, who she mistakenly believes has been stricken by a malady spread from a quarantined ship.

Mr. Antonioni has once more taken his favorite theme—the individual's isolation in modern society—but in "Deserto Rosso"

he has given it new dimension and fascinating variety.

S 8, 1964

WOMAN IN THE DUNES (Suno No Onna), screenplay by Kobo Abe; directed by Hiroshi Teshigahara; produced by Kiichi Ichikawa and Tadashi Ohono for Teshigahara Productions. At Philharmonic Hall. Running time: 123 minutes.
The Teacher..................Eiji Okada
The Woman..............Kyoko Kishida

By BOSLEY CROWTHER

THE first of five Japanese pictures to be shown among the 26 feature entries in the second New York Film Festival went on for the second show last night in Philharmonic Hall. It proved to be a strongly allegorical, strangely engrossing film.

Based on a novel by Kobo Abé called "Woman in the Dunes" (also the title of the picture), it is a long, leaden, grueling account of the arguing and quarreling and lovemaking of a man and a woman trapped in a shack at the bottom af a sand pit amid some remote and desolate dunes. Despite its drabness and some tedium, it grips and agitates the mind.

It begins with the man, an entomologist collecting beetles on the dunes, being directed to the shack by anonymous people from whom he has sought shelter for the night. They lower him into the sand pit with a crude block-and-fall, and there he finds the shabby woman who willingly provides him with bed and board.

But when he is ready to leave the next morning, he finds he cannot get out without having a rope lowered to him by the people above. And they are either absent or are scornful and unwilling to help.

Then the woman tells him that they are eternally caught — or, at least, must remain there at the will of the people above, who send them water and food. She explains, too, that she is resigned to existence under these circumstances. "Last year," she says, "a storm swallowed up my husband and child."

Further, she shows him the necessity of working hard every day to shovel out the sand that has fallen into the shack during the night.

Of course, the man is indignant. He rages and refuses to help. But slowly he makes his adjustment to this frustrating fate. As the picture progresses, he, too, becomes used to the pit, and at the end he does not want to leave it when he has a chance.

This is the barest outline of the plot of this more than two-hour film, which is crowded with harsh and subtle details of the personal relations of the two. But it is in the projection of these details, which have strong emotional and psychological significances, that the director, Hiroshi Teshigahara, has packed a bewitching poetry and power.

●

In describing, for instance, the manner in which the man becomes seduced by the physical presence of the woman, he works such subtle pictorial change that the bare body of the drab widow has a warm and attractive glow; and the physical act is suggested with such closeups of faces and limbs that a strong emanation of passion surges from the screen.

He also draws from his performers, Eiji Okada as the man (he played the lover in "Hiroshima, Mon Amour") and Kyoko Kishida as the woman, some sharp and devastating glints of anger sadness, compassion, gratefulness and despair. In a starkly atmospheric setting and with an eerie musical score,

this drama develops an engulfing sense of spiritual discouragement and decay.

Obviously, it is intended to symbolize the absorption of man and the alienation of his spirit by all the demands and oppressions of his environment. The soul of the individual is clearly challenged in this existentialist realm, and it is reduced to resignation and surrender. Not a happy but a hypnotic film.

"Woman in the Dunes" took the Special Jury Prize at this year's Cannes festival and will be distributed in this country by Pathè-Contemporary. No theater booking in New York is yet set.

S 17, 1964

BAND OF OUTSIDERS (Bande a Part); written and directed by Jean-Luc Godard, from the novel, "Fool's Gold," by D. and B. Hitchins; produced by Anouchka Films/Orsay Films. Running time: 97 minutes.
Odile .... Anna Karina
Franz .... Sami Frey
Artur .... Claude Brasseur
Aunt .... Louisa Colpeyn
and
A WOMAN IS A WOMAN (Une Femme Est Une Femme); written and directed by Mr. Godard; produced by Ponti and Georges de Beauregard; distributed by Pathe Contemporary Films. Running time: 80 minutes. Both films at Philharmonic Hall.
Angela .... Anna Karina
Emile .... Jean-Claude Brialy
Alfred .... Jean-Paul Belmondo
Suzanne .... Nicole Paquin

By EUGENE ARCHER

IF the purpose of the New York Film Festival is to introduce significant new directions in film making, which audiences might not otherwise be able to see, it accomplished its aim last night.

Yesterday's two features at Philharmonic Hall were written and directed by Jean-Luc Godard, the most eccentric and possibly the most gifted representative of the French New Wave. The first, "A Woman Is a Woman," was made three years ago, but is so far out that it still has

382

not opened here. The second, "Band of Outsiders," breaks even more of the conventional story-telling rules.

●

Mr. Godard is not for every taste. Both films are wildly original, stubbornly modern, characteristically French— and often, thoroughly infuriating. They are also very brilliant.

"A Woman Is a Woman," photographed in dazzling color on a wide, wide screen, is the most buoyant and enjoyable movie shown at the festival to date. Superficially, it is a comedy about a pretty stripper, Anna Karina, who yearns for motherhood. When her boy friend, Jean-Claude Brialy, refuses to oblige, she invites their best friend, Jean-Paul Belmondo.

The film has enormous charm, particularly when the characters interrupt the action to imitate actors in a Stanley Donen musical, but it has a serious undercurrent.

"I don't know whether this is a comedy or a tragedy," Mr. Brialy finally remarks to the audience, "but it is a masterpiece."

In a way, it is. The direction and playing have a youthful exuberance that lend a fresh spontaneity even to the film's excesses.

In contrast, "Band of Outsiders," described by Mr. Godard as "Alice in Wonderland meets Franz Kafka," is a mature work by a filmmaker who clearly knows exactly what he wants to do.

This time Miss Karine, who is the director's wife, plays a pigtailed student attracted first to a sinister hoodlum, Claude Brasseur, and later to his more intellectual chum, Sami Frey. The three try to rob the girl's house, where a mysterious lodger has stashed a bureauful of ill-gotten franc notes. As the relationships progress, the robbery changes from a comedy of errors into a fatal escapade.

Aided by a striking set of actors, Mr. Godard indulges in his penchant for paradox through some glittering dialogue, but his greatest talent is for innovation. He likes to intrude his own personality into the narrative, frequently addressing the audience directly to point out the difference between his characters' behavior and their emotions.

By breaking the boundaries of realistic structure, he forcefully reminds the viewer that "a movie is a movie."

A decade from now, Mr. Godard's work will be comfortably at home in a film museum, and it is safe to predict that his reputation will not be minor. Until then, his films offer rich rewards to a limited audience, who will find them stimulating, provocative, controversial— the very essence of the avant-garde.

L'AGE D'OR (The Golden Age); screen play by Luis Bunuel and Salvador Dali; directed and produced by Mr. Bunuel. Running time: 65 minutes.

The Man..................Gaston Modot
The Girl......................Lya Lys

Parlygoers ....
- Max Ernst
- Pierre Prevert
- Jose Artigas
- Cardinal de Lamberdesque
- Jacques Brunius

and

DIARY OF A CHAMBERMAID ("Le Journal d'une Femme de Chambre"); screen play by Mr. Bunuel and Jean Claude Carriere; directed by Mr. Bunuel; produced by Speva Films, Cine-Alliance, Films Sona and Dear Film. Running time: 97 minutes. Both films at Philharmonic Hall.

Celestine ....Jeanne Moreau
Monsieur Monteil ....Michel Piccoli
Joseph ....Georges Geret
Madame Monteil ......Francois Lugagne
Capitaine Mauger........Daniel Ivernel
Monsieur Rebour ..:.......Jean Ozenne

By EUGENE ARCHER

THE New York Film Festival, persisting in its search for a sensation, dug into the vaults last night for "L'Age d'Or," a much-censored 34-year-old classic by Luis Buñuel.

It was an all-Buñuel evening at Philharmonic Hall, with the outrageous old surrealistic comedy followed by his brand-new French version of "Diary of a Chambermaid." This double dose of old-guard moviemaking drew a sellout crowd to both shows at the 2,500-seat auditorium, but disappointment was in the air.

Perhaps too much was expected from the celebrated Spanish director of "Viridiana" and "The Young and the Damned." Teaming him with France's finest actress, Jeanne Moreau, sounded like a good idea, since her erotic gifts would seem an ideal complement to Mr. Buñuel's well-known penchant for perverse themes. No one was quite prepared for the tepid result.

As for "L'Age d'Or," this widely discussed scandal film had been preceded by such a formidable critical reputation that it could scarcely have lived up to expectations.

This 1930 attack on the conventions of society, with particular emphasis on organized religion, was banned in most parts of the world. Its previous screenings abroad were mostly limited to private showings at film clubs and museums, but many critical histories accord it a high place.

The film is still an eye-opener. Its intentions are entirely clear from an early scene. A ceremony commemorating the founding of the Eternal City of Rome is interrupted by a pair of uninhibited lovers writhing in the mud. When the scandalized spectators pull them apart, the frustrated male gives a watching dog a well-aimed kick.

Mr. Buñuel and his co-scenarist, none other than Salvador Dali, have packed just about every surrealist symbol they could think of into this rebellious epic. Their lovers are prevented by society from satisfying their natural instincts.

Finally the hero, called to the telephone from a garden rendezvous, strides furiously to an upstairs window and throws out a donkey, a plow, a feather pillow and an archbishop. A knowledge of Freud is not necessary to get the point.

Since the filmmakers are catholic in their protest, indiscriminately opposing all forms of social conventions rather than specific establishments, it is difficult to take offense. At this late date, the film's outstanding quality is not its defiance of traditional mores but its wit, which is savage, scabrous and frequently hilarious. It is no more shocking than Dada.

If "L'Age d'Or" proved less than a sensation at Lincoln Center, it was in part because of its method of presentation. A French-language print was shown without subtitles, and a translator's voice barraged the auditorium over a loudspeaker, drowning the original sound track. It was not the happiest solution to the dubbing problem.

Sadly, the intervening decades seem to have weakened Mr. Buñuel's powers. His new adaptation of Octave Mirbeau's "Diary of a Chambermaid" suffers in comparison with the strange but memorable version Jean Renoir did with Paulette Goddard in 1946.

He has used the story of a worldly wise domestic in a weird country household as a background for his comment on the changing French social structure before World War I. The provincial chateau is rife with old-fashioned quirks and perversions —a shoe fetishist, a servant-chasing master, a reluctant wife, a sinister overseer who rapes and murders a little girl.

A subdued Miss Moreau gives an able performance as the maid with idiosyncrasies of her own, but she is not aided by unsympathetic direction. Mr. Buñuel has photographed her harshly and scorned any background music that might accentuate her dramatic effects. It seems an ungrateful way to treat a brilliant star whose subtly modulated acting gives meaning to an unresolved and ambiguous script.

S 22, 1964

MY FAIR LADY, screenplay by Alan Jay Lerner, based on the stage musical by Mr. Lerner and Frederick Loewe, from "Pygmalion," by George Bernard Shaw; directed by George Cukor and produced by Jack L. Warner. Presented by Warner Bros. Pictures. At the Criterion Theater, Broadway and 45th Street. Running time: 170 minutes.

Eliza ....Audrey Hepburn
Henry Higgins ....Rex Harrison
Alfred Doolittle ....Stanley Holloway
Colonel Pickering ....Wilfrid Hyde White
Mrs. Higgins ....Gladys Cooper
Freddie ....Jeremy Brett
Zoltan Karpathy ....Theodore Bikel
Mrs. Pearce ....Mona Washbourne
Mrs. Eynsford-Hill ....Isobel Elsom
Butler ....John Holland

By BOSLEY CROWTHER

AS Henry Higgins might have whooped, "By George, they've got it!" They've made a superlative film from the musical stage show "My Fair Lady"—a film that enchantingly conveys the rich endowments of the famous stage production in a fresh and flowing cinematic form. The happiest single thing about it is that Audrey Hepburn superbly justifies the decision of the producer, Jack L. Warner, to get her to play the title role that Julie Andrews so charmingly and popularly originated on the stage.

All things considered, it is the brilliance of Miss Hepburn as the Cockney waif who is transformed by Prof. Henry Higgins into an elegant female facade that gives an extra touch of subtle magic and individuality to the film, which had a bejeweled and bangled premiere at the Criterion last night.

•

Other elements and values that are captured so exquisitely in this film are but artful elaborations and intensifications of the stage material as achieved by the special virtuosities and unique flexibilities of the screen.

There are the basic libretto and music of Alan Jay Lerner and Frederick Loewe, which were inspired by the wit and wisdom in the dramatic comedy, "Pygmalion," of George Bernard Shaw. With Mr. Lerner serving as the screen playwright, the structure and, indeed, the very words of the musical play as it was performed on Broadway for six and a half years are preserved. And every piece of music of the original score is used.

There is punctilious duplication of the motifs and patterns of the décor and the Edwardian costumes and scenery, which Cecil Beaton designed for the stage. The only difference is that they're expanded. For instance, the Covent Garden set becomes a stunningly populated market, full of characters and movement in the film; and the embassy ball, to which the heroine is transported Cinderellalike, becomes a dazzling array of regal splendor, as far as the eye can reach, when laid out for ritualistic emphasis on the Super-Panavision color screen. Since Mr. Beaton's décor was fresh and flawless, it is super-fresh and flawless in the film.

•

In the role of Professor Higgins, Rex Harrison still displays the egregious egotism and ferocity that he so vividly displayed on the stage, and Stanley Holloway still comes through like thunder as Eliza's antisocial dustman dad.

Yes, it's all here, the essence of the stage show—the pungent humor and satiric wit of the conception of a linguistic expert making a lady of a guttersnipe by teaching her manners and how to speak, the pomp and mellow grace of a romantic and gone-forever age, the delightful intoxication of music that sings in one's ears.

The added something is what Miss Hepburn brings—and what George Cukor as the director has been able to distill from the script.

For want of the scales of a jeweler, let's just say that what Miss Hepburn brings is a fine sensitivity of feeling and a phenomenal histrionic skill. Her Covent Garden flower girl is not just a doxy of the streets. She's a terrifying example of the elemental self-assertion of the female sex. When they try to plunge her into a bathtub, as they do in an added scene, which is a wonderfully comical creation of montage and pantomime, she fights with the fury of a tigress. She is not one to submit to the still obscure customs and refinements of a society that is alien to her.

But when she reaches the point where she can parrot the correct words to describe the rain in Spain, she acknowledges the thrill of achieving this bleak refinement with an electrical gleam in her eyes. And when she celebrates the male approval she receives for accomplishing this goal, she gives a delightful demonstration of ecstasy and energy by racing about the Higgins mansion to the music of "I Could Have Danced All Night."

●

It is true that Marni Nixon provides the lyric voice that seems to emerge from Miss Hepburn, but it is an excellent voice, expertly synchronized. And everything Miss Hepburn mimes to it is in sensitive tune with the melodies and words.

Miss Hepburn is most expressive in the beautiful scenes where she achieves the manners and speech of a lady, yet fails to achieve that one thing she needs for a sense of belonging—that is, the recognition of the man she loves.

She is dazzlingly beautiful and comic in the crisply satiric Ascot scene played almost precisely as it was on the stage. She is stiffly serene and distant at the embassy ball and almost unbearably poignant in the later scenes when she hungers for love. Mr. Cukor has maneuvered Miss Hepburn and Mr. Harrison so deftly in these scenes that she has one perpetually alternating between chuckling laughter and dabbing the moisture from one's eyes.

This is his singular triumph. He has packed such emotion into this film—such an essence of feeling and compassion for a girl in an all too-human bind—that he has made this rendition of "My Fair Lady" the most eloquent and moving that has yet been done.

●

There are other delightful triumphs in it. Mr. Harrison's Higgins is great—much sharper, more spirited and eventually more winning than I recall it on the stage. Mr. Holloway's dustman is titanic, and when he roars through his sardonic paean to middle-class morality in "Get Me to the Church on Time," he and his bevy of boozers reach a high point of the film.

Wilfrid Hyde White as Colonel Pickering, who is Higgins's urbane associate; Mona Washburn as the Higgins housekeeper, Gladys Cooper as Higgins's svelte mama and, indeed, everyone in the large cast is in true and impeccable form.

Though it runs for three hours — or close to it — this "My Fair Lady" seems to fly past like a breeze. Like Eliza's disposition to dancing, it could go on, for all I'd care, all night.

O 22, 1964

ZORBA, THE GREEK, screenplay by Michael Cacoyannis, based on the novel by Nikos Kazantzakis; directed and produced by Mr. Cacoyannis; presented by 20th Century-Fox. At the Sutton Theater, Third Avenue and 37th Street. Running time: 142 minutes.

Alexis Zorba	Anthony Quinn
Basil	Alan Bates
The Widow	Irene Papas
Madame Hortense	Lila Kedrova
Mavrandoni	George Foundas
Lola	Eleni Anousaki
Mimithos	Sotiris Moustakas
Manolakas	Takis Emmanuel
Pavlo	George Voyadjis
Soul	Anna Kyriakou

By BOSLEY CROWTHER

IF ever the abundance of life force in man has been poured forth on the screen — and, goodness knows, many efforts to do so have been made over the years—it is done in the brilliant performance given by Anthony Quinn in the title role of the film that Michael Cacoyannis has made from Nikos Kazantzakis's classic novel, "Zorba, the Greek."

Here, in one huge and bold portrayal of a rugged and weather-worn old Greek of uncertain age and origin, indefinite station and career, but of unmistakable self-possession and human authority, Mr. Quinn presents us with a picture of man as he might be if the world were not so much with us and civilization had not forced us into molds.

His Zorba, in this tempestuous picture that opened yesterday at the Sutton, possesses all the energies and urges of the great ones of history and myth. He is Adam in the Garden of Eden, Odysseus on the windy plains of Troy. He is a little bit of Nijinsky and a good bit of Tom Jones.

●

Love for all kindly fellow mortals surges in his breast. Hate and contempt for the mean ones flame in him like a roaring fire. Lust seizes him without resistance. Pathos moves him to tears. When the pressures pile up too much within him—either of joy or of sorrow—he must dance.

To the cliché-accustomed moviegoer, this old tiger is likely to be as much of a surprise and confusion as he is to the mild young Anglo-Greek to whom he attaches himself in the seaport of Piraeus at the beginning of the film. We are not used to so much exuberance, so much landslide persuasiveness, any more than is the young fellow who takes on Zorba (or is taken on by him) to help in restoring an old lignite mine, inherited from his father, on the island of Crete.

And the viewer is likely to be staggered and appalled all the way through the film at the wildly ingenious conceptions and attitudes of the old Greek. His greedy and gallant courtship of an ancient French courtesan who in a cheap little island hotel maintains her memories of conquests; his mad and irreverent maneuver to terrify a monastery full of monks into letting him cut a stand of tall trees off their isolated hillside to provide timbers for shoring up the mine; his spendthrift foray into a brothel and dalliance with a young prostitute—these are grand scale adventures of Zorba that the viewer will not forget.

So large and fantastic is the character that he all but overwhelms the total scene and tends to flatten whatever personal conflicts and dramatic crises occur. This is something that Mr. Cacoyannis has not been able to prevent. Nor does it appear that he really tried to, any more than did Mr. Kazantzakis in writing his book.

●

There are incidents, yes, when the meanness and ignorance of the people of Crete surge up like a flow of molten lava to confront Zorba's cheerfulness and strength. One is when the fierce and angry people rise up in vengeance to destroy a lonely widow who has dared bestow her favor on Zorba's timid friend. The other is when the old women—the old ghouls—strip bare the room and then the house in which Zorba's aged mistress has just died in his comforting arms.

These are incidents that Mr. Cacoyannis has staged with such intense reality—as he has the whole of the picture—that they fairly paralyze the senses for brief spells. Zorba, too, staggers momentarily at such bestial displays. But he quickly recovers from them, as he does from the ultimate collapse of the crazy cable railway he has constructed for bringing the logs down out of the hills. His easy solution for disaster is to go into his wild, defiant dance.

This is the weakness of the picture—as a dramatic exercise, that is. It lacks a significant conflict to prove its dominant character. Zorba is powerful and provocative, but nobody gets in his way. Nothing provides competition, except mob rule for a moment—and the hand of death. The young Anglo-Greek is slightly wary but easily pushed around. He is little more than a smirking straight-man, as played by Alan Bates. The old woman of Lila Kedrova is brilliantly realized, a wrinkled and tacky relic of a once successful coquette, stil hopeful, audacious and courageous. But she's just a passing incident.

●

Irene Papas, who played Electra in Mr. Cacoyannis's memorable film of the Euripides play, is dark and intense as the widow, but she, too, is soon got out of the way. Several other Greek actors are exciting but transient as people of Crete.

Walter Lassally's unfiltered camera gets the hard, barren look of the island scene—the crowded villages, the stark, rocky shoreline and the sunbaked, wind-scoured hills. The musical score of Mikis Theodorakis rollicks and

wails hauntingly. And the editing of Mr. Cacoyannis abets the pace of his direction perfectly.

But out of the whole accumulation of colorfulness and vitality towers the singular, monumental portrait of Zorba, as evolved by Mr. Quinn. And it's this unforgettable portrait that justifies the film.

Incidentally, the principal dialogue is in English—and very rich and racy it is!

D 18, 1964

RED DESERT, screenplay by Michelangelo Antonioni and Tonino Guerra; directed by Michelangelo Antonioni and produced by Antonio Cervi. Presented by Rizzoli Film Distributors, Inc., At the Beekman Theater, Second Avenue and 66th Street. Running time: 116 minutes.

Guiliana	Monica Vitti
Corrado	Richard Harris
Ugo	Carlo Chionetle
Linda	Xenia Valderi
Emilia	Rita Renoir
Max	Aldo Grotti
Son	Valerio Bartoleschi

By BOSLEY CROWTHER

MICHELANGELO ANTONIONI has added color and geometric design to his means of suggesting and conveying the tormenting tensions and morbid moods of another of his neurotic women in an over-industrialized and alien world.

In his latest film, "Red Desert" ("Deserto Rosso"), which came to the Beekman yesterday, the leading existentialist director has abandoned his customary black-and-white for the advantages of Technicolor in defining the volume and hues of massive arrangements of machinery, of modern apartment walls, of buildings in misty landscapes and other aspects of her environment that impinge on the jangled and troubled psyche of his lovely heroine.

●

He has caught the disturbing grotesqueness of the modern industrial scene—here it is in the region of Ravenna—by contemplating a monstrous chemical plant in all its tangle of condensers and piping, like some great, hot, mechanical giant, rising in despotic grandeur amid acres of hideous waste and sludge.

He has captured in graphic compositions of angled and pastel-tinted walls, enclosing odd furniture arrangements, the strange oppressiveness of a modern home. And he has sensed, too, the oblique strain of poetry in this throbbing space age by showing a giant radar antenna reaching with arcing fingers to the sky to hear the sounds of the stars, while near it is a forlorn, abandoned farmhouse and marshes polluted with slag.

In his characteristic fashion, Mr. Antonioni has done a superb job of suggestive image-making — of putting upon the screen compositions of people and places, of situations and atmosphere, that suddenly seize the senses with implications of profound ideas.

When he shows us, for instance, an assortment of men and women, husbands and wives, engineers and their indolent consorts, lolling all together on a huge couch, coaxing one another with caresses and aphrodisiacs, he vividly states the emotional poverty of an over-civilized society and one reason for the distress and frustration of his married but neglected heroine.

●

Furthermore, by placing this strange tangle of human beings in a pale-blue shack by the side of a canal through which huge ships, poetic symbols, pass in the gray-white mist, he creates a haunting conception of the vaporous nature of the lives of the lonely, isolated people who grope so barrenly and pitifully for—call it love.

But, as in his previous pictures — "L'Avventura," "La Notte" and "Eclipse" — the strangely obsessed film-maker tells us little of his tortured heroine, except that she is bewildered and can find no comfort in men. Her husband, an engineer, neglects her—especially in her hour of greatest need, when she is painfully recovering from an automobile accident which has left her in a neurotic state. A friend of her husband with whom she takes up and has a tormented, brief affair, is curiously calm and callous towards her. He has his own existentialist life to live.

Even her small son deceives her, in a classically selfish masculine way. He excites her anxiety by feigning an illness—the symptoms of polio —which almost drives her mad.

And so, at the end, we know little more about this woman than we know at the start. We only learn that she has had a conventional psychic experience as a girl. And we sense that she has learned, like the little birds that fly over the chemical factory, to stay clear of the poisonous vapors of her milieu.

●

Again Mr. Antonioni gives us Monica Vitti in the role of his alienated modern woman, and she plays it with the same congested air, the same tight and withdrawn human aspect, she has made expressive but not too helpful in her previous films. Carlo Chionetti is her husband—a cool, crisp, remote little man—and Richard Harris is the big, awkward lover who does little more than look at her sadly with empty eyes and hands.

The rest of the people in the picture are almost impersonal and vague as the social environment that we are led to construct but never see.

From The New York Times Film Reviews 389

Indeed, they are almost colorless in an engrossingly color-treated film that has more of the quality of painting than of narrative cinema.

Adequate English subtitles are used to translate the Italian dialogue.

F 9, 1965

THE PAWNBROKER, screenplay by David Friedkin and Morton Fine, from the novel by Edward Lewis Wallant; directed by Sidney Lumet; produced by Roger H. Lewis and Philip Langner; presented by Ely Landau and Herbert R. Steinmann. At the Beekman Theater, Second Avenue and 60th Street, the Cinema Rendezvous, 57th Street between Avenue of the Americas and Seventh Avenue, and the RKO 23d Street Theater, near Eighth Avenue. Running time: 114 minutes.

Sol Nazerman	Rod Steiger
Marilyn Birchfield	Geraldine Fitzgerald
Rodriguez	Brock Peters
Jesus Ortiz	Jaime Sanchez
Ortiz's Girl	Thelma Oliver
Tessie	Marketa Kimbrell
Mendel	Baruch Lumet
Mr. Smith	Juano Hernandez
Ruth	Linda Geiser
Bertha	Nancy R. Pollock
Tangee	Raymond St. Jacques
Buck	John McCurry
Robinson	Charles Dierkop
Mrs. Ortiz	Eusebia Cosme
Savarese	Warren Finnerty
Morton	Jack Ader
Papa	E. M. Margolese
Joan	Marianne Kanter

By BOSLEY CROWTHER

ALTHOUGH the tragic character that Rod Steiger powerfully plays in the solemn new film, "The Pawnbroker," is very much a person of today—a survivor of Nazi persecution who has become detached and remote in the modern world—he casts, at it were, the somber shadow of the legendary, ageless Wandering Jew. That is the mythical Judean who taunted Jesus on the way to Calvary and was condemned to roam the world a lonely outcast until Jesus should come again.

For this is a dark and haunting drama of a man who has reasonably eschewed a role of involvement and compassion in a brutal and bitter world and has found his life barren and rootless as a consequence. It is further a drama of discovery of the need of man to try to do something for his fellow human sufferers in the troubled world of today.

To view this remarkable picture, which opened yesterday at the Cinema Rendezvous, the Beekman and the RKO 23d Street, as merely a mordant melodrama of a displaced European Jew who runs a pawnshop in New York's Harlem and is caught up in some evil doings there is to miss the profound dilemma and melancholy of its central character and the broader significance of his detachment and inability to adjust.

This man, played by Mr. Steiger with a mounting intensity that carries from a state of listless ennui to a point of passion where it seems he's bound to burst, has good enough reason for detachment. He has been through the horror of the concentration camps, has lost his immediate family, has seen his best friend tortured and killed. This terrible traumatic experience has left him intellectually drained and emotionally numb. He has a fitful affair with his friend's widow but looks on people as "rejects, scum."

A strange accumulation of events on an anniversary stirs him to painful recollections and causes old words to flash through his mind. An attempt by a woman welfare worker to strike up a friendship with him agitates his resentment with memories of a happier life. The wish of a Puerto Rican Negro assistant to get his help in learning the trade fires him to a violent outburst against the meaninglessness of everything—everything, that is, except money. And an effort by an anguished prostitute to offer her body to him causes him to recall the horrible experience of seeing his wife stripped and raped by prison guards.

●

It is a shattering excess of mental torment and deep self-pity this man must endure. and it shifts him to a level of awareness that lets him see his present life in previous terms. He sees the people on New York's crowded subways as lost souls headed for the concentration camps, the vicious gangsters who actually own his pawnshop as counterparts of Nazi racketeers.

But it is not until he sees his young assistant — Jesus Ortiz is significantly his name—shot dead by holdup hoodlums during a courageous attempt to protect him that he senses the shame of his detachment. Then he slams his hand down on a paper spike to inflict upon himself the stigmata and acknowledge his burden of grief and guilt.

It is not an ennobling picture that Roger H. Lewis and Philip Langner have produced and Sidney Lumet has directed. It is a picture of the shabbiness of man—of the misused, debilitated hero, as well as those among whom he lives. And the whole thing is staged and presented to convey and emphasize the meanness of those environments that would breed such shabbiness.

With the seasoned camera of Boris Kaufman, Mr. Lumet has ruthlessly searched some of the most hideous aspects of Harlem and middle-class life around New York. He has brilliantly intercut flashes of the horrors of the concentration camps . with equally shocking visualizations of imprisonment in a free society. And he has clearly implied in terms of picture the irony of resemblances.

●

In certain respects, the sup-purant screenplay of David Friedkin and Morton Fine departs from the feverish novel of the late Edward Lewis Wallant on which it is based. The detail of medical experiments upon the hero by the Nazis has been removed, thus freeing Mr. Steiger from the onus of playing the character as a sort of golem, as in the book. Now he can make the sad survivor a solid man in command of his own fate, driven with acerbity and cynicism but compelling an eventual sympathy.

Others of the cast are likewise striking—Geraldine Fitzgerald as the woman who tries in a wistful and clumsy fashion to draw the poor man from his obvious loneliness; Jaime Sanchez as the spry Negro assistant who teeters lightly on the fringes of crime; Thelma Oliver as the latter's loyal sweetheart who makes her living as a tawny prostitute; Brock Peters as a brutal Harlem crime boss and many more, including fine old Juano Hernandez in one of the several good small roles.

In his zeal to make sure the point is carried, Mr. Lumet lets his picture run too long. He might have cut out or held down some grim stretches that make for redundancy. But he and his sponsor, Ely Landau, are to to be honored for even attempting this most uncommon film, which projects a disagreeable subject with power and cogency.

Ap 21, 1965

Biblical Film

THE GOSPEL ACCORDING TO SAINT MATTHEW

"The Gospel According to Saint Matthew," a low-budget Italian film acted by non-professionals, is precisely what its title indicates, a literal depiction of the Evangelist's account. It has won several international awards and a number of Roman Catholic film prizes.

Last year there was a special showing of the film in Rome for bishops and others connected with the Ecumenical Council. The showing was arranged by an American Jesuit priest, an authority of films, who gave a short introductory speech, praising the integrity of the picture and lauding the artistry of its young director, Pier Paolo Pasolini.

After the performance, there was general agreement in the audience that the film was more impressive and reverently moving than any of the star-studded, million-dollar Biblical epics recently shown in the city.

The most interesting thing about "The Gospel . . ." is that it is almost entirely a Marxist product. Pasolini is a self-professed follower of Marx and an unabashed atheist. His own mother plays the role of the older Mary. Joseph is played by a Communist lawyer. The Spanish youth who plays Jesus describes himself as a Marxist. Judas is a Communist truckdriver. John the Baptist is a Communist university professor. Peter, the only non-Marxist among the principals, is a Jewish ragpicker.

Inspired by Bible

Pasolini got the idea for the film several years ago when he was forced to spend half a day in an Assisi hotel. Because Pope John XXIII was visiting the town, traffic had been brought to a standstill. There was nothing for the director to do but read, and the only book available at the hotel was a New Testament. He read St. Matthew's gospel, the first time he had looked into it since he was a child, and found it exceedingly beautiful. He decided then and there to make a film from it, he recently told Gunnar Kumlien, Commonweal's correspondent in Rome.

No one has charged Pasolini with tampering with the text, since the only dialogue is taken directly from Scripture, and there have been no charges that he deliberately set out to be irreverent, though some viewers find the

utter simplicity of his Giotto-like settings a shocking contrast with the usual post-Reformation idealizations of the events in the life of Jesus.

He has not, however, escaped criticism. Some Communists have accused him of turning out "religious propaganda," and certain Catholics have accused him of subtly "using" religion to promote Communist ideology.

There was a similar case in Hollywood a few years ago. A popular movie in which the central character was a nun received glowing reviews in the diocesan press. What the reviewers did not know was that its highly lauded script was written under a pseudonym by a blacklisted writer who had been officially eliminated from the industry for years because, in the late 1940's, he refused to tell the House Committee on Un-American Activities whether or not he was a Communist.

Ag 1, 1965

THE SHOP ON HIGH STREET

THE third New York Film Festival scored its first hit last night with the showing of "The Shop on High Street," a Czechoslovak film.

This ironic and heart-tearing observation of one man's cowardly surrender to the hysteria of anti-Semitism in a Slovak town in 1942 greatly surprised and moved the audience at Philharmonic Hall. Although it has not yet been booked for distribution in this country, the consensus was that it would be.

●

Beyond the fact that its directors, Jan Kodar and Elmar Klos, are not well known, even to movie experts in this country, the film was a surprise because of the stunning transition of its story from comedy to stark tragedy, and because of the brilliant performances of its two unfamiliar stars, Josef Kroner and Ida Kaminska.

At the start, it is a drily

humorous look-in upon a good-natured, simple carpenter who is appointed the "Aryan controller" of a Jewish-owned shop by his Nazi gauleiter brother-in-law. The idea is that he will be able, as stupid as he is, to make a tidy rake-off from the business of the shop.

To his chagrin, he discovers not only that it is a profitless button shop run by an aged Jewish woman who is secretly supported by the other Jews in the community but also that the woman thinks he has been put there by her considerate friends to serve as her assistant. And, being a genial fellow, he finds himself falling in with this gentle and humane deception. Indeed, he develops a filial attitude toward the woman.

Up to this point, the film is charmingly humorous, almost Chaplinesque, thanks to the facile performance of Mr. Kroner and the delightful old-worldly graciousness of Miss Kaminska, who, I understand, is a prominent actress in the Yiddish theater in Poland.

Then the blow comes. The order arrives in the community to remove all Jews to the concentration camps, and the little carpenter is put to the dilemma of what to do with his friend—whether to hide her and be her protector or turn her in and protect himself. His comprehension and resolution of this challenge to his humanity constitute the conclusive tragedy—and irony—of the film.

Not since "The Diary of Anne Frank" has there been a drama that has stated the shock and horrible cruelty of Jewish persecution in such overpoweringly close and personal terms. And very few films made in Europe have so subtly and starkly condemned the pusillanimity of the people who allowed these persecutions to take place.

There are some evident flaws in this picture. Some scenes are superfluous or too long. But, by and large, it is finely constructed, directed photographed and played. It is a memorable motion picture about a disgraceful phase of human history.

"The Shop on High Street" was the evening's second offering. The first was the Swedish film "Raven's End," which is a bittersweet observation in a transparent documentary style of a sensitive lad and his pathetic, poor parents living in a lower middle-class area of the city of Malmo. In its gentle and compassionate equating of the relations of the boy with his father there is something of the poignancy of "Death of a Salesman." It was directed by Bo Widerberg, who reveals a humane spirit and a sharp photographic eye. The acting is superbly naturalistic.

This film has not yet been taken for distribution in this country.

S 10, 1965

ALPHAVILLE, screenplay and direction by Jean-Luc Godard; produced by Andre Michelin. A Chaumiane Production (Paris) and Filmstudio (Rome) co-production, released by Pathe Contemporary Films. At the Paris Theater, Fifth Avenue and 58th Street. Running time: 100 minutes.
Lemmy Caution........Eddie Constantine
Natasha Von Braun........ Anna Karina
Henry Dickson . ...Akim Tamiroff
Professor Von Braun......Howard Vernon
The Engineer..............Laszlo Szabo
Asst. to Prof. Von Braun.Michael Delahaye
Professor Eckel........Jean-Andre Fieschi
Professor Jeckel .....Jean-Louis Comolli
Alpha 60.......................Itself

By BOSLEY CROWTHER

NOW it can be stated unequivocally: The trouble with "Alphaville," Jean-Luc Godard's tricky French film, which caused some annoyance and dismay when it was shown as the kickoff picture at the recent New York Film Festival, is that it shifts gears along about the middle.

It begins as a fast-moving prank that combines the amusing agitations of a character on the order of James Bond and the highly pictorial fascinations of a slick science-fiction mystery, and it makes for some brisk satiric mischief when it is zipping along in this vein. Then, half way through, it swings abruptly into a solemn allegorical account of this suddenly sobered fellow with a weird computer-controlled society, and the whole thing becomes a tedious tussle with intellectual banalities.

•

It is lively so long as Lemmy Caution, this secret agent chap who is borrowed from a popular series of cheap French detective films, is moving with eagle-eyed alertness into the mysterious city of Alphaville, casing its robot-like people and the strangely compliant maids in its sleek hotel. And it reaches a high point of excitement when he meets and has a crucial session with a predecessor secret agent, who slips him some vital information and then mysteriously dies.

Up to this point, this offbeat picture, which opened at the Paris yesterday, has all the momentum and promise of a super atomic-age spy film. Lemmy Caution is a cool, efficient tough-guy as played by Eddie Constantine, the sandpaper-faced American actor who has done all his mischief in French films, and Alphaville has the neon-lighted hardness of a modern, city where none but gangsters dwell.

Evil lurks in its shadows. Inhumanity stalks the corridors of the glass-and-metal buildings that seem to immolate a breed of muscular ghosts, and fear signals briefly in the sad eyes of the dying agent, played by Akim Tamiroff. Mr. Godard has set

us up nicely for an onward sweep and entertaining rush of futuristic melodramatics in a modernized Wellsian "Things to Come."

•

And then he goes into low gear. He lets Lemmy Caution get involved with a sloe-eyed, slow-witted maiden who doesn't know the meaning of the word "love," and who seems to be reasonably contented with the technological society of Alphaville. And from here on he leads Mr. Caution—and the viewer—on a slow and painful tour of a complexly automated community that is devoid of conscience and poetry.

Mr. Godard is a great one for making shock impressions with vivid images, and he relies on this technique for achieving the main thematic effects in this film. A scene of people being executed in an airy, antiseptic swimming pool because they have behaved "illogically" — i.e., they have felt emotions—is staggering as a single scene.

But it stands as an isolated image, just as does the fiercely flashing scene of Lemmy Caution penetrating the heart of the computer and easily murdering its master-mind, Professor Von Braun.

What it comes to is simply that the dazzle of Mr. Godard's cinematic style is not matched by the hackneyed idea of a robot society that is expounded in the script. And the mild little tickle of a romance with the daughter of Professor Von Braun is not whipped up to any stirring passion, with Anna Karina meekly playing the girl. Mr. Godard's conclusion that love —good old love—conquers all is a curiously disappointing finish for such an initially promising film.

O 26, 1965

THE SHOP ON MAIN STREET, screen-
play by Ladislav Grossman; directed
by Jan Kadar and Elmar Klos; pro-
duced by Barrandov Film Studios. A
Marie Desmarais-Eurofilm presentation,
released through Prominent Films. At
the 34th Street East Theater, near
Third Avenue. Running time: 128
minutes.
Tono Brtko.................Josef Kroner
Rosalie Lautmann..........Ida Kaminska
Evelina Brtko.............Hana Slivkova
Marcus Kolkotsky.......Frantisek Zvarik
Rose Kolkotska..........Helena Zvarikov
Imro Kuchar...............Martin Holly
Katz, the barber.........Martin Gregory

By BOSLEY CROWTHER

EXCEPT for a slight change in title, "The Shop on Main Street" (formerly High Street) which set up for eminently merited business at the 34th Street East yesterday, is the same stunning Czechoslovak picture that knocked us out of our chairs when it was unassumingly presented at the New York Film Festival last fall.

Nothing in it has been altered. Not a frame of it has been cut, even though there is room for trimming in some of its early and middle scenes —and there is some question, too, about the aptness of its fanciful happy epilogue. It still is for me, on second viewing, away from the crush of the festival, one of the most arresting and devastating pictures I've seen from Europe or anywhere else in several years.

●

The effectiveness of it is clearly in the honesty and simplicity with which it reckons with a great moral issue on the level of small human beings.

Its hero is an average little fellow—an amiable, dullish carpenter living in a small Slovak city in 1942. He doesn't hate anybody (except his nasty, big-mouthed brother-in-law who is the Nazi-installed gauleiter). Some of his best friends are Jews. And he thinks the new political disciplinarians are pompous and absurd.

Yet slowly, as a consequence of taking a favored appointment as the Aryan controller of a Jewish-owned shop in the hopes of getting a rake-off from it, he becomes more and more involved in the gathering moral crisis of abuse and persecution of Jews.

Essentially, he is a good man, and when he finds that the elderly woman who owns the shop doesn't have any money — that she is being secretly supported, indeed, by the charity of the Jewish community — he accepts the fact with wry amusement and becomes the sweet little woman's helper and friend. But he heedlessly commits a cruel injustice by also taking money from the charitable group. And when the day finally comes when the Jewish population is to be transported (to the concentration camps, of course), the weak little man is confronted with the great decision of whether he will protect his helpless friend or betray her to save his own hide.

Out of this simple situation, Jan Kadar and Elmar Klos, who made this film, have constructed a human drama that is a moving manifest of the dark dilemma that confronted all people who were caught as witnesses to Hitler's terrible crime. "Is one his brother's keeper?" is the thundering question the situation asks, and then, as supplement, "Are not all men brothers?" The answer given is a grim acknowledgment.

But the unfolding of the drama is simple, done in casual, homely, humorous terms — until the terrible, heartbreaking resolution of the issue at the end. The little man, played superbly by Josef Kroner, is a cross-cut of human good and bad, a sad and ironic combination of gentle virtues and tragic weaknesses. And the sweet old Jewish lady, played by Ida Kaminska, who is a leading light of the Polish Jewish theater, is a wondrous image of Old World innocence.

●

There are fine scenes and luminous moments in which the culture and social shape of the wartime Slovak city are vividly inscribed. And supporting roles are played as strongly and revealingly as the leads. Hana Slivkova as the carpenter's coarse and sensual wife, Frantisek Zvarik as the wicked Nazi-serving brother-in-law, Martin Holly as a benevolent elder citizen and Martin Gregor as an earnest, patient Jew are unforgettable standouts in an excellent cast.

To my mind, the romantic transport that is tacked on at the end is an obvious and sentimental softening of the picture's intense reality. But it does serve a certain benevolent purpose. As Mr. Kadar was saying here the other day, it does provide him—and, he assumes, his countrymen—the balm of spiritual uplift and hope that the horrible injustices committed against innocent people may bring some realization of the need of brotherhood.

The dialogue is spoken in Slovak, with English subtitles.

Ja 25, 1966

BAND OF OUTSIDERS (Bande a Part); written for the screen and directed by Jean-Luc Goddard; based on the novel, "Fool's Gold" by Dorothy Hitchens; produced by Anouchka Films-Orsay Films and released by Royal Films International. At the Beekman Theater, Second Avenue and 65th Street. Running time: 97 minutes.
Odile ....Ana Karina
Franz ....Sami Frey
Arthur ....Claude Brasseur

A S one of the big wheels churning up France's New Wave, the writer-director Jean-Luc Godard has created a ripple with "Band of Outsiders," which took up residence at the Beekman Theater yesterday. The serio-comic adventure, first exposed to a New York Film Festival audience in September, 1964, is guaranteed to enchant the avant-garde coterie that first took him to its mysterious heart in 1961 with the appearance of "Breathless."

But to the obviously larger body of moviegoers not sensitively attuned to personal jokes and personal statements, "Band of Outsiders" is decidedly outside their ken, and needs fuller explanations and infinitely more credible people.

As was the case in "Breathless," Mr. Godard is concerned with young, footloose types involved in crime. He also is intent on intruding himself on the action via explanations he delivers in off-screen narration that explain both the action and his principal characters. The director has described his film as "Alice in Wonderland Meets Franz Kafka." The description could not be more apt. But his dissections of character and motivation definitely need amplification.

His three leads are a young servant girl and two Parisian hoods she has met in school. She agrees vacuously to accompany them in a robbery of her suburban house. What they are after is a large cache of money, ill-gotten apparently, that a lodger has stashed away. And, as their caper develops, their gay lark turns into a tragic debacle.

As a director, Mr. Godard is well aware of the idea that motion pictures mean motion. His "Outsiders" are constantly on the move in their battered Simca as it swiftly courses from Parisian boulevards to the autumnal suburbs, as one vignette swiftly merges with another. And his views of a misty Paris are truly, as one of the players notes. "Comet-like."

His three principals, on the other hand, are constantly philosophizing about love and loneliness, but show little of

396

either. Mr. Godard, it should be added, is effective in kidding moviemaking styles. This is exemplified in his climactic shooting scene, in which one criminal takes enough bullets to demolish an elephant before expiring. His sense of humor also is apparent when one of the robbers casually snatches a book before proceeding to search for the loot.

Anna Karina, who is Mrs. Godard in private life and has made five films with him, looks amazingly like a youthful Sylvia Sidney. But, as a teen-ager attracted to the rough Arthur and equally to the somewhat tender Franz, she more often projects callow naiveté than charm. Claude Brasseur, as the direct and muscular Arthur, is a vague type despite all of his sardonic, terse talk. He may horse around with his dreamer pal, but one longs for some indications of his background. In a lesser degree this is also true of Sami Frey as the more intellectual of the partners in crime. Dark-haired and with a sense of humor, he is more mysterious than real, a grown-up gamin gone gamy.

Miss Karina and Mr. Frey escape and are happily en route to South America, whence, the English subtitles gaily promise, will come a sequel in "CinemaScope and Technicolor." Mr. Godard obviously is kidding, but the "Batman" TV series, for example, does it infinitely better. Let's just leave them in South America.   A. H. WEILER.

Mr 16, 1966

WHO'S AFRAID OF VIRGINIA WOOLF?—
  Screenplay by Ernest Lehman, based on the play by Edward Albee; directed by Mike Nichols; produced by Mr. Lehman, presented by Warner Brothers. At the Criterion Theater, Broadway and 45th Street and the Tower East Theater, Third Avenue and 72d Street. Running time: 130 minutes.
Martha ....Elizabeth Taylor
George ....Richard Burton
Nick ... .George Segal
Honey ....Sandy Dennis

By **STANLEY KAUFFMANN**

EDWARD ALBEE'S "Who's Afraid of Virginia Woolf?", the best American play of the last decade and a violently candid one, has been brought to the screen without pussyfooting. (It is now at the Criterion and Loew's Tower East.) This in itself makes it a notable event in our film history. About the film as such, there is more to be said.

First things first. The most pressing question—since we already know a great deal about the play and the two stars—is the direction. Mike Nichols, after a brilliant and too-brief career as a satirist, proved to be a brilliant theatrical director of comedy. This is his debut as a film director, and it is a successful Houdini feat.

●

Houdini, you remember, was the magician who was chained hand and foot, bound in a sack, dumped in a river, and then appeared some minutes later on the surface. You do not expect Olympic swimming form in a Houdini; the triumph is just to come out alive.

Which Mr. Nichols has done. He was given two world-shaking stars, the play of the decade and the auspices of a large looming studio. What more inhibiting conditions could be imagined for a first film, if the director is a man of talent? But Mr. Nichols has at least survived. The form is not Olympic, but he lives.

Any transference of a good play to film is a battle. (Which is why the best film directors rarely deal with good plays.) The better the play, the harder it struggles against leaving its natural habitat, and Mr. Albee's extraordinary comedy-drama has put up a stiff fight.

Ernest Lehman, the screen adapter, has broken the play out of its one living-room setting into various rooms in the house and onto the lawn, which the play accepts well enough. He has also placed one scene in a roadhouse, which is a patently forced move for visual variety. These changes and some minor cuts, including a little inconsequential blue-penciling, are about the sum of his efforts. The real job of "filmizing" was left to the director.

With no possible chance to cut loose cinematically (as, for example, Richard Lester did in his film of the stage comedy "The Knack"), Mr. Nichols has made the most of two elements that were left to him—intimacy and acting.

He has gone to school to several film masters (Kurosawa among them, I would guess) in the skills of keeping the camera close, indecently prying; giving us a sense of his characters' very breath, bad 'breath, held breath; tracking a face—in the rhythm of the scene—as the actor moves, to take us to other faces; punctuating with sudden withdrawals to give us a brief, almost dispassionate respite; then plunging us in close again to one or two faces, for lots of pores and bile.

●

There is not much that is original in Mr. Nichols's camerawork, no sense of the personality that we got in his stage direction. In fact, the direction is weakest when he gets a bit arty: electric signs flashing behind heads or tilted shots from below to show passion and abandon (both of them hallmarks of the college cinema virtuoso). But he has minimized the "stage" feeling, and he has given the film an insistent presence, good phrasing and a nervous drive. It sags toward the end, but this is because the third act of the play sags.

As for the acting, Mr. Nichols had Richard Burton

as George. (To refresh us all, George is a fortyish history professor, married to Martha, the daughter of the president of a New England college. They return home from a party at 1:30 A.M., slightly sozzled, drenched in their 20-year-old marital love-hate ambivalence. A young faculty couple come over for drinks, and the party winds viciously on until dawn. In the course of it, Martha sleeps with the young man as an act of vengeance on George. The play ends with George's retribution—the destruction of their myth about a son they never had.

Mr. Burton was part of the star package with which this film began, but—a big but—Mr. Burton is also an actor. He has become a kind of specialist in sensitive self-disgust, as witness the latter scenes of "Cleopatra" and all of "The Spy Who Came In from the Cold," and he does it well. He is not in his person the George we might imagine, but he is utterly convincing as a man with a great lake of nausea in him, on which he sails with regret and compulsive amusement.

On past evidence, Mr. Nichols had relatively little work to do with Mr. Burton. On past evidence, he had a good deal to do with Elizabeth Taylor, playing Martha. She has shown previously, in some roles, that she could respond to the right director and could at least flagellate herself into an emotional state (as in "Suddenly, Last Summer"). Here, with a director who knows how to get an actor's confidence and knows what to do with it after he gets it, she does the best work of her career, sustained and urgent.

Of course, she has an initial advantage. Her acceptance of gray hair and her use of profanity make her seem to be acting even (figuratively) before she begins. ("Gee, she let them show her looking old! Wow, she just said 'Son of a bitch'! A star!") It is not the first time an American star has gotten mileage out of that sort of daring. Miss Taylor does not have qualities that, for instance, Uta Hagen had in the Broadway version, no suggestion of endlessly coiled involutions. Her venom is nearer the surface. But, under Mr. Nichols's hand, she gets vocal variety, never relapses out of the role, and she charges it with the utmost of her powers—which is an achievement for any actress, great or little.

As the younger man, George Segal gives his usual good terrier performance, lithe and snapping, with nice bafflement at the complexities of what he thought was simply a bad marriage. As his bland wife, Sandy Dennis is credibly bland.

Mr. Albee's play looks both better and a little worse under the camera's magnification. A chief virtue for me is that it is not an onion-skin play—it does not merely strip off layers, beginning at the surface with trifles and digging deeper as it proceeds. Of course, we learn more about the characters as we go, and almost all of it is fascinating; but, like its giant forebear, Strindberg's "Dance of Death," the play *begins* in in hell, and all the revelations and reactions take place within that landscape.

What does not wear well in the generally superb dialogue is the heavy lacing of vaudeville cross-talk, particularly facile non sequiturs. (Also, in Mr. Lehman's version, so much shouting and slamming takes place on the front lawn at four in the morning that we keep wondering why a neighbor doesn't wake up and complain.)

More serious is the height-ened impression that the myth of the son is irrelevant to the play. It seems a device that the author tacked on to conclude matters as the slash and counterslash grew tired; a device that he then went back and planted earlier. Else why would Martha have told the other woman the secret of the son so glibly—not when she was angry or drunk—if she knew she was breaching an old and sacred compact with her husband? It obtrudes as an arbitrary action to justify the ending.

The really relevant unseen character is not the son; it is Martha's father, the president of the college. It is he whom she idolizes and measures her husband against, it is his presence George has to contend with in and out of bed. It is Daddy's power, symbolic in Martha, that keeps the visiting couple from leaving, despite circumstances that would soon have driven them out of any other house.

Awareness—of this truth about Daddy, of multiple other truths about themselves and their world—is the theme of this play: not the necessity of narcotic illusion about the son, but naked, peeled awareness. Under the vituperation and violence, under Martha's aggressive and self-punishing infidelties this is the drama of a marriage flooded with more consciousness than the human psyche is at present able to bear.

Their world is too much with them, their selves are much too clear. It is the price to be paid for living in a cosmos of increasing clarity—which includes a clearer view of inevitable futilities. And, fundamentally, it is this desperation—articulated in childless, broken-hearted, demonically loving marriage—that Mr. Albee has crystallized in his flawed but fine play.

And in its forthright dealing with the play, this becomes one of the most scathingly honest American films ever made. Its advertisements say, "No one under 18 will be admitted unless accompanied by his parent." This may safeguard the children; the parents must take their chances.

Je 30, 1966

WHO'S AFRAID OF VIRGINIA WOOLF?

By BOSLEY CROWTHER

AFTER all the initial commotion over "Who's Afraid of Virginia Woolf?" — all the wailing of the censors, the shouting of the reviewers and the mumbling and grumbling of those patrons who have come away stunned and confused — there remains one simple statement to be made about this film: it is a magnificent triumph of determined audacity.

Whatever one thinks about it as a work of art — and that's as moot as a critical judgment of Edward Albee's original play — it does manifest a bold endeavor to put upon the screen material as candid and caustic as that which is put upon the stage. It does represent a thrust of courage and integrity on the part of everyone who risked reputations and money to put it across — and that includes Jack L. Warner, who backed it and stuck to his guns, as well as Richard Burton and Elizabeth Taylor, who play the unglamorous leading roles.

It is, in short, an indication of the kind of determination to come to grips with contemporary human and social problems that our American filmmakers sorely need. It is an example of daring that inspires admiration and hope.

That said — and, believe me, it's a mouthful to be said about an enterprise these days — let's get to a close examination of what has been put upon the screen.

Make no mistake about it being an artful truncation of the play or a subtle Bowdlerization of Mr. Albee's apparent theme. All of the sordid innuendoes, the crudities and the dirty words that flowed on the stage are repeated in this invidious film, and its slant on two tormented persons is the same as it is in the play. Whatever the shortcomings and annoyances in the film, they should be charged against the obscurities in Mr. Albee's work, rather than against the fairness of Ernest Lehman's script or the prescience of Mike Nichols's direction, which is surprisingly good for a first film.

Sharper Focus

Indeed, in my estimation, the major advantage of the film is that it does illuminate a bit more clearly some of the darker obscurities of the play. It does get a closer, sharper focus upon the physical and spiritual agonies of two immature, frustrated persons, a college professor and his middle-aged wife, who have to nourish themselves with wild delusions and strange, masochistic games and myths in order to whip up emotional excitement and give themselves a few sexual kicks.

The crucial point in this drama is that the vulgar and snarling wife is a frightened, inhibited creature for all her brazen profanity and her unbelievable boasting of innumerable infidelities. Why she is frightened and inhibited is one of the niggling obscurities of the play, and it is hard to see it as merely a matter of 'her being the daughter of a tyrannical college president.

Like the poor fellow in "Morgan!", she has to create a fantasy of being something which she isn't — in her case, a wastrel and a slut — in order to give herself character and confidence. She has to bully her husband, use filthy words, pretend to be profligate with her body, affect an air of contempt. And her husband, who is also frustrated — a third-rate intellect, at best — has discovered escape and even pleasure in playing her perverted game.

Therefore he plays it with her. And one gathers — especially from the film which sets up a sense of repetition by its monotonous iterations and peevish moods —that they've been playing it for years. They have been gabbling about the wife's bogus infidelities and the husband's self-pitying boyhood memories and their wholly imaginary child to everybody in the college community who would come to their home and booze it up with them. By now we can well imagine they are the community pests. That's why the wife is excited when they find a new couple come to town, a young, cornball professor and his immature wife, for whom they can do their act — put on their perverted exhibition of verbally flagellating themselves.

All this is clearly presented and developed in the film, and it is made both ironic and poignant by the raw femininity and blowsy charm Miss Taylor is able to communicate in the unattractive role. It is also made significant by the wonderfully subtle blend of sensitive concern and sadism that Mr. Burton gives to the husband role.

The incident on which the continuity of the couple's illusion-act turns is the unprecedented decision of the wife to go upstairs with the physically attractive young professor after a night of boozing with him. (One night of boozing by the two couples is the time-span of the film.)

End of a Game

This startles and angers her husband. This is not playing their game. So he takes the ultimate vengeance. He announces the death of their imaginary child. It is this shattering invention that brings their game to a close.

What is engrossing and appealing about this ugly and tawdry display, outside of the grotesque humor of its blatant vulgarities, is the amount of curious pathos it obliquely generates, the sad and piteous statement it makes about certain sterile types. These are isolated people, wrapped in loneliness. And this is further indicated by a pictorial advantage of the film.

Unlike the stage play, the movie is not played in one room. As the boozing party develops, it tumbles out of doors. And it is surprisingly significant that out on their lawn, in the middle of the night, making outrageous noises and racing about in cars, the couples are awesomely surrounded by only darkness, silence and doom.

Nobody raises a window and angrily shouts, "Shut up!" No watchman arrives to rebuke them. They are totally, terrifyingly alone. And when they go to a road-house for some dancing, the joint is empty. It is a hollow, friendless place in which the continued blathering and the lonely dance of the childish young wife are particularly foolish. The only persons there, a dour proprietor and wraith-like waitress, tell them the place is closed. Even the ordinary privilege of mixing with people in a joint is denied.

It is regrettable that Mr. Nichols was not able to get more from the roles of the other couple, whom George Segal and Sandy Dennis play. As it is, they are crudely affected, theatrical and implausible, so that the hint of two other young people becoming infected with the same perverted urge of the older, frustrated couple is not sufficiently clear.

But Miss Taylor and Mr. Burton are splendid, providing quite as much as the play permits of sharp psychological dissection of the older, corrosive pair. Perhaps Mr. Nichols's direction allows them to punch too hard at times. They do seem to have a disposition to overpound obvious points. And occasionally —such as in a wry scene of Mr. Burton behaving boyishly in a swing—the license and tone developed is that of a comedy act.

When you come right down to it, however, the play invites a mood of harshly contorted black humor. It is almost grotesque comedy. These characters are so wild and aberrant they are close to appearing lunatics. That is why they are frightening and pathetic. They are outcasts of a brutal, baffling world.

Jl 10, 1966

MASCULINE FEMININE, written and directed by Jean-Luc Godard, and produced by Anouchka-Argos-Svensk Film-industri-Sandrews. A Royal Film International release. At the Little Carnegie, 146 West 57th Street. Running time: 103 minutes.
Paul .... Jean-Pierre Leaud
Madeleine .... Chantal Goya
Elisabeth ....:........ Marlene Jobert
Robert .... Michel Debord
Catherine-Isabelle
                 Catherine-Isabelle Duport
Lavinia .... Eva-Britt Strandberg
                         and
                    Brigitte Bardot

By BOSLEY CROWTHER

JEAN-LUC GODARD, a reigning favorite with the New York Film Festival crowd, probably because he is the doggedest of the old new wave cinéists in France, had his first whack at the audience of this year's festival last night, with the showing of his "Masculine Feminine" in Philharmonic Hall.

He will have his next whack with the showing of his "Pierrot Le Fou" on Wednesday night, which will make him and Pier Paolo Pasolini the only directors with two films in this year's festival.

And if that doesn't give accommodation to all the eager admirers of Mr. Godard, "Masculine Feminine" may be seen at the Little Carnegie in a continuous commercial run, beginning today. For the first time in the festival's four years, one of its attractions will go into immediate release, thus taking quick advantage of whatever prestige and momentum it may gain.

The question is how much momentum "Masculine Feminine" may have after its saturation showing to a capacity audience last night. For it is another of those peculiarly vague and elusive Godard films of the sort that he seems to be making at the rate of about two or three a year.

●

It gives a pretense of being a study of the mores of Parisian youth as conducted by a fuzzy-brained young fellow who becomes rather personally involved, especially with a fidgety young woman who seems to lead him to be even more confused than he is at the outset about the attitude of French girls toward sex.

But this is just the pretense of the picture. Mainly it seems to be a movie happening, in which Mr. Godard can play whimsical and sometimes comical stunts, not leading to any clear conclusion as to the stability of youth. He himself, as a motion-picture maker, seems to have little more concentration-span than his saucy, good-looking youngsters, who evidently have none at all.

From lengthy and tedious conversation between his fellow and his girl about themselves, he will jump to scenes of youngsters demonstrating in the streets against Vietnam. In the middle of the random flow of story, he stops for a lengthy interview with a girl who holds the screen for the entire shot, sitting casually on a windowsill. (Evidently this is a put-on of cinema vérité.) Or he turns the screen over for a long and meaningless dialogue between Brigitte Bardot and someone who is apparently a theatrical director, which has nothing to do with this film.

There are some cute things in it, especially Chantal Goya and Marlene Jobert as the most prominent females, and Jean-Pierre Leaud shows that he has grown into a handsome young fellow since he played the tough kid in "The 400 Blows." But it adds up to entertainment of only the most loose and spotty sort.

●

S 19, 1966

PIERROT LE FOU

By BOSLEY CROWTHER

JEAN-LUC Godard dropped his other shoe at the fourth New York Film Festival last night. His second film to be shown—his much-talked-about "Pierre le Fou" ("Peter the Crazy")—was a wet night's sole attraction in Philharmonic Hall. The other film scheduled for the evening, Jean Renoir's 1931 drama, "La Chienne" ("The Bitch"), had been canceled.

The splash caused by Mr. Godard's picture was minor compared with the splashing outside, for it turned out to be a synthetic, repetitious and overlong account of the rambles of two highly elastic lovers who can't make up their minds.

●

The fellow, played by Jean-Paul Belmondo, appears rather gone on the girl; but she, played by Anna Karina, keeps bouncing away from him. Thus they bounce a bit around Paris, until the fellow tosses up his job as a television director. Then they go to the Riviera, where they do a bit of indecisive bouncing around Toulon and St. Tropez.

Since the film is in excellent color, the sight-seeing is good, and that includes some sight-seeing of Miss Karina, whom Mr. Godard photographs lovingly and with great care. But the curious identification of the young woman as a secret consort of criminals and the custodian of a corpse she is compelled to dispose of, intrudes a hint of cryptic symbolism that is unresolved and thus obscure. Of course, this is not uncommon in a Godard film.

From The New York Times Film Reviews

403

Also there are intimations that the young man, a blunt and stupid sort, has romantic illusions about his relations with the girl. He visions themselves as lovers ranging all' the way from the Paul and Virginia of Jean Jacques Rousseau to the melodramatic couples in contemporary comic strips.

●

The concept is mildly amusing, but is not sufficient to sustain the almost two hours of rambling that the couple do. A song or two by Mr. Belmondo, rendered in an unmelodic voice, and some tossed-in impersonations of vulgar Americans seemed to amuse the Godard worshipers in the audience, but the morsels of entertainment were few and far between.

Once again, as in his entry last Sunday, "Masculine Feminine," he fails to build up any feeling for his people. They are just types in an insistently specified film.

S 22, 1966

LA GUERRE EST FINI

THE fourth annual New York Film Festival was brought to a close last night with a film appropriately titled "La Guerre Est Fini" ("The War Is Over"). And in other respects, too, this mood-drenched drama from France's Alain Resnais was appropriate to the windup of the cinema series in Philharmonic Hall.

It is a beautifully made and acted picture, as many in the festival have been. Mr. Resnais has created, from a screenplay by Jorge Semprun, a strikingly realistic and emotionally taut account of the trip that a veteran revolutionary makes from contemporary Spain to report to party headquarters in Paris and to visit his Scandinavian mistress while there.

The drama is on two levels

—first, that of the intrigue and peril of the man getting over the border and avoiding detection in France, and then that of his indecision toward his mistress and toward his work. He is getting on, he is weary, he is disillusioned and he is bored. Perhaps he should give up being a revolutionist and settle down with his mistress and a job.

●

Mr. Resnais blends the drama of both these levels most artfully, moving with sure fluidity from the realistic tensions of his man's political contacts and his activities into the sweet and wistful areas of his own feelings. And the role of the revolutionary is played strongly by Yves Montand, while his mistress is played with serenity and compassion by Ingrid Thulin.

In short—and short is what this notice must perforce be —"La Guerre Est Fini" is artistic and appropriate to close a festival.

Furthermore, it does have the distinction of being something of a cause célèbre at the Cannes festival this year because it was considered inimical to the Spanish Government. It has in it several references to the suppression of workers' demonstrations in Spain and of intransigience toward the leftist opposition. Its showing here upholds the freedom of the screen.

But it must be said that it runs long, tediously long—two hours—and its heavy political orientation may be too slanted and intellectual for general taste. Out of its socialistic sentiments may flow some wistfulness for old loyalties, but its summation is unconvincing.

It is to be distributed by Brandon Films.

BOSLEY CROWTHER.

S 23, 1966

INGMAR BERGMAN TRIES NEW THEME

'Persona' Hailed in Sweden —A Film About Loneliness

By WERNER WISKARI
Special to The New York Times

STOCKHOLM, Oct. 19—Ingmar Bergman has added to what Swedes call his "myth" as a moviemaker with a film about intense personal loneliness, "Persona."

The picture, which opened here last night, was acclaimed today by Stockholm's film critics as one of his simplest, freest and most powerful. The critic of Expressen said that Mr. Bergman, who both wrote and directed the film, had now broken with the "final artistic bond."

Svenska Dagbladet described the movie as a gripping film in which Mr. Bergman evinces his recent trend of focusing on "smaller and smaller circles to people who chance to have the same obsessions."

"Persona," a black-and-white production that occupies a conventional-size screen, is Mr. Bergman's 29th cinematic work. It is without any religious content.

His previous preoccupation with man's relationship with God was last expressed in "The Winter Light," which appeared in February of 1963. It centered on 'a disillusioned clergyman who suffered what Mr. Bergman called the ultimate torment, the silence of God.

With that film Mr. Bergman told associates he was "through" with religious themes. He turned next to a dramatization of the ugliness of human relations when the only contact is physical. "Silence" opened in September of 1963 to the acclaim of critics, and, aided by a controversy over some erotic scenes, it became a box-office hit here and abroad.

There is no eroticism in "Persona," the story of an actress who chooses to turn mute while on the stage. She feels that she is a vampire in a dying world and that there is no use talking when no one is really listening. A nurse undertakes her rehabilitation but in the process takes on the tormented personality of the patient as she succeeds in getting the actress to say only the word "nothing."

The film, which is sprinkled with cinematic tricks, leaves much unanswered. It ends inconclusively with no indications whether the actress will ever speak again. An early version had her returning rehabilitated to the stage. But Mr. Bergman dropped that ending.

The prevailing Swedish aversion to the war in Vietnam is reflected in a scene in which the actress cowers in a corner while watching on television a Buddhist monk burning and toppling over as a newscaster gives details of American bombing raids.

Mr. Bergman got his idea for "Persona" when he chanced to see two actresses together and noted how similar and at the same time how different their faces looked. All the critics here today joined in acclaiming the two stars, Bibi Andersson as the nurse and Liv Ullman as the actress, whose personalities become intermingled.

Mr. Bergman is now completing another film about loneliness. It is entitled "The Wolf's Hour," the Swedish term for the hour just before dawn when most nightmares are said to occur.

O 20, 1966

BLOW-UP; screenplay by Michelangelo Antonioni and Tonino Guerra; directed by Mr. Antonioni; produced by Carlo Ponti and released by Premier Productions Co., Inc. At the Coronet Theater, 59th Street and Third Avenue. Running time: 110 minutes.

Thomas	David Hemmings
Jane	Vanessa Redgrave
Patricia	Sarah Miles
Models	Verushka
	Jill Kennington
	Peggy Moffit
	Rosaleen Murray
	Ann Norman
	Melanie Hampshire

By BOSLEY CROWTHER

IT will be a crying shame if the audience that will undoubtedly be attracted to Michelangelo Antonioni's "Blow-Up" because it has been denied a Production Code seal goes looking more for sensual titillation than for the good, solid substance it contains — and therefore will be distracted from recognizing the magnitude of its forest by paying attention to the comparatively few defoliated trees.

This is a fascinating picture, which has something real to say about the matter of personal involvement and emotional commitment in a jazzed - up, media - hooked - in world so cluttered with synthetic stimulations that natural feelings are overwhelmed. It is vintage Antonioni fortified with a Hitchcock twist, and it is beautifully photographed in color. It opened at the Coronet last night.

It marks a long step for Mr. Antonioni, the Italian director whose style of introspective visualization has featured all his Italian-language films from "L'Avventura" through "Red Desert," and in all of which Monica Vitti has played what has amounted to a homogeneous gallery of alienated female roles. It is his first film in eight years without Miss Vitti. It is his first major film about a man. And it is his first film made in England and in English (except for one vagrant episode in his three-part "I "Vinti," made in 1952).

•

The fellow whose restlessness and groping interests Mr. Antonioni in this new film is a dizzyingly swinging and stylish free-lance magazine photographer, whose racing and tearing around London gives a terrifying hint of mania. He can spend a night dressed up like a hobo shooting a layout of stark photographs of derelicts in a flophouse, then jump into his Rolls-Royce open-top and race back to his studio to shoot a layout of fashion models in shiny mod costumes — and do it without changing expression or his filthy, tattered clothes.

He can break off from this preoccupation and go tearing across the city in his car to buy an antique airplane propeller in a junk shop, with virtually the same degree of casualness and whim as he shows when he breaks off from concentrating on a crucial job in his dark-room to have a brief, orgiastic romp with a couple of silly teenage girls.

Everything about this feral fellow is footloose, arrogant, fierce, signifying a tiger—or an incongruously baby-faced lone wolf—stalking his prey in a society for which he seems to have no more concern, no more feeling or understanding than he has for the equipment and props he impulsively breaks. His only identification is with the camera, that trenchant mechanism with which he makes images and graphic fabrications of—what? Truth or fantasy?

This is what gets him into trouble. One day, while strolling in a park, he makes some candid snaps of a young woman romancing with a man. The young woman, startled, tries to get him to give the unexposed roll of film to her. So nervous and anxious is she that she follows him to his studio. There, because she is fascinated by him and also in order to get the film, she submits to his arrogant seduction and goes away with a roll of film.

'But it is not the right roll. He has tricked her, out of idle curiosity, it appears, as to why the girl should be so anxious. How is she involved?

When he develops the right roll and is casually studying the contact prints, he suddenly notices something. (Here comes the Hitchcock twist!) What is that there in the bushes, a few feet away from where the embracing couple are? He starts making blow-ups of the pictures, switching them around, studying the blow-ups with a magnifying glass. Is it a hand pointing a gun?

There, that is all I'm going to tell you about this uncommon shot of plot into an Antonioni picture—this flash of melodramatic mystery that suddenly presents our fellow with an involvement that should tightly challenge him. I will only say that it allows Mr. Antonioni to find a proper, rueful climax for this theme.

One may have reservations towards this picture. It is redundant and long. There are the usual Antonioni passages of seemingly endless wanderings. The interest may be too much concentrated in the one character, and the symbolistic conclusion may be too romantic for the mood.

●

It is still a stunning picture—beautifully built up with glowing images and color compositions that get us into the feelings of our man and into the characteristic of the mod world in which he dwells. There is even exciting vitality in the routine business of his using photographs—prints and blow-ups and superimpositions—to bring a thought, a preconception, alive.

And the performing is ex-cellent. David Hemmings as the chap is completely fascinating—languid, self-indulgent, cool, yet expressive of so much frustration. He looks remarkably like Terence Stamp. Vanessa Redgrave is pliant and elusive, seductive yet remote as the girl who has been snapped in the park and is willing to reveal so much—and yet so little—of herself. And Sarah Miles is an interesting suggestion of an empty emotion in a small role.

How a picture as meaningful as this one could be blackballed is hard to understand. Perhaps it is because it is too candid, too uncomfortably disturbing, about the dehumanizing potential of photography.

D 19, 1966

LA GUERRE EST FINIE (THE WAR IS OVER); screenplay by Jorge Semprun directed by Alain Resnais; produced by Sofracima of Paris and Europa-Film of Stockholm for release by Brandor Films, Inc. At the Beekman Theater, Second Avenue and 65th Street.. Running time: 121 minutes.
Diego ....Yves Montand
Marianne ....Ingrid Thulin
Nadine ....Genevieve Bujold
Jude ....Dominique Rozan
Juan ....Juan-Francois Remi
Roberto ....Paul Crauchet
Chief ....Jean Daste
Narrator ....Jorge Semprun
Inspector ....Michel Piccoli
Ramon ....Jean Bouise
Yvette ....Yvette Etievant
Carmen ....Francoise Bertin

"**I** A GUERRE EST FINIE" ("The War Is Over") which began an engagement at the Beekman yesterday, is a film that grows on you — and that I can knowingly say, having seen it thrice. (The previous occasions were at the Cannes and New York festivals last year.)

The reason for this is that the fullness of the character that Yves Montand plays — that of an aging revolutionary who has escaped briefly into France from Spain — is much too subtle and complex to be thoroughly understood and emotionally appreciated on the first (or even the second) time it's seen.

Also the snatches of memories and suppositions that Alain Resnais has popped into the picture without any usual punctuation marks to distinguish the mental images from the flow of the narrative are likely to be confusing the first time the film is seen. They sort themselves out very nicely and become much more meaningful, dramatic and poignant when it is seen again. (Remember, the clue to the transitions is in the continuation of the narrative background sounds.)

Further, the intellectual wrangles among Communist theoreticians that occur as this old Spanish left-wing agitator spars with senior and junior members of the Paris cells may be checked off as passages in the picture that you don't have to pay attention to with any strenuous exercise of concentration. They are largely political details.

What is progressively more moving is the sense of weariness, sadness, despair, nostalgia and personal dedication that Mr. Montand communicates in the roil of indecision in this old fellow as to whether he should return to Spain and go on with the "war."

The flow of the drama on the level of political secrecy and intrigue is intense, as I said in my review of the picture when it was shown at the New York festival. Mr. Resnais has done a superb job of getting the realistic look and feel of present-day France in the area of the intellectuals of the working class. And he makes you have stronger comprehension of the operations and intensity of the radical left.

●

But the heart and blood of the drama is in the feelings of Mr. Montand's man—in his attitudes toward his Paris mistress, whom Ingrid Thulin plays with a variety of emo-

tional definition that makes her very real and elusive, too; in his fierce, sudden, nostalgic turning to a politically passionate girl, portrayed by Genevieve Bujold in a most tender, true and convincing way; in his masculine concerns for his associates—indeed, in every respect in which he reveals himself, this picture has meaning and quality.

"La Guerre Est Finie" is a drama above political prejudices. It is a powerful study of a man's commitment to a consuming and bewildering belief.   B.C.

F 2, 1967

PERSONA, written and directed by Ingmar Bergman; an AB Svensk Filmindustri Production distributed by Lopert Pictures Corporation. At the Festival Theater, 57th Street, west of Fifth Avenue. Running time: 81 minutes.
Nurse Alma..............Bibi Andersson
Actress Elisabeth Vogler....Liv Ullmann
Woman Doctor........Margaretha Krook
Mr. Vogler..........Gunnar Bjornstrand
Boy ....Jorgen Lindstrom

By BOSLEY CROWTHER

ONCE again, Ingmar Bergman is bringing us into contact with two strangely troubled women and exploring the sensitive movements of their minds in his new Swedish film, "Persona," which came to the Festival Theater yesterday. And once again he is inviting (or compelling) his public to engage in studious efforts at interpretation or simply outright involvement of themselves, empathically and esthetically, and let the egos and ids fall where they may.

The latter would seem the better purpose with which to approach this lovely, moody film which, for all its intense emotionalism, makes some tough intellectual demands. For its evident contemplation of a singular phenomenon of transfer of personality between an older mental patient and her pretty, lone-

nurse is rich in poetic intimations of subconscious longings and despairs, and it is likely to move one more deeply as poetry than as thought.

Indeed, it appears from the way Mr. Bergman begins his film that he wants us to absorb it as experience conveyed through the mechanical techniques of this illusion-creating medium, rather than as transmitted reality. He wants us to understand clearly that we are looking at images that have their own personal connotations, according to the conditioning of the individual viewer.

He starts his picture literally inside a projection-machine — the arc-light hissing on, the film chattering with its intermittent movement through the gate, images flashing from the blank screen, conventional symbols or ideographs, such as a comic cartoon or a close-up of a hand being pierced by a spike, then shots of the faces of old people lying on slabs under sheets—all indications of the convictions compelled by mechanical images.

One small body lying inert under a seeming shroud, is finally summoned to movement by a persistently ringing telephone (this is an aural symbol), and rises to reveal itself as the boy from Mr. Bergman's "The Silence." He scans a face that comes to form on an opaque screen, runs his hand over the image as though trying to understand it through the sense of touch. The effort is evidently unrewarding.

Thus the emotional experience is introduced.

It is that of a capable young trained nurse, who is given the delicate job of attending a famous actress. The latter has had a trauma of some sort, which has rendered her mute and caused her to withdraw from the world. The two go to spend the summer alone in a cottage by the sea. Here, by some curious osmosis of the actress's attitudes, the nurse takes on her personality and the actress takes on that of the nurse.

At least, I think that's the idea—though, as I say, interpretation is tough, and the impression one gets from the relations of these two images of troubled women may be different. The important thing is that Mr. Bergman has magnificently and sensitively composed a veritable poem of two feminine spirits exchanging their longings, repressions and mental woes against a background of natural beauty and the atmosphere of the sea.

As Mr. Bergman himself has written, "Our work in films begins with the human face," and he has composed much of "Personna" with close-ups of the fascinating faces of Liv Ullmann and Bibi Andersson. Miss Ullmann is the silent patient, whose reactions are in moody pantomime, and Miss Andersson is the nurse, whose strange outpourings come in clouded expressions and many words. picture is that too much is picture is that so much is said with words which, especially for us who have to read them in English subtitles, inject a lot of literary imagery. For instance, there is a lengthy monologue in which the nurse describes a bizarre sexual encounter she and another young woman had with two boys on a beach one summer, from which the nurse became pregnant. It is done with remarkable simplicity and dignity, but it is verbal stimulation, whether listened to or read.

Much finer, more vivid in the medium, is a visual enactment of a dream—or whatever, perhaps a sheer "experience"—in which the two women almost embrace.

That's it. Miss Ullmann and

Miss Andersson just about carry the film—and exquisitely, too. The actress's husband is played in one brief scene by Gunnar Bjornstrand, and Margaretha Krook is very minor as a psychiatrist.

At the end, which is inconclusive, the film goes back into the projection machine and we are left with the haunting wonder: Was this something that happened, or a dream?

Mr 7, 1967

ACCIDENT, screenplay by Harold Pinter; directed by Joseph Losey; produced by Mr. Losey and Norman Priggen; presented by Cinema V Distributing, Inc., and London Independent Producers. At Cinema II, Third Avenue and 60th Street. Running time: 105 minutes.
Stephen .... Dirk Bogarde
Charley .... Stanley Baker
Anna .... Jacqueline Sassard
William .... Michael York
Rosalind .... Vivien Merchant
Francesca .... Delphine Seyrig
Provost .... Alexander Knox
Laura .... Ann Firbank
Bell .... Harold Pinter
Police Sergeant .... Brian Phelan
Plain Clothes Policeman. Terence Rigby

By BOSLEY CROWTHER

IN his new film, "Accident," which opened at Cinema II yesterday, Joseph Losey is in there vying with the English poet, Rupert Brooke. He is graphically and beautifully detailing the things about England he loves — or, at least, those things about Oxford that he finds delightful and serene.

He loves the look out of the college study window of a gentle philosophy don into the courtyard below, where the green grass is kept neatly trimmed by a placid goat. He loves punting on the river, with its lazy ripples and its stately swans. He loves the cricket pitch, with its players lolling through a misty afternoon.

Or, going out into the country, where the don who is his moody hero lives in a pleasant house with a wife and kiddies, he loves just about everything. He loves the way the light falls in the morning on the wide-board, deep-grained floors. He loves the distant sounds of train whistles and the drone of jets high in the sky above the open fields. He makes everything look so mellow and lovely with his color cameras and his way of dwelling idly upon them that you'd think there'd be no fly in the ointment of this most gracious English world.

But there is a fly in the ointment—a very small one—that has been put there by the screenplay's writer, Harold Pinter. The don is mildly in love. At least, he has a vagrant longing for a beautiful Austrian girl to whom he is a tutor, and he is deeply cut when he learns that she has been the mistress of another don.

The fact that this other don is not only one of his oldest friends, but is also an aggravating rival because the other don is a successful television commentator and he is not, doesn't help matters any. Furthermore, our fellow feels he's getting old.

All this is moodily remembered by our hero, whom Dirk Bogarde plays, in a night just after a terrible automobile accident has happened outside his door. The girl he desires, who was driving, is safe but her companion has been killed, and this companion was another of the don's students—a young aristocrat to whom the girl was engaged.

Does that sound a little complicated? Well, it isn't—and it is. It isn't because, actually, the story that Mr. Pinter and Mr. Losey have to tell is simply a frail exploration of the wistfulness and loneliness of this don. It is a conventional study of the

410

minor anxieties of a man who has everything to make him happy, and yet he isn't. He is sad.

But it is complicated from the viewpoint of the person watching the film, because no clues whatsoever are given to the nature of the girl. She is beautiful and quietly mysterious as played by Jacqueline Sassard, but we have no indication of why she so lightly switches men. Her function in the picture is to set up an amoral mystery and serve as an unattainable object of desire for our sad-eyed don.

As played by Mr. Bogarde, he is a conventional type of basically decent homebody, beset by a conventional sentiment. Vivien Merchant is comfortably settled as his only mildly troubled wife, and Stanley Baker is sharp and demanding as the other don. Michael York is mushy and slightly evil as the witless aristocrat, and Delphine Seyrig is softly attractive as the don's old girlfriend in one brief scene.

They all make a slight, incongruous tangle of domestic tensions and sexual mix-ups amid the beauties and graces of Oxford, and now and again one of them will say something amusing or trenchant, thanks to Mr. Pinter's dialogue. But the whole thing is such a teapot tempest, and it is so assiduously underplayed that it is neither strong drama nor stinging satire. It is just a sad little story of a wistful don.

Ap 18, 1967

THE BURMESE HARP, screenplay by Natto Wada, from a story by Michio Takeyama; directed by Kon Ichikawa; produced by Masayuki Takagi for Nikkatsu Pictures; presented here by Brandon Films. At the Fifth Avenue Cinema. Running time: 116 minutes.
Private Mizushima.........Shoji Yasui
Captain Inouye..........Rentaro Mikuni
Old Woman.........Taniye Kitabayashi
Defense Commander....Tatsuya Mihashi

"THE BURMESE HARP" is odd in more ways than one. It won a prize at the Venice Festival in 1956, then reappeared last year for a showing at the New York Film Festival. Yesterday, it began its first run in a United States theater, presented by Thomas Brandon at the Fifth Avenue Cinema.

This poetically photographed Japanese drama is an earnest but extremely circuitous and overstated antiwar film. It moves like a figure 8, making its point at the middle, then looping around for a second, none-too-convincing hour. Under the direction of Kon Ichikawa, it is a stately, almost genteel story of how a soldier, at war's end, turns to the Buddhist priesthood. But in detailing the circumstances — the soldier's inner conflict— barely brushed in and his separation from his Army pals heavily underscored—the picture achieves more sentimentality than spirituality.

The harp of the title is a lovely instrument, ripely plucked by Shoji Yasui, the favorite of his Army unit. He is deputized to pacify some ferocious surrender-holdouts as his company is marched to a British prison camp deep in the Burmese mountains. Isolated, the impressionable soldier stumbles through a horrible aftermath of the war, a wasteland of corpses and bones, stunningly evoked by Mr. Ichikawa's camera on a lunarlike landscape. This is quite the most forceful and forthright part of the film.

What now for the gun-toting harpist?

Abruptly, he turns up outside the prison camp, supposedly a shaven-headed postulant at a Buddhist temple, to the bafflement of his buddies, who peer through barbed wire. The remainder of the film has a cat-and-mouse theatricality, as the prisoners are all obsessed with one question. They are seemingly more concerned with the stranger's shadowy, peek-a-boo appearances than with thoughts of home and family, wanting to know only whether he is or isn't their missing comrade.

They learn, at long last, riding homeward and reading a beautifully written letter from him about the brotherhood of man. The message takes about twice as long as it should, like everything else in the picture.

There are impressive, even skillful nuances in Mr. Ichikawa's drama. But the basic content of one man's spiritual torment remains lengthily sidelined. The key, perhaps, is the photography itself, which brilliantly but methodically dots the players against the looming terrain.

If ever a movie cried out for close-ups, it's this account of a soul-seeking man rent asunder. After the film, it's hard to recall what Mr. Yasui looked like.

HOWARD THOMPSON

Ap 29, 1967

IN THE HEAT OF THE NIGHT; screenplay by Stirling Silliphant, based on the novel by John Ball; directed by Norman Jewison; produced by Walter Mirisch; presented by the Mirisch Corporation, and released through United Artists. At the Capitol Theater, Broadway and 51st Street, and the 86th Street East Theater, east of Third Avenue. Running time: 109 minutes.
Virgil Tibbs...............Sidney Poitier
Bill Gillespie................Rod Steiger
Sam Wood..................Warren Oates
Mrs. Leslie Colbert............Lee Grant
Purdy ....James Patterson
Delores Purdy............Quentin Dean
Eric Endicott................Larry Gates
Webb Schubert..........William Schallart
Mrs. Bellamy (Mama
 Caleba) ....Beah Richards
Harvey Oberst..............Scott Wilson
Philip Colbert................Jack Teter
Packy Harrison..............Matt Clark
Ralph Henshaw........Anthony James
H. E. Henderson.......Kermit Murdock
Jess ....Khalil Bezaleel
George Courtney..........Peter Whitney

By **BOSLEY CROWTHER**

THE hot surge of racial hate and prejudice that is so evident and critical now in so many places in this country, not alone in the traditional area of the Deep South, is fictionally isolated in an ugly little Mississippi town in the new film, "In the Heat of the Night," which opened at the Capitol and the 86th Street East yesterday.

Here the corrosiveness of prejudice is manifested by a clutch of town police and a few weaseling nabobs and red-necks toward a Negro detective from the North who happens to be picked up as a suspect in a white man's murder while he is passing through town. But the surge of this evil feeling is also manifested by the Negro himself after he has been cleared of suspicion and ruefully recruited to help solve the crime. And in this juxtaposition of resentments between whites and blacks is vividly and forcefully illustrated one of the awful dilemmas of our times.

But here Norman Jewison has taken a hard, outspoken script, prepared by Stirling Silliphant from an undistinguished novel by John Ball, and, with stinging performances contributed by Rod Steiger as the chief of police and Sidney Poitier as the detective, he has turned it into a film that has the look and sound of actuality and the pounding pulse of truth.

The line of its fascination is not so much its melodramatic plot. It is not in the touch-and-go discovery by the detective of who it was who bumped off that prominent northern industrialist in town to start an integrated mill, or in the gantlet of perils of bodily injury from snarling red-necks that Mr. Poitier constantly runs. Actually, the mystery story is a rather routine and arbitrary one and it is brought to a hasty conclusion in a flurry coincidences and explanations that leave one confused and unconvinced.

●

The fascination of it is in the crackling confrontations between the arrogant small town white policeman, with all his layers of ignorance and prejudice, and the sophisticated Negro detective with his steely armor of contempt and mistrust.

It is in the alert and cryptic caution with which these two professional cops face off, the white man arrogant and rueful but respectful of the black man's evident skill and the latter enraged and disgusted by the other's insulting attitudes.

And it is in the magnificent manner in which Mr. Steiger and Mr. Poitier act their roles, each giving physical authority and personal depth to the fallible human beings they are.

Fascinating, too, are the natures and details of other characters who swarm and sweat through a crisis in a believable Mississippi town —Warren Oates and Peter Whitney as raw cops, William Schallert and Larry Gates as powerful whites, Scott Wilson as a renegade red-neck and Quentin Dean as a slippery little slut.

The end of it all is not conclusive. It does not imply that the state of prejudice and antagonism in the community is any different from what it was at the start. But it does suggest that a rapport between two totally antagonistic men may be reached in a state of interdependence. And that's something to be showing so forcefully on the screen.

Ag 3, 1967

BONNIE AND CLYDE; written by David Newman and Robert Benton; directed by Arthur *Penn and produced by Warren Beatty; a Tatira-Hiller Production presented by Warner Bros.-Seven Arts. At the Forum Theater, Broadway at 47th Street, and the Murray Hill Theater, 34th Street east of Lexington Avenue. Running time: 111 minutes.
Clyde Barrow .... Warren Beatty
Bonnie Parker .... Faye Dunaway
C. W. Moss .... Michael J. Pollard
Buck Barrow .... Gene Hackman
Blanche .... Estelle Parsons
Frank Hamer .... Denver Pyle
Ivan Moss .... Dub Taylor
Velma Davis .... Evans Evans
Eugene Grizzard .... Gene Wilder

By BOSLEY CROWTHER

A RAW and unmitigated campaign of sheer press-agentry has been trying to put across the notion that Warner Brothers' "Bonnie and Clyde" is a faithful representation of the desperado careers of Clyde Barrow and Bonnie Parker, a notorious team of bank robbers and killers who roamed Texas and Oklahoma in the post-Depression years.

It is nothing of the sort. It is a cheap piece of bald-faced slapstick comedy that treats the hideous depredations of that sleazy, moronic pair as though they were as full of fun and frolic as the jazz-age cut-ups in "Thoroughly Modern Millie." And it puts forth Warren Beatty and Faye Dunaway in the leading roles, and Michael J. Pollard as their sidekick, a simpering, nose-picking rube, as though they were striving mightily to be the Beverly Hillbillies of next year.

●

It has Mr. Beatty clowning broadly as the killer who

fondles various types of guns with as much nonchalance and dispassion as he airily twirls a big cigar, and it has Miss Dunaway squirming grossly as his thrill-seeking, sex-starved moll. It is loaded with farcical hold-ups, screaming chases in stolen getaway cars that have the antique appearance and speeded-up movement of the clumsy vehicles of the Keystone Cops, and indications of the impotence of Barrow, until Bonnie writes a poem about him to extol his prowess, that are as ludicrous as they are crude.

Such ridiculous, camp-tinctured travesties of the kind of people these desperados were and of the way people lived in the dusty Southwest back in those barren years might be passed off as candidly commercial movie comedy, nothing more, if the film weren't reddened with blotches of violence of the most grisly sort.

Arthur Penn, the aggressive director, has evidently gone out of his way to splash the comedy holdups with smears of vivid blood as astonished people are machine-gunned. And he has staged the terminal scene of the ambuscading and killing of Barrow and Bonnie by a posse of policemen with as much noise and gore as is in the climax of "The St. Valentine's Day Massacre."

This blending of farce with brutal killings is as pointless as it is lacking in taste, since it makes no valid commentary upon the already travestied truth. And it leaves an astonished critic wondering just what purpose Mr.

Penn and Mr. Beatty think they serve with this strangely antique, sentimental claptrap, which opened yesterday at the Forum and the Murray Hill.

This is the film that opened the Montreal International Festival!

Ag 14, 1967

THE BATTLE OF ALGIERS, screenplay by Franco Solinas and Gillo Pontecorvo; directed by Mr. Pontecorvo; produced by Antonio Musu-Igor Films of Rome; distributed by Irving Sochin for Rizzoli Film Distributors, Inc. Opening today at Cinema II, Third Avenue at 60th Street. Running time: 120 minutes.
Kader ....Yacef Saadi
Colonel Mathieu ....Jean Martin
Ali La Pointe ....Brahim Haggiag
Captain Dubeis ....Tommaso Neri
Halima ....Fawzia El Kader
Fathia ....Michele Kerbash
Little Omar ....Mohamed Ben Kassen

By BOSLEY CROWTHER

A MOST extraordinary picture for an opener at the New York Film Festival was placed before the first-night audience in Philharmonic Hall last night. It is Gillo Pontecorvo's ferocious "The Battle of Algiers," a starkly realistic re-enactment of events as they substantially occurred between 1954 and 1957 in the rebellion against the French in the capital of Algeria.

It is extraordinary, first, that such a picture—such a literal and traditional account of intra-urban guerrilla warfare in a wasteful conflict that occurred so long ago—should have been picked to open a festival that has been kicked off in the last four years by noticeably avant-gardish and thematically exploratory films.
●

The supposition is that this departure was made because

"The Battle of Algiers" is an uncommonly dynamic picture that has proved its pulling power at festivals. It pulled down the grand prize at Venice and the top award at London last year, and took a blue at Acapulco last winter. On the strength of this, it was acquired for commercial distribution in this country, and was booked to open here at Cinema II tonight.

What could have been more appropriate, then, than to have this much talked-about film rack up two premieres with one show at the New York festival?

But more extraordinary and therefore more commanding of lasting interest and critical applause is the amazing photographic virtuosity and pictorial conviction of this film. So authentically and naturalistically were its historical reflections staged, with literally thousands of citizens participating, in the streets and buildings of Algiers that it looks beyond any question to be an original documentary film, put together from newsreel footage, complemented by staged dramatic scenes.

Startling long shots of people and police fighting in the sun-drenched, tree-lined streets, so familiar and recognizable from the photographs of the Algerian strife; shattering close-ups of thunderous explosions in native quarters and crowded French cafes have all the concrete and vibrant "actuality" of newsreels made during the war.

Yet Mr. Pontecorvo assures us there's not a scrap of newsreel footage in his film —that he and his crews shot the whole thing very much after the facts, with native amateurs and a few professional actors playing the key and leading roles.

This becomes apparent as one follows the narrative account of the violent upsurge of rebellion in Algiers in 1954 and the establishment of a rebel stronghold in the Casbah, from which hit-and-run forays of snipers and women bomb-planters into the French section of the city are made. And it is clear, to anyone who remembers, when the French 'paratroopers move in and begin the systematic clean-out of the Casbah under the command of a Colonel Mathieu.

●

This lean and relentless officer, played by Jean Martin, is obviously not the colorful and memorable Gen. Jacques Massu, whose 10th Paratrooper Division wiped out the rebel opposition in Algiers in 1957. But his manner is so intense and forceful, and his fairness and even respect for the resistance leaders are so well drawn, that one feels as though one is truly watching the spectacular and compassionate Massu.

Likewise, the roles of rebel leaders, played by Brahim Haggiag and Yacef Saadi, are done with such ferocity and fervor that they certainly convince me.

In its melodramatic structure, as well as its staging techniques, this film does have antecedents. The excellent "Four Days of Naples," done with such documentary stylization by Mr. Pontecorvo's fellow Italian, Nanni Loy, back in 1962, is its immediate model. And the prototype for both of them, of course, is Roberto Rossellini's "Open City," a classic neorealistic film.

Essentially, the theme is one of valor—the valor of people who fight for liberation from economic and political oppression. And this being so, one may sense a relation in what goes on in this picture to what has happened in the Negro ghettos of some of our American cities more recently. The fact that the climax of the drama is actually negative, with the rebellion wiped out and its leaders destroyed, has immediate pertinence, too. But eventual victory for the Algerians — and therefore symbolic hope for all who struggle for freedom— is acknowledged in a sketchy epilogue.

I must also mention the very interesting and effective musical score prepared by Mr. Pontecorvo and Ennio Morriscone for this vivid dramatic reportage.

S 21, 1967

CLOSELY WATCHED TRAINS, screenplay by Bohumil Hrabal and Jiri Menzel, based on a story by Mr. Hrabal; directed by Jiri Menzel and produced by Film Studio Barrandov of Prague; a Sigma III Release presented by Carlo Ponti. At the Festival Theater, 57th Street at Fifth Avenue. Running time: 89 minutes.
Trainee Milos ....Vaclav Neckar
Conductor Masa ....Jitka Bendova
Stationmaster ....Vladimir Valenta
Stationmaster's Wife .....Libuse Havelkova
Train Dispatcher Hubicka .....Josef Somr
Station Assistant ......·.......Alois Vachek
Telegraphist ....Jitka Zelenohorska
Councilor Zednicek ......Vlastimil Brodsky
Uncle Noneman ....Ferdinand Kruta
The Countess ....Kveta Fialova
Victoria Freie ....Nada Urbankova
Doctor Brabec ....Jiri Menzel

By BOSLEY CROWTHER

A FILM from Czechoslovakia that is as expert and moving in its way as was Jan Kadar's and Elmar Klos's "The Shop on Main Street" or Milos Forman's "Loves of a Blonde" began a run yesterday at the Festival. It is Jiri Menzel's "Closely Watched Trains," which was presented here in June in a showing of Czechoslovak films at the Museum of Modern Art under the banal title

of "A Difficult Love." That, thank goodness, was discarded after it had been suitably ridiculed by sensible people who saw the picture, and the original title was resumed.

"Closely Watched Trains" —that, too, may call up a commonplace image to the minds of Americans who have no awareness of the significance of the term. But to Czechoslovaks who remember that this was the designation for the German munitions and troop trains that were given priority passage through their occupied country during World War II, it should agitate curiosity—before they see the film. After they—and all others—see it, the aptness of the title should be clear.

•

For this, like "The Shop on Main Street," is a picture that tacitly implies a rueful and lingering contrition for the behavior of some Czechoslovaks during the war—a subtle sort of sardonic comment on the slowness with which they became aware of the annihilating menace of those arrogant, closely watched trains and the casualness with which they pulled themselves together and did something about them in the end.

Also, like "The Shop on Main Street," it begins as a folk comedy, and deceptively it keeps us thinking it is only that right up to the end. Even in its last explosive minute, when a chain of seemingly secondary events build up swiftly and melodramatically to the blasting of a huge munitions train, it is hard for the adroitly diverted viewer to believe he has seen what he has—to realize that he has witnessed a poignant climax to the charming comedy he has been amiably watching.

What it appears Mr. Menzel is aiming at all through his film is just a wonderfully sly, sardonic picture of the embarrassments of a youth coming of age in a peculiarly innocent yet worldly provincial environment. His hero is a thoroughly callow youngster, descendant of a formidable line of small-time braggarts and show-offs, who gets himself a job as an apprentice train dispatcher at a country station somewhere west of Prague, evidently with no greater ambition than to become another uniform-wearing stuffed shirt.

Awesomely and enviously, he watches the nonchalance and dexterity with which his immediate superior. the dispatcher Hubieka, tosses off his modest duties of waving on the trains that come roaring through the station, tending the switches and telegraph instruments, and especially the skill with which he manages to enjoy himself with available members of the opposite sex.

Nervously, our young hero tries to emulate the older man, particularly with a pretty woman train conductor who passes through from time to time. But things don't work out for him as nicely as he realizes they should; he fails at a delicate moment of crisis, and is thrown into a mood of despair. In the end, however, through the interest of his friends and a series of taut events, he is able to meet not one crisis but two and thoroughly prove himself a man.

•

More than that, he and Mr. Menzel prove that the seeming indifference and sluggishness of certain elements of the Czechoslovak people—the provincials who seemed to go through the war in an old, charming, self-indulgent fashion — were deceptive in some brave instances. Unexpected, unimpressive little people heroically grew up.

The charm of his film is in the quietness and slyness of his earthy comedy, the wonderful finesse of understatements, the wise and humorous understanding of primal sex. And it is in the brilliance with which he counterpoints the casual affairs of his country characters with the realness, the urgency and significance of those passing trains.

In Vaclav Neckar he has a most laconic, amusing and touching lad to play his diffident hero, and in Josef Somr he has an actor of lovely skills and very subtle suggestions to play the train dispatcher. Vladimir Valenta as the stationmaster, Vlastimil Brodsky as a Nazi official and Jitka Bendova as the passing conductor are also excellent in a splendid cast.

Jiri Sust's economical yet perfectly applied musical score adds a great deal to the expression of this picture. It has good English subtitles.

O 16, 1967

IN COLD BLOOD

By BOSLEY CROWTHER

THE public hazard in the kind of random violence that is occurring in our communities these days as part of the alarming upsurge of wild, neurotic crime is envisioned in terrifying images in the film Richard Brooks has made from Truman Capote's celebrated reporting of a Kansas murder case, "In Cold Blood." This excellent quasidocumentary, which sends shivers down the spine while moving the viewer to ponder, opened at Cinema I yesterday.

Substantially, the film is a re-enactment in electrifying cinematic terms of the essential events in the case record of that gruesome and mystifying crime in which four members of the modest Clutter family were slaughtered in their home near Holcomb, Kan., by two ex-convicts, Richard Hicock and Perry Smith, one night in 1959.

IN COLD BLOOD, screenplay by Richard Brooks, based on the novel by Truman Capote; directed and produced by Mr. Brooks; released by Columbia Pictures. At Cinema I, Third Avenue and 60th Street. Running time: 134 minutes.

Perry Smith	Robert Blake
Dick Hickock	Scott Wilson
Alvin Dewey	John Forsythe
Reporter	Paul Stewart
Harold Nye	Gerald S. O'Loughlin
Dick Hickock's father	Jeff Corey
Roy Church	John Gallaudet
Clarence Duntz	James Flavin
Perry Smith's father	Charles McGraw
Officer Rohleder	Jim Lantz
Prosecuting Attorney	Will Geer
Herbert Clutter	John McLiam
Bonnie Clutter	Ruth Storey
Nancy Clutter	Brenda C. Currin
Kenyon Clutter	Paul Hough

It is a faithful and absorbing demonstration of how the police, with very few clues and no initial inkling of a motive, patiently investigated the crime while the killers were boldly making an escape into Mexico; how the case was eventually broken, the killers fortuitously caught, then tried, convicted, and executed in a Kansas prison in 1965.

•

Since most of this is now common knowledge, thanks to the circulation of Mr. Capote's book, and since the culpability of the murderers is specified early in the film, the excitement generated in the viewer is not over who committed the murders, but why. Why did two who had originally intended robbery, and who had not committed murder before, suddenly come to the point of slaughtering four innocent persons in cold blood? And what does this single explosion of violence indicate as to society's pitiable vulnerability to the kooks that are loose in the land?

This pervasive concern with the natures and the backgrounds of the two young men who commit the murders and are therefore the symbols of the forces of evil in this dramatic scan accounts for the considerable alteration that Mr. Brooks has made in the substance and structure of Mr. Capote's book.

With a proper disregard for the extraneous, he has dropped out much of the detail of life in the community of Holcomb that Mr. Capote so patiently inscribed, and he has swiftly introduced his two marauders and brought them to the driveway of the Clutter home on that fateful night.

Then, with a rip in the sequence that is characteristic of the nervous style of the film—it is done with frequent flashbacks and fragmentations of continuity—he cuts to the interior of the Clutter home on the morning after the crime and the discovery of the bodies by the housemaid (but unseen by the camera), to her shrieking horror.

Thus the evident hideousness and mystery of what occurred is craftily withheld until the flow of the film has encompassed the investigations by the police, the getaway of the fugitives and their visit to Mexico (during all of which we are treated to grim reflections of their blighted early years), and their capture in Las Vegas, by an extraordinary fluke.

Not until they're brought back to Holcomb do we get in a confession by Smith, a graphic reconstruction of what happened in the house that awful night, and here Mr. Brooks exercises his most admirable skill and good taste. For without once actually showing the raw performance and effects of violence, the shooting and the knifing, he builds up a horrifying sense of the slow terror and maniacal momentum of that murderous escapade.

He makes us see the arrogance of the marauders, the astonishment and disbelief of the awakened Clutters, the fury of the robbers when they find there is no expected hoard of money, and the piteous terror of the victims when they know their lives are to be taken. But, best of all, he makes us understand, on the basis of what he has shown us about these hoodlums earlier in the film, why their wild, smashing outburst of vengeance is inevitable.

From here on, the course of the picture — the barely sketched in trial, the languishing of the men in prison while their case goes through endless appeals, and finally their execution — is but the ironic playing out of society's ritualistic compensation for damage already done. The final scene of the hanging, which is realistically done, is like some medieval rite of retribution. It leaves one helplessly, hopelessly chilled.

•

I have not emphasized the vivid realism and literal quality of this film, which are the product of Mr. Brooks's sharp direction and the black-and-white photography of Conrad Hall; nor have I nailed down the subtle revelations and variations in the performances of Robert Blake and Scott Wilson in the principal roles. Their abilities to demonstrate the tensions,

the torments and shabby conceits of the miserable criminals, give disturbing dimension to their roles.

As dogged investigators, John Forsythe, John Gallaudet, Jim Lantz and others manifest the terminal functioning of the law; Paul Stewart is dry as a reporter and John McLiam plays Mr. Clutter pitiably.

There is sure to be comparison of this picture with the controversial "Bonnie and Clyde," which is also about two killers who are brought to their doom. That one, subjective and romantic, does not hold a candle, I feel, as a social illumination, to this one, which is objective and real.

D 15, 1967

2001 A SPACE ODYSSEY, screenplay by Stanley Kubrick and Arthur C. Clarke; directed and produced by Mr. Kubrick; presented by Metro-Goldwyn-Mayer. At the Capitol Theater, Broadway and 51st Street. Running time: 160 minutes.
Bowman .... Keir Dullea
Poole .... Gary Lockwood
Dr. Heywood Floyd ... William Sylvester
Moonwatcher .... Dan Richter
HAL 9000 .... Douglas Rain
Smyslov .... Leonard Rossiter
Elena .... Margaret Tyzack
Halvorsen .... Robert Beatty
Michaels .... Sean Sullivan
Mission Controller .... Frank Miller

By RENATA ADLER

EVEN the M-G-M lion is stylized and abstracted in Stanley Kubrick's "2001: A Space Odyssey," a film in which infinite care, intelligence, patience, imagination and Cinerama have been devoted to what looks like the apotheosis of the fantasy of a precocious, early nineteen-fifties city boy. The movie, on which Kubrick collaborated with the British science-fiction author Arthur C. Clarke, is nominally about the finding, in the year 2001, of a camera-shy sentient slab on the moon and an expedition to the planet Jupiter to find whatever sentient being the slab is beaming its communications at.

There is evidence in the film of Clarke's belief that men's minds will ultimately develop to the point where they dissolve in a kind of world mind. There is a subplot in the old science-fiction nightmare of man at terminal odds with his computer. There is one ultimate science-fiction voyage of a man (Keir Dullea) through outer and inner space, through the phases of his own life in time thrown out of phase by some higher intelligence, to his death and rebirth in what looked like an intergalactic embryo.

●

But all this is the weakest side of a very complicated, languid movie—in which almost a half-hour passes before the first man appears and the first word is spoken, and an entire hour goes by before the plot even begins to declare itself. Its real energy seem to derive from that bespectacled prodigy reading comic books around the block. The whole sensibility is intellectual fifties child: chess games, body-building exercises, beds on the spacecraft that look like camp bunks, other beds that look like Egyptian mummies, Richard Strauss music, time games, Strauss waltzes, Howard Johnson's, birthday phone calls. In their space uniforms, the voyagers look like Jiminy Crickets. When they want to be let out of the craft they say, "Pod bay doors open," as one might say "Bomb bay doors open" in every movie out of World War II.

When the voyagers go off to plot against HAL, the computer, it might be HAL, the camper, they are ganging up on. When HAL is expiring, he sings "Daisy." Even the problem posed when identical twin computers, previously infallible, disagree is the kind of sentence-that-says-of-itself-I-lie paradox, which—along with the song and the nightmare of ganging up—belong to another age. When the final slab, a combination Prime Mover slab and coffin lid, closes in, it begins to resemble a fifties candy bar.

●

The movie is so completely absorbed in its own problems, its use of color and space, its fanatical devotion to science-fiction detail, that it is somewhere between hypnotic and immensely boring. (With intermission, it is three hours long.) Kubrick seems as occupied with the best use of the outer edge of the screen as any painter, and he is particularly fond of simultaneous rotations, revolving, and straight forward motions—the visual equivalent of rubbing the stomach and patting the head. All kinds of minor touches are perfectly done: there are carnivorous apes that look real; when they throw their first bone weapon into the air, Kubrick cuts to a spacecraft; the amiable HAL begins most of his sentences with "Well," and his answer to "How's everything?" is, naturally, "Everything's under control."

There is also a kind of fanaticism about other kinds of authenticity: space travelers look as sickly and exhausted as travelers usually do; they are exposed in space stations to depressing canned music; the viewer is often made to feel that the screen is the window of a spacecraft, and as Kubrick introduces one piece of unfamiliar apparatus after another—a craft that looks, from one

420

angle, like a plumber's helper with a fist on the end of it, a pod that resembles a limbed washing machine—the viewer is always made aware of exactly how it is used and where he is in it.

The special effects in the movie—particularly a voyage, either through Dullea's eye or through the slab and over the surface of Jupiter-Earth and into a period bedroom—are the best I have ever seen; and the number of ways in which the movie conveys visual information (there is very little dialogue) drives it to an outer limit of the visual.

And yet the uncompromising slowness of the movie makes it hard to sit through without talking—and people on all sides when I saw it were talking almost throughout the film. Very annoying. With all its attention to detail—a kind of reveling in its own I.Q.—the movie acknowledged no obligation to validate its conclusion for those, me for example, who are not science-fiction buffs. By the end, three unreconciled plot lines—the slabs, Dullea's aging, the period bedroom—are simply left there like a Rorschach, with murky implications of theology. This is a long step outside the convention, some extra scripts seem required, and the all-purpose answer, "relativity," does not really serve unless it can be verbalized.

The movie opened yesterday at the Capitol.

Ap 4, 1968, 58:1

LA CHINOISE

"LA CHINOISE," which opened yesterday at the Kips Bay Theater, is a kind of color sequel to "Masculine-Feminine," and Jean Luc Godard's best film by far since "Breathless." It is about a cell of four or five Maoist students in Paris, and Godard uses the technique of the off-camera, almost inaudible interviewer to produce some of the most sensitive and intelligent work on the new young and the New Left that has ever been done in any medium. The talk in the movie is almost entirely of ideas. (Among other things, it is the first instance I have ever seen of ideology used on screen for characterization.) It makes "Tell Me Lies" seem in retrospect a more false and pretentious and even derivative little talk idyll than it seemed at the time.

LA CHINOISE, written and directed by Jean Luc Godard; produced by Productions de la Gueville and released by Leacock Pennebaker, Inc. At the Kips Bay theater, Second Avenue at 31st Street. Running time: 95 minutes.
Veronique .... Anne Wiazemsky
Guillaume .... Jean-Pierre Leaud
Yvonne .... Juliet Berto
Henri .... Michel Semeniako
Kirilov .... Lex de Bruiian
Francis Jeanson.........Francis Jeanson

The question at the heart of the movie is the one at the center of the new radicalism: are things bad enough to make it worth dismantling everything and starting at zero? The young Maoists, more influenced by the idea of Götterdämmerung than perhaps they know, are for burning down and starting over. Anne Wiazemsky, who plays the young lady Maoist of the title, plans to begin by blowing up the Sorbonne and the Louvre. Jean-Pierre Leaud plays her boyfriend (whom Godard, without dwelling on it, calls Guillaume Meister, after Goethe's hero). He also plays an actor—all the characters seem more or less on the verge of playing themselves—very much preoccupied with another problem at the heart of the new radicalism: the relation between politics and theater.

In one of the most dramatically effective moments of the movie—which incorporates the printed word in some extraordinarily interesting ways—Leaud approaches a list of the names of several columns of distinguished writers and erases them one by one, leaving only Brecht. It comes with the shock one might get from the image of Miss Wiazemsky's projected bombing.

There are all sorts of conversations, conversations about making a revolution for the people in spite of themselves, love conversations, suicide conversations, lectures with pauses and repetitions for notetakers in the cell, readings from Mao, a Mao rock song, talks of sincerity and violence. Godard interrupts them with slides of comic strips, slides of engravings of Alice in Wonderland, and slides of commentary. (From several movies lately, it seems film titles, in new forms, are coming back.) There is one almost Socratic conversation between La Chinoise and the famous old French leftist, Francis Jeanson.

But what Godard has caught, in absolutely pure, flat beautiful photography, is the look of these young who are so caught up in the vocabulary of the class struggle of a class to which they do not belong—the look of hurt and intelligence and gentleness quite at odds with what they are saying. (When La Chinoise finally kills a man or two, it seems almost absent-minded.) Also—through something as banal in transcription as clasped hands, or three on a bed, or communal exercises in the morning—the special quality of intimacy between them.

In a way, "La Chinoise" is the perfect companion piece to Gillo Pontecorvo's "The Battle of Algiers." In both films, the sensibility of director and cast is somehow completely gentle, completely fair, and completely engaged. It is as though the cell of children from "La Chinoise" convenes while "The Battle of Algiers" goes on. And both films, in a half-documentary, more-than-half-poetic spirit, permit people to be as complicated as they are.

R. A.

Ap 4, 1968

BELLE DE JOUR, screenplay by Luis Bunuel and Jean-Claude Carriere, adapted from a novel by Joseph Kessel; directed by Mr. Bunuel; produced by Robert and Raymond Hakim and released by Allied Artists. At the Little Carnegie Theater, 57th Street, east of Seventh Avenue. Running time: 100 minutes.
Severine Serizy ......Catherine Deneuve
Pierre Serizy ....Jean Sorel
M.me. Anais ....Genevieve Page
Henri Husson ....Michel Piccoli
Renee ....Macha Meril
Hyppolite ....Francisco Rabal
Marcel ....Pierre Clementi

By RENATA ADLER

LUIS BUNUEL'S particular combination of religion, decay and morbid eroticism has never been my absolutely favorite kind of cinema—although "Viridiana" was great, and people who say they have an interest in the arts, "if only the subject matter were not so depressing," are of a particularly philistine order of square. But "Belle de Jour," which opened yesterday at the Little Carnegie, is a really beautiful movie, and somehow, letting the color in — this is Bunuel's first color film—has changed the emotional quality of his obsessions in a completely unpredictable way. All these clean, lovely, well-dressed people preparing for their unspeakable practices are very attractive; and "Belle de Jour" is, among other things,

Bunuel's first comedy.

The story is a kind of fantasy cryptogram, with countless clues—verbal puns about cats, nonsense syllables, bells, speech with motionless lips, time cues and so on—as to when we are in a fantasy, and whose. Catherine Deneuve plays the young, beautiful but unresponsive wife of a French medical student, Jean Sorel. From a middle-age libertine, Michel Piccoli, she learns the address of a little brothel in Paris, where she goes — or where she appears to go— secretly every afternoon until 5, and where, in a series of afternoons, a young gangster, played by Pierre Clementi, falls in love with her. (Miss Deneuve, Sorel, Piccoli and Clementi are all used by Mag Bodard in "Benjamin," and all but Mr. Clementi will appear later this week in "The Young Girls of Rochefort." They are excellent and they seem to have become a kind of cinema repertory company.)

At the brothel—a wonderfully middle-class household, run by a very kind, sensitive madam, played to perfection by Genevieve Page — Miss Deneuve accommodates a series of gentlemen of eccentric tastes: a jolly, but obligingly sadistic spherical candy manufacturer, an amiable single-minded Japanese, who hopes to pay with his credit card. Just as one thinks the whole movie is about to become a dreary series of sex tableaus by Jean Genêt, a customer—a gynecologist in bellboy uniform, with whip—whose tastes we think we already fully understand, demands an inkwell. The movie becomes comic again.

The young gangster himself is marvelous; a grotesque parody on every young hero,

Jean - Paul Belmondo in "Breathless" included, out of the milieu. And since, in the cinema daydream convention, almost anything goes, Bunuel is able to put in any number of sequences—a thundering herd of bulls, one of which is named Expiation while all the rest are called Remorse, a child refusing the sacrament— that have less of the ring of false profundity to them, since they appear in the minds of his characters this time, and not necessarily in Bunuel's own. The movie ends with a dark ambiguity about how we are to regard what has gone before, but every detail has been so carefully thought out that seeing it again is like seeing it in another key.

Ap 11, 1968

LES CARABINIERS, screenplay by Roberto Rossellini, Jean Gruault and Jean-Luc Godard, from a ploy by Benjamin Joppolo; directed by Mr. Godard; produced by Georges deBeauregard and Carlo Ponti for Rome-Paris Films/Laetitia; presented by New Yorker Films. At the Bleecker Street Cinema, 144 Bleecker Street, and the New Yorker Theater, 2409 Broadway. Running time 80 minutes.

Venus .... Genevieve Gaela
Cleopatra .... Catherine Ribero
Michelangelo .... Marino Mase
Ulysses .... Albert Juross

By RENATA ADLER

'L ES CARABINIERS," which opened yesterday at the New Yorker Theater and Bleecker Street Cinema, is a film of such extraordinary and understated brilliance that it advances the possibilities of film a step. It is an allegory of two men, two women and war, and since it is predictable what course such an allegory must take, one wonders what Jean-Luc Godard, who directs, and Roberto Rossellini and Jean Gruault, who collaborated with him on the script (based on a play by Benjamin Joppolo), can possibly bring to it. What they bring, finally, is a comment that works both at the allegorical level and at the real—on war, symbols, the quality of modern life and the meaning of photography.

The movie opens with titles scrawled, black on white, and a quotation from the great Argentine writer Jorge Luis Borges on "worn metaphors" —which, as it turns out, disarms any criticism one might subsequently wish to make of the film. Then, there are shots of a car advancing, with one headlight burning, across a bleak, flat landscape to a single, isolated hut. Two carabiniers get out and deliver to Michelangelo and Ulysses—two brothers who live with their wives, Cleopatra and Venus, in the hut —a "letter from the King," which asks them to go to war.

Ulysses, the cigar-chomping, weathered older brother (played by Albert Juross on the order of a character from "Tobacco Road") is impressed by the King's expression of friendship and the prospect of spoils—particularly a Maserati—which the carabiniers offer him. Michelangelo, a subliterate spastic (played by Marino Mase, rather on the order of C. W. Moss in "Bonnie and Clyde") looks forward to the "mozibilisation," for the opportunity to steal jukeboxes, to break old men's glasses and children's arms, etc. Venus and Cleopatra (played by Genevieve Galea and Catherine Ribero, like characters nine tenths of the way between Gelsomina and the mad fat lady on the beach in "8½") draw up battle shopping lists. (Godard's lists and inventories are always fantastically selective and intelligent.)

The men send postcards back from the front: "There is no victory, only flags and men falling," but what happens to them there is simultaneously so inventive and inevitable that one begins, by degrees, to trust Godard absolutely. There is a very daring and yet offhand scene in which the brothers, now carabiniers themselves, shoot a young blonde Marxist as she is cooly reciting a long, beautiful poem by Mayakovsky. And then there are scenes just as impressive purely pictorially—a Beckett-charged bleakness and austerity over-all. The photography is by Raoul Coutard, who did "Breathless," "Jules and Jim" and "Shoot the Piano Player!"

The film gets better and better as it goes along, but a very few lapses into the banal (those "worn metaphors") keep the audience wondering whether Godard is going to bring off the turning point and how. The conclusion—what the men bring back from the war—is one of the most impressive sequences in any movie ever. There have been intimations all along—the relationships between the carabiniers and art objects of various kinds— but what they do bring home is no less than Godard's complete pictorial inventory of Western civilization. It is entirely casual, ironic, selective, deep and true. It is about man and film. Yet it holds at the level of bubble-gum wrappers and trading cards. Almost the entire movie is like that.

"Les Carabiniers" played last year at the Lincoln Center Film Festival.

Ap 26, 1968

SENSO

AS an aristocrat proud of his leftist politics, Italy's

424

distinguished opera, stage and screen director, Luchino Visconti, has championed a variety of lost causes on film, including the belated "Senso" now at the Bleecker Street Cinema. Produced in 1954 as a multimillion dollar period piece, it was shown dubbed in English and drastically cut on television as "The Wanton Countess," and the uncut version had a brief, unheralded run last month at the Elgin Theater here.

SENSO, screenplay by Luchino Visconti and Suso Ceccho D'Amico; based on a novel by Camillo Boito; directed by Luchino Visconti for Lux Films and released by Fleetwood Films of Mount Vernon. At the Bleecker Street Cinema, 142 Bleecker Street. Running time: 125 minutes.
Countess Livia Serpieri ......Alida Valli
Lieut. Franz Mahler ......Farley Granger
Marquis Ussoni ....Massimo Girotti
Count Serpieri ....Heinz Moog

Mr. Visconti"s good intentions notwithstanding, there really is no deep mystery about "Senso." As a novel-like depiction of an ill-fated illicit romance intertwined with a momentous chapter in Italy's fight for freedom from the Austrians, it is an obvious, rudimentary operatic approach to amour and an illustration of history that is likely to be fuzzy to anyone but a student of Garibaldi's 1866 campaign in and around Venice and Verona.

●

One must assume that Mr. Visconti, who collaborated on the script, is indicating the moral decay of the aristocracy through his views of the affair between the beauteous Countess Serpieri and her designing, Austrian officer-lover. Set against luxurious sets and actual palazzos that underline the breathtaking beauty of the countryside, their clandestine meetings and incessant protest of passion and fear for the future are repetitious and flamboy-.

ant. It is closer to soap opera than Mr. Visconti imagined.

It is to be expected that the Countess, unloved by her collaborator-husband but sympathetic to the cause of freedom espoused by her aristocratic patriot cousin, will, nevertheless, even give her lover money for the cause entrusted to her. But as expected, the lady can stand just so much two-timing before her heart breaks and she turns him in as a deserter to be shot. All things considered, it appeared perfectly logical, to one viewer, at least, that she seemingly goes mad at the end.

Alida Valli not only is aristocratic and beautiful but also should be credited with carrying an overly heavy romantic role fairly effectively. As the scheming apple of her eye, Farley Granger is merely a handsome, operetta-type of leading man despite a strong climactic confessional scene. And Massico Girotti, as the noble patriotic leader, and Heinz Moog as the Count, are among the principals who simply seem to make many entrances and exits to expound on liberation and its meaning.

To the credit of the late R. G. Aldo and Robert Krasker, the color photography of soldiers advancing in vivid uniforms to the sound of trumpets, firing from behind haystacks or in bloody retreat from the cannonading of the victorious Austrians at the Battle of Custoza enhance the film's historic aspects. But "Senso" means "sentiment" and Mr. Visconti's operatic lovers, who dominate it, date "Senso" more than its history does.

A. H. Weiler.

Jl 19, 1968

THE RED AND THE WHITE, screen-play by Georgij Mdivani, Gyula Hernadi and Miklos Jancso. Directed by Mr. Jancso for Mafilm Studio IV (Buda-pest and Mosfilm Studio (Moscow); distributed by Brandon Films. At the New York Film Festival, Philharmonic Hall. Running time. 92 minutes.
Yelizaveta ....Tatyana Konyukova
Alga ....Krystyna Mikolaiewska
Nestor ....Mikhail Kozakov
Sailor ....Viktor Avdiushko
Tshingiz ....Bolot Beisenalyev
Cossack Officer .....Sergei Nyikonyenko
Tshelpanov ....:......Anatoli Yabbarov
The Commander ....Jozef Madaras

By HOWARD THOMPSON

"THE RED AND THE WHITE" is a splendid picture, with the screen put to thrilling use by Hungary's master director-scenarist, Miklós Jancsó. Using superbly supple photography, razor precision and a marvelous flow of human nuance, Mr. Jancsó has shaped a big, pounding, graphic tableau of warfare that nailed at least one spectator to his seat. The Brandon Films release, a Hungarian-Soviet co-production, was the early evening presentation yesterday at the New York Film Festival.

The conflict, played against the background of the Russian Revolution of 1917, is the murderous entanglement of Red soldiers and Hungarian cohorts and the counter-revolutionary Whites in the hills along the Volga. With a fine, large cast scouring the countryside from a deserted monastery to a riverbank hospital, the conflict is murderous indeed—furtive patrols, wild chases and outright massacres.

The action moves with such skillful speed—and command of the territory shifts so repeatedly—that the viewer must race with it to tell which side is on top. This very thing strengthens the supreme achievement of the film, which is to show both the barbarism and the compassion on each side. The scales tilt toward a valiant group of Hungarian revolutionaries, but there is no ideological spouting. On both sides there are simply people, behaving as such even as they drop like flies while methodically slamming together in the terrible, impersonal irony of war.

There is the aristocratic but not inhuman White officer, casually tweaking his nose before a mass execution and chase that open the film like a dynamic, lunging Western. There is another, younger White officer who executes a lower-ranking colleague for the attempted violation of a peasant girl. There is the stoical head nurse who bravely shelters both White and Red wounded.

There are brilliantly subtle vignettes, such as the tragic liaison of a Magyar and a Polish nurse, and another sequence where the nurses are ordered to a birch grove to waltz together for the diversion of the White officers.

Finally, there is the magnificent panorama near the end where a handful of singing Hungarians march toward the massed enemy dotting the horizon.

"The Red and the White" is quite a picture, about people and war.

S 21, 1968

TWO OR THREE THINGS I KNOW ABOUT HER, written and directed by Jean-Luc Godard; produced by Anouchka Films/Argos-Films/Parc Film Les Films du Carrosse. At the New York Film Festival, Philharmonic Hall. Running time: 90 minutes.
Juliette ....Marina Vlady
Marianne ....Anny Duperey
Robert ....Roger Montsoret
John ....Raoul Levy
Narrator ....,..Jean-Luc Godard.

By RENATA ADLER

JEAN-LUC GODARD's "Two or Three Things I Know About Her," which was shown yesterday at the New York Film Festival, is not one of his better films, although the title, I think, is one of his best. The movie is a kind of treatise on a section of Paris, the 20th Arrondissement, where new lower-middle-class buildings are going up, and a girl (Marina Vlady) who lives there. Godard's voice supplies a partial narration, in a tense whisper, about problems that preoccupy him now: language, politics, comic-strip imagery, appearance and reality. The characters more or less interview one another, or are interviewed by an interlocutor off camera, mainly about questions of identity and sex. The photography, in color, by Raoul Coutard, is beautiful, clear comic-book precise; and the locations—a dress shop, a beauty parlor, the interior of a coffee cup—are informed by Godard's signature.

●

There is an almost intolerable, conscious tension in Godard's work now between word and picture; one's attention is so riveted to the work onscreen that Godard seems to think he can afford to freight it—at one point he speaks of himself as a painter and a writer—with a verbal text that takes off at right angles and includes almost anything that he would care to say.

The trouble is that, except for a few funny pieces of dialogue, the offscreen interview doesn't work too well in this one, and that Godard, as a philosopher and something of a political dogmatist, treats questions of philosophy —How do I know that I exist? Can there be a private language, and so on — as though works from Berkeley to Wittgenstein had not gone before. There are a few interesting reflections about the limits of language and the first principles of the universe, but most of it seems affected and rather tedious. Also, a whisper is not very well suited, over the long haul, to discussions of philosophy.

●

There is certainly enough of wit and beauty, though, to keep the film afloat, and for people who are interested in what interests Godard, there is a particularly patent, conscious (Godard seems always conscious) ambiguity now in what he feels about America. The text is almost detestingly anti, and yet American shoes, and cigarettes, and styles and Cokes are treated by the camera with the feeling that nature lovers reserve for rocks and trees. It is this nailing of attention with something you cannot help wanting to see burdened by a text of words you may not care to hear, that does not work too well this time, seems even superficial, but is a direction worth exploring all the same.

S 26, 1968

WEEKEND, written and directed by Jean-Luc Godard; produced by Co-macico/Copernic/Lira Films (Paris) and Ascot Cineraid (Rome); distributed in the United States by Grove Press. At the New York Film Festival, Philharmonic Hall. Running time: 103 minutes.

Corinne ....Mireille Darc
Roland ....Jean Yanne
Leader of F.L.S.O.....Jean-Pierre Kalfon
His Moll ....Valerie Lagrange
Saint-Just/Man in Phone
  Booth ....Jean-Pierre Leaud
Member of F.L.S.O......Yves Benneyton
Pianist ....Paul Gegauff
Joseph Balsamo ....Daniel Pommereulle
Gros Poucet ....Yves Afonso

By RENATA ADLER

JEAN - LUC GODARD'S "Weekend," which was shown last night at the New York Film Festival, is a fantastic film, in which all of life becomes a weekend, and the weekend is a cataclysmic, seismic traffic jam—with cars running pedestrians and cyclists off the road, only to collide and leave blood and corpses everywhere.

In one tremendously long take, the camera passes along a highway where traffic is stopped by a long line of dead, smashed, burned and stalling vehicles — oil trucks, Renaults, sports cars, Mercedeses, a zoo truck with two llamas in it, recumbent tigers, people playing ball through the tops of their stalled Deux Chevaux, people playing cards, playing chess, honking horns, making gestures, quarreling, crying and ignoring the fact that there is mayhem everywhere. The conception of the movie is very grand. It is as though the violent quality of life had driven Godard into and through insanity, and he had caught it and turned it into one of the most important and difficult films he has ever made.

There are plot fragments at the beginning, betrayals, dire conspiracies to murder, detailed, intimate (and highly comic) sexual anecdotes. They lead nowhere. There are a couple (Mireille Darc and Jean Yanne), who, like refugees from the world of Samuel Beckett, are always looking for a gas station, and later for a town. A lot of the movie is like Beckett, the despair (if this can be imagined) not as it is on stage, simplified and austere, but rich, overloaded, really epic. At one point, as the couple sit by the side of the road, the woman is casually raped in a ditch. No one even bothers to mention it. This would not work in the theater or in prose. It works on film.

The movie is interspersed with little essays, idyllls, jokes, a Mozart sonata, a frantic love song sung by Jean-Pierre Léaud in a telephone booth, noise, rituals, battles with paint sprayers and tennis balls. It ends in slaughter and cannibalism. There are a lot of infantile pretentious touches, punning flashcards (Anal . . . lyse, Faux . . . tographie) and the subtitles seem to have caught a bit of this. "La Paresse" (laziness) is regularly translated as press.

There is a moment near the end when the movie cracks up—long, dogmatic, motionless diatribes on behalf of Africa and the Arab countries with a peroration against black nonviolence, which keeps one thinking Biafra, Biafra, and wanting to walk out. (In fact, it might be advisable to walk out when the speeches begin for a cup of coffee and a cigarette). It's unprofessional, like a musician stopping a concert to deliver a bit of invective to a captive audience. But perhaps, like any serious artist, Godard cannot help including all his preoccupations raw right now, even if they bring his movie down.

●

But the film must be seen, for its power, ambition, humor and scenes of really astonishing beauty. There are absurdist characters from Lewis Carroll, from Fellini, from "La Chinoise," from Bunuel. At many moments the movie, which is in color, captures the precise sense one has about the world, when one is in a city or in a rush, when one reads the headlines or obituary columns, when one drives, when one sets out, for that matter, on a weekend. It is as though the apocalypse had somehow registered on a sensibility calibrated very fine. It is an appalling comedy. There is nothing like it at all. It is hard to take.

S 28, 1968

THE LION* IN WINTER, screenplay by James Goldman, based on his play; directed by Anthony Harvey; produced by Martin Poll with Joseph E. Levine as executive producer; released by Avco Embassy Pictures. At the Lincoln Art Theater, 57th Street and Broadway. Running time: 134 minutes.
King Henry II............Peter O'Toole
Queen Eleanor of Aquitaine
............Katharine Hepburn
Princess Alais ....Jane Merrow
Prince Geoffrey............John Castle
King Philip of France....Timothy Dalton
Prince Richard the Lionhearted
............Anthony Hopkins
William Marshall........,Nigel Stock
Prince John ....Nigel Terry

By RENATA ADLER

IT is a lovely idea to cast Katharine Hepburn as Eleanor of Aquitaine, with and against a very heavy and robust Peter O'Toole as Henry II, in a contest of will. Not a contest for the psychological upper hand, or whether the baby shall have a pacifier and which restaurant to go to tonight, but a contest transposed in 12th-century terms — which son shall inherit the kingdom, who will marry the king's mistress and what will become of the provinces of Vexin and Aquitaine. The dialogue of "The Lion in Winter," taken from James Goldman's Broadway play, is witty and dated in a twenties way—as all wit from drawing room and insult comedy seems dated now. At moments, the parents, sons and visiting royalty at Chinon in 1183 talk so nastily that they seem like a whole household full of men who came to dinner. But the movie, which opened last night at the Lincoln Art Theater is, for the most part, outdoorsy and fun, full of the kind of plotting and action people used to go to just plain movies for.

The film is almost too faithful to the play. It divides neatly into acts, has a long sag in the middle, is weakest in its climaxes—Henry becoming violently upset about the nth time he hears that Eleanor may have slept with his father; Eleanor and her husband's mistress, played by Jane Merrow, falling into each other's arms—and takes it very easy on the cinematic touches, like a marvelous brief jousting scene, or shots of dogs, horses and soldiers in armor (costumes, a kind of Mordor-Romanesque, by Margaret Furse). It has all sorts of intrigue and arguments on questionable grounds — baseless one-upmanship that amounts to, You see, of course, I win. How do you mean? Well, you see, you just put your fork in the butter plate, which is exactly what I planned—and a lot of pointless and vicious conspiracy, as in a game of Diplomacy.

But the acting—Anthony Hopkins, as a queer, manly Richard the Lionhearted; Nigel Terry, as a caricatured, spastic adolescent Prince John; John Castle, as an almost too attractive, scheming Prince Geoffrey; and Timothy Dalton, as a sensitive, regal, embittered Philip of France —is joyful and solid. The relationships between people, though ambivalent, are ambivalent with a certain satisfying ferocity. The only person who directly and unambiguously loves anybody is Henry's mistress and she seems rather beyond her speed with the fierce rest.

Katharine Hepburn, from her first scene when she is briefly taken out of her 10-year imprisonment, shows a wonderful relish for even the most unimpressive sarcastic line. "Well, what family doesn't have its ups and downs," she says, when sodomy, patricide, treason and incest are running their daily course. There is something about an actress with this degree of presence and a wholly distinct, pleasant and idiosyncratic voice that gets her through even misplaced weepy or extravagant scenes.

A lot of the screenplay is in a kind of anachronistic near-verse—"I'm vilifying you, mother. For God's sake, pay attention"; "Hush, dear, mother's fighting"; "I'll have you by me and I'll use you as I like"; "I stole the candles from the chapel. Jesus won't begrudge them and the chaplain works for me"—that Mr. O'Toole, Miss Hepburn and the rest of the cast are somehow able to carry off.

•

The movie is directed with evident pleasure by Anthony Harvey. Its high point—a long scene in which scurrilous revelations are made while characters lurk behind curtains in the bedroom of the king of France—has enough comic and dramatic energy to make even the hard ticket prices worthwhile.

O 31, 1968

THE BIRTHDAY PARTY, screenplay by Harold Pinter, based on his play; directed by William Friedkin; produced by Max Rosenberg and Milton Subotsky with Edgar J. Scherick as executive producer; presented by Palomar Pictures International and released by Continental. At the Coronet Theater, Third Avenue and 59th Street. Running time: 122 minutes.

Stanley .... Robert Shaw
McCann .... Patrick Magee
Meg .... Dandy Nichols
Goldberg .... Sydney Tafler
Petey .... Moultrie Kelsall
Lulu .... Helen Fraser

By VINCENT CANBY

IT is early on a humid summer morning. Striped canvas beach chairs sit facing a calm, blue-gray sea that blends — imperceptibly — into a blue-gray sky. Somehow you feel that the sun may well have risen in the west.

In this brief shot, which opens the movie adaptation of Harold Pinter's "The Birthday Party," William Friedkin, the director, captures in simple visual terms the verbalized purgatory of Pinter's stage play. There are both the hint of menace, never defined, and the suggestion of the dislocation of familiar things, which can be both terrifying and funny.

•

Subsequently, however, the movie becomes an almost literal screen translation of material conceived for the stage. It is beautifully acted and photographed and its soundtrack has a kind of ferocious presence, but it's a movie that doesn't really have a life of its own.

This is more of a tribute to the play, which is a spare, unerring work of words, than a put-down of the movie, which, as any movie must, is constantly commenting, emphasizing and directing one's attention, with every cut and move of the camera. If a play is well written to start with, the faithful movie version inevitably becomes redundant within itself, as if it contained a quietly insistent, built-in echo.

Ironically, "The Birthday Party," which is pure Pinter, cannot hold a candle to either "The Pumpkin Eater" or "The Servant," movies for which Pinter also wrote the screenplays, but which were based on the work of others.

Also, both "The Pumpkin Eater" and "The Servant" take place in worlds that are at least outwardly recognizable, whereas "The Birthday Party," for me, should take place entirely inside a house set in a Krazy Kat landscape—without people, cars, trees or buildings, all of which are seen, if only briefly, in this opened-up screen version.

However, having stated these very real objections, I must say that I enjoyed this "Birthday Party" while always feeling a little out of it.

The movie, like the play, forces us to accept a horror story that has no reasonable antecedents: Stanley (Robert Shaw) is the only guest at a rundown, seaside boarding house owned by Meg (Dandy Nichols) and Petey (Moultrie Kelsall). Into their lives of placid desperation come two strangers, Goldberg (Sydney Tafler), tackily urbane and garrulous, and McCann (Patrick Magee), a faithful goon. They have been sent by someone named Monty and "the organization" to retrieve Stanley.

Just how one interprets their confrontations, alternately joshing and menacing, before, during and after a birthday party for Stanley (who swears it's not his birthday), is not particularly important, though it does have the outline of an operation by a sort of metaphysical syndicate.

Rather it is fascinating as a dramatization of a world in which language never quite matches events, and in which events are rearranged — parsed like the pieces of a sentence—so that logic and sanity never quite hold.

Pinter simply extends to an ultimate absurdity the kind of daily illogic and insanity with which we have all learned to live.

The performances are the-

atrical and superb, especially Shaw as the fanciful paranoid, a little bald, a little mean and not really pathetic even when he's beaten. Miss Nichols also is fine, a sort of summation of all the frumpy chars and landladies who have ever been seen in British films.

For the most part, Friedkin directs the movie without frills, although there are some self-conscious lapses—scenes shot as if seen by one's foot and an irritating view of the party as apparently seen by a fly on the ceiling, but generally plays it straight. "The Birthday Party" may not be a great movie, but it's a good recording of an extraordinary play.

It opened yesterday at the Coronet. Before going, you might call the theater to ask what the weather's like. Yesterday afternoon it was just slightly warmer inside than it was outside.

D 10, 1968

MONTEREY POP, a documentary of the 1967 Monterey International Pop Festival directed by D. A. Pennebaker; photographed by James Desmond, Barry Feinstein, Richard Leacock, Albert Maysles, Roger Murphy, Nick Proferes and Mr. Pennebaker; presented by Leacock Pennebaker, Inc. At Philharmonic Hall, Lincoln Center. Running time: 72 minutes.

By RENATA ADLER

"MONTEREY POP," which was shown last night at Lincoln Center and which will open early in January at the Kips Bay Theater, is a contemporary music film—in the relatively fresh tradition of "Festival" and "Don't Look Back." The movie, filmed by Richard Leacock and D. A. Pennebaker, with the collaboration of Albert Maysles and other independent filmmakers, is an upbeat, color documentary of the

From The New York Times Film Reviews   431

1967 pop-music festival in Monterey, Calif. It stars the Mamas and the Papas, the Jefferson Airplane, Ravi Shankar, the Who and other singing groups. From the moment Scott Mackenzie's "If you're going to San Francisco" comes onto the track and screen, it is clear that this is one good way to do a musical.

•

There is all that shiny hair, orangeade, beautiful hands, shades, watermelon, shoeless feet in tights, flowers papers, dogs, the wrinkled bottom of Ravi Shankar's tapping foot, psychedelic blobs behind the podium, smoke effects behind the infernal Who, mouths approaching microphones, eyes in all those various, distinct, serious young faces, which—10 years ago, before the seriousness of Vietnam began—we didn't seem to have. The photography is pretty well coordinated with the sound, sometimes blinded by strobe lights, so that the screen goes absolutely white, sometimes shifting down lines of audience in a kind of "Rosencrantz and Guildenstern Are Dead" focus of attention on characters other than the main.

There are the lyrical songs, "California Dreamin'" and Simon and Garfunkel's "Feeling Groovy," Janis Joplin straining her voice and being to sing black. Then there is a kind of spot, purely visual interview — a beard and a cop laughing, wordlessly teasing each other; a girl from Champaign, Ill., feeling lucky to be allowed to wipe the folding chairs between performances, a Hell's Angel arriving at the Shankar concert that is the long, wound up climax of the film. There are rock violinists and young

people dressed like pageant potentates.

"We all love each other, right?" Otis Redding shouts, half ironic, half intimidating. "Right," the audience replies. Jimmie Hendrix goes through his thing of somersaulting, then being irreverently, frantically obscene with his guitar, finally destroying it—presaging in a fairly violent way, the quality of the kisses of Tiny Tim.

•

But the nicest thing about the movie is not its musical or nostalgic qualities, but the way it captures the pop musical willingness to hurl yourself into things, without all the What If (What if I can't? What if I make a fool of myself?) joy action-stopping self-consciousness of an earlier generation, a willingness that can somehow co-exist with the idea of cool. Also, musically and photographically, the harmonies, the resolutions of chaos after everything looks as though it is going to fall apart.

"Once you leave here you may not re-enter," a guard at the festival says to some members of the audience at the gate. It is possible that the way to a new kind of musical—using some of the talent and energy of what is still the most lively contemporary medium—may begin with just this kind of musical performance documentary.

D 27, 1968

Belmondo Plays Pierrot to Anna Karina

By RENATA ADLER

"PIERROT LE FOU," which opened yesterday at the 72d Street Theater, is one of the humblest and most gentle of Jean-Luc Godard's films. Shot in 1965, before the cracks in the young French director's composure really opened up, the film has seams, murders, auto accidents, political harangues. The hero ultimately wraps his head in dynamite and blows himself to bits. But Pierrot is the "mon ami, Pierrot" from "Au Claire de la Lune" (a song that occurs uninsistently in the score), and a lot of the film's imagery is of the moon and gentle lunacy. It is in part a delicate, sentimental love story, a little on the order of Truffaut.

PIERROT LE FOU, screenplay by Jean-Luc Godard; based on "Obsession," a novel by Lionel White; directed by Mr. Godard; produced by Georges de Beauregard and presented by Pathe Contemporary Films. At the 72d Street Playhouse, east of Second Avenue. Running time: 110 minutes.
Ferdinand............Jean-Paul Belmondo
Marianne...................Anna Karina
The Brother..............Dirk Sanders
Maria.................Graziella Galvani
The Gangsters ....(Roger Dutoit
(Hans Meyer
and
Raymond Devos, Jean-Pierre Leaud, Samuel Fuller and Jimmy Karoubi.

Jean-Paul Belmondo plays Pierrot, a writer whose girl calls him Pierrot, but whose real name, Ferdinand, is emblazoned on his sweatshirt. (He and the film have some of the sweet loser's ironies of Charlie Brown.) The girl is played by Anna Karina, Mr. Godard's first wife, and no film has ever been more loving in its treatment of a star. Miss Karina makes her particular case for life, clothes, dancing, fields, skies, love and a little violence, and the writer makes his abstract case for "Ambition, love, the movement of things, accidents — everything." They have an affair near the sea, with a fox and a parrot for company. They speak of Bernardin de St. Pierre's innocent "Paul et Virginie."

They despair of each other.

They also have some "Breathless" - style adventures, with many references to Laurel and Hardy, "Johnny Guitar," Michel Simon, "Pepe le Moko" and other cinema presences that are exigently real to the imagination of Godard. The film requires a little patience as it goes its own erratic way. One long drive by night down a highway, with colored lights (the film, shot by Raoul Coutard, is in color) flashing incessantly across the hood and windshield is particularly trying in its affectation. So are the strainings to include a bit of Vietnam and politics. (When Godard is bad, he is terrible.) And the film generates a certain impatience in its oddly felt absence of any scene of sex.

But there is so much that is whimsical and beautiful: Pierrot, painting his face blue before he dies, and fumbling, at the last moment, for the fuse; Miss Karina, parodying musicals, unaffectedly singing (the music, ranging from Beethoven to Duhamel, is a careful, thoughtout comment on the script); an incredible, isolated piece of highway overpass abandoned in a field; Mr. Belmondo putting mustard on an immense piece of cheese, during an authentic, cinéma vérité interview with a frowzy old eccentric who thinks she is the exiled queen of Lebanon; Jean-Pierre Leaud, appearing for one instant, looking baleful, on the screen; a kind of Brechtian bitter, fine misuse of American frames of references, in the "Oh, Moon of Alabama" style; a superb comic turn, about love and refrains in the head, by the Belgian actor Raymond Devos.

The film is poetic, quiet,

introverted, personal. The writer and Miss Karina have funny, despairing things to say to each other. There is no bravado in the part Belmondo plays this time, or any real violence in Miss Karina's. They are both charming and fed up, an idiom that sounds richer in French and that is applied in the film to everyone, including the man in the moon. One moving thing is that a director as proud and forceful, as annihilatingly positivist as Godard should make a film this tentative and forbearing about an artist and his girl in love.

Ja 9, 1969

Truffaut's Lyrical 'Stolen Kisses'

STOLEN KISSES, original screenplay by Francois Truffaut, Claude de Givray and Bernard Revon; directed by Mr. Truffaut; produced by Les Films du Carrosse and Les Productions Artistes Associes; distributed by Lopert Pictures Corporation. At the **Fine Arts Theater,** 58th Street between Park and Lexington Avenues. Running time: 90 minutes.

Antoine Doinel	Jean-Pierre Leaud
Madame Tabard	Delphine Seyrig
Monsieur Tabard	Michael Lonsdale
Christine Darbon	Claude Jade
Monsieur Henri	Harry Max
Monsieur Darbon	Daniel Ceccaldi
Madame Darbon	Claire Duhamel
Catherine	Catherine Lutz
Monsieur Piddy	Andre Falcon

By VINCENT CANBY

FRANCOIS TRUFFAUT'S "Stolen Kisses," which opened yesterday at the Fine Arts Theater, is a movie so full of love that to define it may make it sound like a religious experience, which, of course, it is—but in a wonderfully unorthodox, cockeyed way. Truffaut loves his characters—the well-meaning misfit with

the private integrity, even paranoids; he loves movies —the people who make them and the people who preserve them (this film is dedicated to Henri Langlois of the Cinemathèque Française); he loves the craft of movies, and he loves—or, at least he accepts—the mortality of love itself.

●

Everything Truffaut touches — bookburning ("Fahrenheit 451"), banal adultery ("The Soft Skin"), or monomaniacal revenge ("The Bride Wore Black")—seems to be spontaneously invested with the lyricism that marks his greatest films, "Jules and Jim," "Shoot the Piano Player" and "The 400 Blows."

"Stolen Kisses" is one of his best—strong, sweet, wise and often explosively funny. It picks up the adolescent hero of "The 400 Blows" 10 years later, after his discharge from the Army for being "temperamentally unfit," and details his chaotic adventures around Paris as a hotel night clerk and then as a private eye of spectacular ineptitude.

The movie at first seems to have a rather short focus, but because Truffaut is incapable of doing anything cheaply or flatly or vulgarly, it is soon apparent that "Stolen Kisses" is as humanistically complex as even "Shoot the Piano Player," though more classically ordered in form. The focus is broad and deep and like all fine movies, "Stolen Kisses" has both social and political integrity that seem so casual as to appear unintentional.

Leaud, who has been playing lightweight versions of this role in other movies (most recently in Jerzy Skolimowski's "Le Départ"), is quite marvelous as Antoine, whose face is part predatory

434

cartoon cat, part saint and very, very French. Delphine Seyrig is the cool and beautiful older woman who seduces Antoine in one of the most erotic, nonsex scenes I've ever seen in a movie. Knowing that he has a crush on her she comes to his flat early one morning and points out, quite pragmatically, that since each of them is unique and exceptional, there is no reason they should not sleep together. He has to agree.

•

However, as in every Truffaut film, all the actors are so good one sometimes suspects that they, and not Truffaut, wrote their own lines. Michael Lonsdale is pricelessly funny as Miss Seyrig's husband, a shoe store owner who asks the detective agency to find out why everyone—waitresses, taxicab drivers, his employes and his wife—detest him. He is curious because there can't possibly be any legitimate reason. Claude Jade, who looks like a dark-haired Catherine Deneuve, is Antoine's sometime fiancée, and Harry Max is an elderly detective who sponsors Antoine in the trade.

Antoine (whom Jean-Pierre Leaud plays here, as he did in "The 400 Blows") is a kind of mid-sixties, Parisian Huckleberry Finn, committed to life if not to all of its rituals. Antoine, who is a physical and spiritual projection of Truffaut himself, is a constantly amazed observer and an enthusiastic participant, a fact that gives "Stolen Kisses" the perspective missing from so many other movies about youth seeking to connect.

With what can only be described as cinematic grace, Truffaut's point of view slips in and out of Antoine so that something that on the surface looks like a conventional movie eventually becomes as

fully and carefully populated as a Balzac novel. There is not a silly or superfluous incident, character or camera angle in the movie.

•

Truffaut, however, is the star of the film, always in control, whether the movie is ranging into the area of slapstick, lyrical romance or touching lightly on De Gaulle's France (a student demonstration on the TV screen). His love of old movies is reflected in plot devices (overheard conversations), incidental action (two children walking out of a drug store wearing Laurel and Hardy masks), and in the score, which takes Charles Trenet's 1943 song, known here as "I Wish You Love," and turns it into a joyous motif.

The ending—as in a Hitchcock movie—should not be revealed. It's a twist, all right, but not in plot. It simply italicizes everything that has gone before.

"Stolen Kisses" is a movie I'll cherish for a very long time, a lovely, human movie. Accompanying it on the bill at the Fine Arts is a short subject about cod fishing. It's an industrial fish film that should have been allowed to get away.

Mr 4, 1969

Screen:'If ...'

Tale of School Revolt Opens at the Plaza

By VINCENT CANBY

"IF . . ." is so good and strong that even those things in the movie that strike me as being first-class mistakes are of more interest than entire movies made by smoothly consistent, lesser directors. Lindsay Anderson's second feature (his first, "This Sporting Life," was released here in 1963) is a very human, very British social comedy that aspires to the cool, anarchic grandeur of Godard movies like "Band of Outsiders" and "La Chinoise."

The Cast

IF . . . ., screenplay by David Sherwin, from an original script, "Crusaders," by Mr. Sherwin and John Howlett; directed by Lindsay Anderson; produced by Michael Medwin and Mr. Anderson; a Memorial Enterprises Film presented by Paramount Pictures. At the Plaza Theater, 58th Street, east of Madison Avenue. Running time: 111 minutes.

Mick	Malcolm McDowell
Johnny	David Wood
Wallace	Richard Warwick
The Girl	Christine Noonan
Rowntree	Robert Swan
Denson	Hugh Thomas
Stephans	Guy Ross
Headmaster	Peter Jeffrey

As an artist, however, Anderson, unlike Godard, is more ageless than young. He was born in 1923. His movie about a revolution within a British public school is clear-eyed reality pushed to its outer reaches. The movie's compassion for the individual in the structured society is classic, post-World War II liberal, yet "If . . ." is also oddly nostalgic, as if it missed all that sadism and masochism that turned boys into adolescents for life.

Mick and his two room-mates, Johnny and Wallace, are nonconforming seniors at College House, a part of a posh boarding school that is collapsing under the weight of its 1,000-year history.

"Cheering at college matches has deteriorated completely," warns the student head of College House.

"Education in Britain," says the complacent headmaster a little later, "is a nubile Cinderella, sparsely clad and often interfered with."

As the winter term progresses through rituals that haven't varied since the Armada, Mick, Johnny and Wallace move mindlessly toward armed rebellion. On Speech Day, armed with bazookas and rifles, they take to the roofs and stage a reception for teachers, students and parents—and at least one Royal Highness—comparable to that given by Mohammed Ali to end the control of the Mamelukes.

I can't quarrel with the aim of Anderson and David Sherwin, who wrote the screenplay, to turn the public school into the private metaphor, only with the apparent attempt to equate this sort of lethal protest with what's been happening on real-life campuses around the world. Revolution as a life style, as an end in itself, is the fundamental form of "La Chinoise," but it's confusing and too grotesque to have real meaning attached to what is otherwise a beautifully and solidly constructed satire. In such a conventional context, the revolutionary act becomes one of paranoia.

Anderson, a fine documentary moviemaker, develops his fiction movie with all the care of someone recording the amazing habits of a newly discovered tribe of aborigines. The movie is a chronicle of bizarre details — Mick's first appearance wearing a black slouch hat, his face hidden behind a black scarf, looking like a teen-age Mack the Knife; the hazing of a boy by hanging him upside down over (and partially in) a toilet bowl, and a moment of first love, written on the face of a lower form student as he watches an older boy whose exercises on the crossbar become a sort of mating dance.

As a former movie critic, Anderson quite consciously reflects his feelings about the movies of others in his own film. "If . . . ," an ironic reference to Kipling's formula for manhood, uses a lot of terms most recently associated with Godard. There are title cards between sequences ("Ritual and Rebellion," "Discipline," etc.), and he arbitrarily switches from full color to monochromatic footage, as if to remind us that, after all, we are watching a movie. There is also an enigmatic girl (Christine Noonan), a waitress picked up at the Packhorse Cafe, who joins the revolt. Miss Noonan suggests a plump, English, mutton-chop version of Anna Karina, even without looking much like Miss Karina.

Less successful are visualized, split-second fantasies—or what I take to be fantasies. When the three boys are told to apologize to the chaplain for having attacked him during a cadet field corps exercise, the headmaster withdraws the chaplain's body from a morgue-like drawer. The fantasies just aren't very different from a crazy, believable reality in which a master's inhibited wife wanders nude through a deserted dormitory, lightly caressing objects that belong to the boys.

The movie is well acted by a cast that is completely new to me. Especially good are Malcolm McDowell (Mick), who looks like a cross between Steve McQueen and Michael J. Pollard; Richard Warwick (Wallace), Peter Jeffrey (the headmaster), Robert Swann (the student leader) and Mary McLeod (the lady who likes to walk unclothed).

"If . . . ," which opened yesterday at the Plaza Theater, is such an interesting movie (and one that I suspect will be very popular) that the chances are there will not be another six-year gap between Anderson features. After making "This Sporting Life," Anderson worked in the British theater and turned out two shorts, "The White Bus" and "The Singing Lesson," which will be shown here at the Museum of Modern Art April 30.

Mr 10, 1969

'Lola Montes'

The Cast

LOLA MONTES, screenplay by Max Ophuls, Annette Wademant and Franz Geiger, based on the novel, "La Vie Extraordinaire de Lola Montes," by Cecil St. Laurent; directed by Mr. Ophuls; produced by Gamma Films-Florida (Paris) and Oska Films (Munich); presented by Brandon Films. At the Beekman Theater, 65th Street at Second Avenue. Running time: 110 minutes.

Lola Montes	Martine Carol
Circus Master	Peter Ustinov
King of Bavaria	Anton Walbrook
James	Ivan Desny
Liszt	Will Quadflieg
The Student	Oskar Werner
Mrs. Craigie	Lise Delamere
Maurice	Henri Guisol
Josephine	Pauline Dubost
Lola's Doctor	Willy Eichberger

SEE "Lola Montes."

Yesterday at the Beekman Theater, the late Max Ophuls's 1955 swan-song finally began its first commercial American run in color and with footage restored. The event—and it is indeed an event—trails a case history from Europe almost as legendary as its dancer-courtesan heroine—litigation, cuts, howls of protest and a butchered black-and-white version on a few local screens.

The picture that Brandon Films opened yesterday is one of the loveliest, subtlest, most elegant and haunting movie eyefuls ever devised. Using the lavish unreality of an American circus, where the notorious fallen heroine, played by Martine Carol, pantomimes her life and loves for the masses, Mr. Ophuls embroiders this nightmarish canvas with a series of flashbacks that stunningly evoke the late 19th-century milieu and the enigmatic facade of the amoral heroine. In color, costumes (Karinska), music (Georges Aurio), settings and most of the performances—all of it fused in dazzling imagery—the picture attains the crest of romantic stylization.

But the heart of the picture is the lengthy, exquisitely civilized delineation of the heroine's tender romance with King Ludwig of Bavaria, whose restrained portrayal by Anton Walbrook is the best in the film.

The catch, and the only flaw, is the late Miss Carol, who is front and center virtually every minute as the warm-blooded, doomed Lola. The actress is a beautiful young woman, entirely convincing as a peppery, fatalistic siren but given to vacant-eyed stares with little dimension.

The other strong performance, alongside that of Mr. Walbrook, is the dominant one of Peter Ustinov as the circus ringmaster - owner, whose crackling whip and salty realism continually pull the picture up taut and cue in one of the screen's memorable fade-outs.

For American exposure to "Lola Montes," the mills of the gods have ground slowly but perhaps wisely. Dropping out of the sky now in a film era when anything and everything goes, it gleams like a remote, bygone and genuine jewel.

HOWARD THOMPSON.

Ap 21, 1969

'Midnight Cowboy'

The Cast

MIDNIGHT COWBOY, screenplay by Waldo Salt, based on the novel by James Leo Herlihy. Directed by John Schlesinger; produced by Jerome Hellman; a Jerome Hellman-John Schlesinger Production, presented by United Artists. At the Coronet Theater, Third Avenue at 59th Street. Running time: 113 minutes.

Ratso	Dustin Hoffman
Joe Buck	Jon Voight
Cass	Sylvia Miles
Mr. O'Daniel	John McGiver
Shirley	Brenda Vaccaro
Towny	Barnard Hughes
Sally Buck	Ruth White
Gretel McAlbertson	Viva

JOE BUCK is 6 feet tall and has the kind of innocence that preserves dumb good looks. Joe Buck fancies himself a cowboy, but his spurs were earned while riding a gas range in a Houston hamburger joint. Ratso Rizzo, his buddy and part-time pimp from the Bronx, is short, gimpy and verminous. Although they are a comparatively bizarre couple, they go unnoticed when they arrive at one of those hallucinogenic "Village" parties where the only thing straight is the booze that no one drinks. Everybody is too busy smoking pot, popping pills and being chic. Joe Buck, ever-hopeful stud, drawls: "I think we better find someone an' tell 'em that we're here."

Trying to tell someone that he's there is the story of Joe Buck's life—28 years of anxiety and dispossession fenced off by Priapian conquests that always, somehow, leave him a little lonelier than he was before. Joe is a funny, dim-witted variation on the lonely, homosexual dream-hero who used to wander disguised through so much drama and literature associated with the nineteen-fifties.

"Midnight Cowboy," which opened yesterday at the Coronet Theater, is a slick, brutal (but not brutalizing) movie version of James Leo Herlihy's 1965 novel. It is tough and good in important ways, although its style is oddly romantic and at variance with the laconic material. It may be that movies of this sort (like most war movies) automatically celebrate everything they touch. We know they are movies—isolated, simplified reflections of life—and thus we can enjoy the spectacle of degradation and loss while feeling superior to it and safe.

I had something of this same feeling about "Darling," which was directed by John Schlesinger and in which Julie Christie suffered, more or less upwardly, on her way to fame and fortune in a movie as glossy as the life it satirized. There is nothing obviously glossy in "Midnight Cowboy," but it contains a lot of superior laughter that has the same softening effect.

Schlesinger is most successful in his use of actors. Dustin Hoffman, as Ratso (his first movie performance since "The Graduate"), is something found under an old door in a vacant lot. With his hair matted back, his ears sticking out and his runty walk, Hoffman looks like a sly, defeated rat and talks with a voice that might have been created by Mel Blanc for a despondent Bugs

Bunny. Jon Voight is equally fine as Joe Buck, a tall, handsome young man whose open face somehow manages to register the fuzziest of conflicting emotions within a very dim mind.

Waldo Frank's screenplay follows the Herlihy novel in most of the surface events.

Joe Buck, a Texas dishwasher without friend or family, comes to New York to make his fortune as a stud to all the rich ladies who have been deprived of their rights by faggot eastern gentlemen. Instead, he winds up a half-hearted 42d Street hustler whose first and only friend is a lame, largely ineffectual con artist.

•

As long as the focus is on this world of cafeterias and abandoned tenements, of desperate conjunctions in movie balconies and doorways, of catchup and beans and canned heat, "Midnight Cowboy" is so rough and vivid that it's almost unbearable. Less effective are abbreviated, almost subliminal fantasies and flashbacks. Most of these are designed to fill in the story of the young Joe Buck, a little boy whose knowledge of life was learned in front of a TV set while his grandmother, goodtime Sally Buck, ran a Texas beauty parlor and lived with a series of cowboy-father images for Joe.

•

Schlesinger has given his leads superb support with character actors like Ruth White ((Sally Buck); John McGiver, Brenda Vaccaro, Barnard Hughes and Sylvia Miles. Miss Miles is especially good as the aging hooker Joe picks up under the mistaken impression she is a society lady. The one rather wooden performance, oddly, is that of superstar Viva, who plays a "Village" zombie with none of the flair she exhibits in Andy Warhol's improvisations.

"Midnight Cowboy" often seems to be exploiting its material for sensational or comic effect, but it is ultimately a moving experience that captures the quality of a time and a place. It's not a movie for the ages, but, having seen it, you won't ever again feel detached as you walk down West 42d Street, avoiding the eyes of the drifters, stepping around the little islands of hustlers and closing your nostrils to the smell of rancid griddles.

VINCENT CANBY

My 26, 1969

Wild Bunch

THE WILD BUNCH, screenplay by Walon Green and Sam Peckinpah, based on the story by Mr. Green and Roy N. Sickner; directed by Sam Peckinpah; produced by Phil Feldman; released by Warner Bros.-Seven Arts. At Trans-Lux East Theater, Third Avenue and 58th Street, and Trans-Lux West, Broadway at 49th Street. Running time: 140 minutes.

Pike	William Holden
Dutch	Ernest Borgnine
Thornton	Robert Ryan
Sykes	Edmond O'Brien
Lyle Gorch	Warren Oates
Angel	Jaime Sanchez
Tector Gorch	Ben Johnson

By VINCENT CANBY

SAM PECKINPAH'S "The Wild Bunch" is about the decline and fall of one outlaw gang at what must be the bleeding end of the frontier era, 1913, when Pancho Villa was tormenting a corrupt Mexican Government while the United States watched cautiously from across the border.

The movie, which opened yesterday at the Trans-Lux East and West Theaters, is very beautiful and the first truly interesting, American-made Western in years. It's also so full of violence—of an intensity that can hardly be supported by the story—that it's going to prompt a lot of people who do not know the real effect of movie violence (as I do not) to write automatic condemnations of it.

"The Wild Bunch" begins on a hot, lazy afternoon as six United States soldiers ride into a small Texas border town with all the aloofness of an army of benign occupation. Under a makeshift awning, the good bourgeoisie of San Rafael is holding a temperance meeting. Gentle spinsters, sweating discreetly, vow to abstain from all spirits.

The "soldiers" pass on to the railroad office, which they quietly proceed to rob of its cash receipts. Down the street, a group of children giggle as they watch a scorpion being eaten alive by a colony of red ants. A moment later, the town literally explodes in the ambush that has been set for the outlaws.

Borrowing a device from "Bonnie and Clyde," Peckinpah suddenly reduces the camera speed to slow motion, which at first heightens the horror of the mindless slaughter, and then—and this is what really carries horror—makes it beautiful, almost abstract, and finally into terrible parody.

●

The audience, which earlier was appalled at the cynical detachment with which the camera watched the death fight of the scorpion, is now in the position of the casually cruel children. The face of a temperance parade marcher erupts in a fountain of red. Bodies, struck by bullets, make graceful arcs through the air before falling onto the dusty street, where they seem to bounce, as if on a trampoline.

This sort of choreographed brutality is repeated to excess, but in excess, there is point to a film in which realism would be unbearable. "The Wild Bunch" takes the basic element of the Western movie myth, which once defined a simple, morally comprehensible world, and by bending them turns them into symbols of futility and aimless corruption.

The screenplay, by Peckinpah and Walon Green, follows the members of the Wild Bunch from their disastrous, profitless experience at San Rafael to Mexico, where they become involved with a smilingly sadistic Mexican general fighting Villa. Although the movie's conventional and poetic action sequences are extraordinarily good and its landscapes beautifully photographed (lots of dark foregrounds and brilliant backgrounds) by Lucien Ballard, who did "Nevada Smith," it is most interesting in its almost jolly account of chaos, corruption and defeat. All personal relationships in the movie seem somehow perverted in odd mixtures of noble sentimentality, greed and lust.

Never satisfactorily resolved is the conflict between William Holden, as the aging leader of the Wild Bunch, and Robert Ryan, as his former friend who, with disdain, leads the bounty hunters in pursuit of the gang. An awkward flashback shows the two men, looking like characters out of a silent movie, caught in an ambush in a bordello from which only Holden escapes.

The ideals of masculine comradeship are exaggerated and transformed into neuroses. The fraternal bonds of two brothers, members of the Wild Bunch, are so excessive they prefer having their whores in tandem. A feeling of genuine compassion prompts the climactic massacre that some members of the film trade are calling, not without reason, "the blood ballet."

Peckinpah also has a way of employing Hollywood life to dramatize his legend. After years of giving bored performances in boring movies, Holden comes back gallantly in "The Wild Bunch." He looks older and tired, but he has style, both as a man and as a movie character who persists in doing what he's always done, not because he really wants the money but because there's simply nothing else to do.

Ryan, Ernest Borgnine and Edmond O'Brien add a similar kind of resonance to the film. O'Brien is a special shock, looking like an evil Gabby Hayes, a foul-mouthed, cackling old man who is the only member of the Wild Bunch to survive.

In two earlier Westerns, "Ride the High Country" (1962) and "Major Dundee" (1965), Peckinpah seemed to be creating comparatively gentle variations on the genre about the man who walks alone—a character about as rare in a Western as a panhandler on the Bowery.

In "The Wild Bunch," which is about men who walk together, but in desperation, he turns the genre inside out. It's a fascinating movie and, I think I should add, when I came out of it, I didn't feel like shooting, knifing or otherwise maiming any of Broadway's often hostile pedestrians.

Je 26, 1969

Easy Rider

By VINCENT CANBY

"EASY RIDER," which opened yesterday at the Beekman, is a motorcycle drama with decidedly superior airs about it. How else are we to approach a movie that advertises itself: "A man went looking for America. And couldn't find it anywhere"? Right away you know that something superior is up, that somebody is making a statement, and you can bet your boots (cowboy, black leather) that it's going to put down the whole rotten scene. What scene? Whose? Why? Man, I can't tell you if you don't know. What I mean to say is, if you don't groove, you don't groove. You might as well split.

EASY RIDER, written by Peter Fonda, Dennis Hopper and Terry Southern; directed by Mr. Hopper; produced by Mr. Fonda; presented by the Pando Company in association with Raybert Productions; released by Columbia Pictures At the Beekman Theater, 65th Street at Second Avenue. Running time 94 minutes. (The Motion Picture Association of America's Production Code and Rating Administration classifies this film: "R. Restricted—persons under 16 not admitted, unless accompanied by parent or adult guardian.")

Wyatt .... Peter Fonda
Billy .... Dennis Hopper
George Hanson .... Jack Nicholson
Rancher .... Warren Finnerty
Stranger on Highway ..... Luke Askew
Lisa .... Luana Anders
Karen .... Karen Black

I felt this way during the first half-hour of "Easy Rider," and then, almost reluctantly, fell into the rhythm of the determinedly inarticulate piece. Two not-so-young cyclists, Wyatt (Peter Fonda) who affects soft leather breeches and a Capt. America jacket, and Billy (Dennis Hopper), who looks like a perpetually stoned Buffalo Bill, are heading east from California toward New Orleans.

They don't communicate with us, or each other, but after a while, it doesn't seem to matter. They simply exist —they are bizarre comic strip characters with occasional balloons over their heads reading: "Like you're doing your thing," or some such. We accept them in their moving isolation, against the magnificent Southwestern landscapes of beige and green and pale blue.

They roll down macadam highways that look like black velvet ribbons, under skies of incredible purity, and the soundtrack rocks with oddly counterpointed emotions of Steppenwolf, the Byrds, the Electric Prunes — dark and smoky cries for liberation.

Periodically, like a group taking a break, the cyclists stop (and so does the music) for quiet encounters—with a toothless rancher and his huge, happy family or with a commune of thin hippies, whose idyll seems ringed with unacknowledged desperation.

Suddenly, however, a strange thing happens. There comes on the scene a very real character and everything that has been accepted earlier as a sort of lyrical sense impression suddenly looks flat and foolish.

●

Wyatt and Billy are in a small Southern town—in jail for having disturbed the peace of a local parade—when they meet fellow-inmate George Hanson (Jack Nicholson), a handsome, alcoholic young lawyer of good family and genially bad habits, a man whose only defense against life is a cheerful but not abject acceptance of it. As played by Nicholson, George Hanson is a marvelously realized character, who talks in a high, squeaky Southern accent and uses a phrase like "Lord have mercy!" the way another man might use a four-letter word.

Hanson gets the cyclists sprung from jail and then promptly joins them. He looks decidedly foolish, sitting on the back of Wyatt's bike, wearing a seersucker jacket and his old football helmet, but he is completely happy and, ironically, the only person in the movie who seems to have a sense of what liberation and freedom are. There is joy and humor and sweetness when he smokes grass for the first time and expounds an elaborate theory as to how the Venutians have already conquered the world.

•

Nicholson is so good, in fact, that "Easy Rider" never quite recovers from his loss, even though he has had the rather thankless job of spelling out what I take to be the film's statement (upper case). This has to do with the threat that people like the nonconforming Wyatt and Billy represent to the ordinary, self-righteous, inhibited folk that are the Real America. Wyatt and Billy, says the lawyer, represent freedom; ergo, says the film, they must be destroyed.

If there is any irony in this supposition, I was unable to detect it in the screenplay written by Fonda, Hopper and Terry Southern. Wyatt and Billy don't seem particularly free, not if the only way they can face the world is through a grass curtain. As written and played, they are lumps of gentle clay, vacuous, romantic symbols, dressed in cycle drag.

"Easy Rider," the first film to be directed by Dennis Hopper, won a special prize at this year's Cannes festival as the best picture by a new director (there was only one other picture competing in that category).

•

With the exception of Nicholson, its good things are familiar things — the rock score, the lovely, sometimes impressionistic photography by Laszlo Kovacs, the faces of small-town America. These things not only are continually compelling but occasionally they dazzle the senses, if not the mind. Hopper, Fonda and their friends went out into America looking for a movie and found instead a small, pious statement (upper case) about our society (upper case), which is sick (upper case). It's pretty but lower case cinema.

Jl 15, 1969

Medium Cool

MEDIUM COOL, written and directed by Haskell Wexler; produced by Tully Friedman and Mr. Wexler; released by Paramount Pictures Corporation. At Loew's Tower East Theater, 71st Street at Third Avenue. Running time: 110 minutes. (The Motion Picture Association of America's Production Code and Rating Administration classifies this film: "X—persons under 16 not admitted.")

John .... Robert Forster
Eileen .... Verna Bloom
Gus .... Peter Bonerz
Ruth .... Marianna Hill
Harold .... Harold Blankenship

By VINCENT CANBY

JOHN CASSELLIS (Robert Forster), the hero of Haskell Wexler's "Medium Cool," is a television news cameraman, an instrument that observes, selects, isolates and photographs the reflection of a visible world. With all of the emotional commitment of a highly skilled technician, he moves through the United States in the spring and summer of 1968 mummifying the times as defined by events—such things as automobile accidents, the assassination of Senator Robert F. Kennedy, Resurrection City, riot training at a National Guard camp, the disorders that erupted during the Democratic National Convention in Chicago.

"Jesus," he says as he

watches a TV documentary on the life of the late Dr. Martin Luther King, "I love to shoot film."

For a long time, John Cassellis is able to separate the shooting of film from the meaning of the events recorded. "Medium Cool," which opened yesterday at Loew's Tower East Theater, suspects there is something of this same separation in each of us, especially in the way we cope with TV. The televised image certifies the reality of events and, at the same time, removes them by equating their meaning to that of the commercials — the cheerful haiku—that frame them.

•

"Medium Cool," the first fiction feature to be directed by Wexler, the Oscar-winning cinematographer ("Who's Afraid of Virginia Woolf?"), is an angry, technically brilliant movie that uses some of the real events of last year the way other movies use real places—as backgrounds that are extensions of the fictional characters.

In addition to directing and photographing "Medium Cool," Wexler also wrote it, designing a screenplay to utilize the anticipated demonstrations at the Democratic Convention as the climax of the movie itself. The result is a film of tremendous visual impact, a kind of cinematic "Guernica," a picture of America in the process of exploding into fragmented bits of hostility, suspicion, fear and violence.

The movie, however, is much less complex than it looks. The story of the gradual emotional and political awakening of John Cassellis is somehow dwarfed by the emotional and political meaning of the events themselves, which we, in the audience, experience first hand, rather than through

the movie protagonist. This is a fundamental problem in the kind of movie-making that attempts to homogenize fact and fiction, particularly when the fiction has the oversimplified shape of nineteen-thirties social protest drama and the fact is so obviously of a later, more complicated world.

Wexler has gotten some very good performances from a cast of both professionals and amateurs. Forster, who played the terribly American sounding Coptic Christian Narouz in "Justine," looks and moves like a contemporary technician, a man for whom craft has the meaning of art. Verna Bloom, a stage and television actress, is fine as a sweet Appalachian widow with whom Forster, in a rather unlikely bit of plotting, falls in love. The most convincing performance in the film, however, is that of 13-year-old Harold Blankenship, who plays her small son. The child really is an Appalachian refugee and has the stunted look of generations of deprivation in his physique, in his eyes and in a profile that is as hard as a hickory nut.

•

Wexler has staged some excellent individual scenes—I particularly liked an ecstatic nude romp that should give lust a good name — and vignettes that catch the subsidiary meanings of poverty, such as slum children crawling all over a fancy new automobile as if it were an object from another planet.

The shock of "Medium Cool" comes not from the fiction, but from the facts provided Wexler by Mayor Daley, the Illinois National Guard and the Chicago police. In his use of these events and others, however, Wexler does seem to be somewhat presumptuous, attempting to surpass the devastating live show that television—Marshall McLuhan's "cool medium" — presented as the Chicago riots actually were taking place.

Clever editing and beautiful color can diminish the horror. This occurs, for example, when a nice, tinny, nineteen-thirtyish recording of Franklin D. Roosevelt's theme, "Happy Days Are Here Again," serves as a soundtrack bridge between pious events in the International Amphitheater and the riots outside. That's like pouring catchup on a corpse. "Medium Cool" is an awkward and even pretentious movie, but, like the report of the President's National Advisory Commission on Civil Disorders, it has an importance that has nothing to do with literature.

Ag 28, 1969

Une Femme Douce

UNE FEMME DOUCE, screenplay by Robert Bresson from Dostoevski's "The Gentle Woman." Directed by Mr. Bresson; produced by Mag Bodard; released by Paramount Pictures Corporation. At the New York Film Festival, Alice Tully Hall, Lincoln Center. Running time: 87 minutes.
She .... Dominique Sanda
He .... Guy Frangin
Anna ,.................... Jane Lobre

By ROGER GREENSPUN

"UNE FEMME DOUCE" is the ninth film of the 62-year-old French director Robert Bresson. Of the previous eight, the last three ("The Trial of Joan of Arc," 1962; "Au Hazard Balthazar," 1966; "Mouchette," 1967) have had their premieres in this country at the New York Film Festival. If the festival

had no other justification, merely showing the works of Bresson, and of a few other great and not very popular directors, would be justification enough.

●

Bresson's career has been extensively discussed in film journals and almost totally ignored everywhere else. His movies are austere, relatively static, acted frequently by amateurs whom the director has trained to suppress both facial and vocal expression, and concerned with man's inward life—which they take pains to keep inward. The privileged Bressonian moment is the crisis of the soul's salvation, often, but not always, figured in religious terms.

The Film Festival advertisement asserts that "Une Femme Douce" offers us Bresson's first "real woman" in years—which is not true. The gentle woman of the title, played by Dominique Sanda (17 years old, a model and, like many of Bresson's leading ladies, beautiful) is neither more nor less real than her predecessors. She differs from most of them only in that she has no vocation for her life—except to leave it.

●

In the best critical introduction to Bresson, "Spiritual Style in the Films of Robert Bresson" (1964; reprinted in "Against Interpretation"), Susan Sontag posits a theme common to all his films: "the meaning of confinement and liberty." For the films made since her essay, I should modify that theme to "the meaning of escape." In Bresson's recent movies, "liberty" has meant only the "escape" that is possible through death. The martyrdom of Joan, the dying of the donkey Balthazar, the suicide of the girl Mouchette—all bring to an end unredeemable life situations, and all provide ravishingly beautiful climaxes for their respective films.

The young wife leaps to her death at the very beginning of "Une Femme Douce." The action is then mostly played out in flashbacks, the husband speaking to the maidservant while standing or kneeling over his wife's dead body.

That body may produce mixed reactions. It is distressingly in evidence, and the cuts to it are sometimes shocking. Much of the past action takes place in and around the bed on which the corpse now lies and, because Bresson provides no bridges, you are never sure whether the film will cut to a living wife or a dead one. Nevertheless, the corpse is the residue of something that has escaped, and for that escape we must be glad. At the very end, the husband, a pawnbroker who has helped drive his wife to suicide, begs her to look at him once more. But in Bresson's world a direct look is always a speaking between souls, and this is precisely the sign that can no longer be given.

Just before the young woman's death the audience is given some signs for itself, momentary scenes: the woman's smile in her mirror, her fierce and happy eyes at the door to her balcony, the balcony furniture toppling slowly over, her shawl floating to the ground. Anyone familiar with Bresson will recognize a continuity between these signs and the lovely intimations of grace in his earlier films. You must watch closely. That smile, the film's only smile, lasts a second or two; but in the cinema of Bresson, such seconds are what we go to the movies for.

"Une Femme Douce" is adapted from a Dostoevski novella. Bresson has kept the novella's basic situation and changed everything else. His gentle woman wants to escape not just her husband (as Dostoevski's does) but the very idea of marriage, the tedium of typical life patterns and even the historical continuity of biological forms —by which her bone structure partially reproduces the bone structure of animals long extinct and her nude body duplicates nude bodies throughout the history of painting.

●

Bresson has placed his action in present-day Paris. And he brings in the "modern world"—by which I mean he arbitrarily shows cars, airplanes and race horses on a television screen and introduces the sound of traffic outside the couple's bedroom.

But his world remains mysterious. The pawning of objects, and the paying of money for them, is presented as a secret joint admission of guilt. Empty stairways, doors, street corners repeatedly suggest the absence of the people who have just passed through them. And on her wedding night the new wife simply runs from closet to bath to bed—to indicate (without expression) what there is of pleasure and passion before that fateful smile.

S 18, 1969

Ma Nuit Chez Maud

MA NUIT CHEZ MAUD, screenplay by Eric Rohmer, based on the third of his "Six Moral Tales"; directed by Mr. Rohmer; produced by Barbet Schroeder and Pierre Cottrell. At the New York Film Festival, Alice Tully Hall at Lincoln Center. Running time: 105 minutes.

Jean-Louis .... Jean-Louis Trintignant

446

Maud .... Francoise Fabian
Francoise ....Marie-Christine Barrault
Vidal .... Antoine Vitez

By VINCENT CANBY

ERIC ROHMER'S "Ma Nuit Chez Maud" (literally, "My Night at Maud's") is so French and so Catholic— as well as so fine—that it should prove irresistible to certain Americans, especially to those of us who, having been raised in a puritan tradition, have always been a little in awe of the Roman Church's intellectual catholicism. The French film was shown last night at Alice Tully Hall and will be repeated there tomorrow evening at 6:30. To my way of thinking, it's the first new film to be seen at the current New York Film Festival that achieves with elegance and eloquence the goals it has set for itself.

●

Elegance and eloquence may seem like strange words to use about a film that was photographed entirely in black and white in a French provincial city in the dreariness of winter (mostly in ordinary interior settings) and that concerns four seemingly commonplace people, none of whom renounces a throne or even possesses an inflammatory political pamphlea.

I'd even go so far as to call "Ma Nuit Chez Maud" civilized, except for the fact that that adjective usually recalls some boring film adaptation of a Lillian Hellman play in which people talk canned wisdom as they move from fireplace to settee to French windows, all the while anticipating some melodramatic disaster.

"Ma Nuit Chez Maud" is the first Rohmer feature to be seen in this country. Rohmer, a 40-year-old Cahiers du Cinéma critic, directed one of the episodes in the omnibus

feature "Six in Paris," which was shown at the 1965 New York Film Festival (and which frankly, I don't remember). This new film is described as the third feature in a projected cycle called "Six Moral Tales," of which four have now been completed. Each is a variation on a single situation: a man who is in love with one woman meets and spends some time with another woman, whom he finds supremely attractive, but with whom he does not consummate the affair.

The hero of "Ma Nuit Chez Maud" is Jean-Louis (Jean-Louis Trintignant), an engineer in his early 30's, a solitary but not a lonely sort, a man who at first seems to be something of a prig. He isn't. He just values himself too much—in the best sense —to waste time on superficial sexual or social experiments. Within his abiding Roman Catholicism, he also believes that he will ultimately meet and marry the right girl, who will not only be Catholic but also blonde.

●

By chance one night, he runs into an old friend, a philosophy professor and Marxist atheist, who introduces him to Maud (Françoise Fabian), a divorcee and skeptic (this is the sort of movie in which people's philosophical attitudes are made as immediately apparent as are the birthrights in Shakespeare's histories). Maud, beautiful, wise, tells him about her marriage, her dead lover, her husband's mistress (a lovely young Catholic girl) and tries unsuccessfully to seduce him. The very next day, Jean-Louis meets the girl for whom he has been looking—which is not quite the end of a tale that is as ironic as it is moral.

Rohmer's achievement in "Ma Nuit Chez Maud" is that he has been able to make so much talk so unaffectedly cinematic. Although a quick dip into Pascal's "Pensées" would not hurt before seeing the film, there is so much wit-in-context that it is not absolutely necessary. Most refreshing is the sight and sound of four characters who are articulate, interested, informed, educated, amused, vulnerable, totally free of epigrams and aware of their identities. Their only concern is the manner in which they will realize those identities, and whether it will be by choice, predestination or simple luck.

The film is beautifully played, that is, as written, which is almost as if it were music. The camera literally and figuratively never looks down or up at the characters. It faces them straight on, the better to catch some completely unexpected moments of intimacy and humor.

"Ma Nuit Chez Maud" is set in Clermont, a town of something over 100,000 citizens, southwest of Paris, where Pascal was born in 1623. For more data, you'll have to search your own "Pensées," and the film, both of which might be most agreeable.

S 24, 1969

Le Gai Savoir

The Cast

LE GAI SAVOIR, screenplay by Jean-Luc Godard, loosely based on Rosseau's "Emile"; directed by Mr. Godard; produced by Anouchka Films—Bavaria Atelier (Munich). At the New York Film Festival, Alice Tully Hall, Lincoln Center. Running time: 91 minutes.
Emile Rosseau ....Jean-Pierre Leaud
Patricia Lumumba ....Juliette Bertho

By VINCENT CANBY

IN this time of increasingly personal cinema, the films of Jean-Luc Godard make those of most of his contemporaries look about as original and individual as monogramed Volkswagens.

"Le Gai Savoir," which was shown at the New York Film Festival Saturday evening and again last night, was originally commissioned by the French television network as a modern version of Jean-Jacques Rousseau's "Emile," a treatise on education in the form of a novel.

What Godard finally made is a kind of treatise on the need for de-education, particularly in relation to language and the meaning of words. It is a film whose style is very much its content, which, actually, is somewhat less revolutionary than a description of it makes it appear. I suspect that when Godard ultimately makes his most revolutionary movie, he will have found a way to dispense with camera, film, projector, screen and, perhaps, even audience. In "Le Gai Savoir" Godard is still communicating with us by means of beautiful, comparatively conventional, if fragmented, images and sounds.

Godard is in the same position as Marshall McLuhan, who can only proclaim the end of the old era by means of the old; that is, by placing one word after another in linear sequence. Godard must proselyte for his revolutionary cause in the essentially bourgeois cinema medium in which image and word, though placed on top of each other, must also flow from one to the other, thus immediately assuming a formal structure even when the flow is dictated by chance. Godard, however, seldom makes films by chance.

"Le Gai Savoir" is a very formal film, but one that makes no pretense to having

448

a narrative. A young man, E.nile Rousseau (Jean-Pierre Leaud), and a pretty, intense girl, Patricia Lumumba (Juliette Bertho), are in a television studio ostensibly making a film but actually having a discourse on language, "the enemy," the weapon by which the capitalist establishments confuse liberation movements. Because words condition behavior, they say, man can only free himself by destroying words and their old associations, then building a new, fresh vocabulary.

Like Nana, Veronique, Natasha von Braun, Ulysses, Michelangelo and so many other Godard characters, Emile and Patricia exist in a void, which this time is visual. As they stand, sit, pose, circle one another, they are the only figures to be seen in a liquid black limbo. They are not, however, really removed from a cultural tradition and heritage. Their discourses are packed with literary and film references— Bertrand Russell, Faulkner, Bertolucci, Robinson Crusoe ("a fascist"), Cohn-Bendit, Burroughs, Cahiers du Cinema.

●

At the same time, the camera is constantly cutting to points of visual references— Paris streets, cartoon strips, pop posters—images, which, though fragmented, make complete sense. At one point, the camera moves in to play a word association game with a small boy. Being, in effect, pure, the boy gives responses that illustrate the goal sought by Emile and Patricia. The same game played with an old man brings forth nothing but a lot a quite comic, inanely complex, responses, all, of course, pre-conditioned.

Although I must admit that

I found great patches of "Le Gai Savoir" literally "joyful wisdom" almost unbearably dense and obscure, it is one of Godard's most beautiful, most visually lucid movies, even when the screen goes completely black (key footage, we are told, has been censored) and the whispered dialogue is translated in hypnotically white subtitles.

The movie also is full of puns and typically Godardian whimsey. At the end of a filming session in the TV studio, Emile announces he is off to steal the dreams of two Pop stars to sell to the tabloids, the money from which will go to the revolutionary cause. Patricia admits that she earns extra money by posing for lingerie ads for L'Humanité.

●

Rumors from film circles in Europe to the effect that Godard has gone completely off the cinematic deep end are, I think, dispelled by this film. "Le Gai Savoir" certainly is abstract beyond anything he has done before, but its discourses are simple (or not so simple) extensions of ideas that he has been playing with in films like "Les Carabiniers" "Alphaville," "La Chinoise," "Made in U.S.A." and "Weekend." "Le Gai Savoir" is a sort of finale to those films — where he goes from here, I can't imagine.

S 29, 1969

'In the Year of the Pig,' Documentary, Bows

IN THE YEAR OF THE PIG, directed and produced by Emile de Antonio. Presented by Pathe Contemporary Films. At the New Yorker Theater, Broadway and 88th Street. Running time 103 minutes. (This film has not been submitted to the Motion Picture of America's Production Code and Rating Administration for rating as to audience suitability.)

By **HOWARD THOMPSON**

HAVING made a fine documentary dramatizing the downfall of Senator Joseph R. McCarthy, Emile de Antonio has now assembled "In the Year of the Pig," a documentary on American involvement in Vietnam. It will nail many people to their seats.

There are no frills and few ifs, ands or buts about the stinging, graphic and often frighteningly penetrating movie that arrived yesterday at the New Yorker Theater. Adhering strictly to a dove viewpoint, Mr. de Antonio's picture suggests that we should get out of Vietnam fast. To make his points he uses footage culled from international sources, interspersing, with enormous effectiveness, statements on both sides by political and military leaders, as well as teachers, officials and on-the-spot journalists.

Even with its frank slant, the picture is invaluable on two counts. First, it provides a succinct, backward refresher course on our initial Vietnamese involvement, a needed primer for spectators confusingly numbed by the appalling facts of the present. Second, although some of the footage speaks volumes, it is the statements by the men who led us there and those who went there that cut through to the quick.

With some of the unseen speakers, a good bit of the footage is random and sketchy, such as a portion on the French-Indochinese war, which is repeatedly likened to our involvement. Some of the vignettes are memorable, such as one little drama involving white-suited colonials and rickshaw coolies. In another clip, some husky American soldiers cavorting on a Vietnamese beach scornfully profess disinterest in native girls, described as a "bunch of slant-eyed gooks." Commenting on a memorial service for American troops, Col. George S. Patton 3d smilingly recalls them as "looking determined and reverent," adding: "But they're still a bloody good bunch of killers."

One detailed sequence with a clutter of expressionless natives being firmly shepherded by American soldiers is a microcosm of the Vietnam war. But it is the almost unbroken flow of personal testimonies, for and against our military involvement, that will jolt the viewer, ranging from that given by combat soldiers to those by former President Lyndon B. Johnson and President Nixon.

The film ends with the strains of "The Battle Hymn of the Republic" while an American unit agonizingly hobbles into a clearing in the forest bearing its maimed and wounded.

N 11, 1969

Costa-Gavras Directs 'Z', Topical Drama

The Cast

Z, screenplay by Jorge Semprun and Costa-Gavras, from a novel by Vassili Vassilikos; directed by Costa-Gavras; produced by Jacques Perrin and Hamed Rachedi; distributed by Cinema V Distributing, Inc. At the Beekman Theater, Second Avenue at 65th Street. Running time: 127 minutes. (The Motion Picture Association of America's Production Code and Rating Administration classifies this film: "M—suggested for mature audiences, parental discretion advised.")

Deputy	Yves Montand
Helene	Irene Papas
Investigating Judge	Jean-Louis Trintignant
Manuel	Charles Denner
Nick	Georges Geret
Journalist	Jacques Perrin
Public Prosecutor	Francois Perier
Matt	Bernard Fresson
General	Pierre Dux
Colonel	Julien Guiomar
Vago	Marcel Bozzufi
Sister of Witness	Magali Noel
Yago	Renato Salvatori
Pirou	Jean Bouise

By **VINCENT CANBY**

COSTA-GAVRAS'S "Z," the French film that won the Jury Prize (in effect, the third prize) at this year's Cannes Festival, is an immensely entertaining movie—a topical melodrama that manipulates our emotional responses and appeals to our best prejudices in such satisfying ways that it is likely to be mistaken as a work of fine—rather than popular—movie art.

The film, which opened last night at the Beekman, is based on Vassili Vassilikos's novel, which, in turn, is a lightly fictionalized account of the 1963 assassination in Salonika of Gregarios Lambrakis, a professor of medicine at the University of Athens and a leader of the forces opposing the placement of Polaris missiles in Greece. There is a kind of momentum to democratic processes, and the official investigation of that murder, instigated with some reluctance by the Government, eventually uncovered a plot involving high Government officials as well as a secret right-wing organization of patriotic goons.

●

In the course of the scandal, the Greek Government fell and the men morally and directly responsible for the murder were brought to trial. Within four years, there was a military coup d'état, after which almost everyone connected with the assassination was conveniently "rehabilitated."

The story of the Lambrakis affair is one of national sorrow, of idealism, of bravery, of defeat, of terrible irony. The movie is not one of ideas or ideals, but of sensations—horror, anger, frustration and suspense.

These are communicated —sometimes with all of the subtlety of a hypodermic needle stuck in a nerve— through the extraordinary color camerawork of Raoul Coutard, the man who has photographed just about every important French film of the nineteen-sixties, including Démy's "Lola," Truffaut's "Jules and Jim" and Godard's "Weekend."

Coutard may be unique among cinematographers in the manner in which he adapts himself to the individual demands of his directors without losing his own identity. His work on "Z," shot entirely in an Algiers designed to suggest Salonika, is largely responsible for Costa-Gavras's realization of what is, actually, a dazzling, super-"Dragnet" film, a sort of remarkable newsreel record of events rather than people.

Costa-Gavras, the Greek-born French director ("The Sleeping Car Murder") collaborated with Jorge Semprun ("La Guerre Est Finie") on a screen adaptation that quite consciously subordinates characterization to vivid incident. The cast is large and excellent: Yves Montand as the assassinated doctor, Jean-Louis Trintignant ("Ma Nuit Chez Maud") as the government's investigator, Jacques Perrin as a totally dispassionate newspaper reporter, Pierre Dux and Julien Guiomar as right-wing leaders, and Renato Salvatori and Marcel Bozzufi as the assassins whose patriotism is for hire.

A small part of me, however, tends to rebel against the film's carefully programed responses, including the sight of Irene Papas, who can be a very fine actress, as the doctor's widow. The film thus employs for easy effect Miss Papas's professional image of perpetual bereavement. Without telling us much of what the assassinated doctor believes (except that he is against missiles and for peace), the film makes us grieve by shocking us with graphic details of brutal beatings and civil disorders.

●

Just as the fascists in the film appeal to their audiences by oversimplification, by generalities, by fear, so does the film appeal to us by its use of the techniques of rather ordinary suspense drama—a car speeding crazily down a sidewalk in an attempt to run over a witness. Ever since the days of the swastika, I've been leery of symbols designed to elicit automatic emotional responses — even leery of the peace symbol and of "Z" itself, which, I'm told, stands for the Greek words "he is alive" and is employed by the assassinated doctor's followers in the film.

These are not meant to be major reservations, but I mention them because I think they restrict the film to a genre that is perfectly respectable but incapable of greatness. A lot of people are going to become emotionally unstuck about "Z," seeing it as a strong political statement, which is an unnecessary ruse to ennoble sheer entertainment.

D 9, 1969

They Shoot Horses

The Cast

THEY SHOOT HORSES, DON'T THEY?, screenplay by James Poe and Robert E. Thompson, based on the novel by Horace McCoy; directed by Sydney Pollack; produced by Irwin Winkler and Robert Chartoff; distributed by Cinerama Releasing Corporation. At the Fine Arts Theater, 58th Street between Park and Lexington Avenues. Running time: 120 minutes. (The Motion Picture Association of America's Production Code and Rating Administration classifies this film "M—suggested for mature audiences, parental discretion advised.")

Gloria	Jane Fonda
Robert	Michael Sarrazin
Alice	Susannah York
Rocky	Gig Young
Sailor	Red Buttons
Ruby	Bonnie Bedelia
Rollo	Michael Conrad
James	Bruce Dern
Turkey	Al Lewis
Joel	Robert Fields
Cecil	Severn Darden
Shirl	Alyyn Ann McLerie

By VINCENT CANBY

"CAN I get you something for your feet?" the nurse at the dance marathon asks Gloria (Jane Fonda) who, after approximately 700 hours of continuous dancing, looks like an exhausted Little Orphan Annie. Gloria asks in return: "How about a saw?" And, for a brief moment you can almost see Gloria, propped up on a grimy cot during her 10-minute break, purposefully dismembering her feet as an offscreen band plays something cheerful like "Japanese Sandman."

Gloria, a Typhoid Mary of existential despair, is the terrified and terrifying heroine of Sydney Pollack's "They Shoot Horses, Don't They?", the film adaptation of Horace McCoy's Depression novel that opened yesterday at the Fine Arts Theater. The movie is far from being perfect, but it is so disturbing in such important ways that I won't forget it very easily, which is more than can be said of much better, more consistent films.

●

McCoy's novel, sometimes called "a minor classic" (a patronizing way of saying that something's good but not great), was written and published in its own time (1935). It's a spare, bleak parable about American life, which McCoy pictured as a Los Angeles dance marathon in the early thirties.

The setting is a shabby ballroom on an amusement pier at the edge of the Pacific. The narrator, Robert Syverton, is a gentle, passive nonentity who, as he is tried for Gloria's murder and then as he awaits execution, recalls the events leading up to the murder. When asked why he did it, he answers simply: "She asked me to," adding: "They shoot horses, don't they?" Robert Syverton is the sort of character who, 15 years later, might have sought his fate in an exotic North Africa created by Paul Bowles.

There is, however, nothing exotic about McCoy's novel, which, although lean, is full of the kind of apocalyptic detail that both he and Nathanael West saw in life as lived on the Hollywood fringe.

Gloria, an Angel of Death who wears ankle socks and favors a marcel permanent wave, is too old, too bitter and too gross even to have gotten registered by Central Casting. Robert, who has fantasies of being a great director like von Sternberg and Mamoulian and Vidor, has only played a few "atmosphere bits." In desperation they enter the dance marathon, set, symbolically, at the edge of the Pacific Ocean, the last, impenetrable frontier.

Without actually changing the structure of the novel, told in flashbacks, the movie takes as its principal setting the marathon itself, and flashes forward to the trial in quick, subliminal, highly stylized cuts. Pollack, and his screenwriters, James Poe and Robert E. Thompson, have, necessarily, taken liberties in fleshing out a movie story. They have added characters, some of which like Red Buttons (as an over-age marathon contestant) and Susannah York (as a would-be Jean Harlow with delusions of grandeur) have their prototypes in the sort of nineteen-thirty B-picture microcosms set on submarines or in sorority houses.

Characters who existed in the book as little more than names have been given histories. Rocky, an aging, tank-town Ben Bernie (beautifully played by a no-longer young Gig Young who is the marathon's emcee, now has as much of a past (his father was a faithhealer) as either Gloria or Robert (Michael Sarrazin). ties. The effect of this is to blunt the edge of— and to overstate—the novel's single-minded nightmare-like qualities.

Even with all of the quite marvelous period touches— the songs, the settings, the costumes and the jargon— the movie always looks like a 1969 recapitulation of another time and place. The book, conceived as a contemporary tale, was not so encumbered with artifacts.

Nevertheless, the movie is by far the best thing that Pollack has ever directed (with the possible exception of "The Scalphunters"). While the cameras remain, as if they had been sentenced, within the ballroom, picking up the details of the increasing despair of the dancers, the movie becomes an epic of exhaustion and futility. The circular patterns of the dancers, the movement that leads nowhere, are the metaphors of the movie.

All of the performances are fine — Miss Fonda, Sarrazin, Young, Miss York and Bonnie Bedelia (as a little Okie girl who carries on in the seventh month of pregnancy). There are some small anachronisms, including a new Johnny Green song that recalls the 1940's or 1950's, instead of the 1930's. These are not really important, however.

The most disquieting thing is the movie's stated assumption that people are horses (I don't even think horses should be people, as in "Black Beauty"), an assumption that is somehow denied by the physical opulence (which, in some curious way, represents a kind of optimism) of the production itself.

D 11, 1969

'The Damned' Focuses on Krupp-Like Family

THE DAMNED, screenplay by Nicola Badalucco, Enrico Medioli and Luchino Visconti; directed by Mr. Visconti; produced by Alfredo Levy and Ever Haggiag; released by Warner Bros-Seven Arts. At the Festival Theater, Fifth Avenue at 57th Street. Running time: 155 minutes. (The Motion Picture Association of America's Production Code and Rating Administration classifies this film "X—persons under 17 not admitted.")

Friederich Bruckmann .... Dirk Bogarde
Baroness Sophie von Essenbeck
.... Ingrid Thulin
Aschenbach .... Helmut Griem
Martin von Essenbeck ... Helmut Berger
Elisabeth Thallman...Charlotte Rampling
Olga .... Florinda Bolkan
Baron Konstantin von Essenbeck
.... Rene Kolldehoff
Herbert Thallman........ Umberto Orsini
Baron Joachim von Essenbeck
.... Albrecht Shoenhals
Guenther von Essenbeck...Renaud Verley

By VINCENT CANBY

LUCHINO VISCONTI'S "The Damned" may be the chef d'oeuvre of the great Italian director ("La Terra Trema," "Rocco and His Brothers," "Sandra")—a spectacle of such greedy passion, such uncompromising sensation and such obscene shock that it makes you realize how small and safe and ordinary most movies are. Experiencing it is like taking a whiff of ammonia—it's not conventionally pleasant, but it makes you see the outlines of everything around you with just a little more clarity.

●

"The Damned," called "Götterdämmerung" in Europe, opens like "Buddenbrooks" — with so many characters introduced so quickly that one part of your mind will spend the rest of

the movie just trying to sort them out, which is a rare treat since the decline of the novel-as-genealogy. It also draws on "Hamlet," "Macbeth," the legend of the Nibelungen, on recent history (as it might be fabricated in something like True Detective) and on Visconti's love for the grand cinematic gesture.

Its story is that of a Krupp-like German steel dynasty in the first two years (1933-1934) of Hitler's struggle to consolidate his power. It's not so much that the von Essenecks symbolize Germany — they *are* Germany. The film does occasionally record events in real Germany—the burning of the books, assignations in squalid rooming houses and (for almost a quarter of an hour and with such loving detail that it almost wrecks the balance of the film) the "night of the long knives," when Ernst Röhm and most of his SA (Storm Troops) were assassinated by the SS (Elite Guard).

Most of "The Damned," however, take place within the huge, dark drawing rooms, the bedrooms, corridors, baths and banquet halls of the Ruhr Valhalla where the von Essenbecks, surrounded by silent servants and as isolated as gods, struggle for control of "the factory," the power of the universe.

There's the old Baron, an aristocrat who has made no commitments to Hitler, but only because he regards Hitler with the distaste of a snob. There are also his son, Konstantin (Rene Kolldehoff), a follower of Röhm in matters sexual as well as political; a young cousin, Aschenbach (Helmut Griem), an SS man scheming to keep von Essenbeck arms from the SA; the Baroness Sophie (Ingrid Thulin), the widowed daughter-in-law who likes to see her son, Martin (Helmut Berger), the Baron's heir, dress up in extraordinarily convincing Marlene Dietrich drag, and Friedrich Bruckmann (Dirk Bogarde), a mortal who, with Sophie, plots to acquire the von Essenback fortune, power and name.

If the film can be said to have a protagonist, I suppose it would be Bogarde who, after murdering the old Baron in his bed, finds himself finally destroyed in a bizarre reworking of classic consequences. Visconti, however, keeps the melodrama at such a distance and plays it at such a high pitch that there can't be much thought about protagonists and antagonists.

"The Damned," while having validity as a political and social parable, is mind-blinding as a spectacle of fabulous corruption, detailed within the family organism that so fascinates Visconti. Like "La Terra Trema" and "Rocco and His Brothers," Visconti's new film keeps the audience outside the spectacle, but the von Essenbecks, unlike the families in the earlier works, are not only a family —they create their own social milieu. Nothing that happens outside seems to matter much because despite our knowledge of history, we know that Germany's fate is the von Essenbecks'.

The film triumphs over a number of bothersome things, including too-quick transformations of characters, dialogue of epic flatness ("Complicity grows. I've accepted a ruthless logic and I shall never get away from it"), inconsistency of language (most of it is in English, but some is in German for no apparent reason), self-conscious references to great

moments in history (the Reichstag fire) and scenes of melodrama that would strain even Wagner (as when Martin decides to "destroy" his mother by raping her.

All of the performances are excellent, but at least two are superb, that of Miss Thulin and Berger, a young Austrian actor who gives, I think, the performance of the year.

"The Damned," however, is not a film that depends on dialogue or performance, but on Visconti's vision that capitalizes on what would be theatrical excesses in anyone else's work. He likes to begin scenes in close-up with one character talking to another, who may remain unseen, unknown, for minutes at a time. The entire film evokes a sense of make-up and masquerade, both physical and emotional. Color also is important. The first shot of the movie is a close-up of the orange flames of a blast furnace, after which the light seems to dim progressively to a twilight, set off by splotches of red, first a flower in a buttonhole, then Nazi armbands and flags and, finally, blood.

"The Damned" is a movie of great perversity—so intransigent that I think even von Stroheim would have liked it. It opened yesterday at the Festival Theater where, at the first show, the projectionist had trouble with the projector's arc light and in framing the film so that foreheads or chins weren't lopped off. I trust things improved later in the day.

D 19, 1969

'M*A*S*H'

By ROGER GREENSPUN

To my knowledge Robert Altman's "M*A*S*H" is

the first major American movie openly to ridicule belief in God—not phony belief; real belief. It is also one of the few (though by no means the first) American screen comedies openly to admit the cruelty of its humor. And it is at pains to blend that humor with more operating room gore than I have ever seen in any movie from any place.

The Cast

M*A*S*H, directed by Robert Altman; screenplay by Ring Lardner Jr., from the novel by Richard Hooker; director of photography, Harold E. Stine; music by Jonnny Mandel; produced by Ingo Preminger; released by 20th-Century-Fox. At the Baronet Theater, 59th Street at Third Avenue. Running time: 116 minutes. (The Motion Picture Association of America's Production Code and Rating Administration classifies this film: "R—restricted—persons under 16 not admitted, unless accompanied by parent or adult guardian.")

Hawkeye	Donald Sutherland
Trapper John	Elliott Gould
Duke	Tom Skerritt
Maj. Hot Lips	Sally Kellerman
Maj. Frank Burns	Robert Duvall
Lieutenant Dish	Jo Ann Pflug
Dago Red	Rene Auberjonois
Col. Henry Blake	Roger Bowen
Radar O'Reilly	Gary Burghoff
Sgt. Maj. Vollmer	David Arkin
Spearchucker	Fred Williamson
Me Lay	Michael Murphy
Ho-Jon	Kim Atwood
Lieutenant Leslie	Indus Arthur
Painless Pole	John Shuck
General Hammond	G. Wood

All of which may promote a certain air of good feeling in the audience, an attitude of self-congratulation that they have the guts to take the gore, the inhumanity to appreciate the humor, and the sanity to admire the impiety — directed against a major who prays for himself, his Army buddies and even "our Commander in Chief."

●

Actually "M*A*S*H", which opened yesterday at the Baronet, accepts without question several current pieties (for example, concern for a child's life, but not a grown man's soul), but its general bent is toward emotional freedom, cool wit, and shocking good sense.

Based upon a barely passable novel of the same name (the title stands for Mobile Army Surgical Hospital, but "MASH," of course, stands for a few other things as well.) "M*A*S*H" takes place mostly in Korea during the war. However, aside from the steady processing of bloody meat through the operating room, the film is not so much concerned with the war as with life inside the Army hospital unit and especially with the quality of life created by the three hot-shot young surgeons (Donald Sutherland, Elliott Gould and Tom Skerritt) who make most things happen.

●

But, unlike "Catch-22," with which it has already been incorrectly compared (I mean the novel, not the legendary unfinished movie) "M*A*S*H" makes no profoundly radical criticism either of war or of the Army. Although it is impudent, bold, and often very funny, it lacks the sense of order (even in the midst of disorder) that seems the special province of successful comedy. I think that M*A*S*H," for all its local virtues, is not successful. Its humor comes mostly in bits and pieces, and even in its climax, an utterly unsporting football game between the MASH unit and an evacuation hospital, it fails to build toward either significant confrontation or recognition. At the end, the film simply runs out of steam, says good-by to its major characters, and calls final attention to itself as a movie—surely the saddest and most overworked of cop-out devices in the comic film repertory.

Robert Altman's method has been to fill the frame to a great depth with overlapping bits of action and strands of dialogue. The tracking camera serves as an agent of discovery. To a very great degree, "M*A*S*H" substitutes field of view for point of view, and although I think this substitution has a lot to do with the movie's ultimate weakness, the choice is not without its intelligent rewards.

Insane announcements over the hospital's intercom system, Japanese-accented popular American songs from Armed Forces Radio in Tokyo, bungling corpsmen, drivers, nurses—and again and again the brilliantly understood procedures of the operating room —come together to define the spirit of the film.

In one brief night scene, some MASH-men and the chief nurse meet to divide the winnings of the football game.

In the distance, a jeep drives by, carrying a white-shrouded corpse. The nurse glances at it for a second, and then turns back to her happy friends — and we have a momentary view of the ironic complexities of life that "M*A*S*H" means to contain.

The entire cast seems superb, partly, I think, because Altman (whose previous work, largely on television, I do not know) knows exactly where to cut away.

●

Among the leads, Elliott Gould suggests the right degree of coolly belligerent self-containment, but Donald Sutherland (in a very elaborate performance) supports his kind of detachment with vocal mannerisms that occasionally become annoying. Sally Kellerman plays the chief nurse, Maj. Hot Lips Houlihan—and how she earns her name is the funniest and nastiest sequence of the film. Her character changes—from comic heavy to something like romantic lead — but M*A*S*H really has no way of handling character change,

so she mostly fades into the background.

Early in the film she is the butt of some dreadfully humiliating gags, and with her expressive, vulnerable face, she is disturbing to laugh at. It is as if she had returned from some noble-nonsense war movie of the 1940's to suggest an area of human response that the masterly sophistications of"M*A*S*H" are unaware of.

Ja 26, 1970

The Milky Way

The Cast

THE MILKY WAY, directed by Luis Bunuel; screenplay (French, with English subtitles) by Mr. Bunuel and Jean-Claude Carriere; director of photography, Christian Matras; music by Mr. Bunuel; produced by Serge Silberman; released by U-M Film Distributors, Inc. At the 68th Street Playhouse, at Third Avenue. Running time; 105 minutes. (The Motion Picture Association of America's Production Code and Rating Administration classifies this film: "M— suggested for mature audiences, parental discretion advised.")

Pierre	Paul Frankeur
Jean	Laurent Terzieff
The Man with the cape	Alain Cuny
The Virgin Mary	Edith Scob
Jesus	Bernard Verley
The French Clergyman	Francois Maistre
Maitre d'	Julien Bertheau
The Marquis	Michel Piccoli
The Inquisitor	Michel Etcheverry
The Devil	Pierre Clementi
The Jesuit	Georges Marchal
The Jansenite	Jean Piat
Rodolphe	Denis Manuel
Francois	Daniel Pilon
L'Eveque	Claudio Brook
The Spanish Clergyman	Julien Guiomar
The Prostitute	Delphine Seyrig

By VINCENT CANBY

WOMEN, pronounced St. Chrysostom, are "a necessary evil, a natural temptation, a desirable calamity, a domestic peril, a deadly fascination, and a painted ill."

The good, fourth century mysoginist, just one of the dozens of saints, rascals, nuns, picaroons, inquisitors, heretics, bishops, whores and humble people who are either represented or evoked in Luis Buñuel's marvelous new film, "The Milky Way," clearly had an ambivalent attitude towards women. Because of Buñuel's similar preoccupation with things he professes to abhor, the fine, irascible Spanish film director ("Thank God I'm an atheist!") has often been suspected of ambivalent attitudes towards the Roman Catholicism he has renounced and the God he has denied.

•

While there must always be a certain amount of ambiguity in any proclamation of atheism, there can be no further question about Buñuel and the Church. That is, not after "The Milky Way," which has the form of a lovely fantasy and the density of a theological essay, and which often sounds like the sort of shaggy dog story that might be told in a seminary.

The film, which opened yesterday at the 68th Street Playhouse, is shaped as a sort of surreal Pilgrim's Progress undertaken by two contemporary, not especially pious Frenchmen. Pierre (Paul Frankeur), a bearded, virile, respectful old man, and Jean (Laurent Terzieff), his younger, skeptical companion, are making a pilgrimage (for reasons never specified) to the tomb of the Apostle James at Santiago de Compostella in Spain.

En route, they have a series of extraordinary encounters with personages out of the past, including Priscillian, the fourth century Spanish bishop, martyred for his Manichean unorthodoxies, and the Virgin Mary, who appears to them sitting in a tree.

At one point they meet the devil, lounging in the backseat of a sports car that's just been wrecked. He is a typically Buñuelian devil, both polite and practical, who suggests to the poor Pierre, whose feet hurt, that he take the dead driver's new shoes. Later, they come upon a Jansenist convent whose nuns, not very enthusiastically, are helping one of their order to realize her desire for crucifixion. They also act as seconds in a duel between a Jansenist and a Jesuit, are instructed in the virtues of chasity in marriage, and finally, when they reach Santiago, find, not the Celestial City, but an empty tomb.

While Buñuel is obviously fond of Pierre and Jean, he's not exactly obsessed with them. He doesn't hesitate to drop them from time to time to pursue with greater freedom his principal theme—religion as a man-made phenomenon whose dogmas have been the bases for religious wars, inquisitions and madly irrational theological arguments conducted with the utmost reason.

The movie is constantly side-stepping itself to show, among other things, why Jesus wore a beard (Mary thought it suited him), the Marquis de Sade tormenting a helpless young thing who persists in saying there is a God, Priscillian apologizing to the Communion host ("It was not I who reaped and kneaded Thee").

Through all of the miracles and magical encounters, through all of the deadly nonsensical debates on the true meaning of the Trinity, and through all of the Alice-in-Wonderland-like discussions on the differences between consubstantiation and transubstantiation, Pierre and Jean maintain a saintly sanity that is, in itself, very funny and even moving.

Unlike such an angry film as "Viridiana," in which Buñuel used Freudian psychology to attack the Church (specifically its concept of charity and the subsequent evil of pity), "The Milky Way" goes about its business with a comic, masterly cool that is more remorseless than anything he's done before. The film is closer in tone to his early, surreal "Un Chien Andalou" and "L'Age d'Or" than to the later, non-ironic, malevolent but comparatively gentle "Nazarin" and "Simon of the Desert," which almost persuaded some people that Buñuel was returning to the fold.

One of the nicest things about "The Milky Way," and about the only thing that indicates the director's age (he'll be 70 this year) is its technical facility. Buñuel employs no fantastic effects, though this is a livelier fantasy than, say, "The Wizard of Oz." Everything is photographed straightforwardly, in cheerful but not bilious color, and seen with documentary-like clarity.

•

For what is, in effect, his "Greatest Story Ever Told," Buñuel recruited a large cast of mostly French performers for many cameo roles, including Pierre Clementi (the Devil), Michel Piccoli (de Sade), Bernard Verley (Jesus), Edith Scob (the Virgin Mary) and Delphine Seyrig (the prostitute).

Even if you're non-Catholic, as I am, "The Milky Way" can also be enjoyed as a kind of Pilgrim's Progress through the Buñuel iconography. The film is packed with symbols that repeatedly recur in all of his films (dwarfs, doves, beggars, blind men, religious instruments, graves). And, if you're willing to do a little homework, the film can become so fascinating that you're likely to recall a disturbing remark made by one character, who materializes briefly and is identified in the cast only as The Lecturer. "My hatred of science," he says with bored resignation, "and my horror of technology will finally lead me to this absurd belief in God. . . ."

Ja 27, 1970

Patton

By VINCENT CANBY

"PATTON: A Salute to a Rebel" looks and sounds like the epic American war movie that the Hollywood establishment has always wanted to make but never had the guts to do before. The film, which is now in its premiere roadshow engagement at the Criterion Theater, is 20th Century-Fox's $12-million tribute to the late General George S. Patton Jr., the brilliant, unstable World War II tactician who saw himself as nothing less than the divine instrument for making the world safe for future wars.

It's also an incredible gas, especially in this time and place. "Patton" is a loving, often sentimental, semi-official portrait of a man it characterizes as a near-schizo, a man who admitted that he damn well loved war, was surprised and somewhat taken aback when men near to him were killed, who quoted the Bible, believed in reincarnation, had the political acumen of Marie Antoinette, and, according to the movie, somehow so touched General Omar Bradley with his folksy honesty ("I'm a prima donna—I know it!") that Bradley went through the war looking always as if he were about to weep.

The fact that a supposedly sympathetic character, in a superspectacle such as this, will admit to loving war is, in a negative way, a refreshing change from the sort of conventional big-budget movie claptrap that keeps saying that war is hell, while simultaneously showing how much fun it really is. I don't think that the fact of the existence of a movie like "Patton" necessarily marks an advance in the civilizing processes of our culture, but it's a good deal less hypocritical than most patriotic American war movies. If I sound ambivalent about "Patton," it's because the movie itself is almost as ambivalent about its hero.

"Patton" is, I think, a typical example of a movie of which the production company (Fox) is the real auteur. This is not meant to denigrate the very real contributions of its director, Franklin Schaffner ("Planet of the Apes," "The War Lord"), or of its producer, Frank McCarthy, for whom the film has been something like a 10-year labor of love.

Rather, it's to acknowledge the continuity that, in the good old days, could be detected in the films of an individual studio. In the case of Fox, a large part of that continuity has been provided by the seemingly immortal presence of one man, Darryl F. Zanuck, a founder of the

company over 35 years ago (with Joseph Schenck), for many years its production chief, now its board chairman.

Zanuck always has had a soft spot for the military (as did the former Fox president, Spyros P. Skouras), and Fox has often had military brass on its board of directors. During World War II, Zanuck served briefly in the United States Signal Corps and, I'm told, still doesn't mind being addressed as "Colonel." In addition, Zanuck and Fox have always had a strong affection for the quasi-documentary film, the headline film, and the war film, all of which came together in 1962 in Zanuck's last personal production, "The Longest Day." This was the all-star reenactment of the 1944 Normandy landings, reproduced with all the accuracy that money can buy, but without much cinematic point (which, of course, money cannot buy).

"The Longest Day" was an extremely successful film financially, and ever since its release Zanuck has dreamed of duplicating the success. This is worth pointing out because it describes the context in which the decisions were made to spend $12-million on "Patton" and even more on "Tora! Tora! Tora!," the not-yet-released Fox spectacle in which the Japanese attack on Pearl Harbor is reenacted.

I have no idea of the problems that went into writing a script about Patton, but, after seeing the finished film, it seems that at least some of the people working on the project must have had mixed feelings about the man and the film. So much money and so much care have been spent on the physical production that you might not think it would have an idea in its head. It does, and because the ideas are often contradictory, "Patton" is the first $12-million movie ever made that I could imagine seeing twice.

The opening of the film, which is really a kind of overture, comes very close to being conscious Camp. Patton (George C. Scott) stands on a stage addressing us, the people in the movie audience who have become, apparently, his troops. He is a fine, overly virile figure of a man, riding crop in hand and with so many medals on his chest that he could be a member of the chorus of "The Student Prince." But— and this is important—he is dwarfed by a huge American flag that is pure Rauschenberg, and whose broad red and white stripes form an Op frame around him. He exhorts us, with manic intensity, not simply to kill the enemy, but "to tear his guts out." "All Americans love the sting of battle," he says, and the audience giggles in embarrassment. "That's why we've never lost a war [the giggles stop]. . . We're going to go through [the enemy] like crap through a goose!"

Thus, consciously, I'm sure, the contradictory tone of the film is set. "No bastard ever won a war by dying for his country," he says. "He won it by making some other poor bastard die for his country." Although the military reasoning is sound, the speech is one of astonishing arrogance, a jingoistic tour de force, full of enthusiasm for the butch-

ery to come and reeking with the assumption that there is a God who is, of course, on the side of the Allies. The speech is so wild, in fact, that I'm not completely sure it wasn't written by Robert Downey for use in "Putney Swope."

*

The almost three-hour film follows Patton's career in what is essentially a series of magnificently photographed *tableaux vivants* depicting the North African campaign, the assault on Sicily (including the incident in which Patton slapped a shell-shocked soldier for being a coward), climaxing in the brilliant sweep of his Third Army through France some weeks after the D-Day he was not allowed to participate in.

Patton's private life, his relations with his wife and family, are not even hinted at. Instead, the film presents what could be called an intimate portrait of a public figure. The portrait does not really change in the course of the film; it is simply filled in with additional details. Depending on your point of view, these details show Patton as the embodiment of all of one's fears about the rich, white, Protestant military establishment, a man who confidently believed that America and England should rule the world, or, as a ruthlessly dedicated, eccentric genius, described with great affection as "a 16th-century man lost in the 20th century."

The surprise of the film is not that the weight is clearly in favor of the latter interpretation. Any other choice would be unthinkable for the studio that brought us such films as "A Wing and a Prayer" and "The Fighting Sullivans," along with "The Longest Day " In spite of "M*A*S*H," Fox hasn't become so hip that it would spend $12-million debunking one of our most sacred institutions. "Patton" is meant, I'm sure, as a completely sincere tribute to a man to whom it simply isn't easy to pay tribute.

*

The real surprise is that the film, though long (and, from my point of view, appalling), is so consistently fascinating. It isn't just that Scott's performance is full of odd, unexpected details that compel constant attention. Although you pretty much know the way the movie is going, you can never be sure Scott is going in the same direction, quietly. The film is much more than the one performance that dominates it. Shot in a 70-millimeter film process called Dimension-150, it is extraordinarily, almost unrealistically, beautiful—the epitome of Pop movie epic with lots of broad vistas caught in clear, deep focus. The battle scenes, including desert confrontations as well as Patton's dash through France in the deep of winter, are always more spectacular than bloody. In one frame, you might have Patton in foreground, a tank attack group in the middle ground, and a line of fighter planes flying in over the horizon. A sense of the true horror and panic of battle is thus distanced, replaced by the awe one has of such carefully coordinated, logistically complex filmmaking. Schaffner shoots his interior

scenes—mostly the cavernous castles and baroque palaces in which Patton was bivouacked—with a similar eye for grandeur. More than one scene opens with a shot of a frescoed ceiling, followed by a slow pan that carries the eye down to the action below. It's almost as if the director, like Patton, were constantly paying his respects to God.

F 8, 1970

Zabriskie Point

ZABRISKIE POINT, directed by Michaelangelo Antonioni; written by Mr. Antonioni, Fred Gardner, Sam Shepard, Tonino Guerra and Clare Peploe; director of photography, Alfio Contini, music by Pink Floyd, Kaleidoscope. Jery Garcia, John Fahey, The Grateful Read, the Rolling Stones and the Youngbloods; produced by Carlo Ponti; released by MetroGoldwyn-Mayer. At the Coronet Theater, Third Avenue at 59th Street. Running time: 112 minutes. (The Motion Picture Association of America's Production Code and Ratng Adminstration classifies this film: "R-restricted —persons under 16 not admitted, unless accompanied by parent or adult guardian.")

Mark .... Mark Frechette
Daria .... Daria Halprin
Lee Allen .... Rod Taylor
Cafe Owner .... Paul Fix
Lee Allen's Associate .. G. D. Spradling
Morty .... Bill Garaway
Kathleen .... Kathleen Cleaver
and
Members of The Open Theatre of Joe Chalkin

By VINCENT CANBY

"I DON'T have to prove my revolutionary credentials to you!" an angry young man shouts to—I think—Kathleen Cleaver in the meeting of activists that opens Michelangelo Antonioni's new film, "Zabriskie Point."

Thereafter, revolutionary credentials—beautiful, shiny and largely bogus—are flashed all over the screen at the Coronet Theater, where the film began its run yesterday. They are also there in

462

the film's advertising, which employs the stars-and-stripes motif so favored these days by movies aspiring to sociopolitical significance. You know the ones—"Medium Cool," "Easy Rider," "Patton."

"Zabriskie Point" is Antonioni's first American film and the 11th feature in a filmography that includes "L'Avventura," "La Notte," "Red Desert" and "Blow-Up." Coming to us with those credentials, "Zabriskie Point" demands to be taken seriously, if only by Antonioni buffs for whom no assumption is too outrageous to make in the interests of filling in the blank spaces in the master's plan.

●

I suspect that for the rest of us—with the possible exception of highway engineers (the film includes a lot of lovely aerial shots of macadam roads snaking into blue distances — "Zabriskie Point" will remain a movie of stunning superficiality, another example of a noble artistic impulse short-circuited in a foreign land.

The story is a kind of activists' brief encounter. Mark (Mark Frechette), a young man who may or may not have shot a policeman during a strike in Los Angeles, steals a small plane and flies up to Death Valley where he meets Daria (Daria Halprin, a sweet, pot-smoking postteenybopper of decent inclinations. For several hours they wander through the photogenic Death Valley landscape philosophizing, (She: "It's so peaceful." He: "It's dead."), exchanging political views (She: "There are a thousand different sides to every question." He: "You gotta have heroes and villains so you can fix things up."), and finally making love.

Towards the end of a day in which, from the varying lengths of the shadows we've seen, the sun has spun around on a drunken axis, she helps him paint his plane in psychedelic designs. He returns to Los Angeles and certain arrest ("I want to take the risks," he says by way of explanation), and she drives off to Phoenix where her boss (Rod Taylor), who may or may not be her lover, has a desert Berchtesgaden.

This, of course, is not the real story, as "L'Avventura" wasn't really about a girl who got lost on a craggy island, or "Blow-Up" a whodunit. The story of Mark and Daria is one of options faced and taken—in this case by two young people in a world of such grotesqueness that (according to Antonioni) violence is the only rational response.

The main problem with "Zabriskie Point" is that Antonioni has done nothing with his physical production to illuminate in any meaningful way the emotional states of his two principal characters —if, indeed, they have any.

They are completely instinctive people, but their instincts have been imposed upon them by an intellectualizing Antonioni, rather than by God. Everything in the film is calculated, including the prettily-photographed, conventionally-ironic contrasts between the principal locations—Los Angeles (used-car lots, absurd billboards, glass-and-steel office buildings reaching above the smog) and Death Valley, whose barren hills look like the remains of some cataclysmic oatmeal war of prehistory.

●

Paradoxically, even though everything is calculated, nothing within the film justifies its final, apocalyptic vision of the disintegration of the Western world to the accompaniment of a funky rock tune. It's lovely to look at (books, furniture, food, a copy of Look magazine, all hanging suspended in an emulsion of deep blue), but completely absurd in the context.

So too is a giant specialty number that Antonioni inserts within the film when Mark and Daria make love on the side of a sand dune. All of Death Valley erupts with life and love. Bodies (members of Joe Chaikin's Open Theater), most of whom keep their clothes on, writhe in various kinds of desperate couplings and triplings as we watch as if through a sandstorm. The once austere, puritanical Antonioni seems now to have adopted for erotica, which becomes unintentionally funny. When Antonioni finally returns the air to its natural state, Mark notes quietly: "I always knew it would be like that."

Because of the fundamental emptiness of his American vision, all sorts of flaws that one might overlook in better Antonioni films become apparent. The two young leads, who have never acted before, are beautiful (he, I'm afraid, has the edge), but they move and talk with all the conviction of the life-sized mannequins who perform in a Sunny Dunes television commercial within the film. Only Rod Taylor, a real actor, seems human.

Various Antonioni mannerisms—the blank screen suddenly filled with a face, the endless tracking shots, the pregnant pauses between unfinished thoughts—are finally only tolerable because you remember the times when they were better used. In "Zabriskie Point," Antonioni, like Mark and Daria, succumbs to the hostile terrain.

F 10, 1970

Au Hasard, Balthazar

The Cast

AU HASARD, BALTHAZAR, directed by Robert Bresson; screenplay (French with English subtitles) by Mr. Bresson; photography by Ghislain Cloquet; music by Franz Schubert and Jean Wiener; produced by Mag Bodard; released by Cinema Ventures. At the New Yorker Theater, Broadway and 88th Street. Running time: 96 minutes. (Not submitted at this time to the Motion Picture Association of America's Production Code and Rating Administration for rating as to audience suitability.)

Marie ....Anne Wiazemsky
Gerard ....Francoise Lafarge
Father ....Philippe Asselin
Mother ....Natalie Joyaut
Friend ....Walter Green
Tramp ....J. C. Guilbert
Corn Merchant.........Pierre Klossowski

By ROGER GREENSPUN

ROBERT BRESSON'S "Au Hasard, Balthazar" first played in New York at the 1966 Film Festival, at which time it received mostly unfavorable notices. That it is having a theatrical opening now results largely from the perseverance of Cinema Ventures' Tom Russell and the New Yorker Theater's Dan Talbot—who has done so much for movies in this city that he probably deserves a review of his own.

Actually, Bresson, despite a general critical indifference and commercial failure that puts him in the company of the very greatest filmmakers (Carl Dreyer, for example) has never lacked for serious admirers. And the exceptional popularity of the recently completed Bresson retrospective at the Museum of Modern Art suggests that a much larger audience may be ready for him now than had ever heard of him only a few years ago.

●

Along with the early "Les Dames du Bois de Boulogne" (1944), "Au Hasard, Balthazar" (the title translates literally as "Balthazar at Random") is my favorite among Bresson's nine features. It is at once his most complex and most accessible movie, which should not seem so strange in light of the kinds of films he makes.

His profoundly and unsentimentally religious vision and the severity and self-abnegation of his method set up certain expectations for any Bresson movie in relation to which "Au Hasard, Balthazar" looks like a sudden and gratifying relaxation in style. In fact, it is less austere (though possibly even more severe), than other Bresson films, and the multiplicity of things and themes (and things *as* theme), together with Bresson's most appealing hero, works for an unusual degree of audience empathy.

That hero, Balthazar, is a donkey who, after a happy early life with Marie (Anne Wiazemsky), daughter of a scientific farmer, is sold into harsh toil and exploitation at the hands of a series of masters. Meanwhile, Marie's family suffers through her father's proud stubbornness, and she herself into humiliating liaison with Gérard, leader of the genuinely vicious local young hoods. Periodically Marie and Balthazar are reunited, but at each reunion Gérard reappears (in a sense, Balthazar prepares for Gérard) to take the girl and to torture the donkey.

By the time he has finished, Gérard—whose evil is never explained but who adequately answers one set of his community's needs, just as Balthazar answers another set of needs— has stripped Marie naked and abandoned her in an empty house, and he has loaded the donkey with contraband silks, gold, and perfume, which he means to smuggle across the border.

The ensuing death of Balthazar, less a surprise than a summation, is in its pathos and depth of association the most richly evocative sequence in all of Bresson and surely one of the most affecting passages in the history of film.

Where "Au Hasard, Balthazar" differs from Bresson's other films is in the degree to which it accepts and sustains a multiplicity of actions, objects, even, in an almost traditional sense, "character." Not that Bresson has lowered his vision (the film's range of associations in symbol and dogma should occupy any amateur of Christian theology for some time) but that he has expanded it to include a superbly precise and compassionate awareness of the physical universe.

●

In this film we are given not only the movements of souls and bodies, but also the knowledge of hands and hearts and of the ground we walk on.

"Au Hasard, Balthazar" proceeds by contraries—beginning with the sound track, which opens with a Schubert piano sonata rudely interrupted by a donkey's braying that lead to insights traditionally understandable only in terms of paradox. This is neither an easy film, nor, in the show biz sense, an entertaining one. It makes large demands upon its audience, and in return confers exceptional rewards. It is playing at the New Yorker Theater, and among recent openings it is the only absolutely essential moviegoing in New York.

F 20, 1970

FELLINI SATYRICON

By VINCENT CANBY

IN almost every film Federico Fellini has ever made,

the sea has occupied a very special place, sometimes as the ultimate barrier between confusion and understanding, sometimes as a kind of vast, implacable presence that dimly recalls protozoan origins. "La Strada," "La Dolce Vita" and his newest, most tumultuous movie, "Fellini Satyricon," all end by the edge of the sea.

FELLINI SATYRICON, directed by Federico Fellini; screenplay (Italian with English subtitles) by Mr. Fellini and Bernardino Zapponi; music by Nino Rota; produced by Alberto Grimaldi; released by United Artists Corporation. At the Little Carnegie Theater, 57th Street East of Seventh Avenue. Running Time: 120 minutes (The Motion Picture Association of America's Production Code and Rating Administration classifies this film: "R—restricted, persons under 17 require accompanying parent or adult guardian.")
Encolpius ....Martin Potter
Ascyltus ....Hiram Keller
Giton ....Max Born
Tryphaena ....Capucine
Eumolpus ....Salvo Randone
Fortunata ....Magali Noel
Lichas ....Alain Cuny
Suicide wife ....Lucia Bose
Caesar ....Tanya Lopert
Robber ....Gordon Mitchell
Vernacchio ....Fanfulla
Trimalchio ....Mario Romagnoli
Oenothea ....Donyale Luna
Oriental slave girl......Hylette Adolphe
Suicide husband ....Joseph Wheeler
Scintilla ....Danica La Loggia
Widow of Ephesus.......Antonia Pietrosi

Watching "Fellini Satyricon," which opened yesterday at the Little Carnegie Theater, you suddenly realize that Fellini, unlike the creatures of his extraordinary imagination, has refused to be stopped by the sea. He has pushed on, and there are moments when he seems to have fallen over the edge into the cinema of the ridiculous. You ask yourself: Is this dwarf, or this albino hermaphrodite, or is this latest amputation, really necessary? However, he finally arrives, if not at understanding, then at a magnificently realized movie of his own— and our—wildest dreams.

There have already been lots of pious alarms sounded over the excesses of it all, statements to the effect that it is fascinating to look at, but . . ., and debates about its profoundity—all of which strike me as about as relevant as finding oneself on Venus and complaining that one's Boy Scout pocket compass doesn't work. Even though I feel the film does have meanings, including dozens Fellini himself may be unware of, "Fellini Satyricon" is essentially its own justification, as is any work of art.

The film, which uses the director's name in the title to differentiate it from another Italian film based on the same source, is Fellini's adapation of the satiric novel by Petronius Arbiter, written in the first century A.D. "Satyricon" has survived in such fragmentary form that all scholars do not necessarily agree whether it is a moral essay or simply a catalogue of the sexual achievements, most of them perverse, of its student-hero, Encolpius, his boy-lover, Giton, who has the constancy of a cloud, and his best friend.

Sometimes together, sometimes separately, Encolpius, Giton, and Ascyltus wander across the face of the Roman Empire, either participating in (often as victims) or just observing orgies, feasts, festivals, murders, abductions, you-name-it.

This is the first time that Fellini has based a feature film on a borrowed source, which may be the reason why the movie, although as fragmented in continuity as the literary work, achieves a classic dimension that is new for Fellini. Paradoxically, it is also his most original film. Fellini has done nothing less than create a new world, a kind of subterranean Oz, a world of magic and superstition, without values, without government, without faith, and almost totally without conscience. It has the quality of a drug-induced hallucination, being without past or future, existing only in a present that, at best, can be survived.

"Fellini Satyricon" also has the form of theater, of ritual, to such a degree that there is no difference between the reality of the film and the reality of a play—within-the-film or of the dryly comic legend of the Widow of Ephesus, which is pictured as it is being told by a storyteller at a sulphurous banquet.

This is made apparent from the very first frame, when Encolpius is discovered, back to camera, standing off to one side before a wall that is blank except for some odd graffiti. After a minute or two of rapid-fire, theatrically declaimed exposition, Encolpius turns to face the camera. From that moment on, Fellini fills in the blank wall. Quite literally, he turns his characters into art. The tale never ends. The film simply stops, in mid-sentence, as Encolpius, Giton, Ascyltus and all of the other Fellini phantoms take their places in the fragments of a lovely wall painting that overlooks a serene sea.

●

The most spectacular aspect of the film, which is essentially descriptive rather than narrative, is the décor, the color, for everything has been manufactured by Fellini. Like El Greco, Fellini scorns natural sunlight. Even exterior landscapes have been photographed in such a way as to suggest the exotic fraud of the steamy, hermetic interiors. When Encolpius goes to retrieve his beloved Giton, who has been purchased by an actor, you aren't sure for a moment whether he has wandered into life, or into a play, although everyone seems to be speaking Latin and not Italian.

Even Fellini's casual way of synchronizing dialogue with lip movements works here. Dialogue comes to sound like incantation, instead of information. The individual elements of the film are realized with such conscious style that all of the nonacting, as well as the scenes of violence, or of copulations performed by persons fully clothed, have the effect of ritual, rather than the reality of some gaudy Italian spear-and-sandal epic, to which "Fellini Satyricon" is actually related, as all movies are related, though distantly.

The cast is a typical, multi-national, Fellini mélange of amateurs and professionals, each one of whom exists principally as a face or just as a physical presence rather than as a performer. Most prominent are Martin Potter, an Englishman, and Hiram Keller, an American, who play Encolpius and Ascyltus and who might pass as a couple of Andy Warhol's tough-soft leading men. Max Born, a young Englishman who resembles Joan Collins in drag, is Giton, an existential cupid as might be imagined by Genêt.

●

Although all of the women in the film, with the exception of a patrician's wife (played by Lucia Bose), are harpies of terrifying scale, I don't think Fellini is pushing homosexuality, which he depicts with such noneroticism that the movie looks almost chaste.

"Fellini Satyricon" is no more about homosexuality, than it is about ancient Rome. It is a surreal epic that, I confidently believe, will outlive all its interpretations.

Mr 12, 1970

Mouchette

The Cast

MOUCHETTE, directed by Robert Bresson; screenplay (French with English titles) by Robert Bresson, based on a novel by George Bernanos; director of photography, Ghislain Cloquet; music by Claudio Monteverdi; produced by Anatole Dauman for Argos Films/Parc Films; released by Cinema Ventures. At the New York Theater, Broadway and 88th Street. Running time: 80 minutes. (Not submitted at this time to the Motion Picture Association of America's Production Code and Rating Administration for rating as to audience suitability.)

Mouchette	Nadine Nortier
Mother	Marie Cardinal
Father	Paul Hebert
Mathieu	Jean Vimenet
Arsene	J. C. Guilbert

By ROGER GREENSPUN

WITH the opening of "Mouchette" (1966), at the New Yorker Theater, all the nine feature films of Robert Bresson, except the earliest, "Les Anges du Péché" (1943) and the latest, "Une Femme Douce" (1969), are in current release. Like most great directors, Bressen works within a fairly limited range of themes, and with certain strongly felt and profoundly understood stylistic predilections.

●

He seems always to have made exactly the kinds of movies he pleased, but he has brought to his freedom an unparalleled degree of intellectual self-discipline. All Bresson films move slowly and deliberately, and some of the early films offer a restrained sensuous beauty. But none is relaxed or lyrical. At his best, Bresson constructs dramas of extraordinary tension and adventure, though the tension is scarcely perceptible and the adventure is known only to the soul.

In the late Bresson film, the adventure leads to escape from life, to a moment when nature and the supernatural meet in a fleeting intimation of grace so powerful that even an awareness of what the camera cannot show us is happiness enough.

The suicide of Mouchette, Bresson's most human heroine, is such a moment. Like the ravishing Monteverdi motif that accompanies it ("Deposuit potentes" from the Magnificat to the Vespers of 1610), Mouchette's death is so inexpressibly beautiful that it suggests a kind of theatricalism of the spirit. To my Puritan mind, this is not wholly virtuous.

I think the problem is really in the rest of the film. Although "Mouchette" begins and ends magnificently, its central event, a dreadful night Mouchette spends with the local ne'er-do-well, falls into curious melodramatics that sustain neither the tensions of earlier sequences nor the mystery that pervades the young girl's world. For once the admirable Bresson reticence is abandoned (he even slightly sensationalizes the Bernanos novel upon which his film is based) and the result is not so much an increase in lifelikeness as an acquiescence in the merely commonplace.

Mouchette lives in a world committed to natural causes, a small French village, in which she, a poor, sullen and uncommunicative girl, is treated more as dumb object than as human being. It is a world of heavy sounds and gestures, and Mouchette brings to it a unique and valid insistence on the primacy of mud. She is bumped and battered and pushed and shoved (even the kindness done her takes the shape of insult), and she returns the favors with glaring looks and mud balls. Her looks are always accepted, and her mud balls always hit their marks (a typical Bressonian mundane miracle), and between tormentors and tormented

468

there is a kind of equality that for as long as it lasts is the most exciting aspect of the film.

But that mysterious sense of union is dropped during Mouchette's night of terror and shame, and something very like ordinary human relationship takes its place. The ending, though gorgeous in itself, has too narrow an emotional base to build on. To be accepted into grace one must prepare. Mouchette does prepare. We know this intellectually (though she does not), but we know too much in proportion to what we deeply feel, and the ultimate flight of the spirit loses some of its glory.

Mr 13, 1970

Women in Love

The Cast

WOMEN IN LOVE, directed by Ken Russell; screenplay by Larry Kramer, from the novel by D. H. Lawrence; director of photography, Billy Williams; music by Georges Delerue; produced by Mr. Kramer; released by United Artists Corporation. At the Fine Arts Theater, 58th Street between Park and Lexington Avenues. Running time: 129 minutes. (The Motion Picture Association of America's Production Code and Rating Administration classifies this film: "R—restricted, persons under 17 require accompanying parent or adult guardian.")

Rupert Birkin..................Alan Bates
Gerald Crich..................Oliver Reed
Gudrun Brangwen........Glenda Jackson
Ursula Brangwen..........Jennie Linden
Hermione Roddice........Eleanor Bron
Thomas Crich..................Alan Webb
Loerke ....Vladek Sheybal
Mrs. Crich..........Catherine Willmer
Winifred Crich..........Sarah Nicholls
Laura Crich..............Sharon Gurney
Lupton ....Christopher Gable

By VINCENT CANBY

IF you think of D. H. Lawrence's novel, "Women in Love," as a kind of metaphysical iceberg, then you can accept the film version, which opened yesterday at the Fine Arts Theater, as a loving, faithful, intelligent, visual representation of that part of the iceberg that can be seen above the water. It looks right, and it sounds right, but you can only guess at its actual dimensions.

Lawrence's rhapsodic polemic on behalf of a new form of consciousness, which would allow man to fulfill his sexual nature (and which struck me, when I was in college, as nothing less than Revealed Truth), is now, in this reduced form, an intensely romantic love story about four people and their curiously desperate struggles for sexual power. The polemics can still be heard, but as dim, eccentric echoes.

Because time has served to cool my passion for Lawrence, and especially for "Women in Love," I must admit that, for me, the movie is not a sacrilege.

•

Ken Russell, the director, and Larry Kramer, who wrote and produced it, have transformed the novel-of-ideas into a movie-of-action that is almost as romantic as something by a Brontë sister. By retaining the original locale (provincial England) and the era (circa World War I), they have made a movie that is steeped in nostalgia that has very little to do with the work of a novelist who was ahead of his time — or, at least, thought to be.

The story remains that of two sets of cross-cutting loves, focusing principally on Birkin (the Lawrence figure), an untidy, moody school inspector who aspires to "a free proud singleness" in love, seeking "pure" relationships both with woman and man. Ursula, a sweet schoolmistress, is the somewhat baffled object of his conventional attentions; Gerald, his best friend, is the wealthy son of the local mine owner, and the man to whom he once suggests, quite seriously, a pact of blood brotherhood, and Gudrun, Ursula's liberated sister, is Gerald's love, who completes the quartet.

In the novel, the four are not so much characters as points of view that are constantly shifting. In the film, they remain fixed as they enact various Lawrentian parables about the war between the sexes that can sometimes end in death. Gerald refuses Birkin's overtures to spiritual intimacy and thus winds up in fatal combat with Gudrun, the Female Rampant who is unable to love a man without defeating him.

Although the novel's ideas are necessarily simplified on screen, the movie does capture a feeling of nature and of physical contact between people, and between people and nature, that is about as sensuous as anything you've probably ever seen in a film.

Also faithful to Lawrence is the feeling that the relationship between the two men, who though unfilfilled, is somehow cleaner, less messy, than the relationships of the men with their women. When Birkin first makes love to Ursula, a frantic assignation in the woods, it's a sort of mad scramble of garters, buttons and lust. When, however, he and Gerald strip to the buff to wrestle — in the movie's loveliest sequence— there is a sense of positive grace in the eroticism.

The movie, like the novel, seems to be propagandizing for a kind of bisexuality that looks terribly confused, at least in any Freudian context. Is Birkin, or isn't he? You never really find out. The film, however, evinces a bias in the fact that female nudity is never presented with the same kind of decent simplicity as is male.

I liked all of the performances, although Alan Bates, as Birkin, and Glenda Jackson, as Gudrun, stand out as the two most vivid characters. Oliver Reed, all black brows and piercing eyes, is fine as Gerald, and Jennie Linden, who momentarily threw me because she looks so much like Debbie Reynolds, is a lovely, intelligent Ursula.

•

Russell sometimes gets carried away with his lyric camera, but he shoots, for the most part, directly, letting the scenes play themselves without editorial comment by the camera.

Although this "Women in Love," is not the complete "Women in Love," it is such an appealing movie that I'm not going to worry why someone felt the compulsion to put on screen something that was not made for it. I prefer to think that Russell and Kramer were simply caught up in a passion for a complex novel — a passion they could not control. That, of course, is as romantic a notion as any in the film.

Mr 26, 1970

Woodstock

WOODSTOCK, directed by Michael Wadleigh; photography: Mr. Wadleigh, David Meyers, Richard Pearce, Don Lenzer, Al Wertheimer, Michael Margetts, Ed Lynch, Richard Cheu, Charles Levy, Ted Churchill, Fred Underhill, Robert Danneman and Stan Warnow; produced by Bob Maurice; released by Warner Bros. Inc. At the Trans-Lux East Theater, Third Avenue and 58th Street. Running time: 184 minutes. (The Motion Picture Association of America's Production Code and Rating Administration classifies this film: "R—restricted, persons under 17 require accompanying parent or adult guardian.")
With Joan Baez; Joe Cocker; Country Joe and The Fish; Crosby, Stills, Nash & Young; Arlo Guthrie; Richie Havens; Jimi Hendrix; Santana; Sha-Na-Na; John Sebastian; Sly & The Family Stone; Ten Years After, and The Who.

By **VINCENT CANBY**

"WOODSTOCK" is a record of an extraordinary event, the rock festival that last August drew nearly half a million young people to a 600-acre farm near Bethel, N. Y., for three days of music, mud, grass, love, milk, skinny-dipping, acid, Cokes, hot dogs, love, meth, music and, for those who would stand in line, Port-O-San sanitary facilities.

In effect, the festival is still going on—with stunning good humor and relentlessly —in this movie, which opened yesterday at the Trans-Lux East Theater, and which could become the totem for the benign collectivists who want to save America's soul before worrying about the garbage gap.

The movie, directed by Michael Wadleigh, produced by Bob Maurice and photographed by Wadleigh and 12 other cameramen, is somewhat less extraordinary than the event it preserves—that is, in comparison with a documentary that transforms its subject into cinematic art that is its own justification.

"Woodstock," I think, couldn't care less about such considerations. It is designed, as an entertainment film, to present the performances of its stars—Joan Baez, Country Joe and The Fish, Sly and The Family Stone, Jimi Hendrix, Arlo Guthrie, and the rest—in the context of the event. To this end, it uses a lot of fancy optical effects, including split screens and superimpositions, in aggressive, largely superfluous attempts to interpret performers who are themselves interpreters.

The movie spends, I'd estimate, not quite a third of its time recording the offstage events at what comes to look like Calvary (minus the last act, of course) as it might be staged by a stoned Cecil B. De Mille. An interviewer listens as one totally drenched young man castigates "the fascist pigs" in the helicopters for having seeded the clouds. A pretty little girl, with a face as blank as a pancake, marvels at how beautiful it all is, though she hasn't seen her sister in 24 hours and she must find her to get her to court on Monday morning.

•

Words fail just about everybody, including the interviewer who comments on a statement by one young man by saying: "Great—er, I mean—groovy." An elderly man in Bethel says: "The last time we saw anything like this was at the Rose Bowl Parade." And one lady in the early stages of hysteria pleads for someone to get her out of there—there are just too many people. "We're the third largest city in the world!" exults another girl, and the communicants make love in the bushes, do yoga exercises, say how groovy it all is (thus, perhaps, to protect more private fears), and splash around a nearby pond with (of all things to be found in Bethel, N. Y.) a surfboard.

I can only assume that the film follows the chronology of the festival in the presentation of its stars, who come on for comparatively brief sets in endless procession. Some are better than others. Miss Baez is treated beautifully, without cinematic distortions, singing "Joe Hill" and "Swing Low, Sweet Chariot," as is Jimi Hendrix, who manufacturers his own optical effects as he rocks "The Star-Spangled Banner" to close the festival.

In between are such things as the driving rock of The

Who ("Summertime Blues"), Joe Cocker ("With a Little Help from My Friends") and Sly & The Family Stone ("Higher"). The sheer length of the film (3 hours, 4 minutes), as well as the monotony of its visual rhythm, eventually produces a kind of fatigue that is, I suspect, as close to the feeling of being at an almost nonstop, three-day, togetherness orgy as can be prompted by a film. This effect is magnified, rather than diminished, by those moments when the musicians really do seem to take off for special, secret moments, as when Country Joe sings his Vietnam lament, "Fixin' to Die Rag." There have to be low points if there are any that are high.

●

Wadleigh and Maurice employ various devices to stimulate a feeling of participation on the part of the theater audience. In addition to split screens, which may show a single performer from two or three different angles simultaneously, they use auditorium speakers for "surround" effects. (The sound quality is great, much better, in fact, than that of the 35-millimeter film that has been blown up from 16.)

Although the film never really gave me a sense of experiencing the public ecstasy experienced by those who were at Woodstock, it did make me feel comparatively benign. When a woman sitting in my row got up for the third time to go to the ladies' room, and stepped squarely on my toe with a high heel, I said simply: "Peace."

Mr 27, 1970

TWO OR THREE THINGS I KNOW ABOUT HER
By VINCENT CANBY

JEAN-LUC GODARD'S "Two or Three Things I Know About Her," which opened yesterday at the New Yorker Theater, and which was an entry at the 1968 New York Film Festival, was shot in 1966 concurrently with "Made in U.S.A." He simply arranged his schedule so as to be able to work on one in the morning and the other in the afternoon. Filmographically speaking, it comes after "Alphaville," "Pierrot Le Fou" and "Masculin-Feminin," all made in 1965, and it precedes several short films as well as the features, "La Chinoise" (1967), "Weekend," "Le Gai Savoir" and "One Plus One" (also called "Symphathy for the Devil"), all made in 1968.

I go into this in detail because Godard, in each of his films, constantly directs our attention to the place an individual film takes in relation to his other films, and because the director has repudiated these earlier works and is now reportedly devoting himself to filmmaking as a revolutionary activity, rather than to making revolutionary films. There is a difference.

"Two or Three Things" does not, as some have said, mark the end of Godard's "classical" period (he didn't abandon people and people-in-place until after "Weekend"), but it does dramatize the beginning of Godard as the formal movie essayist.

The film cooly, and in strikingly beautiful images many of which are dominated by the sort of red that would rivet the eye of a child), pictures the situation (it does not tell a story) of Juliette (Marina Vlady), a thirtyish Parisian housewife who becomes a part-time prostitute to help pay for the telly, the clothes, the car and the apartment she shares with her husband and children in one of Paris's new housing projects.

Alternating with these

472

scenes are shots of the construction of the "new" Paris that is arising around Juliette, and all the people like her, to form a concrete and steel environment that effectively makes prostitutes of them all. On the soundtrack, Godard whispers "petites lectures" on everything from politics and the meaning of words to the separation between emotion and thought, between thought and word, and between word and the meaning communicated.

In a similar way is Juliette separated from Paris (actually, the 20th arrondissement), the "her" of the title. Godard's preoccupation with vocabulary and syntax as weapons of political and psychological repression (which is what "Le Gai Savoir" is all about) keeps cropping up throughout "Two or Three Things, in narration, in interviews, in interviews-as-dialogue, and even in posters.

The ideas—which come in the form of Godard's interrogation of himself and of the beliefs that shaped the self-proclaimed Maoist of today—are lucidly, often humorously, presented especially by Raoul Coutard's camera that explores faces, rooms, buildings, cars, Coke bottles and Ajax cans, all with Brechtian dispassion. It's a lovely film and should be seen, particularly by anyone planning to push later on to "One Plus One" at the Murray Hill.

My 1, 1970

'The Passion of Anna'

By VINCENT CANBY

Andreas Winkelman (Max von Sydow) is repairing the roof of the cottage in which he lives as a literate hermit. At one point, he stares off at the sun that hangs low and dim—with its edges made ragged by a telephoto lens—in the Scandinavian sky. Suddenly the sun disappears into the gray-blue haze, but it's as if Andreas had willed it invisible, much as he has tried to will himself invisible without taking the ultimate step.

The Cast

THE PASSION OF ANNA, directed by Ingmar Bergman; screenplay (Swedish with English subtitles) by Mr. Bergman; cinematographer, Sven Nykvist; produced by A. B. Svensk Filmindustri; released by United Artists Corporation. At the Festival Theater, 57th Street at Fifth Avenue. Running time: 99 minutes. (The Motion Picture Association of America's Production Code and Rating Administration classifies this film: "R—restricted, persons under 17 require accompanying parent or adult guardian.")

Anna Fromm .... Liv Ullmann
Eva .... Bibi Andersson
Andreas Winkelman..... Max von Sydow
Ellis Vergerus ....Erland Josephson
Johan Andersson .... Erik Hell
Verner .... Sigge Furst
Verner's wife .... Svea Holst
Katarina .... Ann'ka Kronberg
Johan's sister .... Hjordis Pettersson
First Policeman ......Lars-Owe Carlberg
Second Policeman ....Brian Wikstrom

With this lovely image, Ingmar Bergman begins "The Passion of Anna," which opened yesterday at the Festival Theater and is the concluding film in the "island" trilogy that includes "Hour of the Wolf" and "Shame." As in "Hour of the Wolf," the von Sydow-Bergman character is again pursued by demons, but they are real this time—demons of pride, loneliness and defeat. As in "Shame," he is again framed against a world of war and violence, although the war is miniaturized and distanced (as a fleeting television image from Vietnam) and the violence is the work of a madman who roams the island ritualistically hanging a dog, cutting the throats of sheep and setting horses on fire.

In "The Passion of Anna," Andreas is as much victim as culprit. Living in solitude on the island, after having been abandoned at some earlier time by his wife, Andreas is drawn into a friendship with Elis (Erland Josephson), a successful architect; Eva (Bibi Anderson), his wife, and Anna (Liv Ullmann), their best friend, who is recovering from an automobile accident in which she, the driver, survived her husband and child.

Andreas first has an affair of convenience with Eva, a sad, pretty woman who loves her husband but feels unneeded by him. Later, he shares his cottage with Anna, a voluptuous woman who prattles on about the necessity of striving for spiritual perfection and about the "wholeness" of her lost marriage, although Andreas is perfectly aware of the fact that the marriage was a disaster, that her husband had tried, unsuccessfully, to leave her. Andreas has come upon a letter in Anna's purse in which her husband had warned that her unreasonable demands would lead first to "mental and psychical violence," and then to physical violence. The letter was signed "Andreas," which was also the name of Anna's husband.

Quite relentlessly, Anna's passion leads to the defeat of the second Andreas and, at the end, there is every indication that she will continue to go through life, like some over-zealous Christian missionary, preaching salvation and leaving behind her a trail of lies, compromises, confusion and violence.

"The Passion of Anna" is one of Bergman's most beautiful films (it is his second in color), all tawny, wintery grays and browns, deep blacks and dark greens, highlighted occasionally by splashes of red, sometimes blood. It is also, on the surface, one of his most lucid, if a film that tries to dramatize spiritual exhaustion can be ever said to be really lucid. However, like all of Bergman's recent films, it does seem designed more for the indefatigable Bergman cryptologists (of which I am not one) than for interested, but uncommitted filmgoers.

For example, I am curious about, but am unable to speculate on, the reasons Bergman persists in using the same names for his female characters who are not the same. The names of Eva and Anna turn up in "Shame" and "The Silence," and the names of all his leading female characters in "The Silence," "Persona," Hour of the Wolf," "Shame" and "The Passion" begin with an "A" or an "E," which are the letters tagged on to the name of the von Sydow character in "The Passion."

Does this mean something? I think not, but it is there. I also have the feeling that Bergman, who has a marvelous way of setting his scene and introducing his characters, especially the peripheral ones, becomes, in his role of film creator, rather like one of his own heroes. The director circles in closer and closer to the heart of the film, finally to find a void, or a secret so private that we can only guess its meaning.

●

Getting to the heart of it, however, can be stimulating, and involves its own kind of mounting suspense as one grasps at casual remarks for clues. Elis, the architect, is an amateur photographer, fascinated by faces. When he shows his work to Andreas, he says, with resignation: "I don't imagine that I reach into the soul with these photographs. [They can show] only an interplay of forces."

Of the four principal characters, Andreas is the one on screen the most, and the one least known. He has been in prison (for forgery, striking a policeman) and he has been married, but all we know of the marriage (via a flashback) is that his wife has accused him of having "cancer of the soul . . . you have tumors all over you." He does, however, talk at length about things like "the freedom to be humiliated."

It is somewhat ironic that Bergman, the great humanist, insists that his heroes suffer so profoundly from abstract malaises that they seem positively superhuman.

There is no confusion in "The Passion of Anna" between reality and fantasy—it is all fantasy. That, at least, is the effect of a device by which, at four points in the film, he steps back and asks each of his principal actors about his conception of the role he is playing. The result is not so much enlightenment as it is an expression of Bergman's appreciation to his stars, particularly von Sydow, Miss Ullmann and Miss Anderson, who have contributed so much to so many of his films.

●

They all are superb here, and Bergman gives each of them extraordinary moments of cinematic truth, monologues of sustained richness and drama that are the hallmarks of Bergman's best work, when the camera, without moving, records the birth of a character largely through facial expression and dialogue.

I must admit that ever since "Persona" I've had trouble distinguishing between Miss Ullmann and Miss Anderson (at a certain point, all Bergman actresses look like Jessica Tandy). However, I shall always remember a scene in "The Passion" in which Miss Anderson, a little bit tight on wine, recalls her introduction to God, illustrated in one of her children's book as a handsome old man hovering just above the earth.

She is asked if she still believes in Him. She looks at her husband hesitantly and asks: "Do I?" As in all Bergman films, such moments cut through all the abstractions and make "The Passion of Anna" as vivid and moving as you demand that it be.

My 29, 1970

Catch-22

CATCH-22, directed by Mike Nichols; screenplay by Buck Henry, based on the novel by Joseph Heller; cinematographer, David Watkin; music supervised by John Hammell; produced by John Calley; released by Paramount Pictures. At the Paramount Theater at Columbus Circle and the Sutton Theater, Third Avenue and 57th Street. Running time; 129 minutes. (The Motion Picture Association of America's Production Code and Rating Administration classifies this film; "R —restricted, persons under 17 require accompanying parent or adult guardian.")

Captain Yossarian	Alan Arkin
Colonel Cathcart	Martin Balsam
Major Danby	Richard Benjamin
Captain Nately	Art Garfunkel
Dr. Daneeka	Jack Gilford
Major Major	Bob Newhart
Chaplain Tappman	Anthony Perkins
Nurse Duckett	Paula Prentiss
Lieutenant Dobbs	Martin Sheen
Milo Minderbinder	Jon Voight
General Dreedle	Orson Welles
Hungry Joe	Seth Allen
Captain Orr	Robert Balaban
Captain McWatt	Peter Bonerz
Aardvark	Chuck Grodin
Lieut. Col. Korn	Buck Henry
Colonel Moodus	Austin Pendleton
Nately's whore	Gina Rovere
Luciana	Olympia Carlisli
Old Man	Marcel Dalio

By VINCENT CANBY

Panic, like some higher forms of grief and joy, is such an exquisite emotion that nature denies its casual recollection to all except psychotics, a few artists and an occasional, pre-existential hero like Yossarian, the mad bombardier of Joseph Heller's World War II novel, "Catch-22."

Once experienced by the normal neurotic, panic is immediately and efficiently removed from reality, twice removed, in fact, transformed into a memory of a memory. But Yossarian is not your normal neurotic. At the United States Air Force base on the tiny Mediterranean island of Pianosa, which Heller describes as a defoliated, shrunken, surreal Corsica, Yossarian lives in a state of perpetual, epic panic. For Yossarian, a willing convert to paranoia, panic is a kind of Nirvana.

He is convinced that everyone wants him dead—the Germans, his fellow officers, Nurse Duckett, bartenders, bricklayers, landlords, tenants, patriots, traitors, lynchers and lackeys. If they don't get him, Yossarian is aware that there are lymph glands, kidneys, nerve sheaths, corpuscles, Ewing's tumors and, possibly, Wisconsin shingles that will.

Because mankind is conspiring in his death, and he wants to survive, Yossarian knows that the whole world is crazy—and he's absolutely right, almost. you might say, dead-on-target.

It's the special achievement of Heller's novel, as well as of Mike Nichols's screen version, that Yossarian's panic emerges as something so important, so reasonable, so moving and so funny. In the peculiar, perfectly ordered universe of Pianosa, where the system of rewards and punishments is perfectly disordered, panic is positive and fruitful, like love.

"Catch-22," which opened yesterday at the new Paramount Theater on Columbus Circle and at the Sutton Theater, is, quite simply, the best American film I've seen this year. It looks and sounds like a big-budget, commercial service comedy, but it comes as close to being an epic human comedy as Hollywood has ever made by employing the comic conventions of exaggeration, fantasy, shock, and the sort of insult and reverse logic that the late Lulu McConnell elevated to a fine, low art form on radio's "It Pays to Be Ignorant."

I do have some reservations about the film, the most prominent being that I'm not sure that anyone who has not read the novel will make complete sense out of the movie's narrative line that Nichols and his screenwriter, Buck Henry, have shaped in the form of flashbacks within an extended flashback. Missing, too, are some relevant characters (ex-Pfc. Wintergreen, the dispassionate, God-surrogate who actually rules Pianosa) and relevant sequences, as when Chaplain Tappman learns to lie and thus makes his accommodation with the system).

Great movies are complete in themselves. "Catch-22" isn't, but enough of the original remains so that the film becomes a series of brilliant mirror images of a Strobe-lit reality.

Nichols and Henry, whose senses of humor coincide with Heller's fondness for things like the manic repetition of words and phrases, have rearranged the novel without intruding on it. Most of the film is framed by Yossarian's delirium (after he has been stabbed by what appears to be a German P.O.W.) and is played in the form of funny and sad blackout sketches.

These involve, to name just a few, Colonel Cathcart (Martin Balsam), whose dearest desire is to be featured in The Saturday Evening Post; Captain Nately (Art Garfunkle), the rich Boston boy who is fated to love a mean Roman whore; Major Major (Bob Newhart), the timid squadron commander; General Dreedle (Orson Welles), who likes to say "Take him out and shoot him" when people behave stupidly; Captain Orr (Robert Balaban), who practices crashing in preparation for an escape to Sweden; Milo Minderbinder (Jon Voight), the squadron's mess officer, a sort of one-man, free-enterprise convulsion, and glum old Doc Daneeka (Jack Gilford).

Each one is marvelous, but it is Alan Arkin as Yossarian who provides the film with its continuity and dominant style. Alkin is not a comedian; he is a deadly serious actor, but because he projects intelligence with such monomanical intensity, he is both funny and heroic at the same time.

The film is Nichols's third ("Who's Afraid of Virginia Woolf?", "The Graduate") so it may be safe to say now that he's something more than lucky. "Catch-22" is a giant physical production, even by Hollywood's swollen standards, but the complexities of the physical production never neutralize the personal comedy, even when Nichols has a bomber crash in flames as the background to a bit of close-up dialogue.

There are some things in the film that I wish he had resisted, such as images out of Fellini and a reference to Kubrick's use of "Zarathustra," which is also being used currently in a Swanson's Frozen Foods television commercial.

Nichols's cinematic style now looks almost classic, in comparison with "The Graduate." There is not as much cutting within sequences; he uses real tracking shots; zooms are held to a minimum, and he remains, as he was before, one of our finest directors of a certain kind of controlled comic performance. With the exception of Elizabeth Taylor, nobody in a Nichols film is ever allowed to over-reach himself.

"Catch-22" is so good that I hope it won't be confused with what is all too loosely referred to as black comedy, which usually means comedy bought cheaply at the expense of certain human values, so that, for example, murder is funny and assassination is hilarious. "Catch-22," like Yossarian, is almost beside itself with panic because it grieves for the human condition.

Je 25, 1970

Performance

PERFORMANCE, directed by Donald Cammell and Nicholas Roeg; written by Mr. Cammell; photographed by Mr. Roeg; music by Jack Nitzsche; produced by Sanford Lieberson; released by Warner Bros. At the Trans-Lux East Theater, Third Avenue and 58th Street. Running time; 106 minutes. (The Motion Picture Association of America's Production Code and Rating Administration classifies this film: "X—no one under 17 admitted.")

Charles .... James Fox
Turner .... Mick Jagger
Pherber .... Anita Pallenberg
Lucy .... Michele Breton
Moody .... John Bindon
Rosebloom .... Stanley Meadows
Harry Flowers ....Johnny Shannon
Joey Maddocks ....Anthony Valentine
Tony Farrell .... Ken Colley

By ROGER GREENSPUN

On second viewing, "Performance," which opened yesterday at the Trans-Lux East, seems less pretentiously formidable and more cleverly amusing than on first viewing, and although I'm not sure I want to see it a third time, at least not right away, twice seems an entirely reasonable and even rewarding schedule.

It isn't a very good movie, and without the personalities of its two stars, James Fox and Mick Jagger, it might well prove unendurable. But with those personalities (and they are very much the issue), and with its sadism, masochism, decorative decadence, and languid omnisexuality, "Performance" turns out to be the kind of all-round fun that in the movies oft is tried but rarely so well achieved.

●

Fox (previously best known as the weak young master in Joseph Losey's "The Servant") plays a London protection-rackets hood whose enthusiasm for his work leads him to forget that it's all just a business ("In which," a co-worker explains, "you're a cog, boy—a cog in an organ"), murders a man he should be protecting, and finds it expedient to escape his boss (Johnny Shannon, in a most tender performance). He dyes his hair (equal parts red paint and Bryl Creem), adopts dark glasses, and, disguised as a red-haired, dark-glassed juggler, rents an obscure basement room. His landlord is a former rock star (Mick Jagger) now retired to a fantastic town house where he contemplates life and music, plays with his housemates (Anita Pallenberg and Michele Breton) and his Moog Synthesizer, and watches his mushroom garden grow.

Between Jagger and Fox a complex relationship develops—which compliments the complex relationships that also develop between Fox and Miss Pallenberg, and Fox and Miss Breton; not to mention the relationships long since developed between Jagger and Miss Pallenberg, Jagger

and Miss Breton, and Miss Pallenberg and Miss Breton. The commune is turned on by Fox's pistol and his past. He is turned on by one of their mushrooms. In the end, business calls (in several black cars and with a small army of assassins). But before he goes, Fox has left his mark upon the happy household, and they, we must believe, have done something halfway similar for him.

Into this essentially Abbott and Costello plot, co-directors Donald Cammell (scenarist of the dreadful "Duffy") and Nicolas Roeg (cinematographer for, among others, the gorgeous "Petulia") have introduced every device and attitude known to modern cinema and to the decline of Western Civilization. I believe that the decline of Western Civilization went out of fashion some time back, and modern cinema was never in fashion, and so "Performance" bears a slightly dated, technically preposterous look that hurts it not at all.

For after its initial voluptuous sadism (no sooner are you sure the film prefers the bodies of shiny cars to the bodies of lovely young girls, than it causes James Fox to pour sulphuric acid all over the body of a shiny car), it settles, by way of flashbacks, flashes forward, and, above all, flashes sideways, into a dense mythology of uptight goons and jaded flower children that nobody could ever have taken seriously.

Certainly not the cast. In terms of disguise, James Fox, at one time or another, plays every role in the movie. His performance is unbelievably elaborate, often funny, and devoted in large measure to self-parody of a sort that I think it takes impressive theatrical intelligence to bring off. Mick Jagger, with luxuri-

48

ous black hair and full red lips that suggest an androgynous pre-Raphaelite beauty, has less to do (though he gets the best lines; the dialogue is perhaps 70 per cent "best lines"), but he projects a presence of considerable mystery, and his one big song, "Memo from T" (which sounds a little like a talkthrough version of "Sympathy for the Devil") confirms his own ambiguity and his identity with a role that James Fox embodies and finally leaves behind.

•

But nothing in this film becomes it like the leaving of it. When, near the very end, you get a chance to enter Mick Jagger's brain — literally, in the path of a bullet that penetrates to the innermost source of his wisdom, you know that you are in the presence neither of Caligari nor of Frankenstein, neither Friedrich Nietzsche nor even Dante Gabriel Rossetti, neither East nor exactly West (as at one time or another you will have thought). Rather, you are in the presence of the ultimate metaphysical comic strip—which is what you've always gone to the movies to see.

Ag 4, 1970

'Tristana'

The Cast

TRISTANA, directed by Luis Bunuel; screenplay (Spanish with English subtitles) by Bunuel and Julio Alejandro, based on the novel by Benito Perez Galdos; director of photography, Jose Aguayo; produced by Epoca Films-Talia Film (Madrid), Selenia Cinematografia (Rome) and Les Films Corona (Paris). Released by Maren Films. At the New York Film Festival, Philharmonic Hall, and opening today at the Lincoln Art Theater, 57th Street off Broadway. Running time: 95 minutes. (The Motion Picture Association of America's Production Code and Rating Administration has classified this film "GP—all ages admitted, parental guidance advised.")
Tristana.............Catherine Deneuve

Don Lope.................Fernando Rey
Horacio....................Franco Nero
Saturna.....................Lola Gaos
Saturno..................Jesus Fernandez
Don Cosme..............Antonio Casas

By VINCENT CANBY

Luis Buñuel, the Spanish director who has had to live and work most of his life in exile in France and Mexico, has been making movies since 1928 ("Un Chien Andalou"), but it wasn't until 1961 and the international critical success of "Viridiana" that he could pick his properties with any degree of independence. There has followed a kind of Buñuelian âge d'or, nine years of extraordinarily rich moviemaking of the sort that most fine, idiosyncratic directors—probably unfortunately—pass through before they're 50.

Since "Viridiana," Buñuel, now 70, has made "The Exterminating Angel," "Diary of a Chambermaid," "Simon of the Desert," and, starting in 1967, a series of "farewell," films that include "Belle de Jour," "The Milky Way" and his latest, "Tristana" which is nothing less than the quintessential Buñuel film of all time.

•

This is not quite the same thing as saying that "Tristana." which closed the New York Film Festival last night and opens today at the Lincoln Art Theater, is Buñuel's best. Unlike Tristana, the virginal school girl whose transformation into grand demon Buñuel traces in his new film, I would hesitate to choose the better of two grapes, two bread crumbs or two snowflakes, to say nothing of two Buñuels.

"Viridiana" is his undoubted masterpiece, but "Tristana" is more pure and more consistent, less ambiguous and more complex. It has no "set pieces" to equal "Viridiana's" tumultuous Last Supper, but the entire film moves so swiftly, with such uncompromising concern for the matters at hand, that anything on the order of a "set piece" would have destroyed its practically perfect symmetry.

The film is an adaptation by Buñuel and Julio Alejandro of a novel by Benito Pérez Galdós, the late 19th-century Spanish writer who also wrote the novel on which Buñuel and Alejandro based the screenplay for "Nazarin." The time has been updated from 1892 ·to the early 1920's, and the setting is Toledo, the medieval city whose narrow streets and ancient courtyards (on which a certain amount of restoration is going on, but lethargically) correspond to the Buñuelian view of the social and political scene.

Don Lope (Fernando Rey) is an aging, aristocratic but financially impoverished free thinker, an enemy of all arbitrary authority (except his own) who believes in a gentleman's honor, in those commandments that do not have to do with sex, and in the nobility of only the work that is done "with pleasure." When her mother, an old flame of Don Lope, dies, Tristana (Catherine Deneuve) comes to live with him.

•

Tristana is a dutiful girl who mopes around quite a lot and Don Lope, who is so astute in other ways, assumes that she is in mourning for her mother. Don Lope has compassion, but he is a man. He can't keep his hands off her and calling her "my adored child" with such feeling that it doesn't seem at all unlikely that he may well be her father. With very little fuss, Tristana becomes his mistress, and although she obviously doesn't love him, it is apparent that sex is im-

mensely important to her.

Tristana is not the vacuum she has seemed to be. She puts into practice the freedom Don Lope preaches so loftily. "Smell the sickly odor of marital bliss," Don Lope sneers when they pass a pair of lovers in the street. When the opportunity comes, Tristana runs off with a young artist (Franco Nero), only to return some years later with a malignant tumor on her leg.

Don Lope, now rich with an inheritance, takes her in, nurses her back to health after her leg is amputated with such cheery thoughts as "some men would find you more attractive than ever now." Tristana does become more beautiful, as well as so imperiously perverse that, years later, after they have made "a sinful relationship holy" by marriage, and when he is an old, pathetic man, she can let him die without a gesture of pity.

In what amounts almost to a courtly gesture on his part, as the film's director, Buñuel underscores the terrible inevitability of the events at the very end with a series of quick replays of key moments from the film, unreeling the story backward in a kind of narrative zoom to our first meeting with Tristana, the first scene in the film in which the first words "spoken" are the sign language of deaf mutes.

On this simple tale, Buñuel has made a marvelously complex, funny and vigorously moral movie that also is, to me, his most perfectly cast film. Fernando Rey (Don Jaime of "Viridiana") is splendid—vain, wise, proud, foolish. Catherine Deneuve is beautiful, of course, but never before has her beauty seemed more precise and enigmatic, so that while, at the beginning, there is just the slightest hint of the erotic woman inside the school girl, there is, at the end, an awareness of the saint that once lived within the majestically deformed woman.

●

Like all of Buñuel's films, "Tristana" is a vision of a very special, hermetically sealed world, and although it is fun to recognize familiar items of Buñueliana inside that world (a preoccupation with feet; earnest, misguided clerics; the kind of pragmatism that has Don Lope shout "Long live the living" after a funeral), the film is one that should fascinate even those coming into Buñuel's world for the first time.

The physical production, with color photography by José Aguayo, is uncommonly handsome, and its story is the work of an old master who has such command that he can tell a tale straightforward, without the sort of superficial subtleties and superfluous nuances that, in the work of lesser talents, take the place of primal substance.

S 21, 1970

Montand and Signoret Star in 'Confession'

By VINCENT CANBY

Costa-Gavras's "The Confession," which opened yesterday at the Beekman Theater, is not, I think, a better movie than his prize-winning "Z," with which it will inevitably be compared, not only by the critics but also by those members of the public who may look for a repeat performance. The earlier film was a nearly perfect topical thriller whose form pretty much defined the substance of its liberal politics.

However, because the subject of "The Confession" is much more complex, much more human, I find it vastly more interesting than "Z," even when one is aware of the way Costa-Gavras manipulates attention by the use of flashy cinematic devices that sometimes substitute for sustained drama. It is a horror story of the mind told almost entirely in factual and physical terms, which is something of a contradiction.

These are, however, the terms of which Costa-Gavras is a movie master, and in which Artur London originally wrote his book, adapted for the screen by Jorge Semprun, who also wrote the script for "Z."

●

"The Confession" is the real-life story of Artur London, a loyal Communist who certified his credentials by serving with the International Brigade in Spain and with the Communist anti-Nazi underground in France, and by a long term in a Nazi concentration camp. In 1949, Mr. London returned to his native Czechoslovakia from France to become Under Secretary for Foreign Affairs in the Communist Government of President Klement Gottwald. Two years later, along with 13 other leading Czech Communists (11 of whom were Jewish), Mr. London was arrested for treason and espionage and found guilty in what became known as the "Slansky trial."

The Slansky trial, named for the secretary general of the Czech Communist party, who was also a defendant, was one of the last major gasps of the Stalinist purges that began with the Moscow trials in the 1930's. All of the Slansky defendants were found guilty and all but three, including Mr. London, were executed.

Mr. London lived not only to see the defendants rehabilitated and to write his book but also to return to Czechoslovakia on the day in August, 1968, when Soviet troops invaded his country to end the short Czech spring. "The Confession," with Yves Montand playing Mr. London and Simone Signoret his wife Lise, is the story of a believer's ultimate betrayal by his belief, of intolerable physical torture and psychological harassment (London is urged to confess to crimes he did not commit to prove his loyalty to the party), and, finally, of survival.

It is a harrowing film of intellectual and emotional anguish, dramatized by the breathless devices of melodrama. Costa-Gavras employs abrupt jump cuts and flashes forward as well as back. He underscores the desperation of the meeting of some hunted men in a private apartment with the sounds of children roughhousing in the next room. It may, in fact, be one of the most aurally resonant movies I've ever seen. It is full of ordinary sounds made somehow ominous, like the slamming of doors (car, house, prison) and footsteps (on wood, brick, concrete).

•

Its color photography by

Raoul Coutard is also fine (natural overhead light in all the interiors), even when resorting to the zoom, which can be a legitimate tool in melodrama. Beginning with Mr. Montand and Miss Signoret, it is perfectly cast. One really responds to the faces, the attitudes and gestures in a Costa-Gavras film, as when, during the trial, the trousers of one of the emaciated defendants fall to the floor and he turns to the court with an expression of hopeless, perfectly confused laughter and despair.

"The Confession" is a film of movement and sensation, as was "Z," but there is at its center a complex human being. Like the book, it is an anti-Stalinist rather than anti-Communist polemic (Mr. London has written that he is interested in putting "a human face" on national socialism). One tends to forget the context of the Londons' experience—the totality of a belief that would prompt a wife to denounce a husband that she has loved for almost 20 years, simply because the Party had to be right.

You might not know it from the film, but the Londons are different from you and me—and from Arthur Koestler, whose disenchantment came earlier (1937) and was more complete. In a recent interview, Mr. Koestler recalled the blind party discipline that he eventually denied as he quoted André Malraux: "A life is worth nothing, but nothing is worth a life." Because this is also the essence of "The Confession," I liked it very much, even when its form is in combat with its substance.

PORTRAITS OF STARS

PICTURE CREDITS

Allen, Gracie

Astor, Mary

Bara, Theda

Bardot, Brigitte

Barrymore, Ethel

Bergman, Ingrid

Bow, Clara

Carroll, Madeleine

Christian, Linda

Colbert, Claudette

Crawford, Joan

Davies, Marion

Davis, Bette

De Haviland, Olivia

Del Rio, Dolores

Dietrich, Marlene

Dressler, Marie

Dunne, Irene

Field, Betty

Garbo, Greta

Gardner, Ava

Garson, Greer

Gish, Dorothy

Gish, Lillian

Goddard, Paulette

Harlow, Jean

Hepburn, Audrey

Hepburn, Katherine

Hopkins, Miriam

Kerr, Deborah

Lamarr, Hedy

Lamour, Dorothy

Lanchester, Elsa

Leigh, Vivien

Lollabrigida, Gina

Lombard, Carole

Loren, Sophia

Loy, Myrna

Magnani, Anna

Mercouri, Melina

Monroe, Marilyn

Moore, Constance

Moore, Grace

Negri, Pola

Nissen, Greta

Oberon, Merle

Palmer, Lilli

Pickford, Mary

488

Pitts, Zazu

Reynolds, Debbie

Rogers, Ginger

Russell, Jane

Shearer, Norma

Sidney, Sylvia

Signoret, Simone

Sothern, Ann

Stanwyck, Barbara

Swanson, Gloria

Talmadge, Constance

Taylor, Elizabeth

Temple, Shirley

Turner, Lana

West, Mae

Young, Loretta

Arbuckle, Roscoe

Arliss, George

Bartholomew, Freddie

Blue, Ben

Bogart, Humphrey

Brando, Marlon

Bushman, Francis X.

Cagney, James

Cantor, Eddie

Chaplin, Charlie

Chaney, Lon

Colman, Ronald

Coogan, Jackie

Cooper, Gary

De Sica, Vittorio

Dean, James

490

Fairbanks, Douglas

Fernandel

Fetchit, Stepin

Fields, W. C.

Gabin, Jean

Gable, Clark

Hardy, Oliver

Holt, Jack

Horton, Edward Everett

Howard, Leslie

Huston, Walter

Ingram, Rex

Jannings, Emil

Jolson, Al

Karloff, Boris

Keaton, Buster

Langdon, Harry

Laughton, Charles

Laurel, Stan

Lloyd, Harold

Lugosi, Bela

McLaglen, Victor

Marx, Groucho

Marx, Harpo

Mastroianni, Marcello

Mix, Tom

Montand, Yves

Muni, Paul

Nagel, Conrad

Novarro, Ramon

Poitier, Sidney

Powell, William

Raft, George

Rathbone, Basil

Robinson, Edward G.

Romero, Cesar

Scott, George C.

Simon, Michel

Sinatra, Frank

Stewart, James

Stone, Lewis

Tone, Franchot

Tracy, Spencer

Valentino, Rudolph

Veidt, Conrad

von Stroheim, Eric

Welles, Orson

Young, Roland

TITLE INDEX